A Companion to
# Literature and Film

## BLACKWELL COMPANIONS IN CULTURAL STUDIES

Advisory editor: David Theo Goldberg, University of California, Irvine

This series aims to provide theoretically ambitious but accessible volumes devoted to the major fields and subfields within cultural studies, whether as single disciplines (film studies) inspired and reconfigured by interventionist cultural studies approaches, or from broad interdisciplinary and multidisciplinary perspectives (gender studies, race and ethnic studies, postcolonial studies). Each volume sets out to ground and orientate the student through a broad range of specially commissioned articles and also to provide the more experienced scholar and teacher with a convenient and comprehensive overview of the latest trends and critical directions. An overarching *Companion to Cultural Studies* will map the territory as a whole.

Edited by

# Robert Stam
# Alessandra Raengo

# A Companion to
# Literature
# and Film

**Blackwell**
Publishing

© 2004 by Blackwell Publishing Ltd
except for editorial material and organization © 2004 by Robert Stam and
Alessandra Raengo

BLACKWELL PUBLISHING
350 Main Street, Malden, MA 02148-5020, USA
9600 Garsington Road, Oxford OX4 2DQ, UK
550 Swanston Street, Carlton, Victoria 3053, Australia

The right of Robert Stam and Alessandra Raengo to be identified as the Authors of the Editorial
Material in this Work has been asserted in accordance with the UK Copyright, Designs, and Patents
Act 1988.

First published 2004 by Blackwell Publishing Ltd

2    2006

_Library of Congress Cataloging-in-Publication Data_

A companion to literature and film / edited by Robert Stam and Alessandra Raengo.
    p. cm. — (Blackwell companions in cultural studies ; 7)
  Includes bibliographical references and index.
  ISBN 0-631-23053-X (hardback : alk. paper)
1. Literature and motion pictures.   2. Film adaptations—History and criticism.   I.
Stam, Robert, 1941–   II. Raengo, Alessandra.   III. Title.   IV. Series.

  PN1995.3 C65 2004
  791.43'6—dc22

                                                                2004017778

ISBN-13: 978-0-631-23053-3 (hardback)

A catalogue record for this title is available from the British Library.

Set in 9.75/14pt Bell Gothic
by Graphicraft Ltd, Hong Kong

The publisher's policy is to use permanent paper from mills that operate a sustainable forestry policy,
and which has been manufactured from pulp processed using acid-free and elementary chlorine-free
practices. Furthermore, the publisher ensures that the text paper and cover board used have met
acceptable environmental accreditation standards.

For further information on
Blackwell Publishing, visit our website:
www.blackwellpublishing.com

FSC
Mixed Sources
Product group from well-managed
forests and other controlled sources
Cert no. SGS-COC-2953
www.fsc.org
© 1996 Forest Stewardship Council

# Contents

vii

Contents

# Illustrations

# Notes on Contributors

**Richard Allen** is Associate Professor of Cinema Studies at New York University. He is author of *Projecting Illusion* (1995), and editor of a number of books including, most recently, *Wittgenstein, Theory and the Arts* (2001) and *Camera Obscura/Camera Lucida: Essays in Honor of Annette Michelson* (2002), both with Malcolm Turvey. He co-edited (with Sam Gonzalèz) *Alfred Hitchcock: Centenary Essays* (1999) and is currently completing a book on Hitchcock's films.

**Dudley Andrew** directs Graduate Film Studies at Yale University. His books include *Film in the Aura of Art* (1984) and *Mists of Regret: Culture and Sensibility in Classic French Film* (1995).

**Francesco Casetti** teaches film and television at the Catholic University of the Sacred Heart in Milan, Italy. He has been a visiting professor at Université Paris III, the University of Iowa, and the University of California at Berkeley. His books include *Inside the Gaze: The Fiction Film and its Spectator* (1999) and *Theories of Cinema: 1945–1995* (1999).

**Julian Cornell**, a doctoral candidate at New York University, is completing his dissertation on apocalyptic narratives in recent Hollywood films. He teaches Media Studies at Queens College, CUNY.

**Raffaele De Berti** teaches Film History and Criticism at the University of Milan. He has published various essays on the relationship between cinema, society, and other mass media. Among his books are *Un secolo di cinema a Milano* (1996) and *Dallo schermo alla carta. Romanzi, fotoromanzi, rotocalchi cinematografici: il film e i suoi paratesti* (2000).

**Kamilla Elliott**, who gained her PhD from Harvard University in 1996, is Assistant Professor of English at the University of California, Berkeley, where she teaches Victorian literature and the interdisciplinary study of literature and film. She is the author of *Rethinking the Novel/Film Debate* (2003).

**André Gaudreault** is a tenured faculty in the Département d'Histoire de l'Art at the Université de Montréal, where he heads both the GRAFICS (Groupe de Recherche sur l'Avènement et la Formation des Institutions Cinématographique et Scénique) and the CRI (Centre de Recherche sur l'Intermédialité). He is also the director of the scholarly journal *Cinémas*. He has acted as a visiting professor at the University of São Paulo, the University of Paris III: Sorbonne Nouvelle, the University of Bologna and the University of Paris I: Panthéon-Sorbonne. He has published extensively both scholarly articles and books on filmic narration and/or early cinema, notably *Du littéraire au filmique: système du récit* (rev. edn, 1999) and, with F. Jost, *Le Récit cinématographique* (1990).

**Luke Gibbons**, Professor of English and concurrent Professor in the Department of Film, Television, and Theater at the University of Notre Dame, has lectured widely in Great Britain, Europe, North America, and Australia. His academic interests include film and literature, the visual arts, aesthetics, politics and cultural history, and contemporary debates on postcolonialism. He is the author of *Transformations in Irish Culture* (1996), *Edmund Burke and Ireland: Aesthetics, Politics and the Colonial Sublime* (2003), *Gaelic Gothic: Race, Colonialism and Irish Culture* (2004), co-author of *Cinema in Ireland* (1988), and a contributing editor of the landmark *Field Day Anthology of Irish Writing* (1991).

**Pamela Grace**, a doctoral student in the Cinema Studies Department of New York University and adjunct instructor in the Film Department of Brooklyn College, is completing a book on Jesus films. She has published in *Cineaste* and other journals.

**Tom Gunning** is Edwin A. and Betty L. Bergman Distinguished Service Professor in the Art History Department and the Cinema and Media Committee at the University of Chicago. Author of *D. W. Griffith and the Origins of American Narrative Film* (1991) and *The Films of Fritz Lang: Allegories of Vision and Modernity* (2000), he has written numerous essays on early and international silent cinema, and on American cinema, including Hollywood genres and directors as well as the avant-garde film. He has lectured around the world and his works have been published in a dozen different languages.

**Peter Hitchcock** is Associate Professor at Baruch College, CUNY. His publications include *Working Class Fiction in Theory and Practice: A Reading of Alan Sillitoe* (1989), *Dialogics of the Oppressed* (1993), and *Oscillate Wildly: Space, Body, and Spirit of Millennial Materialism* (1998).

**François Jost** is Professor at the University of Paris III: Sorbonne Nouvelle, where he directs the Center of Studies of the Mediatic Image and Sound (CEISME). He has also been visiting professor in many universities around the world. Among his works are: *L'Oeil-caméra* (1987), *Le Récit cinématographique* (1990, with A. Gaudreault), *Un monde à notre image* (1992), *Le Temps d'un regard* (1998), *Introduction à l'analyse de la télévision* (1999), *La télévision du quotidien* (2001), and *L'Empire du loft* (2002).

**William Luhr** is Professor of English at Saint Peter's College and Co-chair of the Columbia University Seminar on Cinema and Interdisciplinary Interpretation. Among his books as author, co-author, or editor are *Authorship and Narrative in the Cinema* (1977), *Blake Edwards* (vols 1 and 2, 1981, 1989), *World Cinema since 1945* (1987), *Raymond Chandler and Film* (2nd edn, 1991), *The Maltese Falcon: John Huston, Director* (1995), *Thinking About Movies: Watching, Questioning, Enjoying* (2nd edn, 2003), and *The Coen Brothers' Fargo* (2004). He has contributed to a number of journals and is currently writing a book on *film noir*.

**Philippe Marion** is Professor in the Department of Communication (Faculty of Economic, Political, and Social Sciences) at the Catholic University of Louvain, where he is a member of the Unité de Recherche en "Journalisme et Récit Médiatique." He is a co-founder of the Observatoire du Récit Médiatique. Among his publications are *Traces en cases: travail graphique et figuration narrative. Essai sur la bande dessinée et son lecteur* (1993), *Le Documentaire, Cinéma* (edited with André Gaudreault, 1994), and *Image et narration: recherches en communication* (edited with Jacques Polet, 1998).

**Margaret Montalbano** gained a PhD in Cinema Studies from New York University. Her research interests include an examination of the resurgence of the vampire figure in popular culture and a reading of modern vampire myths through the lens of intersubjective psychoanalytic theory.

**Gavriel Moses** teaches Film Studies and the late Renaissance at the University of California, Berkeley. His publications include "Marino's Adonis and the Apparatus to Come," in Francesco Guardiani (ed.), *The Sense of Marino* (1994), *The Nickel Was for the Movies: Film in the Novel Pirandello to Puig* (1995), "*Natural Born Discourse*: soggetto e linguaggi nel cinema americano," in Franco La Polla (ed.), *Poetiche del cinema holly-woodiano contemporaneo* (1997), and "*Damiel Does L.A.*, ovvero: quanti corpi sulla punta di uno spillo?," in Franco La Polla (ed.), *The Body Vanishes: la crisi dell'identità e del soggetto nel cinema americano contemporaneo* (1999).

**Charles Musser** is Professor of American Studies and Film Studies at Yale University, where he co-chairs the Film Studies Program. His books include *The Emergence of Cinema: The American Screen to 1907* (1990), which was awarded the Jay Leyda Prize, the Katherine Kovacs Prize for outstanding book on film and television, as well as the Theater Library Book Award. His long-standing interest in the practice of theater to film adaptation is evident in essays he wrote for *Oscar Micheaux and his Circle: African American*

*Filmmaking and Race Cinema of the Silent Period* (2001), which he co-edited with Pearl Bowser and Jane Gaines.

**R. Barton Palmer** is Calhoun Lemon Professor of Literature at Clemson University. He also serves as one of the founding general editors of *Traditions of World Cinema*. Among other books on film, he has published *Hollywood's Dark Cinema* (1994) and *Perspectives on Film Noir* (1996) and has several others shortly forthcoming, including *Joel and Ethan Coen: Brothers Postmodern*, as well as *Nineteenth-century American Fiction on Screen* and *Twentieth-century American Fiction on Screen*.

**Brigitte Peucker** is Elias Leavenworth Professor of German and Professor of Film Studies at Yale University. She has published widely on questions of representation in film and in literature. Her current book-length project involves the representation of the real in film.

**Ella Shohat** is Professor of Cultural Studies in the departments of Art and Public Policy, Middle Eastern Studies and Comparative Literature, New York University. She has lectured and published extensively on the intersection of post/colonialism, multiculturalism, and gender, both nationally and internationally. Her award-winning works include the books *Israeli Cinema: East/West and the Politics of Representation* (1989), *Unthinking Eurocentrism* (co-authored with Robert Stam, 1994), *Dangerous Liaisons: Gender, Nation and Postcolonial Perspectives* (co-edited, 1997), *Talking Visions: Multicultural Feminism in a Transnational Age* (1998), *Forbidden Reminiscences* (2001), and *Multiculturalism, Postcoloniality and Transnational Media* (co-edited, 2003). A recipient of a Rockefeller Fellowship, she has served on the editorial boards of several journals, including *Social Text*, *Critique*, *Jouvert*, *Public Culture*, and *Meridians*. Her writings have been translated into French, Spanish, Portuguese, Arabic, Hebrew, German, and Turkish.

**Noa Steimatsky** is Assistant Professor of the History of Art and teaches Film Studies at Yale University. Her present contribution draws on a book she is completing on realist landscapes and the claim of the modern in Italian cinema. She has published articles on realism, modernism, and Italian film in several anthologies and journals. She is a winner of the Rome Prize for her current project on the post-war reconstruction of cinematic modernism.

**Chris Straayer** is Associate Professor and Chair of the Department of Cinema Studies at New York University and author of *Deviant Eyes, Deviant Bodies* (1996). Her articles on film and video have appeared in numerous academic journals and anthologies, and she has curated multiple programs, including "Lesbian Genders" at the Whitney Museum of American Art. She serves on the editorial boards of the *Journal of Television and New Media* and *The Velvet Light Trap*, and on the directorial boards of the Consoling Passions Conference on International Television, Video and Feminism and the Lyn Blumenthal Memorial Fund for Independent Video and New Media.

Maria Tortajada is Assistant Professor at the University of Lausanne, where she teaches film history and aesthetics. She is a *docteur ès-lettres* at the University of Geneva, where she has taught for six years. She is currently the editor in charge of the second volume of the history of Swiss cinema (1966–2000) and author of *Le Spectateur séduit: le libertinage dans le cinéma d'Eric Rohmer et sa fonction dans une théorie de la représentation filmique* (1999) and *Cinéma suisse: nouvelles recherches* (with. F. Albera, 2000).

Yuri Tsivian has a PhD in Film Studies from the Institute of Theater, Music and Cinema, Leningrad, and is currently Professor of Film in the Art History Department of the University of Chicago. He is the author of *Silent Witnesses: Russian Films, 1908–1919* (1989), *Early Cinema in Russia and its Cultural Reception* (1994), *Dialogues with the Screen* (with Yuri Lotman, 1994), and *Ivan the Terrible* (2002), and of the CD ROM *Immaterial Bodies: Cultural Anatomy of Early Russian Films* (2000).

Allen S. Weiss is the author of *The Aesthetics of Excess* (1989), *Shattered Forms* (1992), *Perverse Desire and the Ambiguous Icon* (1994), *Mirrors of Infinity* (1995), *Phantasmic Radio* (1995), and *Unnatural Horizons* (1998). He has edited *Experimental Sound and Radio* (2001, a special issue of *The Drama Review*) and produced the CD *Voice Tears*. He teaches in the Departments of Performance Studies and Cinema Studies at New York University.

Zhang Zhen is Assistant Professor in the Department of Cinema Studies at New York University. She has published a number of articles on early and contemporary Chinese film culture, as well as on literature.

# Preface

*A Companion to Literature and Film* forms part of a three-book series devoted to literature and film: more specifically, to the history, theory, and practice of the filmic adaptations of novels; and, more broadly, to the relation between filmic and literary writing. *A Companion to Literature and Film* complements the first two volumes in the series by exploring the broader question of the interface between the literary and the filmic. It features theoretical and analytical essays, previously unpublished, concerning such issues as: (1) the narratology of adaptation; (2) adaptation in the oeuvre of single directors (for example, Alfred Hitchcock); (3) hidden intertextualities (for example, the un-acknowledged presence of *Les Liaisons dangereuses* in the work of Eric Rohmer; and (4) thematic/generic essays on such topics as apocalyptic fiction/film, cross-cultural adaptation, the Hollywood novel/film, *noir* novels and films, and the Bible as cultural object in popular cinema. The *Companion* moves the discussion beyond adaptation per se into broader questions of transtextuality and intermediality.

The first volume in the series, *Literature Through Film: Realism, Magic, and the Art of Adaptation*, approaches the subject from the specific angle of the history of the novel. Arranged according to the chronology of the literary source texts rather than that of their filmic adaptations, *Literature Through Film* highlights key moments and trends in the history of the novel from *Don Quixote* and *Robinson Crusoe* to Nabokov's *Lolita* and Carpentier's *Concierto barroco*. All the novels are treated in their own terms, as novels, but also as seen through their various filmic adaptations. In each case, I stress the historical importance of the novel, its central narrative and aesthetic strategies, and its verbal texture, before moving to the "re-readings" of these same novels as "performed" by film. In sum, I provide an historicized overview of privileged moments in the development of the novel, but as refracted and "rewritten" in the form of cinematic adaptations.

A second volume, *Literature and Film: A Guide to the Theory and Practice of Film* *Adaptation*, consists of a wide range of essays, virtually all previously unpublished, covering a broad spectrum of subjects and problematics. My introductory essay on "The Theory and Practice of Adaptation" is followed by a variety of essays concerning single novels/adaptations, essays that both illustrate and problematize the methodologies.

Although the essays in the two anthologies do not conform to any a priori theory or model, they all share a reflexive awareness of key orienting questions or "problematics." In diverse ways, they mingle the methods of literary theory, semiotics, narratology, cultural studies, and media theory. The totality of the essays moves adaptation discourse forward, through a tour de force of sophisticatedly literate (and cine-literate) readings, performed so as to reconfigure the field of literature/film studies. Cumulatively, the work is highly international, covering novels/films from England, the United States, France, Italy, Germany, Spain, Ireland, Russia, China, India, Egypt, Senegal, Cuba, Brazil, Argentina, Mexico, and Venezuela. The work represented in all three volumes points the way, it is hoped, toward a richly theorized and complexly contextualized and transformalist approach to adaptation. While paying homage to the classics of world literature, the work also highlights the contemporary relevance of adaptation studies in the age of the Internet.

*Robert Stam*

Preface

# Acknowledgments

The editors and publisher gratefully acknowledge the permission granted to reproduce the copyright material in this book:

Tom Gunning, "The Intertextuality of Early Cinema: A Prologue to *Fantômas*." Parts of this essay were previously published as "A Tale of Two Prologues: Actors and Roles, Detectives and Disguises in *Fantômas*, Film and Novel," in *The Velvet Light Trap* 37 (Spring 1996), 30–6. © 1996 by the University of Texas Press. Reprinted by permission.

Figures 14.1–14.4: Collezione G. Garra Agosta. From *Verga Fotografo* (Catania, Italy: Giuseppe Maimone Editore, 1991).

Every effort has been made to trace copyright holders and to obtain their permission for the use of copyright material. The publisher apologizes for any errors or omissions and would be grateful if notified of any corrections that should be incorporated in future reprints or editions of this book.

# Chapter 1

# Novels, Films, and the Word/Image Wars

## Kamilla Elliott

The interdisciplinary study of novels and films has tended to run along two sides of a paradox. On one side, novels and films are opposed as "words" and "images," agreed to be irreducible, untranslatable, a priori entities by most postmodern as well as prior scholars. On the other side, critics propound film's integral formal, generic, stylistic, narrative, cultural, and historical connections to the novel. Somewhat perplexingly, the two sides of the paradox tend to coexist within single critical works: they do not, by and large, represent differing views of opposed critics. This chapter probes the paradox, examines its effects on interdisciplinary discourse on novels and films, as well as on theories and definitions of novels and films within their own disciplines.

## The Celluloid Laocoön

Belief in an essential opposition of words and images holds strongly, even as most other oppositions have been broken down by poststructuralism. Roland Barthes, Michel Foucault, J. Hillis Miller, and W. J. T. Mitchell all support a basic word and image opposition. Barthes concludes that "there is never a real incorporation since the substances of the two structures (graphic and iconic) are irreducible."[1] Foucault presents "statements" and "visibilities," as pure, a priori elements.[2] Hillis Miller argues that "Neither the meaning of a picture nor the meaning of a sentence is by any means translatable. The picture means itself. The sentence means itself. The two can never meet."[3] Mitchell claims that words and images "are not merely *different* kinds of creatures, but *antithetical* kinds."[4] Mitchell has also argued that "The history of culture is in part the story of a protracted struggle for dominance between pictorial and linguistic signs."[5]

In 1957, George Bluestone applied Gotthold Ephraim Lessing's differentiations of poetry and painting to novels and films. Lessing's differentiations had, in the first half of the twentieth century, come to stand for differences between words and images more generally. Thus, Bluestone's application placed novels in the word camp and films in the image camp. In chapter 18 of the *Laocoön: An Essay upon the Limits of Painting and Poetry*, Lessing designates poetry an art of conventional signs, representing temporally and sequentially, and painting an art of natural signs, presenting spatially and statically. On the basis of these differences, Lessing urges poetry and painting to occupy separate representational spheres: poetry should limit itself to representing temporal action; painting should limit itself to depicting static bodies in space.[6] Bluestone entitles chapter 1 of his *Novels into Film* "The Limits of the Novel and the Limits of the Film," after *Laocoön*'s subtitle. In this field-founding chapter, he designates the novel as conceptual, linguistic, discursive, symbolic, inspiring mental imagery, with time as its formative principle, and the film as perceptual, visual, presentational, literal, given to visual images, with space as its formative principle.[7] Like Lessing, Bluestone urges a separation of representational spheres on the basis of these differences: "The film and the novel [should] remain separate institutions, each achieving its best results by exploring unique and specific properties."[8]

Bluestone is as widely cited in his interdisciplinary field as Lessing has been in his. But while poetry and painting studies regularly debate Lessing's premises,[9] by and large, novel and film studies have maintained Bluestone's taxonomy without objection. To cite just a few of the hundreds of scholars who have followed Bluestone, in the late 1970s, Keith Cohen set up detailed and complex narratological categories and codes under which to study novels and films, yet wrote of literary film adaptation more crudely as "seeing words changed into images."[10] In the 1980s, J. Dudley Andrew, one of the most widely reprinted scholars of literary film adaptation, wrote of "the absolutely different semiotic systems of film and language."[11] In the mid-1990s, after acknowledging that film draws on a combination of visual, aural, and verbal signifiers, Brian McFarlane nevertheless designated the novel linear, the film spatial, the novel conceptual, and the film perceptual, after Lessing's categorizations of poetry and painting.[12] Even cultural studies scholars who deplore the political dimensions of formalist agendas cite Bluestone as an authority on formal matters.[13]

One wonders why such categorizations have been challenged in poetry and painting studies, but not in novel and film studies and, more immediately, why categorizations developed for purely linguistic and purely visual arts have been applied to hybrid verbal-visual arts.[14] After all, films abound in words – in sound dialogue, intertitles, subtitles, voice-over narration, credits, and words on sets and props – and written texts form the basis of most films. In the same way, novels have at times been copiously illustrated with pictorial initials, vignettes, full-page plates, frontispieces, and end-pieces and unillustrated novels create visual and spatial effects through ekphrasis.

Intriguingly, no scholar denies that films contain words and that novels, illustrated or not, engage in pictorial and create spatial effects. But most follow Bluestone's justification for classifying them as though they did not: "because neither film nor novel is 'pure,' because the film is suffused with temporal, the novel with spatial, effects, we should not forget the priority of each. For analytic purposes, our emphases will stand. Without visual images there would be no film. Without language there would be no novel."[15] One could object, however, that any thoroughgoing semiotics or theory of cinema must include a substantial consideration of film words and that any critique of an illustrated novel must pay attention to the function of the illustrations, regardless of one's thesis or methodology. Yet what we find when we look at the history, theory, and criticism of film and of the novel is a pervasive tendency not only to treat novels as "words" and films as "images," but to treat films as though they had no words and novels as though they had no illustrations.

Film words suffer a pervasive neglect in film history, criticism, and theory. Ralph Stephenson and J. R. Debrix's *The Cinema as Art* – selected as both representative and widely reprinted – accords a scant five of its 270 pages to verbal language. Much of this scant attention regards words as threats to filmic visuals: words, complain Stephenson and Debrix, "interfere with and disturb the image." Consequently, the authors work to diminish the semantic and narrative functions of words and to subordinate them to other modes of representation. They denude the "shooting script" of its verbal identity by making it "a technical blue-print for putting together bits of sight and sound (of which speech is only one element among several)," the parenthetical reference graphically epitomizing the general attitude to film words. The authors subjugate verbal semantics to their visual and aural packaging: "[visual] beauty in speech and acting apart from the meaning of the words . . . when we do hear the words and their meaning matters, the sound and intonation and the appearance of the characters as they say them may . . . be of as much or more significance."[16] Similar reductions and subjugations of film words appear in other film histories and aesthetics of film.

Even semioticians who found their reputations on their nuanced and detailed attention to varying signs, seeing ten categories of signification where a nonsemiotician sees only one, resist a consideration of film words. Christian Metz, perhaps the most famous film semiotician of the twentieth century, is both representative and influential. Like Bluestone, he acknowledges the presence of film words, but does not allow them to be definitive elements of film:

> [The cinema's] strength, or its weakness, is that it encompasses earlier modes of expression: Some, truly languages (the verbal element), and some languages only in more or less figurative sense (music, images, noise).
>
> Nevertheless, these "languages" are not all found on the same plane with respect to cinema: Speech, noise, and music were annexed at a later time, but film was born with *image discourse*. A true definition of "cinematographic specificity" can therefore only be made on two levels: that of filmic discourse and that of image discourse.[17]

Film theorists since Metz have barely studied film words and continue to subjugate them to image or to the aural more generally. Gilles Deleuze makes the sound of the talkie "a new dimension of the visual image, a new component . . . a fourth dimension of the visual image."[18] The Lacanian psychoanalytic theories that have dominated film criticism since the 1970s privilege scopic processes, with little attention to film words.

In the same way, the novel is discussed as though it had never been illustrated: no theory of the novel integrates the illustrations into its definitions, semiotics, politics, or aesthetics.[19] Indeed, one could argue that criticism has in some sense displaced novel illustrations in twentieth-century re-editions of canonical novels. Taking William Makepeace Thackeray's *Vanity Fair* as a representative example, we observe an older kind of "illustration" taking the place of the illustrations in the subtitles of later editions: "illustration" in the sense of annotation and verbal commentary. While nineteenth-century bibliographical subtitles reference "illustrations on steel and wood by the author,"[20] twentieth-century subtitles substitute verbal for pictorial "illustration": "with an introduction by G. K. Chesterton";[21] "with an afterword by V. S. Pritchett";[22] "with an introduction and notes by Geoffrey and Kathleen Tillotson";[23] "with commentary by Nicholas Pickwoad and Robert Colby";[24] "backgrounds and contents, criticism edited by Peter Shillingsburg."[25] Such editions are typically self-advertised as "a new critical edition," or as "an approved edition," or as an "authoritative text."[26]

This chapter argues that the critical neglect of film words is not unrelated to the critical neglect of novel illustrations, but that each discipline, partly from internal pressures and partly from interdisciplinary rivalry, has worked to press an illusory aesthetic of its form as verbally or imagistically "pure." But before we turn to examine how this unfolds, we must first probe the other side of the interdisciplinary paradox that argues film's integral formal, generic, stylistic, narrative, cultural, and historical connections to the novel, for it too feeds the word and image wars.

## Interart Affinities and Interart Analogies

In 1944, filmmaker and film theorist Sergei Eisenstein forged an influential argument that "from the Victorian novel stem the first shoots of the American film esthetic." Eisenstein argued that the Victorian novel's attention to visual detail, empirical psychology, atmospheric close-ups, alternating omniscient and character viewpoints, and shifts from one group of characters to another, all shaped Western film techniques, which in turn influenced and shaped film art more generally.[27] Subsequent scholars have demonstrated intertextual exchanges between twentieth-century novels and films: Keith Cohen, Claude-Edmonde Magny, Seymour Chatman, and others argue that modern novels were shaped by cinematic techniques, like ellipsis, temporal discontinuity, fragmented vision, cross-cutting, and multiple viewpoints.[28] More recently, cultural studies scholars have been exploring cultural interchanges between modern novels and films.[29]

But twentieth-century novels also diverge from films, scholars maintain. Metz is, perhaps, the best known scholar to argue that:

Inasmuch as it proposes behavioural schemes and libidinal prototypes, corporeal postures, types of dress, modes of free behavior or seduction, and is the initiating authority for a perpetual adolescence, the classical film has taken, relay fashion, the historical place of the grand-epoch, nineteenth-century novel (itself descended from the ancient epic); it fills the same social function, a function which the twentieth-century novel, less and less diegetic and representational, tends partly to abandon.[30]

The idea here is not just that the nineteenth-century novel influenced Western film, but that it in some sense *became* film, while the modern novel evolved in a different direction, both formally and culturally. For this and other reasons that emerge below, this chapter focuses on relations between Victorian novels and twentieth-century Anglo-American films.

In terms of the interdisciplinary paradox with which this chapter is concerned, scholars have tended to represent the formal oppositions between novels and films as more fundamental than their cultural, intertextual, and social interchanges and affinities. Bluestone, again seminal, characterizes novels and films as "overtly compatible, secretly hostile."[31] This phrasing, together with his central argument, represents their alliances and similarities as superficial and deceptive, and their formal oppositions as deeper and truer.

But the designation of novels as words and films as images serves agendas more than analysis. Traditionally, pure arts have been more highly valued than hybrid ones. Therefore, in the battle for representational dominance, novels and films have been pressed toward semiotic and aesthetic purity. Pure arts are not only "better": in the case of hybrid arts masquerading as pure arts, they can also claim territory which another hybrid art has abandoned in order to proclaim its own purity. They do this most commonly by using an analogical rhetoric, in which they speak of themselves in the language of the other. In order to obscure the contradictions between aesthetic practice and critical theory, artists and critics have supported word and image categorizations with an analogical rhetoric that speaks of film images in terms of language and of prose words in terms of painting. This rhetoric claims verbal territory for film images and pictorial territory for novel words at the same time as it obscures and overshadows the literal words of films and the literal pictures of novels.

## Film "Language"

Rooted in the idea, articulated here by Metz, that "visual perception varies less throughout the world than languages do," film images have been regularly and widely proclaimed a "universal language."[32] From the early 1900s, when reviewers heralded film as a cure for the Tower of Babel, to today, when the Landmark Company theaters preface each screening with the words "The language of film is universal," the analogy pervades public, artistic, and academic discourse.

The claim of film images to "language" is an analogical one. It is typically accompanied by a denial, dismissal, and neglect of film's literal words. In 1915, film aesthetician Vachel Lindsay promoted the ascendancy of film's analogical visual language over its verbal language: "Moving objects, not moving lips make the words of the photoplay."[33] In 1923, a film reviewer went further in pressing the linguistic functions of images over their pictorial ones, as well as over literal words and verbal arts more generally: "This picture is not a picture drama, it is an argument, an editorial, an essay . . . No orator, no editorial writer, no essayist could so strongly and effectively present the thoughts that are conveyed in this picture."[34] In 1934, Eisenstein's essay "Film Language" grounded the analogy in academic criticism. The essay argues that montage (editing) constitutes the "language," "diction," "syntax," and "speech" of film images, for it creates syntactic and discursive relationships between them, just as sequencing and spacing do between words. But before he addresses this analogical form of film "language," he begins by roundly dismissing actual film words: "I do not propose to talk of the talking film – or, more exactly, of its talking portions. It speaks for itself. It even screams."[35] For Eisenstein, the analogical "language" of film requires a spokesman precisely because it is not literally language, while film's words are deemed self-explanatory because they are. One sees more of rivalrous agendas than lucid logic in the claim: were such reasoning followed in literary studies, there would be none.

Analogical usurpations continue throughout film history. In the 1950s, the *Cahiers du Cinéma* movement usurped the language of authorship from the screenwriter for the director, who subsequently became the *auteur* of the film. At the same time, the camera metamorphosed into a *caméra-stylo*. In the 1960s and 1970s, Roland Barthes, Marie-Claire Ropars-Wuilleumier, and others extended these analogies to academic criticism, advancing film as *écriture*, labeling films "texts." Such rhetorical shifts have had a mixed effect on word and image rivalries: while film images usurp verbal terminology from film words, film is subjected to critical methods derived from linguistics and literary study that may, ironically, occlude its more pictorial dimensions.[36]

Preceding such high art and scholastic analogies were changes in mainstream industry nomenclature practices, changes that combined analogy with synecdoche to redefine film as "images." In the early days of film, the term "Screen Play" referred to the entire film (the film was a screened play): subsequently it came to reference only the written text on which a film was based, the screenplay. In the process, the whole was reduced to a part (Screen Play to screenplay, the capitals removed and the words run together). Accompanying this synecdochal shift, what was once perceived as only a part of film, the cinematography, was cropped of its verbal half (-ography) and inflated via synecdoche to represent the whole film – cinema. Such synecdochal displacements moved film nomenclature away from theatrical and verbal terms to imagistic and technological ones.

Subsequent criticism of the relationship between Screen Play (film) and screenplay (script) work to diminish the importance of the latter. John Harrington's account is typical: "Necessary as a blueprint is, the film image is of ultimate importance . . . film scripts receive scant attention. Primarily only film buffs read scripts . . . The fact that few people read scripts signals the rightful dominance of the medium of film."[37] The final phrase raises Bluestonian notions of the image's rightful dominance in film aesthetics and Metzian exclusions of verbal elements from semiotic definitions of film. Subsequent critics represent filmmaking as a triumph of cinematography over screenplay. In 1998, Bernard F. Dick put it this way: "the script recedes into the background as it changes from a verbal to a visual text, so that by the time the film has been complete, the words have been translated into images."[38] Like those film adaptations that begin with dissolving shots of their founding novels, this aesthetic represents the displacement of the film word by the film image as a cardinal principle of filmmaking. Such an aesthetics is partial and false: the bulk of most screenplays consists of dialogue, which enters film directly as words; again, word and image rivalries overshadow objective analysis. Such rhetorical displacements did not, however, originate with the discourse on film. Discussions of the Victorian novel engage in similar rhetoric, fostering a similar war between words and images.

## Prose "Painting"

Although film discourse inherited the film "language" analogy more directly from a centuries-old rhetoric that figured painting as a language, its use of analogy to claim verbal properties for its images while denigrating its literal words far more closely resembles efforts by nineteenth-century novelists and critics to claim pictorial capacities for prose words while denigrating the novel's literal pictures – its illustrations.[39] Analogies that represent a novel's prose as "painting" were as ubiquitous in the nineteenth and early twentieth centuries as film language analogies have been in the twentieth and early twenty-first centuries. Everywhere one turns, one finds novel writers aspiring to painting by analogy. To cite just a few, in the preface to the 1838 edition, Charles Dickens insisted that he had "painted" *Oliver Twist*.[40] In 1843, Edward Bulwer-Lytton declared: "To my mind, a writer should sit down to compose a fiction as a painter prepares to compose a picture."[41] In 1859, George Eliot opened *Adam Bede* with a claim of the magical hieroglyphic powers of her pen and ink.[42] In 1872, Thomas Hardy subtitled his novel, *Under the Greenwood Tree*, "A Rural Painting in the Dutch School." In 1881, Henry James published his prose *Portrait of Lady*. In 1897, Joseph Conrad wrote that fiction "must strenuously aspire . . . to the colour of painting."[43] References to prose as painting are so pervasive that Mario Praz nominated *ut pictura poesis* as "the golden rule . . . of nineteenth-century narrative literature."[44]

Prose painting analogies pervade nineteenth-century periodical reviews of novels to such an extent that it is difficult to find one that does not speak of prose in terms of painting, or of characterizations as portraits, or of the novel as a canvas, or of prose style in terms of painting schools, or of writers by analogy to well-known painters. Reviews of *Vanity Fair* offer representative examples. In 1848, Elizabeth Rigby praised Thackeray's verbal characterization by analogy to *plein air* portraiture: "There is that mutual dependence in his characters which is the first requisite in painting every-day life: no one is stuck on a separate pedestal – no one is sitting for his portrait."[45] George Henry Lewes agreed: "We feel that he is painting after Nature."[46] Robert Bell in the same year extended the analogy to the novel as canvas: "Into this picture all sorts of portraits are freely admissible. There is nothing too base or too low to be huddled up in a corner of the canvass [sic]."[47] A writer for the *North British Review* comparing Dickens to Thackeray in 1851 determined that "it will assist us very much in our discriminations if we call to mind, by way of illustration, the leading distinctions of style and faculty in the kindred art of painting." Likening Thackeray to Hogarth, Wilkie, Maclise, and Watteau, and comparing Dickens to Landseer, Leech, Wilkie, Rembrandt, and Maclise, this reviewer designates Thackeray an artist of the "Real School of Low Art" and Dickens a writer in the "Ideal School of High Art."[48]

Just as film's literal words have suffered critical neglect as film language analogies have flourished, so, too, the novel's literal illustrations suffered a similar neglect even as prose painting analogies proliferated. In 1848, Robert Bell devoted thirteen pages to the prose of *Vanity Fair*, but only a brief paragraph to the illustrations. His account of the prose abounds in analogies to painting:

> The life that is here painted is not that of high comedy, but of satiric farce . . . He knows his sitters well and has drawn them to life . . . he seizes upon the small details which make up the whole business of the kind of life he paints with a minuteness, precision, and certainty, and throws them out with a sharpness of outline and depth of colour rarely if ever equalled.

When Bell turns to the illustrations, he represents them in generic or technological terms, in much the same way as screenplays become "blueprints" in film criticism:

> We ought to say something about the illustrations of our artist-author, for he gathers laurels in both fields. The humour of the plates is broad and sketchy, and full of the same cynical spirit which pervades the text. The characterization is equally keen and striking. Becky is especially excellent . . . [and] the grotesque Dobbin, the surly Osborne, the radiant O'Dowd, are all capital, and hit off at the top of their peculiarities with a bold and brilliant pencil.

In this account, drawings of characters are not "portraits" (the prose has usurped that term), but more generally and generically "characterization."[49] Neither are the illustrations "drawings"; they are instead "plates," a term emphasizing their technological modes of reproduction over their artistic means of production. This term further casts them hierarchically below prose "painting" as an applied rather than a fine art. The reference to the "sketchy" qualities of the plates alternatively renders them cruder visual forms than painting – even a preliminary stage of painting.[50] Gleeson White noted in 1897 the widespread condescending admiration that decreed a novel illustration to be "a composition worthy of being painted."[51]

Prose painting analogies, however, worked more effectively to excise illustrations in publication practice than film language analogies did to eradicate words. While critics like Harrington and Dick make the destruction of the word a cardinal principle of film art, few films have proved willing or able to excise their words. But a century earlier, critics like Henry James marshaled prose painting analogies to argue successfully for the eradication of book illustrations from adult novels.[52] In 1884, James claimed that "the analogy between the art of the painter and the art of the novelist is, so far as I am able to see, complete."[53] Here he refers to a one-sided completion, in which prose has aspired and attained to all the functions of painting. Twenty-five years later, as new styles of illustration increasingly drew popular attention away from their accompanying prose, James urged a more annihilating analogical triumph, declaring prose sufficiently pictorial to do without illustration at all. Conceding the popular and critical consensus that "The essence of any representational work [verbal or visual] is of course to bristle with immediate images," he declared "a [drawn] picture by another hand on my own [prose] picture" to be "a lawless incident . . . That relieves responsible prose of the duty of being, while placed before us, good enough, interesting enough and, if the question be of picture, pictorial enough, above all *in itself*."[54] Although other factors certainly contributed to the excision of illustrations from novels, these and similar analogies played their part. One could posit that the refusal and/or failure of film to excise its words accounts for the persistence and prevalence of the film language analogy, while the prose painting analogy died concurrently with novel illustration, its task of dominating literal pictures complete.

Moreover, that authors, critics, and publishers grew most eager to excise illustrations from novels precisely as film was gaining ascendancy in popular culture suggests that word/image wars within these hybrid arts intersected with interdisciplinary rivalries fought in the name of words and images, as film and prose fiction vied for cultural dominance in the early years of the twentieth century. Even as prose proponents like James pressed for the excision of book illustrations, film advocates strained film toward an aesthetic of pure images. Filmmakers and scholars from the earliest days of film to the present have exalted the pinnacle of filmic representation as one entirely free from verbal language. David Bordwell, Janet Staiger, and Kristin Thompson document that film without verbal intertitles was a prevalent filmic ideal between 1913 and 1916 in America.[55] At the other end of the twentieth century, film historian James Card rhapsodizes over "silent films so eloquent in their pantomime that they needed no intertitles whatsoever – no dialogue, no explanatory titles, just pure, uninterrupted images. What a boon to international distribution – no language barrier anywhere!"[56] Yet silent-film historian Kevin Brownlow attests that "Eliminating titles . . . could be done . . . it *was* done; but the results were invariably grossly overlength. Tortuously explanatory visual passages were needed to dispense with one simple title."[57] If film was winning the battle for cultural dominance, it was losing the race toward semiotic purism. It is in this context that interdisciplinary analogical rhetoric joins intradisciplinary word/image analogies, casting early film as "book illustration" and early film words as "literature." In so doing, each art claims owner-ship of the other and denies eschewed aspects of itself in the name of the other, though not in exactly similar ways.

## Film as Book Illustration

Although novel prose had won the battle with novel illustrations, by the 1910s, a new, super-illustration had arrived. Wherever we turn in the early days of film, we find first literary film adaptation heralded as a superior form of book illustration, then film more generally, and beyond that, worded films set in rivalry with illustrated books as pictorial narratives. A reviewer of the 1915 *Vanity Fair* adduces that "the reels make a set of illustrations superior to the conventional pen-pictures of a deluxe edition."[58] In 1921, a *New York Times* reviewer heralds a film that is "much more worth seeing than all the illustrated novels and plays turned out in a year."[59] Increasingly, the rhetoric evolves into one of word against image, with novels and theater cast into the word camp and film into the image camp. (The rhetorical battle was still, however, film against "litera-ture.") A review of Ernst Lubitsch's 1925 *Lady Windemere's Fan* asserts that "a good story can be made a better picture . . . sheerly through cinematic qualities . . . when it does this, it is doing what is beyond the power of the written word in books and the spoken word on the stage."[60] Here, the word becomes cinematic image and trumps the word.

Culturally speaking, historians of Western book illustration largely agree that film replaced the illustrated book. In 1947, illustration historian Philip James assessed: "Illustrated fiction, once a source of rivalry between all the great publishing houses and the illus-trator's main occupation, has now given way to screen fiction."[61] Although prose had won the battle with illustrations over the production of images in the novel, increasingly in the first half of the twentieth century, literary voices cede images to film.[62] Not only were novels being adapted to film, novelists were also having to adapt to film. Leo Tolstoy wrote on his eightieth birthday in 1908:

> You will see that the little clicking contraption with the revolving handle will make a revo-lution in our life – in the life of writers. It is a direct attack on the old methods of literary art. We shall have to adapt ourselves to the shadowy screen and to the cold machine. A new form of writing will be necessary. I have thought of that and I can feel what is coming.[63]

Bluestone ascertains that, in the wake of film's ability to so vividly and immediately represent visual and dramatic narrative, "The novel has tended to retreat more and more from external action to internal thought, from plot to character, from social to psychological realities."[64] Although literary critics continue to argue the superiority of mental images derived from words over actual pictures,[65] Ellen J. Esrock documents a relinquishment of even mental images by numerous twentieth-century writers.[66] Such concessions, together with widespread assertions that the high modern novel is unfilmable, have sought to carve out new word and image territories for novels and films. The novel's retreat from its own pictorial aspirations is followed by a taunt that film cannot follow.[67]

When films do try to follow books by filming them, literati turn the very rhetoric they had once used to so successfully diminish and eradicate book illustrations against these adaptations. William Luhr's essay, "Dickens's Narrative, Hollywood's Vignettes," makes MGM's 1935 adaptation of *David Copperfield* a plural miscellany of that clinging vine of illustration, the vignette, in contrast to the prose, which alone is accorded narrative status.[68] The essay continually asserts the book's superiority and mocks the film's narrative pretensions. More central to interdisciplinary discourse, Geoffrey Wagner's influential categories of literary film adaptation rank "transposition" – scornfully referenced as "book illustration" – lowest as the "least satisfying," and the most common form of adaptation. In denigrating transposition, Wagner cites literary criticism of book illustrations, namely I. A. Richards's comment that "all illustrations are disappointing," and he notes condescendingly: "They usually are, except to children; and Hollywood was for long making films for children of all ages."[69] The literal banishment of illustration to children's books in publishing practice here analogically fuels the critical relegation of popular films and their consumers to the nursery.

Analogies that represent adaptation as book illustration continue. In 1992, John Orr suggested the term "picture-book" to replace the more common nomenclature, "literary film adaptation." His essay gives no indication that adapted novels themselves may be illustrated, but represents the novel as pure prose. The picture-book in his formulation is subservient to the novel and words: "At its most powerful, [a picture-book] illustrates the power of the text by persuading us to read it . . . it graphically reminds us of textual power." The purpose of the literary film adaptation is less to "illustrate" the story and characters and more to promote the cultural "power of the text."[70] It is to lead viewers away from picture-books to pure prose. It is thus more book jacket than book, blurby praise of the text, a pictorial hook leading away from itself to pure prose. In diametric opposition to aesthetics that makes the displacement of the word by the image a founding principle of film art, Orr's theory of adaptation restores the primacy of the word over the image. Orr and the other critics who speak of film analogically as book illustration wage interdisciplinary word and image wars with intradisciplinary rhetoric. It is a rhetoric that proved successful against illustrations. But it is a spectral rhetoric fighting ghosts rather than realities.

---

## Film Words as Literature

Just as film and film adaptation have been figured as book illustration, so too film words have been figured as literature. Just as film-as-book-illustration analogies ceded literature's pictorial territory to film, so too film-words-as-literature analogies ceded film's verbal territory to literature. In 1923, filmmaker Ernst Lubitsch wrote: "In our titles we borrow from the stage or the novel. Later we will have discovered the motion picture style . . . I try to exclude titles wherever possible . . . [and] have every scene speak for itself."[71] The word "borrow" implies that words do not belong to film, but rather constitute temporary literary loans until film's images can speak for themselves. In 1928, Ukrainian theorist Leonid Skrypnyk complained: "Cinema has to humiliate itself and seek compromises [with literature]. Intertitles constitute the first major compromise."[72] In 1925, a reviewer complained that verbal intertitles were "literary hemorrhages" sullying film art.[73]

When intertitles give way to spoken dialogue, critics and filmmakers attack it as a reinfestation of film by literature, rather than a new technology or an integral component of film. Historian Gerald Mast is typical: "Although the post-Griffith silent film had declared its independence from the stage, the early sound film became the vassal of the theatre once again . . . The moving picture stopped moving and stopped using pictures. Critics and directors sang a requiem for film art and said amen."[74] In other accounts, synchronized sound is simultaneously hailed as a rescue from the tyranny of intertitles and resisted as a new verbal oppressor: "the sound film had liberated the cinema from its thirty-year bondage to the printed word," says one historian. "The task now was not to re-shackle the medium to the spoken word of the talkie."[75] Strikingly, no such objections emerge regarding the music or sound effects that synchronized sound also brought to film. Arthur Knight's account is representative. Before sound can be Knight-ed as a *bona fide* part of film art under the subheading "The Art of the Sound Film," it must first traverse Knight's other subheadings: "The Tyranny of Sound," "Liberating the Camera," "Mastering the Sound Track," and "Exploring the New Medium," a rhetoric of emphatic subjugation, glorious revolution, power reversal, and venturesome colonization.[76]

The designation of film words as "literary" other, to be resisted, mastered, and colonized continues in other decades and discourses over other film words. Sarah Kozloff documents "the conventional notion that films caught voice-over (like the measles?) from novels."[77] Richard L. Stromgren and Martin F. Norden represent two among hundreds of critics who declare any kind of verbal narration in film to be an "uncinematic" throwback to literary modes of story-telling.[78]

At times, film-words-as-literature analogies combine with film-images-as-language analogies to further relegate film words. In "Film Language," Eisenstein castigates film words both as uncinematic and as bad literature. The talking film, he claims, "even before cinematically appraising it, contains so much poverty of a purely literary sort that its film claims may be put aside." A few pages later he urges "film-workers" to emulate the "speech and word" of "the great masters of literature" in their "montage and shots," developing each "montage sequence with as much care as a line of poetry is admitted into a poem."[79] Film words are denied "film claims" both on grounds of not being cinematography and of being poor literature, while filmic visuals are hailed as cinematic and as analogical purveyors of great "literature."

When intertitle writers did try to improve their art, it was figured as a literary affair. As a 1921 essay notes:

> Picturegoers of to-day who can recall the early days of the kinema industry will retain memories of the crude and ugly explanatory sub-titles that once disfigured the silver sheet. In those days the sub-title was regarded as a necessary blemish on the face of the film, and no attempt was made towards either literary or artistic improvement.[80]

Producers of the 1920s and 1930s sought to improve the quality of film scripts by importing literary luminaries, like James Barrie, Joseph Conrad, and F. Scott Fitzgerald, with little or no success. Accounts of these efforts also indicate interdisciplinary wranglings over the word. Literary critic Edmund Wilson blamed Hollywood for the early deaths and wasted talents of Fitzgerald and Nathaniel West: "both West and Fitzgerald were writers of conscience and with natural gifts rare enough in America or anywhere and their failure to get the best out of their years may certainly be laid partly to Hollywood, with its already appalling record of talent depraved and wasted."[81] However, film critic Bernard F. Dick takes the opposite tack, attributing Fitzgerald's failure to his lack of talent as a screenwriter.[82] Elsewhere, literature/film word rivalries took more politicized forms. A 1920 advertisement for the Irving System of Photoplay Writing decrees: "Millions of People Can Write Stories and Photoplays and Don't Know It! Don't you believe the Creator gave you a story-writing faculty, just as He did the greatest writer?"[83]

Early film adaptations of Victorian novels point to additional interdisciplinary rivalries between films and novels over the word. Edison's 1915 film of *Vanity Fair* does not include a single line of Thackeray's prose (only place and character names remain): here, filmic attempts at "literary improvement" take on the added sense of improving on the literary text. Readers must judge for themselves whether intertitles like "George's love for Amelia has commenced to wane" or "A cold grey dawn and a dark brown taste" improve on Thackeray's prose. Other attempts at improvement on literary originals range from puns – "Mr Sowerberry, the Undertaker, whose need of five pounds provides Oliver a chance to study a grave occupation" – to metaphors – "And each night Oliver sought rest amid the terrifying souvenirs of eternal sleep"[84] – to moralistic, melodramatic prose:

> Eighteen years have passed since Honoria Barbary became Lady Dedlock. In the magnificence of her surroundings, and under the soothing touch of time, her former romance has faded into a sad memory. [scene shot] The impulsive girl of years ago is now a cold and haughty leader of society, concealing her womanly emotions behind a mask.[85]

We see, then, that analogies that make film words "literature" run along various lines to foster various interdisciplinary rivalries: from resenting film words as literary encroachments, to castigating film words as bad literature, to subjecting film words to "literary" modes of improvement, to film words striving to outdo literary words.

The final sections of this chapter turn to test such analogical rhetoric against the evidence of aesthetic practice. The first considers connections between book illustration and film's analogical "language," montage; the last examines the role of verbal intertitles in the development of film's montage.

---

## Book Illustration and Film "Language"

For all the discussions of the Victorian novel's influence on film, no scholar has credited its illustrations with shaping film techniques. John L. Fell's *Film and the Narrative Tradition* points to a host of influences on film: advertisements, woodcuts, comic strips, stereograph cards, chromoliths, dime novels, dioramas, sheet music, and more, but it does not mention novel illustrations.[86] Some scholars of literary film adaptation have noted the influence of novel illustrations on the visuals. Publicity for MGM's 1935 *David Copperfield*, for example, juxtaposes life-sized enlargements of Phiz's illustrations to stills of the film's actors, cast, costumed, and positioned to appear like *tableaux vivants* of the drawings.[87] In 1948, David Lean defended his ultra-racist caricature of Fagin (Alec Guinness) by its resemblance to George Cruikshank's illustrations for *Oliver Twist*. In 1999, Marc Munden, director of the BBC's most recent televisation of *Vanity Fair*, described the production as "gritty . . . like a caricature by the cartoonists of the time, men like Cruikshank and Rowlandson."[88]

But no one has yet noted that certain Victorian novel illustration practices offer precursors of film montage. As we have seen, it is montage more than any other aspect of film that forms the basis of film images' claim to language, for, scholars argue, montage creates syntactic relationships between images. Filmmaker D. W. Griffith said that he gleaned editing techniques from Charles Dickens. Yet Griffith does not credit the illustrations of these books.

The standard version of film history[89] traces a progression from single-shot scenes filming whole bodies with static cameras to multiple-shot scenes combining shots of various sizes at various angles filmed with both static and moving cameras. It argues that montage within and between scenes differentiates film from static visual arts and forms a pictorial equivalent of verbal language, as in the novel. While most of the illustrations for *Vanity Fair* depict characters from head to toe, after theater and portrait conventions, as do the earliest films, some illustrations create montage sequences within a chapter. The pictorial initial that opens chapter 1 of *Vanity Fair*, for example, depicts a carriage waiting outside Miss Pinkerton's academy. A page turn produces a reverse angle and shows characters in the interior of this building: one looks out of the window at the waiting carriage. Subsequent illustrations in this chapter provide additional angles and perspectives of the carriage and characters in various sizes and from various angles. The full-page plate of Becky throwing the dictionary offers a larger, closer "shot" of the carriage than the pictorial initial; the end-piece reduces the size of the carriage and changes the angle of view yet again, showing its back as it drives from the school and out of the chapter, a technique common in Western films (in both senses of the word "Western"), as horse-borne heroes ride off into the horizon. Many other similar examples can be found in other illustrated Victorian novels. But the point here is less to multiply examples than to argue that the lack of critical commentary on such readily apparent, simple continuities cannot derive from their rarity, complexity, or obscurity. Rather, it must result from the word and image rivalries that have so clouded critical objectivity for more than a century. It emerges as almost comical that critical rhetoric insists on film as book illustration analogically, yet overlooks ways in which actual illustrations may have directly influenced film techniques. To do so, however, would require a reconsideration of film images' claim to language and undermine the rivalries that it fosters.

---

## Film Words and Film "Language"

---

Aesthetic practice also supports an opposite and equally disruptive challenge to standard theories of how film montage developed and of its purely pictorial operations. Another view of film montage history runs thus: intertitles constituted a temporary crutch while film fumbled toward its manifest destiny, the development of a purely visual language through montage. The historical and aesthetic task of early film was to shake off its dependence on verbal language to narrate and replace it with an analogical visual "language" in montage. Editing within and between filmed scenes produced a visual syntax that lessened the need for verbal intertitles.[90] André Gaudreault is typical: "until the narrative faculties of *editing* had been further developed – this narrator would carry out the work of narration through the use of words, of articulated language, either in written form (intertitles) or oral form (speaker)."[91]

The evidence, however, does not support the argument. While some films used fewer intertitles, the vast majority of Anglo-American dramatic films used more frequent and more prolix intertitles as montage developed. Two films of *Oliver Twist* made in 1912 and in 1922 exemplify the general trend and offer especially focused points of comparison, since they purport to adapt the same novel. The 1912 Thomas Bentley adaptation bears between seven and eight intertitles per reel, while the 1922 First National version carries eighteen per reel. The cards are not only more frequent, but also lengthier. The 1912 "Rose saves Oliver, who is adopted by Mrs Maylie" becomes "Bill's murderous purpose was thwarted by the Providence of a just God and Oliver quickly recovered from the slight wound in his shoulder."[92]

Adding to this perplexing discrepancy between film history and the evidence of aesthetic practice, not one historian contests that the intertitles grew longer and more frequent during the late silent period: they simply do not see the contradiction. Instead, they focus on filmmaker efforts to make shifts between intertitles and scenes – between words and images – less jarring. Yet none addresses montage techniques designed to do exactly this: montage sequences that interweave intertitles and filmed scenes to form hybrid verbal-visual "sentences" governed by verbal syntax. In this practice, another substantial challenge to theories of film "language" and of montage emerges.

In the late silent period (generally set at 1918–26), narrative intertitles do not always form complete grammatical sentences, but are often fragments or dependent clauses for which filmed scenes function as main clauses. The final two cards of Nordisk's 1924 *Little Dorrit* read: (1) "Beyond the sombre shadow of the Marshalsea . . ." and (2) "And that was one hundred years ago." Between these sentence fragments, the scene of Little Dorrit's wedding to Arthur Clennam forms the main clause of a hybrid visual-verbal filmic sentence.[93] Far from begrudged necessities explaining the plot, as critics so often construct intertitles to be, these intertitles are informationally dispensable. But they provide rhetorical and rhythmic effects, closure and enclosure for filmed scenes within a verbal structure. Such practices were widespread in this period. In the 1920 *Bleak House*, for example, of the forty-nine narrative intertitles that are not introductory descriptions of characters, thirty-three begin with conjunctions or dependent clauses or constitute incomplete sentences.[94]

What we see is that editing between intertitles and scenes in the late silent period is frequently constructed according to verbal syntax and speech rhythms, rather than to the syntax of image narrative that traditional film histories privilege. The intertitles of the 1922 *Vanity Fair* are punctuated (as are many late silent film intertitles) with ellipses that can only suggest declamatory pauses. One card from the film reads:

> The seeming ease with which Becky obtained her entrée into the exclusive society of "Gaunt House" . . . rather alarmed her husband . . . but he had no suspicions . . . It was natural that she should shine in society . . . she was made to shine there . . . Was there any woman like her?[95]

Some later silent films replace such ellipses with scene shots. In *The Only Way* (a 1926 adaptation of *A Tale of Two Cities*), as Carton waxes earnest in his courtroom defense of Darnay, his speech is punctuated with scene shots:

> England hated Evrémonde as much as he loves France! [*scene shot*] All that a man can do for France, that man has done. [*scene shot*] He renounced his name, title, wealth, estate – he flung them to the wind [*scene shot*] and went to earn his living in a strange land. [*scene shot*] That was like a man – a real man, [*scene shot*] a man who loved his country much, but liberty and manhood more! [*scene shot*] You, Builders of a New World, will you not forgive that man? [*scene shot*] His fault is a Name – his atonement a Life. [*scene shot*] This man who we all know, the Prisoner of the Bastille, [*scene shot*] DOCTOR MANETTE!!! [*scene shot*] He has given him his gentle daughter, Lucy [sic].[96]

The shots here do more than indicate speaker and auditors, since they repeatedly show the same speaker and auditors. They function rhetorically, conforming the rhythms of film editing to the rhythms and pauses of speech.

Such rhetorically based modes of editing are not limited to dialogue cards: they extend to narrative intertitles. Another sequence in this film runs as follows:

*Intertitle*: Then, sixteen years . . .
*Long shot*: *Marquis and guests feasting*
*Intertitle*: . . . Years that to Evrémonde recorded only the passing of Time
*Midshot*: *Marquis and guests*
*Intertitle*: Years that so changed another, that even, freed from the Bastille, the twilight of his mind held him prisoner
*Midshot*: *Manette holds a shoe, stares vacantly at the camera, then lowers his eyes*
*Long shot*: *a concerned Defarge, Lorry, and Lucie standing near Manette*
*Intertitle*: Years that burned the hatred of a decadent aristocracy into one having reason to hate
*Midshot*: *Defarge speaks*[97]

Here, the semantic and syntactic relationships of the sequence are established by the run-on verbal sentence of the intertitles rather than by visual syntactic relationships between scene shots (between looker and looked at, actor and reactor, actor and object). The shots perform both visual and aural functions, doubling as illustrations of and as rhetorical spacers between the intertitles.

Even from these brief examples, it is clear that the illustrations of Victorian novels and the intertitles of silent films complicate standard theories of film montage and call for new investigations of film's relationship to the Victorian novel and its influence on film's aesthetic history. This chapter as a whole demonstrates that the casting of novels and films into word and image camps, respectively, may have done more to obscure and falsify interdisciplinary study than to elucidate it, and that interdisciplinary rivalries, together with broader word and image wars, may have falsified film theory and novel theory separately as well. In these tanglings, the interdisciplinary paradox that simultaneously opposes and connects novels and films begins to clarify and points the evidence of aesthetic practice that contradicts it to more complex word and image engagements both within and between the two media.

--- Notes ---

1   Roland Barthes, "The Photographic Message," in *Image–Music–Text*, ed. and trans. Stephen Heath (New York: Hill and Wang, 1977), p. 205.
2   Elsewhere he writes: "The drawing of the pipe and the text that ought to name it cannot find a place to meet," in Michel Foucault, *This Is Not a Pipe*, trans. James Harkness (Berkeley, CA: University of California Press, 1981), p. 36.
3   J. Hillis Miller, *Illustration* (Cambridge, MA: Harvard University Press, 1992), p. 95.
4   W. J. T. Mitchell, "Going Too Far with the Sister Arts," in James A. W. Heffernan (ed.), *Space, Time, Image, Sign: Essays on Literature and the Visual Arts* (New York: Peter Lang, 1987), p. 1 (emphasis in original).

Novels, Films, and the Word/Image Wars

Chapter 1

5   W. J. T. Mitchell, *Iconology: Image, Text, Ideology* (Chicago: University of Chicago Press, 1986), p. 43.

6   Gotthold Ephraim Lessing, *Laocoön: An Essay upon the Limits of Painting and Poetry* (1766).

7   This taxonomy builds on a more expansive set of poetry and painting differentiations developed since Lessing. George Bluestone, *Novels into Film* (Berkeley, CA: University of California Press, 1957), pp. vi–vii, 61.

8   Ibid., pp. 218, 1–64.

9   E. H. Gombrich, for example, contests the naturalness of the visual sign and advances the temporality of painting, Murray Krieger propounds the spatiality of literary representation, while W. J. T. Mitchell has brought the space–time continuum to bear on the temporal/spatial dichotomy. See E. H. Gombrich, "Moment and Movement in Art," *Journal of Warburg and Courtauld Institutes* 27 (1964) and "Meditations on a Hobby Horse," in *Meditations on a Hobby Horse and Other Essays on the Theory of Art* (London: Phaidon, 1963); Murray Krieger, "The Ekphrastic Principle and the Still Movement of Poetry; or *Laokoon* Revisited," in *The Play and Place of Criticism* (Baltimore, MD: The Johns Hopkins University Press, 1976); W. J. T. Mitchell, "Spatial Form in Literature: Toward a General Theory," *Critical Inquiry* 6 (Spring 1980). More recently, an issue of *Eighteenth-century Fiction* 10: 4 (July 1998) was devoted to spatiality in literature.

10  Keith Cohen, *Film and Fiction: The Dynamics of Exchange* (New Haven, CT: Yale University Press, 1979), p. 4. See also Keith Cohen, "Eisenstein's Subversive Adaptation," in G. Peary and R. Shatzkin (eds), *The Classic American Novel and the Movies* (New York: Ungar, 1977), p. 255.

11  J. Dudley Andrew, *Concepts in Film Theory* (Oxford: Oxford University Press, 1984), p. 103.

12  Brian McFarlane, *Novel to Film: An Introduction to the Theory of Adaptation* (Oxford: Clarendon Press, 1996), pp. 26–8. An earlier book by McFarlane is entitled *Words and Images: Australian Novels into Film* (Melbourne: Heinemann, 1983).

13  See, for example, Deborah Cartmell and Imelda Whelehan (eds), *Adaptation: From Text to Screen, Screen to Text* (New York: Routledge, 1999), p. 11.

14  I am keenly aware that most films are more than word and image arts, incorporating elements of music and other art forms as well. However, within the confines of this chapter, I am interested only in word and image dynamics.

15  Bluestone, *Novels into Film*, p. 211.

16  Ralph Stephenson and J. R. Debrix, *The Cinema as Art* (London: Penguin, 1978; first published 1965), pp. 199, 202, 200. Most of the chapter on film sound deals with music and nonverbal sound; the five pages on film words do not run continuously.

17  Christian Metz, "The Cinema: Language or Language System?," in *Film Language: A Semiotics of the Cinema*, trans. Michael Taylor (Chicago: University of Chicago Press, 1991), p. 58 (emphasis in original).

18  Gilles Deleuze, *Cinema 2: The Time-Image*, trans. Hugh Tomlinson and Robert Galeta (Minneapolis, MN: University of Minnesota Press, 1989), pp. 226, 233. Elsewhere, Deleuze advocates a dialectic of sound and image that builds on early Russian theories of film, but even here, the term "sound image" replicates, though to a lesser degree than prior theories, the definition of film as "images" and the subordination of sound to a rubric of "image."

19 Some scholars have addressed novel illustrations, arguing their essential and integral role, but they constitute a decided minority. See, for example, Joan Stevens's numerous essays on Thackeray's illustrations to *Vanity Fair*.

20 London: Bradbury, 1847.

21 Oxford: Oxford University Press, 1931.

22 New York: New American Library, 1962.

23 Boston: Houghton Mifflin, 1963.

24 New York: Norton, 1994. This edition restores Thackeray's illustrations, but includes verbal annotations and commentaries as well.

25 New York: Garland, 1989.

26 These words appear in the subtitles of the Norton and Garland editions.

27 Sergei Eisenstein, "Dickens, Griffith, and the Film Today," in *Film Form: Essays in Film Theory*, ed. and trans. Jay Leyda (New York: Harcourt, Brace and World, 1949; first published 1944), pp. 195–255, quotation on p. 195.

28 See, for example, Keith Cohen, *Film and Fiction: The Dynamics of Exchange* (New Haven, CT: Yale University Press, 1979); Claude-Edmonde Magny, *The Age of the American Novel: The Film Aesthetic of Fiction between the Two Wars* (New York: Frederick Ungar, 1972; first published 1948); and Seymour Chatman, *Story and Discourse: Narrative Structure in Fiction and Film* (Ithaca, NY: Cornell University Press, 1978).

29 See, for example, Deborah Cartmell, I. Q. Hunter, Heidi Kaye, and Imelda Whelehan (eds), *Pulping Fictions: Consuming Culture Across the Literature/Media Divide* (London: Pluto Press, 1996) and Deborah Cartmell and Imelda Whelehan (eds), *Adaptations: From Text to Screen, Screen to Text* (New York: Routledge, 1999).

30 Christian Metz, *The Imaginary Signifier: Psychoanalysis and the Cinema*, trans. Celia Britton, Annwyl Williams, Ben Brewster, and Alfred Guzzetti (Bloomington, IN: Indiana University Press, 1977), p. 110.

31 Bluestone, *Novels into Film*, p. 2.

32 Metz, *Film Language*, p. 64.

33 Vachel Lindsay, *The Art of the Moving Picture* (New York: Macmillan, 1915), p. 161.

34 "The Screen: A Movie of the Prairies," *The New York Times* (March 17, 1923), 9; review of D. W. Griffith's *A Corner in Wheat*, "Reviews of Licensed Films," *The New York Dramatic Mirror* 62.1618 (December 25, 1909), 15.

35 Sergei Eisenstein, "Film Language," in *Film Form*, pp. 108–21.

36 Roland Barthes also writes of the "rhetoric of the image." Marie-Claire Ropars-Wuilleumier, *De la littérature au cinéma: genése d'une écriture* (Paris: A. Colin, 1970).

37 John Harrington (ed.), *Film and/as Literature* (Englewood Cliffs, NJ: Prentice-Hall, 1977), pp. 102–3.

38 Bernard F. Dick, *Anatomy of Film*, 3rd edn (New York: St Martin's Press, 1998), p. 220. Like Harrington, he sees screenplays as of primarily archival and scholarly interest: "Still, a serious student of film will always look for the screenwriter's name in the credits."

39 Rensselaer W. Lee, in his *Ut Pictura Poesis: The Humanistic Theory of Painting* (New York: Norton, 1967), notes that the idea of painting as a universal language appeared in the Renaissance. It had a particularly robust airing in the nineteenth century: in 1843 John Ruskin wrote: "Painting, or art generally, with all its technicalities, difficulties, and particular ends, is nothing but a noble and expressive language." John Ruskin, "The Theory of Expression,"

chapter 2 of *Modern Painters* (London: Smith, Elder, 1843). Mary Barton referred to painting in 1890 as a "universal language," a phrase Edmund J. Sullivan extended to book illustrations in 1921. Mary Barton cited in Gerard Curtis, "Shared Lines: Pen and Pencil as Trace," in Carol T. Christ and John O. Jordan (eds), *Victorian Literature and the Victorian Visual Imagination* (Berkeley, CA: University of California Press, 1995), p. 37; Edmund J. Sullivan, *The Art of Illustration* (London: Chapman Hall, 1921), p. viii.

40   Charles Dickens, *Oliver Twist* (London: Penguin, 1966), pp. 34, 479.

41   Edward Bulwer-Lytton, *The Last of the Barons*, preface. Cited in Richard Stang, *The Theory of the Novel in England, 1850–1879* (New York: Columbia University Press, 1959), p. 12.

42   The opening sentence reads: "With a single drop of ink for a mirror, the Egyptian sorcerer undertakes to reveal to any chance comer far-reaching visions of the past. This is what I undertake to do for you, reader. With this drop of ink at the end of my pen I will show you the roomy workshop of Mr Jonathan Burge, carpenter and builder in the village of Hayslope, as it appeared on the eighteenth of June, in the year of our Lord 1799."

43   Joseph Conrad, preface to *The Nigger of the "Narcissus"* (London: Penguin, 1987), p. xlix. Although Conrad defers to the Aesthetic Movement's claim that music is "the art of arts," his emphasis on vision renders his painterly aspirations more central. Music appears nowhere in his conclusion that "the aim of art [is] to arrest, for the space of a breath, the hands busy about the work of the earth, and compel men entranced by the sight of distant goals to glance for a moment at the surrounding vision of form and colour, of sunshine and shadows; to make them pause for a look, for a sigh, for a smile – such is the aim, difficult and evanescent, and reserved only for a very few to achieve" (p. li).

44   Mario Praz, *The Hero in Eclipse in Victorian Fiction*, trans. Angus Davidson (London: Oxford University Press, 1956), p. 29.

45   Elizabeth Rigby, *Quarterly Review* 84: 167 (December 1848), 162.

46   George Henry Lewes, *The Athenaeum* (August 12, 1848), 795.

47   Robert Bell, *Fraser's Magazine* 38 (September 1848), 320.

48   *North British Review* 15 (May 1851), 68.

49   Bell, *Fraser's Magazine* 38 (September 1848), 320–2, 333.

50   Edmund J. Sullivan is one of many to write of illustration as a "form of applied art" (*The Art of Illustration*, p. v).

51   Gleeson White, *English Illustration: The Sixties, 1855–1870* (Westminster: A. Constable, 1897), p. 10.

52   John Harthan's *The History of the Illustrated Book: The Western Tradition* (London: Thames and Hudson, 1981) provides a succinct overview of the virtual end of novel illustration in the early twentieth century.

53   Henry James, "The Art of Fiction," in *Partial Portraits* (New York: Haskell House, 1968; originally published 1884 in *Longman's Magazine*), p. 378. He continues: "Their inspiration is the same, their process (allowing for the different quality of the vehicle) is the same, their success is the same. They may learn from each other, they may explain and sustain each other. Their cause is the same, and the honour of one is the honour of another."

54   Henry James, preface to *The Golden Bowl: The Art of the Novel*, ed. R. P. Blackmur (New York: Scribner's, 1947; originally published 1909), pp. x–xi.

55   David Bordwell, Janet Staiger, and Kristin Thompson, *The Hollywood Classical Cinema: Film Style and Mode of Production to 1960* (London: Routledge and Kegan Paul, 1985).

56    James Card, *Seductive Cinema: The Art of Silent Film* (New York: Knopf, 1994), p. 60. Such claims make dubious assumptions regarding the language of objects. Cultures contain many objects specific to themselves, requiring translation or explication for other cultures.

57    Kevin Brownlow, *The Parade's Gone By* (New York: Ballantine, 1968), pp. 334–5.

58    *Boston Transcript* (January 11, 1916), cited in Robert A. Colby, "'Scenes of All Sorts . . .': *Vanity Fair* on Stage and Screen," *Dickens Studies Annual* 9 (1981), 178.

59    Review of *Shattered*, "Screen: Pictorial Efficiency," *The New York Times* (December 11, 1921), section 6: 3.

60    Anon, "Exceptional Photoplays: *Lady Windemere's Fan*," *National Board of Review Magazine* 1: 1 (March–April, 1926), 11–12.

61    Philip James, *English Book Illustration 1800–1900* (London: King Penguin, 1947), p. 9. See also Harthan, *History of the Illustrated Book*.

62    Henryk Markiewicz notes similar tendencies in the twentieth-century branch of the poetry/ painting debate. See his "Ut Pictura Poesis . . . A History of the Topos and the Problem," *New Literary History* 18: 3 (Spring 1987), 535–59.

63    Cecile Starr, *Discovering the Movies* (New York: Van Nostrand Reinhold, 1972), p. 32.

64    Bluestone, *Novels into Film*, p. 46.

65    Donald Hannah's 1966 evaluation of *Vanity Fair*'s illustrations, which assesses that "the pen does not really need (and can even be hampered by) the pencil" and attacks illustrations in general as one-dimensional, lacking implication and complexity, distracting the reader, and as too explicit to allow for imagination, is typical. Donald Hannah, "'The Author's Own Candles': The Significance of the Illustrations to *Vanity Fair*," in G. R. Hibbard (ed.), *Renaissance and Modern Essays* (New York: Barnes and Noble, 1966), p. 120.

66    Ellen J. Esrock, *The Reader's Eye: Visual Imaging as Reader Response* (Baltimore, MD: The Johns Hopkins University Press, 1994), p. 32.

67    Most critics concur with Bluestone's argument that "Proust and Joyce would seem . . . absurd on film" (*Novels into Film*, p. 61). See also Ghislaine Géloin, "The Plight of Film Adaptation in France: Toward Dialogic Process in the *Auteur* Film," in Wendell Aycock and Michael Shoenecke (eds), *Film and Literature: A Comparative Approach to Adaptation* (Lubbock: Texas Tech University Press, 1988), p. 136, on the unfilmability of the high modern novel, pp. 135–48.

68    William Luhr, "Dickens's Narrative, Hollywood's Vignettes," in Michael Klein and Gillian Parker (eds), *The English Novel and the Movies* (New York: Frederick Ungar, 1981), pp. 132–92.

69    Geoffrey Wagner, *The Novel and the Cinema* (London: Tanting Press, 1975), p. 223.

70    John Orr, "Introduction: Proust, the Movie," in John Orr and Colin Nicholson (eds), *Cinema and Fiction: New Modes of Adapting 1950–1990* (Edinburgh: Edinburgh University Press, 1992), pp. 1, 4. In another essay, Orr insists: "The book comes first, the film second despite the current temptations of our audio-visual culture": John Orr, "*The Trial* of Orson Welles," in Orr and Nicholson (eds), *Cinema and Fiction*, p. 27.

71    "Lubitsch on Directing," *The New York Times* (December 16, 1923), section 9: 5.

72    Leonid Skrypnyk, *Narysyz teorii mystetstva kino* (Kiev: Derzhavne vyd. Ukraine, 1928), p. 20, trans. and cited in Bohdan Y. Nebesio, "A Compromise with Literature? Making Sense of Intertitles in the Silent Films of Alexander Dovzhenko," *Canadian Review of Comparative Literature* 23: 2 (September 1996), 679–80.

73    "A situation calling for a simple fact such as the passing of a night is liable to blossom forth in such a literary hemorrhage as: 'Came the sweet-voiced harbingers of a new day, putting to rout the somber blackness of the night.'" Peter Milne, *Photoplay* (October 1925), 132.

74   Gerald Mast, *A Short History of the Movies* (Indianapolis, IN: Bobbs-Merrill, 1981), p. 185.

75   David A. Cook, *A History of Narrative Film* (New York: Norton, 1981), p. 252.

76   Arthur Knight, *The Liveliest Art: A Panoramic History of the Movies* (New York: Macmillan, 1957), p. 142ff.

77   Sarah Kozloff, *Invisible Storytellers* (Berkeley, CA: University of California Press, 1988), p. 23.

78   Richard L. Stromgren and Martin F. Norden, *Movies: A Language in Light* (Englewood Cliffs, NJ: Prentice-Hall, 1984), p. 173.

79   Eisenstein, "Film Language," pp. 108, 115. Eisenstein extends the literary analogy from practice to criticism. Lamenting that "in comparison with analyses of [literature] . . . my analysis is still quite descriptive and easy," he offers analogical remedies: "An analysis of the very lenses employed in filming . . . with camera angles and lighting . . . would serve as an exact analogy to an analysis of the expressiveness of phrases and words . . . in a literary work" (p. 120).

80   "The Art of the Sub-Title," *The Picturegoer* (May 1921), 21.

81   Edmund Wilson, *The Boys in the Back Room* (San Francisco: Colt Press, 1941), p. 56.

82   Dick, *Anatomy of Film*, p. 215.

83   Cited in Brownlow, *The Parade's Gone By*, p. 316.

84   Both examples are from the British intertitles written for the First National 1922 *Oliver Twist*, dir. Frank Lloyd, USA. (The American titles differ.)

85   *Bleak House*, Ideal Pictures, 1920.

86   John L. Fell, *Film and the Narrative Tradition* (Norman: University of Oklahoma Press, 1974).

87   I am indebted to Guerric DeBona for this information.

88   Astonishingly, he does not mention Thackeray's illustrations, which are in the same school. A disclaimer of his literary background elsewhere in the interview suggests that he may not be too familiar with the novel (interview on http://www.bbc.co.uk/education/bookcase/bookworm/vanity/vanity5.shtml).

89   I use David Bordwell's term here from his *On the History of Film Style* (Cambridge, MA: Harvard University Press, 1997).

90   As early as 1913, Adolph Zukor, president of Famous Players, informed audiences: "We are trying to let the story tell itself as far as possible. To do this we are introducing more scenes and connecting links." "Telling itself" here implies that story and filmed scenes are synonymous while words are extraneous. Cited in Bordwell et al., *The Hollywood Classical Cinema*, p. 186.

91   André Gaudreault, "Showing and Telling: Image and Word in Early Cinema," in Thomas Elsaesser and Adam Barker (eds), *Early Cinema: Space, Frame, Narrative* (London: British Film Institute, 1990; essay originally published in 1984), p. 277 (emphasis in original).

92   *Oliver Twist*, prod. H. A. Spanuth, Eclair, USA, 1912; *Oliver Twist*, dir. Frank Lloyd, First National, USA, 1922.

93   *Little Dorrit* (*Lille Dorrit*), dir. A. W. Sandberg, Nordisk Films, DN, 1924.

94   *Bleak House*, dir. Maurice Elvey, Ideal Films, UK, 1920.

95   *Vanity Fair*, dir. W. C. Rowden, GB, 1922.

96   *The Only Way*, dir. Herbert Wilcox, UK, 1926.

97   I have omitted actor credits for Manette and Defarge that appear on two of the intertitles.

# Chapter 2

# Sacred Word, Profane Image

## Theologies of Adaptation

## Ella Shohat

Poststructuralist discourses about translation challenge the idiom of "fidelity" and "betrayal" that assumes an innocent correspondence or symmetry between two textual worlds. Rather than a transparent and coherent presentation of an already-existing source, or a process of mimicking an originary text, translation always already involves acts of mediation, constructedness, and representation. At the same time these mediations do not escape the gravitational pull of geography and history; they are shaped and produced within specific cultural contexts that imply a "take" on the very act of translation. As a mode of translation, the adaptation of words into images, or novels into film, has often been seen as an aesthetic challenge involving the movement across two differing, even clashing, media. Yet, the displacement of written text onto a cinematic space, I will suggest here, cannot be appreciated solely in its formal dimension; rather, it must be seen within a larger, millennial movement across philosophical traditions and cultural spaces.

Given that the status of words and images varies widely within and across cultures, how can we speak of adaptation without addressing the veristic substratum haunting both novel and film? What happens, for example, in the movement from word to image within aesthetic traditions where verism has *not* occupied center stage, and where the very act of visual representation has been enmeshed in taboos and prohibitions? Here I want to explore both the multifaceted relations between texts and images as shaped within a Judeo-Islamic space, and the implications of these relations for film as a medium and adaptation as a practice. In fact, the tenuous and problematic dichotomy of image versus word was itself produced within a specific moment of monotheist rupture from polytheism. Yet, over millennia, the word/image clash has never resulted in "pure" religious practices, as is evident from certain syncretisms found even within monotheism. Such syncretism is due, perhaps, to the impossibility of an isolationist approach to the senses. Any negation of the very interdependency of the senses, becomes, to an extent, a futile philosophical endeavor. Since the Enlightenment, the separation of the senses – each endowed with essential qualities, and placed within a hierarchy – acquired a significant scientific meaning; that is, the privileging of the abstract over the concrete, and mind over body. Kant's preference for the sublime of pure reason, for example, secularized, as it were, the monotheist investment in the disembodied God.[1]

The novel's veristic procedures, one might argue, came into existence in an era pressured by two related and diacritical forces: on the one hand, the grounding of modern science in visuality, in the objective gaze, for example in Cartesian perspectivalism that supposes an observing standpoint "outside," and, on the other, a certain aniconism gaining philosophical importance, culminating in the twentieth-century sciences of "language."[2] And yet, unlike figurative representations, the novel as medium retained an a priori affinity with the religion of the word and scripture. Might the denigration of the cinema and adaptation be partially linked to the biblical phobia toward the apparatuses of visual representation? Could some of the hostility to filmic adaptations of novels, one wonders, be traceable in some subliminal and mediated way to this biblical injunction against the fetish of the image, the cult of star worship, and the fabrication of false gods? In what ways has faith in the sacred word provoked contemporary iconoclastic anxiety, perceiving adaptation as an inherently idolatrous betrayal? And how do we begin to account for adaptation when it is not of a book but rather of *The Book*, and one that virtually decrees that it *not* be adapted?[3]

Born in a kind of righteous rage against the fetish of the image, monotheism explicitly prohibited the practice of "graven images" as part of the Ten Commandments, the first "contractual" agreement, or the covenant between God and the People of Israel as mediated by Moses. The first commandment – "Thou shalt have no other Gods before Me" ("*Lo yihie lekha elohim aherim al panai*") – is immediately followed by the second commandment: "Thou shalt not make unto thee any graven image, or any likeness of any thing that is in heaven above, or that is in the earth beneath, or that is in the water under the earth" ("*lo ta'ase lecha pesel kol tmuna asher bashamayim mima'al va-asher ba-aretz mitahat va-asher bamayim mitahat la-aretz*)" (Exodus 20: 3–4). Yet Deuteronomy's verbal mediation in the expression of the taboo on visual representation paradoxically elicits in the reader's mind the very image of what is prohibited:

> Lest ye corrupt yourselves, and make you a graven image, the similitude of any figure, the likeness of male or female, the likeness of any beast that is on the earth, the likeness of any winged fowl that flieth in the air, the likeness of any thing that creepeth on the ground, the likeness of any fish that is in the waters beneath the earth: and lest thou lift up thine eyes unto heaven, and when thou seest the sun, and the moon, and the stars, even all the host of heaven, shouldest be driven to worship them, and serve them, which the LORD thy God hath divided unto all nations under the whole heaven. (Deuteronomy 4: 16–19)

The passage that stipulates the interdiction of visual representation contains its own violation. The description elicits mental moving images of, for example, flying birds and swimming fish, while at the same time asking the reader to negate the very visuality elicited.

The concept of a god who is at once One and indivisible is imbricated from the outset in the admonition both against worshiping other gods and against the very medium utilized in worshiping them, to wit any medium generating visual representations. Here, then, we find one of the ancestral sources of the demonization of visual media. The biblical prohibition of graven images, furthermore, comes with a positive corollary: the affirmation of the Holy Word. In fact, Judaic culture is thoroughly predicated upon concepts having to do with the "word" and "hearing." Central to the "covenant" (*brith* in Hebrew) between God and his Jewish people, for example, is the duty of male circumcision – a ritual of purity and loyalty to God – known as *brith mila*, or the covenant of the word. The linguistic genealogy of the Ten Commandments, or *aseret ha-dibrot*, similarly, derives from the root "d.b.r," signifying "speak," while the Torah imperative phrase "*na'ase ve-nishma*" (we shall do and listen), along with the daily prayer "*Shma Israel adonai alohenu adonai ehad*" (Listen Israel, adonai our God, one God), places words, written and spoken, at the center of the believer's act. In contrast to the ancient Egyptian and Greek visual representations of gods, which often attached a human head to animals' bodies – for example, sphinxes or centaurs – the Jewish God could neither be represented in animal form, nor be miscegenated as a cross between the human and the animal. With the Hebrew, as with the Arabic alphabet, an aesthetic of abstraction informs even the theological conception of a non-representational alphabet, a feature contrasting with Egyptian hieroglyphs based on resemblance, where the relation between signifier and signified was as much iconic as symbolic.

Within the monotheistic tradition all souls are equally created in the image of God. But the biblical formulations, which on one level seem democratizing vis-à-vis polytheism, also embed a series of hierarchies: man over woman (whose existence derives from Adam's rib), humans over animals, and animate over inanimate. God endows Adam – whom He created from "Adama" or earth in Hebrew – with the power of the word, the power to name, and thus granted him a verbal dominion over a world entrusted to him by his creator. Although man constitutes an imagistic representation of God, the divine itself was not to be represented in imagistic form. The very origins of monotheism are rooted in the idea, not only of the indivisibility of God but also of his invisibility, whence the prohibition of visual representation, that is, the censure on making any representation of an eternal God from perishable materials fashioned by mortal human beings. The original prohibition of "graven images" is motivated by a double hostility, first to idolatry – the worship of idols – and second to polytheism – the worship of many gods. The words formulating the prohibition are also significant. One common biblical phrase in Hebrew to designate the practice of graven images is *avodah zarah*, literally, "alien," "foreign," or "strange" work, but figuratively "false worship." The other phrase is *akum*, an abbreviation for *ovdei kokhavim u'mazalot*, that is, workers/worshipers of stars and constellations (a phrasing oddly reminiscent of the Hollywood Dream Factory and its worship of stars and love of astrology). Truth thus lies in the worship of the invisible, where believing in *not* seeing.

A favorite within biblical filmic adaptations, precisely because of its spectacularity, the Torah story of the golden calf (*egel hazahav*) bears on these issues. In that story, the People of Israel, soon after their exodus from Egypt, wait for Moses to bring his message from God, but his extended absence on the mountain triggers their skepticism about the novel idea of a single invisible God. Their erection of a golden calf provokes Moses' outrage upon his return, culminating in his violent act of smashing the idol. A foundational narrative for the iconoclastic tradition, the golden calf has initiated generations of Jews and other monotheists into the theological anomaly constituted by monotheism vis-à-vis polytheism. Moses leads *Benei* Israel forty years in the desert in order to cleanse them of their Egyptian habits, ensuring the death of "*dor ha-midbar*" (the desert generation) *prior* to entering Canaan, a land to be filled with a new generation that "did not know Egypt."

Idolatry was prohibited in Christianity too, as expressed in St Paul's cautioning against the *speculum obscurum* – the glass through which we see only darkly – or in the iconoclastic controversy of the eighth-century Byzantine church. Roman Catholicism, meanwhile, tended to accommodate the "pagan" penchant for animal symbolism by figuring Christ as lamb or fish. The iconoclasm of Protestantism, with its repugnance for crucifixes, saints' statues, and ecclesiastical artifice, in a sense constitutes a partial re-Judaization of Christianity.[4] Islam, for its part, also reinforced iconoclasm, highlighted through descriptions of the Prophet Muhammad's battle against the idolaters in the Qa'aba, while also recounting the smashing of idols by Abraham, the father of monotheism (Qur'ān, surah 21: 53/52 to 70). Arab history prior to the revelation of Islam is defined negatively as "*al-Jahiliyah*," the early period of worshiping idols ("*ansab*"), only to be transcended by the ensuing prohibition of iconic representation; for no object ("*sanam*") can be venerated next to God.[5] Although the wall-painting decorations of palaces could portray the rulers' battles, hunts, drinking, and dancing, figural representations of living creatures were to be avoided within designated spaces of worship. Some Persian manuscripts, however, did contain winged figures accompanying Muhammad's ascension to Paradise, and in some cases the Sh'ites produced pictorial representations of the holy family and of Muhammad himself.[6] The Qur'ān does not explicitly state that the representation of living creatures is forbidden, yet most Muslim legal scholars viewed it as a violation, since it entailed a usurpation of the uniquely creative power attributed solely to God.[7]

The prohibition of graven images condenses a number of theological arguments having to do with interrelated anxieties circling around God's image: (1) the fear of substituting the image itself for God, and thus committing idolatry – worshiping the object "standing in" for God, rather than God; (2) the fear of portraying God inaccurately in a kind of failed mimesis or wrongful representation; (3) the fear of embodying an infinite God in finite materials; (4) the fear of portraying God in shapes and forms made by finite humans; (5) the fear of giving "flesh" to God; and, ultimately, (6) the fear of representing the unrepresentable, that which is above and beyond representation.[8] The prohibition of graven images, furthermore, linked the religious condemnation of representing deity with the assertion of the epistemological impossibility of actually knowing the deity. How can the unknown and the transcendent be represented visually? Although man is created in God's image, this same supposedly God-like man, paradoxically, cannot know God. The knowledge is unilateral and non-reciprocal. Any attempt at representation thus amounts to a sacrilege, precisely because it would force God's invisible abstractness to "descend" into the "bad neighborhood" of the visible and the earthly.

While visual representation is the main object of the taboo, *verbal* representations of God are not regarded as entirely innocent either. The Sephardic philosopher Maimonides (Ibn Maimun), in his *The Guide of the Perplexed* (*Dalalat al-ha'irin*), concludes, after a thorough investigation, that representing God in words can *also* be a sacrilege, if figurative biblical language is understood literally.[9] Maimonides' blurring of the distinction between the visual and language is rich in implications for adaptation practices, for aesthetic theory, and for word/image relations. Extrapolating Maimonides' argument, as we shall see, would place most of cinema's five tracks under a cloud of suspicion, the visual track most obviously but also the phonetic speech and written materials track. The very act of representation, of translating, as it were, from the verbal to the visual, entails an anxiety, for to represent God is to contain and diminish him. Maimonides censured verbal descriptions of God because they might elicit images in the responding human mind. God could only be spoken about in the negative – that which he is not. Given this theology, it is noteworthy that both Hebrew and Arabic lack any exact equivalent for the word "representation," in which, by definition, something "stands for" something else. The very act of semiotic substitution is at the core of monotheistic anxiety. The prefix "re" in the word "representation" implies an absence, since "representation" by definition is not direct, that is, present; it entails invocation of absence through an act of repetition, of presenting anew that which is not present.

Within Judeo-Islamic theology, the importance of the word was predicated on its paradigmatic substitution for the visual. The desire for the visual and for a translation of the sacred into the perceptible was sublimated and displaced, as it were, onto other objects, images, and senses. Within these objects, the word still reigned, whether in the form of the *mezuzah* (a small case nailed to the doorframe containing a scroll of parchment inscribed with the words of "*shma*," along with the words of a companion passage from Deuteronomy); or in the *tefillin* (phylacteries – a leather case also containing a scroll designed for Jewish men to bind words to their hands and between their eyes during prayer); or in *aron hakodesh* (the sacred space in the synagogue containing the biblical scrolls). Judaic culture's enthusiastic embrace of textuality as a generative (and regenerative) matrix founded a way of life. It has cultivated the mystique and even the erotics of the text in its physicality: the touch of the *tefillin* on the male body, the kissing of the *mezuzah* at the threshold, and the dance around the Torah scroll. Allegorical expressions are often linked to the idea of a sacred language – the language of the Bible delivered by God – involving various degrees of concealment, especially the Torah as a fragmentary discourse, virtually soliciting the hermeneutic deciphering which typifies, for example, the talmudic commentaries. The historical narrative of the Jewish people has been deeply imprinted and "engraved" by texts. The messianic verses of the Sephardic poet Edmond Jabes describe Judaism as pre-eminently a passion for writing. For the homeless Jew, Jabes argues, the book is the fatherland and home is Holy Writ. Jabes anticipates, in this sense, not only George Steiner's idea of a textual homeland, but also the glorification of the text and writing in the work of Jacques Derrida. In his essay on Jabes, Derrida speaks of the "pure and founding exchange" between the Jew and writing: the Jew chooses the scripture (writing, *écriture*) and Scripture chooses the Jew.[10]

In both Judaism and Islam, letters themselves become signs of the sublime as well as a site of visual pleasure, developed particularly within the art of calligraphy. In Islam writing was crucial, since God communicated and revealed himself through his Word, in the Arabic language – itself a subject for a major theological debate about whether the divine language is *haliq* (creator) or *mahluq* (created). The genealogy of the word "Qur'ān" derives from "q.r.a," the linguistic root of the word "read." "Read," says the Qur'ān, "And thy Lord is the Most Bounteous, Who teacheth by the pen, Teacheth man that which he knows not" (Qur'ān, 96: 3–5). At the same time, the Qur'ān states: "O believers, wine and games of chance and statues and (divining) arrows are an abomination of Satan's handiwork; then avoid it!" (Qur'ān, 92).

Whereas the art of writing was revered, the art of figurative images was more controversial. The visual artist was seen as usurping God's prerogative as the sole "author" of life. The production of the visual, as with Judaism, was displaced onto other mediated forms. The surfaces of mosques and public buildings, for example, were covered with Arabic writing shaped in forms that would enhance the architectural design of a building. Calligraphy turned letters into a sensual visual medium, designing myriad geometric or vegetal forms created out of words, either through repetition or through sentences, often highlighting the greatness of God, his eternity and glory. Calligraphy had gradually become the most important Islamic art, deployed even in non-religious contexts, adorning coins, textiles, and pottery. The Judaic and Islamic censure of "graven images," and the preference for abstract geometric designs, known as arabesques, cast theological suspicion on directly figurative representation and thus on the ontology of the mimetic arts. While Roman Catholicism shared the Judaic prohibition of substituting an image of God for God, it also accommodated the desire for a visual, for the visible God. Brilliant paintings and frescos representing sacred scenes, including of individual saints and even some pictorial adumbrations of the deity, adorn churches. Within the Judeo-Islamic ethos, a visible carnal divinity, such as that shown in Michelangelo's painting on the ceiling of the Sistine Chapel featuring a bearded male God in the process of creating Adam, would be quite unimaginable.

Marking the beginning of the so-called "modern encounter" between Europe and the Muslim world, the arrival of French forces in Ottoman Alexandria in 1789, along with the nineteenth- and twentieth-century imperial domination of North Africa and the Middle East, triggered a complex aesthetic dialogue, revolving around issues of mimesis and verism.[11] Initiated both by individuals and institutions, a growing movement of translations of European literature (largely French and English) impacted upon the production of modern Arabic literature (the realist novel, in particular) as a syncretic site, mingling diverse Arabic literary traditions with veristic "Western" procedures. On one level, the idea of mimetic art, as we have seen, would seem almost inherently alien to the monotheistic tradition and to Judeo-Muslim aesthetic regimes. Within this perspective, Judeo-Muslim culture, partial to the abstract, would be essentially antithetical to the diverse techniques and movement of reproducing the real: the Renaissance perspective in the arts, the nineteenth-century rise of realism and naturalism as literary "dominants," and the ever-more-refined technologies of verism, specifically the still and cinematographic cameras with their built-in Renaissance perspective.

Verism did indeed pose an interesting challenge to cultures where mimesis had not constituted the norm. At the same time, however, Judeo-Muslim civilizational space cannot be reduced to the taboo on graven images, or seen as completely disallowing the representation of living creatures, or as devoid of all mimetic practices. The Umayyad mosque in Damascus, for example, utilized mosaics that portray, for instance, houses and the natural world within a relatively realistic fashion. In palaces, as suggested earlier, the visual taboo was not fully respected, whence the decoration of walls in tiles, wood, or stucco, as well as wall-painting, depicted human beings engaged in parties, wars, or hunting. Miniature art invited sensual pleasure, and illustrative images drawn in manuscripts – for example, the stories of *Kalila wa Dimna* from the twelfth and thirteenth centuries – contain pictures of birds and animals.[12] A more dialogic view of the relationship between so-called "East" and "West," furthermore, would allow for spaces of hybridity, such as the uncovering of the traces of Arabic literature and art within Iberian culture, and through it, within the European Renaissance. In the wake of the modern colonial re-encounter between Europe and the Arab world, meanwhile, verism as a modern Western norm entered a new geopolitical semantics. It came to occupy a far more central role in Arab aesthetic practices, whose genealogy is clearly placed within ideologies of modernization – a discourse shared by both imperialist and nationalist ideologies.

As appendages to the modernization project, art schools were founded in places like Istanbul, Alexandria, and Beirut. Artists of the "Orient" were learning to "disorient" traditional aesthetics by mimicking Western styles of mimesis. Figurative art signaled a world-in-transition, in contrast to the largely abstract art of Islam, rendered "traditional," an obsolescent practice that inevitably would have to be abandoned in favor of the forces of progress. In this metanarrative of progress, mimesis conveyed not merely a learning mode of an artistic technique, but also the process of becoming conversant with the aesthetic and cultural norms of so-called Western modernity.[13] In this strange rendezvous between "East" and "West," realistic aesthetics signified modernity, while non-figurative art was implicitly cast as past times. Yet such an encounter has generated some fascinating paradoxes. During the same period that the "Orient" was learning realism, the "Occident" was unlearning it.[14] The ideology of political and economic modernization found its aesthetic corollary not in avant-garde modernism, but rather in realism, and in modernizing through mastery of up-to-date veristic techniques. In the same period that the modernist avant-garde was rebelling against mimesis, opting for new modes of abstract, geometric, and minimalist representation, Arab-Muslim aesthetic practices were moving toward mimesis as an integral part of modernity. Verism as artistic practice was gaining importance around the same place and around the same time that Auerbach wrote his magnum opus *Mimesis* concerning the Western tradition of mimesis. In Turkey, a site of syncretism between Greek mimesis and Islamic arabesque, Auerbach, the German Jew refugee, contrasted the Hebrew Bible and Hellenic mythology, whose central figures had lived in the same region millennia earlier. Indeed, his book *Mimesis* itself was premised on a dichotomy between Hebraism, associated with ethics, depth, equality, and the word, and Hellenism, associated with aesthetics, superficiality, hierarchy, and the image.[15]

Discourses about aesthetic modernization in the Middle East, then, were hardly linked to modernist experimentation with the new languages of Futurism, Surrealism, Cubism and so on. The miniature's non-spatial painting or the arabesque's geometrical composition were not "translated" to the screen. Rather, the novel's mimetic qualities seemed more appropriate to a technology whose "essence" seemed to be equated with the "real." The tendency for adapting novels reached its paroxysm in the 1950s, as the work of celebrated Egyptian writers such as Ehsan Abdel Qouddous, Tewfik al-Hakim, and Youssef al-Seba'i was brought to the screen. Well-known French, English, and Russian novels were also adapted by filmmakers of French cultural background, such as Togo Mizrahi, Youssef Wahbi, Henri Barakat, and Hassan al-Imam, who Egyptianized the non-Egyptian novels and re-made films already adapted to the screen in France or Hollywood. Among such readapted novels were Emile Zola's *Thérèse Raquin*, Anatole France's *Thais*, Dostoevsky's *Crime and Punishment* and *The Brothers Karamazov*, and Tolstoy's *Resurrection* and *Anna Karenina*. At least fifteen French novels were adapted numerous times, including Victor Hugo's *Les Misérables*, Balzac's *Le père Goriot*, Dumas' *The Count of Monte Cristo*, which was actually adapted seven times, and Pagnol's *The Trilogy*, which was adapted four times.[16] Verism was propelled to center stage, signifying the double-edged sword of modernity: assimilation to Western culture as well as resistance to its aesthetic regime.

Representations of living creatures within the diverse technologies of verism were becoming a virtual lingua franca within a modernizing aesthetic trend in the Arab-Muslim world. Photographic and cinematographic images, interestingly, were not categorically prohibited. Based on theological interpretations of the *hadith*, or the Prophet's sayings – "Angels do not enter a house where an image is stored unless it is a sign on fabric" (*inna al-mala'ika la tadkhulu baytan fih suratun illa raqamun fi thaubin*) – photography was not considered a creation but rather a sign, produced in a pattern or a formula.[17] Photography and the cinema, however, were defined not as creating souls in the likeness of God, but rather as presenting God's creation, and thus reinforcing his power rather than competing with him.[18] Yet, treating holy matters within the profane space of novels and films did provoke tensions, themselves allegorizing the diverse force-fields shaping contemporary identities in Arab-Muslim spaces. The question of the novel as a "modern" literary form, adapting religious subjects within veristic fiction, became in itself a contested terrain. And in the colonial and neocolonial context of the negative portrayal of Muslim religion, the adaptation of the Holy Text onto the screen triggered clashes. Thus, even apart from the problem of cinematic adaptation, novels already formed a conflictual space. To take a recent example, *Satanic Verses* did not have to wait for screen adaptation to trigger an Islamicist *fatwa* against author Salman Rushdie.

In the contemporary Middle East, the colonial clash has also left its imprint on the image/word debate. From its outset, Egyptian cinema was the site of cultural tensions, especially when European film companies attempted to produce films touching on Islamic themes. The film *Al Zouhour al-Qatela* (Fatal Flowers, 1918), for example, offended the Islamic community by garbling several phrases from the Qur'ān, thus provoking the first case of censorship.[19] A more severe case occurred in 1926, around the anticipated production of a film about the grandeur of the early days of Islam. The Turkish writer Wedad Orfi, who initiated the idea, approached the Egyptian director and actor Youssef Wahbi to play the role of the Prophet Muhammad in a film to be financed by the Turkish government and a major German producer. Within a modernizing vision that characterized the new Turkish nation, it is not surprising that Atatürk, as well as the Istanbul council of `ulamas (scholars of religious law), gave their approval. Upon learning of the plan, the Islamic Al-Azhar University in Cairo alerted Egyptian public opinion, and published a juridical decision, stipulating that Islam categorically forbids the representation of the prophet and his companions on the screen. King Fouad sent a severe warning to Wahbi, threatening to exile him and strip him of his Egyptian nationality.[20] The protests resulted in the abandoning of the adaptation of the Qur'ān, for while the representations of living creatures within the framework of the relatively profane could be tolerated, such representations within the realm of the sacred were unacceptable.

These protests triggered the 1930 prohibition against portraying the prophet and the four righteous caliphs, while, later, the 1976 censorship law explicitly stated that "heavenly religions [i.e. the monotheistic religions, known in Arabic as *ahel al-kitab*, or the People of the Book] should not be criticized. Heresy and magic should not be positively portrayed."[21] Suspicion of the cinema led some religious scholars in Saudi Arabia to oppose even the building of movie theaters, although films have been watched within the private sphere. With the growing power of Islamicists in Egypt, in 1986 the prohibition was expanded to include all the biblical figures and prophets – for example, Abraham, Moses, Jesus – mentioned in the Qur'ān. And, more recently, Youssef Chahine's film *Al-Muhajir* (The Emigrant, 1994), a loose adaptation of Joseph's story, angered the Islamicists due to the representation of one of the Qur'ān's prophets, obliging the director (of Christian background) to defend his cinematic reading of the biblical story in court.[22] Although its presumed "dubious morality" as a social institution has stirred much apprehension, the cinema's intrinsic capacity to violate a deeply ingrained taboo has also contributed to its guilty status.

The spread of veristic and mimetic practices has not, for the most part, interrupted the millennial aesthetic code governing sacred spaces, which has continued to resolve the problem of visual pleasure and the censure of graven images through a complex mode of aesthetic abstraction. If over the past two centuries images of living creatures have inundated Arab-Muslim visual culture, this limited verism could exist only because it was reserved for the realm of the mundane, and thus did not interfere with the more deeply ingrained taboo. Arab novelists and filmmakers have often respected the spatial division between the sacred and the profane, drawing the contours of the realist novel and film so as to exclude religiously prohibited visual representations. In contrast, film history in Christian-dominated societies has frequently presented prominent religious figures such as Christ. It was not the mere act of representing Christ or Christian figures that provoked official Catholic wrath against Buñuel's work but rather the films' satirical stance toward Christianity. Similarly, Mel Brooks's satirical adaptation of the Bible's tale of the Tablets of the Covenant (*luhot ha'brith*) on Mount Sinai in *History of the World, Part I* (1981) was at odds with Orthodox Jewish perspective. The Brooks film has Moses, who receives three rather than two tablets, reduce the number of the commandments after he drops one of the tablets, thus calling attention to the arbitrariness of the Torah's number ten. In a reflexive moment, the film also calls attention to its own transgression of the commandment condemning *any* visual representation of the sacred.

Despite the political marginalization of religious parties during the decades of Labor Party rule in Israel, satires of the Bible in the public sphere were usually met by political pressures for censorship. A mid-1970s' TV program, *Nikui Rosh* (Head Cleaning), re-enacted the biblical story of the Torah deliverance, casting a funny-looking comedian (Dubby Gal) as Moses. Barefoot on the hot desert sand, as God delivers an interminable message, Moses hops from foot to foot, his suffering exacerbated by the heat of the burning bush. Shown on the state-owned TV station, the scene provoked the protests of the religious parties for having subsidized offensive images. Apart from the satire of the grand monotheistic moment, *Nikui Rosh* transgressed another taboo by endowing Moses with an image, within a culture where the grave of the Hebrew leader was intended to remain unknown. Unlike Hollywood's "map of the stars" which guides the vision of pilgrims in search of local deities, Jewish tradition obscures the location of Moses' burial place to ensure that his grave does *not* turn into a site of idolatrous worship.

In the case of Judeo-Muslim tradition, even a respectful visual representation of prophets and of God comes under suspicion, and the act of mimetic visualization itself is subjected to surveillance. Interpreting the graven images prohibition strictly, the Jewish Ashkenazi faction of *Naturei Karta*, for example, has for the most part resisted the camera, shielding their faces with hats or hands to ward off any photographer. Given this context of a deeply ingrained taboo, it is no coincidence that the screens of both Israel and the Muslim world have not proliferated in adaptations of the Bible or the Qur'ān. In Egypt, most films about Islam were produced in the wake of Nasser's revolution during the 1950s and 1960s, and constituted a vehicle for promoting and staging national cohesion.[23] Most were set in the early days of Islam, such as *Bilal, Mu'adhin al-rasul* (*Bilal, The Prophet's Muezzin*, 1953)[24] by Ahmad al-Tukhi, who also directed *Intisa al-Islam* (*The Victory of Islam*, 1952) and *Bayt Allah al-haram* (*The House of God*, 1957), while only a few were produced about later-day Arab Muslim figures such as Salah-a-Din (1961) who fought against the crusaders, or about mystic figures such as al-Sayed Ahmed al-Badawi (1953 by Baha Eddine Charaf) who spread Islam in the thirteenth century in Egypt.[25]

At the same time, the largely veristic procedures of Arab, Israeli, Turkish, and Iranian cinemas have performed a certain rupture with the non-veristic visual tradition, tending instead to adhere to the rules of mimesis and realism. Thus, within a film culture that has largely departed from the Islamic principles of visual representation, a faithful adaptation of the Qur'ānic narrative has posed serious aesthetic challenges.[26] While the Qur'ān can be said to possess narrative qualities that the historical realist genre can easily accommodate, the scriptural taboo places obstacles to its "translation" into the cinema. Arab films that sought the historical genre to tell of Islam, resolved the problem of representing holy figures by avoiding it, even while the narrative unfolds all in the name of God and his prophet.

Mustafa Akkad's film *Al-Risala* (*The Message*, 1976), however, represents a rare mode of adaptation of the Qur'ānic narrative concerning the prophet's life. The script received the theological imprimatur of Al-Azhar University, partly due to the filmmaker's innovative approach to evoking the sacred without actually visually representing it. Never shown in the film, Muhammad's presence is only implied. The film's images show what is relatively unsacred, acknowledging, as it were, the inferiority of the visual, and its fallibility in the face of the holy. As announced at the film's opening, *The Message* was submitted to the scholars and historians of Islam at Al-Azhar University in Cairo and the High Islamic Congress of the Shi'at in Lebanon, who approved the "accuracy and fidelity of this film." After a short prelude, the intertitles inform us that:

> THE MAKERS OF THIS FILM HONOUR THE ISLAMIC TRADITION
> WHICH HOLDS THAT THE IMPERSONATION OF THE PROPHET
> OFFENDS AGAINST THE SPIRITUALITY OF HIS MESSAGE.
> **THEREFORE, THE PERSON OF MOHAMMAD
> WILL NOT BE SHOWN.**

Written in capital letters and in bold to underline this crucial piece of information, the warning addresses various publics, especially those fearful of blasphemy as well as those expecting a spectacular epic film in the Hollywood biblical tradition. On the one hand, the film's grand scale, its high production values, its "location" shooting (with Morocco and Libya standing in for the holy cities of Mecca and Medina), its international crew, its wide-screen cinematography, its ostentatious commentative music, along with its larger-than-life heroes, would seem to point to a multiple generic affiliation with a number of spectacular genres: the biblical epic, the historical film, and the war film. The story of God's revelation to Muhammad, and Islam's triumph over the idolaters of Mecca, would seem to offer the celebrated hero as a vehicle for spectatorial identification. While traditional identification is facilitated via recognized stars, especially Anthony Quinn in the role of Hamza, one of Muhammad's close followers, the truly central hero remains incognito. The film's introductory intertitles undercut any possible desire or anxiety concerning the visual representation of the hero of both religion and film. Against the grain of the spectacular epic tradition, the intertitles announce a conspicuous lack, that of the visual (and aural) pleasure of getting to know our hero and star: Muhammad himself. In this sense, religious fidelity – to the text and to religious values – paradoxically entails *in*fidelity to certain fundamental features of the film medium; the intertitles seem to promise nothing but frustration of the scopophilic cinematic experience.

In the context of adaptation, the word "fidelity" is often associated with the expectation of an exact correlation between the "original" literary text and its filmic representation, with the word "infidelity" suggesting a betrayal of the canonical text. In the context of adapting the Qur'ān, "infidelity," however, takes on serious overtones, as it involves a betrayal of God's word in the most literal sense, since the Qur'ān, like the Bible, is believed to be an unmediated delivery of the sacred word. The burden of fidelity in the case of Qur'ānic screen adaptation is multifold. First, within the theological stricture concerning visual representation, the film's capacity to represent is not equated with the act of interpretation; the filmmaker is expected to play a "neutral" role, and cannot presume to offer or "add" interpretations, an act reserved to the scholars of the Qur'ān. Yet, the very permission given for making *The Message* inadvertently does imply some form of interpretation, since the Qur'ān, as we have seen, is ambiguous on the subject of making images.

Second, the filmmaker is expected to abide by the tradition of avoiding imaging the prophet, never using the cinematic space to represent the non-visualizable. Even if little is revealed about his appearance, Muhammad acts, speaks, and is talked about in the Qur'ān. In the film, third-person speech about the prophet does not pose a theological problem since it does not involve his immediate presence on the screen. However, although Muhammad is an absent-presence in the film, on a number of occasions he is addressed in the second person, as "you." In a few rare instances, the spectator is even placed within the subjective point of view of Muhammad himself. In one early sequence set against the backdrop of Ka'aba, for example, we witness myriad idolatrous practices. A few of the leading pagans suddenly turn their gaze in the direction of the camera/spectator, their faces manifesting awed respect and anxiety, underlined by a gentle murmur of wind on the sound track. The idolaters briefly suspend their activities, followed by a visitor's question: "Who is that man who looked into my soul?" The visual, the sound, and the dialogue tracks are all orchestrated to imply a holy presence, which we infer to be that of Muhammad himself. The observing of the sinful activities by "the prophet" constitutes the film's first instance of deploying a disembodied gaze. The ensuing dialogue proceeds to orient the spectator, affirming that *The Message* employs an unconventional language to signify the screen presence of an invisible presence.

*The Message* negotiates this dialectics of presence/absence through a highly unusual deployment of point-of-view shots, over-the-shoulder shots, and shot/counter-shots, all unconnected, as it were, to any "visible" subject who might "anchor" these shots within a specific body and face. While the film *Lady in the Lake* (1947) sutured the spectator into a total viewpoint of an unseen subject, *The Message*'s new twist on cinematic language entails a positioning of the spectator within multiple modes of address. In one instance, we hear a dialogue to the effect that Muhammad is now on a mountain, followed by an aerial shot that carries us to the mountain and into the darkness of a cave, as well as to what we assume to be Muhammad's presence, all accompanied by the now familiar sound of rushing wind. The black screen is reigned over by an acousmatic voice enunciating: "Muhammad, Read! In the name of thy Lord who created Man from a sensitive drop of blood, who teaches Man what he knows not . . . Read!" An image of a flame, slowly moving up from the bottom to the center of the screen, conjures up what literally becomes light out of darkness. We have not seen Muhammad or heard his voice, but we did hear *a* voice, implied to represent the words of the angel Gabriel. Is this voice an enactment of Gabriel's voice or does it merely relay quotations excerpted from the Qur'ān, and read by the film's sporadic voice-over? *The Message*'s codified language tempts the spectator into inferring that the voice could not possibly be diegetic, since that would denote an explicit re-enactment of Gabriel, when the film never even provides the mortal prophet with a literal voice. Such denotation would amount to an acoustic corollary to the re-presentation in flesh of a divine figure. The very act of an actor lending his voice to a prophet, or to an angel, not to mention God, would be construed as sacrilege. However, despite the spectator's initiation into the film's governing theological logic and aesthetic code of effacing holy figures, the cinematic status of Gabriel's voice remains ambiguous. Even if we feign that the film's narrator is not performing the voice of an angel, his acousmatic presence ironically places him at the apex of the sound track's vocal hierarchy. His deep and sanctimonious male voice, as well as his non-diegetic position, elevate him to the privileged slot of the omniscient narrator with a radiating God-like authority.

Placing us within Muhammad's subjectivity, some sequences, as we have seen, suture the spectator into a static literal point of view. Others, meanwhile, engage the viewer in the prophet's dynamic movement across space as well as in his interaction with diverse interlocutors. When Muhammad escapes the idolatrous Meccans into a cave, for example, the film cuts from the searching Meccans riding in the wide, open desert to the claustrophobic darkness of a cave, as "Muhammad" glances through the unbroken spider's web at the approaching enemies. The film deploys an over-the-shoulder low angle shot, as if looking from Muhammad's sitting position inside the cave at the standing Meccans who wonder over his whereabouts. In this over-the-shoulder shot, however, the spectator is deprived of a literal shoulder over which he or she could "lean" his or her cinematic gaze. Yet, since the spectator is cognitively already accustomed to the film's coded language, he or she makes the visual leap and "fills in" the gap. The Meccans at the cave's entrance, illuminated by the bright sun, are seen within Muhammad's point of view; the spectator's senses, perceptions, and knowledge are confined to the trapped hero's "eyes" and "ears." The overlapping between primary and secondary identifications enhances the increasing suspense, happily resolved through an additional thrill of a "first-hand" experience of a deus-ex-machina intervention: the unbroken web convinces the persecutors to leave, since Muhammad could not possibly be hiding inside the cave. Human logic fails the antagonists, and, allegorically, the *kafir*, the infidel or unbelieving spectator; for God's hand possesses different rational, dictating scenarios written from above (*maktub*).

In other sequences, characters speak to Muhammad, or more precisely to the camera, from diverse angles, furnishing the spectator with a sense of the prophet's corporeality and bodily kinesis: sitting, standing, getting off a camel, building a mosque, or walking away from an offensive enemy. In these sequences, the deployment of the conventional shot/counter-shot only highlights the unequal status of the two interlocutors vis-à-vis the camera: the seen/heard and the unseen/unheard. In contrast to Christian theological acrobatics to explicate the Holy Trinity, Jesus in Muslim tradition is revered not as a deity but only as a prophet, who, like Muhammad, is thought of as a mortal figure, with the difference that the latter is said to be the *last* prophet. Yet, despite the film's endorsement of Muslim theology, its formal procedures for rendering Muhammad as a visual absence, ironically only endow him with God's own attributes as the invisible deity. At the same time, in spite of Muhammad's concealment, the film offers the spectator another inadvertent blasphemous experience: the vicarious power of "being" the prophet. The diverse characters approaching the prophet address the camera directly, having the effect of conflating Muhammad with the viewer. As a result, the spectator is converted, as it were, *into* Muhammad – a cinematic act that paradoxically would seem even more sacrilegious than simply revealing a corporeal prophet on the screen. To put it differently, while such aesthetic paradigms observe the prohibition, they also betray tensions rooted in the challenge of translating across differing media.

Unlike the cinema in the Muslim world, where adaptation was bound to frustrate any desire to gaze at God and his prophets, Hollywood's biblical films emerged from a long history of Christian visual representation of divine figures, even if some of the producers were of Jewish descent. Often happily endorsed by Christian denominations, biblical films represented holy figures such as Moses or Christ in a way that gave an additional twist to the phrase "larger-than-life." At the same time, in Hollywood, too, biblical narratives were subjected to a surveillance regime. The Hays Office Code and the Production Code of 1934 explicitly forbade the negative depiction of religious figures. For the Church, adaptation – as in the case of Arab cinema – was judged in terms of its faithfulness to the original text. Quite in contrast to a poststructuralist stance concerning the ubiquity of mediation, the theological expectations about biblical and Qur'ānic adaptation for the screen have tended to be dominated by a non-reflexive discourse in which an adaptation does not form a mode of "reading" and "writing;" the filmmaker is conceived as faithful "follower" or disciple who offers no exegesis on the holy text.

Often deploying the spectacular epic, biblical adaptations, however, were inevitably mediated by narrative and generic codes, located within the space of both the fantastic and the testimonial. The cinema's apparatus of the "real," of nurturing the illusion of facticity, absorbed the biblical story into the aura of the moving image, where the history of God and his people was reincarnated, unfolding before the spectator's eye in a kind of a ghastly repetition of time past. The Christian concept of the Holy Trinity facilitated the practice of visually representing the Father and the Son, for God always already comes re-presented, reincarnated though his Son, dressing himself in flesh, as it were, in order to reveal himself to his flock. (Could Jesus be thought of as a filial form of adaptation?) Rather than a violation of God's decree, the artistic procedure of endowing God with an image is accepted as a homage, a mimesis of God's own descent to earth in perceptible human form.

God himself first made his debut in silent cinema, and his presence over the next century of film has been felt in diverse genres, including the spectacular epic, the quotidian drama, and the satirical comedy. Although according to the Bible God made man in his own image, a few films have projected God in man's image, making casting an unusually difficult challenge. Adapted by Larry Gelbart from Avery Corman's novel, Carl Reiner's film *Oh God!* (1977) has George Burns play a sympathetic 80-year-old man/God, who chooses a supermarket manager (John Denver) to spread the Word to the rest of the world. Vittorio de Sica enacts the role of God in the fantastic Italian comedy *Ballerina e buon dio* (*Ballerina and the Good God*, 1958) directed by Antonio Leonviola. In Yvan Le Moine and Frederic Fonteyne's Belgian comedy, *Les Sept Péchés capitaux* (*Seven Deadly Sins*, 1992), Robert Mitchum reincarnates an American God who smokes cigars and speaks English. In the animated NBC series *God, the Evil, and Bob* (2000), James Garner gives voice to a laid-back aging hippie God clashing with Satan, the slick and British-accented voice of Jonathan Crow. Antonio Fagundes performs an exhausted down-to-earth God, resting from his labors in the northeast of Brazil, in Caca Diegues's *Deus é Brasileiro* (*God is Brazilian*, 2003). Morgan Freeman plays God in Tom Shadyac's *Bruce Almighty* (2003), about a man (Jim Carrey) who always complains about God, until God appears, and gives him extraordinary powers for a 24-hour period. (The casting of a black God is interesting in light of the historical whitening of the figure of Christ.) Alanis Morissette appears as God/woman at the end of Kevin Smith's unorthodox satirical film *Dogma* (1999), although she does not exactly become a humanized god. Playing God also constitutes a rare challenge for actors. How would a method actor prepare for the role? Since omnipotence and omniscience are not available to most actors, what "sense memory" does the actor draw on to recreate the feeling of creating the universe?

God's cinematic incarnation requires concrete choices involving complexion, facial features, and figure. Unlike in novels, appearance and description in the cinema are grounded in the concrete and the specific; phrases such as "sad face," "seductive eyes," or "God's hands" have to be translated into the shape, color, and features of a particular performer. The visual adaptation of oral and written narratives, including biblical ones about God, forces the painter, photographer, or film director to take a stance, as it were. Cinematic production necessitates a selection of actors, and a casting process that inevitably locates face and body in concepts of gender and race. In Western iconography, for example, Christ was gradually de-Semitized, his appearance remodeled as an Aryan, deemed more appropriate for a supreme being within a white normative ethos. This image of Christ has persisted in contemporary visual culture, including in Hollywood, in the cinemas of the Americas and in the European film. In Franco Zeffirelli's epic *Jesus of Nazareth* (1977), the blue-eyed Robert Powell was cast for the role of Jesus, and Olivia Hussey for the role of Mary, also spared any overly Semitic appearance.

Filmic adaptations of the New Testament, from the respectful silent film *From the Manger to the Cross* (1912) to more irreverent films like Godard's *Hail Mary* (1985) and Scorsese's *The Last Temptation of Christ* (1988), have featured Christ on the screen, while those based on the "Old Testament" (i.e. the Jewish Bible) have tended to focus on the signs and symptoms of God's works without attributing an actual face and body. Thus, in a sense, these films remained "faithful" to the biblical narrative that eschews any description of God's corporeality as well as to the prohibition against visualizing God. Given that the classical narrative film places its hero at the center as a vehicle for spectatorial identification, the biblical film was faced with an unusual challenge. Even if mediated via one of his messengers, such as Moses, the main protagonist, the usual *raison d'être* of the story and its teleology, the force behind Moses, remains invisible throughout such films. One might understand the affinity of the biblical film with the spectacular epic genre as a form of compensation for the absence of the One in whose name the narrative unfolds. The excessive visuality of the spectacular in most Hollywood biblical films thus displaces two "lacks" – the verbal nature of the Book and a central character devoid of visual traits. Generally, filmic adaptations draw on the novel's descriptions of characters, translating the visuality of the verbal into film language. In the case of biblical adaptations, however, the written word of the source text itself denies access to the visuality of the protagonist, believed to be the very creator of the word.

While Hollywood's biblical adaptations can be said to remain faithful to this de-visualization of God, they can simultaneously be seen as subverting it by reversing the biblical hierarchy of word over image. The "ontologically" kinetic status of the filmic image, its place as a technology of truth, endowed cinema with reality effect over the written word. Cinema lent indexical credibility to the Bible, authenticating and arming it with visual evidence, as it were. At the same time, cinema implicitly celebrated its own technological superiority over the Bible's "mere" verbality. In a kind of ironic reversal, it was now the Word that depended on a totemic image. Moses' name and words have exercised their awe for millennia, but now millions, when they hear the name, conjure up the figure of Charlton Heston. As a modern fetish, cinema has provided a secular form of star-worship cults, while substituting its storytelling for the traditional narrator mesmerizing his tribe around the fire in the dark of night. The ability of cinema to chart the world like the cartographer, to chronicle events like the historiographer, to "dig" into the distant past like the archeologist, to anatomize "exotic" customs like the anthropologist – all have propelled it to the role of a powerful, popular storyteller. Manifesting its cultural legitimacy, cinema borrowed the Bible's aura through the act of adaptation, but simultaneously staged its own pre-eminence through an extravagant visuality.

Despite their forms and themes constituting a major break with both the literary canon and popular narrative traditions, novels written in Arabic and Hebrew have possessed a certain prestige by virtue of working with and through the sacred languages of the Bible and the Qur'ān. The unfolding of nationalist modernization teleologies in the Arabic and Hebrew realist novel, and specifically their role in the larger project of language standardization, could not nevertheless erase the historical traces of the sacred inscribed in the word. The twin product of science and entertainment, cinema had to struggle for its seventh art status within various cultural geographies. Early on, cinema enacted an historiographical and anthropological role, writing (in light) national and religious myths. The penchant of Hollywood's silent films for graphological signifiers, such as hiero-glyphs (as in the diverse versions of *Cleopatra*), Hebrew script (*Intolerance*, 1916), or the pages of an open book (as in "The Book of Intolerance"), highlights cinema's role as an archivist and historiographer. By associating itself with writing, and particularly with the "original" writing, early cinema granted a grand historical and artistic aura to a medium still associated with circus-like entertainment.

In a search for identity, early theory was also concerned with the written word. Film theorists saw hieroglyphs, for example, as anticipatory of the cinema. Eisenstein envi-sioned cinema in relation to the iconicity of both Egyptian hieroglyphs and Japanese ideograms. Eisenstein's view seems to bring us full circle; cinema resembles the visual conceptual logic of the ideogram or the hieroglyph where writing is motivated, mimick-ing its referents. Unlike language, which inhabits the realm of the abstract and arbitrary word, cinema exists within the realm of the concrete and the visible resemblance. For the contemporary mind, meanwhile, the very phrase "graven images" conjures up Bazinian notions of the cinema itself as registering or "engraving" images. Certain notions within postwar film theory, for example, the ideas of *auteurism* and camera-stylo and film-writing or *écriture*, in contrast, gesture toward restoring the sacred aura of the word.

The transformation of the sacred word into the realm of the visual has produced paradoxes in Hollywood films as well. Although not explicitly an adaptation of a biblical narrative, Steven Spielberg's *Raiders of the Lost Ark* (1981) can be seen as an anachron-istic adaptation of the clash between the monotheist Moses and pagan Egyptians, as well as between Jewish and Christian readings of the Bible. *Raiders of the Lost Ark* reveals a hidden Jewish substratum, even in the absence of Jewish characters. By liberating the ancient Hebrew ark from illegitimate Egyptian Arab possession, the American hero also rescues it from Nazi sequestration, allegorically reinforcing American and Jewish solid-arity against the evil Nazis and their Arab collaborators. That *Raiders of the Lost Ark* ends with the US army guarding the "top secret" ark – with the ark's active complicity – further buttresses this sense of geopolitical alliances. Just as the ancient Egyptians dis-possessed the Hebrews of their ark, so do the Nazis in the film's putative present (the 1930s). But in a kind of time-tunnel, Harrison Ford can be seen as fighting the Nazis in the name of a Jewish shrine, although the word "Jewish" is never uttered. In this fan-tasy of liberation from a history of victimization, biblical myths of wonders wrought against ancient Egyptians are now redeployed against the Nazis – miracles conspicuously absent during the Holocaust. The Hebrew ark itself magically dissolves the Nazis, saving Indiana Jones from the Germans, who, unlike the Americans, ignore the divine injunction against looking at the Holy of Holies. The Jewish prohibition against looking at the sacred, and the censure of "graven images," triumphs over the Christian predilection for religious visualization. Instantiating the typical paradox of cinematic voyeurism, the film punishes the hubris of the Christian-German who dares to gaze at divine beauty, while also generating spectacular visual pleasure for the spectator, who is able, thanks to the cinema, to have a God-like power to see even what the heroes themselves cannot see.

While the imaging of God's body was censured in the Judeo-Islamic tradition, in both the Bible and the Qur'ān, God does speak, and his voice is heard, although it is never described. Yet in the cinema, in contrast to a written text, the voice raises the problem of embodiment. The voice, not unlike body and face, is inevitably specific – it is gendered and accented, and sometime classed and raced, it has a grain, an accent, an intonation, a timbre, a pronunciation, and even a vocal mannerism, all of which may remain "inaudible" in a text. While silent biblical films could simply cite God's words in the form of intertitles, talking films were compelled to lend specificity to an audible voice. Adaptations for the screen, by definition, then, imply descriptive attributes, obliging an audible embodiment of God's voice. The voice, furthermore, has to be mediated via a specific language. In biblical spectaculars the ancient Egyptians and the Israelites all speak English, as, for that matter, does God. All have as their lingua franca the English of Southern California, with a touch of a British accent to convey greater prestige. (In fact, the English of God and of the ancient Hebrews does not in itself constitute a sacrilege to traditional or Orthodox Judaism that maintains Hebrew's sacredness, a language to be solely retained for holy rituals.) In biblical films God's voice – deep, masculine, serious, resonant – delivers a kind of authority conventionally associated with the documentary off-screen narration, symptomatically called "Voice of God" narration.

The aura of the disembodied voice is genealogically traceable to the biblical paradox of the invisibility of the omnipresent. Playing on a primordial monotheist awe toward the unseen creator, dystopian science fiction and suspense films have often deployed an omniscient incorporeal voice. In the TV series *Mission Impossible*, the recorded voice of an all-knowing boss ordering a top-secret, cold-war mission appears and disappears at the beginning of each program. Identifying with the heroes carrying out his mission, the viewers are left in the dark as to the actual face of the authority who, thanks to miraculous technology, has all the traces of his own voice – the recorded tape – vanish in a cloud of smoke.

Literary critical discourse refers to the "omniscient narrator," or to the "invisible narrator," imperceptible like God, to the point, as Flaubert suggested, of being "refined out of existence." The special kind of authority exerted by the unseen voice has not gone unnoticed in film theory, as when Michel Chion speaks of the acousmatic voice as the voice that is heard but whose source is not detectable in the shot, as in the case of the off-screen narrator in the *Wizard of Oz* (1939).[27] Biblical films, more specifically, endow cinema itself with an aura of magically reproducing the voice of the all-seeing omnipotent deity. Although God remains intangible on the screen, his voice is subjected to a mimesis that re-presents the scriptural "spoken" words. Within traditional Judeo-Muslim space, meanwhile, enacting God's voice provokes anxieties similar in nature to his visualization, since the disembodied voice is acknowledged in its corporeality. The film *The Message*, as we have seen, resolved this dilemma by avoiding any direct enactment of the voice of God or of his prophet Muhammad. The film intermittently uses a male voice-over narrator, who recites scenes and sayings from the Qur'ān that do evoke the presence of an authority beyond the spectator's perceptible senses. At other instances, God's "spoken" words are "heard" via the visual, that is, through the representation of written material quoted from the Qur'ān.

The epic-spectacular generic space, meanwhile, cannot be seen as the antithesis of the biblical representation, since the Bible itself constitutes a mélange of genres.[28] Indeed, the Bible proliferates in spectacular scenes on an epic scale: "And all the people saw the thunderings, and the lightnings, and the noise of the trumpet, and the mountain smoking: and when the people saw it, they removed and stood afar off" (Exodus 20: 18). God's visuality is absent but the visual symptoms of his power are omnipresent, and grand in scope, virtually constituting a visual language. It would be misleading, in other words, to contrast the cinema as a purely visual medium with the Bible as a purely verbal medium. Spectacular moments in biblical passages offer nature's sublime disturbances, such as lightning and floods, as signs of the divinity behind them, while God himself remains obscure and unintelligible. His "appearance" through cloud and fire has traditionally been interpreted as a manifestation created by God for the purpose of revelation, rather than as a display of God himself, or even of something resembling him.[29] Deuteronomy describes the Israelites' experience on Mount Sinai as a matter of hearing the voice of God without perceiving any shape (Deuteronomy 4: 12). The God who decreed the prohibition of graven images, the biblical text suggests, does not reveal himself to his chosen people. The adaptation of biblical stories, even by Hollywood's image-making machine, is itself constrained by a source text, the Bible, which obscures God's image. The adaptation theology of most biblical films has only partly respected the source text's anti-visual injunction, relaying God's words along with some indirect visual manifestations, yet leaving the precise nature of his image an unresolved enigma.

The aniconism typical of monotheism has been echoed in discourses about the cinema, which, especially since the introduction of semiology, Marxism, and psychoanalysis, have been concerned with obsessive mimesis, fetishistic voyeurism, the fixating gaze, star worship, and idolatrous iconicity. The powerful apparatus of cinema was said to produce reality effects that delude the spectator into believing in the three-dimensionality of the moving image. Spellbound and transfixed in the dark, the spectator was paradigmatically imagined as somnambulating in a shrine, a hypnotized believer in a false god. The pseudo-ancient Egyptian and Greek architectural designs of the movie palace only intensified the association of cinema with ritual and pilgrimage. As in the Mosaic rejection of graven images, apparatus theory inclined to view cinema as an iconic space that entraps the spectator in an illusionistic primal error – substituting a representation of an object for the actual object. Echoes of monotheist anxiety about the substitution error are detectable in what I call the "literarist" ambivalence toward filmic adaptation. From this perspective, while the act of adaptation might seem, on the one hand, to affirm the desirability of the word, on the other hand, the actual adaptation is despised as merely a surrogate icon incapable of surpassing the true god, the supreme textual being. Films based on novels are regarded as doubly iconic both in relation to a pre-existent reality and also vis-à-vis the novel. Within this literarist theology, film incarnates an earthly embodied object, inferior to heavenly words, while the practice of adaptation remains always already an act of inauthenticity and deviance.

Literarist adaptation discourse has also been haunted by creationist and originary theologies. In the beginning was God who created Adam in his image, but Adam is constitutionally incapable of seeing the all-perceiving creator who, in any case, warns against even thinking of creating his image. Imitation of God and a reproduction of his image, to evoke Walter Benjamin, would diminish his aura, premised on uniqueness and inaccessibility. Seen as mere repetition of the authentic word, film, in literarist adaptation discourse, is often assigned the actantial slot of the corporeal body vis-à-vis the novel's "faceless" abstractness. If, in the beginning, there was always the word and the novel, film is then bound, within this logic, to re-enact the novel as divine creation to be refashioned in the creator's image. Defined as a lack, cinema becomes a mere speculum that registers a copy of the originary word, just as man is God's fallible reflection, and just as all creators ultimately mimic, on a smaller scale, the creator. Rather than another mode of mediation, cinema's visual facility is reduced to an iconic object deemed to forever orbit around the holy text. Novels, furthermore, enjoy a certain aura derived from the very seniority of the medium of the word, through which God and monotheism are said to bring order out of chaos. Literarist discourse about the novel/film inscribes the creator/created dualism, in which the author of the world always remains the primeval source from which everything else emanates and back toward which everything refers. But, within another perspective, the adapted novel can be seen as the creature of the film, just as God can be seen as the copy of man. In sum, monotheism's conception of God and his representation in a sense allegorizes the relationship between novel and film.

The aniconism of literarist adaptation discourse is premised on numerous misconceptions about the complex nature of cinema. Adaptation has been conventionally viewed as a transition from what is wrongly understood to be a uniquely verbal medium (the novel) to what is understood, again wrongly, to be a uniquely visual medium (film). The visual and the written remain locked within a rigid discursive dichotomy uninterested in the languagedness of the image, nor in the visuality of the word, whether literally through its graphic image or through the images it elicits in the reader and the viewer. Although the word/image dichotomy is inscribed at the very beginnings of monotheism, even the biblical hermeneutic tradition itself, as we have seen, has at times acknowledged that images and words are not easily separable. Words may elicit images, while narrative, as we know, offers the unfolding of a movement in verbal time and space, which triggers imagery in the mind of the reader (and the viewer.) God's own scriptural name, commonly pronounced as *yehova*, constitutes the Bible's most sacred word. Yet, his name also inscribes the very prohibition on its utterance, thus paradoxically producing God's textual presence as a merely visual mark, discernible only to the eye that sees. Images, for their part, may elicit words in the mind of the viewer, whether in the form of proverbs, metaphors, or concepts.

An imprecise and reductive discourse about cinema as merely a visual medium, then, underestimates the potential of film language to transform "The Book" into multiple realms in which the word, images, sounds, dialogue, music, and written materials all constitute, together, the complex space called the cinema. Transcending such false dichotomies as the "visual" and the "verbal" is crucial for criticizing the orthodoxy of literarist adaptation theologies. To write complexly about the "translation" of "The Book" for the screen thus requires moving beyond an iconophobia rooted in the adoration of the word, and beyond a logophobia rooted in the fetishism of the image. Theological anxiety concerning the adaptation of sacred texts thus allegorizes the very discourses about adaptation: the anxiety of moving from the sacred and the canonical to the flesh-and-blood incarnation, grounded in the concrete and the specific – and, inevitably, the profane.

## Notes

1 "Perhaps the most sublime passage in the Jewish Law," writes Kant, "is the commandment: Though shall not make unto thee any graven image . . . This commandment alone can explain the enthusiasm that the Jewish people in its civilized era felt for its religion when it compared itself with other peoples, or can explain the pride that Islam inspires. The same holds also for our presentation of the moral law, and for the disposition within us for morality": Immanuel Kant, *Critique of Judgment*, trans. Werner S. Pluhar (Indianapolis, IN: Hackett, 1987), p. 135.

2 For an account of the visualist inclination of Western modern science, see Walter J. Ong, *The Presence of the Word* (New Haven, CT: Yale University Press, 1967). On anti-ocularism, see Martin Jay, *Downcast Eyes: The Denigration of Vision in Twentieth-century French Thought* (Berkeley, CA: University of California Press, 1993).

3 For more on the literary prejudices toward cinema, see Robert Stam, "Introduction: The Theory and Practice of Adaptation," in Robert Stam and Alessandra Raengo (eds), *Literature and Film: A Guide to the Theory and Practice of Film Adaptation* (Oxford: Blackwell, 2005), pp. 1–52.

4 On Protestant iconoclasm, see, for example, Carlos M. N. Eire, *War Against the Idols: The Reformation of Worship from Erasmus to Calvin* (Cambridge: Cambridge University Press, 1986).

5 On Islam's iconoclasm, see, for example, G. R. Hawting, *The Idea of Idolatry and the Emergence of Islam: From Polemic to History* (Cambridge Studies in Islamic Civilization; Cambridge: Cambridge University Press, 1999).

6 Similarly, when 'Ala ad-Din Kay-Qubad (1219–1236) built the walls around his city Konia in Asia Minor, he set up on each side of one of the great gates a winged figure. Thomas W. Arnold, *Painting in Islam: A Study of the Place of Pictorial Art in Muslim Culture* (New York: Dower, 1965), p. 24

7 For a fuller discussion, see Bishr Fares, "Philosophie et jurisprudence illustrées par les Arabes: la querelle des images en Islam," *Melanges Lois Massignon* (Institut de Damas, 1957), and Ahmad Muhammad, "Muslims and Taswir," *The Muslim World* 45: 3 (July 1995), 250–68.

8    For more on the theological and philosophical dimensions of this debate, see Jan Assmann, *Moses the Egyptian: The Memory of Egypt in Western Monotheism* (Cambridge, MA: Harvard University Press, 1997); Moshe Halbertal and Avishai Margalit, *Idolatry*, trans. Naomi Goldblum (Cambridge, MA: Harvard University Press, 1992).

9    Moses Maimonides (Ibn Maimun), *The Guide of the Perplexed*, 2 vols, trans. Shlomo Pines (Chicago: University of Chicago Press, 1963).

10   See Jacques Derrida, "Edmond Jabes and the Question of the Book," in Jacques Derrida, *Writing and Difference*, trans. Alan Bass (Chicago: University of Chicago Press, 1978), pp. 64–78. See also George Steiner, "Our Homeland the Text," *Salmagundi* 66 (Winter–Spring 1985), 4–25. Here one may want to note the intersection between the twentieth-century "linguistic turn" and the revalorization of Jewishness as the religion of the word.

11   On the "modern" beginnings of the movement of translation into arabic, see Ibrahim Abu-Lughod, *Arab Rediscovery of Europe: A Study in Cultural Encounters* (Princeton, NJ: Princeton University Press, 1963).

12   On these elements of mimesis in the history of Arab art, see Albert Hourani, *A History of the Arab Peoples* (New York: Warner Books, 1991).

13   A photograph in the January 1939 issue of the *National Geographic* magazine inadvertently captures some of these paradoxes resulting from the intertwined arrival of verism and nationalist modernization in Muslim spaces. The photograph shows mostly female students drawing a nude female model in a "life class" in the Academy of Art in Istanbul. Although the photo does not show the nude model, the reader/viewer receives a glimpse of her image through the various canvases. In a kind of *mise-en-abyme*, this photograph not only captures the process of making realistic images but also makes the viewer aware of the very process of viewing via the photographic lens, since the viewer's ability to see is inscribed in the mechanics of the camera itself as the scientific reincarnation of Renaissance perspective and of the mimesis of three-dimensionality. Several hundred years after the introduction of Renaissance perspective, and almost a century after the introduction of the camera, there should be nothing unusual about such a scene. Yet, the novelty of a life class in a *Muslim* space merits the *National Geographic* gaze. The photo celebrates the apprenticeship of the young Turkish women in the creation of figurative art, while also signaling that a world-in-transition is unfolding in front of the reader/viewer's eyes. The largely abstract art of Islam is implicitly rendered "traditional," replaced by the new of the modern movement. The photo's caption – "From Veiled Women to Life Classes with Nude Models" – explicitly links aesthetic and gender moments of transition. Wearing white gowns and standing in front of their canvases, the modern Turkish women – symbolic daughters of the new father of the Nation, Atatürk – abandon both Muslim aesthetics, associated with the fallen Ottoman Empire, along with the veil. Mimesis here conveys the process within a *telos* of becoming "like" and "repeating" the aesthetic and cultural norms of "Western modernity." On a critique of the metanarrative of art history, see Ella Shohat and Robert Stam, "Narrativizing Visual Culture: Towards a Polycentric Aesthetics," in Nicholas Mirzoeff (ed.), *The Visual Culture Reader* (London: Routledge, 1998), pp. 27–49.

14   On this problematic geographical imagining of the world, see Ella Shohat and Robert Stam, *Unthinking Eurocentrism: Multiculturalism and the Media* (London: Routledge, 1994).

15   Auerbach, in fact, registered an intellectual debate that began in the nineteenth century, in which Jewish-German intellectuals, such as Heinrich Heine, Hermann Cohen, Heinrich Graetz, and Frantz Rosenzweig, have responded to a diverse anti-Semitic denigration of Hebraism

and the veneration of Hellenism, the latter for possessing visual art and the former for its lack. See Erich Auerbach. *Mimesis: The Representation of Reality in Western Literature*, trans. Willard R. Trask (Princeton, NJ: Princeton University Press, 1953); and Kalman P. Bland, "Anti-Semitism and Aniconism: The Germanophone Requiem for Jewish Visual Art," in Catherine M. Soussloff (ed.), *Jewish Identity in Modern Art History* (Berkeley, CA: University of California Press, 1999).

16  Mahmoud Kassem, "Adaptation, égyptianisation et 'remake'," in Magda Wassef (ed.), *Egypte: 100 ans de cinéma* (Paris: Editions Plume, Institut du Monde Arabe, 1995), pp. 238, 241.

17  For a discussion of the aesthetic concerns raised by the Islamic prohibition on graven images, see Allen Terry, "Aniconism and Figural Representation in Islamic Art," *Five Essays on Islamic Art* (Sebastopol, CA: Solipsist Press, 1988), pp. 17–37; Barbara Brend, *Islamic Art* (Cambridge, MA: Harvard University Press, 1991); Oleg Grabar, *The Mediation of the Ornament* (Princeton, NJ: Princeton University Press, 1992); Viola Shafik, *Arab Cinema: History and Cultural Identity* (Cairo: The American University of Cairo Press, 1998); Hamid Dabashi, "In the Absence of the Face," *Social Research* 67: 1 (2000), 127–85.

18  Shafik, *Arab Cinema*, p. 49.

19  Samir Farid, "La censure mode d'emploi," in Wassef (ed.), *Egypte: 100 ans de cinéma*, pp. 102–17.

20  Ibid., p. 102.

21  Shafik, *Arab Cinema*, p. 34.

22  Ibid., pp. 49, 221. For further discussion of the history of censorship in Arab cinema, see also Viola Shafik, "Egyptian Cinema," in Oliver Leaman (ed.), *Companion Encyclopedia of Middle Eastern and North African Film* (London: Routledge, 2001), pp. 23–129.

23  Shafik, *Arab Cinema*, pp. 170–2. Shafik also shows that the production of Muslim religious feature films shifted at the end of the Nasser era to television.

24  While *Bilal, The Prophet's Muezzin* is the correct translation of the Arabic title, the film was distributed in English-speaking countries with the title *Bilal, the Prophet's Call to Prayer*.

25  See Ahmed Rafaat Bahgat, "Cinéma et histoire: du Baiser dans le désert à l'Émigré," in Wassef (ed.), *Egypte: 100 ans de cinéma*, p. 176.

26  On the Qur'ānic narrative, see, for example, Mustansir Mir, "Qur'ān as Literature," *Religion and Literature* 20: 1 (Spring, 1988), 49–66. I thank Ahmad Dallal for his insightful comments on this issue.

27  Michel Chion, *Audio-Vision*, ed. and trans. Claudia Gorbman (New York: Columbia University Press, 1993).

28  On genres of the Bible, see Robert Alter, *The Art of Biblical Narrative* (New York: Basic Books, 1981).

29  Onkelos, the Bible translator/commentator, interpreted God's "appearance" as merely a manifestation of his presence, not to be confused with God.

# Chapter 3

# Gospel Truth?

## From Cecil B. DeMille to Nicholas Ray

## Pamela Grace

Of all films based on written texts, those about the life of Jesus may make the loudest claims of "fidelity" to their source. "Based on the Gospels" and "great attention to historical accuracy" are typical promotional phrases. However, since the Gospels are not historical documents (although they contain some historical material), claims of textual fidelity and historicity are mutually exclusive. Moreover, the story told in the canonical Gospels (ignoring for the moment the many contradictions in the four versions) is not one that most filmmakers would want to put on the screen unaltered. The Gospels, as printed in our household Bibles, tell us that God sent his chosen people, the Jews, a messiah, who walked on water, raised the dead, and offered eternal salvation to those who believed in him. The Jews rejected their own savior, arranged to have him crucified by the Romans, and cried out "His blood be on us and on our children!" God showed his displeasure (and his preference for Christians over Jews) by darkening the earth for three hours at midday and sending lightning to rend the Jews' sacred temple veil. Three days later, the messiah rose from the dead and ascended bodily into heaven, from where he will some day judge the living and the dead.

The story confronts filmmakers with a number of problems: it is grotesquely anti-Semitic (written by members of a small, endangered sect, who were at odds with mainstream Jews, terrified of the Romans, and eager to make converts); it contains reports of several miracles that most respected biblical historians now regard as pure inventions inspired by passages from the Hebrew Bible and intended to prove the divinity of Jesus; it represents a worldview that is virtually incomprehensible to modern people; and there is no agreement about the meaning or even the substance of the texts. Even if it were possible for a film to "illustrate" or "replicate" a literary source – which, of course, it cannot do – films based on the Bible would, of necessity, always be interpretations or readings. Ironically, the films that make the most claim of adherence to their written sources are usually those that best demonstrate the impossibility of such a claim – and the undesirability of such a goal.

If some films deliberately avoid certain aspects of the Gospel texts, many more movies steer away from some of the interpretations offered by historians. Most large-budget movies do not explore readings that would be upsetting to audiences. The possibility that Jesus was a highly skilled magician, or that his body was stolen after the crucifixion, or the grisly probability that his body, like that of many other crucified men, was left on the cross to be eaten by birds and wild dogs, tend not to be incorporated into popular films. The only widely distributed picture courageous enough to take on issues of this kind is Denys Arcand's *Jesus of Montreal*, made in Quebec in 1989, and this film deals with uncertainties and conflicting interpretations by means of commentary by diegetic narrators. Usually when filmmakers are faced with uncertainty or unpleasantness they resort to traditional representations of scripture, no matter how historically inaccurate these familiar scenes may be.

This chapter examines two influential cinematic interpretations of the life of Jesus: *The King of Kings* (Cecil B. DeMille, Pathé, 1927) and its contrarian descendant, *King of Kings* (Nicholas Ray, MGM, 1961), both of which attempt to be true to the spirit of the Gospels. The later film, aiming to correct the errors of its predecessor, reversed nearly every major artistic decision of the earlier one, but oddly, in the end, produced its own versions of many of the original *King*'s problems.

The way in which popular films interpret the Gospels is of more than theoretical interest, especially in an era that is experiencing a dramatic rise in fundamentalist power throughout much of the world. In Islamic countries, the resurgence of fundamentalism has been linked with literal – and, according to many scholars, inaccurate – readings of the Qur'ān; similarly, in the United States, the rise of the religious right has been justified by traditional – often literal – interpretations of the Bible. Conservative Christian politicians, anti-abortion organizers, creationists, and even violent, white supremacists find biblical passages that they believe support their positions. Public arguments that seem to contradict the Bible often result in confrontation since the "Good Book" is regarded as the sacred text of Western culture. In the United States, the Christian Bible is the book on which citizens swear to tell the truth, the whole truth, and nothing but the truth; and the God in whom "we trust" on every dollar bill is implicitly the God of the Hebrew Bible and the New Testament.

At a time when only a small number of people read the Bible, and only a fraction of those have any familiarity with biblical scholarship, popular knowledge of the text most central to Western culture is increasingly dependent upon representations in movies and television programs. Many Americans find it difficult to think of Moses without imagining Charlton Heston in flowing robes, and cannot contemplate the crucifixion without hearing Hollywood thunder and music. Many others, who do read the Bible or parts of it, are likely, perhaps involuntarily, to "see" and "hear" some passages through the filter of well-known films. If the sights and sounds of the popular cinema have influenced our

Gospel Truth?

Chapter 3

concept of the biblical world, the *values* conveyed in movies about biblical figures have undoubtedly seeped even more deeply into our sense of biblical right and wrong.

Interpretation of the Gospels has been a work in progress for nearly two thousand years. Participants in this continuing effort have included translators, theologians, preachers, painters, hymnists, playwrights, and filmmakers. In our era, filmmakers have begun to take on the popularizing role once occupied by painters and stained-glass artists: they supply images and "bring the stories to life." DeMille's *The King of Kings* defined Jesus for vast numbers of people who saw the film in theaters or church halls or on television. The movie was the most often-screened film of the first half of the twentieth century, and continued to be shown on television into the 1970s. Some critics still consider it the best Jesus movie ever made.

Produced before the Holocaust, before archaeological findings such as the Nag Hammadi manuscripts (1945) and the Dead Sea Scrolls (1947) helped to place Christian writings in historical context, and before advances in biblical scholarship led to a better understanding of early Christian literature, *The King of Kings* expresses anti-Semitic ideas that were widespread for hundreds of years (ideas that, when portrayed in passion plays, roused audiences to go on killing sprees in Jewish ghettos after performances). Images, along with intertitles such as "Spies of the High Priest — driven by the fury of religious hatred," associate Jews with hypocrisy; and in one well-crafted dissolve, a cross miraculously emerges from a menorah just as the Jewish symbol evaporates into smoke!

The final cut of *The King of Kings* is not as anti-Semitic as it might have been. During the production process Jewish groups and other concerned citizens pressured DeMille to eliminate or at least tone down the film's negative portrayal of first-century Jews, and the director made some concessions. The most notable is a personally signed prefatory statement that attempts to explain away what follows in the rest of the film:

> The events portrayed by this picture occurred in Palestine nineteen centuries ago, when the Jews were under the complete subjection of Rome – even their own High Priest being appointed by the Roman procurator.
>
> Cecil B. DeMille

The statement is interesting – and entirely unconvincing – for a number of reasons. (1) It asserts historical veracity ("the events portrayed . . . occurred . . ."), which is quickly contradicted by the opening scene, an obviously fictional depiction of Mary Magdalene with her lovers. (2) The claim that the Jews were under Roman control does not in any way explain why they are portrayed as venal, underhand, and cruel. (3) The attempt to shift blame from the High Priest to the Romans who appointed him does not tell us why Caiaphas seems to have many loyal followers. (4) The statement is historically inaccurate. As the biblical historian E. P. Sanders explains in detail, Rome allowed the Jews a large measure of independent rule as long as they paid taxes and did not rebel against the empire. The film itself contradicts the introductory statement, portraying the daily life of the Jews as regulated by religious authorities and the temple police, who had to turn to the Romans only for administration of the death penalty.[1]

DeMille's film is as striking for its truth-claims as it is for its anti-Semitism; and, tragically, the combination is extremely powerful. Following the preface, the film itself opens with an intertitle: "This is the story of Jesus of Nazareth." Like many of DeMille's titles, this one allows for more than one reading (is it *the* story or the *story*?). Having provided a faux apology and truth-claim in quick succession, DeMille next identifies the film as a specifically Christian work (a sectarian project). An intertitle states: "He Himself commanded that His message be carried to the uttermost parts of the earth. May this portrayal play a reverent part in the spirit of that great command."

DeMille was so eager to give his film a religious aura that he blurred the line between the Hollywood lot and the world it represented. While the actors were on location, he organized daily prayer sessions (with representatives of several religions) and stipulated that Henry B. Warner, who played Jesus, take his meals alone and travel to and from the set in a closed car when in costume. He also had Mass celebrated on the set each morning, commenting that it was "like a constant benediction on our work" – and was also "a good insurance policy against future attacks on the film."[2] During the production period, all the actors were ordered to lead exemplary private lives and Warner was forbidden to appear in public.[3]

In order to ensure fidelity to the Gospels and ward off criticism from religious groups, DeMille hired as an adviser one of the people responsible for the Motion Picture Production Code – Daniel A. Lord, a Jesuit priest.[4] With Jeannie McPherson as scriptwriter, DeMille arranged to use biblical quotations for much of the dialogue and many of the explanatory intertitles. He drew attention to the sacred source of the words by adding a biblical citation after each quote. Throughout the film, we read titles such as:

> Tarry ye here, and watch with Me, while I go yonder and pray.
> Matthew 26: 36.

The style of the titles constitutes a central semantic element of the film. By preserving the words of the Authorized Version in written form, uninflected by the voice of an actor, and by following most of the lines of dialogue with citations, the titles repeatedly emphasize the film's supposed fidelity to the ancient texts; and the graceful pauses for each title impose a dignified pace that reinforces the "reverent" feel of the movie.

It is in this carefully constructed environment of "reverence" and "authenticity" that the film's anti-Semitic elements appear; the movie's truth-claims make its assaults on Jews more convincing than they would be in a less "serious" film. Scholars have examined the relationship between DeMille's religious/ethnic insensitivity and his own unacknowledged part-Jewish background, an instance of the intersection between a largely Jewish Hollywood and the general anti-Semitism of the United States in the 1920s (the decade in which Henry Ford had *The Protocols of the Elders of Zion* printed in *The Dearbourn Independent*). The larger and more significant context of the film's production, of course, is the combination of two patterns of thought that have persisted for thousands of years: the idea that there can be only one "true" religion and the Christian bias against "deicidal" Jews.

DeMille's second effort at toning down the film's negative portrayal of Jews as a group was his decision to concentrate as much evil as possible on the single figure of Caiaphas. The over-fed High Priest is consistently smug, conspiratorial, and venal. Near the end of the film, DeMille even dresses him in a headpiece that suggests two horns – a piece of costuming that recalls a tradition of the passion play. Caiaphas gleefully counts out the thirty silver pieces to pay for Judas's betrayal of Jesus (another image reminiscent of the passion play) and orders his spies to bribe the people to cry out for the savior's death. What DeMille creates, as he tries to shift blame away from the Jews as a people and onto one person, is, in the words of Bruce Babington and Peter Evans, "an anti-Semite's dream caricature of wickedness."[5] This single, memorable, cartoon-like character may be as effective in its anti-Semitism as any image of a faceless evil mob.

DeMille's attempt to modify the Gospels' negative image of "the Jews" is complicated by his desire to adhere to the New Testament portrayal of Pontius Pilate. All four Gospels, in their eagerness to appease the Romans, go out of their way to exonerate the man who ordered Jesus's death. They describe Pilate (who, according to most historians, was removed from office for the extreme cruelty of his regime) as giving Jesus every opportunity to justify himself, but then finally giving in to the pressure of the crowd. DeMille, needing to avoid portraying a Jewish mob calling for Jesus's death, makes Pilate give in to the urgings of one man, Caiaphas. The film portrays the conventional scene in which Pilate washes his hands of responsibility, telling the crowd to "see to it yourselves." DeMille then replaces the crowd's response – the most shocking verse of the Gospels: "His blood be on us and on our children" (Matthew 27: 25) – with a statement from the High Priest. The intertitle reads: "If thou, imperial Pilate, wouldst wash thy hands of this Man's death, be it upon me – and me alone." Moments later, in an aside, the High Priest adds a brief prayer: "Lord God Jehovah, visit not thy wrath on thy people Israel – I alone am guilty." The placement of Caiaphas' response and the particular words selected almost force the viewer to hear a chorus of scriptural accusations against the Jews. "Be it *upon* me" echoes the older translation of Matthew 27: 25 – "His blood be *upon* us and *upon* our children;" and "visit not thy wrath on thy people Israel" recalls numerous verses about God's punishment of his people in the Hebrew Bible as well as the later Christian claim that God "visited his wrath" on the Jews by destroying the temple in 70 CE. The High Priest's line in the film, with its many biblical echoes, gives the impression that something too horrible to mention is being covered up.

Although shockingly anti-Semitic by post-Holocaust standards, *The King of Kings*, when released in 1927, took a moderate position compared to that of most Christian churches. A year after the film's release, Pope Pius XI suppressed a Catholic organization, called Friends of Israel, which worked toward reconciliation with the Jews and reformation of church positions on issues such as God's "curse" on the "deicidal" Jews. In a statement against the Friends, the Pope asserted that the organization did not recognize "the continual blindness of this people" and that its approach was "contrary to the sense and spirit of the Church, to the thought of the Holy Fathers and the liturgy."[6] As Garry Wills points out, the "thought of the Holy Fathers" included many references to the Jews as "devils;" and the liturgy mentioned was undoubtedly a reference to "the perfidious Jews," which remained in the Holy Week liturgy until the 1960s when it was finally removed by the forward-looking Pope John XXIII.

Nicholas Ray's *King of Kings* (1961) illustrates the ease with which the focus of demonization can slip from one religious or ethnic group to another. Setting out with the laudable intention of providing a correction to the typical New Testament-based movie images of deicidal Jews, and especially committed to reversing many of the decisions made by his predecessor, DeMille, Ray strangely recreates the most unfortunate element of the 1927 film: he makes his movie's most despicable character an ethnic stereotype.

Herod the Great, described by historians and the Scriptures as the son of an Idumean Jew and a Samaritan mother – the half-Jewish descendant of a family whose rule of Idumea went back for generations – is presented in Ray's film as an Arab. Ray's Herod and his son, Herod Antipas (implicitly also an Arab) have no redeeming qualities; they are embodiments of irrational cruelty, degeneracy, perversity, and orientalized otherness. It is the elder Arab who orders the massacre of the innocents (an order that a Roman soldier tries to resist) but his cowardly, superstitious son is even more repulsive. Costumed in jewels, elaborate robes, and hundreds of little curls, he kicks his own father down a flight of stairs to his death, drools over his stepdaughter, Salomé (a blood-thirsty, sadistic, bored child), and personally places a red cape across Jesus's shoulders, taunting him with "Does he not look like a king?"

The false claim that the Herods are Arabs functions more as a slur than a structuring element in the film. Antipas, although a significant character, does not have the centrality of Caiaphas in DeMille's movie. The film's central concern is not conflict between different religious or ethnic groups but between violent and non-violent methods of dealing with tyranny. A working title of the film – *The Sword and the Cross* – was abandoned, but the final version contains numerous references to the two alternatives. Jesus is called "the Messiah of Peace," while his heroic but misguided counterpart, Jesus Barabbas, is called "the Messiah of War."

Ray's film – perhaps more correctly described as the film that Ray directed for a time before he lost control to the studio, which added and subtracted characters and scenes and re-edited sections that Ray had completed[7] – self-consciously responds to its 1927 father-figure through a series of reversals. Whereas DeMille's Jesus emphasizes the hero's divine nature and fatherly qualities (upright, patriarchal, and somewhat distant, he is played by the nearly fifty-year-old Henry B. Warner), Ray's Jesus focuses on the savior's human side and son-like qualities (the youthful, warm, outgoing Jesus is played by the blue-eyed, teen-idol Jeffrey Hunter, a casting choice that led to the film's nickname, "I was a teenage Jesus").

Gospel Truth?

Chapter 3

Caiaphas, DeMille's villain, becomes a minor character in Ray's film. He consorts with Herod and Pontius Pilate in several non-historical, extra-biblical scenes, but he is honest, straightforward, and articulates the needs of his people. Like the Caiaphas of John's Gospel, he decides that Jesus must be given over so that the Romans will not use him as an excuse to massacre the Jews. Pilate, who helplessly washes his hands in DeMille's movie, becomes a character of some complexity in Ray's version: he gives Jesus ample opportunity to defend himself, but eventually shouts "Scourge him, make him confess." And Judas, DeMille's slimy, greedy betrayer, becomes an idealist who gives Jesus the kiss of death hoping to "force his hand" and make him establish himself as an earthly leader.

Ray's choice of familiar scenes to portray or omit also contrasts with DeMille's. The earlier movie, which presents the apostles as proto-Christians prepared to "fight the good fight," omits Peter's denial of Jesus after the arrest in the garden. Ray, on the other hand, emphasizes the human weakness of the man considered the "rock" of the church, showing Peter's denial of his beloved teacher and his agonized face when he realizes what he has done. DeMille's temple is a center of money-changing and animal sacrifice and is the place where Caiaphas interrogates Jesus. In the Ray film, no sacrificial animals are shown, and there is no depiction or even mention of Jesus's "cleansing" the temple by overturning the tables of the money-changers. Ray has Pilate make brief reference to Jesus's interrogation by Caiaphas, but does not portray the scene. More significantly, he entirely omits any suggestion of a Jewish crowd shouting "Crucify him" or "His blood be on us and on our children."

Despite these differences and many others, the two *Kings* have several traits in common. Like its predecessor, Ray's film announces its seriousness, its historical claims, and its cultural pretensions from the outset. The narrative is preceded by a long musical introduction presented in high Hollywood-biblical style: the orchestral piece is sumptuous, anticipatory, and repetitious, and the wide screen is filled with an image of the sky at sunset. Imposed in large, gold letters over the after-the-crucifixion sky is a single word: "Overture." The written announcement is, in effect, a title; it immediately recalls the silent movie of almost the same name. (Later, the movie provides a long "Entr'Acte" and "Exit Music" in the appropriate places, complete with titles identifying them.)

Ray's opening shot and accompanying voice-over, like DeMille's inserted but unconvincing preface, immediately identify the Romans as the source of all harm. As hundreds of helmeted, red-caped soldiers file into an ancient city to the sound of triumphal military music, the unmistakable (but uncredited) voice of Orson Welles sonorously announces, "And it is written that in the year 63 BC, the Roman legions, like a scourge of locusts, poured through the east . . ." The initial phrase, like the citations in DeMille's intertitles, suggests the Bible, and the historical information evokes its source, Josephus, but the anachronistic "BC" proclaims the voice-over as an invention that cobbles together a variety of ancient phrases (a technique that was used repeatedly by DeMille). Welles's voice serves the same purpose as DeMille's intertitles: it lends a feeling of authority and associates the words with a sense of justice.

The voice now quotes Josephus directly. As we watch Pompey riding his horse through a crowd of Jewish worshipers, silently ordering the death of all the priests, and then continuing *on horseback* into the temple, we hear: "Where no pagan had ever stood, in the court of the priests, most irreverent Pompey stood himself down." Having dramatically depicted the Roman evil that DeMille only mentions in his preface, Ray now attributes to Pompey the greed and materialism that DeMille attached to the high priest (and thus to the Jews). Pompey enters the sanctuary "burning for the touch of precious metals," hoping to find "great statues of gold, bright as the sun." To his dismay, he finds "just a scroll of parchment" – proof of the Jews' ethical, non-materialistic values.

The scene in the sanctuary is a pointed and highly significant reversal of a DeMille passage. After the crucifixion, DeMille indicates God's displeasure with the Jews by showing the sacred veil being torn by the wind – in other words, by an act of God. In Ray's film, the gauzy curtain is cut by a human hand: Pompey slashes it with his sword. Ray's powerful image does more than blame the Romans for desecration. It eliminates one of DeMille's (and the Gospels') most dramatic indications of God's alliance with one people against another. Ray's scene states that a highly symbolic act traditionally attributed to God was in fact carried out by humans, *if it occurred at all*. The suggestion that the act may never have occurred is implied in three ways: the chronological displacement (the Gospels locate it on Good Friday, whereas Ray places it many years before Jesus's birth); the fact that the whole Pompey scene is a schematic depiction of the Roman invasion, with no pretense at portraying specific events; and the fact that the voice-over narrator speaks with obviously fictional omnipotence (no historian was present to see exactly what Pompey was doing inside the inner sanctum, and no one could have known Pompey's inner thoughts and feelings). The condensed and exaggerated quality of the scene is echoed in Pompey's highly stylized use of excess force: unsheathing a large sword to cut through a piece of delicate, semi-transparent cloth.

The epic tone continues in voice-over: "Thus for more than fifty years after Pompey's invasion, the history of Judea would be read by the light of burning towns . . . There was a harvest of people to be brought in . . . Like sheep, they went to the slaughter." The accompanying images show long lines of people being herded by soldiers and a body being thrown onto a fire – self-conscious evocations of the Holocaust. It is in this context that Ray introduces his Arab accusation. Voice-over: "But Caesar could find no Jew to press Rome's laws on this fallen land. So Caesar named one Herod the Great, an Arab of the Bedouin tribe." When the Jews rebelled against his rule, Herod crucified them, creating "forests of crosses." The screen shows Herod looking out from his carriage with an evil smile on his face, as the voice-over explains that he was "passing pleased."

Released only thirteen years after the creation of the state of Israel, and five years after the Suez Crisis, the film strives to unify Judaism and Christianity as a continuous tradition. Herod, gazing over the implicitly Judeo-Christian land, is associated with the "Arab threat." He is linked with the Roman form of execution (crucifixion, which is used to torture and kill the Judeo-Christian messiah) and with the Holocaust-like burning of Jews, who are closely associated with Christians. Whereas DeMille has Jews and Romans plotting against Christians, Ray has Arabs and Romans persecuting Jews and proto-Christians. Ray even uses the crucifixion theme to explain the poetic justice of the death of Herod the Great. As the king lies at the bottom of the stairs, kicked by his son, the voice-over says: "So Herod the Great, self-crucified by his many murders, fell dead."

In keeping with contemporary Christian thinking, *King of Kings* emphasizes Jesus's Jewishness. Jesus is addressed as "Rabbi" far more often than "Lord" or "Master." At the Last Supper, which is pictured much like a Passover Seder, he utters a traditional Jewish prayer, "Blessed art thou our God, King of the Universe;" he makes statements such as "I am come not to destroy the law and the prophets, but to fulfill them;" and he ends the Sermon on the Mount with an affirmation of the ancient tradition: "This is the law of the prophets." When Pilate asks: "What is truth? Can there not be more than one truth?" Jesus answers: "There is only one – be true to God."

Ray's Jewish community is emphatically not a faceless mob of highly religious people in long robes, irrationally awaiting a savior. The film emphasizes the community's diversity of opinion (although the alternatives are greatly simplified – "to run with the messiah of war or walk with the messiah of peace"). Barabbas and his fellow zealots are a fearless group of extremely muscular men, who are shown, shirtless, forging their own weapons and then bravely attacking the heavily armed Romans. The shots of the zealot fighters are rich in associations. In one scene, the men very effectively use the ancient form of slingshots against the Romans, fighting David and Goliath style. Another scene alternates between shots of the leather-clad fighters emerging from the land like "Indians" in a Western and low-angle shots of individual fighters standing alone against the horizon like triumphant white settlers on the frontier. The film thus associates the zealots with courageous figures on both sides of the battle over the American West. In these sequences, the Romans, in their red capes, add another association: they recall the British during the American Revolution, battling in a territory they did not belong in or understand. Ray's zealots seem to be fighting for more than their own people; they give the impression that they are fighting for the dignity of all oppressed people everywhere.

In dealing with the miracles, Ray's film clearly intends to counter DeMille's but, by the end, its portrayal of miraculous deeds serves the conventional purpose: affirming Jesus's divinity, God's ultimate control of the world, and the ever-present possibility of divine intervention. The DeMille film, always intent on proving its close tie to its sacred source and its supposed historical truth, accompanies most of its miracles with citations from the Gospels. To the same end, it also draws upon a popular idea that originated with Papias (c.130 CE) and was propagated by the Church Father, Eusebius (d. 325): the notion that the author of the Gospel of Mark was a follower of the apostle Peter. The film incorporates a child, identified as "Little Mark," who is an eyewitness to the miracles and crucifixion. One of DeMille's most convincing methods of giving the impression of a direct link between historic events and the Gospels, and between the Gospels and his film, is arranging for us to "see" the author of the earliest Gospel as he witnesses important events in Jesus's life.

Ray's film, which focuses on Jesus's humanity, attempts to minimize the miracles. It eliminates the most dramatic one, the raising of Lazarus, and avoids direct representation of the voice and acts of God. One of the film's techniques is an extremely effective use of reported speech. At Jesus's baptism, an extra-diegetic, anonymous voice-over (commonly called a "voice-of-God") *reports* the words of the deity. The Orson Welles voice-over states: "A voice said, 'This is my beloved son.'" In the scene, present-tense visual representation and past-tense oral description are simultaneous: we seem to be witnessing an event and looking back upon it at the same time. The high moment in *King of Kings*, with regard to the miracles, is a scene in which a very appealing Roman centurion, Lucius (Ron Randell) – a fictitious character who serves as the viewer's surrogate – reads a report about Jesus to Herod Antipas, Pontius Pilate, and Pilate's wife. The scene expresses several levels of belief and disbelief about the material that is reported. Holding a scroll, Lucius reads: "he cast out a demon from a madman, brought a dying child back to life." There is an interruption from Pilate's wife: "Lucius, these things – can they really be true?" Lucius: "I don't know, my lady – I myself have never seen a miracle." Pilate cuts in abruptly: "There are no such things as miracles, only fools who believe in them." Lucius continues: "It is reported that from a basket containing a fish and two loaves of bread, the man fed the entire multitude." Pilate cuts in again: "I've never heard such absolute nonsense!" Lucius goes on, as if Pilate had not interrupted: "The day after the Ides of July, Jesus was seen to walk on the water of the Sea of Galilee." Pilate now snatches away the scroll, sputtering "Ridiculous!" The steady Lucius continues as if still reading, but without the scroll, mentioning Jesus stilling a storm. Pilate, reaching for a golden goblet offered by his wife and contemptuously tossing the scroll into a shallow pool, says "Does Lucius mock me?" Lucius ends the exchange with a non-committal line that sums up the position taken by a number of movies and even some biblical historians: "So it is reported."

In this contradictory film, however, a few miracles are portrayed in a more convincing way. We see the healing of a paralytic and a blind man effected by the shadow of an off-screen Jesus; and the film half-heartedly affirms the resurrection and refers to the ascension. The effective representation in *King of Kings* of these healings – the creation of a miraculous atmosphere, where anything could happen – contradicts the film's general skepticism about miracles. It temporarily lures the viewer into a dream realm where the ills of the world can be remedied by a visitor from heaven who merely needs to cast his shadow on worldly sufferers. The film's adherence to the gospel message – the good news – in these moments departs from the ideas conveyed in the opening scenes, which focused on the political situation.

A movie that set out to counter DeMille's approach, *King of Kings* in the end reproduces many of the earlier film's weaknesses. It rejects anti-Semitism, but villainizes an orientalized Arab; it lionizes the muscular activist, Barabbas, but then depicts the futility of his uprising and the massive loss of life it causes, ultimately condemning the "messiah of war;" it presents Jesus as youthful and non-authoritarian rather than old and distant, but nevertheless makes him a super-human being who works miracles and rises from the dead; and it replaces Christian evangelism with political passivity. One of Jesus's most memorable lines, spoken with reference to John the Baptist, is: "I come to free him within his cell." *King of Kings* implies that the only real need of those imprisoned by poverty and injustice is spiritual freedom.

Ray's film was certainly not the last to fragment and oversimplify the message of Jesus (or the message as we now understand it from the limited evidence available), but it did suggest a move away from the anti-Semitism and pseudo-reverence of earlier films such as DeMille's *The King of Kings*. However, the year 2004 saw a revival of several issues associated with the DeMille picture – and one of the most dramatic phenomena in the history of Jesus films. Mel Gibson's self-financed *The Passion of the Christ,* a two-hour depiction of torture and death filmed in Aramaic and Latin and subtitled in modern languages, became the top-grossing picture in the United States and several other countries. Several aspects of *The Passion* and the controversies surrounding it hark back to the production of *The King of Kings*. Like DeMille, Gibson asserted that his film had a spiritual purpose. The introductory title states the theme of the film and implies that we should take responsibility for what will appear on the screen – "He was wounded for our transgressions, crushed for our iniquities. By his wounds we are healed" – but the movie then concentrates on images of Jesus being tortured by Roman soldiers at the urging of Jews, who watch the bloodletting with satisfaction. As in DeMille's film, blame and piety are interwoven; and in *The Passion,* self-blame and blame of the Jews overlap. Gibson, like DeMille, claimed both biblical and historical authenticity despite the fact that both claims were blatantly untrue. Just as DeMille began his film with an overtly fictitious scene, Gibson straightforwardly acknowledged his use of extra-biblical material, especially the many details taken from *The Dolorous Passion of Our Lord Jesus Christ*, a description of the bloody, anti-Semitic visions of an early nineteenth-century nun, Anne Catherine Emmerich, who is now being considered for canonization. And, as DeMille had done, Gibson sought out religious authorities as advisers in order to bolster his claim of authenticity. Tragically, within this environment of truth claims – half a century after the Holocaust and three-quarters of a century after the release of DeMille's picture – Gibson revived some of the anti-Semitic imagery and language that has long been associated with passion plays.

During production, both directors resisted pressure to tone down their film's negative portrayal of Jews. As mentioned above, DeMille made some accommodations. He inserted a prefatory statement about Roman control of the Jews, focused blame for Jesus's death on the high priest alone rather than the Jewish people as a whole, and changed the "blood curse" from "His blood be on us . . ." to Caiaphas's request that God blame him alone. Gibson, a "traditional Catholic," who rejects the reforms made by the church during the Second Vatican Council in the 1960s, was far more resistant to change. Again, the "blood curse" was a major focus of contention. After considerable pressure, Gibson agreed to remove it, and when the film was released, the English subtitle was, indeed, gone. However, the line was retained in Aramaic, available to be subtitled in other languages.

Gibson's film repeats the anti-Semitism of *The King of Kings* in several other respects as well: the Jewish priests (with the exception of two briefly glimpsed dissenters) are depicted as evil (a Satan figure floats among them); the trial before Caiaphas is emphasized (and involves humiliation and torture); the significant "good" characters are portrayed as proto-Christians (the two Marys look like nuns); and the film as a whole strongly implies that God prefers Christians to Jews.

In the mid-twentieth century, a still from DeMille's *King* was a popular image of Jesus: a somber, kindly, bland, fatherly figure. Pictures of Ray's Jesus, played by Jeffrey Hunter, never achieved that status. Suddenly, in 2004, *the* dominant image of Jesus – appearing on posters and book covers and sold in framed pictures – is *The Passion*'s Jim Caviezel, wearing a crown of thorns and dripping with blood. It is a sacrificial Jesus, who suffered willingly for our sins, at the hands of the Jews. DeMille gave us the triumph of Christianity over Judaism; Ray gave us a simple form of peace and unity (with a sideline of blame for the Arabs); and Gibson takes us back to DeMille's malevolent priests, now associating them with cruelty and torture. The popular Jesus film has gone full circle, adding early twenty-first century blood and gore to ancient biases.

---

## Notes

1 As E. P. Sanders points out in *The Historical Figure of Jesus* (New York: Penguin, 1993), p. 24, the Jews were allowed to administer the death penalty in one situation: temple police could immediately kill any non-Jew who entered the well-marked forbidden area of the temple.

2 Les and Barbara Keyser, *Hollywood and the Catholic Church: The Image of Roman Catholicism in American Movies* (Chicago: Loyola University, 1984), p. 22, cited in Lloyd Baugh, *Imaging the Divine: Jesus and Christ-figures in Film* (Kansas City: Sheed and Ward, 1997), p. 12.

3 Baugh, *Imaging the Divine*, p. 12.

4 Ibid.

5 Bruce Babington and Peter William Evans, *Biblical Epics: Sacred Narrative in the Hollywood Cinema* (Manchester: Manchester University Press, 1993), p. 122.

6 Georges Passelecq and Bernard Suchecky, *The Hidden Encyclical of Pius XI*, trans. Steven Rendell (New York: Harcourt Brace, 1997), pp. 138–9, cited in Garry Wills, *Papal Sin: Structures of Deceit* (New York: Doubleday, 2000), p. 32.

7 For details of the many problems during the production of the film, see Bernard Eisenschitz, *Nicholas Ray: An American Journey* (London: Faber and Faber, 1993), pp. 360–76.

# Chapter 4

# Transécriture and Narrative Mediatics

## The Stakes of Intermediality

## André Gaudreault and Philippe Marion

Adaptation, mediality, and intermediality: these are the issues engaged in our text. Our original aim was to demonstrate that, in moving from one medium to another, the "subject" of a story – we will return to the issue of what we mean by "subject" – would necessarily undergo a series of informing and deforming constraints linked to what might be called the new medium's intrinsic configuration, since each subject would be presumably endowed with its own configuration. This configuration, in our original conception, would be always already more or less compatible with a particular medium and would thus preprogram, as it were, any process of adaptation. Beginning from these early intuitions, we decided to develop a deeper reflection concerning adaptation, rewriting, transécriture, and trans-semioticization. The first question we confronted is at the very kernel of the whole problematic: is it possible for the story (*fabula*) to exist outside any and all media? Or, to put it differently, is it possible to imagine a story in a kind of original virgin state, prior to any mediatic incarnation?

### The Means of Expression as the Occasion for a Physical Encounter

We can begin our investigation by looking at the issue of expressive production and creation. When the artistic "subject," and here we use "subject" in a different sense, in the sense of the expressive artist, when this "subject" decides to express him or herself, he or she is always confronted by a kind of resistance specific to the chosen medium of expression. Human thought, as it "materializes" itself, always undergoes an encounter with the world of contingency. There is no incarnation that does not brush up against the flesh that actualizes the very process of incarnation. In one of his novels, Paul Auster describes the uncertain writerly materialization of the thoughts of his narrator:

> When I first started, I thought it would come spontaneously, in a trance-like outpouring. So great was my need to write that I thought the story would be written by itself . . . No sooner have I thought one thing than it evokes another thing, and then another thing, until there is an accumulation of detail so dense that I feel I am going to suffocate. Never before have I been so aware of the rift between thinking and writing. For the past few days, in fact, I have begun to feel that the story I am trying to tell is somehow incompatible with language, that the degree to which it resists language is an exact measure of how closely I have come to saying something important.[1]

Here Auster evokes the resistance of the expressive material in relation to the artist's desire to inscribe in that material whatever ideas come into the artist's mind. The thoughts of the narrator – since we are dealing here with a novelistic representation – will remain incommunicable, merely playing with their own opacity, if they were not incarnated in a given expressive form, in this case writing. But perhaps it is also true that the said form – that is, literature – is inadequate to the project envisioned by the narrator. But could it not be that the inadequacy attributed to the incarnational resistance of thought itself as a floating aura, might in the end be nothing more than a refusal of cooperation on the part of the material of expression? One might go even further and see the issue from a more positive angle: perhaps all these vague ideals which throw themselves endlessly against the breakwater of scriptural language are mistaken in persisting in this direction. Might they not find a better semiotic incarnation in another medium, in music for example?

We can also note that if these thoughts escape the narrator, it is also because those thoughts have hardly yet been formulated. That idea obviously evokes the question of the possibility of the existence of thought "before" or "beyond" (depending on one's point of view) prior to its formulation. Can thought exist without being always already formulated, that is to say, mediated, if only for oneself alone, inside one's head? This question is a momentous one, touching on such diverse fields as epistemology, philosophy, and ethics, and we will return to it later, but for the moment our project is more modest. We would like to establish the propositional foundations for what we would call a narrative mediatics, a project "nourished," as it were, by transdisciplinary intuitions.[2]

Within this train of thought, and along the same lines as suggested by the Auster text cited above, is the notion that all expression is first of all an encounter with opacity. In order to become transparent, communication has to be measured against the fundamental opacity inherent in any material of expression. As in the famously clear line attributed to Hergé: we know the extent to which its "ideality" comes only from work transcended, from the graphic drudgery of erasures, hesitations, and corrections. We also know that narrative as well as graphic clarity is the ideal product generated by a wrestling with the graphic-figurative material, but that the finished work tries to muffle that conflict in favor of transparency in the expression-representation. In the case of graphic design, or of the image in general, transparency is obviously linked to what is represented, to the real or imagined referent. Transparency means that the material image is effaced in favor of what it evokes beyond itself. Which is to say that monstration, at least when it tends toward figuration, is transitive. Every analogical *simulacrum* needs such transitivity; that is, every image strives to make itself forgotten as a contingent means of representation.

Any means of expression, and especially any means of artistic expression, then, has to be framed in relation to the constraints of the chosen materials of expression. That is the sense in which expression is always a quasi-physical encounter, a *"corps à corps."* At the same time, a constraint is not a limit, because a constraint is also the source, and even the condition, of creativity. If one were to create – we can always dream – an "imaginatics," a transversal discipline which would study the genesis of creative works in so far as they emerge from the interactive encounter of a subjective imaginary opened up by a means of expression, then this discipline would have to take into account the role of this material opacity within the creative process.

If one looks at the example of literary creation, for example, theorists normally take into account the stimulation that comes from the writer's encounter with language, with writing in its very materiality. The writerly encounter is linked to what one might call "fictional germination." Commenting on his own literary genetics, Claude Simon points out that: "What one writes . . . is the product not of a conflict between a vague initial project and language itself, but rather of a symbiosis between the two . . . which makes the result infinitely richer than the first intention."[3] In literature, writing, in the specificity of its opacity, becomes itself a material for fiction, "the singular adventure of a narrator who never stops searching, touchingly discovering the world by groping in and through writing."[4]

We might equally draw our example from musical creation. If one studies the genesis and evolution of the sonata form in Beethoven, one notices an intense interaction between musical form and mediating material, notably in relation to the new pianoforte. In that period, the composer discovered the timbre and potentials of this "avant-garde" instrument, which prefigured the emerging new symphonic orchestra. Thus, in several sonatas, for example Opus 27, Number 1, Beethoven develops a strong interactive confrontation with the percussive element and the specific resonating capacities of the pianoforte, as one can attest by examining Beethoven's successive manuscripts and by the name "sonata quasi una fantasia" (as if one were improvising). As Beethoven himself revealed, musical scenarios conceived on paper are often profoundly modified through interaction with the sonority and dynamics of the instrument which opened up extraordinary new horizons.

The example of Beethoven is not meant to imply a form of cultural elitism implicitly linked to the image of the classical composer as musical demiurge. We can also draw our example from the realm of popular culture. The *Jimi Hendrix Experience* constitutes a complex cocktail: the creative intuitions of an improviser in interaction with a specific instrument, the guitar, in dialogue as well with the whole phenomenon of electrified, amplified, and saturated sound, as well as with the social-cultural-anthropological moment of mass pop concerts. To put it ironically, how can one convert Jimi Hendrix into an English flute? Or, better, how can one convert Jimi Hendrix into an English flute without performing a veritable adaptational re-creation? Here we encounter the fundamental and very Hegelian problematic of the interaction of human beings with their means of expression. Human beings invent expressive or technical means and devices which allow them to have a certain grasp and understanding of the world, but these means also resist human intervention and thereby offer, as part of the specific confrontation with this resistance, inexhaustible possibilities for creativity.

This physical encounter between idea and material, or in terms of the narrative arts the encounter between the story (*fabula*) and the medium, has important consequences because it assumes that any process of adaptation has to take into account the kinds of "incarnations" inherent in this encounter in terms of the materiality of media. Whence our desire to reframe this problematic within a new "transversal" discipline – narrative mediatics – which would deal with questions of intermediality, transécriture, and trans-mediatization, and whose goal would be to study the encounter of a narrative project – that is, a story not yet fixed within a definitive matter of expression – with "the power of inertia of a given medium."[5] Indeed, in order to be communicated, any real or imaginary narrative substratum is obliged to deploy a means of mediation allowing for finding the configuration within which the coherence of story making or *mise-en-intrigue*, this crucial act which Ricoeur calls "second mimesis,"[6] can be constructed.

---

## Fabula, Syuzhet, Media

---

But before proceeding in this direction, we have to disentangle a rather tangled skein, bringing to the surface a notional pair quietly present in this article since the very beginning, to wit the distinction between *fabula* and *syuzhet*, inherited, as everyone knows, from the Russian Formalists. The exercise, as we shall see, is very revealing. But first a warning. In what follows, we will be using not the translation but rather the transliteration of the words "*fabula*"and "*syuzhet*," as is the custom in the Anglo-Saxon world, in order to better mark off their differential character than their French equivalents – "*fable*" and "*sujet*" – which are too polysemic and tarnished by ill usage. We must point out from the outset that for the Russian Formalists the "*fabula*" exists absolutely independently of any specific medium. It is, by definition, external to any actual work; it is not at all incarnated. Tomashevsky is very clear on this point:

> We call [*fabula*] the ensemble of linked events which are communicated to us by a given work. The *fabula* can be exposed in a pragmatic manner by following the natural order, i.e. the chronological and causal order of events, independently of the manner in which they are placed and introduced in the work itself.[7]

The question of the independence of the *fabula* for an adept of narratology can be clarified through Bremond's famous formulation suggesting that a narrative is a "layer of autonomous signification, whose structure can be isolated from the message as a whole" and that the structure of the recounted story is independent of "the techniques which are used to express it."[8] It seems possible, and legitimate, at first glance, to extract from a narrative work a kernel of actions quite apart from the means of expression through which this kernel of actions is relayed. The pedagogic and canonical process of the synopsis, or narrative summary, is based on precisely such an idea. But what are the limits of such a procedure? How much of the original work remains in the summary and how much is lost? Although we cannot give a definitive answer to this question, we can clarify some elements of an answer.

At the same time, we cannot accept the overly categorical claim that a *fabula* cannot exist except as it is embodied in some medium or other. All we need to do, to realize the limitations of such a view, is to close our eyes and imagine the story of "Little Red Riding Hood." The *fabula* of "Little Red Riding Hood" clearly exists, in each of our brains. More accurately, it exists as it is deformed and informed by each of our brains, or even more precisely by the powers and limitations of our brains which play the role, in this case, of media, or better of pseudo-media since their perception is not shared with other people, unless one turns to a "medium" in the other, more magical, sense of that word.[9] To share our *fabula*ting experience with another subject, we have to rely on a real medium such as language, mime, or design. Which implies as well the ways in which the media inform and deform any given *fabula*.

But when the Formalists argue that the *fabula* is independent of the media, it does not mean it is possible to refer to that *fabula* without thinking of a medium. To think, or express, the *fabula* in its very independence in relation to media, we still need to express or think the *fabula* in relation to some medium. In most cases, the medium will be verbal language as a kind of integrated medium closely linked to our own thought processes. A *fabula* like "Little Red Riding Hood," moreover, is more easily separated from its mediatic actualization insofar as it has a mythic dimension as a kind of psychic landmark indicative of collective social identity, and even of the human race.

Beyond the *fabula*, there is also the *syuzhet*, which has always been difficult to define, insofar as the Formalists have always defined it as both distinct from the *fabula* and at the same time in some sense not so distant from it. One might even suggest that the *syuzhet* includes the *fabula* or at least includes diverse elements of the *fabula*, but only after having passed through the crucible of what one might call the *mise-en-syuzhet*, or a process of, to use a rather barbarous neologism, "*syuzheticization*." A later passage in the Tomashevsky text clarifies the point: "The [*fabula*] is opposed to the [*syuzhet*], which is constituted by the same events, but which respects their order of appearance in the work itself and the sequence of informations that designates them."[10]

One part of this statement – "the sequence of informations that designates" the events – is intriguing, and Tomashevsky does not elaborate on it, except for one note: "In short, the [*fabula*] is what really happened, and the [*syuzhet*] is the manner in which the reader learns about what happened." If we take Tomashevsky seriously, then, the *syuzhet* is, in a way, the text as it is incarnated in a specific medium. We encounter the same idea in a text by Tynianov: "It [the *syuzhet* of the story] represents a kind of dynamics which takes form on the basis of all the material links . . . having to do with the style of [the *fabula*] and so forth."[11] And again, this time in relation to the cinema: "The script usually provides the '[*fabula*] in general' together with a few elements linked to the 'bouncing' character of the cinema. How the *fabula* will be developed, what will be the *syuzhet*, is something the scriptwriter knows nothing about, any more than the director before the projection of the fragments."[12] Thus the *syuzhet* would be the equivalent of the *fabula* insofar as it is mediated. In other words, the same *fabula*, the same anecdotal substratum, could undergo various "*syuzheticizations*." So "Little Red Riding Hood" could undergo a writerly *syuzheticization*, an oral *syzheticization*, a filmic *syuzheticization* and so forth, all of which would be quite distinct.

David Bordwell would disagree, since for him: "The structuration of the *syuzhet* is, in logical terms, independent of the media, since the same *syuzhet* structures could be materialized in a novel, a play, or a film."[13] One might think that Bordwell here commits the error denounced by Chklovski decades before: "Many people confuse the notion of [*syuzhet*] with the description of events, with what I propose we call the [*fabula*]. But in fact the [*fabula*] is nothing but a material in the service of [*syuzhet*]."[14] But Bordwell, in fact, does clearly distinguish *between fabula* and *syuzhet*, which he defines as "the concrete disposition and representation of the *fabula* within the film."

Bordwell's error, in our view, lies in not taking into account the range of phenomena that the Formalists include within the wide net of their *syuzhet*. In fact, their notion of *syuzhet* is in a way too broad, since it includes both (1) what Bordwell sees in it, i.e. the specific structuration of the *fabula* within a specific work – and it is not clear that structuration in this sense has anything to do with the media in question – and (2) the diverse aspects of mediatic incarnation implied by structuration. As formulated by the Formalists, in other words, *syuzhet* comprises two very different phenomena, even though the Formalists are not entirely wrong to connect them. Yet within our project here it strikes us as useful to distinguish the two points and consider them as enjoying a relative autonomy.

It is true that the *syuzhet* represents the ensemble of the motifs of the *fabula* according to, as Tomashevsky puts it, "the succession of events in the work itself."[15] But for us the definition of the *syuzhet* cannot be limited to such factors since, as Tomashevsky also points out, it is not insignificant that: "The reader becomes aware of a specific event at a specific point in the work and that the event is communicated directly by the author himself, or by a character, or with the help of indirect allusions."[16] There can thus be no doubt about the textual nature of the *syuzhet*. Thus at one end of the spectrum we have the *fabula*, the story as pure virtuality, the abstract story prior to any mediatization. At the other end of the spectrum we have the medium, the expressive support, the semiotic vehicle, also abstract in its way, insofar as here it is being considered in its virtuality. *Fabula* and medium are completely independent in relation to each other, while the *syuzhet* mediates a kind of rendezvous between the two, a product of the incarnation in media of a narrative substratum.

And this *syuzhet* has two faces or aspects. One turns toward the *fabula*, the other toward the medium. We will call one aspect the *syuzhet*-structure and the other the *syuzhet*-text, partly inspired by Thierry Groensteen's enumeration concerning the various "levels of accomplishment" of a work of fiction (he uses the French word "*sujet*," while we, following the Formalist usage, prefer *fabula*):

> For my part, I would distinguish three levels of accomplishment in any work of fiction. A fiction is the result of an effort at invention, producing what in French is called a "*sujet*" (theme) [and in Russian the *fabula*]; of an effort of organization, producing a *structure*; and an effort of expression, productive of a *text* . . . We can therefore – and indeed this is what usually happens – be faithful to the "*sujet*" (the theme) while modifying the other two levels. The term "adaptation" emphasizes the modifications in the structure as a result of technical constraints (for example the operation of time in the various media). The word "transsemiotization," meanwhile, emphasizes the replacement of one text by another, whose mediatic materiality is *essentially* different.[17]

Groensteen concludes with a very important question, to which we shall return, to wit: "To what extent can structure and text be literally transposed?"

A fiction, then, is the product of three kinds of creative intervention: (1) an intervention in terms of invention, the famous *inventio* of classical rhetoric, which generates the diverse elements of the story being told; (2) an intervention having to do with organization, bearing on the structuration of the story, which can be identified with the *dispositio* of classical rhetoric; and, finally, (3) an intervention at the level of expression, through a medium, of the narrative elements already "invented" and "disposed." This tripartite division in terms of the levels of accomplishment – theme, structure, and text for Groensteen; *fabula*, *syuzhet*-structure and *syuzhet*-text for us – allows us to pose in a much clearer way the question of the relation between narrative ideas and the constraints specific to the diverse media. When we move from one level to another, in the order that we have established, we discern a progressively greater implication of media in terms of the text being constructed. Which suggests to us that the *fabula* is already implicated by the media in question. Indeed, it matters little that the *fabula* is independent of specific media, since the *fabula* only exists as such insofar as it is on the side of "thought," for as soon as we imagine the *fabula* being on the side of the constructed, we are in the realm of the media.

Anyone who doubts this idea need only try to adopt the *fabula* of "Little Red Riding Hood" in a "unipunctual" medium such as still photography. Specifically mediatic questions like 'pluripunctuality' " quickly come to the surface.[18] Every *fabula*, in fact possibly every event, in its configuration, even before its "medial incarnation," already has certain features which are in a certain sense "medial." Furthermore, the relationship between a given story or event and a given medium already carries a certain meaning, which at least partially confirms our basic feeling that each *fabula* is intrinsically endowed with its own configuration which is always already compatible with the various media and thus preprograms, as it were, every process of adaptation.

As for the *syuzhet*, which would then occupy an intermediate terrain between *fabula* and medium, and which we prefer to regard in a theoretical sense as the place of securing of the told and the telling, in this sense the *syuzhet* is deeply implicated in the media. The *syuzhet*-structure already implies a minimum of medial consciousness, to the extent that, as Groensteen suggested in the text cited above, the technical constraints inherent in specific media impose a certain dimension or calibration on the structure of the *syuzhet*, in terms of the treatment of time, for example. Whence some of the specific challenges of adaptation. As for the *syuzhet*-text, it exists in symbiosis with the media in the sense that it can only be developed as it is poured into medial form, resulting in serious problems for adaptation.

--------------------- *Médiagénie* and Adaptation ---------------------

Up to this point, we have dealt with media in terms of *fabula* and even more of *syuzhet*. Now we have to move in the opposite direction, beginning from the media. Our goal is to show that if one wants to grasp the genesis and the status of a mediatized story, one cannot remain at the level of a simple logical consecution articulating the sequence of "*inventio*," "*dispositio*," and a mediatic-expressive structuration. For that reason, we will now further explore the idea of narrative mediatics introduced earlier.

We have already stressed the extent to which the encounter, or better the profound interaction, with the resistant opacity of the chosen matter of expression is itself generative, even decisive, within the process of creation. This general proposition needs to be further developed, especially in terms of the narrative arts insofar as they are fashioned within the crucible of the media which serve as a vehicle for them and even define them. Obviously, when one thinks of narratives, one spontaneously thinks of them in terms of their "natural" materialization in verbal language. But, even on this level, think for a moment of the very different character, and even the different meaning, of a story, or more precisely a *syuzhet*, when it is expressed orally as opposed to when it is expressed through the work of writing. And these differences proliferate even more when the *syuzhet* surfaces within such complex media as the cinema, television, and the comic strip.

Each medium, according to the ways in which it exploits, combines, and multiplies the "familiar" materials of expression – rhythm, movement, gesture, music, speech, image, writing (in anthropological terms our "first" media) – each medium, to recapitulate, possesses its own communicational energetics. Such is the nature of the power of inertia invoked earlier. The metaphor of inertia, borrowed from physics, perhaps brings with it overly negative connotations. One might prefer concepts such as "the force of gravity" or even "force of attraction." Such appellations doubtless point more effectively to the expressive and narrative potential of a given medium when, as they say, one looks at it in the abstract. This observation recalls the distinction, proposed a few years ago, between intrinsic and extrinsic narrativity.[19] Thus the film and the comic strip by their very nature have a certain narrative *je ne sais quoi* when they are defined in terms of the manner in which they activate and trigger a succession of images, as well as the manner in which they stimulate the possibility of introducing a principle of transformation within that succession. It is the responsibility of this intrinsic narrative potential to receive an extrinsic narrative content.

To receive or, better, to interact with the aforementioned content. To draw once again on the archive of metaphors drawn from the sciences, but this time from chemistry, the media "react" with the *fabula* that chooses that medium. Or to put it in a way more in keeping with what we have argued up to this point, the media can only take on the responsibility of communicating a *fabula* by developing a *syuzhet*-reaction whose scope, obviously, can vary a good deal. As a narrative project, the *fabula* is incarnated through interaction with a medium. This interaction is manifested first of all in and through the *syuzhet*-text, but also in and through the *syuzhet*-structure to which it is intimately linked. Narrative transparency therefore always brushes up against the opacity of a reaction-*syuzhet* secreted by the medium. The goal of the classical fictional story is, of course, to win over the public by trying to hide its status as artifact, but the media and the means of expression mobilized by such stories resist the attempt. This resistance, this opacity – we can recall again the example of Beethoven – can be the sources of creation, offering the *fabula* fabulous opportunities for *syuzheticization*.

Narrative mediatics requires more work on these issues in order to clarify the possible limitations and developments, while also defining more precisely the idea of media. It seems to us that this discipline should apply first of all to the mass media, that is, to complex media which gather together various basic materials of expression.

Alongside the extrinsic and intrinsic features already mentioned, we might also distinguish two broad conceptual categories: mediativity[20] (or perhaps mediality) and narrativity. The first would bear on the expressive power (much as one speaks of the power of an engine) developed by the media. This ontological potential is medium-specific and depends on the intrinsic features of the means of expression or representation that the medium requires or combines. Comic strips, for example, generally combine a designed image with a written text, both of which are poured into a homogeneous graphic dynamic. More generally, the potential of a medium derives from a double interaction: not only the interaction that allows a coded opening of an internal space where different materials of expression can be combined, but also the interaction that is produced by the encounter, or the (chemical) reaction of these first means of expression with the technical apparatuses designed to relay and amplify them. How many possibilities, for example, in the encounter of a single voice with the sonorous modulations made possible by the microphone! Mediativity would refer then to a medium's intrinsic capacity to represent – and to communicate that representation. That capacity is determined by the technical possibilities of the medium, by the internal semiotic configurations that it calls up, and by the communicational and relational apparatuses that it is able to put in place. A cinematic example: in its manner of representing the pro-filmic (that which the camera records), the *filmographic*, in its specificity, has everything to do with mediativity.[21] The same is true of "*graphiation*,"[22] the basic instance of enunciation of the comic strip. And the same point applies for the mediatization-narration of events by direct transmission as one of the specific features of television.

As a necessarily more narrow category, narrativity refers to the character or the quality of that which is narrative. But this definition becomes inadequate in the context of narrative mediatics. It might be preferable to give narrativity a pragmatic, virtual meaning. One can observe the narrative character of a given object (for example, of a fiction film), but one can also discern the narrative "seed" or potential within a given object (for example, the photograph which suggests a possible story without actually being that story). We therefore have to distinguish between an explicitly affirmed narrative and a virtual narrative as a possible dimension inherent in a given configuration of an object (whether a sign, a message, or, more basically, a medium). In a sense, narrativity is included within the larger category of mediativity; it is in this sense a particular modality of mediativity.

Intrinsic narrativity, then, has to do with the ontological narrative potential of media which it possesses as a function of its own mediativity (for example, the contiguity and consecution of the images of a comic strip). Supposing that the media generate their own illusion, intrinsic narrativity shapes and conditions the *syuzhet*.

Extrinsic narrativity, meanwhile, has to do with the narrative disposition, stronger or weaker as the case may be, manifested in the anecdotal substratum on which the *fabula* is based. Thus, some real-life events, such as a horrific crime, the suicide of a star, or the Tour de France with its progressive stages, seem to slide more easily than other events into a story; such events seem to spontaneously ask to be rendered as stories. Such would be the object of study of narrative diegetics: to study what in reported events, whether real or imaginary, lends itself to narrative. Or, to put it differently, to study the question of a narrative virtuality of events which precedes even the formation of the narrative. If we push this thinking even farther, is it not this intuited narrative virtuality that enables us to "construct" an event? Diegetics could thus conceive of a downstream and an upstream approach to the media, since some *fabula*s seem less susceptible to the force of attraction of the media, and some are more easily detached from their mediatic *syuzhet* (think, for example, of the propensity for emancipation, even autonomy, of the little story in Lumière's *L'Arroseur arrosé* [The Waterer Watered]).

But here we touch on one of the most important consequences of narrative mediatics, having to do with questions of intermediality, transécriture, and adaptation. Each narrative project, in our view, can be considered in terms of *médiagénie*.[23] Fables and stories have the possibility of being brought to life in the best possible way by choosing the most appropriate mediatic partner. Perhaps this explains why some works seem "unadaptable." Being literally poured into the form a specific medium, these stories suffer enormous losses in the transition from one medium to another. The burlesque episodes lived on the screen by a Buster Keaton or a Harold Lloyd only realize their full expressive potential in and through the silent film. One might make the same point about the intimate confidences of Proust in *A la recherche du temps perdu*, the various adaptations of which have generally been seen as scandalous. We find the same situation with the *Adventures of Tintin*, whose *fabula* is of a body, almost literally, with its *syuzhet*, and its *syuzhet* with the medium, and whose adaptation in the form of an animated cartoon is criticized, somewhat paradoxically, for freezing its characters in place. Here we have a strange paradox, indeed, since the model, despite the intrinsic stasis of its fixed images, seems less static than its adaptation into moving images. *L'intermedialité*, it seems, has its reasons, that reason itself does not know.

It is true that, basically, the reader who immerses him or herself in the story of a comic strip will always be disappointed when the story is transposed into film. The disappointment is perhaps exacerbated by the kind of false proximity of the relationship between these two means of telling stories through images. But the processes of fictionalization, the phenomenology of reading, and the modes of participation in the two media are quite different. With its way of displaying images across the space of a page, with its obvious deficiencies in terms of realistic illusion, the comic strip actively calls on the reader's participation. Readers have to draw on their own imagination to mentally represent what has not been given in perceptual terms (sound, movement, temporality). Once we have supplanted this lack, filled in the void, the comic strip world communicates the idea that our imaginary is indirectly responsible for the experience. Tintin, Haddock, and Castafiore all have a grain of voice which is the one that we have mentally ascribed to them. The Dupondt have their attitude, their own gawkiness. When the same characters, in a film, become endowed with real voices and movement, the fans of these comics are almost necessarily disappointed. The incarnated voice of Captain Haddock will never be "realistic" or authentic for the person who knows the character through prior experience of the comic strip. To grasp this phenomenon even better, we can think of the experience of radio, which in some ways constitutes the opposite situation. When we know a voice through radio, when the medium has made it familiar, we are almost always surprised and often disappointed when we encounter the same voice accompanied by the body to which it belongs. Here we touch on the question of what one might call the localization of the foyer or place of the impression of reality, a localization which can be more or less internal or external to the medium, depending on the fictional configurations generated by the medium.

It might be useful, in this sense, to imagine a class of texts which consists of those works (plays, films, novels, comic strips, and so on) which are more or less unadaptable without major upheavals or without "breaking up" entirely. This hypothetical repertory would include those works that use the media to express the last entrenchments of the medium. In the comic strip, such would be the case of the stories of Marc-Antoine Mathieu whose plots integrate and dramatize the internal workings of the "ninth art" along with the process of reading that the work demands. In this sense, certain forms of *mise-en-abyme* would be a way of rendering both the *syuzhet* and the medium irreplaceable. A number of works nourish themselves by accepting this mediatic opacity as a kind of necessary rustle. Others reveal their genius by the exemplary manner in which they inextricably mingle their narrative with the spectacular emancipation, and therefore the opacity, of the medium in question.

How does one find the forms of fidelity to the spirit of a medium? That kind of fidelity is probably more productive than the famous notion of fidelity to an author, or to a story. Every self-respecting adaptation needs to organize the violence done to the *fabula* and to the *syuzhet* of the source work, for in a way the new *syuzheticization* involves not only a *mise-en-sujet*, that is, the shaping of a story, but also and especially a *mise-en-sujétion*, and its "subjectedness" to a specific medium.

The weight of a story, like that of a body, is only imaginable in relation to a mediatic force of attraction. The more intense the *médiagénie*, the more awkward the attempts to free oneself from this force of attraction. In order to move in the direction of another medium, the "being" of the story, insofar as it exists, has to dress up in a space suit, as it were, which can allow it to confront a temporary but dangerous state of weightlessness. If the translation succeeds, the story will accept a greater weight, or a loss of weight. And even, at times, accept profound modifications in mass and aspect. All of which opens up, as on the moon, hitherto unsuspected developments and perspectives.

*Translated by Robert Stam*

---

### Notes

1 Paul Auster, *The Invention of Solitude* (New York: State University of New York Press, 1982), p. 32.

2 For more on this subject, see Phillipe Marion, *Cours de communication narrative* (Louvain-la-Neuve: DUC, 1992).

3 Claude Simon, *Discours de Stockholm* (Paris: Minuit, 1986), p. 25 (translation of quotation by Robert Stam).

4 Claude Simon, *Orion aveugle* (Paris: Minuit, 1981), p. 5 (translation of quotation by Robert Stam).

5 See Philippe Marion, "Le Scénario de bande-dessinée: la différence par le média," *Études Littéraires* (Quebec) 26: 2 (1993), 77.

6 Paul Ricoeur, *Temps et récit*, 3 vols (Paris: Seuil, 1983, 1984, 1985); English translation by Kathleen McLaughlin and David Pellauer, *Time and Narrative*, 2 vols (Chicago: University of Chicago Press, 1984, 1985).

7 Boris Tomashevsky, "Thematique," in Tzvetan Todorov, *Théorie de la littérature* (Paris: Seuil, 1973), p. 268.

8 Claude Bremond, *Logique du récit* (Paris: Seuil, 1973), pp. 11–12.

9 Our brain might itself be conceived of as a medium if we remember that it allows different parts of the body to communicate with one another and exchange information.

10 Tomashevsky, "Thematique," p. 268.

11  Yuri Tynianov, "Des fondements du cinéma," *Les Cahiers du Cinéma* 220–1 (May–June 1970), 67.

12  Ibid., 69.

13  David Bordwell, *Narration in the Fiction Film* (Madison: University of Wisconsin Press, 1985), p. 50.

14  V. Chklovski, quoted by B. Eikhenbaum, "La Théorie de la 'méthode formelle'" in Todorov, *Théorie de la littérature*, p. 54.

15  Tomashevsky, "Thematique," p. 269.

16  Ibid.

17  Thierry Groensteen, in a text appended to a letter to André Gaudreault, dated February 25, 1991.

18  Notions of "unipunctuality" and "pluripunctuality" are developed in André Gaudreault, *Du littéraire au filmique: système du récit* (Paris/Quebec: Méridiens/Klincksieck/Presses de l'Université Laval, 1988). To be published in English by University of Toronto Press in 2005.

19  Ibid., p. 43.

20  For more on this concept, see Philippe Marion, "Narratologie médiatique et médiagénie des récits," *Recherches en Communication* 7 (1997), 61–87.

21  Gaudreault, *Du littéraire au filmique*, passim.

22  Philippe Marion, *Traces en cases: travail graphique et figuration narrative. Essai sur la bande dessinée et son lecteur*, vol. 1 (Brussels/Louvain la Neuve: Bruylant/Academia, 1993).

23  For the first formulations of this concept, see Marion, *Traces en cases*, and "Petite mediatique de la peur," *Protée* 21: 2 (1993), 47–56.

André Gaudreault and Philippe Marion

Chapter 4

# Chapter 5

# The Look: From Film to Novel

## An Essay in Comparative Narratology

## François Jost

Born at the beginning of the twentieth century, the relations between novel and film have often been thought of in hierarchical terms. To the extent that filmic adaptations of novels are much more frequent that novelistic adaptations of films (commonly called "novelizations"), scholars tend to reflect more on the transformation of written texts into images than on the converse transformation. There is certainly much to learn from comparing a given novel with its filmic adaptation, both in ideological and narrative terms. But what I am proposing here is something quite different. Here, it will not be a question of studying film–novel relations, but rather cinema–literature relations. I will not be discussing the relation between two specific texts; rather, I will practice a kind of shuttle between cinema and novel in order to better comprehend a narrative category which functions equally well for the analysis of written as well as filmic narrative. In sum, it will be a question of what I call "comparative narratology." But how can we define such a field? To put it concisely, comparative narratology is less a matter of pointing up resemblances or differences between two semiotic systems than of deploying the cinema–literature shuttle in order to forge more precise and productive concepts.

Our itinerary will take us from what Metz calls a "universal code" – that is, a code found in multiple semiotic systems; for example, a narrative which could be literary, cinematic, or sung – to more restricted codes, concretely linked to the specificities of the materials. For comparative narratology, transcodification will be a heuristic method for understanding a certain concept of narrative. In this back and forth, we will begin with literature in order to find the origin of the concept, then move to the cinema to clarify it, and finally return to literature.

# The Theory of Literature and Vision: The Metaphor of the Camera

François Jost

Chapter 5

This chapter is oriented around the concept of what literary theorists call "point of view," or, following Genette, "focalization." It is curious that this notion, which evokes the look or the gaze, was first formulated by *literary* theory, since within the novelistic field, vision per se does not exist; it is only a transcription, the rough equivalent of a physical phenomenon, more metaphoric than actual.

Even in cases where a description is introduced by a verb of perception, such as "see," "observe," or "regard," the equivalence between a series of words and the described referent will always be a result of convention, of an implicit contract of transcodification in which the author participates. The expression of the thought or intellectual point of view of a character, meanwhile, is more simple and direct, since then it is a matter only of exchanging the verbal for the verbal – if we put aside for the moment the case of non-verbalized psychic movements translated or transposed by authors such as Joyce or Sarraute. What is called "point of view" thus covers two very different phenomena: on the one hand, perceiving, and on the other, thinking and knowing. Yet literary theorists generally use the same labels for the two activities: "vision," "point of view," and "focalization."

It is striking, then, that despite the purely conventional character of the gaze in the novel, literary theorists tend to look to the cinema to explain the functioning of vision in the novel. Thus we often read that the narrator of Camus' *L'Etranger* registers external events in the manner of a camera. As Lintvelt puts it, "the novelistic action is not perceived by one of the actors, but rather focalized, so to speak, by a camera."[1] But, for a film theorist, this use of the camera metaphor is shockingly imprecise. What does it mean to distinguish between actions perceived by an actor and actions perceived by a camera? In films, frequently enough, what is seen by the character is also what is shown by the camera. The idea of the camera's neutrality is also surprising, since both filmmakers and theorists often speak of the "subjective camera." Indeed, what is most bizarre is that literary theorists, who need the cinematic model in order to think through novelistic procedures, do not bother to study either the functions of the camera or the ways in which the look is constructed in film. For those theorists, the camera is first and foremost an apparatus for objectively registering the world, little more than a tool without any narrative function. It plays no active role in the representation; it merely copies reality without changing it. But no informed contemporary scholar still believes in the old dream of automatic filmic transparency formulated by Bazin.

The camera metaphor unfortunately also triggers a kind of sliding from the idea of vision to the idea of objectivity or impartiality. And this sliding, in its turn, transforms a simple perceptual attitude into a mental attitude. Perception and mental attitude are presumed to function together. Literary scholars assert, for example, that if in a novel one follows the events through a character's point of view (Genette's "internal focalization"), one should not see the character from outside, since it is impossible to be simultaneously inside and outside the character. For example, in *La Chartreuse de Parme*, the description of the Battle of Waterloo is reduced to what the character Fabrice knows – i.e. very little – and he should not be described from the outside. Following the same logic, if one does not know a character's thoughts, they suggest, one should also not know his or her perceptions.

Indeed, a careful reading of Genette's *Figures III* reveals a sliding between the moment where Genette defines "focalization" and the moment, a few pages later, where he explains it. In the first instance, point of view is defined in cognitive terms, through equality or non-equality. For example, Genette claims that a narrative features internal focalization when "the narrator only says what that character knows." In this formulation, the knowledge of the narrator is equal to that of the character. Genette argues further that a narrative features external focalization when "the narrator says less than the character knows," a formulation where the knowledge of the character exceeds that of the narrator. He speaks further of "zero focalization," where the narrator knows more than all the characters, or, more precisely, reveals more than any one of the characters knows. Here the knowledge of the narrator exceeds that of the characters. A few pages later, however, Genette deploys perceptual criteria – vision – to define point of view. Genette speaks, for example, of the traveling carriage in *Madame Bovary*, "told from the point of view of an external witness." Genette also speaks of a scene in which the "witness is not personified but is only an impersonal observer," or again of a situation in which "internal focalization implies the disappearance of the character." This sliding from the cognitive to the perceptive reaches a kind of climax when Genette chooses, as his example of internal focalization, a film, *Rashomon* (1951), which actually shows characters externally, from the *outside*.[2]

Even more curiously, this same confusion between seeing and knowing is found even in the work of some very reputable film theorists. Thus Jean Mitry defines the "subjective camera" as follows: "The image is called subjective because it allows the spectator to occupy the place of the heroes, to see and feel like them."[3] Once again, perceptions and sensations have been conflated. Yet even the slightest reflection on the matter suggests that in the cinema the seen and the known do not always go hand in hand. What happens precisely, then, in that art for which point of view is a fundamental semiotic feature?

## The Roles of the Camera in the Cinema: The Construction of the Look

The cinema has two physical tracks – the image track and the sound track – so one easily imagines that film can simultaneously express what is seen – through the image track – and what is thought – through voice-over. The difference between seeing and feeling and knowing is almost a semiotic difference: it is possible to show someone or something and at the same time express something completely different through the voice.

In order to differentiate visual point of view, on the one hand, which once again is not a metaphor in the cinema but rather a narrative reality, and cognitive point of view on the other, I would propose the following terminology: *ocularization* has to do with the relation between what the camera shows and what the characters are presumed to be seeing; *focalization* designates the cognitive point of view adopted by the narrative, with the equalities or inequalities of knowledge expressed at their full strength. In a film, focalization is a complex product of what one sees, what the character is presumed to be seeing, what he or she is presumed to know, what he or she says, and so forth. Here I will restrict myself to the first problem, to wit the problem of determining the narrative value of what is shown by the camera, which I have referred to as ocularization.

Depending on the context, every photograph can be called objective or subjective. A photograph of a landscape can be related to the landscape itself (the referential function) or to the photographer (expressive function). That is why the same photographs are sometimes published as part of a report on a given country, and sometimes as part of a report on the work of a given photographer. And that is why any shot from any film can be transformed into a look simply by juxtaposing it with an image of someone looking. But how can we go beyond this "undecidability," this apparent neutrality? We get a glimpse of how in a small 1900 film, by the British filmmaker Hepworth, entitled *How it Feels to Be Run Over*. In the film, a horse-drawn carriage comes toward the camera and then moves off-screen, followed by an automobile, which also moves toward the camera, after which the screen goes black. White spots spread around the darkness, while we read the following words: "Oh! Mother – *will* – be pleased!"

In viewing this film, one at first has the impression that one is seeing an ordinary Lumière-style "view," a monstration, without any special twist. But then, when the automobile heads straight toward the spectators, their identification with the camera becomes more important than what is viewed. Finally, on reading the title "Oh, mother will be pleased!" one has the clear impression of having shared a particular look. In fact, catalogues from the period inform us that white spots against a black background were designed to signify the stars as seen by the unfortunate victim of an accident.

In order to interpret this shot, then, we have to situate it in relation to the imaginary axis of the camera-eye. Either one regards the image as being seen by specific eyes, in which case one assumes that those eyes belong to a character, or the status or the position of the camera becomes more important, in which case we attribute it to an entity external to the world portrayed, to what has been called the "grand imager." Or we can overlook the existence of this axis, in which case we have the famous illusion of transparency. These three possible attitudes in fact boil down to a binary choice: either a shot is anchored in the regard of an instance internal to the diegesis – what we have called "internal ocularization" – or it is not so anchored, and is therefore a case of "zero ocularization." We can chart this opposition in the following manner:

$$
\text{Ocularization}
\begin{cases}
\text{internal}
\begin{cases}
\text{primary} \\
\text{secondary}
\end{cases} \\
\text{zero}
\end{cases}
$$

"Primary internal ocularization" may be defined by several configurations. In the first instance, it is marked in the signifier by the materiality of a body, whether immobile or not, or the presence of an eye which allows us, without relying on context, to identify a character not present in the image. It is a question of suggesting a regarding look without necessarily showing it. To this end, one constructs the image as an index, as a trace which allows spectators to establish an immediate link between what they see and the camera which has captured or reproduced the real, through the construction of an analogy with the spectator's own perception.

We find most of these configurations in the shot from *The Lady in the Lake* (1947) where Marlowe visits a man named Lavery: a slightly trembling forward tracking shot advances toward a sign on a door where we discover the name of the person being sought; another camera movement takes us from the sign to the hand pressing the buzzer, followed by another movement toward the name. Then the hand pushes open the door and sweeps over the house. We also discern the character's shadow.

Other criteria sometimes suggest the presence of a regarding look; for example, an unusually low angle or an out-of-focus background, or the deformation of the image in relation to what cinematic convention regards as normal in a given period (superimposed double images, out-of-focus effects) which suggest conditions such as drunkenness, strabismus, myopia, and so forth: for example, the road which becomes doubled during "Kaplan's" (Cary Grant) drunken ride in *North by Northwest* (1959); masking effects which suggest the (sometimes unnamed) presence of an observing eye (keyhole, binoculars, microscope). If masking effects, perceptual deformations, and the foregrounded presence of a part of the body almost invariably construct a character's point of view, the case of the shakily subjective tracking shot is more ambiguous. The shaking camera could signify the bodily experience of the person seeing, or could be merely an accident due to unfavorable shooting conditions which prevented a more stable image. The question is not always easy to answer since in semiotic terms nothing allows us to make an absolute distinction between a shot which simply elicits primary identification with the camera on the spectator's part, and a point-of-view shot linked to an unidentified character. With some films, it is possible to posit the difference, but in other cases we only know thanks to extrafilmic information concerning genre, period, mode of production. If the camera shakes in a big-budget Hollywood blockbuster, one can assume that it is not a question of technical ineptitude and that therefore the shaking implies an observing character. If the camera trembles in a 1960s' low-budget "direct cinema" militant documentary, on the other hand, one can assume that this stylistic "defect" has to do with the conditions of production as well as the "narrator" who "speaks cinema."

"Secondary internal ocularization" occurs when the subjective image is constructed through editing (as in shot/counter-shot); that is, through a contextualization of an image. Any image that is edited together with a shot of a person looking, within the rules of cinematic "syntax," will be "anchored" in the visual subjectivity of that person or character.

"Zero ocularization" occurs when the image is not seen by any entity within the diegesis. The "zero" here is not pejorative but technical; it simply signifies seen by no one,

The Look: From Film to Novel

Chapter 5

"nobody's shot," or, as Eisenstein puts it: "the action which would be depicted without any author's relation to it (the subject) of any kind." In our modern terminology, we would say that this kind of ocularization has to do with the narrator; that is, the instance which seems to organize and execute both the representation and the story. But zero ocularization can be more or less marked: a normal angle seems transparent, while a bizarre or surprising angle more clearly unveils a narrating presence organizing the fiction. "Zero," then, simply means that it is not possible to assign an image to any specific gaze. Most shots of most films use zero ocularization, even in the case of characters or narrators telling their own stories in flashback.

## Looking Relations in the Novel

Our little detour through the cinema has taught us the following. First, that seeing and knowing are two different things. A story can be limited to what a character knows (internal focalization) even while at the same time we see the character from outside (zero ocularization). The converse is also possible, as the case of Beckett's *Film* suggests. When a shot is in primary internal ocularization, we know less than the character – for example, we do not know his or her identity, as in the beginning of *Dark Passage* (D. Davies, 1947). The point is that in the novel as well, it is likely that the cognitive and the visual criteria do not always function together and in tandem; they can move in opposite directions.

Secondly, we have learned that the concept of ocularization or the determination of point of view assumes that it is possible to localize that point of view. When the positioning of the camera is not linked to the regard of a character within the diegesis, that positioning reveals the presence only of the cinematic narrator (zero ocularization). In the novel, then, it is likely that some moments allow us to identify an ocular position and others do not allow us to do so, and where we are not obliged to do so. Thirdly, we have learned that in the cinema there are semiotic criteria which enable us to posit with precision the relation between camera position and a character's (or the film's narrator's) point of view. And one suspects that we might also find in the novel some equivalent of this articulation of the narrative and the semiotic at the linguistic level.

With this in mind, let us examine an utterance such as the following: "Toward ten in the evening, the poker players began to show signs of fatigue." When Mieke Bal speaks of a "narrator-focalizer" and concludes that the word "signs" means "that the behavior of the characters may be seen and interpreted by a spectator . . . and that the narrative is obviously told by an extra-diegetic narrator and also focalized by an extra-diegetic focalizer" she fails to carry out the operations that I have been recommending here.[4] Although the word "signs" does imply exteriority in relation to the poker players, one cannot limit oneself to such imprecise approximations when it is a question of defining a "focalizer." Within the utterance, there is no indication of the virtual looking position.

And if the idea of ocularization is to have any conceptual value at all, only this criterion – the question of looking position – should operate, as we have seen in our detour through the cinema. Moreover, if one imagines the filmed version of this poker scene, it becomes quite clear that the camera could be placed in any number of "correct" positions: low angle, high angle, behind the players, in front of the players, and so forth. If you are outside the scene, it is a case of zero ocularization; which does not imply that the scene is observed by someone. In the case of this quotation, then, there is no point of view but only a narrator who tells the story, in the third person, and who is only implicitly present. The choice that confronts the writer, then, is whether he will emphasize the narrative action or choose to make the narrator more or less perceptible to the reader.

The fact that an image is seen by a spectator does not necessarily imply that it is oriented by a point of view in the diegesis. Distinctive indices and/or contextual information are necessary to say whether such an utterance moves toward a subjective intention. The example of cinema – where the look is definitely a fact of language – prods us into clarifying the question of novelistic point of view by articulating both narrative and semiotic criteria. Readers should try to determine, through and beyond the words, whether or not what they read is filtered through the eyes or through the ears. And just as one requires semiotic methods (concerning the material of expression) to analyze these questions in the cinema, one requires linguistics to analyse looking relations in the novel.

Let us examine, for example, the following utterances:

> But the noise of the high heels cannot be heard here. (from Robbe-Grillet's *Dans le labyrinthe*)

> Thus, on my right, the somber and silent image of death; and on my left, the decent bacchanalias of life. (Balzac's *Sarrasine*)

> Above the Hotel Recamier (far behind?) a crane stands out in the sky. (It was there yesterday, but I don't remember any longer having noticed it.) (from Georges Perec's *Tentative d'épuisement d'un lieu Parisien*)

> A luminous rectangle stands out against the wall, in the back and to the right, just in front of the staircase, and an illuminated zone from that point on . . . (Robbe-Grillet's *Dans le labyrinthe*)

In all four of these utterances, space is organized around a viewing position. The first example separates two spaces: inside and outside. The last three examples all lend a sense of laterality or depth to the described space, but the ocular position is not produced in the same way in the three cases. In the first example, the eminently deictic adverb "here" implicitly calls attention to what C. Kerbrat-Orecchioni calls a "locutor-observer."[5] (The fact that the observer is an ear changes nothing.) In the case of the first sentence, "auricu-larization" is deduced in the same manner as ocularization, in the sense that it is a deictic subjectivity, that is, a subjectivity characterized by a spatio-temporal situation, that constructs the text. In the second sentence, it is the possessive adjective "my" that relativizes the spatial description in function of the narrator. In the third sentence, it is the parenthetical sentence that allows us to attribute the sentence to the narrator. In the fourth sentence, we need more contextual information to determine whether we should attribute description to a character or a narrator.

The first point to make about these examples is that the vectorization of perception is more easily determined than the anchorage of a look. It is no exaggeration to speak of a narratological "law:" the existence of ocularization precedes its identification. This observation is not surprising, furthermore, given the difficulties of localization in lan-guage. To resolve the question of attribution of a point of view in any given instance, we have to solve two problems. First, the question of orientation in space. If the word "here" necessarily points to a locutor, it is not the same with paradigmatic oppositions like "left" and "right" and "behind" and "in front of." Kerbrat-Orecchioni demonstrates that such words can be used in very different ways. To say that "X is to the right of Y" changes meaning depending on whether Y is oriented in a lateral sense or not. "Go sit to the left of the chair" refers to the side which is "my" left. "Sit to Pierre's left" means to sit at the left side of Pierre, not to my left. Moreover, some objects presuppose a given orientation. The tops and bottoms of a building are the same for everyone, independent of viewing position, whence the need for the parenthesis in statement 3 above.

Second, we need to solve the problems linked to displayed speech. The fourth utterance is difficult to interpret because "in the back" and "to the right" can be deictic or can have to do with the position of a character about whom one is speaking, since "it often happens that when the space is the one where evolves, not the subject of the enunciation but an actant of the utterance, that the relation of the localization is determined in func-tion of S1, the place where the actant is supposed to be."[6] In that case, only a contextual analysis can allow us to determine positionality.

For the moment, we can bypass the problems relating to textual analysis. The list of textual indicators can be enriched through particular analyses. Be that as it may, linguistic reflection, based on a method culled from semiotic film analysis, allows us to offer a tripartite account of ocularization:

*Primary internal ocularization* occurs when spatial adverbs are deployed as deictics because we are sure that these adverbs bear on the one who is telling the story and on the one who is seeing the scene. As in the cinema, this configuration can be deduced from the signifying traces of the enunciation. Primary internal ocularization thus refers back to a first-person narrator, whereas in the cinema we can only affirm that it refers back to someone seeing the scene, but who is not necessarily telling it. In the cinema, there is no equivalency or solidarity between the observer and the speaker.

*Secondary internal ocularization* occurs when the description is anchored in the eyes of a character (once we have resolved the kinds of problems addressed above).

*Zero ocularization* is reserved for cases where the description is oriented in some way but without gaining meaning in relation either to the narrator or to the character. For example, when a painting is described in such a way that there is an orientation, that is, a specific attitude in relation to the painting, but without that attitude being ascribable to a specific narrator or character. In that case, the third-person utterance points to an implicit narrator, but not to a visual positioning. Zero ocularization in a novel is therefore closer to an *absence* of point of view, which is hardly surprising since point of view is not one of the inherent semiotic mechanisms of literature; it can therefore only be indirectly suggested or evoked.

*Geographical ocularization,* finally, characterizes those descriptions which do not point either to a narrator or to a character but rather to a kind of anonymous traveler of the kind one finds in touristic guidebooks or in Stendhal, with his famous definition of the novel as "a mirror traveling down a road."

Indeed, if literary theorists have often confused knowing and seeing, it is because the language uses the same words to express both attitudes, the cognitive and the perceptive. This process becomes manifest in the following utterance. "James Bond seems astonished." The sentence could either describe a deduction based on the visible appearance of the character or convey the idea that one does not really know the inner feelings of the character. Only the "detour" through cinema can definitively clarify this kind of situation. But the literary detour has also allowed us to bury a series of preconceived ideas from literary theory. First, in terms of the famous "objectivity of the camera." The notion of the "camera eye," often used by critics to evoke a neutral and objective description, is now revealed as a dangerous and baseless metaphor. Secondly, to speak of the looking position in a novel requires us to inquire into localization. In this sense, the concept of "focalizer" is more or less useless, since it adds nothing to the concept of "narrator." Third, the relationship between seeing and knowing is not obligatory. We can see a character *and* be inside his or her head. Ocularization does not always go hand in hand with focalization.

The semiotic materials of film and novel are not the same, and one cannot mechanically transfer concepts forged in one domain to another domain. But it is also useless to try to solve these problems through imprecise metaphors. If one has to define the point of view, which obviously has to do with the visual, it is important to look to those arts, such as cinema, which point concretely to an ocular position, as long as one takes into account the material differences of the two media. Thus transcodification is not only a prod for innovatory theoretical reflections but also a means for forging the more solid and rigorous concepts needed for comparative narratology.

*Translated by Robert Stam*

The Look: From Film to Novel

Chapter 5

1  Jaap Lintvelt, *Essai de typologie narrative: le "point de vue"* (Paris: Librairie José Corti, 1981), p. 79.

2  Gérard Genette, *Figures III* (Paris: Editions du Seuil, 1972), pp. 206, 208, 209.

3  Jean Mitry, *Esthétique et psychologie du cinéma* (Paris: Editions Universitaires, 1965), vol. 2, p. 61.

4  Mieke Bal, "Narration and Focalization," *Poétique* 29 (1977), 121.

5  C. Kerbrat-Orecchioni, *Lénonciation* (Paris: Armand Colin), p. 49.

6  Ibid., p. 106.

François Jost

Chapter 5

# Chapter 6

# Adaptation and Mis-adaptations

## Film, Literature, and Social Discourses

## Francesco Casetti

_____ **Film and Literature: From Modes of Expression** _____
**to Spheres of Discourse**

The relationship between literature and film has been the subject of numerous reflections and analyses. Despite their diversity, most of these researches have a common starting-point. Both literature and cinema have been regarded essentially as *modes of expression*, sites and ways of manifestation of an ability to give shape to ideas, feelings, and personal orientations; in other words, as sites in which an individual's perceptions are combined with the person's will/necessity to offer an image of him or herself and of his or her own world. As a consequence, many of these contributions employ, as their key concepts, notions such as "work," "author," "poetics," and "intention." These notions focus on the presence of an individual's work and, simultaneously, on the fact that a text testifies to it; they emphasize the unfolding of personal actions and a personal universe, and the additional idea of being the repository of the text's deepest identity.

Among the reasons that have permitted this approach to become dominant, one in particular stands out: the desire to "valorize" cinema as an art form and as an object of inquiry; that is, the recognition of its "artistic value," a privilege that other fields, and in particular literature, have had for a long time. This desire, which is apparent in critical writings from the 1920s to the 1980s, has led to the application of categories used in literary studies – such as author, work, poetics, and so on – and in aesthetic theory to the cinema. Such an approach has contributed to the partial disregard of some of cinema's specificities; for instance, the fact that it is a mass-communication medium. Conversely, film studies have failed to extend the application of some peculiarly cinematic categories to other fields in order to provoke them into questioning their own aesthetic assumptions.[1] Had that been done, the state of crisis in those categories would have become apparent; that is, the fact that they are no longer capable of sanctioning a medium's "artistic value." Benjamin had seen it coming: for him, the advent of photography and cinema was going to change the parameters of art, to the point that, retroactively, we appreciate how inappropriate it is to employ categories for film that should be undergoing re-formulation even in other fields. Rather, it is necessary to move in the opposite direction: cinema and photography should be used as new frames of reference for the critical assessment of other fields.[2] The Benjaminian path, however, has rarely been followed.

In keeping with this approach, I would like to suggest another perspective: both film and literature can also be considered as *sites of production and the circulation of discourses*; that is, as symbolic constructions that refer to a cluster of meanings that a society considers possible (thinkable) and feasible (legitimate). Consequently, film and literature are more revealing of the ways in which subjects interact with each other as either addressers or addressees, than of an author's ability to express him or herself. I therefore suggest regarding audiovisual and literary texts as one would regard conversations, newspaper reports, public speeches, research reports, stories and anecdotes; that is, as discursive formations which testify to the way in which society organizes its meanings and shapes its system of relations; or else, as events, as Foucault defines them,[3] which punctuate social life, functioning, on the one hand, as reservoirs of meaning, and, on the other, as vectors of relations. This perspective, which does not exclude a more aesthetically concerned approach, leads to a reformulation of the conceptual framework usually activated in understanding the relationship between film and literature, and to a reconsideration of the notion of *adaptation*.

---

## Adaptation as the "Reappearance" of Discourse

Within this perspective adaptation is no longer seen as a work repeating another work, nor as an expressive intention that juxtaposes itself to another expressive intention. We are no longer confronted with a re-reading or a re-writing: rather, what we are dealing with is the *reappearance, in another discursive field, of an element (a plot, a theme, a character, etc.) that has previously appeared elsewhere.*

A reappearance is a new discursive event that locates itself in a certain time and space in society, one that, at the same time, carries within itself the memory of an earlier discursive event. Within this reappearance, what matters is the development of a new communicative situation, more than simply the similarity or dissimilarity between the later and earlier events. Otherwise said, what matters is the new role and place that the later event takes on within the discursive field, more than the abstract faithfulness that it can claim with respect to the source text. In fact, the text's identity is defined more by this role and this place than by a series of formal elements.

An initial consequence is the fact that the analysis of adaptations should do more than compare the former with the latter text. It should instead focus on what changes in the passage from one to the other; that is, the frame within which they are located. Therefore, analyses devoted merely to formal aspects should not be trusted. Too often the analysis of adaptation is reduced to pointing out the narrative structure of the two texts in order to establish what changes have been made from one to the other, when in fact we understand that the passage from the source text to its adaptation is not simply a formal variation. There is something else going on, something deeper: the fact that the source text and its derivative occupy two entirely different places in the world scene and in history. Therefore, when we talk about adaptations, transformations, remakes, and so on, we should not simply focus on the structure of those texts – their form and content – but on the dialogue between the text and its context. Evidently, adaptation is primarily a phenomenon of *recontextualization of the text*, or, even better, of *reformulation of its communicative situation*.

Discussions about displacement are appropriate here:[4] in an adaptation we always need to identify the background of a story – for instance, in Luhrmann's *Romeo and Juliet* (1996) the story of Romeo and Juliet is moved from Verona to Los Angeles – and, especially, we need to redefine the background within which the text locates itself – from Elizabethan theater to youth culture, its cult movies, and MTV. A displacement has taken place, specifically from one space–time to another, from one geographical location to another. As I suggested earlier, the passage from text 1 to text 2 involves – always and most importantly – a transition from a "situation 1" to a "situation 2." Therefore, consideration needs to be given not only to the text as such, but also to its conditions and modes of existence.

## The Communicative Situation

The notion of the *communicative situation* is rather complex. Let us consider a conference panel: there are words bouncing from the table to the room; subjects, some of whom talk while others listen, ready to take the floor when the others have stopped talking; actions connected to the circulation of texts, such as the act of speaking, or gestures that accompany it in order to emphasize important sentences or even less serious ones; circumstantial actions, such as doodles drawn in the margin of one's notebook, or the winks of people that already know each other; circumstances, that is, the time and place of this communication; an organization that is responsible for the event, whether it is a university or a researcher's association; established rules that govern the conference; and again, in Schütz's words, a "life world," the existential framework within which we are located; and, finally, a "paper world," the universe of texts and discourses that circulate around us and give weight to what we say. A communicative situation is the result of the interrelationship among all these factors; it cannot be reduced to the sum of a text and a context. Rather, it is the complex, and often contradictory, interplay of all these elements.[5]

Adaptation and Mis-adaptations

Chapter 6

Simplifying, the communicative situation involves the presence of a text, a series of elements that guarantee the communicative interaction (interactional frame), a set of institutionalized rules and manners (institutional frame), a series of background discourses (intertextual frame), and a set of personal and collective experiences that operate as a reference (existential frame). These factors work together and determine each other. Each one of us has experienced communicative situations in which the existential frame exerted influence, for whatever reason. I read Flaubert's *The Sentimental Education* when I was sixteen, or so. Naturally, I did not consider the writing style as I was reading it. Rather, at that time, I read it as a novel that explained to me how hard it was to become an adult and, in this case, the real world "won." However, in my French Literature class the paper world, the intertextual frame, would be the winner: there, one is required to explain the author's stylistic choices and their relation to the choices of other authors of the same period. What this means is that in a communicative situation the elements that I listed above do not merely interact with each other, sometimes one of them overcomes the others and determines the whole. The role and the meaning of the text are consequently changed. If, for example, we want to proclaim our love to a woman with whom we are deeply in love, the style of the delivery does not concern us much; on the other hand, if we are poets, missing the rhyme is a great failure, regardless of the outcome of our declaration.

Calling attention to the communicative situation does not just imply considering a text and its surroundings, but, more importantly, it means dealing with the relationship between these elements and the way in which they, together, bend the text one way or another. What is at stake is the way in which a text appears as an event within the world. In some cases, texts appear to provide us with useful information for our life-world; at other times they entertain us (the institutional frame of cinema demands entertainment); other times they establish connections with previous discourses; finally, at other times, they simply ensure continuity within communicative interactions. The direction taken by the communicative situation therefore appears to be crucial.

The perspective I have just outlined carries precise consequences for the study of the recontextualization implied by adaptation. Let us consider the incredible number of adaptations in early cinema. Besides responding to the assumption that culture is an archive and that cinema works within it as the possibility to circulate its "symbolic capital," early cinema manifests the desire to challenge film's institutional frame: to present a story that has already been told, means to explore how cinema is capable of renewing and intensifying the relationship between text, representation, and spectatorship. The presence of a system of attractions, as emphasized by Tom Gunning, confirms that cinema relies on its ability to re-propose a new and more intense "spectacular experience."[6]

Let us then consider the famous adaptations of classical cinema, starting from Laurence Olivier's adaptations of Shakespeare. In these cases cinema is celebrated for its storytelling ability as much as theater, and with equal artistic value. Therefore, the intertextual frame is predominantly activated, and the adaptation rests on a situation that refers primarily to the "paper world." Finally, let us consider some contemporary adaptations, such as Ang Lee's *Sense and Sensibility* (1995): if the question we pose is not so much what changes in thematic and formal terms between Jane Austen's novel and the film, but rather the change in terms of the communicative situations that the two texts construct and operate within, then the answer is that, while the novel appears to be referencing primarily a life-world, the film employs the same plot to explore the possibility of constructing a melodrama in the postmodern era. Ultimately, the film refers to the institutional and cultural framework within which cinema operates today. These examples, admittedly tentative, serve as indications of how to approach a new consideration of adaptation.[7]

———————— **Adaptation as "Re-programming" the Reception** ————————

To adapt, to move from one communicative situation to another, entails a number of things, most significantly, to re-program the reception of a story, a theme, or a character, and so on. The second life of a text coincides with a second life of reception. Let us go back to an example already mentioned: *Romeo and Juliet*. The link between Luhrmann's film and Shakespeare's tragedy is established by the reappearance of the same title and by the repetition of original lines. However, while the lines are the same, their reading changes. It changes first and foremost because Luhrmann's film presents an entirely different communicative situation, especially in the way in which it positions the spectator. In the move from play to film, what changes is the social function of the spectacle: while in the Shakespearean version an entire society recognized itself, in Luhrmann's film only the youth subculture can recognize itself. As a consequence, the reception of the film depends upon a sense of belonging and on exclusionary mechanics that have no relation to those activated by the shows at the Globe theater. Luhrmann then can claim faithfulness to Shakespeare, while in reality he re-programs the text's reception in a totally different way.

Ironically, society's self-recognition in the face of tragedy is nowadays activated by other films, which do not derive directly from Shakespeare. For instance, Abel Ferrara's *The Funeral* (1996) stages a somewhat Elizabethan story. More importantly, it forces all its spectators, without subcultural distinction, to question the meaning of life vis-à-vis the pervasiveness of evil. In this sense, I would go as far as to say that while Luhrmann's film keeps Shakespeare's lines unchanged, while shifting their meaning, Ferrara's film does not refer to Shakespeare yet, by reproposing a theme reminiscent of his work, and by activating a communicative situation in some ways similar to the one activated by Shakesperean tragedies, acts as a faithful adaptation in its own way (although not in an explicit, intentional way). In sum, *The Funeral* re-programs the "same" reception, while *Romeo and Juliet* programs a reception that is foreign to the original.

Along these lines we can naturally look for more complex examples. Consider Visconti's *La terra trema* (1948), an adaptation of Verga's novel *I malavoglia*, which originated in the desire to make a film about Sicily on behalf of the Italian Communist Party, in preparation for the 1948 national election. Lino Miccichè has successfully reconstructed, on the basis of unpublished documents, the long process of preparation for Visconti's film,[8] and has effectively shown what we could define as a double dislocation: from the militant project to Verga's novel – on which there had been heated debate in the pages of the film journal *Cinema*, and in which Visconti had to some extent participated; and from Verga's book to the film. On the basis of Miccichè's findings, we could say that *La terra trema* is composed of two different texts that work in two different communicative situations. It is a commissioned film within a communicative situation in which the reference to the life-world has priority (to make a film that would show the class struggle in Sicily in support of the election) and in which the life-world itself was to be the element emphasized by the film. However, if we analyze the history of the critical reception of *La terra trema,* we see that from the very beginning the film becomes the manifesto of Neorealism: the attention is shifted from the horizon of reality (which fades away into a generic dimension) to the system of discourses that support the cinematic movement to which Visconti's film belongs. After all, even today this is the prevalent reading: the film is not regarded as a documentary on Aci Trezza or on the social and political condition of the Sicilian people (nor as an essay on social injustice or class struggle, although the opening epigraph encourages us to see it thus), but as the greatest, though problematic, example of a specific poetics. In other words, the guiding principle of the contemporary reading of the film's communicative situation is represented by the paper world more than by the life world. In this case, the relationship with Verga, which should be kept in the background in the case of the documentary reading of the film, comes instead into the foreground as an interesting element. We should remark that this re-programming of the reception is not the result of someone's intention (a change of mind by the Italian Communist Party or Visconti's will), but the outcome of a set of processes occurring around the film.

## Postmodern Discourses

The perspective that I have been presenting raises issues ignored within the traditional debate on the relationship between cinema and literature; it makes it apparent, I hope, that the old issues need to be re-formulated.

Let us consider the idea of "faithfulness" and "unfaithfulness," or "closeness" and "distance," between the source and the derivative text. Within our perspective, it becomes clear that the main issue is no longer that of the permanence of a certain number of common elements, but rather that of re-proposing (or failing to do so) homologous or similar communicative situations. On this ground, if we ask: what of Shakespeare is present in Luhrmann? Then the answer is nothing, besides lines from *Romeo and Juliet*. We can also ask: what of Shakespeare is in Ferrara? And the answer will be everything (maybe via Artaud), except the lines. We can even wonder whether *The Jerry*

*Springer Show* is the most Shakespearean of all, given that, in this day and age, it is the place where *The Merry Wives of Windsor* and family tragedies across generations are celebrated. The question remains open, but what is certain is that by changing our approach, the idea of closeness or distance between texts transforms radically.

Within this framework we also need to address another question: whether the discursive areas to which literature and cinema belong, and, more generally, the discursive space of postmodern culture have a role in the redefinition of such concepts as faithfulness or closeness. This is a substantial theme which I will only briefly explore.

One initial observation is that media present different "stages of maturity." Let us consider cinema: its regime of representation is changing as a consequence of the increasing use of digital images; the images on the screen that once stood for traces of reality are now images without a referent, mere graphic inventions, despite efforts to attain the highest degree of similarity with the world. Adaptation has to take this into account too: the "truth" of the sign matters (and this "truth" as a trace of reality is stronger in sound media, radio for example, or written media, such as books or Internet pages, than in visual media). At the same time, today's media tend toward convergence. If we consider cinema again, we can see how the advent of VHS, and then of cable television, led to a greater degree of proximity between cinema and television. The widespread use of digital signs will bring these two media even closer, and this will spread to other media. The technological base of different media will become increasingly homologous, thus fostering the process of contamination of genres and formats; we will witness an increasing hybridization of texts and the construction of increasingly universal formats, which can move without mediation (without adaptation) from one medium to another.

This osmosis between cinema, television, and other media also finds confirmation in the tendency toward uniformity in their use. Cinema-going is becoming closer to watching television (for example, it is losing its "festive" character and its ability to encourage processes of socialization), while television is "radiofied," insofar as "listening" is preferred to "viewing." These tendencies within the system of mass communication suggest an increasing synergy among media, and maybe a homologization of apparatuses, both in terms of the typology of products and in terms of reception. Within this framework, the short circuits that adaptations used to provoke between different discursive spaces appear quite insignificant vis-à-vis the interplay of references, and the nomadism of postmodern texts. For this reason, perhaps the most interesting instances are those in which adaptation functions as a site of resistance, as a block and filter; that is, when adaptation is in fact mis-adaptation.

## Mis-adaptations and Resistance

If adaptation involves the reformulation of a communicative situation, we can foresee instances in which the adapted work does not really fit because it is too contrived, out of place, or inadequate. Indeed, "second lives" are not always successful (and that is also true for the "first"). There are, however, some failures that are revealing in terms of the initial and final communicative situations. A first case of adaptation is very famous: *Les Parents terribles* (1948). Here, Cocteau adapts his own play by shooting it as if on stage. In this case the mis-adaptation is caused by the fact that the film does not distance itself enough from the source play: rather, it remains literally attached to it. However, as Bazin suggests in one of his best essays ("In Defence of Mixed Cinema"),[9] this fact is very revealing: by shooting a play in a claustrophobic way, as if on stage, without adding cinema's artistic specificity, Cocteau manages to highlight the essence of the cinematic gaze: its voyeurism, its ruthlessness, its key-hole aspect. Consequently, Cocteau's mis-adaptation tells us something that an adaptation could not say: it unveils the functioning of the filmic device, the institutional frame of cinematic reception. This is the way cinema works, and that is the way things are in a movie theater.

The second case is the opposite, and it is caused by an excess of distance, not of closeness. In it, the transformation has been too ambitious, and the journey from the source text to the derivative text too long, so that the connection between the two has been lost. It is a mis-adaptation that occurs because of a "too-much," not because of a "not-yet." I am referring to Kubrick's *Eyes Wide Shut* (1999). We can legitimately ask what of Schnitzler's *Double Dream* is left in this film, and probably realize that there is nothing left but a hint of the narrative. However, it seems to a lot of people that Schnitzler can reappear within our discourses only in this way: in a masquerade, as if in a party where he does not belong, deprived of his knowledge and his control. (With Branagh's adaptations of Shakespeare, the case is very similar, although with opposite outcomes: a distance of mis-adaptation which is not revealing . . . )

--- New Perspectives ---

Without wanting to attribute to adaptation a value and a significance that it does not have, especially when compared to social phenomena of different weight – consider, for example, the processes of cultural hybridization of diasporic experiences – I still think that a more attentive, perhaps less orthodox analysis of this practice can offer precious insights into the social and cultural spheres. Naturally, to do so, we should go beyond the brief observations I have made so far. It is clear that this kind of orientation requires us to go beyond dry comparisons between film and literature in order to construct a corpus of discourses that comprise all kinds of social discourses, which in turn appear as unqualified and unqualifiable *écritures* revealing tendencies in taste, value orientation, and social obligation. This corpus must then be examined according to an explorative principle – whether thematic, stylistic, axiological, aesthetic, and so on – in search of a system of inner relations that does not necessarily privilege proximity over distance, nor coincidence over tensions; in fact, it is sometimes useful to read a discourse on the basis of what it denies. Finally, from this system of inner relations, we need to extrapolate a plot which, while it might not be the most apparent, can be the one that would allow us to bring to the surface what is unsaid together with what is said, what is repressed together with what is apparent, and what is denied together with what is practiced. The goal is to give an account of a *network of discourses*, their connections and their intersections; and within this network, the coming together and the coming apart of some entities and configurations.

This is the bulk of the analyst's task, which is very far from the traditional, comparative approach based on an interplay of references, although not immediately apparent. Rather, it is closer to Foucault's project in *The Archaeology of Knowledge*, which he defines as "a *pure description of discursive events* as the horizon for the search for the unities that form within it."[10] Foucault's perspective is crucial here both for its purpose and for the methodological issues it raises. Some of Foucault's goals – the will to "grasp the statement in the exact specificity of its occurrence," and, at the same time, to discover "relations between statements and groups of statements and events of a quite different kind," in order to "constitute . . . discursive groups that are not arbitrary, and yet remain invisible,"[11] as well as some of the operational concepts and some of the analytical procedures that he proposes, such as the idea of discursive formations, or discursive practices, and the methodology of analysis of utterances or the retrieval of an episteme – can be very useful here as methodological guideposts. Besides, the perspective that I have been describing is less of a sociology of symbolic constructs than an "archeology of knowledge" as Foucault proposed it, and as it has developed in recent scholarship.

One more point needs to be added. If we consider cinema and literature as social discourses to be connected to a broader network of other discourses, we need a way to contain our analysis, or else we would undertake a never-ending project. Personally, I have been exploring the notion of negotiation, which is based on the assumption that every node in the network "confronts itself" with other nodes, while trying to maintain its peculiarity, on the one hand, and to connect with the rest of the network, on the other hand. As a consequence, each node either "connects" or "mis-connects" with the whole. This negotiation occurring at the intertextual level is then accompanied by a negotiation taking place at the level of reception (the text confronts its addressee, the latter's expectations, its readership, its previous knowledge, and the tension between the two poles creates an interpretation), a further negotiation on the institutional level (the text confronts the rules and principles of use in its own realm and at the same time it renews and explores their viability: often texts work this way), and a negotiation taking place on the broader social level (the text confronts itself with the life-world of a group and, in particular, with the social practices, the needs, and the processes of reception that characterize it; in this way the text presents itself as an individual and collective resource). In the case of cinema – that is, in the case of a medium that has had such a strong impact on the forms of discourse, reception, and social habits of the past century – to emphasize the processes of negotiation of some films permits us to focus on them while considering the broader network to which they belong, which can then be used as a background or as a generic whole.

By way of conclusion, let me point out that I have been trying to show the possibility of changing the orientation of scholarship devoted to the relationship between cinema and literature. In particular, I have suggested that we should consider these two realms as sites of production and circulation of discourses and connect them to other social discourses in order to trace a network of texts, within which we can identify the accumulation or dispersion, the coming forth or the reformulation, the emergence and the disappearance of some themes and issues. This is not an easy task, even if it has an already established tradition in other disciplines. At any rate, this approach allows us to raise new questions, and to regard cinema and literature as two large "construction sites" where every society experiments with its values, meanings, and systems of relations – in other words, what it deems visible, thinkable, shareable. In these "construction sites" society challenges itself and to some extent the destiny of its members. In this sense, they are crucial to all of us.

*Translated by Alessandra Raengo*

---

## Notes

1  The insistence on the nature of the cinematic medium has, of course, always been present: from Morin to MacLuhan, this tendency has grown stronger in recent years. However, this line of thinking has been largely absent in comparative studies, in the exploration of cinema's relationship with other "arts." For an attempt to resume this approach in a comparative context, see my "Il cinema come arte, il cinema come medium," in L. Quaresima (ed.), *Il cinema e le altre arti* (Venice: La Biennale di Venezia/Marsilio, 1996).

2  In this respect Benjamin is bitterly ironic: "It is instructive to note how their desire to class the film among the 'arts' forces these theoreticians to read ritual elements into it – with a striking lack of discretion." Walter Benjamin, "The Work of Art in the Age of Mechanical Reproduction," in Hannah Arendt (ed.), *Illuminations: Essays and Reflections* (New York: Schocken Books, 1968), p. 227.

3  Michel Foucault, *L'Archéologie du savoir* (1969), trans. A. M. Sheridan Smith, *The Archaeology of Knowledge* (New York: Pantheon, 1972).

4  See S. Bernardi (ed.), *Storie dislocate* (Pisa: ETS, 1999).

5  For a more detailed definition of the communicative situation, see my "Communicative Situation: The Cinema and the Television Situation," *Semiotica* 1: 2 (1996), 35–48.

6  Tom Gunning, "The Cinema of Attractions: Early Film, its Spectator and the Avant-garde," in Thomas Elsaesser and Adam Barker (eds), *Early Cinema: Space–Frame–Narrative* (London: British Film Institute, 1990), pp. 56–61.

7  The role of performance as agent of mediation between the paper world and the real world deserves mention and would require an investigation beyond the scope of this chapter. It is nevertheless important to point out that performance and performativity do contribute to the

make-up of the communicative situation and alter the balance among its various structural elements.

8   Lino Miccichè, *Visconti e il neorealismo: Ossessione, La terra trema, Bellissima* (Venice: Marsilio, 1990).

9   André Bazin, "In Defence of Mixed Cinema," in *What is Cinema?*, vol. 1, trans. Hugh Gray (Berkeley, CA: University of California Press, 1967), pp. 53–75.

10  Foucault, *Archaeology of Knowledge*, p. 27 (emphasis in the original).

11  Ibid., pp. 28 and 29.

Adaptation and Mis-adaptations

Chapter 6

# Chapter 7

# The Invisible Novelty
## Film Adaptations in the 1910s

## Yuri Tsivian

Early film histories have a special taste for the new. We rank inventions above borrowings; we look tenderly at little things like trick films, chase films, scenic pictures, or early actualities, while often giving the cold shoulder to screen adaptations – not because we deny them their share in film history, but rather because, deep down, we believe that the former are truer children of the film medium than are works begotten of other arts. Our dislike of canned theater and filmed novels is akin to the prejudice some cultures have against illustrated books.

Not that I do not share this taste, but I quarrel with its universality. I think that in our attempt to outline the trajectory of early cinema we too readily identify innovation with invention – two things that do not necessarily entail each other. Novelty is a relational and often invisible value. There are epochs for which the new does not associate with the medium-specific, as there were filmmakers whose sense of novelty was different from ours. In European film history such is, roughly, the spell between 1910 and 1920, a relatively quiet season in terms of conventional inventions, though truly innovative in a less-visible sense. It is with an eye to elucidating those elusive innovations that I turn to Yevgeni Bauer, the most resourceful figure among Russian filmmakers of the 1910s, and his 1915 attempt at a screen version of a literary classic.

There exists a curious document left to us by Bauer – his answer to a peevish letter from a cultivated filmgoer containing a list of grudges – of the sort that I am sure many screen versions of classics have elicited. The letter is apropos Bauer's film *After Death*, a 1915 screen version of a story by Ivan Turgenev, "Klara Milich" (1883). Let me quote an editorial that appeared in a 1916 issue of *Pegas* (a mixture of trade journal and fan magazine financed by the Khanzhonkov production company):

Y. Bauer has passed on to us the following letter, which is addressed to him: "The Khanzhonkov company's picture *After Death* was shown the other day in Petrograd and environs. I would be most grateful if you could clear up my bewilderment: why was it necessary to re-christen the universally known *Klara Milich* in such a way? Why change the names, and more importantly, the characters? I should particularly cherish your replies to these questions. Why depict the small spindly figure of Zoya Kadmina instead of the strapping beauty Klara? . . . And instead of the miniature and sickly Yasha, the wonderful Andrei Bagrov, spick and span at any time of the day or night? And why the stout Kapitolina instead of the "tall" Platosha? As someone with a great love for cinema I find it frustrating to encounter such apparently inexplicable phenomena. I am therefore turning directly to you, for who, if not the director, could explain it all? Assume these to be "questions from the public." It is not long since you became the company's chief director, and it may be that this drama was not produced under your direction. But it is not an isolated instance – I mention it only as one recent example of a phenomenon that interests me. Perhaps you could, all the same, find a few minutes to reply."[1]

It is rather unusual for a director to use his own company's press vehicle to publicize a viewer's critique of his film, but the answer that came from Bauer is even more surprising. One would expect a defensive or explanatory kind of response; instead, we read a disarmingly self-effacing, almost self-deprecating statement, the sole extenuating circumstance it cites being the state of the film medium and the plight of filmmakers condemned to be dealing with trash:

On handing the letter to us, Mr Bauer made the following statement: "I totally agree with Mme N. I., and we think that her observations are applicable to all pictures illustrating Turgenev's works. It is our view that the cinema has still not found the movements and pace required to embody Turgenev's delicate poetry. Nor, alas, will it find them soon, since film directors have been educated in conditions allowing them to take barbarous liberties with the authors. Since, in the initial phase of their career, they are involved merely with works that are hopeless from the literary point of view, they grow accustomed to doing as they wish, to altering arbitrarily the intentions, the situation and even the heroes invented by the author. Turgenev should be approached in a different spirit and with different habits."[2]

In his attempt to pay tribute to Turgenev, Bauer does an injustice to his own work. I do not think it will surprise anyone (except for a die-hard literalist like Mme N. I.) if I say that *After Death* is at its best not when it repeats, but rather when it deviates from the source. Many screen versions are like that, but there is an added historical interest which makes it worth pausing to ponder what could be the possible reason – a problem, a stopgap device, a tempting alternative solution – for some of Bauer's deviations from the letter of Turgenev's book. Although, for the sake of simplicity, I will use phrases like "Bauer wanted" or "Bauer needed," I will be using those expressions as historical explanation, not as historical descriptions: they say as little about the real Bauer as pieces moved on a chessboard tell us about what is happening in the player's mind.

---

## Story Synopsis

In a nutshell, the Turgenev story is about a young man and a dead girl. Yakov Aratov is a loner who avoids human company except for a gregarious friend and his loving, old aunt who lives in the same house as he. One day, the friend convinces Aratov to go out. There is a social meeting at which our recluse feels quite ill at ease, and a charity concert that makes him even more uncomfortable because of the inexplicable attention on the part of an actress whose strange beauty stays in his mind. Her name is Klara Milich. In a few days Aratov receives a note asking him for a rendezvous; shocked, he rebuffs what he interprets as an inappropriate advance, but again, is surprised at the sincere and tragic grief of her reaction. The girl disappears from Aratov's life, but only until he chances upon a newspaper obituary telling that a young talented actress, Klara Milich, has killed herself while performing on stage. This news and a vague sense of guilt upset Aratov's staid life; from Klara's sister he obtains the diary of the deceased, which confirms that his rejection of Klara did, indeed, cause the death of this pure and romantic soul. Klara begins haunting Aratov's dreams; the dreams become more and more real; finally, the girl answers Aratov's entreaties to let him stay with her. In the morning, the distressed aunt finds the nephew dead, his face filled with bliss. The story takes fifty pages; the film is four reels long.

---

## Names and Title

Let me begin by addressing the question that nonplussed Mme N. I.: why alter names and the very title of the work? Normally, such things were done (as in the famous case of the later *Nosferatu*) to safeguard the studio against possible copyright litigation; and it may have been, indeed, that some authority or other at the Khanzhonkov Studio had apprehensions of that sort. These worries do not fully account, however, for Bauer's changes, which are less arbitrary than they may appear at first. Bauer's title *After Death*, for instance, is originally Turgenev's: shortly before the manuscript went to the printers, Turgenev changed it to "Klara Milich" in reluctant compliance with the publisher's suggestion (to whom "After Death" sounded too "*lugubre*").[3] Some critics found the change unfortunate; one even wrote in a letter to Turgenev in 1887: "I defy Stasiulevich [the publisher] and his change of the title of your story. Nothing he could think of could be more stupid. Did it never occur to this ass that titles derived from *proper names* point to the author's intention to present this or that *type*, whereas here the question is not the type, but a unique and remarkable mental phenomenon?"[4] From this perspective, what Bauer did by changing the title was to revert to the original version of the original, as it were.

The game of name changes is somewhat similar, at least insofar as the heroine is concerned. In Bauer's film Turgenev's Klara Milich becomes Zoya Kadmina. This was a "knight's move" – away from the story ("Zoya" is a random forename) and behind its scenes, as it were, for "Kadmina" is the last name of a real person, the drama actress and opera singer Evlalia Kadmina (1853–1881) whose sensational on-stage suicide (still hot off the press when the story came out) inspired Turgenev to write "Klara Milich."

## Suicide

In this regard, there is an oddity about Bauer's treatment of Kadmina's suicide that merits discussion. Turgenev's story presents it as a conundrum, not in the sense that its motives were obscure, but because the author does not quite let his hero (and the reader) decide what to make of it. Klara's death is never depicted directly: Aratov learns about it from a brief, matter-of-fact obituary he stumbles on halfway through the story; later on (well into its second half) Aratov's "sanguine friend" Kupfer supplies a more detailed version of how it happened; still later, he sees her die in one of his nightmares. While the first news strikes Aratov as tragic, Kupfer's affected rendering makes Klara's suicide look so stagey that for the rest of the day our hero "tried not to think about it, fearing that it might give in him a feeling akin to repulsion."[5] This is Kupfer's story:

> What happened was this. She had to perform that day and perform she did. She took a vial of poison to the theatre and just before the first act started she drank it. And she stayed on stage till the end of the act – with the poison inside her! What a strong will! What strength of character! And they say she'd never acted before with such feeling and passion. The audience suspected nothing and kept clapping and calling her back. But as soon as the curtain went down she collapsed right there on the stage, writhing around in agony, and an hour later she'd given up the ghost. Surely I told you about it, didn't I? It was even mentioned in the papers.[6]

Now, if we look at all this through the eye of a 1915 screenwriter, Klara's suicide is clearly the "punch" of the whole story (to borrow the term from screenwriting manuals of the 1910s). What made the scene foreign to introvert Aratov (and, on another level, to Turgenev-style prose) – its panache, its intrinsic theatricality, the last melodramatic embrace of play and life – made it, one would think, a perfect match for stage and screen. Here, for once, was a story situation whose dramatic potential would only gain when transposed from the written to the staged, a *coup de théâtre* no film star could refuse. And yet, we find no theater stage, no convulsions behind the curtain, no raving and

**Figure 7.1** The dead girl materializes with a little bottle of poison.

clapping theater crowd in Bauer's *After Death* – nothing, aside from a brief, almost informative, flashback (backstage, Klara expires surrounded by fellow actors) inserted in the story Aratov hears from Klara's sister, and one unpretentious dream in which the girl materializes with a little bottle of poison clasped in her fist (figure 7.1), more an attribute than a prop. Did Bauer miss his chance or was something else going on?

To answer this question, we need to look beyond a mere comparison of the film and the text. As mentioned earlier, Turgenev's Klara had a real-life prototype: the actress Evlalia Kadmina who poisoned herself (using some makeshift stuff prepared from the sulphur scratched off the tips of matches) after seeing in the audience the handsome army heel who had jilted her for a rich merchant's daughter, and whom he had the nerve to bring along to see her play. This actually occurred on a Kharkhov theater stage in 1881; Kadmina took the poison between acts and collapsed in the middle of her scene, subsequently being carried home where she died in less than a week.[7]

Instantly, this news became the sensation of the day. "Klara Milich" was not the only literary version of Kadmina's suicide. The event left in its wake two popular plays of the 1880s: *Evlalia Ramina* by N. N. Solovtsov and *Tatyana Repina* by Aleksei Suvorin (and a one-act skit by Anton Chekhov in which the ghost of the suicide – "A Lady in Black" – haunts the church and foils the villain's wedding). In prose, Turgenev's story was followed by two more: Nikolai Leskov's "Theatrical Character" and "The Last Debut" by Aleksandr Kuprin. The reasons for the heroine's suicide could vary, but its method – or rather its setting – was common to all.

Some thirty years later – not long before Bauer's screen version of "Klara Milich" – some ripples from Kadmina's death reached the world of filmmaking. As far as I can tell, the first film star whose character killed herself on stage was the Italian diva Lyda Borelli in *Ma l'amor mio non muore* (1913, American distribution title *Love Everlasting*). In this remarkable film, Borelli plays a singer who commits suicide to save the man she loves from disgrace, a noble-hearted crown prince whom we see among the spectators of her last show. In Russia (where, after all, it had all started) Borelli's film gave birth to a fine imitation, the 1914 hit *Chrysanthemums,* which perhaps helps to explain why death on stage, so prominent a theme in Turgenev's original, is all but absent from Bauer's 1915 screen version. The problem was one of overproduction: people can take the same lurid act seriously only so many times. Some four or five months before Bauer set out to make his *After Death,* a screen version of Suvorin's stage play *Tatyana Repina* (written, we recall, in the wake of Kadmina's death) was released by Khanzhonkov. Four on-stage suicides in three years were enough to make this kind of "punch" look like worn-out cinematic currency rather than anything out of Turgenev. Worse, Vera Karalli, the "Zoya Kadmina" of *After Death,* was the same person who had played the suicidal ballerina of *Chrysanthemums* – a memorable debut in which Karalli (the former ballet star of the Moscow Imperial Theater) graciously passes away in the middle of her solo dance, to the acclaim of unsuspecting ballet fans and the culprit, the calculating ex-lover. After *Chrysanthemums,* any such scene with Vera Karalli was bound to appear self-replicating and anti-climactic. For the moment, to save the game it was wiser to sacrifice the queen.

---

## The First Dream

---

Naïve viewers (the likes of Mme N. I.) and occasional scholars tend to place screen adaptations in a mimetic space, leaving the filmmaker the dismal task of "living up to the book" and the researcher to the drudgery of comparing "adaptations" with "originals." For them an omission is a sin and a side-step a crime. Not even for the sake of argument would such purists admit that an obscure filmmaker in 1915 might remain unimpressed by this or that aspect of a nineteenth-century literary classic and therefore try to slip in an improvement. For these intellectual jailers, mimesis is a penal code.

The impression one gets from Bauer's screen version is that he left mimesis for savants and laymen to ruminate over. Despite the humble note (no doubt sincere) found in his response to the incensed spectator, practice shows that Bauer put himself on a par with the author – a game partner, an opponent, rather than a model. For instance, he obviously found Turgenev a poor dreamer. In the story, the first meeting after death is set in a conventionally morose dreamscape:

> He dreamt he was walking across bare steppe lands strewn with stones under a lowering sky. A path wound among the stones and he followed it.
>
> Suddenly something like a thin cloud rose up before him. As he peered at it, the cloud became a woman in a white dress with a light-coloured sash round her waist. She was hurrying away from him. He could see neither her face nor her hair. They were covered by a long veil. But he felt an intense desire to catch up with her, and to look into her face. Yet however fast he went, she proved swifter than he.
>
> There was a wide, flat stone lying on the path, similar to a gravestone. It blocked her way. The woman stopped. Aratov hurried up to her; she turned to him – but he still could not see her eyes – they were closed. Her face was white, as white as snow; her hands hung lifeless. She resembled a statue.[8]

If we compare this gothic dream scenery from Turgenev to its counterpart in the film we will be surprised to discover that these dreams are quite dissimilar. We may even say they are opposite; so much so that it almost seems that Bauer has decided to take Turgenev's description and read it by contraries. Turgenev's afterworld is barren and stony; Bauer's is fertile. Note the vast field with wheat-ears almost reaching your shoulders; Aratov's back is visible in the foreground; and the girl, dressed in shining white tunic, approaching it slowly down a narrow path in the wheat (figure 7.2). This is not a location shot: the wheat field is studio-made, so the "live" ears of wheat we see ripple in the foreground (evidently they used a wind machine) merge with a pastoral landscape (hills and sheaves) painted on the backdrop. There is no trace of a gravestone or anything that looks remotely sepulchral; instead of abiding by Turgenev's "her hands hung lifeless," Bauer makes the sleeves of Kadmina's pre-Raphaelite tunic flutter in a Botticelli-like breeze (figure 7.3). Her hair twined with flowers, the dead girl looks something like Persephone, the goddess of fecundity, the mistress of an underground kingdom.

Why all these changes? A closer look at what was going on in film art around 1915 will be needed to get to specific answers; but, first, a quick establishing view. There are three general ways in which we account for changes like this. Sticklers, we have seen, find them simply outrageous. People who treat film as art and art as a form of expression will look for some inner, individual reasons; their conversations will pivot around Turgenev and Bauer (and their "artistic visions"), though not around literature and film. Scholars versed in structuralist approaches will counter, saying that changes like this are often decided not by the artist but by the medium this artist works in. This third assumption sounds workable, but there lies a pitfall I want this study to avoid. It seems immensely plausible to go on from there and to say that Turgenev's dream had been written for a book, and was not cinematic enough for Bauer's film – but it is exactly here that we must watch our step. "Cinematic" is a smug, scanty concept; to say "cinematic" of a

**Figure 7.2** Aratov's figure is visible in the foreground; the girl, in shining white tunic, approaches slowly down a narrow path in the wheat.

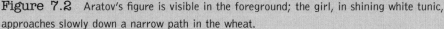

movie is like saying "poetic" of a poem or praising a landscape for being picturesque. Our mental pictures of media derive from the stalest of their conventions. Bauer's dream was new, not cinematic; looking at Bauer, forget the medium-specific and look for the medium-innovative.

Novelty, as I suggested earlier, is a relational matter. In the mid-1910s, regular — "cinematic" — dreams and apparitions, which as a habit took the form of semitransparent superimposed images, were becoming (along with a number of other photography tricks — the novelty of the previous decade) a thing of the past. In 1915, "effects" lighting (as distinct from the then-current practice of having your spaces evenly lit), creative (as opposed to functional) staging, and fanciful camera movements were in. Lighting was key for the dream: that Bauer went to the expense of having its open-air landscape built in the studio was, I am sure, in order to buy full control over lighting equipment needed to achieve, among other things, that peculiar spotty quality of light which art historians (speaking of Edouard Vuillard, for instance) term "dappled." To bring in new lighting effects was enough of a reason for Bauer to pay no attention to the "lowering sky" of Turgenev's prose; instead of its uniform dimness, we see sun-spotted wheat

**Figure 7.3** Bauer makes the sleeves of Kadmina's pre-Raphaelite tunic flutter in a Botticelli-like breeze.

quivering in the wind from an off-screen wind machine; by the same token, rather than cover the girl's head with Turgenev's "long veil" Bauer leaves her head uncovered, and tells the cinematographer (Boris Zavelev) to put so much light on the girl's face that it becomes a blurry irradiant lump (figure 7.4) – a daring, state-of-the-art lighting effect of the kind called "blooming" by present-day technicians.

And yet, despite deviations, Turgenev was integral to Bauer's game – integral in a sense specific to the 1910s. To see how a literary classic – a past master of letters, but of letters only – could be of use to a predominantly visual filmmaker like Bauer, we must imagine something that may seem to put the cart before the horse. Normally, we picture a filmmaker shooting a silent screen version of a book as a sort of translator, a person that takes a handful of literary images and provides them with visual equivalents. Forget for a moment this natural order of things, and pretend our filmmaker is a maker of visuals in need of a writer to tell us what they mean – this picture will be closer to the way in which Bauer's mind worked. What follows is an attempt at such a reverse perspective. I shall take another two scenes from *After Death* (one from the beginning of

**Figure 7.4** Bauer told his cinematographer, Boris Zavelev, to put so much light on the girl's face that it becomes an irradiant blur.

the film, another from the middle), asking not what Bauer did (or did not) to deliver Turgenev, but what made Turgenev interesting for Bauer in terms of Bauer's film.

## Door in the Dark

The scene I want to begin with is from the first reel. It starts in full darkness. A chink of light splits the dark screen around the middle (figure 7.5), growing to the width of a narrow door. The woman whose rotund silhouette appears in the door (figure 7.6) is Aratov's aunt (not to confuse them, I will refer to the film's characters by Turgenev-given names); she is shown entering her staid nephew's study with a cup of tea in her hands. No sooner than her silhouette unblocks the doorway, we glimpse Aratov at the far end of the study absorbed in a book (figure 7.7). The whole take lasts for around ten seconds (the time it takes the aunt to reach Aratov's armchair), during which time

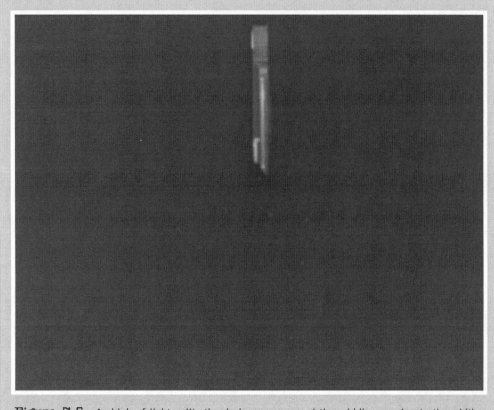

**Figure 7.5** A chink of light splits the dark screen around the middle, growing to the width of a narrow door.

the camera setup stays unchanged, and our field of vision narrowed down to about one-fifth of the screen's width. Next, a brief cut-in into the room (figure 7.8) enables us to see how the aunt offers Aratov some more buns, and his impatient gesture of refusal; then, as the aunt is about to leave the study, the camera resumes its earlier position, taking us back to that dark antechamber and the bright slot through which to observe the aunt crossing the same ground in the opposite direction (figure 7.9). As she finally closes the study door behind herself, we are back to where it began – to another brief moment of darkness.

My plan is to place this scene in two different contexts: first, to measure its novelty against mid-1910s' film practice; second, to explore its link with Turgenev. To explain what made the door in the dark visually exciting, we will need to connect it to two techniques I will refer to as "foreground flanking" and "silhouette lighting." By foreground flanking, I mean the particular staging scheme when a segment of the set (a curtain, a doorway) is used to reduce our field of vision; as for silhouette lighting, the term is self-explanatory. Both schemata were trends of the 1910s, mostly in Europe;[9] both are found in some of Bauer's films of 1913–14, and, earlier on, in Danish and Swedish cinema,

**Figure 7.6**  The rotund silhouette of Aratov's aunt appears in the door.

though rarely in tandem; the door in the dark from *After Death* is uncommon because here the two novelties work to reinforce each other.

Why would Bauer (or other filmmakers like him) want to do such relatively compli-cated things? In other words, what was there about foreground flanking and silhouette lighting that made them attractive and worthwhile? Let me suggest a quick retrospec-tive hypothesis that helps to account for this fashion. First of all, as I said, there was the question of novelty. Silhouette photography, and the use of contrivances like doors or curtains to screen off a section of the acting ground, presented a novel alternative to frontal lighting and frontless setups prevalent in the 1900s and still common in the 1910s.[10] Secondly, there was a question of cultural gravitas. Both foreground silhouetting and foreground flanking had – and this was an important advantage in the eyes of a culture-minded film director of the 1910s – antecedents in fine arts: the former, for instance, in dark human shapes found on the fringes of some prints by Jacques Callot; the latter (another example) in a door-framed scene found in the 1670 oil *The Love Letter* by Jan Vermeer (figure 7.10). We can go even further and say that, by shooting through doors, Bauer and his European predecessors were creating for their viewers a new, more involved

**Figure 7.7**  We glimpse Aratov at the far end of the study absorbed in a book.

subject position, for this is exactly what art historians claim that Vermeer's *Love Letter* did for the seventeenth-century beholder. This is how Arthur K. Wheelock, the student of Vermeer, explains the effect of the technique:

> A recurring concern of Vermeer was the creation of the semblance of privacy in his paintings. To achieve this effect he used many devices. He placed figures behind large pieces of furniture, tables, or chairs to separate them from the viewer. He hung curtains in the foreground or placed his figures on the far side of the large room. Invariably he portrayed people in moments when they were preoccupied with some activity or with their own thoughts and were unaware of being observed. The culmination of this interest in portraying those private, unguarded moments in life is *The Love Letter*. In this remarkable painting Vermeer, in a way that anticipates the "keyhole" realism of Degas in the nineteenth century, portrayed the figures through a doorway.[11]

Visual analogies are deceptive, particularly of things compared across media and across centuries, but the analogy I am talking about is not between visual facts, but between

**Figure 7.8** A brief cut-in into the room enables us to see how the aunt offers Aratov some more buns, and his impatient gesture of refusal.

visual effects. What matters for us is not the fact that Bauer, as Vermeer before him, placed his actors behind that shaded door, but the effect that this new trick produced upon Bauer's film viewer who, much like a seventeenth-century person before Vermeer's picture, was all of a sudden a peeper into characters' private lives.

Now that the visual family to which Bauer's door belongs has been established, it is time to see how this image marries with Turgenev. There are no through-the-door views mentioned anywhere in "Klara Milich," which fact is not surprising, knowing as we do that this was Bauer's pet staging arrangement. A cup of tea is the only factual evidence that links Bauer's scene to the source story: in a subordinate clause on the third page Turgenev says that the aunt had the habit of placing on Aratov's desk a cup of medicinal (*grudnoi*) tea "each time she thought he was showing signs of sickness."[12] However, if we agree – here, too – that the links we are looking for are not between facts, but between effects, there could be a less-visible thread in Turgenev that leads to Bauer's door. Recall that the scene shot through the door is among the opening scenes of *After Death*. Now, if it is true, as I have just argued, that around the time this film was made similar peeping vistas were sometimes used to lend to scenes a sense of peeped-at privacy; then, given

Yuri Tsivian

**Figure 7.9** The bright slot through which we observe Aratov's aunt.

Chapter 7

all this, such a thread is the seclusion motif woven into Aratov's portrayal found on the very first page of "Klara Milich:"

> He held himself aloof from his fellow students and made friends with almost nobody. He was particularly shy of women although he was very tender-hearted and was captivated by beauty. He even acquired a splendid British keepsake album and, shameful though it was, used to take pleasure in the pictures which adorned it of various enchanting Gyulnars and Medores. However, innate bashfulness kept him in check.[13]

I realize that this connection may sound pretty tenuous with only a few stills to check it with. The only thing I can do to help is to advise the unconvinced reader to repeat the experience I had as I read the above passage against the film sequence running on the video monitor (a video version of *After Death* is commercially available).[14] It could, of course, be in part the effect of any voice-over, but it is amazing to observe Turgenev's words "aloof," "shy," "bashfulness," "in check" echo in Bauer's clever visuals: in Aratov's placement at the far end of his room; in the door which confines the inquisitive viewer

**Figure 7.10** *The Love Letter* by Jan Vermeer (oil, 1670).

to a narrow view; and in the way in which the whole sequence is enclosed between two brief moments of darkness. For me, this reading-while-watching experience proved helpful not only as a self-check, but also as a makeshift semiotic experiment showing that the way in which texts and images translate into each other is not necessarily object-to-object (a cup of tea here, a cup of tea there), but often through various intermediary agencies – like functions, or effects. This is not surprising, for words and pictures are not semiotic siblings but rather semiotic partners; pictures cannot "mean" in the same sense as verbal utterances do. Meaning is integral to words; pictures thrive on found or borrowed meaning (found in books, for example, or borrowed from the onlooker). Visual tools like Bauer's door may be used to reflect Turgenev's meaning, but hardly to generate it in the way Turgenev's words do.

This helps to explain Bauer's interest in screen adaptations, and, wider, the import-ance of screen versions for ambitious filmmaking of the 1910s. Filmmaking has always been a leapfrog race between art and technology, where the supply of technical novel-ties regularly outstripped artistic demand. In the 1910s – the decade of visual *Sturm und Drang* – it often happened that new visual tools became available to filmmakers before they saw a clear need for them. Speaking of Bauer, semantic deficit by visual surplus had always been the balance of his style, for Bauer was not a person to wait for a nar-rative need to come by to try out a new visual device. It is in view of this balance that a writer – the provider of meanings – could be seen as a useful investor.

## Movement and Pace

Adaptation is a reciprocal process: a gambit, a give and take. To say "story adapted to suit the medium of film" is ahistorical. Bauer's screen version is an example of the opposite: here the game is rather to adapt the film medium to the need of the story. *After Death* lends "Klara Milich" visual forms in exchange for semantics, as it were. Whether this worked to Bauer's satisfaction was another matter, as we recall him admitting in his answer to Mme N. I.: "It is our view that the cinema has still not found the movements and pace required to embody Turgenev's delicate poetry."

"Movement and pace" were indeed among the main resources whose potential to make meaning (to "reflect" it, as it were) Bauer had hoped Turgenev would help him refine. Bauer's work is remarkable for its lack of emphasis on titling and acting – two crutches habitually used by silent filmmakers to surmount (or, rather, bypass) a "literary" obstacle. (Players complained that Bauer forbade them to emote, which made them feel he treated them as mere elements of design.) Take, for instance, a brief passage in "Klara Milich" describing sedentary Aratov ill at ease at the social gathering where he gets the first glimpse of Klara:

> Aratov did not stay long, however. In the first place, the twenty or so guests he found there, both men and women, may have been nice people but they were strangers, and this made him uncomfortable, despite the fact that he was put in the position of having to converse very little – and it was this he was most afraid of.[15]

It is not hard to imagine an average (non-Bauer) screen version in which a compressed variation of this passage would appear in explanatory intertitles; or, otherwise, Aratov's state of mind might be conveyed by the player enacting another description found a few lines below: "Huddled in a corner, he spent his time either casting glances over the faces of the guests, without really distinguishing between them, or else staring at his feet."[16]

This would seem a scene tailor-made for the screen, but Bauer does not like obvious solutions. Instead of boxing the actor into a Turgenev corner, he stages an unusually

**Figure 7.11** Aratov introduces himself to interminable groups of guests who watch his progress with curiosity.

long take (*plan-sequence*) in the duration of which our recluse is shown moving amidst a considerable crowd, introducing himself to interminable groups of guests who watch his progress with understandable curiosity (figure 7.11). There is practically no acting in the usual 1910s' sense (facial reactions, telltale postures, significant glances) on the part of either Vitold Polonsky who plays Aratov or the extras playing the guests. All we see is an endless (more than three minutes long) repetitive ordeal of bows and handshakes.

The way this is staged is that, as Aratov advances, the camera moves backwards, keeping the hero in view and revealing more and more strangers to be met. This was new – not in the sense that moving cameras had not been used before (Bauer, and some of his most inventive contemporaries like the Italian Giovanni Pastrone, had been experimenting with studio-set mobile framing as early as 1913) – but in the sense that in the period shots of this kind had an air of novelty about them. For a tracking shot, furthermore, three minutes was a record duration, a trick especially difficult to work out with the camera traveling through a crowd scene. All this, one could argue, was challenging enough for someone like Bauer; but again, there could also be a Turgenev connection. True, Polonsky does not look at his toes or otherwise enact Aratov's uneasiness, but there is little need for facial acting, for something of that (Bauer thought) could be evoked by means of "movement and pace" – the excruciating pace of the event, for instance, or the pace of the camera which moves abreast of the character as if to empathize with Aratov or to eye him with the rest of the crowd.

## To Conclude

The aim of this chapter has been to appreciate the genre of screen adaptation in terms of its unique experimental value. One of the less-noticed aspects of the cinema of the 1910s was its covert penchant for artistic experimentation, seen as the selection of tasks and the use of solutions with no predictable outcome. I say "covert" because, oddly for us, in that period experimentation mostly falls to "respectable" genres – such as film versions of classics. Things that originate within the workaday world of pragmatic filmmaking are often more pedestrian than those borrowed from other arts. It was rather well known how to write and direct an original script: the first thing screenwriting manuals warned one against were themes and subjects difficult to visualize. And to embark on an adaptation of a literary work like Turgenev's spelt exactly that – things difficult to visualize. The only known recipe for such cases was to trim the literary work down to what is "cinematic" – that is, visual in the old sense. Many still think of screen adaptations this way, but for Bauer adaptation works the other way round: instead of adapting the story to the film medium, he sought for ways to adapt the medium to the story. The success was hard to guarantee, but that is what we pay for novelty.

## Notes

1 *Pegas* 4 (1916), 103–4; reproduced in Yuri Tsivian, *Silent Witnesses: Russian Films, 1908–1919* (London: British Film Institute, 1989), pp. 289–90.

2 Ibid.

3 See I. S. Turgenev, *Polnoe sobranie sochinenij i pisem* [*Complete Works and Letters*] (Moscow: Nauka, 1982), p. 426.

4 Ibid. (emphasis in the original). The story of the changed title (though not this letter) was known to literati at Bauer's time.

5 "Klara Milich," in *The Mysterious Tales of Ivan Turgenev*, trans. Robert Dessaix (Canberra: The Australian National University, 1979), p. 184.

6 Ibid., p. 183.

7 For more on Evlalia Kadmina's life and death, see Boris Yagolim, *Kometa divnoi krasoty* [*The Comet of Wondrous Beauty*] (Moscow: Iskusstvo, 1969).

8 "Klara Milich," p. 163. To bring it closer to the original I have modified Dessaix's translation using an older English version: *The Novels of Ivan Turgenev*, vol. 10, trans. Constance Garnett (London: William Heinemann, 1897), pp. 54–5.

9  On the history of cinematic lighting, see Barry Salt, *Film Style and Technology: History and Analysis* (London: Starword, 1992), pp. 40–4 (on lighting in 1900–1906); pp. 62–78 (on lighting in 1907–1913); pp. 114–26 (on lighting in 1914–1919); Lea Jacobs, "DeMille, Belasco and the Development of Lasky Lighting," *Film History* 5: 4 (December 1993), 405–18; Kirstin Thompson, "The International Exploration of Cinematic Expressivity," in Karel Dibbets and Bert Hogenkamp (eds), *Film and the First World War* (Amsterdam: Amsterdam University Press, 1995), pp. 65–85.

10 On shooting through doors and on deep staging in general, see the corresponding sections in Salt, *Film Style and Technology* as note 9; Thompson, "International Exploration of Cinematic Expressivity," and Ben Brewster, "Deep Staging in French Films 1900–1914," in Thomas Elsaesser and Adam Barker (eds), *Early Cinema: Space–Frame–Narrative* (London: British Film Institute, 1990), pp. 45–55.

11 Arthur K. Wheelock, Jr, *Jan Vermeer* (New York: Harry N. Abrams, 1988), p. 110.

12 "Klara Milich," p. 133.

13 Ibid., pp. 132–3.

14 It is part of the Bauer DVD/VHS selection under the general title *Mad Love* released by the British Film Institute in 2002.

15 "Klara Milich," p. 137.

16 Ibid.

Chapter 7

# Chapter 8

# Italy and America
## Pinocchio's First Cinematic Trip

## Raffaele De Berti

─────────────── Collodi's Book ───────────────

In 1883, just a few years after the unification of Italy, the first edition of *The Adventures of Pinocchio* by Carlo Collodi (pseudonym of Carlo Lorenzini) was published by Paggi in Florence.[1] The book enjoyed an immediate success which has lasted to this day. In addition to innumerable Italian editions, there have been scores of translations into many different languages and more or less free adaptations in all kinds of expressive forms: cinema, theater, comic books, and television.[2] In literature alone, *Pinocchio* has generated an astonishing number of derivative texts, among which are those that expand on the original story by adding new adventures for the wooden marionette, those that continue the story beyond the original ending in which Pinocchio transforms into a child, parodies, and texts that are entirely independent of the original story. In the latter, the fictional character of Pinocchio is principally used as a "mask" (in the tradition of the Italian *commedia dell'arte*) characterized by specific features – such as a long nose and the tendency to get into trouble – and is then placed in the most diverse situations: for example, the world of journalism (*Pinocchio Newspaperman*, 1911), an underwater world (*Pinocchio Diver*, 1911), and the exotic world of Africa (*Pinocchio in Africa*, 1907).

Such a wealth of transpositions, including Disney's famous adaptation, present many variations from the source novel and thus make it necessary to recall the outline of the original story. The book is divided into thirty-six chapters and opens with Master Cherry, a carpenter, who, finding a piece of wood that weeps and laughs like a child, gives it to his friend Geppetto, so that he can make himself "a Marionette that will dance, fence, and turn somersaults." The marionette immediately appears to be very rebellious, quite a rascal, with little interest in school. Annoyed by the preaching of the Talking Cricket,

Pinocchio smashes him against a wall with a hammer. And so his adventures begin, taking him from trouble into more trouble. Pinocchio sells his school books to pay his way into the Marionette Theater where he meets the frightening Fire Eater, who is unexpectedly moved by him and lets him go after giving him five gold pieces for Geppetto. On his way home, Pinocchio meets some assassins who hang him to an oak tree, only to be saved by the Blue Fairy. The marionette lies to the Blue Fairy and his nose grows longer. The Fox and the Cat rob Pinocchio of some money the Fairy has given him and, in punishment, the poor marionette is sentenced to four months in prison in the City of Simple Simons.

Meanwhile, Geppetto is looking for him on a little boat which, tossed about by the waters, disappears into the sea. Pinocchio promises the Fairy that he will be good and will study because he wants to become a real boy. Instead, he runs away to the Land of Toys with his friend Lamp-Wick. After five months of play, his ears grow and he transforms into a donkey. Pinocchio is bought by a circus and, after injuring himself, is sold to a man who wants to use his skin for a drumhead. Thrown into the sea, he is eaten by fishes and becomes a marionette once more. He is swallowed by a Terrible Shark in whose stomach he finds Geppetto. The marionette and Geppetto manage to escape. Pinocchio, who has saved his "father," dreams of the Fairy and she forgives all his pranks and transforms him into a boy.

Given the enormous success of the story, the vast critical literature on it presents a multiplicity of critical approaches. It has been pointed out, quite consistently, that *The Adventures of Pinocchio* is much more than a piece of pedagogical literature for children, teaching them how to behave in life and become adults. Grotesque situations, bordering on parody, combine with a sometimes sinister atmosphere akin to Gothic literature. The recurrence of mythical elements, such as his being swallowed by a fish, and his metamorphosis into different bodies (Pinocchio goes from being a piece of wood, to being a marionette, to a donkey, back to a marionette and, finally, he is transformed into a boy), intermingle with elements of the classic fairy tale exemplified by the Blue Fairy and the anthropomorphic animals. *Pinocchio* also bears the influence of travel literature about real or imaginary lands, which was very popular in the nineteenth century. Because of its polymorphic nature, and its ability to act as a "container" of heterogeneous cultural materials, Collodi's book supports the most diverse readings and transformations. Indeed, as early as the second decade of the twentieth century, Pinocchio had become a symbolic figure, a universal myth, embodying, in each period, the rebel and the restless child – who is ultimately a good boy – creating a metaphor for the ideal journey toward adulthood.

--------------------  Methodological Perspective  --------------------

Confronted with the innumerable possibilities offered by the literature on Collodi's book and on its derivative texts, it becomes necessary to narrow this research by raising some preliminary questions. My interest is not in the reconstruction of the critical literature on *Pinocchio*; nor do I intend to add new interpretations to this already impressive body of work. Neither am I interested in making a comparative study of the degree of fidelity between what, according to Genette's categories, is defined as the literary hypotext and the cinematic hypertext.[3] The following analysis will try to raise the question as to why there are specific variations in the films considered. The answer, as we shall see, relies on their connection to the medium employed and the different communicative contexts in which these films operate. My goal is not so much to highlight the semantic and syntactic transformations of the source novel, but rather to understand what the new communicative situation is, to which the text belongs. As Robert Stam points out:

> One way to look at adaptation is to see it as a matter of a source-novel hypotext's being transformed by a complex series of operations: selection, amplification, concretization, actualization, critique, extrapolation, popularization, transculturalization. The source novel, in this sense, can be seen as a situated utterance, produced in one medium and in one historical context, transformed into another, equally situated utterance, produced in a different context and in a different medium.[4]

Thus, the methodological perspective employed here is that of intermediality, whereby the film under consideration will be analyzed as a complex cultural product, resulting from an interaction between texts originating in different media within a specific historical and social context.[5] In this sense, *Pinocchio* presents an extreme case of intermediality insofar as Collodi's book itself, due to its multiple illustrated editions, appears from the beginning as a "multimediatic" text in which word and image are strictly interwoven.

The attention to intermediality has to be further combined with an idea of communication as the stipulation of an implicit pact between addresser and addressee. As Francesco Casetti puts it, "negotiation aims at creating or refining the communicative pact, which seems to support the action of the communicators, and also involves the conditions and functions of communication."[6] Within this framework, any transposition, or even simply any translation or illustrated edition of *Pinocchio*, re-formulates the communicative pact existing with the reader-spectator, thus creating the opportunity for other interpretations, while simultaneously affecting the cultural and social context of its reception. My goal, therefore, is to present the first film adaptation of *Pinocchio*, produced in 1911 by the studio Cines in Rome, under the direction of Giulio Antamoro, as a case study within the theoretical perspective outlined above.

--- Giulio Antamoro's *Pinocchio* (1911) ---

Antamoro's *Pinocchio*,[7] besides being the first film adaptation of Collodi's novel, is also one of the first feature-length films in the history of Italian cinema. In 1911 cinema was moving toward the feature-length film. Burch has identified this phase as the transition from early cinema to the classic era, characterized by the consolidation of the institutional mode of representation.[8] The year 1911 was a very important one for Italian cinema because, a few months prior to the release of *Pinocchio*, another important adaptation was released: *Inferno*, a film version of Dante's *Divine Comedy*.[9] It is not by chance that the first features produced in Italy refer to well-known texts that the public considered to be the cultural capital of Italian national identity. This production strategy responded to the need to attract wide audiences and, more importantly, to ennoble the cinematic institution via an association with high art.[10] Both films, however, still present a strongly pre-institutional structure.[11] The overall narrative structure proceeds as a chain of *tableaux* and autonomous shots, combined with the use of depth of field and the movement of actors within the filmic space. It is a far cry from the linear narrative structure of the institutional mode of representation.[12]

The pre-institutional nature of Antamoro's *Pinocchio*, as of all early cinema, presents an ideal case study for intermedial analysis, which would allow appreciation of all the cultural series so far neglected because of the assumed superiority of literature. According to André Gaudreault, early cinema is an intermediatic web which contains and shapes various cultural series, such as "the *féerie*, the wax museum, the stage or circus number, and the theatrical play."[13] The copy of the film I have screened was restored in 1994 by the Cineteca Nazionale in Rome from a negative provided by the Cineteca Italiana in Milan. In their insightful and precise analysis of the film, Giacomo Manzoli and Roy Menarini point out that the restored copy is 1086 meters long as opposed to the 1203 meters acknowledged in the censorship documents. The two scholars suggest that the loss of 10 percent of the film is distributed along the entire length of the film rather than resulting from the cancellation of individual episodes.[14]

The film is a free adaptation of Collodi's novel and, although it presents the fundamental episodes, it also varies in many significant ways: some characters and events are eliminated, and the place they occupy in the narrative is different from the book. In particular, a surprising addition has been made to the original, featuring the adventure of Pinocchio and Geppetto in the Land of the American Indians. I will focus on this part of the film, while trying to understand the reasons for such an apparently eccentric addition. Before moving to the textual analysis, some general information about the film and the context in which it was produced is necessary.[15]

As has been previously pointed out, the book's enormous popularity is responsible for a number of derivations and adaptations of Pinocchio's character as early as the beginning of the twentieth century. By 1911, parodies and corruptions of the marionette's story with materials deriving from other cultural series – travel narratives, comic and fantastic literature (such as the books of Jules Verne and Albert Robida),[16] film comedies and Méliès – had become a well-established practice on the eve of Italy's culture industry. Among the many titles of new stories featuring Pinocchio – the so-called "Pinocchiate" (the "Pinocchio thing") – were *Pinocchio's Secret: Neglected Trip by the Famous Collodi's Marionette* (1894), *Pinocchio's Friend: Lamp-Wick* (1900), *The Astonishing Adventures of Pinocchio Policeman* (1910), *Pinocchio on the Moon* (1911), *Little Pinocchio at the Beach: That is, Strange Illustrated Adventures* (1910), *Little Pinocchio, the Explorer* (1910), *Little Pinocchio, the Diver* (1910), *Little Pinocchio in Egypt* (1910), *Little Pinocchio at the North Pole* (1910), and *Little Pinocchio, Newspaperman* (1911).[17]

The theme of travel appears central in this series of publications. In *Little Pinocchio Newspaperman*,[18] for instance, the protagonist is not a wooden marionette, but a clumsy youth, a little eccentric with a big nose, so as to recall the original Pinocchio. The newspaper director, who is Little Pinocchio's boss, sends him to the United States to report on the New World. The American section of the story is set in New York and follows quite faithfully another famous book, titled *An Italian in America* by writer Adolfo Rossi (1892).[19] The web of filiations and corruptions proves to be whirling and unpredictable, and Antamoro's film, at least in the episode of the Land of the Indians, belongs to this tradition, making it appear less eccentric than it may have seemed at first glance.

Other elements worth considering in relation to the iconographic sources of the film are the illustrated editions of Collodi's book. Specifically, the film displays a clear relationship with the illustrations realized in 1891 by Attilio Mussino for a new edition of the book for the publisher Bemporad in Florence. Mussino's drawings were to become, for many years, the most popular point of reference for the imaginary universe created by Collodi. Compared to previous editions, Mussino re-invented the iconography of Pinocchio whose appearance displays a number of similarities – both in physique and costume – with Guillaume, the title character in Antamoro's film.

With respect to the relationship between Mussino's illustrations and Antamoro's film, Manzoli and Menarini do not establish a hierarchy between the two texts, and rightly so. Rather, they suggest the hypothesis that the similarities between the two texts are a result of a "combined act," an attempt to "use the character with a 'multimediatic' angle, across film, literature and illustrations, in which both Cines and Bemporad try to exploit the power of the Pinocchio trademark, which needs to be fixed in a stable form so as to be immediately recognizable."[20] Another element characterizing the film version vis-à-vis the book is the emphasis on the fantastic and adventurous elements, as well as the parodic and burlesque tone of Pinocchio's story. In Antamoro's film, this comic element is strictly linked to the casting of Ferdinand Guillaume in the role of Pinocchio.

In 1910, after years of working in the family circus, Ferdinand Guillaume and his brother Natale were hired by Cines. Under the pseudonym Tontolini, Guillaume appeared in 135 comedies, produced between 1910 and 1911, the majority of which were directed by Antamoro.[21] Later, upon leaving Cines and moving to Pasquali Film in Turin, Guillaume's career as a comedian continued under the pseudonym Polidoro.[22] When shooting *Pinocchio*, then, Antamoro and Guillaume represented a well-established pair of artists, whose work together in comedies is clearly reflected in this film. The effect of the comedy form on the film can be seen in the undermining of the moralistic and pedagogical elements of the story. Some intertitles bear reference to Pinocchio's duty to be a good boy, but at no point is there a clear-cut contrast between good and evil. It is consistent with this approach that the Talking Cricket does not appear in the film. Guillaume's

Pinocchio is basically very similar to a restless rascal with the tendency to get himself into trouble, very much as Tontolini would have done. The Guillaume–Tontolini "mask" is adapted to Pinocchio's character, while often maintaining its clown-like attributes, such as acrobatic agility, mimicry, and a penchant for gags and chases. From the very beginning, the film encourages the identification of Guillaume with Pinocchio: the first scene features the stage curtains opening to reveal Guillaume in plain clothes. After greeting the audience, the actor does his typical somersault and transforms into Pinocchio. This strikes a chord with the audience as they know the comedian and his films very well.[23]

In short, Antamoro's film presents itself as a syncretic text in which Collodi's book, travel cinema and literature, fantasy literature, the series of "Pinocchiate," the iconography of Pinocchio's illustrations, and Guillaume's physical comedy come together. Within the film's multifaceted framework of cultural and intermedial references, the addition of the episode portraying Pinocchio in the Land of the Indians appears plausible and consistent. Moreover, in Collodi's book itself there is a brief reference to America, identified as "The New World," where Geppetto, aboard a boat, looks for Pinocchio and ends up being swallowed by a big shark.

<hr>

### Pinocchio, the Whale, and the Indians

The episode of the meeting with the Indians occupies almost a fifth of the length of the film and is connected to the episode in which Pinocchio is swallowed by the whale. It is noteworthy that, as early as 1911, what is described in the book as a shark becomes a whale in the film, as it will in many other future "translations," including the popular 1940 Disney version. Because of its biblical references – Jonah is swallowed by a whale – the whale is more suitable, within popular imagery, for containing men in its stomach than a shark. Moreover, Mussino's illustration for the book shows a big fish that looks more like a whale than a shark. Another probable element adding to these cultural references is the popular iconography surrounding *The Adventures of Baron Münchhausen*, in which the title character is also swallowed by a big fish.[24] This variation, therefore, is not casual; rather, it is consistent with a widely known cultural series, independent of Collodi's text.

Since the film cannot readily be seen, a description, in outline, of the essential events and shots of this episode, is added below. Camera movements are rather rare and intertitles usually have a proleptic function, introducing the action about to unfold. Indeed, the intertitles appear to be performing the role of the *bonimenteur* or popular storyteller who describes the *tableaux vivants* and often anticipates what the following images will show. This element confirms the extent to which *Pinocchio* still adheres to the pre-institutional phase of cinema, which privileges "monstration" over a linear narrative.[25]

After having escaped from jail in the City of Simple Simons, Pinocchio dives into the waters and begins to swim:

*Intertitle*: "Pinocchio and the Whale."

*Intertitle*: "After swimming for 99 days, Pinocchio arrives at the Land of the Indians."

Pinocchio swims.

*Intertitle*: "Hurry! Hurry! Here comes the Whale!"

Pinocchio keeps on swimming and, in the background, the whale approaches the marionette.

*Intertitle*: "The Indians, who saw the Whale, prepare to capture it . . ."

On their canoes, the Indians hurry toward the Whale.

*Intertitle*: ". . . but before they get there, Pinocchio is swallowed."

The Whale catches up with Pinocchio and swallows him.

Brief shot of the Whale on the waters.

*Intertitle*: "In the Whale's stomach"

The inside of the Whale's stomach.

Brief shot of the Whale on the waters.

Pinocchio moves about in the Whale's stomach.

*Intertitle*: "The Indians have captured the Whale."

The Indians attack the Whale.

Inside the Whale, Pinocchio meets Geppetto.

*Intertitle*: "Father! Why are you here? . . . Son, I went looking for you and the Whale swallowed me!"

Pinocchio and Geppetto hug.

*Intertitle*: "Let's escape this way!"

Pinocchio and Geppetto walk inside the Whale.

*Intertitle*: "Pinocchio and Geppetto are captured by the Indians."

Pinocchio and Geppetto exit from the blowhole of the whale and are captured by the Indians who turn their boats toward the land.

*Intertitle*: "Pinocchio, who is made of wood, is considered a magician and made chief of the Indians. Geppetto is put on the grill.

Pinocchio, with the typical Indian headgear on his head, exits a tent and is worshipped by the Indians at the camp.

*Intertitle*: "I am the boss!! Set that man free!!"

Indians dancing around a wooden grill where Geppetto has been tied up. Pinocchio talks and gestures to the Indians who then untie Geppetto.

*Intertitle*: "Go away! I will save my own skin!"

In the foreground Geppetto and Pinocchio talk to each other while the Indians stand in the background. Pinocchio gestures to Geppetto to run away.

*Intertitle*: "Pinocchio escapes. He is followed. Arrives at the Canadian soldiers' camp."

Pinocchio peeks out of a tent. An Indian sees him and wakes up the whole camp.

Pinocchio is chased by the Indians.

Pinocchio arrives at the Canadian soldiers' camp and asks for help.

The Indians arrive and fight against the Canadians.

*Intertitle*: "The Canadians kill all the Indians and send Pinocchio home . . . as you will see."

The soldiers put Pinocchio in a cannon and shoot him with a cannon ball. Pinocchio flies, riding the ball above the sea. The ball explodes and Pinocchio falls on the land.

*Intertitle*: "My Pinocchio, are you not back yet?"

Geppetto is sitting at home and looks very concerned. Pinocchio lands, crashing through the roof. The two hug with affection.

In dealing with an episode such as the one just described, having rejected the hypothesis of simple eccentricity on the part of the filmmaker, we are compelled to wonder from what cultural series or medium the "Indian" imagery could have been derived. Given the popularity of the film, it would have to have been a widely known and accepted source. Besides, as has been already noted, Pinocchio's story and the character itself function as an ideal "container" for various imageries. A possible hypothesis is that these references belong to the American Western cinematic genre, which are chosen here among many possible adventures. Certainly, the world of the Wild West, as we shall see, already occupied an important place in Italian children's imagination at the beginning of the twentieth century. Yet, at that time, it was not established as an autonomous film genre. Until 1910, according to Rick Altman, "Western sceneries" were merely a part of other genres:

> in fact, it might reasonably be claimed that many of the pre-1910 films produced in the west by Essanay, Kalem, and Selig were actually not westerns. They may have imitated the outward trappings of the currently popular Wild West shows, and offered identifiably western scenery, but always in association with a dominant already existing genre, and without the civilization versus savagery plot motifs that later come to characterize the genre . . . A careful study of the Western's early development would certainly point to a combination of the travel genre's exotic locations . . . with the crime genre's suspenseful situations (and their melodramatic trappings).[26]

## Western Sceneries

Following Altman's observations, the Western scenery in *Pinocchio* appears, undoubtedly, as part of the wider travel genre and exotic themes that were very popular in Italy at the end of the nineteenth and beginning of the twentieth centuries, both in books and periodicals. This exotic vein is characterized by a readiness to combine real people and places with fantastic ones. The episode considered here is proof of this as it contains iconographic elements belonging to different cultural traditions and countries. Specifically, the attempt to grill Geppetto refers to a cannibalistic practice usually linked to generic tribes of savages rather than the American Indians and the world of the Western. Interestingly, the film, analogous to the popular literature of its time, displays a colonialist viewpoint whereby all people who are different from the "white man" are considered savage and cannibals, whether they live in America, Africa, or Asia. In the film, the Indians appear almost as props, deprived of any true identity. They are mean and dangerous, act irrationally and can be easily killed – a stereotypical portrayal of Native Americans that will dominate the cinematic Western for many years to come. Moreover, the Canadian soldiers, who quickly kill all the Indians and save Pinocchio, do not wear the popular "Red Coat," but the outfit of Italian colonial troops, who in 1911 were engaged in the conquest of Libya.[27]

Finally, with reference to the travel genre, Pinocchio's return home astride a cannon ball is a clear citation from *The Adventures of Baron Münchhausen* by Rudolf Erich Raspe. The book, as previously noted, which was very popular and had various illustrated editions, also probably influenced Collodi in the episode of the big fish swallowing Pinocchio. Raspe's book narrates marvelous travels by land and sea and can therefore be considered as one of the models of reference for Antamoro's film in creating the episode in the Land of the Indians. If this hypothesis holds true – that the film's main reference is not so much the Western genre as the exotic genre of adventurous travels – then we are left with the task of inquiring into the origin of what Altman calls the "Western sceneries." Thus, we need to identify what other sources, available to the general public, could have contributed to the intermediatic circulation of Western sceneries.

The first scenery was popular both in Italy and in the United States: William Frederick Cody's show "Buffalo Bill's Wild West" exhibited Native Americans as circus freaks, depriving them of any cultural or historical identity, just as they are portrayed in the film. In Europe, too, Buffalo Bill embodied the legend of the West. In 1890 his show arrived in Italy. The entire crew's meeting with Pope Leo XIII was given great attention in the Italian press. In the same year, Buffalo Bill's "circus" successfully toured the entire peninsula, south to north, stopping in the main cities, such as Naples, Florence, Bologna, Milan, Verona, and Mantua. In 1906, Buffalo Bill and his Rough Riders toured again in Italy.

From the substantial official program of the Italian show (75 pages), accompanied by a number of photographs, it is possible to obtain some interesting information about the European and Italian success of the show. Colonel Cody spectacularizes the Wild West and contributes to the creation of a series of myths and stereotypes that would later find their way into the film. Among the twenty acts of the 1906 show are the following titles: "Life in the Far West," "General Custer's Last Battle," "Cow-boys and their Entertainments," "The Pony Express and its Rider." The program also specifies that the performance is an "exact reproduction of real episodes, it is a living story." At the current stage of my research, however, I have not been able to determine to what extent films featuring Buffalo Bill circulated in Italy. Nevertheless, given the popularity of the protagonist, they must have had a wide circulation.[28] The Buffalo Bill character becomes a mythical figure, identified with the West itself, which circulated across media with extreme ease: from the live show to film and popular literature. In Italy, as far as popular literature goes, Buffalo Bill's adventures were published in serial form for the first time in 1890, while the show was touring the country with the title *Buffalo Bill/Frightening Adventures among the Savage Indians*.[29] The widest literary circulation of Buffalo Bill's adventures, though, occurred between 1908 and 1910, when the American publisher in Milan published, in 150 weekly episodes, the translation of the dime novels published in the United States.[30]

The fact that the publication of the dime novels featuring Buffalo Bill barely anticipates the release of Antamoro's film cannot therefore be considered a coincidence in explaining the presence of the Indian episode. In Italy, the circulation of Western sceneries in literature is not confined merely to Buffalo Bill. There are many other materials and figures that I will now briefly consider. In 1828, for instance, the first translations of James Fenimore Cooper's novels, such as *The Pioneers* and *The Last of the Mohicans*, appeared in Italy, as well as the Italian edition of *A Tour on the Prairies* by Washington Irving in 1837. From 1868 on, the Italian editions of Thomas Mayne Reid's novels also proved to be very successful.[31] In the late nineteenth century, as a consequence of the popularity of travel literature, characterized by a penchant for exoticism and interest in African settings, the West, with its peoples and prairies, began to be discovered. Travel literature, whether in the form of books, serials, or episodes published in magazines such as *World Tour* or *The Illustrated Journal of Travels and Adventures by Land and by Sea*,[32] was always accompanied by illustrations, which began to popularize the iconography of the West and the Indians. This Wild West imagery and iconography was finally consolidated within Italian culture and society, not only by the wealth of translations, but also through the use of these scenarios by Emilio Salgari, the most influential and popular Italian writer of adventure novels at the turn of the century. Shortly before killing himself, Salgari began to write a cycle of novels set in the Far West (*On the Far West Frontier*, 1908; *The Female Scalp Hunter*, 1909; and *The Burning Woods*, 1910).[33]

Thus, before the release of Antamoro's *Pinocchio*, the imagery of the Western world had already become part of the best-known popular literature in Italy. Indeed, Salgari's novels were known and loved by the Italian public as much as Collodi's book. The film confirms the Italian tendency to be open toward foreign cultures in order to creatively adopt them[34] – often with a parodic slant – within an attempt to foster forcefully the peculiarity of the national culture. An example of this tendency is the Spaghetti Western, which, in the 1960s and 1970s, also began to establish itself abroad. (Incidentally, it is interesting to note that, like many Spaghetti Western directors, Giulio Antamoro directed *Pinocchio* under an American-sounding pseudonym – Gant.) Consistently, Antamoro's *Pinocchio* is a highly syncretic text that appears to function as a relay within an intermediatic network of references, adopting and re-shaping the various cultural series employed. Not only is it one of the many hypertexts originated by Collodi's hypotext, but it leans over, as it were, toward the broader cultural sphere, thus helping to prepare the Italian public for the imminent penetration of the Western as an autonomous film genre.

Finally, this film entered the intermediatic network partaking of the new iconography around Pinocchio, which Mussino's illustrations had contributed to creating, and became itself a model for popular "Pinocchio-like" literature. As an example, consider the fact that in 1930 the publisher Nerbini of Florence published – within a series featuring Pinocchio (in this case he was a real boy, a living, breathing rascal) – an episode titled *Pinocchio the Explorer: Extraordinary Adventures By Land and Sea*.[35] This episode features a variation on the meeting between Pinocchio and the Indians, clearly modeled on its prior film version. In Italy, Antamoro's film was periodically and successfully screened in small provincial theaters until the late 1920s. The differences between the short story (only 24 pages) and the film are revealing with respect to the political climate determined by Mussolini's government. This time it is not Geppetto who is nearly barbecued, but a missionary father. He is saved by a feisty Pinocchio who alone kills the Indians with a shotgun and declares himself a follower of *Balilla* (the fascist youth organization). As late as the 1930s, the stereotype of the Indians, analogous to that employed in the film, still survives. The Indians are savage people in need of civilization and, accordingly, Geppetto has to be replaced by a missionary father. This last case shows how Pinocchio, as a mythical figure, easily crosses over into different media, originating new adventures and all sorts of transformations. Moreover, his metamorphic nature allows him to wear ever-changing masks, reflecting different social and cultural contexts, as well as being ubiquitous and transhistorical.

## Conclusion

It has been established how productive it can be to analyze the relationship between the literary hypotext and its hypertext, not simply from a philological perspective that points to similarities and differences, but in order to understand the choices made by a certain text and the causes of its transformations when adapted into different media and new sociocultural contexts. Consequently, within this perspective, it does not matter so much whether the film "respected" the "spirit" of Collodi's book or whether it is a faithful rendition of it. The cinematic hypertext, in this case Antamoro's *Pinocchio*, besides being a symptom of the society in which it is produced, also becomes the hypotext for later adaptations by entering an intermediatic chain that interacts with and influences the culture in which it belongs. Intermedial analysis, therefore, allows us to inquire into the social discourses that texts activate through their constant negotiation of the communicative pact that they establish with their audience.[36] This explains why in 1930 in Italy Pinocchio can identify with a young *Balilla* and at the same time remain the rascal that he is.

In conclusion, among the many possible ways of addressing the relationship between the literary and the film text, the intermedial approach employed in the analysis of *Pinocchio* can unravel the working of a text from an historical and pragmatic perspective, and so offer interesting insights about its social and cultural functions.[37] Lastly, the intermediatic analysis proves to be a useful theoretical tool for the history of cinema, insofar as it has emphasized how the film *Pinocchio* articulates a tendency within Italian cinema to continue some communicative forms of pre-institutional cinema much longer than, for instance, American cinema. Forms such as "monstration," the autarkic shot, and the use of depth of field – as opposed to the fragmentation of a scene into different shots to facilitate narrative editing – are examples of the persistence of the pre-institutional mode in Italian cinema at this time.[38] Other case studies[39] of Italian and European cinema within a comparative perspective could also shed new light on American films of the same era.

*Translated by Alessandra Raengo*

Raffaele De Berti

Chapter 8

I am indebted to a number of generous people who have helped me with this chapter by providing me with sources, information, and suggestions. In particular, I would like to thank Piermarco Aroldi, Francesco Casetti, Ruggero Eugeni, Giacomo Manzoli, Elena Mosconi, Matteo Pavesi, and Alessandra Raengo.

## Notes

1   The 1883 volume includes the series of episodes published between 1881 and 1883 in the *Giornale per i bambini*, which had been very successful with young readers.

2   An in-depth study of Pinocchio's character in different media, which I have drawn upon extensively for this chapter, is G. Bettetini (ed.), *La fabbrica di Pinocchio: le avventure di un burattino nell'industria culturale* (Turin: VQPT-Nuova ERI, 1994). See also Isabella Pezzini and Paolo Fabbri (eds), *Le avventure di Pinocchio: tra un linguaggio e l'altro* (Rome: Meltemi, 2002). Also important is the work of the Collodi Foundation in Pescia, both in terms of archival research of materials on Pinocchio and in terms of activities such as conferences, studies, exhibitions, and so on.

3   See G. Genette, *Palimpsestes: la littérature au second degré* (Paris: Editions du Seuil, 1982).

4   R. Stam, "Beyond Fidelity: The Dialogics of Adaptation," in James Naremore (ed.), *Film Adaptation* (New Brunswick, NJ: Rutgers University Press, 2000), p. 68.

5   For a good theoretical and bibliographical treatment of the issue of intermediality see, among others, the special issue of *CiNéMAS*, "Intermédialité et cinéma," 10: 2–3 (Spring 2000). Consistent with my approach is Jurgen E. Muller's "L'Intermédialité, une nouvelle approche interdisciplinaire: perspectives théoriques et pratiques à l'exemple de la vision et de la télévision," pp. 105–34 in the special issue of *CiNéMAS*. For Muller, "there are variable mediatic relations between media, and their function arises from, among other causes, the historical evolution of these relations . . . A medium contains within itself structures and possibilities which belong to it alone. Which does not mean that the media plagiarize one another mutually, but rather they absorb into their own context certain questions, concepts, and principles which developed over the course of the social history of the media and of Western figurative art" (translation of quotation by Robert Stam), pp. 112–13.

6   F. Casetti, "Film Genres, Negotiation Processes and Communicative Pact," in L. Quaresima, A. Raengo, and L. Vichi (eds), *La nascita dei generi cinematografici* (Udine: Forum, 1999), p. 27.

7   Technical information and data about the film can be found in V. Martinelli (ed.), *Il cinema muto italiano 1911*, Biblioteca di Bianco & Nero-CSC, vol. 2 (Turin: Nuova ERI, 1996), p. 65. *Pinocchio*, directed by Gant (Giulio Antamoro); story from the novel *Pinocchio* by Carlo Collodi; starring: Ferdinand Guillaume (Pinocchio), Augusto Mastripietri (Geppetto), Lea Giunchi (Blue Fairy), Natalino Guillaume (Lamp-Wick); produced by Cines; released in December 1911; length 1350 m. There is a difference in length between Martinelli's account (1350) and the credits of the copy restored by the Cineteca Nazionale, Rome and the Cineteca Italiana, Milan, which report a more feasible length of 1203 m.

8   Cf. N. Burch, *Life to Those Shadows* (London: British Film Institute, 1990).

9   *Inferno* was produced by Milano Films and directed by Adolfo Padovan, starring Francesco Bertolini and Giuseppe De Liguoro. The length of the film is 1200 m.

10  Vittorio Martinelli cites a meaningful comment by an anonymous writer announcing the film's forthcoming release: "The new film will confirm once again the usefulness and effectiveness of the moving pictures applied to the education of heart and mind. It could probably be the first film to be used in our schools since the book by Collodi has been already adopted as a textbook," *La Cinem-Fono e la Rivista Fono-Cinematografica* (May 1911). This comment suggests an awareness of the tendency to seek the integration of film and literature with a pedagogical function and in order to foster national identity in education. See G. P. Brunetta, *Storia del cinema italiano*, vol. 1 (Rome: Editori Riuniti, 1993), pp. 151–73.

11  The term "pre-institutional" is derived from Burch and is not meant pejoratively.

12  See E. Dagrada, A. Gaudreault, and T. Gunning, "Lo spazio mobile del montaggio e del carrello in Cabiria," in P. Bertetto and G. Rondolino (eds), *Cabiria e il suo tempo* (Milan: Museo Nazionale del Cinema, Editrice Il Castoro, 1998), pp. 151–83, subsequently published in French as "Regard oblique, bifurcation et ricochet, ou de l'inquiétante étrangeté du carrello," *CiNéMAS* 10: 2–3 (Spring 2000), 207–23. This is an exemplary study which emphasizes the differences in film style in the early 1910s in the United States (space is explored through fragmentation for narrative purposes) and in Europe (space is explored in depth for non-narrative purposes).

13  A. Gaudreault, "Il cinema tra intermedialità e letterarietà: postfazione 1998," in A. Gaudreault, *Dal letterario al filmico: sistema del racconto* (Turin: Lindau, 2000), p. 182; originally published in French as *Du littéraire au filmique: système du recit* (Paris: Meridiens Klinksieck, 1988).

14  This hypothesis has been reinforced by the analysis of a "photostory" version which does not show any significant variation from the restored copy of the film. See G. Manzoli and R. Menarini, "Pinocchio, comico muto," in M. Canosa and A. Costa (eds), *A nuova luce / cinema muto italiano, Fotogenia* (special issue), 4/5 (1997–8), 211–22.

15  Besides Manzoli and Menarini's work mentioned above, see also E. Mosconi (ed.), *L'oro di Polidor* (Milan: Quaderni Fondazione Cineteca Italiana, Editrice Il Castoro, 2000).

16  An insightful analysis of the influence of Verne's and Robida's fantasy literature on Italian cinema can be found in Antonio Costa's critical study of the film *The Most Extraordinary Adventures of Saturnino Farandola* (M. Fabre, 1914, produced by Ambrosio). See A. Costa, "Il mondo rigirato: Saturnino versus Phileas Fogg," in P. Bertetto and G. Rondolino (eds), *Cabiria e il suo tempo* (Milan: Museo Nazionale del Cinema, Editrice Il Castoro, 1998), pp. 295–310.

17  These titles are quoted in P. Marchese, *Bibliografia pinocchiesca* (Florence: La Stamperia, 1983).

18  *Little Pinocchio Newspaperman* belongs to the series called "The Astonishing Adventures of Little Pinocchio," published by Bietti (Milan) in the early 1910s.

19  A. Rossi, *Un italiano in America* (Milan: Treves, 1892). The great immigration of Italians into the United States, which occurred at the end of the nineteenth and the beginning of the twentieth century, was partially responsible for a growing interest and curiosity about America on the part of the Italian public.

20  Manzoli and Menarini, "Pinocchio, comico muto," p. 216.

Raffaele De Berti

Chapter 8

21  Among the many titles are *Tontolini Makes a Somersault* (1910), *Tontolini Toreador* (1910), *Tontolini Hypnotized* (1910), and *Tontolini at the Circus* (1911).

22  On Ferdinand Guillaume, see Mosconi (ed.), *L'oro di Polidor*, and G. Marlia, *Polidor: storia di un clown* (Empoli: Ibiskos, 1997).

23  See Manzoli and Menarini, "Pinocchio, comico muto."

24  Among the best-known illustrators of Raspe's book is Gustav Doré, who was responsible for a famous edition of the *Divine Comedy* whose illustrations inspired the authors of *Inferno* (1911).

25  See Gaudreault, "Il cinema tra intermedialità."

26  R. Altman, *Film/genre* (London: British Film Institute, 1999), pp. 36–7.

27  I owe this observation to Paolo Fabbri who, with Isabella Pezzini, coordinated the Conference on *The Adventures of Pinocchio*, organized by the International Center of Semiotics and Linguistics, Urbino University, July 16–18, 2001.

28  Among the Buffalo Bill films, reproducing his shows, are *Buffalo Bill's Wild West Parade* (1900), *Buffalo Bill's Wild West Show* (1902), and *Buffalo Bill's West and Pawnee Bill's Far East* (1910).

29  This book was published by Edoardo Perino, a small publisher in Rome. Information on popular publications featuring Buffalo Bill can be found in C. Gallo and G. Bonomi (eds), *Buffalo Bill and Tex Willer: storie e miti dall'Ovest americano* (Verona: Colpo di Fulmine Edizioni, 1996). See also E. Detti, *Le carte rosa* (Florence: La Nuova Italia, 1990).

30  The Italian edition faithfully reproduces the American model. These are 32-page booklets, sold at a popular price (25 cents) covering an entire episode. The publication of dime novels featuring Buffalo Bill in the United States was promoted by Street and Smith in 1869. Buffalo Bill stories circulated in other European countries. In fact, the first dime novels were published in Germany in 1905. See Gallo and Bonomi (eds), *Buffalo Bill and Tex Willer*.

31  Some titles are *The Scalp Hunters* (Sonzogno, 1868), *The White Chief* (Muggiani and Guigoni, 1878, reprinted in 1887), and *The Mortal Gunshot* (Treves, 1886).

32  *World Tour* was the Italian edition, published by Trevesa from 1863, of the French Magazine *Tour du Monde*, while *The Illustrated Journal of Travels and Adventures by Land and by Sea* was published by Sonzogno in 1897. The former was designed for a cultured public, while the latter was geared toward the lower classes and combined travel reports with adventure novels. For further information on this subject, see F. Colombo, *La cultura sottile* (Milan: Bompiani, 1998).

33  Another two adventure cycles are responsible for Salgari's notoriety. They are the Indo-Malese cycle centered around Sandokan, and the Corsars cycle. Among the books set in America are *2000 Leagues under America* (1888), *The King of the Prairies* (1896), *Adventures among the Red-Skins* (1900,) under the pseudonym G. Landucci, and *The Queen of the Golden Field* (1905), in which, for the first time in an Italian book, Buffalo Bill appears. Reporting for the daily *Arena*, Salgari followed Buffalo Bill's 1890 show in Verona. See V. Sarti, *Nuova bibliografia Salgariana* (Turin: Sergio Pignatone Editore, 1994) and C. Gallo and G. Bonomi (eds), *Buffalo Bill and Tex Willer*.

34  See Colombo, *La cultura sottile*, and D. Forgacs, *Italian Culture in the Industrial Era 1880–1980: Cultural Industries, Politics and the Public* (Manchester: Manchester University Press, 1990).

35  Epaminonda Pravaglio, *Pinocchio the Explorer: Extraordinary Adventures By Land and Sea* (Florence: Nerbini, 1930). Thanks are due to Piermarco Aroldi for pointing out this text to me.

36  On the communicative pact, see Casetti, "Film Genres." On the subject of film genres, Casetti introduces the complex relationship between "genre film and the discursive space," suggesting that "if the negotiation is successful the film could reach a new agreement with the spectator in which new generic traits are accepted, their legitimacy being assured by the viewer's recognition and acceptance of uncommon intertextual references" (p. 31).

37  For this analysis, I have drawn on the analytical tools employed, with Elena Mosconi, in a reading of Italian films about Saint Francis: R. De Berti and E. Mosconi, "L'icona del santo: serialità francescana nel cinema muto italiano," *La Valle dell'Eden* 6 (2000), 35–51.

38  Another interesting comparative analysis of the cinematic style in early Italian cinema and other contemporary national cinemas (especially French and American) is by Barry Salt in "Il cinema italiano dalla nascita alla grande guerra: un'analisi stilistica," in R. Renzi (ed.), *Sperduto nel buio: il cinema italiano e il suo tempi (1905–1930)* (Bologna: Cappelli, 1991). Salt shows that in 1913 American films of the same length had at least twice as many shots as Italian films (p. 53). This appears to confirm the Italian cinema's tendency to maintain some resistance toward the institutional mode of representation.

39  See, for example, Dagrada et al., "Lo spazio mobile del montaggio."

# Chapter 9

# The Intertextuality of Early Cinema

## A Prologue to *Fantômas*

## Tom Gunning

——————————————— Before Adaptation ———————————————

I would claim that there was no such thing as film adaptation of literary works during the first decade of the cinema's existence. Cinema emerged at the end of the nineteenth century within a welter of popular entertainments recently transformed by new technologies of mechanical reproduction into a complex environment of mass entertainment. In spite of the best efforts of film historians to identify the personnel behind the first films issued by the Lumière and Edison companies (and a flood of individual film companies around the world), these films were issued as unauthored works, in most countries barely protected by copyright. For the most part, films in the 1890s functioned as the software used by exhibition companies (such as the Lumière Company and the American (or British) Biograph Company) to demonstrate the hardware of their projecting machines. The first film audiences crowded into exhibition halls and vaudeville theaters to see the Biograph, the Vitascope, or the Cinématographe, rather than a particular film, let alone the work of a specific filmmaker. This was an era of technical marvels and mechanical novelties, rather than of individual authors or texts.

Yet far from being a primitive form of folk art, this modern form of entertainment issued primarily from highly capitalized and sophisticated corporations, who utilized cutting-edge technology and were well aware of the business practices of high capitalism. During cinema's first decade, while films were hardly regarded as individualized works of art, their production companies aggressively sought to guarantee their profit-making potential and employed legal means to protect their right to their exclusive exploitation. Conceiving of films as commodities rather than authored works, early film companies utilized trademarks (included in film intertitles and sometimes actually placed within sets themselves) and company brand names to legally claim ownership, rather than employing discourses of authorship or claims of intellectual property. The copyright law in the United States, for instance, did not recognize films as examples of dramatic or narrative work. Before the law was amended in 1912 to include motion pictures, films were copyrighted as photographs, and it was their exact visual appearance that was granted legal protection.[1] It is nearly impossible to "adapt" a photograph.

Thus when the Edison Company was sued by the American Mutoscope and Biograph Company in 1904 for having produced a film entitled *How a French Nobleman Found a Wife through the New York Herald Personal Columns*, which re-staged shot by shot their successful film comedy *Personal*, the court found that no copyright was violated, since the Edison film, while containing the same plot, characters, and action, did not actually reproduce the photography of the earlier Biograph film.[2] It was not until 1909, when a lawsuit brought against the Kalem Company for their 1907 film version of *Ben Hur* was finally decided, that a United States court recognized the possibility of copyright violation by a film version of a copyrighted narrative work in another medium.[3] This date corresponds with the period in which the film industry worldwide underwent an enormous economic reorganization (typified by the Motion Pictures Patents Company in the USA and by the Congress de Paris and formation of the Comitè Internationale de Editeurs de Films in Europe), bringing economic organization and predictability to the film market.[4]

It was also at about this time that film production companies recognized the fictional narrative as the major genre of film and storytelling and as the stylistic dominant guiding how they were made. The nickelodeon revolution had begun a very few years earlier in the United States, as thousands of film theaters opened nationwide charging a cheap admission price and attracting a mass audience. This transformation in film exhibition paralleled a marked rise in the popularity of story films over the actualities, magical trick films, and brief gags that had dominated film programs during cinema's first decade.[5] With the appearance of new character-driven stories, filmmakers began to employ styles of editing, staging, and acting, as well as intertitles, that made the stories and their characters easier to follow and emotionally involving even to unsophisticated audiences. Thus a cinema of narrative integration arose in which the idea of adaptation from literary sources became a possibility.[6]

My claim that there was no literary adaptation in cinema before roughly 1907 does not mean that there were no films based on famous novels or plays before that date. On the contrary, scores of films took their action or characters from such classic or popular works as *Ten Nights in a Ballroom*, *Faust*, *Uncle Tom's Cabin*, *Hamlet*, *Robinson Crusoe*, or *Rip Van Winkle*. However, calling these early films "adaptations" only confuses things and threatens to superimpose later categories onto an early practice with a different cultural background and intention. Rather than attempting to realize a literary work in the new medium of film, these early films *make reference* to famous works, often relying on what Charles Musser calls "audience foreknowledge."[7] Thus a film version of

*Ten Nights in a Ballroom* might only include five famous, but rather brief, moments from the well-known temperance drama, each a separate film (*The Death of Little Mary, The Vision of Mary, The Fatal Blow, The Murder of Willie*, and *The Death of Slade*, all copyrighted by the American Mutoscope and Biograph Company in 1903 and none lasting more than a minute). A film might be made of only the duel scene from *Macbeth*[8] or a series of scenes from *Rip Van Winkle*.[9] This "peak moment" approach, excerpting a famous action from already well-known works, paralleled similar treatments of well-known material in vaudeville programs (which might present a famous speech, song, or action-packed moment from a famous play, usually performed by the actor who made it famous), or even the illustration of famous gestures or *tableaux* from plays in journal illustrations and popular prints. We might call this strongly intertextual practice, which has little interest in the integrity of the text, a cinema of reference rather than adaptation, the goal being to recall a famous work or even a specific performance, rather than give a treatment of its narrative or dramatic content.

Even the longer films that seem at least to summarize (usually in a ten-minute version) the whole action of a work (such as Edison's film of *Uncle Tom's Cabin* from 1903 or Méliès' 1904 *Faust and Marguerite*) would be best approached as traditional adaptations. Instead of a relation to a single ur-text, such films relate to a process and history of absorption and reference in which the original novel or verse drama can only be glimpsed (sometimes much transformed) through a variety of appropriations, including stage melodramas or operas and a variety of other popular forms (parodies, popular songs, visual illustrations, and prints). Porter's *Uncle Tom's Cabin* or Méliès' various Faust films work less as adaptations than as palimpsests of references caught within an echo chamber of popular memory.[10]

Further, one should not focus exclusively on the relation of early film to literature, as the lens of adaptation would encourage us to do. Early films find inspiration and material in diverse sources: vaudeville acts, dance crazes, political cartoons, comic strips, musical revues, popular songs, famous paintings, commercial advertisements, catch phrases, minstrel shows, verbal jokes, and clown gags. Such a range of sources affirms not only the place of early film within an unstable environment of popular commercial entertainments, but also the process of multiple reflection and reverberation, creative appropriation, self-conscious parody, and unconscious theft that dominated this world, blurring distinctions between individual works in favor of a promiscuous intermingling. Thus a Biograph film, *Foxy Grandpa and Polly in a Little Hilarity* (1902), not only refers to a popular comic strip of the era (about which the Biograph company made a series of films besides this one), but also to a musical review based on the comic strip (whose star, Joseph Hart, appears in the film) and to a popular dance (the "little hilarity") which he performs in the film. To trace an early film back to a single source would not only be difficult, but also efface the actual context of free borrowing across and within media which characterizes early film production and much early popular commercial entertainment.

But with the transformations (which Yuri Tsivian, tracing a similar change in Russian cinema of the time, calls a "reception shift")[11] that occurred around 1909, the meaning of adaptation changed. Literary rights were recognized legally in the USA, and, internationally, the prestige of an adaptation for a burgeoning industry desirous of middle-class acceptance became obvious. The French *Films d'art* premiering in 1908 produced both original works and filmic adaptations of classics, proclaiming that cinema was a new art form (whose artistry was based not so much on its originality as on its pedigree, with the new company employing actors and authors well known from the theater).[12] During 1909 nearly every film company around the world was influenced by the *Films d'art* innovations and produced what William Uricchio and Roberta Pearson have called "quality films" whose mark of distinction came from the cultural capital of either portraying events of history or mounting adaptations from literature.[13]

However, these same film companies (especially in the USA) generally recognized the need to retain a large, popular, working-class audience, even as they pursued their middle-class aspirations, playing to the masses while attracting the classes, to paraphrase early film entrepreneurs. Thus, adaptations began not only of classic or culturally recognized works, but also of the popular literature with which cinema had much in common. Somewhat redefining the promiscuous intertextuality of the previous era, popular film genres emerged – Westerns, melodramas, and detective films – whose repetitive formulas reference a domain of shared plots, character types, and situations that exceed the boundaries of one-to-one adaptation from a single text. But the prestige of certain works of popular fiction, along with the tightening of legal protection against unacknowledged adaptation, led to film versions of, for instance, the Sherlock Holmes stories of Arthur Conan Doyle (often filtered through the various stage adaptations of Holmes) and of the work I will focus on in this chapter, the serial novel *Fantômas* by Marcel Allain and Pierre Souvestre.[14] Here the one-to-one comparison of the literary text to its filmic adaptation shows both the elements that film genres were absorbing from popular literature and also the difference in narration that film, as a visual form, seemed to offer filmmakers such as Louis Feuillade in 1913.

## Spreading Terror: Popular Crime Fiction and Cinematic Narrative

"Fantômas."
"What did you say?"
"I said 'Fantômas.'"
"And what does that mean?"
"Nothing . . . Everything."
"But what is it?"
"Nobody . . . and yet, yes, it is somebody."
"And what does the somebody do?"
"Spreads terror."[15]

With this unattributed dialogue, Marcel Allain and Pierre Souvestre began the first chapter of the first volume of their narrative of the exploits of Fantômas, a narrative which would extend to thirty-two volumes. As the source of such a Niagara of literary production, it is worth lingering over. In fact, the authors withhold the identity of the speakers in this dialogue for two pages, delaying their appearance through an accumulation of Balzac-like details of setting and character description. Through this separation from its enunciating characters, the opening dialogue seems suspended above the narrative, functioning almost like an epigraph, a prologue, or the argument for the piece.

And this is undoubtedly the intention. The stylistic device accomplishes, with great economy and elegance, a number of narrative tasks. By avoiding immediate identification of the speakers, it announces formally, through a sort of mini-enigma, its allegiance to the genre of mystery stories, tales of suspense. Further, the lack of attribution of the words spoken raises in narrative form the very issue discussed in the conversation, the tremulous nature of identity and names – the phantom-like obscurity of the figure Fantômas, who appears in much of the novel as little more than a name. The terror that name produces derives to a large degree from the mystery that surrounds its uncertain identity so well described by this opening dialogue: nobody, yet somebody, nothing and everything.

The initial speaker is eventually identified as President Bonnet, a retired magistrate (and fairly minor character in the tale). He soon extends his opening enigmatic remarks with a further description of this mysterious figure:

> It is impossible to say exactly what or to know precisely who Fantômas is. He often assumes the form and personality of some particular and even well-known individual; sometimes he assumes the form of two human beings at the same time . . . That he is a living person is certain and cannot be denied, yet he is impossible to catch or identify. He is nowhere and everywhere at once.[16]

But the exact identity of Bonnet's interlocutor in the opening dialogue is never firmly established. It could be any one of the guests whom the president regales with his description of the mysterious criminal at the dinner party given by the Marquise de Langrune that evening. This lack of a specifically named addressee seems designed to encourage the reader to insert him or herself in this unknown questioner's position. Like the interrogator, he or she knows nothing yet of Fantômas, is curious to know more, and is eager to formulate the enigmas which express this curiosity and which will fuel the act of reading and decoding that the mystery genre demands.

However, among the assembled audience of guests for Bonnet's invocation of the name of Fantômas, a young man named Charles Rambert expresses the greatest interest, paralleling the ardent questioner of the opening dialogue. Charles displays a curiosity so intense that Bonnet finds it excessive and even distasteful. "I fail to understand your attitude, young man," he says reproachfully. "You appear to be hypnotized, fascinated."[17] And, indeed, that night, trying to sleep at the Marquise's chateau, Rambert seems to be haunted, not simply by the name Fantômas, but by a protean series of images it summons up:

> In his imagination Charles saw all sorts of sinister and dramatic scenes, crimes and murders. Hugely interested, intensely curious, craving for knowledge, he generally was given to concocting plots and trying to unravel mysteries. If for an instant he dozed off, the image of Fantômas took shape in his mind, but never twice the same way. Sometimes he saw a colossal figure with bestial face and muscular shoulders; sometimes a wan, thin creature, with strange and piercing eyes; sometimes a vague form, a phantom-Fantômas.[18]

Rambert, in fact, awakes in the morning to find his hostess, the Marquise, dead. Wakening into a nightmare, as the latest victim of Fantômas's histrionic machinations, he becomes the key suspect in her murder. As if immersed in the hallucination brought on by his fascination with Bonnet's invocation, he loses his own sense of identity, becoming an accused murderer, forced for a time to hide disguised as a chambermaid, while a drowned body without a recognizable face is identified as his own. Eventually taken under the protection of Detective Juve, his new mentor fashions for him a new identity and a new name. He asks Juve to make it "something arresting – like Fantômas"[19] and takes on the name Jerome Fandor, the investigative journalist sidekick of Detective Juve in many of the succeeding volumes. However, this rescue through the agency of Fantômas's detective nemesis only underscores Charles's brush with oblivion, a fitting punishment perhaps for his over-susceptibility to Fantômas's fascination.

If the reader seems at first to be identified with this too-impressionable victim of Fantômas's spell, readers familiar with the genre soon recognize their preferred surrogate in Detective Juve, who sees through appearances in order to sketch with clarity the shadowy figure of the master criminal. The opening of the novel, therefore, first proposes a dangerous way to receive its tale of villainy: Charles's dream-like submission to its thrill of evil; then the proper alternative: Juve's both rational and intuitive scrutiny and detection. Following genre tradition, it is Juve who at the climactic trial of Fantômas (under his alias of Gurn) will provide the interpretation which converts the events of the mystery *syuzhet* into a solution *fabula*, the position of final knowledge which the reader shares with satisfaction.[20]

To note that *Fantômas* makes use of shifting identities simply fixes its place in the already established genre of detective adventures in which both criminals and detectives ply their trades through a mastery of disguise. But the particular care with which Allain and Souvestre keep the actual identity of Fantômas intangible beneath his various avatars produces an elaborate and somewhat unique game for mystery readers, focused less on the traditional mystery riddle of naming the culprit than on recognizing the already named villain beneath a succession of aliases: Etienne Rambert, Gurn, Professor Swedling, plus a variety of unnamed walk-on (or rather run-through) parts. Throughout the first two volumes at least, Fantômas remains a truly ambiguous figure, little more than a name whose presence is suspected behind his actions. The novels present a series of crimes and a cast of characters, and only gradually is the figure of Fantômas revealed beneath his disguises. As Juve laments to another police officer in the second volume in the series, *Juve versus Fantômas*:

> "We see the puppets moving – Loupart, Chaleck, Josephine, others maybe – but we don't see the strings."
>
> "Perhaps the strings that move them are none other than – Fantômas," ventured Michel.[21]

This conversation provides the structure of the first eight novels.[22]

Through a restrictive narration, which is designedly uncommunicative, readers are kept in the dark about the true nature of characters. In *Juve versus Fantômas*, for instance, Chaleck and Loupart turn out to be the same character, and both of them are revealed to be disguises assumed by Fantômas. However, they are presented on the *syuzhet* level as if they are separate characters, and their identity with Fantômas is only revealed toward the very end of the tale. Allain and Souvestre supply in the first installment of *Fantômas* a wonderful image for this now-you-see-it-now-you-don't figure (which appears in the first of the Feuillade film series as well): the initially blank calling card he leaves with Princess Danidoff after stealing her jewels and cash which after a time slowly displays the legend "Fan-to-mas."

In adapting Allain and Souvestre's novels to the screen, Louis Feuillade skillfully stream-lined a plot designed for extended reading in a serial publication into a series of fast-paced, semi-independent, multi-reel films. As Jacques Champreux points out,[23] Feuillade cannily eliminated the complex plot elements dependent on interlocking railway time-tables (a frequent device in turn-of-the-century detective novels). Even more crucial to the simplifying of the narrative line, he also cut the complicated plot of Charles Rambert and his supposed father, picking up the character already transformed into the journalist Fandor. But perhaps most fundamentally, Feuillade transformed the narrative role of the reader/viewer by immediately imaging Fantômas beneath (and alongside) his disguises.

He does this by opening both of the first two installments of Gaumont's Fantômas series, *Fantômas* and *Juve contre Fantômas*, with prologues which play a complementary role to the opening dialogue of the series of novels. Like the opening dialogue, these sequences deal with events and characters within the fictional world yet stand outside them. They also rehearse for the audience, before narrative events get under way, the films' themes of identity and illusion and formally indicate the reader's relation to these mysterious transformations. In the films these sequences act as peritexts[24] on the threshold of the diegesis. They function more as title sequences than as part of the unfolding narrative. Each of these opening sequences introduces the actor Rend Navarre as Fantômas and presents Fantômas in the disguises he uses in the film. In *Fantômas* these are Dr Chaleck, an unnamed hotel porter, and Gurn, and in *Juve contre Fantômas* these are the apache Loupart, Chaleck, and the hooded and robed "man in black." In the second film, a similar sequence is also devoted to Breon, the actor who portrays Juve, who is shown in several of the disguises he employs in his pursuit of Fantômas.

What are we to make of this essential change in narrative address between film and novel? I believe that, like all significant textual nodes, it reflects the intersection of several concerns. First, the most frequent narrative approach in early feature films is one that rarely withholds knowledge from its audience. Although enigmas occur in early feature films, they tend to result from questions about the proairetic events (in other words, questions about how things are going to turn out) rather than from withholding knowledge from the audience, particularly "back stories" of events shown on the screen.

This narrative strategy undoubtedly has several motivations. A linear story line is easier to follow in a medium whose use of flashbacks in this period remains primarily limited to brief inserts of character (or viewer) memory. Apparently, early filmmakers had doubts about the ability of audiences to follow a nonchronological exposition of earlier events via an extended flashback (which could actually reconfigure the meaning of events already shown) and therefore limited the play in early films between *fabula* and *syuzhet* on which mystery narratives often depend. The narration of early features tends to be extremely communicative. Therefore, films adapted in the 1910s from literary sources often unscrambled the events of the *syuzhet* and presented them in a chronologically linear fashion. For instance, the 1919 adaptation that Leonce Perret (Feuillade's former colleague at Gaumont) made in the United States of Wilkie Collins's *The Woman in White*, entitled *The Twin Pawns*, begins with the separation of identical twins, which forms one of the final climactic revelations of the novel. Likewise, Vitagraph's *A Tale of Two Cities* begins with the romance which causes the imprisonment of Dr Marinette, an enigma the novel reveals only gradually.

Further, as Richard Abel reveals in his treatment of the French crime film in his work *The Cine Goes to Town*, crime films were subject during this period to special scrutiny by censors and government officials. It is possible that Feuillade's opening could reassure censors by providing viewers with a more secure orientation toward this rather anarchistic drama than its literary source provided.[25] One might return to the novel's original dialogue on Fantômas. The lack of a secure identity for this master criminal sparks Charles's fascination and brings on the disturbing hallucination/nightmare of Fantômas's protean power. A film with a similarly disorienting narrative address might threaten to turn viewers into victims of fascination (if they were not undone by narrative confusion). Instead, Feuillade immediately places them into a secure and knowing reading position, like that of Detective Juve, who sees the figure behind the disguises and is able to see through Fantômas's powerful visual illusions.

The legal apparatus of the Third Republic showed great concern to maintain stable identity, particularly of malefactors. The Bertillon method of identification through carefully cross-indexed photography and anthropometry was aimed primarily at establishing scientifically certain identification of those arrested in spite of attempts at disguise or false names. Such clear identification would allow law enforcement officials to isolate recidivists, the repeat offenders who so obsessed the criminologists of a society terrified of "degenerate" criminal types.[26] Fantômas plays on these fears with delight and thumbs his variety of nose types at any attempt to fix identity and culpability. However, the opening sequence of the Gaumont film reveals what the criminal conceals, and creates for the film viewer a reassuring sense of the underlying unity of Fantômas's character, whose equivocal nature in the original novels provides many of their narrative enigmas. Important as this play with the social regulation of the identity of social deviants is in explaining the structure of *Fantômas*, this film sequence appears overdetermined. As a prologue it strikes viewers familiar with the devices of early feature films less as a unique opening than as a variation on a form of prologue quite frequent in this period in both American and French films: the introductory sequence that presents both actors and their roles. The sequences in the first two Fantômas films not only reveal Fantômas beneath his disguises; they also introduce the actor Navarre alongside his fictional roles. Indeed, one could argue that the identity the prologue reveals as underlying the various roles embodied by these disguises is less that of the character Fantômas than that of the actor Navarre who plays all these roles, including Fantômas.

These actor-centered introductory film sequences seem to appear first in France and to serve several functions. Most obviously, they mark a change in modes of production and reception, moving from the previous anonymity of players to a new emphasis on the presence of actors, often stars previously known from theatrical careers, in films. Following the logic of the *Films d'art*, these prologues announce the importance of the actor and bring to films the imprimatur and cultural capital of theater, while they instruct audiences that they should receive the film partly as a performance in which the actor's skill is appreciated beneath the role.[27] In the *Fantômas* films, this relatively new protocol of film viewing as actor watching becomes doubled (or tripled) as one admires not only the actor's but also the character's skill at role-playing. If film viewers (at least in France) had already learned to recognize performers, a film like *Fantômas* redoubled these pleasures by cueing them to recognize actors like Navarre or Breon in a variety of roles and also to note the power of make-up and costuming, elements of showmanship fully recognized in theater.

After the initial introduction of the concept of the actor (that is, a person recognizable from several roles, not simply a performer) to cinema around 1908–9, a number of techniques in early feature films from around 1912–14 seem to renew this novelty of actor recognition through a series of baroque variations. Actors play multiple roles or even appear as twin characters through devices of re-photography in a number of highly publicized early features. The multiple disguises of Fantômas and Juve can be seen as one of the ways in which early feature films drew audience attention to the still relatively recent phenomenon of the film actor separate from (or underlying) specific roles.

Yet, at the same time, the position of Navarre in these prologues remains somewhat paradoxical. The opening shot of the actor without disguising make-up asserts his stable identity as a performer. But the succession of disguises seems to progressively obscure his identity as much as it affirms his skill as an actor and his ability to merge with his role. This sense of a vanishing identity is clearest in the prologue of *Juve contre Fantômas* as we move from the undisguised, hairless face of Navarre to the hirsute disguises of Loupart and Chaleck. It then reaches its climax (marked by a change in lighting and possibly tinting) with his apotheosis as the "man in black" when he pulls the hood over his face and becomes concealed from the viewer. This figure, masked and hooded with all individual features concealed, stands in the film series as the ultimate image of Fantômas, even more than the domino-masked titan looming over Paris that Gaumont adapted from the cover of the first *Fantômas* volume for the film poster.

We find in these film prologues, then, two identities being formulated for audiences to follow. On the one hand, they inscribe the figure of Navarre the actor, who might be remembered from a number of previous performances at Gaumont (and who could be followed in a number of non-Fantômas roles to come). On the other hand, they also fix the image of Fantômas, criminal genius and master of disguise, who can also be followed in a series of films. If the identification of actors as figures existing beneath their roles is a general strategy of the French film industry of this period, the creation of a consistent character, tied to (but not restricted to) a performer, was also essential to achieving the equally important marketing strategy of the film "series."[28] The series appears in its most obvious form in the comic films produced in the 1910s by French studios. Gontran, Onesime, Rigadin, Bebe, Rosalie, and others all name characters in series of films whose titles invariably included their character names.

The early French detective film genre also used recurring characters to define series. Several studios had recurring detective heroes (occasionally based on a literary proto-type) with a string of separate film adventures: Eclair's Nick Carter, Pathe's Nick Winter, Eclipse's Nat Pinkerton. This genre dealt in a more complex way with the nature of a recurring character than the comedies were able (or needed) to. Most of the detective characters employed disguises which endowed their recurring characters with a range of appearances. The fairly simple approach to recurring characters in the comedies, the immediately recognizable physique and physiognomy of rotound Rosalie, goofy Rigadin, or dapper Max which quickly established audience familiarity and expectations, was given a baroque variation in the detective genre as audiences recognized an established figure often hidden beneath a deceptive appearance.

Further, the dangers endemic in the detective genre made the detective's continued appearance from film to film the result of a nearly preternatural invulnerability, rather than the irrepressible suite of reappearance of the comedians. The dramatic overcoming of death by detectives or criminals provided a way of intensely dramatizing the continuation of the series. Recall that both the last lines of *Juve contre Fantômas* and the final title of Feuillade's film version (which comes after Fantômas triggers the dynamite explosion of Lady Beltham's villa with Juve and Fandor within) equivocally close their narratives with the words: "But were Juve and Fandor among the dead?"

Thus, Eclipse's publicity announced in December 1911, after a series of Nat Pinkerton adventures: "No. He is not dead. The famous detective, the police agent so loved by the public continues the series of his exploits in *Nat Pinkerton l'emmure*."[29] Eclair also announced a new film in its Nick Carter series with a full-page advertisement containing a dramatic black-bordered announcement stating simply: "Nick Carter is not dead."[30] Similarly, when Eclair began its publicity for its second *Zigomar* film, it immediately addressed the fact that in its first feature Zigomar had seemed to perish in the explosion of his subterranean criminal lair. The first advertisement hinting at the second Zigomar film addressed this question to its readers: "Who, then, has claimed that Zigomar was dead – under the smoking rubble of his mysterious hideout – after the explosion of the crypt? A slight noise . . ."[31]

We recognize here a familiar narrative device of both the adventure film serial and the character-based thriller series: the redefinition of narrative closure in which what seemed in one film a definitive demise becomes redefined in a sequel as somehow less than fatal. In this structure, character recognition and popularity overrule credibility and discrete narrative form. The heroes of these crime film series display not only an ability to appear in various roles and guises, but also a near immortality based less on verisimilitude than on popularity and profitability. The mysterious identity and powers of these characters could be used to motivate their continued appearance in a succession of films even when their mortality appeared to have been tested to the limits. But the longevity of such characters, especially of the master criminals such as Zigomar or Fantômas, was partly naturalized by the very malleability of their ambiguous identity. They could *play* dead because they were so good at disappearing under assumed identities. They could be resurrected because their power of disappearance entailed a complementary ability to materialize unexpectedly.

If Feuillade avoided the incommunicative narrative structure that defined the ambiguous nature of Fantômas's character in Allain and Souvestre's novels, he nonetheless found in the figure of the "man in black" (Fantômas in his tight-fitting leotard and *cagoule*) a visual correlative to an anxiety-causing effacement of individuality. While the visual appearance of this figure undoubtedly has many antecedents, at least one of these would seem to be the dark-robed and hooded figures of the theater of illusions that allowed the magical manipulation of props in the "black box" magic practiced by Méliès and others. With the proper lighting, these dark-shrouded figures remained invisible to the audience against the black backgrounds of the stage sets, thus creating magical illusions of levitation and disappearance.[32] This ancestry is particularly clear in Eclair's predecessor to Fantômas, Zigomar, whose robed henchmen use their dark habits to literally disappear into the darkness of the unlit backgrounds of their hideouts. What in the magic film functioned as a technical device intended to remain invisible to the viewer, in the crime thriller became a dramatized process as these dark-robed figures merge into darkness to become invisible or emerge from the shrouded background like terrifying apparitions. Once again the genre discovers a visual means to play with identity and presence.[33]

The terror inspired by Fantômas and Zigomar resides not only in the ability they share to become a range of other characters but in their apparent power of disappearing entirely, leaving only their name, like Fantômas's mysterious calling card. In fact, the literary source for Zigomar, Sazie's *feuilleton* in *Le Matin,* was launched by a publicity campaign which plastered posters inscribed with the mysterious and vaguely distressing name of the anti-hero in nearly every public place without further explanation. Like the opening dialogue of *Fantômas*, the lack of attribution or context for the name inscribed the enigmatic structure essential to the mystery genre in the very form of its publicity.

Eclair's first publicity for its film of *Zigomar* continued this announcement of a name rather than a character, showing against a black background a contorted face shouting, "Zigomar."[34] The name of Allain and Souvestre's Fantômas was conceived to have a similarly anxiety-causing effect on both characters and readers, as skeptical police agents speculate that Fantômas is nothing but a legal fiction, as phantasmatic as his name.

Other than for publicity purposes, a name without a body remained a literary conception of dubious value to a filmmaker in the early 1910s. But the creation of a character whose face, identity, and even name remained malleable and uncertain provided devices of mystery which could have a direct visual impact. The fascination that the crime films of the period showed with nameless and often faceless characters certainly reflects not only the inherent mystery convention of uncertain identities but also a cinematic play with establishing and complicating the viewer's ability to recognize consistent characters and actors. This is evident in the recurring icon in the genre of the masked figure with a mysterious name (see, for instance, Eclair's advertisement for Tom Butler[35] or Lux's advertisement for "*X le mysterieux*"[36]). However, Feuillade (and Jasset in *Zigomar*) achieved something with more visual power than the domino masks that disguise these figures: an image of an actor whom we see transform himself into a variety of identities and ultimately efface himself into darkness through his dark *cagoule*.

It is certainly true that the viewer of the *Fantômas* series possesses, via the prologues to these films, knowledge of the identity underlying Fantômas's disguises, a knowledge denied the mystery reader. However, we might also point out that the visual power of these shifting identities, and especially of the "man in black" (so much more important in the film than in the novels), possesses an unsettling impact which the security of narrative knowledge may not entirely outweigh. The approach of the mystery film genre in the early 1910s seems to rely more on the power of visual transformations than on the unraveling of carefully crafted enigmas. It remains a genre based on visual effects and attractions rather than intricately crafted plotting. The visual effect of such scenes may have been such that film viewers felt more like Charles Rambert, subjected to his nightmare hallucination of shifting images, rather than sharing the sangfroid and perspicacity of Inspector Juve. How many of us, even today, can imagine the nightmares provoked in a darkened theater by the triumphant gesture of the "man in black" at the explosion which ends *Juve contre Fantômas*?

The first volume of *Fantômas* climaxes with the guillotining of the criminal under his alias Gurn. However, the deceptive nature of this public demonstration of justice is subverted by one of Fantômas's most devious ruses. The scandalous nature of Gurn's crimes and trial has prompted Valgrand, a Parisian actor, to star in a theatrical recreation of the criminal's career employing a detailed make-up patterned on the actual criminal. Valgrand is manipulated by Fantômas when Lady Beltham convinces him to meet her in his make-up near the prison for a romantic tryst. The vain and somewhat perverse actor remains unsuspicious, seeing this arrangement as "a positive refinement in erotic delight. See? The lady and I – the double of Gurn – and right opposite, the real Gurn in his cell."[37]

Like Charles Rambert in the opening, only more seriously, Valgrand pays for his fascination with devious role-playing. He is drugged and, with the aid of a corrupt prison guard, replaces the real Gurn in his cell. Despite his protests ("I am not Gurn . . . I am Valgrand the actor. Everybody in the world knows me"),[38] it is Valgrand who loses his head on the scaffold. On examining his remains, Juve alone discovers the greasepaint that reveals Fantômas's final disappearing act. Feuillade uses this climax as well but substitutes a milder ending as Valgrand is saved at the last moment. However, seemingly inspired by Valgrand's perverse scenography of the tryst in the novel, Feuillade adds an original element: Fantômas and Lady Beltham watching the execution from a nearby window, their spectatorial position underscoring the theatrical nature of the scene. While both endings complicate the theme of the genre's identity through play-acting, Feuillade's film gains an additional complication, in spite of its seemingly more conventional moral ending. This film, which begins with a nondiegetic prologue demonstrating the actor's skill in assuming identities, ends with a fictional sequence demonstrating the danger of playing roles too well, while also visualizing the perverse pleasures of spectatorship. Again, while the film version may possess a more reassuring narrative, the cinematic context complicates and plays with the new regimes of film viewing and actor recognition, arousing anxieties from other sources.

## Conclusion: Adaptation, Identity, and Genre

The *Fantômas* series, like many other features, serials, and films in series released in the era of cinema's increased narrativization, acted out a drama of mysterious disguises and multiple identities. The prologue to the *Fantômas* films, like many similar prologues displaying actors and roles that open films from this period, seemed designed to assist viewers to recognize the actors beneath the roles. As such, these prologues stimulated the newly appearing star system in which recognizable actors became a major attraction to audiences. But the *Fantômas* prologue reveals, not only René Navarre, but also the mysterious Fantômas, the phantom-like presence that underlies all the disguises, in some ways like an actor underlying roles. But, as we have seen, with a master of disguises, this relation becomes more complex and fraught with peril. It might not always be so easy to divide actor from role, and one might not be sure whether there was something tangible left over once the disguises were torn away.

In a curious way this paradox of actor/role and disguise/identity parallels the act of transformation that literature was about to undergo at the hands of cinema. On the one hand, in search of middle-class respectability and cultural capital, the cinema worked its newly founded publicity machines to stress that works of classical literature were now being offered in cinema versions. Thus, individual film adaptations (and cinema in general) gained status through relation to a higher art form. In fact, filmmakers responded to more complex narrative material with developments in film language in order to express subjectivity of characters and the temporal re-organizations of literary plot. But, like issues of disguise raised by the detectives and mysterious super-criminals brought from the dime novels to the cinema, issues of adaptation might confound issues of identity rather than resolve them. Was a successful adaptation one in which, as in one under-standing of the actor's responsibility to role, faithfulness to an original model was paramount? Or, as the film of mystery hinted, was such faithful imitation only a sign of clever deception, and the truly cinematic adaptation in fact a film in which the original source material has been wholly absorbed by the new medium, so that no original identity could be said to persist? Generations of argument about the relation of identity and adaptation, faithfulness and invention and the interrelation of media appear here.

It is perhaps important, however, to recall that cinema's borrowing from pulp literature provided it with some of its most powerful visual metaphors and filmic practices. Visualizing the detective or mystery story opened up for cinema a tradition of narrative so attuned to the visual devices of the medium – and often so distant from the emphasis on character psychology of the realist novel – as to seem to be inherently cinematic rather than "literary." But it all depends on what literature one refers to. In adapting the devices of the mystery story, the cinema created a genre rather than, primarily, a reference to singular pre-existing literary works. Thus, the single identity of a source dissolves into a series of devices, plot templates, character types, and dramatic situations. Instead of the body of a singular canonical work, the cinema appropriated parts and elements from many works, much like the scene in *Fantômas contre Juve* in which Dr Chaleck escapes from the police who have grabbed him, leaving them astonished, holding only an evening coat and a pair of artificial arms.

### Acknowledgment

Parts of this chapter were previously published as "A Tale of Two Prologues: Actors and Roles, Detectives and Disguises in *Fantômas*, Film and Novel," *The Velvet Light Trap* 37 (Spring 1996), 30–6. © 1996 by the University of Texas Press.

### Notes

1  The copyrighting process which resulted in the Library of Congress Paper Print Collection is discussed in detail in Patrick Loughney, "A Descriptive Analysis of the Library of Congress Paper Print Collection and Related Copyright Materials," unpublished dissertation, George Washington University, 1988.

2  André Gaudreault, "The Infringement of Copyright Laws and its Effects," in Thomas Elsaesser and Adam Barker (eds), *Early Film: Space–Frame–Narrative* (London: British Film

Institute, 1990), pp. 114–22, covers this and other early copyright suits in early cinema. He places the emphasis somewhat differently from the way I do. The lawsuit over *Personal* is also discussed in Charles Musser, *Before the Nickelodeon: Edwin S. Porter and the Edison Manufacturing Company* (Berkeley, CA: University of California Press, 1991), pp. 280–2. As Musser notes (p. 281), there was another solution, which the Biograph Company followed after this lawsuit, which was to copyright the scenario for the film as a dramatic work as well as the film roll itself. However, this was a separate and – importantly – a *written* document, filed with the copyright office.

3   See the decision in this case by K. S. Hover reprinted in *Nickelodeon* (September 1909), 81–2.

4   On the Motion Picture Patents Company, see Robert Jack Anderson, "The Motion Picture Patents Company," unpublished PhD dissertation, University of Wisconsin, Madison, 1983. On the CIDEF, see Georges Sadoul, *Histoire général du cinéma*, vol. 2: *Les Pionniers du cinéma* (Paris: Denoel, 1948), pp. 483–96.

5   On the rise of the story film, see Charles Musser, *The History of American Cinema*, vol. 1: *The Emergence of Cinema* (New York: Scribners, 1990). Musser dates this slightly earlier than I do, but does not include in his conception of the story film the importance of character-driven action. With this in mind I stick with the later date of 1906–7.

6   I discuss the change from an earlier cinema based in attraction to one founded on narrative integration in my *D. W. Griffith and the Origins of American Narrative Film* (Urbana: Illinois University Press, 1991).

7   Charles Musser, "The Nickelodeon Era Begins: Establishing the Framework for Hollywood's Mode of Representation," in Elsaesser and Barker (eds), *Early Cinema*, pp. 256–73.

8   *The Duel Scene from Macbeth*, American Mutoscope and Biograph Company, copyrighted 1905.

9   In 1896 the American Mutoscope and Biograph Company filmed the famous aging actor Joseph Jefferson in his signature role as Rip Van Winkle. Again, a series of peak moments were shot: *Rip Meeting the Dwarf*, *Rip and the Dwarf*, *Rip Leaving Sleepy Hollow*, *Rip Passing over the Hill*, *Rip's Toast*, *Rip's Toast to Hudson and Crew*, *Rip's Twenty Years' Sleep*, and *Awakening of Rip*.

10  On *Uncle Tom's Cabin* particularly, see the discussion of dramatic sources by Janet Staiger in *Interpreting Films: Studies in the Historical Reception of American Cinema* (Princeton, NJ: Princeton University Press, 1992), pp. 105–19.

11  Yuri Tsivian, *Early Cinema in Russia and its Cultural Reception* (London: Routledge, 1994), pp. 23–4.

12  On the *Films d'art* as a company and as a movement, see Sadoul, *Histoire général du cinéma*, pp. 497–512.

13  William Uricchio and Roberta E. Pearson, *Reframing Culture: The Case of the Vitagraph Quality Films* (Princeton, NJ: Princeton University Press, 1993).

14  For background on *Fantômas* as a literary source, see Robin Waltz, "Serial Killings, *Fantômas*, Feuillade and the Mass-culture Genealogy of Surrealism," *The Velvet Light Trap* 37 (1996), 51–7.

15  Marcel Allain and Pierre Souvestre, *Fantômas* (New York: William Morrow and Co., 1986), p. 11.

16  Ibid., p. 14.

17  Ibid., p. 19.

18  Ibid., p. 21.

19  Ibid., p. 210.

20  My point in using these terms from Russian Formalism is that as *syuzhet,* that is, the mystery story as actually written, the mystery genre needs the re-reading of events by the detective to provide the actual story (*fabula*), with the elements previously withheld now filled in by the detective's interpretation. The most thorough discussion of these terms in relation to the mystery narrative in film is given in David Bordwell, *Narration in the Fiction Film* (Madison: University of Wisconsin Press, 1985), esp. pp. 64–5.

21  Marcel Allain and Pierre Souvestre, *The Silent Executioner* (translation of *Juve contre Fantômas*) (New York: William Morrow and Co., 1987), p. 106.

22  Robin Walz's chapter on *Fantômas,* "The Lament of *Fantômas*: The Popular Novel as Modern Mythology," in his "Imaginary Paris: Surrealism and Popular Culture in Early Twentieth-century France," unpublished dissertation, University of California at Davis, 1994, pp. 80–137, provides an excellent overview of the series of novels as a whole. In his section "Modern Masks" (pp. 106–12), he details the complex exchanges of identity which pervade the whole series, with at points even Juve being taken for Fantômas or masquerading as Fantômas. I thank Professor Walz for sharing this chapter with me.

23  Jacques Champreux, "L'Année du maître de l'effroi," *1895,* numéro hors série *L'Année 1913 en France* (October 1993), 256.

24  The term *peritext* comes from Gérard Genette, who uses it to refer to aspects of a work which are on the threshold of a text, such as the title, preface, and so on. See Genette, *Seuils* (Paris: Editions du Seuil, 1987).

25  Richard Abel, *The Cine Goes to Town: French Cinema 1896–1914* (Berkeley, CA: University of California Press, 1994), p. 364, makes the point that in 1912 the coincidence between actual anarchist violence (for example, the Bande à Bonnot) and films supposedly celebrating criminal heroes led to the banning of a number of crime films. This may have caused Gaumont to be cautious in their adaptation of *Fantômas*. Champreux indicates that the *Fantômas* films did encounter bans in some areas of France (p. 262).

26  For a thorough discussion of Bertillon and the use of photography to establish identity in France, see Christian Pheline, "L'Image accusatrice," *Cahiers de la Photographie* (Paris) 17 (1985). For a discussion of French concerns about degeneration and recidivism, see Robert A. Nye, *Crime, Madness and Politics in Modern France: The Medical Concept of National Decline* (Princeton, NJ: Princeton University Press, 1984).

27  My thoughts on these prologue sequences have been influenced by a very fruitful exchange with Livio Belloï of the University of Liège who is undertaking a study of such sequences. I have found our correspondence invaluable and thank him for sharing his insights with me.

28  Abel discusses both the comic series and the detective and crime series and their role in the French film industry in *The Cine Goes to Town*.

29  Eclipse advertisement in *Ciné-Journal* (December 19, 1911), n.p.

30  Eclair advertisement in ibid. (November 25, 1911), n.p.

31  Eclair advertisement in ibid. (July 29, 1911), n.p.

32  Méliès describes one instance of his use of such shrouded manipulators of props in his description of his illusion "Les Phenomenes du spiritisme" performed at the Theatre Robert Houdin, reprinted in Pierre Jenn, *Georges Méliès cineaste* (Paris: Albatros, 1984), p. 165.

Tom Gunning

Chapter 9

33  I have discussed the use of devices from the magic theater in Zigomar in my article "Attractions, Detection, Disguise: Zigomar, Jasset, and the History of Film Genres," *Griffithiana* (May 1993), 111–36.

34  Eclair advertisement, *Ciné-Journal* (March 25, 1911), n.p.

35  Eclair advertisement in ibid. (April 27, 1912), n.p.

36  Lux advertisement in ibid. (May 11, 1912), n.p.

37  Allain and Souvestre, *Fantômas*, p. 299.

38  Ibid., p. 308.

A Prologue to *Fantômas*

Chapter 9

# Chapter 10

# Cosmopolitan Projections
## World Literature on Chinese Screens

## Zhang Zhen

Somewhere in the middle of *A Spray of Plum Blossoms* (*Yi jian mei*; Lianhua, 1931; dir. Bu Wancang), a Chinese silent film inspired by Shakespeare's sixteenth-century comedic play *Two Gentlemen of Verona*, something takes place that would probably have made Shakespeare's jaw drop (if he had held it in place so far). Hu Lunting (a Chinese incarnate of Valentine), played by the erstwhile "China's Valentino," Jin Yan, and Shi Luohua (for Sylvia) begin to compose a classical poem together as a token of love, with a brush pen, on a rock in Miss Shi's plum blossom-filled garden. The poem (generating the poetic Chinese film title), like many other things in the film not found in the original, is one of the points where the film takes on a life of its own. One can no longer treat the film merely as an adaptation of a classical European text about fidelity and betrayal in friendship and love. A different mode of appreciation is called for.

The film, up to this point, may have given its informed contemporary viewers, that is, those who had read or attended the performance of the play, a sense of familiarity with the central structure found in the original play: the vicissitudes in the love life of two romantic pairs. This familiarity begins to erode with the insertion of the poem-writing scene and the ensuing drama that employs the plum motif as a narrative vehicle. What motivated the translator (in this instance, the screenwriter Huang Cuoyi and the director Bu Wancang) to structure the plot with the plum poem and its referent, a spray of plum blossoms? How could a Renaissance tale of "two gentlemen of Verona," who go to Milan to fulfill their masculine training, turn into a romance of two modern girls and boys traveling from Shanghai to Canton in 1931? (Why not, say, to Beijing?) On the level of reception, one ponders also for whom the film, with its ensemble of stellar actors of the nascent Lianhua Studio (in English, the United Photoplay Service Company) in Shanghai, was intended.

Obviously, these questions cannot be tackled simply by taking the film apart in order to sort out original and added ingredients, which I nevertheless will attempt selectively, for the reasons to be explained below. This particular case proffers rather a unique instance and opportunity (as the silent film is luckily extant) for outlining a practice in the history of Chinese silent film that few scholars have paid serious attention to. The theoretical implications of this historical project are twofold. On the one hand, I will engage and evaluate existing models for describing not just screen adaptation but cross-cultural adaptation, such as in *A Spray of Plum Blossoms*, and explore new avenues for talking about such border-crossing cultural practices. On the other hand, the question of cross-cultural adaptation necessarily invokes other related issues such as translation, equivalence, and power dynamics in the production and, importantly, the consumption of knowledge and desire. Thus, a more viable model than that of national (or for that matter transnational) cinema may, following the adapters who created *A Spray of Plum Blossoms* and other films, be conceived. This possibility falls within the realm of "cosmopolitan projections" to be delineated in this chapter.

---
## Terms of Discussion
---

In China, cinema's symbiotic relationship with literature has been strong since at least the 1920s, after the consolidation of narrative cinema.[1] While the bulk of silent cinema in China is heavily indebted to the rich tradition of classical Chinese literature, as well as the modern vernacular literature that flourished in the early decades of the twentieth century, a number of attempts were made to adapt world literature to the Chinese screen for local as well as cosmopolitan audiences. These adaptations derived in part from the highly institutionalized practice of translating world literature into Chinese, which flourished from the late Qing period. But the process and the results of these cinematic productions are complicated, not merely by what Lydia Liu has termed the "translingual practice" that defines the intercultural literary transaction,[2] but also by the thorny problem of intermedia transfers of words, gestures, and emotions. Beyond the level of literary transcription, cinematic adaptations constitute the *performance* and *embodiment* of both the original and the translation. As is commonly known, the symbiotic relationship between literature and cinema has been an ambivalent one because of the institutional and cultural divide between the "high" (literature) and the "low" (cinema/mass culture) forms that each medium is perceived to stand for. Scholars have been obsessed with the question of fidelity and authenticity, often motivated by purely aesthetic and formal concerns, projected from the "high" end of the spectrum of the arts in which the cinema is not only the youngest but also regarded as the ambivalent "bastard."[3]

This divide, when placed in the intercultural field of translation and adaptation, generates a new set of questions. It is a commonplace that the technology of cinema was developed in a number of locations on both sides of the Atlantic, the seat of the industrial revolution and attendant cultural and political movements that contributed to the formation of what is known as modernity. The spread of cinema to the rest of the world was, directly and indirectly, part and parcel of the colonial expansion of modern world history. The reception of this novel communicative technology and aesthetic medium, unlike industrial and military machinery, however, precipitated complex reactions due to cinema's manifold identity as technology, commodity, entertainment, and a powerful instrument of mass enlightenment and democratization. The redemptive power and democratic potential imbued in the medium, a "blue flower" in the land of technology, as underscored by Walter Benjamin, have the potential for waging a possible "revolution" in the industrialized Western world.[4] It has also been deployed by people in the colonized or semi-colonized nations not only as a viable form of national industry, but also as an instrument of political and cultural empowerment.[5] The new representational technologies, such as photography and cinema, have been appropriated by the so-called "primitives" and developing nations who, through intentional or non-intentional "misuses" of the machines at hand, replenish their own cultural repertoire while forging critiques of the colonial presence and domination.[6]

Recent historical and theoretical inquiries into the early years of cinema have greatly expanded the theoretical potential of the notion of reception, extending it beyond the more familiar ground of passive textual digestion. Yuri Tsivian's pioneering study of the "cultural reception of cinema" in pre-revolutionary Russia contributes a notion of reception as "reflective rather than reactive response." He expounds, "by 'reflective' I mean a response that is active, interventionist, or even aggressive."[7] Tsivian is here primarily concerned with the response of Russian culture to, and its internalization of, the cinematic medium. The "reflective" mode underscored by Tsivian, however, is not to be confused with "reflection" as an unmediated form of mimetic representation, or a "mirror image," nor as the more individuated and interiorized modernist metacritical stance toward representation in the wake of modernity and industrial capitalism. It is rather grounded on a specific cultural terrain in which cinema inspires and forges a productive aesthetic experience. On this ground, the "high" and "low," imported and homegrown cultural forms and sensibilities converge as much as they collide. Remarkably, such convergences and collisions – or "confluences of cultural forces"[8] – often take the "embarrassing" form of mis-reception, whereby expected or assumed responses do not occur, or obverse reactions make the original intentions or intended effects irrelevant.

However, due to its received passive baggage or "reactive" connotations, the term "cultural reception" cannot fully account for the bilateral or even multidirectional construction of cultural meaning taking place in intercultural screen adaptation of literature and drama. The often "aggressive" acts of translation involved in screen adaptation across vastly different languages and cultures entail anxiety as well as excitement, the combination of which generates what I call "cosmopolitan projections" of visual pleasure and cultural experience. For such "projected" acts not merely "translate" one culture for and in terms of another in a linguistic sense, they in fact create a space in which the original and the adaptation coexist with tension. At the same time, they generate a surplus of meaning that cannot be subsumed by either the source language/culture or the target language/culture. Adaptations of Western literature by non-Western filmmakers run the risk of mimetic identification yet also may seize opportunities to "reflect" on that mimetic act and appropriate the source material by mobilizing the aesthetic and expressive possibilities of cinema.

In the late Qing period, China's intensified contact with the rest of the world, especially the colonial powers of the West and Japan, ran parallel with a booming translation enterprise. During the second half of the nineteenth century, government-sponsored institutions conducted systematic translations from Western languages and Japanese, primarily on the subjects of law, the military, governmental politics, and statecraft, with the explicit aim of serving the purpose of "enriching the nation and strengthening the military." Hardly surprising, Yan Fu, the late Qing reformist and leading intellectual who coined this slogan, was one of the pioneers of translation in both practice and theory. In a preface to his 1898 Chinese translation of Huxley's *Evolution and Ethics*, Yan presented his famous three-tiered phraseology on translation: *xin/da/ya*, or fidelity/comprehensibility/grace. The last category has exercised critics in the past who often found it to be evidence of Yan's privileging of style over fidelity, form over content, translation over the original. His adherence to a "graceful" classical prose is unfailingly cited as proof of his theory of "unfaithfulness." A recent study re-examines Yan Fu's translation theory and practice not simply in terms of translation technique but more in light of political exigencies, readership, patronage, and the ambivalent position from which the late Qing intelligentsia negotiated their split cultural and linguistic (Chinese and foreign, classical and vernacular) identities.[9] One telling illustration of Yan Fu's creative technique in achieving the effect of "comprehensibility" is the method of "example exchange" (*huanlifa*) whereby examples used by the author of the original text which are obscure to the Chinese reader are replaced by those taken from the familiar local environment.[10] Yan Fu's method is instructive for understanding the insertion of the classical poem in *A Spray of Plum Blossoms*, with which the adapters smoothly translated the motif of love-letter writing and exchange in the original play to the Chinese context. The amorous "exchange" is thus made relevant to an audience who reads the classical poem as an approximate but reasonable "equivalent" (for its archaic connotation) of the Elizabethan verse.

The late Qing period was also a time when world literature became widely (and often wildly) translated into Chinese. Sporadic efforts had been made since the Opium Wars; however, the translation of world literature for popular consumption allegedly began with Lin Shu's (1852–1924) "translation" of Dumas fils' *La Dame aux camélias* in 1898. In collaboration with Wang, a friend who was well versed in French literature, Lin Shu, who knew next to nothing of foreign languages, rendered Wang's oral translations into elegant classical Chinese prose. The commercial success of the book spurred a craze for translated foreign literature. Within the next two decades, Lin Shu emerged as the most prolific and popular translator of foreign literature, despite his lack of knowledge in any foreign tongue. By 1907, the number of translated literary works had reached as many as 126, far exceeding works of fiction written directly in Chinese.[11] An early survey found that about two-thirds of the 1,500 literary works published in the last decade of the Qing dynasty (1900–10) could be considered translation (including many "aggressive" adaptations and appropriations).[12] Like Lin Shu, many translators hardly knew foreign languages. Some worked with secondary translations, via translations in Japanese or classical Chinese. Translating as such is considered no less honorable or creative than writing an original story, just as scholars in the past would partake in a genealogy of a collective authorship through commenting on existing canons. Such approaches to translation and adaptation were by and large carried over into the theater and later on into cinema. The original literary screenplay as an independent entity was not institutionalized until as late as the early 1930s.[13]

In recent years, several Chinese scholars have productively engaged Western theories of translation for constructing a new conceptual apparatus and methodology for understanding the historical genesis of modern Chinese language and literature. Of particular interest to me are Lydia Liu and Hu Ying's works about the linguistic as well as cultural transactions that gave rise to a "translated modernity" (Liu) and a "composite" image of the "New Woman" (Hu) as a cosmopolitan subject. In her attempt to correct the assumptions of "hypothetical" cultural equivalence or commensurability commonly found in the theory and practice of translation, Lydia Liu proposes the term "translingual practice" for grasping the "practical" as well as discursive nature of the "initial interlingual contacts between languages." For her, the late Qing and early Republican periods in China are significant moments for such contacts:

> Broadly defined, the study of translingual practice examines the process by which new words, meanings, discourses, and modes of representation arise, circulate, and acquire legitimacy within the host language due to, or in spite of, the latter's contact/collision with the guest language. Meanings, therefore, are not so much "transformed" when concepts pass from the guest language to the host language as invented within the local environment of the latter.[14]

Furthermore, Liu underscores the fact that the application of the notions of "host language" and "guest language" allows a shift of focus onto the "host" language (or onto translation rather than the original). However, this changed emphasis is not meant to be a simple reversal of opposites in power relations but rather to spell out the complex layers of mediation in the translation process, including subversion as well as complicity.[15] "Translingual practice," as such, is thus not limited to the study of language and literature but may be extended to discussions of other representational and cultural practices.

In her study of the "composition" of the image of the New Woman in China in the late Qing period, Hu Ying finds that this highly gendered representational practice takes place in the field of translation and constitutes the core of a collective production of the modern imaginary. The Chinese New Woman is, in fact, a translated cosmopolitan product, bearing resemblance to La Dame aux Camélias, Sophia Perovskaia, and Madame

Roland de la Platière. Yet, as she is being composed in(to) Chinese, she takes on features and behaviors of her would-be literary ancestors and sisters in the Chinese literary tradition.

It is thus not surprising for the reader to find a revolutionary who is also a filial daughter and a "chaste widow recite a poem from *Romeo and Juliet*" – in short, a composite figure that is neither "original" nor "coherent."[16] In light of this, Shi Luohua's (Sylvia) ability to dash off a classical poem while wearing a military uniform would come across as quite natural in the eyes of the contemporary spectator. Hu's study demonstrates that translation practice of one kind or another, just as with the creation of the Chinese New Woman, "bristles with implications about the difficulties in presuming either 'fidelity' of translation or adequacy in representing cross-cultural experience." Translation as such, beyond the literal and literary domains, is thus "a tension ridden 'contact zone.' "[17]

The difference between cinematic and literary translation, however, begins where their similarity ends.[18] The advent of cinema in China coincided with the aforementioned massive translation enterprise in urban China, particularly Shanghai. As a new and synthetic form of representation, the cinematic experience was deeply implicated in the "translation" and domestication of Western technology and ideas beyond the realm of print. This makes sense also because early film practice, particularly in the arena of exhibition, as elsewhere in the world, more often than not involved the instrumental presence of a simultaneous "interpreter" who provided a running commentary on the motion pictures which they also usually programmed or compiled. These commentaries could be very far from what the images "intended" to say and often served as a means of mediation between the foreign sights and local tastes. In the process, the exotic images were infused with a set of new meanings and became, to use Hu's wording, a "composition." Because each "interpreter" could do very different things with the same pictures, due to dialect, regional difference, and personal taste, the number of their performative oral translations could be infinite. Their "translingual practice" had to cross not merely linguistic barriers but cultural thresholds, on an experiential level.

For many years, before the Chinese began to make films with imported equipment, early film experience in China consisted mostly of exhibition or projection of the "foreign electric shadows." The irreducibility of the materiality of "guest" film technology, in both production and exhibition, never entirely disappeared as it could with a book in a foreign language in the process of translation. This calls for a medium-specific approach that also addresses the question of spectatorship. I insert the notion of "projection" into the discussion in order to understand the cultural politics and poetics governing the adaptation of world literature in Chinese silent film in particular and intercultural adaptation practice in general. Terms with the prefix "trans-" (transfer, transplantation, transmogrification, transaction, and transformation) have dominated the recent discourse on cultural translation. While "trans" aptly accounts for the crisscrossing of objects and meaning, and implies a certain measure of "transgression" of cultural or textual boundaries, it stops short of explaining the complex mechanism behind exchange and change, even less so with the transitions between one medium and another in the cross-cultural arena.

World Literature on Chinese Screens

Chapter 10

I mobilize the term "projection" for its double meaning and rich resonance in film studies. First, projection is deployed as a basic but defining cinematic element, a crucial stage that bridges production and reception, technology and society, thereby constituting cinema as an exhibition-bound practice in a public space. When this process involves the transplantation of a text and commodity from one culture to another, from one time to another, and from one medium to another, projection as a cinematic as well as a cultural event entails a complex web of losses and gains. The role of the translator or adapter in this conception is thus intertwined with the role of the "projectionist" in a metaphoric sense; for it is only through the act of projection that words and images are brought to life on the silver screen, generating pleasure, meaning, and identification. In early exhibition practice, the showman who functioned as a simultaneous "translator" of the pictures, foreign as well as domestic, may be seen as a prototype of this adapter-projectionist in one.

Secondly, yet connected with the first point, projection as used in the domain of psychology signifies the subjective imposition of ideas, attributes, and emotions onto the other (person or collective entity) and brings to relief on the surface of life the undercurrents of consciousness and perception. Most translators and adapters of foreign literature into Chinese for print and the screen in the first three decades of the twentieth century took great liberty in their treatment of foreign sources. Their creative – or "irreverent," depending how one sees it – approach to the original was, however, not whimsical or due to a lack of translation skills. Nor can it be simply explained away by resorting to the diametrically different perceptions of authorship and the integrity (or "copyright" in modern terms) of a text that Chinese culture has in the past fostered. The bold omissions and additions rampant in much early translated literature, as well as in some silent films produced in the 1920s and 1930s, demonstrate a translation and adaptation method encapsulated in the spirit of "projection" – far-fetched yet close to home. The seemingly idiosyncratic creative choices involved in turning the original text into something that speaks or appeals to a Chinese reader or viewer are predicated on a broad understanding of the cultural forces behind the translation and reception of the chosen texts and images at a given historical moment. Far more than with print, popular cinema requires a particular kind of imagination to create an even more vernacularized version of the original for a mass audience, through the palpable visual (and verbal) language of silent cinema.

## Texts and Intertexts

Compared to the abundance of films adapted from Chinese literature and drama, the number of foreign adaptations on the Chinese silent screen is more modest. A perusal of existing filmographies of roughly three decades of silent film in China reveals only a few dozen or so foreign adaptations. It was nevertheless a persistent strand, which runs from the 1910s to the early 1930s, when sound was gradually implemented by the Chinese film industry. I have identified about twenty films that are apparent adaptations, although some original sources remain obscure. I say "apparent" because, as Hu Ying's example of *Yu Li Yun*, a popular novel second-handedly based on *La Dame aux camélias* shows, there are often "opaque" translations and derivatives that do not directly correspond to their sources of inspiration. Adaptation can take many forms with some having more visible umbilical cords linked to original sources and others outlandishly incarnating into something nebulous or different.

The modest amount notwithstanding, the range of sources covered is rich in geographic as well as thematic distribution. It is hard to pinpoint the earliest screen adaptation as the concept of such was not yet quite in place. Given the proliferation of the image of La Dame aux camélias in China following Lin Shu's first translation in 1898, the non-extant *Xin chahua* (New Camellias), one of the shorts made by the Asia Company in 1913, is likely to have been the first cinematic incarnation of a literary subject of foreign origin. *Che zhong dao* (Great Train Robbery, 1920, 7-reel), the first title from the Film Department of the Commercial Press, was allegedly based on a detective novel translated by Lin Qingnan (Lin Shu). *Hongfeng kulou* (Red Skeleton; Xinya/Commercial Press, 1921), also a detective film, is about a female Mafia gang who seduce and kidnap rich young men for ransom. The film was liberally adapted from a French novel, *Ten Sisters of the Life Insurance Company* (literal translation of the Chinese title, *Shijiemei baoxiandang*), by director Guan Haifeng, who applied his expertise and experience in mechanical theater to the *mise-en-scène* of the film. The film was a commercial flop, but the costumes for the *femmes fatales* designed by Guan were so popular that they quickly appeared on the streets of Shanghai, becoming a fad among modern girls.[19]

In the mid-1920s, when a vibrant domestic film industry emerged in Shanghai, demand rose for scripts for feature-length films. This attracted a number of writers of popular fiction, particularly the so-called "Mandarin Ducks and Butterflies" school, including Bao Tianxiao, Shen Zhengya, Zhu Shouju, and Zhou Shoujuan. Not surprisingly, the screen adaptation of Shen Zhengya's *Yu Li Hun*, a novel in classical prose derived from the Camellia story, was a huge box-office hit in 1924. Shen's serialized story is a far cry from the French original. The famous Parisian courtesan is transfigured into a Chinese widow who, painstakingly trying to obey the Confucian codes of chastity, renounces her desire for the child's teacher, a young scholar, only to die of depression and melancholy.

A number of films adapted from both Chinese and foreign sources in this period address the "question of woman" brought to the foreground of the debate over national culture from the last decade of the Qing dynasty. A notable example is *A String of Pearls* (*Yichuan xianglian*; Great Wall, 1926; dir. Li Zeyuan) adapted from Guy de Maupassant's well-known story, "The Diamond Necklace." In the film, diamonds are supplanted by pearls, a jewel that carries the staple meaning of tears and sorrow in the Chinese aesthetic tradition. Hou Yao's script transplanted Maupassant's story to a Chinese setting, turning it into a "family problem drama" set in Shanghai's emergent urban culture. The original short story is about a young Parisian couple who borrow a diamond necklace from a rich friend, so that the wife can wear it to a ball. But the necklace is lost on their way home, and the couple have to work very hard for ten years before they can repay the debt. Only then, after all the hard work and social degradation they have endured, is the truth revealed. The lost necklace was, in fact, made of mock diamonds. They have paid 35,000 francs to purchase a new necklace whereas the fake one only costs 350 francs.[20]

In Hou Yao's version, not only do all the characters assume ordinary Chinese names, but the setting of the story also changes from an official function in Paris to a private party in Shanghai during the Chinese Lantern Festival. Several key elements are also changed, to enhance not only the narrative function of the necklace and its nature as a commodity, but also its cultural and cinematic appeal to the Chinese audience. Instead of diamonds, the necklace is now a string of pearls, a more familiar motif in traditional Chinese folklore and literature. The round shape of pearls (and the "string" or *chuan*) and their literary association with tears combine to make the necklace a pertinent narrative vehicle for a melodrama about the circulation of commodity and desire in a Chinese metropolis. A *String of Pearls* underscores the danger a nuclear family is exposed to in a modern city by adding a child to the picture, foregrounding the moral conflict encountered by the urban woman, who is poised between the private and public spheres. The husband's workplace is changed from a government bureau to an insurance company, which allows the narrative to unfold in a different direction. Instead of working hard to repay the debt, the husband in Hou Yao's film resorts to a "short-cut" – by "borrowing" the money in the company's safe. Hou Yao also made bold alterations to the second half of the story, spinning a subplot into a circular tale of moral retribution. With that resolution, the sexual imbalance caused by the (woman's) desire for material display is readjusted and the family and social order restored. A *String of Pearls* makes visible the cultural and economic presence of the West and attendant forms of a "cosmopolitanism of extraterritoriality" in Shanghai in the early twentieth century.[21] Hou's script is as much a result of "borrowing" as of adaptation. Circulating in a global sphere of mass culture, wandering from Paris to Shanghai, from a brief piece of fiction in French to a feature-length film scripted in Chinese, the film is implicated in a larger circle of exchange and consumption.[22]

By placing the centerpiece of the *mise-en-scène* – the string of pearls – in a prolonged trajectory of circulation and exchange, Hou Yao's revision of the original story produces a highly dramatic effect of reversal and accentuates the uncanny logic of repetition, reciprocity, and social reproduction in a modernizing city. Throughout the film, the necklace, now appearing, now vanishing, functions as an organizing device that links different narrative elements and characters. As an enigmatic object of desire and an ornamental artifice that wreaks havoc on a nuclear family of the emerging urban middle class, the necklace lives out its full life as a quintessential commodity form as it keeps haunting those who come into contact with it.

Other world literature that made its way to the Chinese silent screen include a Tolstoy novel (*Liangxinde fuhuo*, 1926), an Oscar Wilde play (*Shaonainaide shanzi*, 1928), a German folktale (*Feixingxue*, 1928), Conan Doyle's detective stories (*Fu'ermusi zhengtan* an, 1931), Polish fiction (*Lian'ai yu yiwu*, 1931), and Japanese fiction (*Konggulan*, 1926; *Sanzimei*, 1934). These productions were created by adapters and directors associated with different studios. The adaptations tend to be "Chinese" in their basic outlook, meaning that little if any effort was made to "faithfully" recreate the originals in terms of cast, costume, and setting. The original plots would usually have been deconstructed and reconstructed beyond recognition by the time their Chinese screen incarnations met the Chinese audience. In making *Liangxinde fuhuo* (Resurrection of Conscience), for instance, the director Zheng Zhengqiu insisted on adding *liangxin*, or conscience, a cornerstone in the Chinese moral universe, to the title. This gesture was not only in line with Zheng's production philosophy, "business plus conscience," coined for his Mingxing company, but also aligned with his belief in ethical redemption and transformation (*jiaohua*) through cinema.[23] Zheng's emphasis on "conscience" is akin to Hou Yao's resort to "retribution" in his "borrowing" of de Maupassant's "Diamond Necklace" mentioned above. A predominant theme shared by most of these adaptations is the question of women and their status within the family and in a society undergoing drastic changes in the wake of modernization. The fate of women in these works of disparate cultural origins, through Chinese cinematic *mise-en-scène*, acquires a local visage as well as a cosmopolitan dimension.

A *Spray of Plum Blossoms* is one of the few known Shakespeare adaptations in Chinese silent film history, and it is worth asking what in this particular play attracted the Chinese filmmakers and what differences in the Chinese screen version from the play appealed to Chinese audiences of 1931. As with *A String of Pearls*, this film, also extant, provides us with a rare glimpse into the "look" of adaptation films produced in the silent period. Besides the plum blossom motif that endows the love story with a touch of the "Butterfly" fiction, the overall changes are more structural than this seemingly trifling flourish suggests. The film retains the plot of two pairs of troubled lovers, but their ties are strengthened by added family connections. Hu Lunting (Valentine) and Hu Zhuli (Julia) are made into siblings (as their Chinese surname indicates), while Shi Luohua (Sylvia) becomes Bai Lede's (Proteus) cousin because Shi's father happens to be Bai's uncle, who is the governor of Canton (instead of the Duke of Milan). With this familial take, the film sheds some of the picaresque flavor of the Renaissance tale about individual formation (of which the friendship between two men outweighs heterosexual love).[24] The film excised Lance and Speed, two clownish and talkative characters, who would not only be hard for a silent film to manage but the comedic effect of whose lengthy and allusion-rich speeches would have been lost in translation and presentation. The adaptation emphasized and expanded, however, on Hu Lunting's exile into the domain of the "outlaws." The leader of the outlaws is given a real name while their headquarters bear the allusive name of "Plum Blossoms Village" in the borderland between Canton Province and Jiangxi Province.[25]

The domestication of the play is above all evident in the geographic setting. Hu Lunting and Bai Lede are two recent graduates of a military academy in Shanghai. Hu is described as "an ambitious newly graduated cadet" and Bai as a playboy who "knows girls better than soldiers." Hu Lunting is assigned to Canton to serve under Bai Lede's uncle while the latter stays in Shanghai and courts Hu's sister Zhuli. The kinship between the characters is thus matched by the "kinship" of the two most prosperous Chinese treaty ports. Given that Canton is the gateway to Hong Kong and the Nanyang region (Southeast Asia), which was at the time the largest market for Chinese cinema, this narrative itinerary effectively links Shanghai, the center of Chinese film production, and the Nanyang market. The bilingual intertitles, common in Chinese productions of the time, while serving Shanghai's non-Chinese residents as well as Chinese cosmopolites, also catered to the Chinese diaspora communities, especially those in the European-ruled colonies in Southeast Asia. Thus the domestication of a Western play turns inversely into a process of making and marketing a cosmopolitan film.

The film departs further from the play in gender representation, in both a playful manner and "militant fashion" (I will explicate this double entendre shortly). This change is imbricated with the shift of emphasis from romance to kinship, but with a significant twist. The original tale of "two gentlemen of Verona" is, beyond the complete change of title, supplanted by a tale of two modern girls of China. Ruan Lingyu, the actress best known for her roles as a tragic heroine in films such as *Spring Dream of the Old Capital* (1930), *Little Toys* (1933), *Goddess* (1933), and *New Woman* (1935), offers here a surprising performance as the witty and intelligent Hu Zhuli. In the play, Sylvia is the more important female role between the two young amorous women; *A Spray of Plum Blossoms*, however, enhances the importance of Julia by casting in the role Ruan Lingyu, who ranked higher in star stature than Lin Chuchu (Sylvia). As two leading stars, who often appeared together, Ruan Lingyu and Jin Yan's sibling roles in the film take precedence over the romantic relationships among the two pairs of star-crossed lovers.

As if to complicate the matter further, Ruan's Julia and Lin Chuchu's Sylvia attain far stronger androgynous qualities than their counterparts in the play. Romance in the film is not so much the end as the means by which the two modern Chinese girls learn more about themselves and forge an alliance with one another. In much of the film we see the two leading ladies flaunt their male attire or, to be precise, military garb. Luohua, the daughter of the Governor-general, is no love-starved maiden locked away in the deep recesses of an aristocratic palace but an officer with a rank. An early intertitle card describes her as "a maiden with a spirit of masculinity." (She does, however, retain her long hair.) We see her riding horses in breeches and walking around the interior scenes with a horsewhip in hand. Whether in public or in her private quarters, she confidently commands her male as well as female underlings. After Hu Lunting is dismissed from his post, she takes over the position and in turn appoints the recently arrived Zhuli to be her "right-hand *man*."

Zhuli (Julia), for her part, outperforms Shakespeare's Julia on many counts. In the play, planning with the maid Lucetta her trip to Milan to track down Proteus, Julia would travel "not like a woman, for I would prevent the loose encounters of lascivious men."[26] The modern girl from Shanghai undergoes a metamorphosis after arriving in Canton. The piano-playing, singing, and dancing girl dressed in a white feminine dress that we see at the beginning of the film may be Sylvia's modern incarnation in Shanghai's foreign concessions, but it is no longer the case when she arrives in Canton. Luohua takes Zhuli under her wing and the two quickly form a sisterly bond. Rather than serving Bai Lede as his page in disguise as in the play, Zhuli joins Luohua to carry on their war with the opposite sex. Ruan Lingyu dons a masculine military form, hair tucked in under an officer's cap – a far cry from her typical tragic and pitiful screen persona. The star text here both invokes and parodies the prevalent expectations of Ruan's (tragic) star image.[27]

The move toward conspicuous androgyny and the forging of a sisterhood in masculine disguise is not merely an update of the masquerade trope found in several of Shakespeare's plays. The cult of the modern girl in urban China on the cusp of the 1930s is an important indicator for understanding the two young Chinese women flaunting their fashion of breeches and military caps. The subplot of sisters-in-arms should also be viewed with regard to the martial arts film that rose at meteoric speed in the late 1920s. The martial arts film craze not only exponentially expanded the market for Chinese cinema in Nanyang but also generated a widespread social discourse on the empowerment of marginalized subjects, including women. The large bulk of films with martial heroines, or *nüxia*, as protagonists constituted a sizable subgenre. Films like *Red Heroine* (1929) and *Female Knight-errant of Huangjiang* (1929–31) feature a maiden turned knight-errant who serves as the arbiter of a community; in the process, the heroine usually rescues another maiden in distress. In many films, the veteran heroine also initiates the other maiden into the world of martial arts and knightly grace.[28] In Shakespeare, the picaresque itineraries of the two interweaving romances are meant to be part of the education of the two (supposedly) knightly gentlemen. In the Chinese film, the women groom and train themselves to be knightly subjects, both in heart and in style. They take control of their circumstances rather than being dictated to by them. Meanwhile, the men they love to hate (Bai Lede and Diao Li'ao) are relegated to the background or serve as mere foils to the two "gentlewomen," while the true "gentleman" Hu Lunting languishes in his exile among the outlaws.

The wilderness where Hu is turned into a knight-errant and where the narrative reaches its denouement is also the place where the film further betrays its indebtedness to the martial arts genre. While the play does contain a digression in which Valentine is banished and chosen by the nameless outlaws as their leader, and indeed this must have been part of the "raw material" that attracted the adapters, the film extends and transforms this digression. The leader of the outlaws is given a real name, Li Fei, and their headquarters, the "Plum Blossoms Village," is complete with decorative motifs corresponding to Shi Luohua's residence. After the gentleman from the city is adopted as the head of the wild bunch, he decrees that their gang will not do anything harmful to the poor or to women. Rather, they will live by the principle of "Eradicating the Powerful and Aiding the Weak," a motto in the world of knight-errantry made popular by martial arts fiction and film in the 1920s. More local color is laid over the play with the insertion of a minor character, Feizhu (homophone for "fat pig" played by the well-known character actor Liu Jiqun, nicknamed "Fatty"). To entertain the gang, Feizhu sings Peking Opera songs associated with the famous female impersonator Mei Lanfang, adding a further twist to the gender-bending element in the film.

Why did Lianhua Studio, a new player in the Chinese film market, which advocated a radical departure from existing Chinese film practice and aesthetics, play with elements taken from genres that it tried to distance itself from? How may we further explain the uninhibited translation and refashioning not just of the play to the Chinese screen but also of perceived Western lifestyle and sensibilities? What is the cinematic and social infrastructure that supports the making and marketing of a popular film of foreign adaptation, which existing scholarship has singularly failed to address?

## National Cinema and Cosmopolitan Projections

Films adapted from foreign sources in China have received very little scholarly attention. While Chinese literary critics and translation theorists have been embroiled in debates on fidelity, style, cultural equivalence, and other conceptual issues in translation discourse since the late Qing period, the same critics and writers have hardly concerned themselves with a popular medium like cinema and the question of adaptation. In cinema, the adaptation of Chinese literature to the screen, both classical and contemporary, has been taken for granted in a culture with an entrenched tradition of writing.[29] The lack of scholarly interest in foreign adaptations, I think, has less to do with the seeming insignificant number of such productions and a lot to do with a preoccupation with the ideological construct of a national cinema. The adaptation of native literature and drama has always, as with other nations, been perceived to be indispensable for the making of an indigenous cinema, although certain kinds of literature, for example, the martial arts genre, may be censored for political as well as commercial reasons at certain times. The making and reception of films like *A String of Pearls* and *A Spray of Plum Blossoms*, however, proffer opportunities whereby the tension between the desire to construct a national cinema as a buttress against the domination of foreign cinema (in particular, Hollywood), on the one hand, and the desire to achieve a cosmopolitan identity through cinema, on the other, becomes apparent.

The early 1930s marked a turning point in Chinese film history. By 1931, the Nationalist censors had put a stop to the mass production of the martial arts film, which they saw as a dangerous outlet of anarchic social energy. With the Japanese looming dangerously in Manchuria and the Communists fortifying their base in the southern mountains, the Nationalists found it imperative to assert tighter control over the newly "unified" nation and its cultural life. As a result, most of the small studios, which had been surviving by making low-budget martial arts copycats, quickly vanished. After a year, only a few large studios carried on, for a brief period, their major martial arts series. This change coincided with a major reconfiguration in the Shanghai film industry, most prominently marked by the rise of the Lianhua Studio. In the midst of the martial arts craze and the ensuing censorship, this newcomer emerged as the self-appointed "savior" of Chinese cinema with a pompous slogan: "Promote Art, Disseminate Culture,

Enlighten the Masses, Revive the Film Industry."[30] To gain a spot in the limelight of the very competitive film scene in Shanghai, Lianhua recruited a contingent of high caliber directors (notably Sun Yu and Bu Wancang) and actors (such as Jin Yan, Ruan Lingyu, Lin Chuchu, and Gao Zhanfei), launching a campaign of producing quality films of mostly contemporary subjects. Within only a year, with several box-office hits to its credit, including *Spring Dream of the Old Capital* and *Wild Flowers*, both starring Jin Yan and Ruan Lingyu, Lianhua established itself as one of the three most influential companies (the other two being the veterans Mingxing and Tianyi). More importantly, the carefully cultivated modern look and patriotic flair (notice, for instance, the reference to "national distress" in *A Spray of Plum Blossoms*) of its productions give Lianhua a cutting edge in the transformation of Chinese cinema and its spectator. Beyond the "petty city dwellers" (*xiaoshimin*) and members of the working class, Lianhua was also eager to recruit the more educated and cosmopolitan strata of society as part of its target audience, who would, for instance, welcome such a Shakespeare adaptation, albeit thinly disguised as a partial martial arts film.

Unlike other studios established previously, Lianhua distinguished itself as the first vertically and horizontally integrated corporation. Its founder, Luo Mingyou, started as a distributor and exhibitor in Northern China. In the wake of the Japanese invasion of Manchuria and the intensified onslaught of American cinema, he decided to move south to establish an enterprise that would save both the nation and its film industry. Well connected in the political, business, and even military world,[31] Luo quickly built up a film empire by acquiring small or medium-sized companies (including the rights to their films) and theater chains, and set up branches in Shanghai, Hong Kong, as well as many other cities inland. A native of Canton and son of an influential Canton–Hong Kong merchant, Luo was aware of Hong Kong's geopolitical and commercial significance as an entrepôt of the Southeast Asia region.[32] The company was registered both with the Nationalist government and the Hong Kong colonial administration. In fact, its head office was based in Hong Kong, whereas Shanghai served as the main site of production. Li Minwei, a pioneer of Hong Kong cinema who moved to Shanghai in the mid-1920s, joined Lianhua with his Minxin company; so did his uncle Li Beihai with his Hong Kong Film Company in Hong Kong, which became Lianhua Studio No. 4. The strong Hong Kong connection readily explains the Canton setting of *A Spray of Plum Blossoms* (or the movement from Shanghai to Canton) and Li Minwei's role as its production manager.

Lianhua Film Production and Printing Limited Company (also known as United Photoplay Services Co.) was established as a multimedia company, which enabled a close link between film and publishing, including the necessary publicity arms and literary resources. Luo's other major partner, Huang Yicuo (also known as Jeffrey Y. C. Huang), joined Lianhua with his publishing, translation, and printing company (*Shanghai Lianye bianyi yinshua gongsi*). In charge of Lianhua's publicity sector, Huang also served as the chief editor of the company's trade journal, *Yingxi zazhi* (*The Film Magazine*). The magazine engaged in the promotion of the "film novel" (*dianying xiaoshuo*) – a cross-pollinated genre between screenplay and ordinary fiction – and, among other things, called for a screenplay contest for a sequel to the first Lianhua hit, *Spring Dream of the Old Capital.*[33]

Huang Yicuo himself wrote many film novels and scripts, most of them being primarily meant for print, a practice shared by many writers at the time. *A Spray of Plum Blossoms* is one of his successful and realized attempts. A reader of the magazine sent in the following letter about his viewing experience of the film:

> I finally got a chance to see the long-awaited *A Spray of Plum Blossoms* on the 23rd (of September?). Because it was raining I decided to see it in the capital [Nanjing, instead of going to Shanghai]. I want to inform you of the Chinese people's enthusiasm for Lianhua's productions!
>
> It was raining so hard that day. We arrived at the theater two hours in advance but there were already many waiting for tickets. As soon as the door opened, people rushed in. Many got their clothes and umbrella torn up . . . And this was only the case in the south. If not for the simultaneous national release, it would have been more crowded.[34]

Interestingly, *The Film Magazine*, Lianhua's most effective publicity channel, marketed the film as one with an "original screenplay by Huang Yicuo" and one of the "ten great works" (*shida weipian*) from Lianhua.[35] On the same page, however, *Love and Duty* is indicated as an adaptation (*gaibian*) of a novel by Madame Horose (Hua Luoshen in Chinese transliteration).[36] The advert reveals that Huang's script was originally called "True and False Love," and the release title was advertised as "The Amorous Bandit alias 'A Spray of Plum Blossoms'" under the genre rubric "A Great Picture of Knightly Love" (*xiayi aiqing jupian*). The "original" packaging and the variations on the title spell out some of the ambiguities in the making and marketing of the film as both a "national film" (*guopian*) and a commodity catering to a cosmopolitan market. The two couplets that frame the advertisement are telling indications of this Janus-faced production ideology:

> [Upper]
> Resist Foreign Cultural and Economical Invasions;
> Propagate the Essential Virtues of our Nation.
>
> [Lower]
> Down with Films that are Non-artistic and Harmful to Society;
> Gain Back the International Status of Domestic Films.

Straddling, at the same time, art, politics, and profit, the rise of Lianhua in the early 1930s not only signaled the emergence of a new cinema but also a new brand of cosmopolitan film culture. Infused with nationalist fervor and cosmopolitan ideals, Luo, who was also a practicing Christian, emerged as a patriotic "cosmopolitan capitalist" in the culture industry.[37] Lianhua's acquisitions and expansions practically put an end to the era of filmmaking as a cottage industry. While veteran companies like Mingxing and Tianyi tried to catch up with the changes in the local film industry and global market by investing much of their resources in sound experiments, Lianhua focused on the perfection of silent film. Its productions, commercially viable, artistically refreshing, and politically "correct," filled the lacuna in a film market that was slow in embracing American talkies, for a combination of technical, linguistic, and cultural reasons.[38]

Beyond an intertextual reading of *A Spray of Plum Blossoms* in the previous section, I have delved into the historical context of both film industry and national culture in the early 1930s that gave rise to such a seemingly anomalous adaptation. To this end, engaging sources, such as the studio's trade journal, proves a useful methodology. Neither an "original" nor a "copy," the method of adaptation here is more of a *projection* – cinematic and cultural appropriation and re-production – than translation and adaptation in the usual sense. In the process, it is no longer about a truthful *mise-en-scène* of a Shakespeare classic on the Chinese screen, but the creation of a new cosmopolitan product. The retaining of the bare bones of the dramatic plot and the English names of the characters, appearing in the intertitles, allows, however, the film to be read as a transnational text. The audience could see the film as *at once* a "national film" and an exotic incarnation of the Occidental other. While the actors become de facto "bilingual" cosmopolitan subjects on the screen (thanks to the "translatability" of silent film's intertitles) the audience could shift between different linguistic communities and cultural identities, and form fleeting but still meaningful new ones. Cosmopolitan projections, of which "aggressive" adaptations like *A String of Pearls* and *A Spray of Plum Blossoms* are but two pronounced cases, are about synchronicity and tangentiality, whereby the local is wedged in the global (and vice versa), and the contemporary absorbs or remakes the past.

Cross-cultural screen adaptation, more than the kind adapted from literature in a native language, brings to relief the contradictions inherent in modern cosmopolitanism irrevocably tinged with colonialism and industrial capitalism. Such a form of cinematic cosmopolitanism is conditioned not simply by specific social and political circumstances that produce a film like *A Spray of Plum Blossoms* and a company like Lianhua. It is also shaped by available representational technologies that both constrain and, often unwittingly (as with the absence of sound technology), revitalize a struggling national cinema caught up in multiple demands and ideologies. The "golden age" of Chinese silent cinema took root precisely in this period of technological as well as cultural sea change, with Lianhua contributing a large body of films that are now considered the silent classics. On the level of textual inscription, the kind of genre bending, irreverent mixing or juxtaposition of scrambled elements from unrelated time and space, frequently found in such adaptations, is an articulation of a cosmopolitan imagination that is not shy about its "superficial" or reproduced originality. This attitude explains why a film like *A Spray of Plum Blossoms* could contain a discernible patriotic rhetoric and gender politics while its sets bristled with art deco motifs and its stars could pen a love poem in classical idiom. It also explains why the pages of *The Film Magazine* were at one and the same time filled with lavish advertisements for Lianhua-owned theaters and slogans advocating a strong and popular national cinema, as well as copious photos of Hollywood starlets and utopian eulogies of the future of film technology.

---
## Epilogue
---

In subsequent decades of the twentieth century, the adaptation of world literature to the Chinese screen became sparser and more random. Substantial historical research has to be undertaken in order to determine the nature of this diminished investment in foreign literary sources. Here I would venture to offer a few speculative points. First of all, the complete implementation of sound in Shanghai theaters by the mid-1930s created an advantageous market for Hollywood and European talkies. This in turn forced the domestic industry to woo Chinese audiences by concentrating on productions that capitalized on cultural and linguistic difference. If the bilingual intertitles of a film like *A Spray of Plum Blossoms* made it possible for the Chinese actors, and spectators as well, to "pose" as translingual and transcultural subjects, the linguistic imperatives of the talkies would have significantly reduced, if not obliterated, the indeterminate space for such a playful, cross-over subjectivity and spectatorship.

Secondly, the surge of patriotic passion and nationalism in the wake of the all-out Japanese invasion of China in 1937, and the subsequent occupation of Shanghai, greatly altered the landscape of Chinese film culture. While a domestic film industry in Shanghai struggled to survive under the occupation through or beyond "collaboration," political exigencies impelled Chinese filmmakers to turn once again, to a large extent, to "escapist" historical subjects and costume dramas.[39] In the late 1940s, recovering from the devastation and trauma of war, the Shanghai film industry experienced a revival: interestingly, screen adaptations of foreign literature reappeared precisely in this period, along with realist films that depicted postwar social fragmentation and reconstruction. Two prominent examples are *Night Shop* (*Yedian*; Wenhua, 1947) and *The Watch* (*Biao*; Wenhua, 1949), both from Russian sources (the former based on Gorky's play, *Lower Depth*), adapted and directed by Huang Zuolin, a well-known playwright and stage director as well as translator of Western plays and drama theory. The collective portrayal of a group of petty urban subjects residing in a small hotel presents a vivid microcosm of confused and anarchic postwar Chinese society. Rather than the flamboyant and fashionable adaptations of the earlier period, these cross-cultural projections reflect rather a somber vision of a war-torn urban landscape and a traumatized social body.

After the Communist take-over of China in 1949 and the subsequent nationalization of the Chinese film industry, arbiters of the overarching ideology of socialist nationalism and related cultural policies regarded the kind of cosmopolitanism embodied by the Shanghai cinema of the Republican period as "poisonous weeds" (*ducao*) that spread Western or colonial lifestyles, values, and worldviews. As a result, exhibition of these films was, in most instances, outlawed. The adaptation of non-Chinese sources ceased almost completely, while Chinese filmmakers, working exclusively for state-owned studios, were given the responsibility to portray, and promote, the struggle of the young People's Republic. It was not until the revival of Chinese cinema in the 1980s, which coincided with the "re-opening" of China and the translation or reprinting of foreign literature and other texts on an extensive scale, that world literature began to return to the Chinese screen. *Bloody Morning* (*Xuese qingcheng*, 1991), adapted from a novella by Gabriel Garcia Márquez, and directed by the Fifth Generation woman director Li Shaohong, won both Chinese and international critical acclaim.[40] Re-set in a mountainous rural village in China, Li's version of the drama of sexual repression is played out against the backdrop of China's tortuous journey toward modernity. The death of two young people, suspected of illicit premarital sexual relations, is made into an allegory of the violence and sacrifice involved in the process. Shot and released shortly after the suppression of the student protests in Tiananmen Square in June 1989, it is astonishing that the film, especially with its suggestive title, managed to pass the censors and went on to become a success in China. Perhaps the format of adaptation in this particular instance might have worked the magic – or, better, the magic realism. It gave the poignant story both a sense of defamiliarizing distance, due to its Latin American origins, and a sense of proximity and urgency conveyed by the Chinese "look" of the film. The choice of a Third World author's work (one extremely influential on the Chinese intelligentsia of the 1980s) for articulating the troubled vision of Chinese modernity and the attendant gender politics, after nearly a century-long struggle, indicates, perhaps, the emergence of a new and more self-reflective cosmopolitan cinema from China in relation to world literature and world cinema.

---

## Notes

1. For a discussion of the genesis of Chinese cinema and the emergence of narrative cinema, see my "Teahouse, Shadowplay, Bricolage: *Laborer's Love* and the Question of Early Chinese Cinema," in Yingjin Zhang (ed.), *Cinema and Urban Culture in China, 1922–1943* (Stanford: Stanford University Press, 1999).

2. Lydia Liu, *Translingual Practice: Literature, National Culture, and Translated Modernity in China, 1900–1937* (Stanford: Stanford University Press, 1995). See also her introduction in Lydia Liu (ed.), *Tokens of Exchange: The Problem of Translation in Global Circulations* (Durham, NC: Duke University Press, 1999), pp. 1–12.

3. For an instructive critique of adaptation discourse based on "fidelity" and moralistic judgment, see Robert Stam, "Beyond Fidelity: The Dialogics of Adaptation," in James Naremore (ed.), *Film Adaptation* (New Brunswick, NJ: Rutgers University Press, 2000), pp. 54–76.

4. Miriam Hansen, "Benjamin, Cinema, and Experience: The Blue Flower in the Land of Technology," *New German Critique* 40 (Winter 1987), 179–224.

5. Andrew Higson, "The Concept of National Cinema," *Screen* 30: 4 (Autumn 1989), 36–46. See also Roy Ames, *Third World Filmmaking and the West* (Berkeley, CA: University of California Press, 1987).

6 See Michael Taussig, *Mimesis and Alterity: A Particular History of the Senses* (New York: Routledge, 1993). See also Ella Shohat and Robert Stam, *Unthinking Eurocentrism: Multiculturalism and the Media* (London: Routledge, 1994), esp. ch. 7, "The Third Worldist Film," and ch. 8, "Esthetics of Resistance."

7 Yuri Tsivian, *Early Cinema in Russia and its Cultural Reception* (London: Routledge, 1994), p. 1.

8 Tom Gunning, foreword to ibid., p. xvii.

9 Wang Hongzhi, "Chongshi 'xin/da/ya': Lun Yan Fu de fanyi lilun [Reinterpreting "xin/da/ya": On Yan Fu's Translation Theory]," in his *Chongshi "xin/da/ya": Ershi shiji Zhongguo fanyi yanjiu* [Reinterpreting "xin/da/ya": Studies on Translation in Twentieth-century China] (Shanghai: Dongfang chuban zhongxin, 1990), pp. 79–111.

10 Ibid., pp. 104–5.

11 Chen Pingyuan, *Ershi shiji Zhongguo xiaoshuoshi xiaoshuoshi* [History of Twentieth-century Chinese Fiction], vol. 1 (1897–1916) (Beijing: Beijing daxue chubanshe, 1989), pp. 24–42. Cited in Wang Hongzhi, *Chongshi "xin/da/ya*," p. 148.

12 Cited in Liu, *Translingual Practice*, pp. 26–7. Wang also uses the term "baolide" (violent or aggressive) to characterize the translation enterprise in modern China in general.

13 Zhong Dafeng, "Foreword," in Zheng Peiwei and Liu Guiqing (eds), *Zhongguo wusheng dianying juben* [Chinese Silent Film Scripts] (Beijing: Zhongguo dianying chubanshe, 1996), pp. 1–17.

14 Liu, *Translingual Practice*, p. 26.

15 Ibid., p. 27.

16 Hu Ying, *Tales of Translation: Composing the New Woman in China, 1899–1918* (Stanford: Stanford University Press, 2000), p. 5.

17 Ibid., p. 12.

18 See Richard Allen, *Projecting Illusion: Film Spectatorship and the Impression of Reality* (New York: Cambridge University Press, 1995).

19 Guan Haifeng, "Wo paishe *Hongfeng kulou* de jinguo" [How I Shot *Red Beauty and Skeleton*]," *Zhongguo dianying* [Chinese Cinema] 5 (1957), 60–1.

20 Guy de Maupassant, "The Diamond Necklace," in Saxe Commins (ed.), *Selected Tales of Guy de Maupassant* (New York: Random House, 1950), pp. 137–44.

21 The term is from Acbar Abbas, "Cosmopolitan De-scriptions: Shanghai and Hong Kong," *Public Culture* 32 (2000), 774.

22 The film was reportedly exported to and shown in France, along with other Great Wall productions. The Cinémathèque Française holds a rare print of the film.

23 For a discussion of Zheng Zhengqiu's career and the ethical preoccupations in his filmmaking, see Tan Chunfa's biographical study, *Kai yidai xianhe: Zhongguo dianying zhifu Zheng Zhengqiu* [The Pathbreaker: Zheng Zhengqiu, the Father of Chinese Cinema] (Beijing: Guoji wenhua chuban gongsi, 1992).

24 See Kurt Schlueter's introduction to William Shakespeare, *The Two Gentlemen of Verona*, ed. Kurt Schlueter (Cambridge: Cambridge University Press, 1990).

25 This could be an oblique reference to the base of the Red Army, as they were also seen as the "outlaws" by the Nationalists.

26 *Two Gentlemen of Verona*, II. vii. 22.

27 This is more interesting considering that Ruan played, against Jin Yan, a woman caught between desire and societal constraints in another foreign adaptation, *Love and Duty*, released earlier that year.

28 See my "Bodies in the Air: The Magic of Science and the Fate of the Martial Arts Film in China," *Post Script* 20: 2–3 (2001), 43–60.

29 For a general discussion of film adaptations of Chinese literature, see Yan Chunjun, *Wenhuade jiaoxiang: Zhongguo dianying bijiao yanjiu* [Cultural Symphony: A Comparative Study of Chinese Cinema] (Beijing: Zhongguo dianying chubanshe, 2000), pp. 327–34.

30 Cheng Jihua, *Zhongguo dianying fazhanshi* [History of the Development of Chinese Film] (Beijing: Zhongguo dianying chubanshe, 1981 [1963]), p. 148. The slogan was ubiquitous in *The Film Magazine*. In one interesting presentation, the slogan was placed at the center of a whole-page advertisement under the general rubric: "Lianhua's Great March." Lianhua's stars (with their faces framed in the shape of a star) are "scattered" throughout and the top and bottom of the page are decorated with airplanes and marching soldiers: *Yingxi zazhi* 2: 2 (1931).

31 For instance, the director of Lianhua's board of trustees was He Dong, a powerful Hong Kong businessman with close ties in Canton. Li Suyuan and Hu Jubing, *Zhongguo wusheng dianyingshi* [History of Chinese Silent Film] (Beijing: China Film Press, 1997), p. 204.

32 Gary Hamilton, *Cosmopolitan Capitalists: Hong Kong and the Chinese Diaspora at the End of the Twentieth Century* (Seattle: University of Washington Press, 1999), p. 38.

33 *Yingxi zazhi* 2: 2 (October 1931). In his "*Bianzhe shuominghua* [The Editor's Words]," Huang thanks Luo for the idea of the contest "which significantly increased the value of the magazine."

34 *Yingxi zazhi* 2: 2 (October 1, 1931), 42. This reader goes on to comment on the film in some detail, including the presentation of translated intertitles: "Compared to *Love and Duty* which has a couple of flaws, *A Spray of Plum Blossoms* is perfect. From the beginning to the end, I watched contentedly with my mouth open. My only misgiving has to do with the English translation of the [diegetic] announcements and letters. They should have been put in intertitles consistently, and not projected on the wall sometimes in Chinese and sometimes in English."

35 *Yingxi zazhi* 1: 11–12 (April 1931).

36 This is probably because Horose was still living in Paris when the film was released in China. Madame Horose had lived in China and the novel is supposedly based on her experience of China. See her article (in Chinese translation), "Progrès du cinéma dans la Chine moderne," which details her knowledge of Chinese film and the exhibition of some Chinese films, especially Lianhua productions, in France; *Yingxi zazhi* 2: 2 (October 1930), 36–7.

37 The term is from Hamilton, *Cosmopolitan Capitalists*.

38 In an article, Huang Yicuo stressed the "golden opportunity" afforded by the unpopular American talkies for perfecting the art of silent film in China. Huang Yicuo, "Guonei de xin yingye [The New Domestic Film Industry]," *Yingxi zazhi* 1: 10 (January 1930), 29–31.

39 On the complexity and political ambiguity of film culture in this period, see Poshek Fu, "The Ambiguity of Entertainment: Chinese Cinema in Japanese-occupied Shanghai, 1941 to 1945," *Cinema Journal* 37: 1 (Fall 1997), 66–84.

40 See the section on Li Shaohong and her works in Yang Yuanyin, Pan Hua, and Zhang Zhuan (eds), *Jiushi niandai de "Diwudai"* [The Fifth Generation of Chinese Filmmakers in the 1990s] (Beijing: Beijing guangbo xueyuan chubanshe, 2000), pp. 53–86.

# Chapter 11

# The Rhetoric of Interruption

## Allen S. Weiss

Mallarmé – representing the inner limit of that great surge of lyricism in French poetry of the late nineteenth century, extending from Verlaine and Rimbaud through Valéry – well understood the exigencies of the relation between sound and image in Wagner. In his celebratory text, "Richard Wagner: rêverie d'un poëte français," Mallarmé writes of the sublime, totally generative aspect of Wagner's music: "an audience would have the feeling that, if the orchestra were to cease exercising its control, the mime would immediately become a statue."[1] As the myth of Galatea offers the scenarization of an ontological category error transformed, through wish-fulfillment, into aesthetic delight, its inversion is particularly telling.

Cinema is the art of animation par excellence, which is why the immobility of the frozen moment is particularly disquieting. Luis Buñuel, in the chapter of his autobiography preceding the discussion of *L'Age d'or* (1930), recounts that in his dreams he was never able to make love in a satisfying manner: "sometimes, when the climactic moment arrives, I find the woman sewn up tight. Sometimes I can't find the opening at all; she has the seamless body of a statue."[2] This anti-Galatean moment informs the (almost) climactic garden scene of *L'Age d'or*, when, just as the lovers are separated yet again, the woman, naturally frustrated, finds some meager substitute gratification by sucking on the toe of a nearby statue. In a bizarre reaction shot, the face of the statue remains unmoved, expressionless, a sign of the futility of sublimation, a note about the ridiculousness of the film itself in the face of desire.

It is not, however, a foot – fetishistic symbol of base, perverse materiality – that is being kissed, but cold marble, the simulacrum of a foot. This image is an ironic condensation of the major theme of the film: the sublimated aestheticism of classic statuary and the perverse desire of erotic substitutions merge to depict the malaise of civilization, where sublimation operates as a system of substitutions, deflections, deferrals, and differences to metamorphize and channel desire. Frustrated or sublimated Eros is deflected from the body onto inanimate cultural objects and formations, such that culture provides a symbolic system of substitutions and representations that is nothing other than a matrix of symbols for the body. All defenses are tropes that dissimulate the origins and aims of the libido in perpetual displacement; culture is but a vast ellipsis between moments of desire.[3]

Perversion, to the contrary, is the substitution of individual desire for the symbolic law; perversion contests the Oedipal order of the symbolic, effecting a wasteful erotic expenditure, where the reign of the symbolic is circumvented, the sexual laws of the socius shunned, and a desublimated, heterogeneous, autonomous desire reigns. In perversion, desire is the law.[4] The substitute erotic gratifications and violent displacements of emotion in *L'Age d'or* are motivated by the continual coitus interruptus that determines the course of the narrative. They are not simply signs of protest against those repressive forces that would crush individuality and desire, but are rather an integral aspect of a logic of perversion that contests sublimation itself. The paradox of the film – allegorized by the scene with the statue – is to narrate untold intimacy, to sublimate passion, to track the libido.

The "revue programme" for *L'Age d'or*, signed by numerous members of the Surrealist group, contains a section on "Amour" [love]: "Buñuel formulated a hypothesis on revolution and love that touches, through the most pathetic of debates, the most profound recesses of human nature, and he fixed, through a profusion of beneficial cruelties, that unique moment when, with tight lips, one follows that most distant, most present, slowest, most urgent voice, to a shout so strong that it can barely be heard: Love . . . love . . . love . . . love . . ."[5] Here, the ellipses would seem to indicate a mere pause in the enunciation. However, in the context of the film, the entire structure of sublimation – with its ironic correlate, its foundation in deferred satisfaction – is called into play. This theme is symbolically doubled by the soundtrack, where the music from Wagner's *Tristan und Isolde*, a tale of passion worked through by deflection, postponement, substitution – including that most orgasmic of musical statements, the *Liebestod* – is itself ultimately interrupted. In rhetoric, the ellipsis is the fortuitous or intentional omission of a linguistic element, capable of signifying the entire gamut of meanings: from an evident suppressed statement or scene to the vagueness and paradox inherent in conflicting interpretations, to total agrammatism, aphasia, silence, death. The modalities of the ellipsis are as endless as the catalogue of rhetorical figures. In the form of the montage cut, the ellipsis is the key articulatory form of cinema, and by extension the central trope of modernism. Existentially, it is the very form of human existence, of dialogue and thought itself.

The film ends on a supremely poetic ellipsis, between one chateau and another, as the feathers falling out of the window of the chateau (in the diegetic present of 1930) are transformed into snow falling on the chateau of D. A. F. de Sade's *120 journées de Sodome*. To the musical accompaniment of the drums of Calanda, the scandalous libertine, the Duc de Blangis, leaves the Chateau de Silling in the form of Christ – a kinetic icon conflating Rome and Silling, church and bordello, sublimation and desublimation, repression and desire, mystical and lustful union, Eros and Thanatos. *Here, only within the ellipsis, is desire satisfied in the film*, a desire signified by the entirety of Sade's recently rediscovered text of *120 journées de Sodome*, the necessary textual supplement to the film. For, in the novel, by the time the Sadean libertines leave the chateau, a vast panoply of desires have been satisifed without restraint, without guilt, without sublimation: the 150 simple passions, 150 complex passions, 150 criminal passions, 150 murderous passions. (Indeed, by the end of the tale, nearly everybody in Silling is murdered.)

Sade's eroticism is highly ordered as the events of these a hundred and twenty days unfold according to strict protocols: each category of the passions has its own story-teller, and the tales – specifically conceived to inflame the imagination – begin at 6.00 p.m. every day, to be interrupted at any moment, for whatever time necessary so that the libertines may fulfill their desires. As the storytellers' lubricious tales inflame the imagination, the narrated scenes are interrupted by the activities of the masters and their victims: interruption begets concupiscence, a tale begets a tale. In most narratives (except the explicitly pornographic), between the desire and the spasm is an ellipsis, a tale. In Sade, desire drives the narrative, and the storytellers' frame narratives are interrupted precisely for the more profound tales of the fulfillment of the libertines' desire. There transpire, however, untold events in this seemingly panoptical mechanism.

Recent Sade scholarship has focused on the profound, coherent, and constant theatricality of Sade's writing, where the artifice of spectacle informs literary style, cultural critique, and seductive technique. Architectural historian Anthony Vidler suggests that the Chateau de Silling constitutes a solipsistic architecture, reversing standard modes of eighteenth-century theatricality, since the staging of desire by the elite brotherhood that rules Silling conflates author, spectator, and actor.[6] In Sade, sexuality is raised to the level of epistemology, such that language = theater = architecture = eroticism. Indeed, only through this conflation of ontological realms can a true eroticism exist. This was already hinted at by Roland Barthes in *Sade, Fourier, Loyola*, where he explains that in Sade the enclosure that permits the imaginary system is constituted in order to "reciprocally contaminate the erotic and the rhetorical, speech and crime, to suddenly introduce the subversions of the erotic scene into the conventions of language . . . he always places himself on the side of *semiosis*, not of *mimesis*."[7] Therefore, the Chateau of Silling is "the sanctuary not of debauchery, but of the 'tale' [*histoire*]."[8] This is precisely the "space" – invisible, unrepresentable, undecipherable, ineluctable – alluded to in the final scene of *L'Age d'or*: the cut where everything is possible, the cut that signifies desire, the cut that marks death. In the *120 journées de Sodome*, the Chateau of Silling constitutes the real site of the most radical liaisons; in *L'Age d'or*, it denotes its utopian double.

In *L'Age d'or*, the entirety of the *120 journées de Sodome* is condensed into a single ellipsis, forced into a pregnant invisibility. Yet even in Sade's erotic combinatory mechanism, there is an unstated, unstable dimension that is elliptically suppressed in the narrative. The apparently panoptical organization of the chateau is ultimately belied by its secret chambers – literal *chambres closes* within a *maison close* – where invisible pleasures and unspeakable horrors are enacted. These sequestered, dark, unnarrated activities constitute a textual supplement, which, if determinable, would totalize the erotic combinatory system. But such totalization is impossible. No panopticon exists to reveal all the paths of the libido. Whence the extraordinary richness and mystery of the Sadean cut in *L'Age d'or*, its fidelity to Sade in revealing that no textual supplement can fully discern the secrets of Eros. Erotic closure is impossible, for not all things erotic have their *place*: Eros exists as the aporia between the imaginable and the unimaginable, gesture and speech, desire and act. Here, the full richness and ambiguity of eroticism reigns, with all its terrors and delights. Sade wrote of spaces obscene, because haunted by death; sites fascinating, because ruled by pure metamorphosis; scenes of excess, because they necessarily extend beyond the limits of any single imagination; realms of seduction, because they permit phantasmatic projection; theaters of pornography, because of an unspeakable promiscuity; domains of transgression, because symbolic articulation is no longer possible.

The gap is the place of the tale. One might well compare that grandest example of literary invention, *The Thousand and One Nights*. To avenge the infidelity of his wife, King Shahryar married a virgin every night, to deflower her and, after a night of love (or rather debauch), have her decapitated at dawn, so as not to leave any time for betrayal. After three years – nearly exhausting the city's supply of virgins in a protocol as strict as that of the systematic deflowerings in the *120 journées de Sodome* – Shahrázád, his Minister's daughter, offers herself up, harboring a scheme to stop the slaughter. It is at this point that the tales begin: three years of sex and terror motivate a thousand and one nights of sex and tales. After Shahrázád, too, is deflowered, she begins a tale that – over the course of a thousand and one nights – she always interrupts at a crucial point certain to cause curiosity about what follows, thus perpetually postponing her execution. (It might be added that the narrative structure establishes implicit ellipses: the tales are varied in length, some long enough to take up an entire night, others very short, implying that other activities, notably erotic ones, would have filled the rest of the night in question.) Indeed, these narrative interruptions, this perpetual creativity, do not continue only for the thousand and one nights suggested by the title, but indefinitely, as one of the epigraphs of the translator, Richard Burton, suggests. Quoting Crichton's *History of Arabia*: "The pleasure we derive from perusing the Thousand-and-One Stories makes us regret that we possess only a comparative small part of these truly enchanting fictions." Indeed, there are enough for a lifetime. The stay of execution, the postponement of death, is the principle of literature itself.

In a sense, the narrative mechanism of the *120 journées de Sodome* is the inverse of the *Thousand and One Nights*. In the latter, the deflowerings and murders are punctual gestures, never described, and the death sentence is interrupted only by the potential victim's narrative, with its 1001 interruptions occurring either simply *in media res* or through a complex system of subtle imbrications and allegorical doublings. To the contrary, in the *120 journées de Sodome* the victims are required to remain totally silent, and the storytellers' tales are interrupted only by accounts of the libertines' subsequent debauches. In Sade, the tale is interrupted not to forestall, but to motivate, death. Contrast Buñuel's last film, *Cet obscur objet du désir* (1977), where a single tale is generated by virginity

The Rhetoric of Interruption

Chapter 11

maintained, and the protagonist's erotic obsession limits the story to a single passion. However, death, that *malin génie* of interruption, played a role in the narrative of the film, in the form of random terrorist acts, introducing the principle of fortuity. The *Liebestod* of unsatiated passion arrives in the form of a bomb, this time to the strains not of *Tristan und Isolde,* but of *Die Walküre.* While the meaning of *L'Age d'or* is generated by the interruptions of the narrative, the nonsense of destiny depicted in *Cet obscur objet du désir* is marked by the finale, where the ultimate interruption, death, elegantly coincides with the end of the film. That it also marked the imminent death of the filmmaker is a cruel irony worthy of Buñuel, one that only enhances the effect.

Narrative is always susceptible to the effects of a deus ex machina; whether it be an incomprehensible act of God, the imperious command of an absolute monarch, or the director's imperative cut, a moment of pure volition and unlimited power generates the narrative. Buñuel transforms the Surrealist practice of generating fortuity through collage and montage into the cinematic practice of narrativizing fortuity *within* montage, of diegetizing chance. In the triangulated matrix of discourse–sex–death, the inexpressible limit of pleasure is linked to the nonsensical limit of death, precisely through the variegated structures of rhetoric. The narrative code is ultimately regulated by the gaps between *desire and spasm* or *desire and death*.

These reflections on the ellipsis, the invisible, and the untold touch the core of the aesthetics and rhetoric of cinematic adaptation. Might it not be that the most faithful adaptation is that which is not depicted but merely implied? Might the issue of adaptation ultimately be a function of the phantasmatic, and not, strictly speaking, the cinematic? In *The Uses of Enchantment*, Bruno Bettelheim argues that one should never read illustrated fairy tales to children, so as to better stimulate the child's imagination, permitting the characters to take on the lineaments of each child's unique desires, anxieties, wonderment.[9] This principle suggests a most radical role for the ellipsis in cinema, that exceedingly visual art, arguing for the primacy of the cut and the blank screen as being potentially the richest moments in film. An ellipsis may contain a missing word or gesture, a lengthy scene, a whole book, or an entire universe.[10] But every great filmmaker already knows this . . .

In his theorization of early film as a "cinema of attractions," Tom Gunning draws on Saint Augustine's notion of *curiositas,* "the lust of the eyes." In contrast to the visual aspects of *voluptas, curiositas* combines scoptophilia and epistemophilia in a desire "that draws the viewer toward unbeautiful sights, such as a mangled corpse, and [as Saint Augustine claimed in the fifth century] 'because of this disease of curiosity monsters and anything out of the ordinary are out on show in our theaters.'"[11] The cinema of attractions is thus a cinema of astonishment, of shock. But in eroticism, the essential is what is not shown, what escapes narrativization, what cannot be reproduced. Buñuel realized that the cinematic cut is more than a narrative articulation; it is a veritable sign of the most intimate realms of individuality, desire, rebellion. While *Un chien andalou* (1928) epitomized the desire to invoke the oneiric, the irrational, through a fortuitous Surreal montage, *L'Age d'or* revealed the cut as a revolutionary, critical mechanism. Dali, too, understood this. In an article of 1927 dedicated to Buñuel, he wrote: "I would speak of a blind, deaf, silent cinema, since the best cinema is the one we can see with our eyes closed."[12] Buñuel, like all great filmmakers, and like all great artists of concupiscence, would use this invisibility *within* his films.

There are many means of interrupting films. André Breton practiced a Surrealist mode of spectatorship, creating a veritable cinematic montage by entering different theaters to partially and consecutively view segments of randomly chosen films. On a darker note, the notorious right-wing riot that interrupted the screening of *L'Age d'or*, as well as the legal interdiction that censored it for decades, made no less a political statement than the content of the film itself. But there are other means of experiencing cinema by interrupting the narrative, other use-values for cinema than the scoptophilic, other ways to cinematically satisfy desire.

During the 1960s there existed numerous second- and third-run cinemas in Paris, specializing in monster and horror films. In the wings, one could witness, or even participate in, provocative scenes of intense, often anonymous, erotic activity. Here – as in much nineteenth-century Parisian bourgeois theater, though with much less inhibition – the spectators became the spectacle, and the eroticized body became the scene. Several of these sites – such as Le Brady at Chateau d'Eau and Le Mexico near the Place de Clichy – offered a peculiar architectural feature, insofar as the bathrooms (where the private scenarios usually culminated) were located behind the movie screen. Thus, within these scatological *maisons ouvertes* (to ironically coin a phrase), the caresses and couplings of rapid love were dubbed with the inarticulate, inhuman, disembodied screams of monsters and mutants, vampires and ghouls. Indeed, the talking film radically transformed the destiny of Eros.

### Acknowledgment

This chapter was originally presented as "La Rhétorique de l'interruption" in the colloquium "Luis Buñuel" organized by La Revue Parlée and Jean-Michel Bouhours at the Centre Georges Pompidou, May 24, 2000.

### Notes

1   Stéphane Mallarmé, "Richard Wagner: rêverie d'un poëte français" (1885), in *Oeuvres complètes* (Paris, Gallimard/Pléïade, 1945), p. 543.

2   Luis Buñuel, *My Last Sigh*, trans. Abigael Israel (New York, Vintage, 1984), p. 97.

3   On desublimation in *L'Age d'or*, see Allen S. Weiss, "Between the Sign of the Scorpion and the Sign of the Cross," in Allen S. Weiss, *The Aesthetics of Excess* (Albany, NY: State University of New York Press, 1989), pp. 166–70; for an excellent overview relating the aesthetic to the political, see Paul Hammond, *L'Age d'or* (London: British Film Institute, 1997).

*The Rhetoric of Interruption*

Chapter 11

4   See Guy Rosolato, "Étude des perversions sexuelles à partir du fétichisme," in *Le Désir et la perversion* (Paris: Le Seuil, 1967), pp. 9–40; and Allen S. Weiss, "Iconology and Perversion," in Allen S. Weiss, *Perverse Desire and the Ambiguous Icon* (Albany, NY: State University of New York Press, 1994), pp. 11–31.

5   "*L'Age d'or*: revue programme," in Daniel Abadie (ed.), *Salvador Dali* (Paris: Centre Georges Pompidou, 1979), p. 113.

6   Anthony Vidler, "Asylums of Libertinage," in *The Writing of the Walls* (New York: Princeton Architectural Press, 1987), p. 108. See also Chantal Thomas, *Sade* (Paris: Le Seuil, 1994), pp. 205–28; Allen S. Weiss, "The Libidinal Sublime," in *Unnatural Horizons* (New York: Princeton Architectural Press, 1998), pp. 64–82; and Annie Le Brun (ed.), *Petits et grands théâtres du Marquis de Sade* (Paris: Paris Art Center, 1989), passim.

7   Roland Barthes, *Sade, Fourier, Loyola* (1971), in *Oeuvres complètes*, vol. 2 (Paris: Le Seuil, 1994), pp. 1063, 1065.

8   Ibid., p. 1066.

9   Bruno Bettelheim, *The Uses of Enchantment: The Meaning and Importance of Fairy Tales* (London: Thames and Hudson, 1976).

10  *L'Age d'or* contains another vast ellipsis in the scene of the founding of Rome; see my analysis in "Between the Sign of the Scorpion and the Sign of the Cross," pp. 166–9.

11  Tom Gunning, "An Aesthetic of Astonishment," *Art and Text* 34 (1989), 38–9.

12  Salvador Dali, "Film-art, film antiartistique," in Abadie (ed.), *Salvador Dali*, p. 65. On the differences between Breton's and Dali's aesthetics, from the rhetorical point of view, see Laurent Jenny, "From Breton to Dali: The Adventures of Automatism," *October* 51 (1989), 105–14.

Allen S. Weiss

Chapter 11

# Chapter 12

# Visualizing the Voice

## Joyce, Cinema, and the Politics of Vision

## Luke Gibbons

In one of the few biographical glimpses of James Joyce's relationship to film, Lucie Noel, the wife of his literary executor Paul Leon, relates how the writer often asked her to accompany him to the cinema. One such film was the controversial *Ecstasy* (1933) in which the beautiful Austrian actress Hedy Lamarr was shown swimming in the nude, and in which there was also, as Noel recounts, "a very realistic love scene between horses":

> The film was quite erotic and I was quite embarrassed, because I had to explain much of the action to Joyce . . . At that time his eyesight was really bad, and every few minutes he would ask, "What are they doing now?" I would try to tell him in as general a way as I could, and he would say "I see," obviously amused by my fumbling explanation. But we both thought it was a very fine picture.[1]

Listening to the words, however "fumbling," of his female companion, Joyce did not answer "I understand" or "I follow" but "I *see*," as if words were sufficient by themselves to enable him to view the world — even the world as flesh.

It is perhaps not coincidental that this verbal "gaze" is grounded in female speech for such were the cadences of a woman's voice in Joyce's acoustic imagination that they functioned as an optical unconscious. The sonorous qualities of language for Joyce possessed the erotic allure of the image but without its voyeuristic associations, or its controlling designs over the figure of desire. Such "scopic regimes" or mastery of fields of vision do not come easily to individuals in Joyce's fiction, and not just because of bad eyesight, whether on the part of the author, or the characters themselves. In *A Portrait of the Artist as a Young Man*, even Stephen's experience of sexual pleasure with a prostitute seems to elude the nets of vision. In his moment of rapture, we are told that he "closed his eyes" as the sensuality of the word merged with the other senses: during the kiss "he read the meaning of her movements," and the "dark pressure of her softly parting lips . . . pressed upon his brain as upon his lips as though they were the vehicle of a vague speech . . . softer than sound or odour."[2] It is not just Stephen who "surrenders" here but the image itself falls under the aural and olfactory spell of language. This dispersal of vision becomes a permanent condition of the colonial city, as experienced by Stephen on his amorous encounters through its streets. When the unattainable E_ C_ rejects his sexual overtures later in *Portrait*, he seeks consolation for her shattered image in half-remembered snatches of female speech and song.

> Rude brutal anger routed the last lingering instant of ecstasy from his soul. It broke up violently her fair image and flung the fragments on all sides. On all sides distorted reflections of her image started from his memory: the flowergirl in the ragged dress with damp coarse hair and a hoyden's face who had called herself his own girl and begged his handsel, the kitchengirl in the next house who sang over the clatter of her plates with the drawl of a country singer the first bars of *By Killarney's Lakes and Fells* . . . (p. 239)

It is not just that the woman has scorned his advances: she has taken someone else into her confidence, entrusting her inner life and such "innocent transgressions" as she has ventured to "the latticed ear of a priest": "To him she would unveil her soul's shy nakedness" (p. 240). Nakedness is again exposed through the medium of language: for Stephen, the most radiant, erotic vision is filtered or rather intensified through speech, even if, in this case, the darkened auditorium is that of the confessional rather than the cinema.

It is not, then, as if the graphic and the visual do not feature prominently in Joyce for, as was evident from the earliest critical responses to his work, the cinematic nature of his prose and narrative techniques was already such as to place him among the pre-eminent literary exponents of the twentieth-century "society of the spectacle." What is at stake here, however, is precisely spectacle, if by that is meant the drive toward pure opticality or "ocularcentrism," cleansing the doors of perception of all extra-visual components to do with language, narrative, time or, indeed, history.[3] Joyce's writing is indeed visual throughout, but the modes of experience he is interested in, and the ones which lend themselves to his distinctive modernist sensibility, are those that question the sovereignty of sight, and the privileged position of the eye among the senses. In twentieth-century philosophy, Merleau-Ponty did much to dethrone the eye from its centrality in perception, arguing that other senses, and the carnality of the body as it moves through space and time, are as important in negotiating our experience of the external world.[4] Joyce takes this a stage further, showing that eyesight is not only embedded in the erotics of the body but also in the force-field of history, in a *politics* as well as a phenomenology of perception. Even the most elementary responses to the visual environment, such as color, are already intercepted by what Stephen in *Ulysses* calls "the nightmare of history" in Ireland.

These intonations are given to sight by virtue of the fact that its precocious – or perhaps traumatic – entry into history is inflected by the human voice, as is clear from Stephen's dawning awareness of both language and perception in the opening pages of *Portrait*. The difficulty for pictorial representations, and particularly for cinematic adaptations, is how to orchestrate the image to register these subtle modulations of the voice. Through a brief discussion of one motif in *Portrait* and a more extended analysis of John Huston's cinematic adaptation of "The Dead," I intend to show that there is a sense in which the image can capture the cadences of a voice, and by extension, the somatic traces of history, whether registered in the tonalities of speech or glimpsed through the off-narratives of peripheral vision.

## The Politics of Perception

In one of the early scenes in *Portrait*, the young Stephen Dedalus arrives home for Christmas from the wintry cold of Clongowes College, and experiences the warm glow of the dining room:

> A great fire, banked high and red, flamed in the grate and under the ivytwined branches of the chandelier the Christmas table was spread. They had come home a little late and still dinner was not ready; but it would be ready in a jiffy, his mother had said. They were waiting for the door to open and for the servants to come in, holding the big sides covered with their heavy metal covers. (pp. 25–6)

It is not too difficult to imagine a camera evoking this scene on film: indeed, it is the stuff of sentimental Christmas cards and Dickensian evocations of seasonal cheer. If we attend closer to the description, however, it may be precisely this archetypal image that is the problem, for it is largely of our own making, and not in the prose itself. Joyce, practicing his own "scrupulous meanness," is very sparing on the specific details of the scene, mentioning the only two features of the room that catch Stephen's eye: the fire, flaming in the grate, and the ivy on the chandelier. The distinguishing feature here, as we shall see, is one of color, a contrast between *red* (of the fire) and *green* (of the ivy) that recurs on several occasions when the narrative is refracted through Stephen's visual sensibility: "But Clongowes was far away; and the warm heavy smell of turkey and ham and celery rose from the plates and dishes and the great fire was banked high and red in the grate and the green ivy and holly made you feel so happy" (p. 28).

Why, then, is the chromatic range of Stephen's perception so disposed as to alight on the colors of red and green whenever they enter his field of vision? If we revert to the beginning of the book, to the account of his earliest sensory experiences, we are told of his aunt Dante that she "had two brushes in her press. The brush with the maroon velvet back was for Michael Davitt and the brush with the green velvet back was for Parnell" (pp. 3–4). That the colors associated with Michael Davitt (1846–1906) and Charles Stewart Parnell (1846–1891) – the towering figures of the Land League and the Irish Nationalist movement at the end of the nineteenth century – become the organizing codes of Stephen's universe is clear in the account given of his geography book when he moves to Clongowes as a small boy:

> There was a picture of the earth on the first page of his geography: a big ball in the middle of clouds. Fleming had a box of crayons, and one night during free study he had coloured the earth green and the clouds maroon. That was like the two brushes in Dante's press, the brush with the green velvet back for Parnell and the brush with the maroon velvet back for Michael Davitt. But he had not told Fleming to colour them those colours. Fleming had done it himself. (p. 12)[5]

For Stephen, it is as if Fleming gives an objective confirmation of his highly colored vision of the world. Politics, and the fraught narratives of the nation under the charismatic leadership of Parnell and Davitt, are not confined to current affairs or the public sphere, moreover, but frame his inner life, shaping the very contours of his consciousness: "It pained him that he did not know well what politics meant and that he did not know where the universe ended" (p. 14). In the opening lines of *Portrait*, the primordial basis of this elementary color scheme is traced back to "baby tuckoo's" (Stephen's) lisping response to the plaintive ballad sung to him by his father:

> *0, the wild rose blossoms*
> *On the little green place*
> He sang that song. That was his song.
> *0, the green wothe botheth*. (p. 3)

In the father's version, red and green are separated, but the infantile craving for order and unity is so pronounced that Stephen fuses them together, as if the world – whether physical or political – would fall apart were these colors sundered. This impulse surfaces again at Clongowes when Fr Arnall's division of his classroom into the white and red factions of the "War of the Roses" induces a reverie on whether roses might come in other colors: "Lavender and cream and pink roses were beautiful to think of. Perhaps a wild rose might be like those colours and he remembered the song about the wild rose blossoms on the little green place. But you could not have a green rose. But perhaps somewhere in the world you could" (p. 9).

The War of the Roses was a civil war, and such is the catastrophic impact of the fall of Parnell, and the defection of Davitt from the Parnellite camp, on the young Stephen, that it is as if a civil war has entered his sensorium. The traumatic news of the death of Parnell comes to him when he is lying in the sick bay of the college in a semi-delirium:

> He is dead. We saw him lying on the catalfaque.
> A wail of sorrow went up from the people.
> Parnell! Parnell! He is dead!
> They fell upon their knees, moaning in sorrow. And he saw Dante in a maroon velvet dress and with a green velvet mantle hanging from her shoulders walking proudly and silently past the people who knelt on the water's edge. (p. 25)

This sequence immediately precedes Stephen's return home from the college in which he sees the "great fire, banked high and red," and the "ivytwined branches of the chandelier" which made "you feel so happy" – as if the surge of desire for healing the wounds of the Parnell split is such that the red and green are magically united again. The happiness, however, is short-lived for a tumultuous row breaks out at the Christmas table as a frenzied Dante sides with the church against the "uncrowned king," leaving Mr Casey reduced to sobs of pain:

> Poor Parnell! He cried loudly. My dead king!
> He sobbed bitterly and loudly.
> Stephen, raising his terror stricken face, saw that his father's eyes were full of tears. (p. 39)

Given the importance of the leitmotif of color in the early sections of Joyce's *Portrait*, it is clear then – to revert to the earlier description of Stephen's arrival home from Clongowes – that the spare descriptive detail of the scene is not simply a matter of narrative economy but is central to understanding the framing perspectives of Stephen's vision. How, then, might a camera be expected to highlight these "signatures of the visible," giving them pride of place in the *mise-en-scène*? One could perhaps envisage – borrowing from the artificial luster of Christmas advertisements – a point-of-view shot from Stephen's position, using lighting, color, and compositional techniques to compose the shot so that the eye would be drawn immediately to the fire, and then, perhaps with a slight tilt of the camera, to the chandelier. But, even at that, more would be included in the domestic interiors than is necessary for Joyce's prose – a visual surplus that may inundate the underlying anxieties behind Stephen's stifled and highly selective vision. As Seymour Chatman writes of Jean Renoir's adaptation of Maupassant's story "A Country Excursion," discussing a scene in which the excursion cart passes over a bridge:

> The number of details in Maupassant's sentence is limited to three . . . Thus the reader learns only those three and can only expand the picture imaginatively. But in the film representation, the number of details is indeterminate, since what this version gives us is a simulacrum of a French carriage of a certain era, provenance, and so on. Thus the number of details that we could note is potentially large, even vast. In practice, however, we do not register many details.[6]

In Joseph Strick's adaptation of *Portrait* (1977), something similar happens as Stephen arrives home. The episode opens with a shot of young Stephen knocking at the front door and being welcomed by his parents, followed by a cut to the dining-room depicting his father (T. P. McKenna) and Mr Casey (Desmond Perry) imbibing whiskey in front of a mirror placed over a sideboard. The mirror (or "pierglass") is garlanded with holly and red berries (recalling perhaps the earlier evocation of the room in Stephen's imagination at Clongowes: "There were holly and ivy round the pierglass and holly and ivy, green and red, twined round the chandeliers" [p. 18]). There is no red fire banked high, but during the Christmas dinner, Stephen's mother (Rosaleen Linehan) is dressed in maroon and framed against closed curtains of a matching color. These items are undoubtedly surrounded by a surfeit of other details, but it is not clear that this by itself is sufficient for the film to lose sight of the Parnellite color-coding threaded through the narrative.

Chatman proceeds to make a distinction between the capacity of language to *assert* a statement and the more limited capacity to simply *name* a quality or present it. "The cart was tiny: it came over the bridge" corresponds to the former, an assertion. "The green car came onto the bridge" corresponds to the latter, in which greenness is not asserted but included as an incidental detail. In this latter case:

> The greenness of the cart is not asserted but slipped in without syntactic fuss. It is only named. Textually, it emerges by the way. Now, most films seem to be of the latter textual order: it requires special effort for films to assert a property or relation. The dominant mode is presentational, not assertive. A film doesn't say. "This is the state of affairs." It merely shows you that state of affairs.[7]

It is this latter use of "filmic" language that corresponds to Joyce's practice, for it is precisely as throwaway details, or incidental references, that the narrative voices and sensibilities structuring the novel reveal their barely discernible presence. Over and above the more familiar uses of montage and "parallel-editing" in *Ulysses* that are usually taken to exemplify his cinematic sensibility, Joyce's prose is at its most visual, paradoxically, when it is most acoustic, if by that we mean the kind of peripheral vision that best serves to register the intonations of a voice. Voice, in this case, has to do with the multiple framing perspectives through which the story is told, and is less concerned with mimetic realism than with the cultural and subjective intonations given to our everyday world. In Strick's version of *Portrait*, attention is paid to period detail to give a reasonably accurate rendering of a late nineteenth-century upper-bourgeois household, but Joyce's fiction is not interested in surroundings so much as the points of view of those who inhabit them. As Robert Stam argues: "Less important than a film's 'accuracy' is that it relay the voices and the perspectives – I emphasize the plural – of the community or communities in question . . . an appeal to voice over image, *or better in conjunction with image*, disputes the hegemony of the visible and the image-track by calling attention to sound, voice, dialogue and language."[8]

This emphasis on the voice may be most effective when the image is at its most optical, as when, for example, the tinctures of red and green are picked up in the *mise-en-scène* of Strick's *Portrait* on Stephen's arrival home. But the failure to relate this to a narrative voice, and to the submerged narratives of Parnell and Davitt that orchestrate Stephen's moral universe, is clear from Strick's depiction of the climactic Christmas dinner-table scene, in which Stephen's father wears a red/maroon cravat (aligning him with Davitt) while, equally at odds with Joyce's text, Dante (Maureen Potter) is dressed in green, which would ally her with her arch-enemy Parnell.

The muted Parnell subtext is given a literal textual expression – it is introduced through intertitles, silent movie fashion, at the beginning of the film, and discussed out loud by priests when Stephen is in the sick-bay – but it is not relayed visually as it is in Joyce's acoustic imagination. Politics remains in the public sphere, narrowly conceived, whereas the underlying impulse of Joyce's narrative suggests that it is part of the innermost structures of feeling of the characters in the Dedalus household. In Chatman's terms, the Parnell theme is *asserted* in the film – often crudely – but not "slipped in" through the modality of the visible; by contrast, Joyce, though narrating in language, makes words perform the work of images, "displaying" the details that matter most through the nuances of the voice.

So far from the image achieving its effects in film, moreover, at the expense of voice and intonation, it may be the camera's very ability to attend to throwaway details, and "the surfaces of things," that captures the resonances of inner speech – often, indeed, while departing from a literal or pedantic fidelity to the original work. This is of interest not just for literary narration but for cinema itself, for, as Stam suggests, the ultimate test of an adaptation of a literary work lies not in a scrupulous adherence to the "letter" of the original, but more to its "spirit" – or spirits, if by that we mean the colloquy of voices or perspectives that frame the story, giving it its emotional and tonal coloring. While recourse to voice-over, or related verbal devices, provides one obvious method of registering these narrative viewpoints, cinema is often most evocative when "the look" of a film, and its optical qualities, are used to convey these tonal effects. Through editing and camera movements, set design, pictorial composition, lighting, color-coding, costume, and other techniques, the visual architecture of a film may ventriloquize apparently absent voices, the image functioning as an echo-chamber of inner speech.[9]

Even with the subjective camera, as Chatman notes above, there is always more included in the shot than could possibly be noticed by the character, and it may be precisely this quality of cinema that appealed most to Joyce's distinctive modes of narration. Though uniquely attuned to the idioms of a character's voice, the narrative is seldom confined to their consciousness, the use of "free indirect discourse" or "third-person presentation" always suggesting, as with the cinematic image, something beyond the singular self. This "third-person" vantage point, as Weldon Thornton argues, belongs to the authorial voice, but:

rather than expressing either a traditional "omniscient author" or a distinct persona/ character, simulates the social or collective psyche that Stephen constantly, implicitly participates in, thus illustrating the inextricable interrelatedness of "individual" and "social," conscious and unconscious . . . Perhaps the most distinctive feature of Joyce's presentation of his characters' psyches both in *Portrait* and in *Ulysses* is the persistent merging of figural consciousness and exposition . . . of individual psyche and collective psyche.[10]

For a powerful exploration of this merging between the figural and the literal, the individual and collective psyche, we may turn to Joyce's story "The Dead," and to John Huston's attempt to visualize the colloquy between inner and outer worlds in his remarkable adaptation of the story, *The Dead* (1987).

Luke Gibbons

### "The Dead": The Voice from below the Stairs

Huston's *The Dead* differs markedly from Strick's *Portrait* in that its narrative voices are most pronounced when language and speech are absent, and the image speaks for itself: the image, as it were, being most optical when it is mediated by occult speech. Throughout Huston's film, the *mise-en-scène* is haunted by off-screen, inaudible voices that bear witness to one of the underlying themes of the story: the capacity of unrequited sorrow to assume a palpable, almost other-worldly force in the minds of the living. The facility with which the cinematic image evokes these voices is evident in its relaying of the presence of the overlooked, the cast-off objects or indeed people at the margins of the action. It is fitting therefore that it is the voice of the servant, Lily (Rachael Dowling), with all its hesitations and infelicities, that introduces – and, as it were, infiltrates – the action in Joyce's story. Huston's achievement was to find visual expression for this tremulous voice and, by linking it to other characters and events, gesture toward what may be called the cultural underworld of "The Dead," the fugitive and endangered undercurrents of Irish society caught in the force-field of a servant's story.[11]

Joyce's story "The Dead" is unusual in that a servant's voice is not only heard but, in its different idiomatic frequencies, assumes a narrative intensity that will not go away, despite the best attempts of other controlling voices to silence it. The servant's voice is that of Lily, the maid in the Misses Morkan's household, but her idiomatic English is not only heard in the first person but also breaks through the feigned detachment of the third-person narration which introduces the story: "Lily, the caretaker's daughter, was literally run off her feet."[12] According to Clive Hart, "This sloppy, market place use of 'literally' is Lily's language; or perhaps we should say that the language of the story is attracted into Lily's linguistic aura."[13] "Sloppy" this language may be, in the sense that it is Lily no doubt who empties the slops of the Morkan household each day, but it is far from being inaccurate or inappropriate, and Hart is correct to insist that the story thereafter resonates with the echoes of her voice. What we learn from Lily's idiomatic

Chapter 12

expressions is not just that she is extremely busy but also that the "literal" has lost contact with the ground in more ways than one, and merges with the figural in her consciousness. It is in this sense that the rest of the story is indeed attracted into her "linguistic aura," for it is the contested ground between literal and imaginative truth that will come to preoccupy the minds of those present at the Morkans' party as the events of the night unfold. Reality is not so much obscured as viewed, in Stephen's famous description in *Ulysses*, through the cracked looking glass of a servant,[14] reflecting a world in which memory finds no refuge in nostalgia and truth itself offers no consolation.

The second sentence of the story is again inflected by Lily's voice, concerned as it is with such commonplace details as unadorned spaces and malfunctioning doorbells: "Hardly had she brought one gentleman into the little pantry behind the office on the ground floor and helped him off with his overcoat, than the wheezy hall-door bell clanged again and she had to scamper along the bare hallway to let in another guest" (p. 173). We suspect that it is Lily who is wheezy and out of breath, thus foreshadowing the fate of bronchial Michael Furey at the end of the story. Since Lily's voice introduces the story, the problem facing a prospective filmmaker is how to attract the image into the "linguistic aura" of her speech; how, that is, to sift the *mise-en-scène* through the minds of characters who are not, at first sight, even the main focus of the story.

At one point in Huston's *The Dead*, a guest at the dinner, Mr Grace (Sean McClory), takes to the floor to recite one of the many party-pieces that punctuate the action of the story. The recitation in question, "Broken Vows," is, Mr Grace explains, a translation by Lady Gregory from the Gaelic original, "Donal Og," and it relates a tale of love and betrayal in which a young woman is seduced by a lover who promises her unimaginable riches and happiness, only to abandon her in her hour of need. As the penultimate verses of the poem express it:

> You promised me a thing that is not possible;
> That you would give me gloves of the skin of a fish;
> That you would give me shoes of the skin of a bird
> And a suit of the dearest silk in Ireland
>
> My mother said to me not to be talking to you,
> Today or tomorrow or on Sunday.
> It was a bad time for telling me that,
> It was shutting the door after the house was robbed.

The poem, as critics of Huston's film were not slow to point out, is, in fact, an interpolation into the story, and is thus, like the ghost of Michael Furey, something of an uninvited guest at the party. But its centrality in Tony Huston's screenplay, and its eerie premonition of what is to come, is made clear from the mention of the name "Gregory" in relation to the translator of the work. In the context of what is to unfold later in the night, this also alludes to the name of the ignoble seducer, Lord Gregory, who betrays "the Lass of Aughrim" in the haunting ballad sung at the end of the party. As the young peasant girl in the ballad stands in the rain and snow with her baby in her arms, she pleads at the door of the castle of her seducer, Lord Gregory, to be admitted, and for the father to acknowledge his paternity of her baby:

> The rain falls on my yellow locks,
> And the dew it wets my skin;
> My babe lies cold within my arms:
> Lord Gregory let me in.[15]

Nor are the reverberations of the name "Lord Gregory" confined to the ballad. In Irish popular memory, Lady Gregory's husband was the author of the notorious Gregory clause in the Poor Law Act of 1847 which was responsible for the eviction of thousands of destitute peasants during the Great Famine of 1845–8.[16] The lass of Aughrim, it would seem, was not the only victim to be thrown onto the roads by a callous Lord Gregory, and the ironic inclusion of his widow's translation of a lament from the Irish introduces an ominous political undertow to the personal narratives of many of those present at the Misses Morkan's party, not least those whose "people," as the central character Gabriel Conroy describes it, are from the west of Ireland. It is notable in Joyce's story that while others serve the meat at the Morkans' dinner, Lily's function is to serve the potatoes "wrapped in a white napkin," keeping three especially for Gabriel. In Huston's film, this is brought forward to the beginning when Lily complains of her difficulty in watching the potatoes and answering the hall-door as the guests arrive.[17] That Lily hails from the west of Ireland is hinted at by her three-syllabic idiomatic pronunciation of Gabriel Conroy's (Donal McCann) name – "Mr Con-er-roy" – when she proceeds to the pantry to help him take off his overcoat on his arrival at the party.[18]

In the short story, this sets in motion a chain of associations with the plight of the abandoned peasant girl in "The Lass of Aughrim," as Gabriel first recalls Lily as a child "nursing a rag doll" and then notices that she is no longer the child he used to know, but "a slim, growing girl." This dawning awareness of her sexuality allows his thoughts to run in a direction which he seems not aware of, but which Lily is not slow to pick up. He asks her jocularly, in a scene re-enacted in the film, "I suppose we'll be going to your wedding one of these fine days with your young man, eh?" (p. 175), only to be met with the rejoinder from the beleaguered girl ("said with great bitterness" in the story): "The men that is now is only all palaver and what they can get out of you." "Gabriel coloured," we are told in the story, "as if he made a mistake . . ." (p. 176). It would seem that Lily has been emotionally bruised, if not actually sexually exploited, in conformity with the vulnerability of maids, servants, or nurses in respectable bourgeois households. "There's that Lily," says her employer, Aunt Kate, "I'm sure I don't know what has come over her lately. She's not the girl she was at all" (p. 179).

As recent histories of the domestic underworld of bourgeois households have shown, one of the main casualties of the sexual propriety of the respectable classes upstairs were the servant classes downstairs, objects of both intense affection and anxiety for the repressed fantasies of their superiors. As Mona Hearne has observed of the condition of servants in Ireland during that period:

> The most prevalent problems concerning servants, apart possibly from petty theft, were those involving illicit sexual relations . . . The mothers of illegitimate children were frequently domestic servants . . . If the servant complained to her mistress she not only lost her job but was probably blamed for the indiscretion that had occurred. Unlike other workers, servants had no private life. They were often lonely, deprived of the companionship of members of the opposite sex and so were particularly vulnerable; employers and their friends frequently took advantage of this situation.[19]

The projecting of a displaced eroticism onto the servant was not unrelated to the fact that it was mainly the servant who had physical contact with children in households, including the intimacy of bathing and wet-nursing, with their attendant first flushes of bodily pleasure. Freud's earliest sexual awareness was induced by his nurse (who was later replaced by the figure of the mother when reformulated for the Oedipus complex), and it was this suspicion of servants as "teacher[s] in sexual matters" (as Freud described his own nurse) that conveniently allowed their superiors to blame them for the sexual transgressions which befell them.[20] In an Irish booklet, published as late as the 1940s, the anxious Jesuit author Robert Nash warned respectable Catholic mothers of the necessary precautions in choosing a maid (one wonders whether he had James Joyce's maid in mind):

> The importance of the choice can hardly be overstated. It is possible for the children you love to be ruined by a maid. From her and from her companions they have been known to hear for the first time filthy suggestive stories and foul expressions. Through her influence they have been led to the garbage heap and taught to gather scraps of knowledge from the gutter.[21]

There is little here about arousing suggestive thoughts in adults, or – more likely – of being the objects of the repressed sexual desires of the male members of the household.

For Joyce, the nursemaid was also one of the main portals of discovery in sexual matters, and his attempt to woo one of the many women he became infatuated with in Trieste was hardly helped by his confession that his first sexual arousal was induced by a nursemaid who asked him to avert his gaze when she urinated. Some years later, a young maid was dismissed from the Joyce household when she was discovered carousing in the bedroom with James. Lily in "The Dead," like her counterpart, the exploited "slavey" in "Two Gallants" in *Dubliners*, would also seem to be running this risk of dismissal on account of her "back answers" to her employers, a disposition clearly evident in her caustic riposte to Gabriel. His blushing response implicates him in the "palaver" of "the men that is nowadays" and, as if out of guilt, he hands Lily a coin which she warily accepts as a tip – or perhaps, as Margot Norris speculates, as hush money.[22]

Gabriel comes off no better in his next encounter with the feisty Miss Ivors, except that now reminders of the west of Ireland embrace a political as well as a personal agenda. It is difficult to know whether Gabriel's unease with Miss Ivors has to do with her flirtatious behavior or her political sentiments – or both. When she asks him to come to the west of Ireland to renew contact with his own culture, she lays "her warm hand eagerly on his arm." Gabriel balks at the suggestion (or the gesture), and when Miss Ivors reminds him that his wife, Gretta, is from the west of Ireland, he replies curtly: "Her people are." When Gretta herself exclaims that she would love to see Galway again, Gabriel dismisses her desire: "You can go if you like." In keeping with his anxious civility, Gabriel is attempting to sever Gretta's emotional ties with her cultural background, and her less than desirable (to his mother at least) class origins. Gabriel here is distancing himself from the rhetoric of the Irish Literary Revival (as represented by Miss Ivors) which looked to a mystique of the West as a replacement for the compromised modernity of the East, but – unlike Joyce – he fails to see that this may be a false opposition in the first place. An image of the West that places it outside modernity is no different from that version of civility and urbanity, espoused by Gabriel, that turns away from the past. Gabriel's mental journey westward is one in which modernity is released from its own amnesia, and the history locked away in the heart comes back to haunt the living. History is not simply content or superadded to the *mise-en-scène*: as in Stephen's homecoming in *Portrait*, it is part of the politics of perception, and the texture of both visual and aural experience.

## Visualizing the Voice

It is in this manner that Lily's voice – and her barely concealed plight – acts as a narrative thread bringing together many of the seeming loose ends in the story: Lady Gregory's translation of "Broken Vows," Lord Gregory and the experience of eviction, the ballad of "The Lass of Aughrim," and both Lily's and Gretta Conroy's association with the west of Ireland. But if the grain of this voice – and its tonal echoes in the lives of other characters in the story – is relayed through the idiomatic inflections of Joyce's prose, Huston's task in his film adaptation was to ventriloquize these through the visual medium of cinema.

In the "Cinema of Poetry," Pier Paolo Pasolini argues that, while cinema has no grammatical equivalents of linguistic idioms, the use of stylistic markers, having to do with framing and composition, camera movements, focus, editing, and so forth, allows it to give visual expression to "free indirect discourse" through the "look" of the camera. By means of such techniques, the camera simulates the "disoriented, disorganized, beset by details state of mind of the protagonist":

> The intense moments of expression in the film are, precisely, those "insistences" of the framing and montage-rhythms, whose structural realism . . . is charged . . . till it explodes in a sort of technical scandal. Such an insistence on details, particularly on certain details in the digressions, is a deviation in relation to the system of the film: *it is the temptation to make another film.*

It is as if another set of narratives or voices are impinging on the action, threatening to throw it off course by "the obsessive attachment to a detail or a gesture."[23]

As if taking his cue from Pasolini, R. B. Kershner, in his insightful discussion of Joyce's story, calls attention to a mysterious, narrative agency at the Misses Morkan's party, which seems to interrupt or cut across a character's train of thought, giving it an emphasis other than the one they intended. Hence in Gabriel Conroy's final grief-laden exchanges with Gretta in their hotel bedroom, as Kershner describes it:

> Another voice constantly mitigates the effect he intends, as when "a kinder note than he had intended went into his voice" or "he tried to keep up his tone of cold interrogation but his voice when he spoke was humbler and indifferent" or even when a "strange friendly pity for her entered his soul." [This] second inner voice, the one associated with [Michael] Furey and the ghosts, has begun to creep into his thought and his speech, causing him to pull his conversational punches.[24]

When Gabriel first comes in from the cold and stands in the hallway of the Morkan household, we are told that "as the buttons of his overcoat slipped with a squeaking noise through the snow-stiffened frieze, a cold fragrant air from out-of-doors escaped from crevices and folds" (p. 175). As the story develops, it is as if this air has ushered in the spectral form of Michael Furey, for as the singing of "The Lass of Aughrim" transfixes Gretta on the stairs, Gabriel reverts to his original position in the hallway: "He stood still in the gloom of the hall, trying to catch the air that the voice was singing and gazing up at his wife" (p. 207). The air, in both senses of the word, has at this point almost become visible: "The voice, made plaintive by distance and by the singer's hoarseness, faintly illumined the cadence of the air with words expressing grief . . ." (p. 207). The "gloom" in the hallway recalls the "gloomy moralizing" in his after-dinner speech "on the absent faces that we miss here tonight," but that it is also linked to Lily is evident from his response to "her bitter and sudden retort" in the pantry: "It had cast a gloom over him which he tried to dispel by arranging his cuffs and the bows of his tie . . . He had taken up a wrong tone" (p. 176).

The challenge presented to any adaptation of "The Dead" is how to capture "the right tone," and the "faintly illumined" cadences it sends through the Morkan household. The stylistic achievement of Huston's adaptation of the story derives from the manner in which these ghostly echoes – constantly oscillating between the inner and outer worlds of the characters – is conveyed by the choreography of the camera. When Miss Julia sings "Arrayed for the Bridal" in another of the party-pieces in the story, the camera appears to assume a life of its own as it leaves the room, exploring the keepsakes and mementos of Julia's past scattered throughout the house – porcelain angels, faded photographs, old war medals, a needlework sampler, a crucifix with beads. This could also be a journey into the deepest recesses of her mind, a transition between "inner" and "outer" states that recalls Eisenstein's scheme for a form of "inner monologue" that would emulate "the dissolution of the distinction between subject and object undertaken in the novels of Edward Dujardin and fulfilled in *Ulysses*":

racing visual images over complete silence. Then linked with polyphonic sounds. Then polyphonic images. Then both at once. Then interpolated into the outer course of action, then interpolating elements of the outer action into the inner monologue. As if presenting inside the characters the inner play, the conflicts of doubts, the explosions of passion, the voice of reason, rapidly or in slow-motion, marking the different rhythms of one and the other . . .[25]

As Aunt Julia sings, the intimations of mortality captured by the camera anticipate the fate of both the "Lass of Aughrim" and Michael Furey, but "Arrayed for the Bridal," with its theme of a bride jilted on her wedding day, also refers back to Mr Grace's recitation of "Broken Vows." Throughout Mr Grace's recitation, the camera cuts to the reactions of various members of the audience as they express a mixture of awe and incomprehension at the sentiments of the verse. When it comes to the final stanza, the editing homes in not only on the central players of the story but integrates the barely noticed figure of Lily into its field of vision:

You have taken the east from me,
You have taken the west from me,
You have taken what is before me
And what is behind me;

You have taken the moon,
You have taken the sun from me,
And my fear is great
You have taken God from me.

As Mr Grace invokes "the east," the camera cuts to a taciturn Gabriel, devotee of all that lies to the east (Britain, Belgium, Europe), who reacts with a suspicious glance toward Gretta. With the invocation of "the west," the focus shifts to Gretta (Angelica Huston), who appears to be lost in a world of her own, her eyelids closed as if to protect a slumbering world within. At the precise moment Mr Grace utters the words "and what is behind me," Lily suddenly emerges in the dark space of the stairs in the background of the shot, accompanied by the muffled sound of her footsteps and the faint rustle of her clothes. Immobilized in the half-light, Lily presages Gretta's epiphany later in the night when she stands in a reverie on the stairs, enraptured by the singing of "The Lass of Aughrim" – a connection picked up in the stage directions for the screenplay:

> *Gabriel. Slightly baffled by the look on his wife's face. There is movement behind him. He looks round. It is Lily.*

As Mr Grace reaches the last despairing lines of "Broken Vows," Lily steps out of the frame of the stairway and into the room, unwittingly intruding on the dramatic space of the performance.

It is the rendition of "Broken Vows" that first induces a trance-like reverie in Gretta, and as the sound of applause brings her to her senses, the camera cuts immediately to Lily, who informs Aunt Kate in a quivering voice that the goose will be ready in half-an-hour: "And, Mam, I've just put fresh towels in the toilet." In this sequence, the images seem to carry the weight of Lily's voice, bringing the matrix of associations bound up with the servant's story into the emotional aura of Gretta's inner world. As if to underscore this connection, Gretta is again shown passing into a trance during the meal when Aunt Kate pays nostalgic homage to the sweet tenor voice of a forgotten singer, Parkinson, only to be awoken once more by Lily's voice over her shoulder, announcing that the pudding is ready to be served. Parkinson is an English tenor, and this prefiguring of the tenor voice of Michael Furey associates the west of Ireland and Gretta, through the figure of the servant, once more with the "East" and modernity. As Huston frames this shot, the profiles of both Gretta and Lily are superimposed on one another, as if Lily were a flashback to Gretta in her youthful days. This visually evokes the underlying affinities drawn in the story between the heads of Lily and Gretta, both of which are described as being illuminated by gaslight (pp. 175, 209), which links them to Michael Furey who worked in the gasworks – the tropes of gaslight (mentioned several times also in connection with the lighting of the city) and gasworks once again underscoring the relationship between modernity and the West. Though some critics accept at face value Gretta's middle-class airs, her background may not be too different from that of the servant girl: her idiomatic English, and the fact that, as a "country cute" Galway girl, she insinuated herself (in his mother's opinion) into Gabriel's affections, explains his mother's "sullen opposition" to their marriage. The triangulation of desire between Gabriel, Gretta, and Lily culminates in the sequence leading up to Gretta's rapt response to the singing of "The Lass of Aughrim." Lily, once again, introduces the shot, and is in the process of helping Gabriel to put on his galoshes in the hallway when the strains of the song transfer his attention from the girl at his feet to his wife on the stairs.

In Joyce's writing, voices are all pervasive but they are far from being authoritative, let alone omniscient. The voices that matter are barely audible, and, in an important sense, are not entitled to speak, or, at least, are not used to being listened to. Lily, we are told, got on well with her three mistresses "but the only thing they would not stand was back answers." As Margot Norris suggests, "we are prompted here . . . to think of the text of 'The Dead' as a narration itself unwilling to allow a series of back answers that nevertheless disrupt it."[26] Hence Lily's mispronunciation of "Conroy," though mentioned, is not actually voiced in the text though it is in the film, and when she does break into speech directly, it has the effect of unsettling Gabriel and, indeed, the night's proceedings in the Morkan household. By the same token, the politically incorrect word that enables Gretta to link "galoshes" with the New Christy Minstrels – "gollywog" – is not actually mentioned, and not only does she forget the name of the ballad that in one sense has orchestrated her inner life, but only two and a half lines are given in the text, before an ellipsis fades into silence. It is striking that when Gabriel apprehends Gretta listening to the ballad on the stairs, his response is to translate sound into spectacle, and music into the still formality of an image:

> asked himself what is a woman standing on the stairs in the shadow, listening to distant music, a symbol of. If he were a painter he would paint her in that attitude. Her blue felt hat would show off the bronze of her hair against the darkness and the dark panels of her skirt would show off the light ones. *Distant Music* he would call the picture if he were a painter. (p. 207)

In Huston's *The Dead*, Gabriel's attention is drawn to the ballad as Lily is fitting on his galoshes, his gaze switching from the servant to his wife on the stairs, entranced for the third time on the night of the epiphany. As if reversing the silence of a still life, Huston's achievement is to create an acoustic image, infusing the film at key moments with the sound at the top of the stairs. In a remarkable shot in Chris Sievernich's documentary on the making of Huston's *The Dead*, "John Huston's Dubliners," we catch Lily in silhouette looking in at the night's proceedings through a lace-curtained window. As soon as Lily glides out of shot, the camera moves toward the window and occupies her position, as if framing the action from her point of view. Like the movements of a camera, the labor of the servant is all but invisible and, as if in sympathy with each other, the camera and the servant collude at several points in Huston's *The Dead* to bring out the "inner speech" of the image, the language through which, like Joyce at the cinema, we view the world.

---

### Notes

1  Lucie Noel, *James Joyce and Paul L. Leon: The Story of a Friendship* (New York: Gotham Books, 1950), p. 19, cited in Thomas Burkdall, *Joycean Frames: Film and the Fiction of James Joyce* (New York: Routledge, 2001), p. 6.

2  James Joyce, *A Portrait of the Artist as a Young Man* (London: Penguin, 1992), pp. 107–8. All further references in parentheses in the text are to this edition.

3  For wide-ranging discussions of the drive toward "ocularcentrism" in Western culture, and its critics, see Martin Jay, *Downcast Eyes: The Denigration of Vision in Twentieth-century*

French Thought (Berkeley, CA: University of California Press, 1994), and David Michael Levin, Modernity and the Hegemony of Vision (Berkeley, CA: University of California Press, 1993).

4   See Maurice Merleau-Ponty, The Phenomenology of Perception, trans. Colin Smith (London: Routledge and Kegan Paul, 1962).

5   For an illuminating discussion of these aspects of Portrait, see David Lodge, The Modes of Modern Writing: Metaphor, Metonomy and the Typology of Modern Literature (London: Arnold, 1977), pp. 130ff.

6   Seymour Chatman, "What Novels Can Do That Films Can't (and Vice Versa)," in W. J. T. Mitchell (ed.), On Narrative (Chicago: University of Chicago Press, 1981), p. 121.

7   Ibid., p. 124.

8   Robert Stam, "Bakhtin, Polyphony and Ethnic/Racial Representation," in Lester D. Friedman (ed.), Unspeakable Images: Ethnicity and the American Cinema (Urbana, IL: University of Illinois Press, 1991), p. 256.

9   For the relationship between the cinematic image and inner speech, see Paul Willemen, "Cinematic Discourse: The Problem of Inner Speech," in Look and Frictions (London: British Film Institute, 1994).

10  Weldon Thornton, The Antimodernism of Joyce's Portrait of the Artist as a Young Man (Syracuse: Syracuse University Press, 1994), p. 109.

11  For the cultural underworld of Joyce's story and Huston's film, see the more extensive discussion in my "'The Cracked Looking Glass of Cinema': James Joyce, John Huston and the Memory of the 'The Dead'," in Dudley Andrew and Luke Gibbons (eds), "The Theatre of Irish Cinema," special issue of The Yale Journal of Criticism 15: 1 (Spring, 2002), on which the present discussion is based. See also the related articles in the same issue by Kevin Whelan, "The Memories of the Dead," and Marjorie Howes, "Tradition, Gender and Migration in 'The Dead', or: How Many People has Gretta Conroy Killed?," and the insightful monograph by Kevin Barry, The Dead (Cork: Cork University Press, 2000).

12  James Joyce, "The Dead," in Dubliners [1914] (Harmondsworth: Penguin, 1976), p. 173. All further references in parentheses in the text are to this edition.

13  Clive Hart, Joyce, Huston, and the Making of The Dead (London: Colin Smythe, 1988), p. 14. Hart is turning Joyce's earlier jibe at the "sloppy English" of D. H. Lawrence against himself. The extensive debate on the implications of Lily's idiomatic English for Joyce's narrative technique was sparked off by Hugh Kenner's influential analysis in Joyce's Voice's (London: Faber and Faber, 1978), pp. 15ff.

14  James Joyce, Ulysses (New York: Vintage, 1961), p. 6.

15  For a meticulous historical analysis of "The Lass of Aughrim" and its many variants, see Hugh Shields, "A History of the 'Lass of Aughrim'," in Gerard Gillen and Harry White (eds), Irish Musical Studies, vol. 1 (Dublin: Irish Academic Press, 1990), pp. 58–73.

16  For interpretations of the Gregory Clause, see Christine Kinealy, This Great Calamity: The Irish Famine 1845–52 (Dublin: Gill and Macmillan, 1994), pp. 216–27.

17  Leopold Bloom, of course, carries a potato around in his pocket in Ulysses, which acts as a memento mori of the Famine throughout the text.

18  See Donal Torchiana, Backgrounds for Joyce's Dubliners (Boston: Allen and Unwin, 1986), p. 227. Torchiana is drawing on John Kelleher's suggestion that Lily's three syllabic pronounciation links the story to the Old Irish legend of King Conaire.

19  Mona Hearne, *Below Stairs: Domestic Service Remembered in Dublin and Beyond, 1880–1922* (Dublin: Lilliput, 1993), pp. 96ff.

20  Sigmund Freud, "Extracts from the Fliess Papers" (1897), cited in Peter Stallybrass and Allon White, *The Politics and Poetics of Transgression* (London: Methuen, 1986), p. 157.

21  Robert Nash, SJ, *Marriage Before and After* (Dublin: Browne and Nolan, 1947), p. 163.

22  Margot Norris, "Not the Girl She Was at All: Woman in 'The Dead'," in Daniel R. Schwarz (eds), *James Joyce: The Dead* (Boston: Bedford Books/St Martin's Press, 1994), p. 200.

23  Pier Paolo Pasolini, "The Cinema of Poetry," in Bill Nichols (ed.), *Movies and Methods*, vol. 1 (Berkeley, CA: University of California Press, 1976), p. 554. Pasolini tends to link the stylistic voice to that of the director or *auteur* but allows for cases (e.g. Antonioni's *Red Desert* [1965]) where a character's voice takes precedence, or, alternatively (e.g. Bertolucci's *Before the Revolution* [1964]), where a "contamination" takes place "between the vision [a character] has of the world, and that of the author, which are inevitably analogous, but difficult to perceive, being closely intermixed, having the same style" (pp. 553–4.)

24  R. B. Kershner, *Joyce, Bakhtin, and Popular Culture: Chronicles of Disorder* (Chapel Hill, NC: University of North Carolina Press, 1989), p. 142.

25  Sergei Eisenstein, "A Course in Treatment," in *Film Form: Essays in Film Theory*, trans. Jay Leyda (San Diego: Harcourt, Brace and Co., 1977), p. 105. It is important to remember that Eisenstein here is relating his advanced "modernist" methods to more conventional naturalistic novels such as Dreiser's *An American Tragedy* – a strategy that can also be extended, as I argue in this chapter, to some of Joyce's earlier naturalist fiction.

26  Norris, "Not the Girl She Was at All," p. 193.

Luke Gibbons

Chapter 12

# Chapter 13

# Adapting Cinema to History
## A Revolution in the Making

## Dudley Andrew

——————————————— I ———————————————

Late in 1937, buoyed by the unprecedented international acclaim that *La Grande Illusion*
was just then garnering, Jean Renoir was planning *La Bête humaine*, while putting *La
Marseillaise* in the can. The press brimmed with enthusiasm, for in the first case he promised
to deliver a classic but torrid novel written by Zola, whom he could claim as practically
a family acquaintance; and, in the second, he had put himself more humbly at the service
of a patriotic venture which would at once celebrate the 150th anniversary of the storming of the Bastille and fan enthusiasm for the beleaguered government of a beleaguered
nation. These were national, nearly civic projects, and anticipation bubbled over, as the
many stories and interviews in the papers attest.

I link this pair of films to stand between the twin giants that flanked them in 1937
and 1939 (*La Grande Illusion* and *La Règle du jeu*) since both of those came from original scripts. When asked by reporters to characterize and promote his work, Renoir's
rhetorical task had to differ from one pair to the next. Rather than give his prospective
audience a tantalizing preview of a plot, characters, and themes born of his imagination,
with *La Bête humaine* and *La Marseillaise* he could bank on their keen knowledge; and
so he took care to justify his particular access to these public treasures and explain how
he would exploit them. *La Bête humaine* attracted him for personal reasons. (He claims
he made it to have done with the naturalism that had caught him in its grip even before
*Nana* in 1925; and who knows the relation of this erotic nightmare to his complicated
relations with women at the time?) *La Marseillaise*, on the other hand, advertises itself
as the very model of collective filmmaking. Yet both films depend on treasured sources,

cinema vivifying something that stands before and above it. This brace of films, then, forces the question this chapter means to address: does the historical film adapt its material in the same way as a film from a noted literary source does?

At stake in this question lies the reputation of standard cinema, for a high percentage of films are based on literary or historical sources. Often denigrated as a facile, mechanical, and inevitably compromised practice, the transformation of well-known sources into movies deserves the sustained attention recently given in literary scholarship to the *longue durée* of genres over the singular events of masterpieces; that is, to the ordinary life of literature rather than to those rare revolutionary moments where its direction changes utterly.[1] "The Revolution and the Ordinary" is, in fact, the theme of *La Marseillaise* and the title of an essay I published on the film some years ago,[2] an essay which I adapt now to address the very question of adaptation. The conclusion of that essay still holds: Renoir produced an exceptional film by driving the medium's penchant for the everyday to a limit that is in no way ordinary. Following André Bazin, I mean to shed the light of an extraordinary example, Renoir's film, on a common cinematic practice, "mere adaptation." Bazin, of course, would never denigrate "adaptation," given the defining role it plays in biological and social organisms of every sort. Creatures, people, and entire cultures adapt to circumstances, changing themselves so as to persist *as* themselves. Cinema recapitulates this process; certain powerful films figure it indelibly.

## II

Let us begin with the ordinary. Taken as a particular instance of cultural adaptation, the updating of literature in cinematic form refreshes and broadens the reach of a source text that some producer or institution deems both pertinent and ripe for exploitation. *Exploitation* is an apt term, since a certain amount of built-in insurance and advertising makes investing in adaptations so attractive that this practice amounts to a very high percentage of all films made. Insurance derives from the success of the pre-tested narrative, while the title and author of the original provide automatic advertising to the degree that either has been controversial or beloved. Mixing Pierre Bourdieu's vocabulary with that of the film industry, we might say that "cultural capital" accrues to a given "property" through the discourses of criticism and education that extend its reputation and identify its relevance to the current moment. *Current* indeed. Adaptations traffic in *currency*, in the two senses of that term. And comparisons of films to their dramatic or novelistic sources – the most common species of adaptation study – grasp this implicitly, as they manipulate the market with insider information, currency exchange, and trading in futures.

As for the commodities themselves, the celluloid of an adaptation resembles that of other films: meaning rises from the images and sounds inscribed on its surface. However, the value of an adaptation's meaning (its *significance*, to use E. D. Hirsch's handy, though questionable, distinction)[3] depends on an additional dimension, the dimension of depth provided by the substrate text that supports what is on the celluloid. A palimpsest, we might say, but a peculiar one, in that the surface layer engages, rather than replaces, a previous inscription. When the layers appear nearly congruent – the film filling in with vibrant colors the fading skeletal lines of the original – the effect and the value of the adaptation are greatly multiplied, as Bazin would claim of brilliant adaptations.

Architecture offers a more suggestive analogy. Many Romanesque churches, themselves built on previously consecrated sites, found themselves incorporated into Gothic structures in the thirteenth century, some of which in turn underwent Mannerist, High Renaissance, and Baroque updatings. Each century of Christians wanted to make use of, yet modernize, their particular places of worship. This utterly common architectural practice became truly notable when the original structure bore special prestige, as when the site was an episcopal center (a cathedral or a church whose reliquaries drew pilgrims). We might say that the everyday activity of renovating churches led ineluctably to those exceptional examples that tourists take such pleasure in exploring from crypt to belfry: Saint Geminiani in Modena, for instance. Similarly, while fully 50 percent of Hollywood's output in the early 1930s derived from literary sources, attention was drawn (then as now) to such renowned cases as *A Farewell to Arms* and *Les Misérables*.

In sum, be they churches or stories, adaptations express the liveliness – indeed, the life principle – of cultural production. Persistent issues that arise with each notable adaptation (such as fidelity of execution, respect for the original, creative elaboration, or historical relevance) depend on and specify the way in which a culture inhabits the physical and mental spaces adapted by and for it. Adaptations may have been diverted into the sloughs of both filmmaking and scholarship, particularly when compared to the cascade of radical and avant-garde work, so exhilarating to experience; nevertheless, these quiet waters seep into the vaster fields of cinema and culture, irrigating them year after year, decade after decade. The critic cannot help but function as an historian of everyday life when tracking continuities in values or gradual shifts in tastes that even the most mediocre adaptation makes evident.

As the prominent retracing of vital expressions of the past, the practice of adaptation inevitably opens onto historiography. The link that Paul Ricoeur forged between the writing of history and of fiction[4] becomes far more evident in the case of adaptation where the debt owed to the traces of the past by the historian is analogous to the onus felt by the filmmaker to respect some text from the cultural storehouse. And so why not treat historical films as adaptations, particularly now that so many historians, following on Hayden White's *Metahistory*,[5] consider their work to be largely that of re-creation, re-presentation, and textual elaboration? As was argued for adaptation, the key cases to consider would be those films daring to take on prominent historical topics. Low-profile period films, like the innumerable movies drawn from fiction, may be crucial to the overall economy of cinema, but they do not initiate a practice of comparison. However, the viewer (and certainly the critic) of films based on subjects as well known as, say, Abraham Lincoln, Joan of Arc, the American Civil War, or – in this case – the French Revolution, will almost certainly measure the film at hand in relation to other interpretations of these familiar events or personages. The French Revolution has been so often examined by historians that Jean Godechot catalogued the differing attitudes and methods it had inspired in his aptly titled meta-history, *Un jury pour la Révolution*.[6] Godechot might well have included in his catalogue the dozens of films using the Revolution as dramatic background or at least those key instances when films have claimed to forge epic history. To test the value of treating historical films as adaptations, this chapter will be concerned only with the latter.

Let André Bazin fund this inquiry. In his celebrated essay on Robert Bresson's *Le Journal d'un curé de campagne*, Bazin arrives at an image of the relation of film to literary source that may hold for the historical film as well. "It is hardly enough to say of [Bresson's film], once removed, that it is in essence faithful to the original because, to begin with, it *is* the novel . . . the resulting work is not certainly better but 'more' than the book," for the film reminds us of "all that the novel has to offer plus, in addition, its refraction in the cinema."[7] Might not these words apply full force to an historical film like *La Marseillaise* which delivers scenes quarried from the period of the Revolution while it builds a separate creation, the national anthem of its title? An earlier passage from Bazin encourages this view by addressing the question of script design. Bresson treats the Bernanos novel as

> a cold, hard fact, a reality to be accepted as it stands. One must not attempt to adapt it to the situation in hand, or manipulate it to fit some passing need for an explanation; on the contrary it is something to be taken absolutely as it stands. Bresson never condenses the text, he cuts it. Thus what is left over is a part of the original. Like marble from a quarry, the words of the film continue to be part of the novel.[8]

Renoir, too, never condenses what he shows us of 1792, and he cuts out so many characters and events that *La Marseillaise* scarcely traces the political drama that is, in any case, familiar to all French citizens. (For this he would be excoriated.) Instead, he shoots the past like a newsreel cameraman, locating peripheral characters and events, then sliding past them to investigate their surroundings which may not be directly relevant to Grand Political History but which vividly belong to this world swept by history. Renoir puts us inside revolutionary times, making us sense ourselves still part of its moment. He lends us its momentum. Bresson's achievement, Bazin believes, is analogous: his film does not transform Bernanos's novel, since in the first place, "it *is* the novel," the novel as seen from a certain time, place, and point of view, "a secondary work with the novel as foundation. In no sense is the film 'comparable' to the novel or 'worthy' of it. It is a new aesthetic creation, the novel so to speak multiplied by the cinema."[9] Analogously, has not Renoir given us the French Revolution multiplied by the Popular Front and by his (and the medium's) democratic aesthetic? But I get ahead of myself. How do we register and calculate this effect of multiplication? Only by looking simultaneously at style and at history within the problematic of adaptation, a problematic best laid out in its two essential dimensions: design and texture.

Every adaptation invites investigation first into its congruence with the shape of its source (the design or structure of characters and plot) and next into the appropriateness of its "feel" (the texture of details, point of view, tone). An earlier era might have termed these inquiries into the "matter and the spirit" of adaptation, a quaint formulation that still aptly applies to those rare cases, like the French Revolution and the life of Christ, that continue to exert undiminished moral pressure on individuals and on culture as a whole.

With the tenacity, the vivacity of their historical referents in mind, let us compare Renoir's task to that of Pier Paolo Pasolini as he prepared his *Vangelo secondo Matteo* in 1963. Pasolini immediately restricted himself to one of the four authorized biographies of Christ, the one credited to Matthew, a text of around 20,000 words. This helped him pare his film to its most important elements and to adopt the humility of his source (allegedly the tax collector Matthew) and of his subject (Jesus Christ). Pasolini's film caused a stir in part because it flew in the face of a tradition of films that vied with each other in glorifying Christ's exploits, embellishing, sensationalizing, and sentimentalizing every incident, speech, character, and prop without restraint. As we will see, Pasolini's *cinema povere* aligns itself with Renoir's populist vision of the Revolution, and in doing so runs into an inevitable conundrum: how to express the formulation of a message (Christian in one case, revolutionary in the other) which demands that every human being continue in his or her own humble sphere the universal transformation begun in a moment so cataclysmic it brought about a completely new calendar. Both of these events changed the social landscape in a virtually cosmic way, yet both address themselves to "everyman" in everyday circumstances.

For his part, Pasolini took care to present the characters and incidents Matthew recounts with simplicity; that is, in their appropriate scale and generally in the order found in his sacred source. But the point of view and tone of this presentation — the texture of the film — is dense and complex. Pasolini means to display not just the bare story, but the incalculable impact it has had in the nineteen intervening centuries by rendering it through references to a variety of famous depictions. We see Matthew's Christ as the Renaissance, the Baroque, and the classical painters saw him, and we hear the feeling wrung from Christ's passion in Bach, Mozart, Prokofiev, and in gospel music.

Despite its inherent fascination, we must leave the Pasolini case, having used it just to set off by contrast Renoir's. There exists no authorized gospel of the French Revolution. Nor has anything comparable to an immutable Church been able to adjudicate genuine from apocryphal anecdotes; for, unlike the papacy, France has had a succession of governments, each taking a different official position in relation to the nation's founding moment and each fostering variant depictions of it. But there quickly developed a litany most school children could recite of signal moments in the tumultuous final decade of the eighteenth century.

Renoir must have felt less free than usual in planning this film, for *La Marseillaise* developed as a genuine Popular Front undertaking; that is, as an experiment in collective representation. Dutifully he began by considering every angle, imagining as complete a cinematographic treatment of the Revolution as possible. The initial outline he submitted to the Writers' Syndicate in April 1937 consists of thirty-two sequences in chronological order, opening in 1787 and concluding with the Battle of Valmy in September 1792.[10] Following an opening sequence involving a destitute peasant family being ground under by the local lord, all subsequent scenes pit key political players against one another. It is not until the second half of this preliminary script outline that another commoner is encountered, an artisan; and he serves only to move the movie forward to what is explicitly labeled "*le scène principal du film*," an unusually lengthy dialogue between the architects of the revolutionary government, Robespierre and Brissot, to be played by Louis Jouvet and Pierre Renoir respectively. Renoir estimated that, if actually filmed and edited, this would have constituted over twenty hours of screen time.[11] Unfeasible, this design was also unimaginative: a set of illustrated flashcards of the events of the Revolution as commonly laid out. More than this was needed by the flagging Popular Front, and so Renoir and his collaborators began to narrow the focus to pertinent themes, effectively adapting that portion of the immense "text" of the Revolution that suited the situation at hand.

Two months later, a second submission to the Syndicate lists a hundred and thirteen scenes grouped into six large sections. While the lives of common people now receive far more attention, this outline retains the essentially pedagogic ethos of the first. For instance, a prologue, disguised as a newsreel documentary, lays out the chief causes of popular unrest in the eighteenth century. The formation of the Third Estate dutifully follows, though on the heels of a telling incident in which a peasant is caught and tried for poaching a nobleman's pigeon. (As in the final filmed version, the peasant manages to escape and meet up with a progressive priest.) Next comes the storming of the Bastille. This version concludes with the thwarting of the king's escape at Varennes, an action that shows the people's ratification, in word and deed, of nation over monarch. Despite this rousing populist finale, most scenes in this script pit famous orators against conniving aristocrats or against one another in a conventional manner. This would have been a digest of the Revolution, like those educational versions of novels by Dickens.

Truly radical by comparison, the final version – the one actually filmed, starting in September 1937 – swept virtually every illustrious politician off-screen. As for the aristocrats, Renoir treats them with bemused detachment, observing the peculiarities of their reactions to their ill fortune rather than tracking their nefarious counter-insurgency measures. This change in Renoir's orientation from politics to everyday life can be glimpsed already in two lengthy sequences of the second script outline (the version of June 28). One takes place in a Parisian beauty salon and the other in a clothing store in Germany. In both cases, details of the political crisis emerge as merchants and clients discuss and bemoan fads, prices, and moral behavior. While the intent of these scenes remains homilitic, they give Renoir room to exploit his archive of information about daily life. In the final version, such free-standing scenes proliferate within the loose structure he calls "A Chronicle of some events leading to the fall of the Monarchy."

A "chronicle" that becomes an "anthem": this is the flexible design Renoir settled upon and within which he then had great freedom to select and order characters, incidents, and dialogue. We can see this particularly if we compare *La Marseillaise* to the two competing versions of the revolutionary period representing, respectively, the epic and the dramatic traditions: *Napoleon Bonaparte* (Gance, 1935) and *Danton* (Roubaud, 1932). Both versions are constrained to repeat a well-known sequence of actions, encounters, and speeches, striving to enliven them with a panoply of media flourishes. For a sonorized re-cut of his inimitable silent life of the emperor, Abel Gance synchronized classical music to add still another layer of homage to the heroic trajectory he never wavers from. This is the sort of national history Renoir's critics pined for when they expressed their disappointment at the clumsiness of *La Marseillaise*. History should soar as does Napoleon's eagle in Gance's films, whereas Renoir's history seems pedestrian, content to saunter alongside the common folk.

The other competitor, *Danton*, is a different story altogether, or rather several stories. Renoir and his countrymen were exposed to a 1932 French remake of a German *Danton* shot in 1930. This, in turn, may have been based on the play *The Danton Case*, published in 1928 by Stanislawa Przybyszewska, which was explicitly written in dialogue with Georg Büchner's famous *Danton's Death* of 1835.[12] Whether or not Renoir knew Przybyszewska's play, it is telling to set these works beside one another. *The Danton Case* unrolls as a taut duel between Danton (sensualist, libertarian, a figure adored by the people) and Robespierre (intellectual, recluse, a model for the elite). The few ancillary characters of the play's early scenes disappear in its central confrontation of these two men – representing two interpretations of history – over a superb dinner. Brilliantly upholding their respective positions, both of which seem not just plausible but necessary, Danton eats and drinks beyond capacity, while Robespierre scarcely lets the wine touch his lips. Przybyszewska designed her play to fatally interlock two opposing aspects governing human experience; in their mutual self-destruction she senses a tragic impasse in government altogether. An emperor will be needed to clear the corpses off the stage.

The first representation of the French Revolution to incorporate clear references to the Soviet Revolution, *The Danton Case* prudently went underground after its 1933 production in Warsaw, the year of Przybyszewska's death at 31 years of age. After waiting out the Stalin era, the play re-emerged in the same year as did *La Marseillaise*, 1967, then was discovered by André Wajda who staged it to great acclaim in 1975 and again in Gdansk in 1980. His famous film, starring Gerard Depardieu and Wojciech Pszoniak, made under martial law in 1983, tailored the drama to the suppression of the workers' rebellion, tilting the balance in favor of Danton, who loses his head but wins all our sympathy. Adapting Przybyszewska's adaptation, Wajda delivers the kind of French Revolution Renoir scorned as hopelessly clichéd, a Revolution full of edifying speeches by characters (and actors) bigger than life, caught in a classic dramatic net.

Przybyszewska, it is true, had no patience with the masses. A recluse and an anorexic, not so different perhaps from her beloved Robespierre, she believed that the Revolution came from the minds and wills of heroic individuals, only later penetrating society. Minds and wills clarify themselves best in the theatrical crucible she chose, neoclassical tragedy. Renoir, more like Danton in his love of life and his apparent willingness to negotiate and compromise, trusted the people, offering them in the baggy design of his chronicle and the amiable tone of his anthem, an "everyman's revolution" that they might identify with and pursue in their own day.

---

IV

---

*La Marseillaise* aimed to rally decisive support for the flagging Popular Front, forging history even while representing it. Yet decisiveness characterizes historiography in the grand, virile mode (sagas of actions and virtue), precisely what Renoir always avoided. Unlike the actual participants in the Revolution, Renoir hesitates to condemn and is seldom judgmental. His harmony with the Popular Front can be felt in their shared tone of reconciliation. Even before he himself, as Octave in *The Rules of the Game*, uttered the memorable phrase "Everyone has his reasons," he had promoted understanding among rich and poor, Jew and Catholic, even Frenchman and German in *The Lower Depths* (1936) and *Grand Illusion*. The play of interests and values under a guiding rule, a "unity of conception" characterizes Renoir's method and style. *La Marseillaise* carries the tone of the Jacobin meetings it represents where many have their say, where they all react enthusiastically in their own manner, and where a song uniting them seems bound to emerge, sung in various registers but sung together. Decisiveness without dictation could be seen in July 1789, August 1792, and on the fields of Valmy, all moments swelled by an upsurge of national feeling, that came about not despite differing views, but because of debates in the Jacobin clubs, heated exchanges on hastily printed broadsides, and respectful altercations in public squares. Could this unity in diversity be recovered in 1938 to save the Popular Front? Arguments there will be, but the differing voices holding forth in different registers must in the end intone a national anthem; and in moments of genuine crisis, the anthem (or the unity and nation it represents) can carry a people forward into the history they make.

It was at a highly publicized meeting in March 1937, blessed by the presence of the Education Minister of the Popular Front government, that Renoir announced he would coordinate *La Marseillaise*, making use of volunteers drawn from the top writing and directorial talents of the industry. The likes of Jean Gabin, Eric Von Stroheim, and even Maurice Chevalier had signed on. The bravura of the declaration, however, masked deep anxieties about the precise nature of the film. Those anxieties soon precipitated the defection (or release) of two famous co-writers, Henri Jeanson and Marcel Achard. Although personal squabbles, including arguments over money, seem behind the breakup, the fact is that neither writer could have furnished Renoir with what he needed in his determination to jettison the clichés of history and to involve spectators in a new relation to their past and present.

Anxiously working without these studio writers, Renoir and his close assistants furiously drafted and redrafted script ideas. Imagine the near panic among the producers of this three million franc experiment when shooting commenced in August with a third script that retained from the earlier ones only the prologue. Yet Renoir thrived in the indeterminacy of this atmosphere; in this case he felt stabilized by his explicit point of view, which he characterized as Popular Frontist, and by the solidity and value of the archive on which he drew. Even if specific anecdotes, characters, and dialogue fell to the wayside, even if every scene were dispensable, Renoir believed that the film would succeed so long as a populist attitude ran like a current through a suite of events pulled from that archive. His humility before the overwhelming "text" of history is like that of Mary Ellen Bute in *Passages from Finnegan's Wake* (1967). Both films derive from sources so immense they can at best be sampled. Bute's term "Passages," like Renoir's "A Chronicle of some events," abjures totality from the outset. All scenes bear the same weight.

And, indeed, no scene was sacrosanct for Renoir save the prologue which survived each rewrite and was the first to be shot. It stands in every respect as an epigraph for the entire project, particularly in the line on which it fades out: during the changing of the king's guard in the palace, the Duke de La Rochefoucauld arrives and politely but urgently pushes his way into the king's private chambers, interrupting his breakfast in bed. The king rambles on about his recent hunt, his hunger, and about the food on his plate, particularly the fowl, but he listens at last to the news of the taking of the Bastille and ingenuously asks: "*Alors, c'est une révolte?*" "*Non,*" replies La Rochefoucauld, "*C'est une révolution.*"

What can this mean for Renoir, and for us? While dangerous and unwanted, *revolts* were to be expected by a sovereign who ruled millions of subjects through a complex network of subordinates and protocols. Revolts were like fevers, indicating imbalances and unhealthy practices that needed correction once the fever was reduced. But La Rochefoucauld portends far more in uttering the word *revolution*.[13] He foresees the entire system rolling over, including the meaning of health and balance, of sovereignty and subjects. Yet here lies the paradox that drives Renoir's film. Revolts may be willed by heroes and martyrs who make history, but "The Revolution" is a name for history itself, history passing through the innumerable agents who accept the moral pressure it exerts.

Like Christ, indeed in imitation of him, the French Revolution claimed to inaugurate a new epoch, and signaled this by instituting a completely new calendar, as though sidereal time had been altered at an historic juncture. And yet, speaking astronomically, a revolution is not a juncture at all – and thus not a revolt – but a cycle. To spin around, to come around, to orbit, time and again. How is it possible to break from accustomed patterns that return annually, and then are repeated generation after generation? What power can remain in a French Revolution that has been repeatedly represented, updated, adapted, and effectively institutionalized. Renoir answered this question with a film he continued to believe in but that most viewers have found unconvincing.

Adapting Cinema to History

Chapter 13

Its many harsh critics in 1938 and in our own day dismiss *La Marseillaise* for its flaccid politics. To them, Renoir's decentralized aesthetic, ready to adjust to circumstances and to the impulses of the moment, produced a quaint film that disarmed the dynamite within the Revolution of 1792 and compromised it as a model for the Popular Front. Renoir was said to have betrayed the hopes that had made him the key leftist filmmaker of the day.

> There is little disagreement over the verdict: *La Marseillaise* was a failure; the critics didn't like it, spectators did not support it, and historical judgment has not redeemed it . . . Critics across the spectrum, with the Communist critics such as Sadoul and Aragon notable exceptions, found the film dull, boring, mediocre, fatiguing . . . To a large degree, I believe this objection was directly proportional to the inflated hopes with which the project had been inaugurated . . . Rather than extending the mobilization of the masses which was responsible for the victory of the Popular Front, as *La Vie est a nous* certainly did, *La Marseillaise* looked backward, thematically and formally, basking in the glow of victory.[14]

To use La Rochefoucauld's distinction, *La Marseillaise* can be called a film of the *revolution*, perhaps even a *post-revolutionary* film made on the downslide of the Popular Front, while *La Vie est a nous*, shot frantically in 1935, was a film in *revolt* against the ruling state of affairs. Clumsy and brash, it lashed out against French society and simultaneously against the constraints of standard cinematic form. It opens with a school teacher reciting at length to his pupils (and to us) the reasons for France's social inequities. This literally dictatorial set-up is repeated in the finale when the leaders of the PCF preach from a podium behind which are draped the sacred photographs of Marx and Lenin. Audacious, to be sure, and agitational, *La Vie est a nous* stands closer to the anti-aesthetic of *revolt* that fueled successive avant-garde movements from Dada to Artaud's *Theater of Cruelty*. Only the political emergency born of the February 1934 riots brought Renoir into working relations with this avant-garde fringe and led to his coordinating *La Vie est a nous* as a Communist Party propaganda film for the May 1936 elections. Audacious and insolent, the film was refused an exhibition license by the very socialist government it helped elect. Like Buñuel's *L'Age d'or* (1930) and Vigo's *Zero de conduite* (1933), such censorship only confirmed its purity and fame. In Renoir's case, this fame came at the expense of *La Marseillaise*, a mellow film by contrast, and one that I must argue stands much closer to what is "radical" about his approach. That approach is tied precisely to "adaptation" rather than experimentation and to revolution, not revolt.

Here we strike a paradox: despite promoting the commonplace and the routine, *La Marseillaise* was produced in a revolutionary manner by the most exceptional filmmaker of the times and at a moment when he believed his métier could serve lasting social goals. Renoir bluntly stated: "I have chosen the Revolution because one cannot make a film directly about the political affairs in France today." In an address pronounced in Los Angeles on the eve of D-Day,[15] he said that he had adapted events of the Revolution to fit in allegorical fashion the crisis of the Third Republic and the Popular Front. *La Marseillaise* proved unpopular because his avant-garde critics found the film tame, while the larger public was attuned to representations previously monumentalized in official, intellectual, and popular culture. Renoir did not represent heroic events in the heroic style that those events were said to demand, a style that most other versions felt authorized and pleased to unleash.

Confident that the Popular Front had digested revolutionary history and that his film had adopted its tone, Renoir felt no need to retrace the story of the Revolution, and thus no need to include cornerstone occurrences and obvious characters. Instead, he recorded representative activities from a period of exceptional social awareness, a period he rigorously re-imagined from the documents and facts he collected. Sweeping his mobile camera across the country, he situated and interrelated various events to constitute an imagined newsreel of an impassioned time. As did Bresson in his literary adaptation *Le Journal d'un curé de campagne*, Renoir took on the ethos of a documentarian, one whose subject matter lay neither in the contemporary world nor in his imagination, but in a rock-hard record (the novel of Bernanos in the one case, the archives of the late eighteenth century for Renoir).

---

V

---

Having apologized for Renoir's rather shapeless design so as to honor the remarkable texture and tone of *La Marseillaise*, have I not bartered whatever credit is potentially invested in the notion of the film as an adaptation? It is one thing for Bresson to pick and choose among the scenes of a 300-page novel; it is quite another for Renoir to rummage through an archive of indefinite size. The answer turns on a single word: style. Disinclined to simply retrace the standard story or to add to the positivist accumulation of the storehouse of knowledge about those times, Renoir wanted instead to make something whole out of what are admittedly just small parts of the period. The song signifies the wholeness of outlook of the Renoir project to which it lends itself as a title. The achievement of this style invites one to scan not just the Revolution's past, but its still unfinished future. This style, and Renoir would add "this Revolution," is applicable to life today and tomorrow.

With this in mind, Renoir's film may at best adapt the *parti pris*, not the content or structure of some earlier historians of the Revolution. His sympathy for the lower classes, for instance, reminds us of Michelet a century before him, but *La Marseillaise* in no way looks like the two-volume *Histoire de la Révolution Française* that was simultaneously being re-published in the prestigious Pléiade series.[16] Godechot would more likely place Renoir within the Marxist tradition of Albert Mathiez and Georges Lefebvre, the dominant historians of the Revolution of Renoir's time, and men whose viewpoint coincided with people in his circle. But Mathiez's three-volume study has nothing in common with Renoir's film; moreover, Przybyszewska, whose play stands at the antipodes to *La Marseillaise*, relied on Mathiez as her "principal source," quarrying her characters and their speeches from its bedrock.[17] If a work in one literary genre can be adapted from the material of another (Verdi's *Otello* based on Shakespeare), then *The Danton Case* may be considered an adaptation from Mathiez's *Histoire de la Révolution Française*. But not so Renoir's film. His canticle responds to the Revolution as Mathiez, and more pertinently, Lefebvre recount it, but it does not imitate their, or any, authoritative historical rendering.

Lefebvre is surely the historian whose leftist but inclusive attitude Renoir can best be seen to adapt to his film. Remarkably, this man, who ranked among the most prominent historians of the day, actually contributed his own personal research to *La Marseillaise*. He was at the time finishing *Quatre-vingt neuf* for the 150th anniversary of the Revolution, a project taken on at the behest of Jean Zay, the same socialist Minister of Education who sat beside Renoir to announce the production of *La Marseillaise*. Zay might very well have brought the two men together. Renoir certainly did not follow Lefebvre's structure in that book (a chapter each to the revolutions of the aristrocracy, the bourgeoisie, the popular class, and the peasants), but he did adopt an ethos that would suppress all signs of scholarly superiority (the book is without footnotes) and that "used the occasion to delineate the revolutionary legacy common to all Frenchmen and to issue a call for its defense."[18]

Lefebvre must have found it easy to contribute in a small way to Renoir's Popular Front film, especially since he need only supply him with notes on topics about which he had in his life amassed mountains of information. Among the files he submitted is a dossier on the Army of the Coalition that helped turn the tide at Valmy. Just as Renoir would want, Lefebvre meticulously establishes the diverse geographical and social backgrounds of the hundred thousand men who went out to face the Prussians. Other entries informed Renoir about the wheat famine and the concomitant "great fear" that helped foment the strikes and other actions of 1789. Lefebvre's most arcane entry tells of an entourage of women from Les Halles who approached Louis XVI but were mistreated by the Swiss guards. Lefebvre goes so far as to identify six of these women by name and occupation. Here he shows himself not just a social historian, but one who was becoming a partisan of the growing trend toward recounting daily life, something he pursued as editor of the *Annales Historiques de la Révolution Française*.

Lefebvre was the most illustrious of a group of consultants who put together an impressive set of notes, hundreds of pages in length, on an amazing array of topics.[19] Renoir cared less about the structure of the Revolution, than about the texture of the period's forms of life, insofar as this could be gleaned from the nearly random facts he pored over. Catalogued into topics like "Elegance," "Food," "Costs of living," he learned about changes in wigs, hats, and handkerchiefs, and about social differences in the vocabulary used for these fads. Information about military and aristocratic lifestyle survives plentifully. Four full pages detail a banquet of the "Regiment of Flanders," including prices for food and wine. New dietary fads – of special concern for women – included milk and a variety of juices and concentrates. The basis of the prologue scene jumps out of this section of the archive in an entry signed by the historian Caron, concerning protocol at the king's table. Louis XVI boasted an enormous appetite. A single meal could consist of twenty separate items. Before hunting, he was said to eat a breakfast of a *poulet de grain,* four cutlets, and poached eggs with ham, quaffing this with a liter of champagne; then he would return from his hunt once again famished. A note in the margin of the file questions the wine service. Does the servant serve the king only after tasting the wine and washing the goblet in front of him? In any case, and as in the film, goblet and carafe are brought in together on a platter.

Information about the middle and lower classes, no doubt harder to come by, helped Renoir imagine sets he might want built. He learnt, for instance, that the materials used for barriers in Paris were logs rather than iron; he found out just how much difficulty the new government had in rationalizing Parisian street names, for the people refused to give up their picturesque vocabulary. The price of salt in three different French cities is compared, but the dossier also reminds Renoir that only two of France's twenty-three million people inhabited the cities. Perhaps the most detailed section of the entire dossier concerns types of entertainment available in Paris, from serious theater to Italian comedy, variety shows, and fairs with circus acts. Included here are the names and reputations of actresses. As for audiences, documentation indicates that they frequently applauded performances by stomping their feet. Details like this bolster individual scenes, such as the one at the shadow play; they also helped Renoir in countless ways to bring politics into a concrete world. Renoir knew, for instance, that when Camille Desmoulins declaimed against the Brunschwig manifesto it was in a salon above the café de Chartres, a notorious gathering spot. This bit of information may not have been lifted from the archive into the film, but having it in his mind could only help Renoir solve the cinematic problem of presenting something as abstract as this manifesto.

We can see now why Renoir disappointed his viewers by refusing to put on the screen Danton, Robespierre, or Marat, for there is no version of the French Revolution that does not feature such key players. What could Renoir have been thinking? His idea was to show the king being replaced by the nation, his sacred head falling to the feet of his anonymous former subjects. But actually these men are not anonymous at all, for Renoir proudly attests that his patriots (Bomier, Arnaud, Moissan) are documented in the registry of Marseilles. Attending to these ordinary people in their extraordinary times, attending to their daily, as opposed to their exceptional, activities (to their food, their banter, their entertainment, their music), Renoir adapted the situation French people faced 150 years earlier to that which they faced in 1938.

Bazin lauded adaptation as a practice that in principle should expand the possibilities of the medium by putting it at the service of something whose pre-established shape must be respected. But most adaptations of novels and of historical situations put convenience or a misguided belief in the integrity of the film medium ahead of the integrity of their subjects. They feed exceptional material into the sawmills of studio cinema and turn out movies of standard length, a standard look, and standard sentiments. Renoir joins Bresson and those few other filmmakers who use the singularity of each adaptation project as a license to abandon the very idea of standard cinema; they adapt the medium

Adapting Cinema to History

Chapter 13

to the remarkable source that justifies the undertaking. Among extraordinary undertakings, *La Marseillaise* stands out because, paradoxically, its mission is to represent the ordinariness, not the spectacular nature, of revolutionary times.

Renoir's hopes for the Popular Front scarcely lasted beyond the premiere of the film, but his hopes for cinema, in part because of this film, were soon fulfilled in what now goes by the name of the modern cinema: on the heels of *La Marseillaise* came *La Règle du jeu*, opening the way for the projects of Rossellini (*Paisan, The Flowers of Saint Francis*), Jean Rouch (*Jaguar, Chronique d'un été*), Godard (*Vivre sa vie, Deux ou trios choses que je sais d'elle*). Preconceived notions of script and cinematography could now be put aside, as the medium adapted itself to the rudderless conditions of a postwar modernity. A variety of very different films and directors were felt at the time by Bazin and his followers to participate in "A Chronicle of some events contributing to the fall of the Classical Hollywood Cinema."

---

### VI Epilogue

---

The battle for control over the French Revolution has been joined most recently by one of Renoir's most sympathetic allies, Eric Rohmer.[20] In *The Lady and the Duke* (2001), however, he seems to relish this opportunity to have it out with French historiography in general and Renoir's *La Marseillaise* in particular. It is true that Rohmer's startingpoint could not be further from recent directions in historiography. Not only does he focus on the privileged classes and on the great events of the time (the film being broken into chapters such as "July 14, 1790: the anniversary of the storming of the Bastille," "August 10, 1792: the storming of the Tuileries," and so on), but the source of his work is unique, the memoirs of a foreign eye-witness, the lady of the film's title. Where Renoir combed through a plethora of accounts and facts, striving to bring out the feel of momentous times as they affected countless unnamed citizens, Rohmer's attention and artistry go entirely into adopting the singular perspective of a woman who was in every respect "exceptional." This he does without the irony characteristic of his moral tales, where first-person accounts (think of Frederic in *L'Amour l'aprés-midi*, for example) are intermittently held out at arm's length for wry inspection by Rohmer's crystalline camerawork. But Grace Elliott is never second-guessed, perhaps because her views are so alien to the modern mentality. From start to finish her memoirs and their attitude control what is shown, even when, on occasion, her commentary is supplemented by material Rohmer took from the memoirs of the Duke.[21] Lucy Russell, who played Lady Grace, appreciated her intelligence and courage, recognizing that her views developed in the closed drawingroom world of the aristocracy of the times. She had virtually no contact with the people who make up Renoir's cast of characters. And if Rohmer prefers the drawing-room to the streets, it is because, like so many of his characters across four decades, he treasures solitude and reflection.[22]

The film's personal and political climax justly pushes the question of point of view to its limit. On a hillside, some miles from Paris, Grace and her serving woman attend the execution of Louis XVI. In fact, Grace cannot look, refusing the telescope her servant offers. But she hears the cries of the crowd and the retort of the cannon, signaling the fallen head, the fallen monarchy, and a fallen way of life. Her own head bows sadly in response. All this is filmed with the city spread out before her, in *repoussoir*, a painting literally come part way to life. But only part way, for the film, like the characters, seem detached from their moment. "Detachment," Philippe Azoury reminds us, was just the way Michelet spoke of the real "actors in the time of the Revolution." And so Rohmer renders "a silhouette of the Revolution played on a fantasmagoric stage by bodies who appear taken in their dreams."[23] The bodies that Renoir films, on the contrary, are earthy and have nothing of the fanstasmagoric about them, even when attending a genuine shadow play. Practical, pedestrian, and sensual, they seem most at home when chatting and eating. In their mountain hideout, four of them (priest, peasant, artisan, and lawyer) cook a rabbit and consolidate their grievances and their hopes. Like Renoir, they seem closer to Danton than to the coolly intelligent Robespierre, whom Rohmer portrays with sympathy.[24] Robespierre, the incorruptible, is also, despite his many disquisitions, a man of silence, the one who wanted to clear the stage of politics by shortening debates and trials, and by insisting on the absolute simplicity of judgment. Remaining hidden from the people as much as possible, he inspired the terror that stands sublimely above discourse, like its symbol, the guillotine.

Lady Grace witnesses the king's decapitation in silence and from a sublime, literally artistic distance, above Paris in Meudon. Rohmer must have thought of Renoir's house in the same town, a place famous for conviviality, where much of *La Marseillaise* was planned. Surely Renoir's biography made him equally sensitive to the passing of refinement. In the films just preceding *La Marseillaise* he registers feelingly the decline of the world of the Baron (*Les Bas Fonds*) and that of Raufenstein and Boldieu (*La Grande Illusion*). But Rohmer boldly accuses Renoir of being "partial" to the lower classes, and "[t]hey were a violent people, largely manipulated. Let's face it they weren't amicable," their excesses laying civility to waste.[25] In adapting the memoirs of Grace Elliott, Rohmer has given us something that is precisely precious, a time of trouble reflected in a delicate sensibility. Whereas Renoir, in adapting his cinema to the daily life of the ordinary classes past, present, and future, has given himself over not to a viewpoint but to the inevitability of history. *La Marseillaise* is indeed "partial," partial to history. Such allegiance to something that has shaped culture is the surest motive and the very sign of every adaptation worthy of the name.

---

### Notes

1   Franco Moretti, "Introduction," in *Signs Taken for Wonders* (London: NLB, 1983).
2   Dudley Andrew, "Revolution and the Ordinary: Renoir's *La Marseillaise*," *Yale Journal of Criticism* 4: 1 (1990), 53–84.

3   E. D. Hirsch, *Validity in Interpretation* (New Haven, CT: Yale University Press, 1967). For Hirsch, "meaning" refers to that which the author meant to convey at the time he or she wrote the text. "Significance" refers to the way(s) in which the text has been read over time.

4   Paul Ricoeur, *Time and Narrative*, vol. 3 (Chicago: University of Chicago Press, 1987), p. 154.

5   Hayden V. White, *Metahistory: The Historical Imagination in Nineteenth-century Europe* (Baltimore, MD: The Johns Hopkins University Press, 1975).

6   Jean Godechot, *Un jury pour la Révolution* (Paris: Robert Laffont, 1974).

7   André Bazin, *What is Cinema?*, vol. 1, trans. Hugh Gray (Berkeley, CA: University of California Press, 1967), p. 143.

8   Ibid., p. 128.

9   Ibid., p. 142.

10  Jean Renoir, *La Marseillaise: inédits*, ed. Claude Gauteur (Paris: CNC, 1989). This pamphlet contains the two early script outlines dealt with here plus an early and revealing draft of the prologue sequence when the king learns of the fall of the Bastille while eating. The Renoir archives at UCLA contain a typescript that seems to combine both versions. More ample than either, it makes frequent use of the wealth of information gathered for the project.

11  Jean Renoir, "La Forme et l'esprit: *La Marseillaise*," *Les Cahiers de la Jeunesse* 7 (February 15, 1937), reprinted in Jean Renoir, *Le Passé vivant* (Paris: Cahiers du Cinéma, 1989), p. 30.

12  Thanks to Sally Shafto for introducing me to Przybyszewska and her "theater of revolution."

13  See Marc Ferro, "Introduction," in *Révoltes, révolutions, cinéma* (Paris: Centre Pompidou, 1989), p. 9.

14  Jonathan Buchsbaum, *Cinéma engagé* (Champaign, IL: University of Illinois Press, 1989), p. 270.

15  Jean Renoir archives, UCLA.

16  Jules Michelet, *Histoire de la Révolution Française*, ed. Gerard Walter (Paris: Nouvelle Revue Français, 1939).

17  Daniel Gerould, "Introduction," in Stanislawa Przybyszewska, *The Danton Case*, *Thermidor* (Evanston, IL: Northwestern University Press, 1989), p. 11.

18  Ben Kennedy, "France's Celebration of the Cent-cinquantenaire of the Revolution in 1939 and Georges Lefebvre's *Quatre-vingt neuf*," unpublished paper presented at the NEH Summer Seminar on France between the Wars (Summer 1991).

19  These materials are conserved in the Jean Renoir archives of the Special Collections at UCLA.

20  Rohmer's collected film criticism, *The Taste for Beauty* (New York: Cambridge University Press, 1987) concludes with an entire section devoted to Renoir's films.

21  Eric Rohmer, interview in *Libération* (September 7, 2001), 29.

22  Philippe Azoury, *Libération* (September 7, 2001).

23  Ibid.

24  Frédéric Bonnaud, in *Film Comment* (October, 2001), 11.

25  Rohmer, interview in *Libération* (September 7, 2001), 29.

# Chapter 14

# Photographic *Verismo*, Cinematic Adaptation, and the Staging of a Neorealist Landscape

## Noa Steimatsky

> With perfect stylistic coherence the realism in this tale gradually becomes more emphatic until it surpasses itself and becomes metaphor and meaning: a manner of seeing the world that, in manifesting itself, becomes art.
>
> Umberto Barbaro, 1939[1]

> By the power of photography, the natural image of a world that we neither know nor can know, nature at last does more than imitate art: she imitates the artist.
>
> André Bazin, 1945[2]

Although it would seem that the adaptation of a literary work from another era would be an anathema to realist cinema, we find in key works emerging from the paradigmatic realist schools just such undertakings. Jean Renoir's 1938 adaptation of Emile Zola's novel *La Bête humaine* (1890) in the era of French "poetic realism" is a celebrated example; it foreshadows the Italian Neorealist example of Luchino Visconti's 1948 production *La terra trema*, adapted from a novel by Giovanni Verga, *I malavoglia* (1881).[3] Though Visconti does not acknowledge his source text as Renoir, his mentor, has so emphatically done – with Zola's portrait and signature accompanying the epigraph – there is a way in which both adaptations serve their makers as occasion to examine realist precedents via the established medium of literature, bringing those precedents to bear on the question of realism in cinema. For both filmmakers were profoundly indebted throughout their careers to European realist traditions in literature and the visual arts, a debt which remains inseparable from their concern with theater, melodrama, and the staging of history.

Interestingly, Renoir and Visconti focused on the related variants of, respectively, Naturalism in France and *verismo* in Italy – literary movements informed by a social-scientific ambition to record and analyze the determinant causes of human action via the fatal stamp of heredity, and of social, historical, and geographical milieux upon the subject.[4] These "scientistic" aspirations appear to have been tied, more or less consciously, in the filmmakers' imagination to cinema's privileged indexical claim: its photographic but also auditory capacity to register, to preserve, its evidentiary force that transpires even in the work of fiction. Thus both filmmakers place their adaptations in contemporary milieux, making use of location shooting to inform their charting of the social and economic relations that drive the narratives. Their realism is informed, then, both by the indexical/documentary claim of their medium – always fraught with pitfalls yet never quite possible to dismiss – and by historical precedents and conventions that have molded realist traditions in their respective national cultures. Delving into the intersection of these realist fronts, even at its most problematic, proved remarkably fruitful as both filmmakers achieved therein an enhanced consciousness of their craft and have taken that lesson well beyond these specific adaptations.

In this chapter I wish to focus on Visconti's *La terra trema* as an exemplary project that delves into the foundations and complexities of realism in the cinema. General debates on realism – with all its pitfalls and fallacies – in literature, art, and film constitute a wider ground than can be summarized here. Yet the Italian postwar revival of the term (as of its contradictions) makes manifest in *La terra trema* a paradigmatic instance in which some of realism's key questions – as a historical movement, and as a continued impulse in cinema – can be examined. My interest in Visconti's film as a work of adaptation lies less in a detailed comparison with its source text,[5] and is primarily focused on the film's tackling of the question of realism *vis-à-vis* that source and other, related models. Giovanni Verga, a key reference for the Neorealist school at large, himself aspired to bring literature's realist ambition to its limits, raising at those limits the possibility of the new medium of photography as potentially fulfilling these ambitions. In analyzing this aspiration and its repercussions, one comes to acknowledge the paradoxical productiveness of the realist fallacy as such: the epistemological ambition of the work to define itself vis-à-vis reality *tout court*. We shall see how Visconti's reworking of such issues squarely confronts the fragile question on the "representation of reality" with the historical resonances and wealth of the realist tradition brought to consciousness in this formative moment that was to prove so influential for postwar cinemas at large.

## Verghian Premises

When Luchino Visconti undertook in 1947 the production of his second feature film, he was ostensibly committed, under the auspices of the Italian Communist Party, to a documentary rendering of the labors and hardship of Sicilian fishermen. This was to be the first in a projected trilogy on Sicilian workers which, following the *Episodio del mare* – the "Episode of the Sea," a subtitle that still follows *La terra trema* in the opening credits – would treat the experience of peasants, and finally of sulphur miners with whom the revolutionary struggle would be resolved. Francesco Rosi, an assistant on the production, attests to Visconti's commitment to the documentary project, but he also asserts that it was, above all, Giovanni Verga's *I malavoglia* that Visconti always had in mind for a film set in the specifically designated location of the novel, the fishing village of Aci Trezza, on the shore of the Ionian Sea.[6] An avid reader of the European novel, well versed in French, German, and Russian literature and in the nineteenth-century Lombard novelist Alessandro Manzoni, Visconti sought to redefine for postwar Italian cinema a realist aesthetic drawing on regionalist sources in literary and pictorial traditions. Although realist and regionalist trends persisted under Fascism, they were largely geared toward rural folk mythology, seeking to forge an heroic union with the Italian soil rather than expose gaps and conflicts between national and regional orders.[7] One might say that Visconti sought to reconstruct a realist genealogy that would bypass this immediate, tainted past, and yet exhibit historical and social awareness.

Verga's late nineteenth-century realism, in the specific mode of *verismo*, came to be a paradigm for what began to be defined in the late 1930s as a Neorealist school in literature and cinema. Visconti and his colleagues sought to adopt Verga's synthesizing of sociological and linguistic data in the attention to hitherto neglected milieux, on the margin of Italy's slow entry into European modernization, as the subject for art. But it was also the epic bent of Verga's work, its tragic-heroic pathos and original linguistic texture that were salient for Visconti when he traveled along the eastern coast of Sicily, still during Fascism, years before *La terra trema*'s production, in the footsteps of Verga's narratives.[8] This was the period of Visconti's encounter with the group of early Neorealists associated with the magazine *Cinema*, including Giuseppe de Santis, Mario Alicata, Gianni Puccini, and others who came to constitute Visconti's professional and intellectual milieu in Rome from around 1940. Their collaboration in fact resulted in several treatments of Verga's writings toward possible adaptation. Visconti's first script of a Verga narrative in that period, "L'amante di Gramigna" ("Gramigna's Mistress") was flatly rejected by the Fascist minister of popular culture who had written on it with a red pencil: "Enough with those bandits!"[9] Tales of bandits and their mistresses over the background of a scorched, primal Sicilian landscape seemed hardly adequate to the desired image of a centralized, imperially ambitious Fascist Italy as it was entering the war: an Italy that denied the voice of indigenous, marginal cultures that might corrupt the standard language, question the Europeanized progress of the North, critique – as Antonio Gramsci had already done – the virtual colonization of the south, and mar the workings of a Fascist rural mythology as well as the "White Telephone" studio production of Cinecittà.

Verga is reluctant to burden "Gramigna's Mistress" with extensive descriptive detail. What makes this short story so vivid, nonetheless, is his interweaving of Sicilian dialect expressions, as if to let the material "speak for itself" – though not before it is translated into high literary Italian. Close to *I malavoglia*'s adapted language of gossip, superstition, proverbs, and epithets, "Gramigna's Mistress" is marked by a synthetic, layered style – at once distancing from and engaged with the voices of the place – which achieves remarkable pathos. The heroic dimension of primal passions in the rough, humble milieu is punctuated by the laconic irony of understatement as narration is stripped to bare outline. Curiously, almost a third of Verga's story is taken up by an expository prologue, a *verista* credo of sorts. We know that Visconti must have studied the text of "Gramigna" and considered carefully its implications for cinema. For its subtle evocation of all the realist terms that were to animate the cinematic sensibility of Visconti and his colleagues, it is worth citing the prologue at some length. Thus, Verga, 1880, addressing the story to his contemporary and colleague Salvatore Farina:

Dear Farina, here is not a story but the sketch of a story. It will at least have the merit of being very short and of being very factual – a human document, as they say nowadays . . . I shall repeat it to you just as I picked it up along the paths in the countryside, with nearly the same simple and picturesque words that characterize popular narration, and you will certainly prefer to find yourself face to face with the naked and unadulterated fact, without having to look for it between the lines of the book, through the lens of the writer.

The simple human fact will always make one think; it will always have the force of what *has really been* . . .

We willingly sacrifice the effect of the denouement to the logical, necessary development of passions and facts leading to the denouement, which is thus rendered less unforeseen, less dramatic perhaps , but not less fatal . . . [T]he demonstration of this obscure tie between causes and effects will certainly not be less useful to the art of the future. Shall we ever reach such perfection in the study of passions that it will become useless to continue in this study of the inner man? Will the science of the human heart, which will be the fruit of the new art, develop so much and so generally all the powers of the imagination that in the future the only novels written will be *faits divers*?

When in the novel the affinity and cohesion of its every part will be so complete that the creative process will remain a mystery, like the development of human passions, and the harmony of its elements will be so perfect, the sincerity of its reality so evident, its manner of and its reason for existing so necessary, that the hand of the artist will remain absolutely invisible, then it will have the imprint of an actual happening; the work of art will seem *to have made itself*, to have matured and come into being spontaneously, like a fact of nature, without retaining any point of contact with its author, any stain of the original sin.[10]

A native of those same eastern Sicilian parts in which "Gramigna's Mistress" and *I malavoglia* are located, Verga in fact composed the major part of his Sicilian writings in distant Milan. Having accumulated lists of dialect expressions and studies of Sicilian folklore, he cut short a career of composing romantic novels on society life to write his *verista* work about the people of his native region from the distance of the northern, modern metropolis. This biographical fact suggests a nostalgic outlook: the removed scene of writing may have facilitated the wide embrace of the varied materials, Verga's grafting of the literary fiction's epic grandeur upon linguistic and sociological documentation. The "scientific" ambition declared in the "Gramigna" prologue is partly fulfilled in that Verga's texts contain specific and accurate geographical descriptions complete with place names, and veritable catalogues of Sicilian habit and idiom. The critic Romano Luperini notes that Verga's portrayal in *I malavoglia* of the overlapping of archaic modes of life alongside the advent of modernity is itself historically informed; a sense of stasis and cosmic circularity intersects with the emerging social and spatial mobility of the town's inhabitants.[11] But in the linguistic texture of Verga's work, particularly in the use of free indirect discourse, Luperini locates an inherent yet fruitful ambiguity that comes to characterize his understanding of *verismo*. For Verga does not simply transcribe or "repeat," as his credo would have it, the popular language of the countryside, but rather, out of the particular Sicilian dialect incomprehensible to most Italians, and the narrator's high literary language, he establishes a synthetic construct all of his own, one that departs both from sources in actual speech *and* from Italian poetic convention. Narrator and character speak a language that fuses speech and reflection, concrete local idiom and ironic commentary or poetic turn: Verga's mastery enables the many voices to mingle in a resonant "chorale."

Certainly, the realism of this chorale cannot be quite "transparent": even as Verga's translation renders Sicilian idiom comprehensible, he infuses his literary Italian with the vivid concreteness of distinctive regional voices, but the result is intricate artifice. Verga's hope that "the hand of the artist will remain absolutely invisible" in the process of literary synthesis is surely frustrated thus. The desired authenticity of linguistic sources, data, and sentiment undergoes a poetic transfiguration, effecting fruitful contradictions that are echoed, as well, on other levels of the text. For example, Luperini notes, Verga's precise geographical indications are countered by elusive descriptions of the inner spaces of the village: these remain indistinct, idealized in an effort to have them conform to a mythical image of an archaic, serene world where persons and their environment merge: this in nostalgic contrast to the modern, urban Milanese environment from which Verga was actually writing. Similarly, a linear realist narration that would conform to the quotidian, horizontal world of Aci Trezza – a mode that would be adaptable to Visconti's prospects for a Marxist trilogy of an impending revolution – is disrupted already in Verga by an enclosed, cyclical, rhythmic sense of time, a mythical order of fate. In this "vertical" order Aci Trezza appears unchanging and unchangeable, obeying the cycles of nature, itself mythicized to include the constellations above, the volcano behind, and the repetitive rhythm of the sea opposite. In fact, the year following "Gramigna," Verga's brief prologue to *I malavoglia* betrays some intimation that his removed and encompassing vision seeks at the same time an aesthetically satisfying epic or tragic grandeur in the transition from a premodern to a modern life, the eclipse of an archaic world in the face of progress.

> The fateful, endless and often wearisome and agitated path trod by humanity to achieve progress *is majestic in its end result, seen as a whole and from afar*. In the glorious light which clothes it, striving, greed and egoism fade away, as do all the weaknesses which go into the huge work, all the contradictions from whose friction the light of truth emerges.[12]

In literary practice, Verga's orchestration of contradictions was perhaps too rich to fit the theoretical mold of his own *verista* ideals. Written language as such appeared unsatisfactory, as the "Gramigna" prologue already intimates, in Verga's declared search for the work of "art of the future." Could the novel reveal *directly* – without the mediation of the artist's hand or voice – the determinant causes for the *denouement*, as if those were already written upon the face of the earth, waiting to be simply "picked . . . up along the paths in the countryside?" Searching to resolve this difficulty, Luperini cites Verga's notion of "intellectual reconstruction" performed from an objectifying distance and informing the written work. But what we also find here is an opening to an altogether different practice, perhaps more radical in its implications than that acknowledged by Luperini. Planning to revisit his chosen location of Aci Trezza, after having worked on *I malavoglia* in Milan, Verga writes to his *verista* colleague Luigi Capuana: "Don't you think that, for us, the aspect of certain things cannot be dealt with unless *seen from a specific visual angle*? And that we never succeed in being genuinely and effectively true [*veri*] unless we do a work of intellectual reconstruction *not with our mind but with our eyes*?"[13] "Intellectual reconstruction" here is no abstract conceptual analysis but, interestingly, a labor for the eyes, pertaining to vision as a specific, concrete, even if subjective practice – vision grasped, moreover, as an intellectual processing of the optical imprint of phenomena "from a specific visual angle."

The substitution of verbal conceptualization by an optical intellect is in other writings qualified as approaching the "perfect impersonality of the work of art," positivistically inflected by scientific or technological means.[14] In this turn to the visual as possibly capable of fulfilling that which remains frustrated by language, it is perhaps the example of contemporary painters that Verga may have initially had in mind. The school of the *Macchiaioli* forms with Verga and his colleagues the larger range of the Italian nineteenth-century culture of realism.[15] For in the aesthetic of this quasi-Impressionist movement, as well, we identify the desire for a spontaneous artistic creation whose imprint of reality is understood as self-manifesting through the effects of light in the painting. These optical impressions the *Macchiaioli* professed to capture *all'aperto* and express in brushstrokes, patches, and spots – "*macchie*" – which have given the movement its name. The effect of the painting upon the eye was understood to repeat the perceptual imprint of reality itself. Verga's thinking may have been informed by such a definition of the *macchia* as appeared in an 1852 dictionary:

> Painters use this word to express the quality of certain drawings and sometimes paintings done with extraordinary facility and with such harmony and freshness, without much finish or color, and in such a way as to seem not made by the artist's hand but *to have appeared by itself* on the sheet of paper or canvas.[16]

Verga's trust in a manifest and objective "truth" of the visible must have been informed, as well, by a consideration of photography as revolutionizing the status of images and the notion of artistic reproduction via the causal, indexical charge of the photograph, understood as an unmediated impression upon the plate by nature itself.[17] The photographic effects achieved by some of the *Macchiaioli* and their occasional use of actual photographs in the work process is particularly suggestive in view of Verga's search for an art of the future that will fulfill the realist vision. With photography in mind, the "Gramigna" prologue now appears in a new light.

> [Y]ou will certainly prefer to find yourself face to face with the naked and unadulterated fact . . . The simple human fact will always . . . have the force of what *has really been* . . . [When] the hand of the artist will remain absolutely invisible, then [the work] will have the imprint of an actual happening; the work of art will seem *to have made itself*, to have matured and come into being spontaneously, like a fact of nature . . .[18]

Like its French Naturalist model, *verismo* grasped the determinant causes of action as manifest, materially or optically inscribed upon reality, and in this sense available to representation which would surpass in revelatory power, so Verga suggests, the novel's speculations on "the inner man." Can one identify, then, in Verga's utopian notion of realist art something that can be approached only outside of literary discourse, in work that indexically traces the premises – or shall we say referents – of literature "from a specific visual angle," in a nonverbal, nonsymbolic form of representation? The impasse of the *verista* ambition, which the novel could not overcome (and remain literature), is what, one may postulate, contributed to Verga's eventual suspension of his literary production. For his biography is sharply marked by a retirement from literary work that roughly coincides with the return to his native Sicily.

It was then that he discovered photography. After the publication of *Maestro Don Gesualdo* in 1889, followed in 1891 by a volume of short stories, Verga began writing the third novel in his *I vinti* cycle, but never completed it. The coinciding of his suspension of literary work and his growing engagement with photography suggests several hypotheses. It may suggest that specific difficulties with the third novel in the cycle led him to photography as an aide, an artist's tool. Or perhaps Verga perceived photography as a self-sufficient fulfillment of that which literature could not accomplish, and hence altogether a substitute for the written text. But yet another ambition may have driven Verga's photographic project. For in the choice of subject matter Verga's camera yielded a visual re-interrogation, an *adaptation* as it were, of materials and modes derived from his own writings. The letter to Capuana concerning the fulfillment of the *verista* project from "a specific visual angle" already suggested the optical, photographic return to the scene of literature by way of verification and reconstruction. The photographic project now replaces the precise topographical detail that informs Verga's work, as well as his lists of linguistic and sociological data assembled in preparation for writing.

Verga's turn to photography links him with other Italian promoters of *verismo*, such as Capuana and De Roberto,[19] but also, clearly, with his Naturalist contemporaries, most famously Emile Zola in France. Zola, too, devoted himself to photography *following* the writing of his major work, and often as a return to its subjects and sites. Yet while Zola's interest in photography, evidenced by his friendship with Nadar, might have been triggered early, Verga's photographic *practice* precedes Zola's by some fourteen years. Verga's photographs – some 400 of them were discovered by his archivist in 1970 – date from 1878 to 1911.[20] He was most prolific in the 1880s and early 1890s, that is, contemporary with but mostly following his late literary production. Among Verga's photographs there are, alas, none of Aci Trezza, the designated location of *I malavoglia* and the theater of its adaptation in *La terra trema*. But the interest in the reciprocity of places and persons, the impact of setting on expression, is consistent with that of the writings. One witnesses in the photographs, as well, the organization and grouping by classes, occupations, types: men, women, and children are examined in relation to their habitat and work place; they are characterized by contiguity with domestic objects or tools of labor, animals, clothing, and other props.

Here are workers and farmhands, in work clothes and Sunday clothes, posing against the scorched landscapes, hilltown views, fields, houses, alleys, or just plain walls. The frontal poses suggest an interest in the typical and the evident, the documentable physiognomies and expressions of people in their native habitat – enclosed courtyards are a favorite setting – with no suggestion of shadow or mystery enfolding them. Rather these are fully illuminated human features, with no touch-ups, often contorted under the strong sunlight, confronting the camera among everyday objects: against a blind arch or a stone wall enclosing a courtyard, a chair carved out of a tree trunk, a bowl of beans waiting to be sorted complete the family portrait (figure 14.1). In several portraits, a piece of cloth stretched clumsily behind a posing figure determines the flat and functional simplicity of the composition, supporting the clear outlining of the human figure as its proper object. Such compositions suggest that the likeness was intended as record of an "interrogated" object, set up to eliminate distraction, narrativizing links, the complexity of spatial depth, and striving instead for a standardized identity photograph.

But even where the views are panoramic they are usually not of the sweetest or touristic sights of Sicily. Towns and villages are most often registered in their vernacular, unmonumental aspect, through specifically named streets, houses, or courtyards. Two 1892 views of the hilltown of Vizzini from slightly different angles register, as in a topographic survey, the town's nested position within the landscape, the particular angularity of its roofs that complement its forms and rhythms on the hillside, the relationship of the human

**Figure 14.1** Giovanni Verga: Tébidi, 1892.
Collezione G. Garra Agosta. From *Verga Fotografo* (Catania, Italy: Giuseppe Maimone Editore, 1991).

habitat to its natural setting. In other photographs, people are grouped or altogether distanced as they are fully inserted in deep, detailed, revealing surroundings, as if to enhance all possible ties – practical, social, sentimental – with the milieu, a sense of integrity and continuity of persons and places. In a photograph of 1897, a crowd of people turn to face the photographer at a crossroads in the town of Mascalucia (figure 14.2). The camera captures the townspeople at a distance, as if they had just paused and turned around for a moment in the public place; yet the groupings of posing figures against the surrounding buildings also suggests the deliberate blocking of characters, or the positioning of a chorus upon the stage, as perhaps for a scene in the Mascagni opera of Verga's own *Cavalleria rusticana*.

And so we witness the tensions of literary *verismo* persist through these images, duplicating the inherent denotational/connotational bind of photography itself.[21] The documentary, "factual," even *functional* aspect of the photographs, coupled with the impassive disposition of the human figures, is inflected by an expressivity that one might call dramatic, even theatrical in orientation. For instance, while Verga's organization of the frame and

**Figure 14.2**  Giovanni Verga: Mascalucia (?), 1897.
Collezione G. Garra Agosta. From *Verga Fotografo* (Catania, Italy: Giuseppe Maimone Editore, 1991).

Noa Steimatsky

Chapter 14

choice of angles often appear straightforward and simplified, sharp contrasts of light and shade, unsoftened by the lens or in processing, eloquently impart the subjugation of these Sicilians to the Mediterranean climate, the punishing sun, the arid earth, in dramatic terms. The drama of the light and the textured contrasts become as much *objects* of the representation here as they are the means *by* which we see what the camera has enframed. Does Verga's work reveal some consciousness of, does it acknowledge the *bind* between fact and expression, reference and *poesis*, denotation and connotation in photography's ontological constitution? Under the violent sunlight and harsh shadows that mark their faces, three Sicilian farmers from Tébidi are frontally grouped, from the waist up, in an 1897 photograph (figure 14.3). Such an image clearly exceeds the neutralizing function of cataloguing or of the identity card. The subtle low angle of the camera just suffices to endow these figures with an heroic aspect that is made more eloquent by the unsoftened light, enhancing the shiny, deeply marked foreheads, the hands looming large in the front, the depth of the glances right into the camera, confronting the lens in defiance of the sunlight, each from a slightly different position.

A late photograph (1911) of a little girl at the window in Novalucello (figure 14.4) is reminiscent of some of Visconti's most memorable framing in *La terra trema*: the elegance of its composition seems dictated by the window's "natural" enframing of the girl, just as the theatrical organization of other photographs appeared naturally dictated by the given setting. Yet precise choices determine these graceful images of Sicily. For here, again, the slight angle and harsh contrasts enhance the texture, indeed the expressivity,

**Figure 14.3**  Giovanni Verga: Tébidi, 1897.
Collezione G. Garra Agosta. From *Verga Fotografo* (Catania, Italy: Giuseppe Maimone Editore, 1991).

of the wall surrounding the girl, who emerges into the sunlight dramatically defined against the dark interior of the room behind her. But even in such compositions – so evocative of pictorial renderings of "the woman at the window" as a conventional trope – the inter-framing seeks to present actuality as itself already fully expressive, "naturally" poetic, and *as such* ready to lend itself to the photograph. These Sicilian photographs – like Verga's literary chorale of factual, documentary sources and poetic embellishment – aspire to render reality-as-art by sheer, spontaneous self-manifestation. The *verista* yearning for unmediated registration invariably results in an aesthetically satisfying chorale, com-posed from "a specific visual angle."

The case of Verga as photographer reveals an impulse behind a nineteenth-century realist school as it aspires toward and is taken up by photography and film. While he must have contemplated cinema in corresponding with several institutions concerning prac-tical and economic possibilities for the adaptation of his work, Verga's thought on this front is not as developed as that on photography.[22] Yet as associative threads that lead from *verismo* to Visconti's cinematic return to the sites of *I malavoglia*, Verga's photo-graphs speak most eloquently. For they themselves constitute an adaptation, a visual

**Figure 14.4** Giovanni Verga: Catania, Novalucello, 1911.
Collezione G. Garra Agosta. From *Verga Fotografo* (Catania, Italy: Giuseppe Maimone
Editore, 1991).

revisitation by modern technological means to the literary project of *verismo*, affording
insight into a realist fantasy of art as an "imprint of an actual happening." And while
such photographic work may have seemed to Giovanni Verga capable of superior neutrality of impersonal documentation, it inevitably repeats the contradictions of the *verista*
text that precedes it. Neorealism was to rehearse a similar, and comparably rich, play
of contradictions some half a century later.

Dwelling on the revival of interest in Verga in the 1940s, Romano Luperini draws attention to the oxymoron "*verità e poesia*" – "truth and poetry" – in the title of an influential article by Mario Alicata and Giuseppe De Santis, published in *Cinema* in 1941.[23] In this early Neorealist credo Alicata and De Santis define the cinema as driven in principle by a documentary impulse, but also as an inherently narrative form, bound to the novel and to realism as the novel's most powerful mode. Verga's project is taken as a prime model for the new cinema; but the ambition to reconcile documentary sources with a so-called "poetry of truth" resulted in Neorealism's inevitable rehearsal of the contradictions of *verismo*.

> [I]nstead of the more habitual use of back doors to realism, there is a main entrance . . . Giovanni Verga . . . Since we believe in an art which above all creates truth, the Homeric, legendary Sicily of *I malavoglia, Maestro Don Gesualdo,* "L'Amante di Gramigna," and "Jeli il pastore" . . . could give inspiration to the imagination of our cinema which looks for things in the space-time of reality to redeem itself from the easy suggestion of a moribund bourgeois state.[24]

And in the second installment of the article:

> We too want to take our movie camera into the streets, into the fields, into the ports, into the factories of our country; we too are persuaded that one day we shall make our finest cinema by following the slow and weary pace of the laborer as he returns home, narrating the essential poetry of a new and pure life, that contains within itself the secret of its aristocratic beauty.[25]

Such romantic glorification of the humble worker in the heroics of the everyday is the most salient feature shared by *verismo*, Neorealist ideology, and its postwar variants, ranging from Christian humanist to overtly Marxist outlooks. Yet in some of the later Neorealist theorizations the shift to a more outspoken social and political commitment often resulted, paradoxically, not in a strictly analytic model but in what is often cited as the school's somewhat naïve, self-defeating notion of capturing "life as it really is." A few years after the "Truth and Poetry" articles, Alicata came to condemn the digressive, "lyricizing" elements – "the sound of the waves . . . the sublime narrative rhythm" – in an adaptation of Verga, prescribing instead a linear, progressive structure advanced by the emblematic conflict of types and wills in the social drama, in place of the mythical temporality of *I malavoglia*.[26] But in 1941 Visconti is frankly explicit in his fascination with, precisely, the archaic, tragic rhythm and pathos of *I malavoglia*. His notes in an article for *Cinema* titled "Tradizione e invenzione" are of a piece with Alicata and De Santis's earlier outlook. Visconti dwells on:

> the religious and fatal tone of an ancient tragedy [that Verga gives] to those humble facts unfolding in everyday life, to that story apparently consisting of scraps, of refuse, of matters of no importance, to that shred of a peasant "chronicle," enframed by the monotonous sound of the waves that break on the *Faraglioni*.[27]

Early Neorealism appears in these excerpts as neither unconscious of nor denying the artistic heritage and aesthetic drive that would inflect its ideological program and epistemological claims. The synthesizing of "scraps" of "everyday life" with high poetic grandeur will keep its hold on Visconti's imagination even after the war, as he will commit himself to a documentary project sponsored by a political party on the eve of elections.

Gianni Puccini, Visconti's colleague in the *Cinema* group, tells of an evening spent in conversation on the subject of Giovanni Verga between the aspiring filmmaker and Gianni's father, Mario Puccini, himself a writer who had known Verga personally. Puccini the elder gave Visconti an old picture postcard of the rough landscape of Aci Trezza, which Visconti hung in his study. Though dating some fifty years before Visconti's film, the postcard might have looked like a frame enlargement. He would later say that it was this image that bred in him the desire that led to *La terra trema*.[28] And it was this image that first drew him to explore the eastern shores of Sicily and visit Aci Trezza. Upon his return he asked the painter Renato Guttuso to prepare a series of drawings of Sicilian fishermen, with Verga's characters in mind. Visconti's thinking about an adaptation of *I malavoglia* evolves, from the start, via a notion of cinema as capable of dismantling the abstracting, symbolic mediation of language in favor of what he identifies as the "visual and plastic" sensory concreteness of cinematographic realism.

Like the self-exiled Verga writing on Sicily from the north, the Lombard Visconti gone south acknowledges that an artist's distance from the regional landscape informs his sense of its expressivity, affording a unifying visionary perspective. He notes, also in "Tradizione e invenzione," the figurative suggestiveness of Sicily: an enclosed geographic form defined against the sea and the mainland, the Mediterranean island itself becomes an anthropomorphic presence in its embodiment of Verga's world. Indeed, rather than deny a mythicizing outlook, Visconti acknowledges it fully, naming its sources. And it is in these glowing terms that he contemplates the cinematic possibilities of the novel:

> To me, a Lombard reader, accustomed by tradition to the limpid rigor of the Manzonian imagination, the primitive and gigantic world of the fishermen of Aci Trezza . . . always appeared exalted in the fantastic and violent tones of an epic: to my Lombard eyes content with the sky of my native land that is "so nobly fair in fair weather," Verga's Sicily appeared truly as the island of Ulysses, an island of adventures and ardent passions, lying immobile and proud opposite the waves of the Ionian Sea. That is how I thought of a film on *I malavoglia*. From the moment I decided not to discard this thought as the improvised fruit of a solitary rapture but to seek in every way possible to realize it, the intimate doubts, the councils of prudence, the estimate of difficulties, always surrendered before the excitement of being able to give a visual and plastic reality to those heroic figures that have the allusive and enig-matic force of a symbol but not its abstract and austere frigidity.[29]

The Northern aesthete's mystified grasp of the south partakes of traditional patterns of Italian regionalism. Sicily's geographical and historical separateness, its unstable, intricate history, its shifting status as the garden of the Mediterranean but also as a colonized, exploited, vanquished land – these contribute to the rich imaginative texture of the place. Visconti's consciousness of these cultural connotations intersects with the realist's privileging of neglected subject matter or milieu. It is in this way that the humble Sicilian fishing village of contemporary, post-Fascist Italy may somehow enfold no less than the gigantic world of *The Odyssey*. This imaginative resonance comes to fuel, as well, the nascent consciousness of its own backwardness and, thereby, its awakening to and participation in modern history. Even as it tendentiously differs from Verga's text, Visconti's treatment maintains the epic-heroic pathos, investing it in his script's progressive ideological prospects that thus acquire depth and import. Yet, while endorsing the developing class consciousness of his fisherman-hero and his preliminary moves toward an open, dynamic, revolutionary order, Visconti endows the suffering of his characters with an aura of grace and grandeur that draws on an opposed, morbid impulse to maintain an earlier, archaic state of being. The tensions that inform Visconti's aesthetic at this historical moment are thus articulated in the specific conditions of this Sicilian arena. Rather than profess to expose a singular, solid "reality beyond the myth" of Sicily's aesthetic appeal – as some postwar Neorealists imagined they might achieve – Visconti embraces his location's wealth of connotations, even at the cost of certain tensions in his progressive project, that one must now acknowledge as fully conscious of the traditions of which it partakes and to which it now contributes.[30]

To achieve this complexity, Visconti, the Milanese aristocrat, reversed Verga's removal of the site of writing from the site of the fiction and came to immerse himself for many months in the designated location of *I malavoglia*. But this ostensibly documentary-driven choice – informed by a Gramscian awareness of "The Southern Question"[31] and of the intellectual's role in the world of labor, bridging both regions and classes – mingles with an imaginative grasp of Aci Trezza as poetic entity. Accounts of the production of *La terra trema* reveal the binding of "truth and poetry," the documentary aspiration and elaborate literary, pictorial, and emphatically theatrical artifice at every level of the work. Hence the use of authentic dialect, incomprehensible to most Italians, is only in part designed to serve a realist epistemology. Dialogues were based on what were initially improvised responses in local idiom of the participating townspeople of Aci Trezza. Yet, once satisfied with the selected expressions, Visconti would fix them in the script, to be as carefully rehearsed as a composed text in a perfectly contained and controlled performance. Inseparable from the commitment to authentic sources is Visconti's fascination with the dialect's archaic-Homeric auditory quality, whose incomprehensibility itself contributed to its musicality, transcending verbal contents toward a quasi-operatic quality. The use of standard Italian in the voice-over narration – which initially connotes documentary practice – itself serves to enhance poetic and musical values, as well as irony, by way of repetition and variation on the spoken/subtitled dialogue. Such layering is specific to the possibilities of cinema, echoing the complexity of Verga's literary composition in what critics have described as Visconti's adaptation of Verga's *chorale*.[32]

The discipline Visconti demanded from his performers was echoed in the degree of preparation and control that he exercised on all planes of the image. It is here that one locates the larger dimensions of Visconti's well-wrought realism, well exceeding the linguistic and thematic planes of adaptation. For the kind of attention to detail of *mise-en-scène* in this icon of Neorealist cinema does not fall short of the elaborate construction of Visconti's theater and opera productions. While he insisted on the use of authentic exterior as well as of interior locations, sites were altered either architecturally or by the simulated conjunction of disparate spaces in editing. Interiors and other built spaces were redesigned to serve not so much a sense of spatial integrity as a composed and molded theatrical order that would lend itself to the choreography of the actors' motions and blocking. Windows were added, while interiors and exteriors across from windows – as with Mara's basil plant window appearing to overlook the bricklayers' workplace – were matched in synthetic editing of what were in fact two different parts of the town.[33] An intricate binding of planes via figure and camera movement across windows or thresholds is afforded by depth of field cinematography, always in the service of a theatrical order grafted out of the location's conditions. The vernacular Mediterranean architecture, the light and weather by which it is seen, as well as the preindustrial economy and tightly interlaced community that goes along with it are all taken up by Visconti's camera, as they were by Verga's own, and elevated to an aesthetic principle.

The sequence of the selling of the anchovies to the wholesalers in the family's court-yard is a paradigmatic instance of the deterministic theatricalization of architectural spaces in Visconti's film. The camera's position *vis-à-vis* the surrounding walls makes salient here a centripetal enclosure[34] that is echoed by the inter-framing of the women at the window in the background early in the sequence. Reframing, afforded by camera move-ment and the shifting of position of the figures, is designed to consummate dramatic situ-ations, end sequences, and connect different phases of the emblematic *tableaux* in relation to the setting, to the frame, and to each other. This is epitomized in the summary image of the family's failure at the anchovy sale negotiations at the end of the season (figure 14.5). Formal repetition of such enclosed compositions at different phases of the economic process is clearly understood to reflect the prefigured fate and deterministic sense of inevitable outcome. These virtually static group compositions of the family in its native habitat, against the bare walls of the courtyard, call for comparison with the photographic family portrait that makes its appearance in key instances in the film. Standing for an idealized and lost past that precedes the narrative time frame, set in a photographer's studio with fringed theatrical curtains enframing a backdrop of snow-tipped Etna, the studio portrait, with its sentimental vision of harmonious continuity and integrity, may also be juxtaposed with Verga's photography *all'aperto*, where the principle of grouping and choice of milieux partake of a relatively functional, documentary, even cataloguing project as a new realist-poetic order. Visconti's static group shots oscillate between

**Figure 14.5** Conclusive *tableau* of the anchovy sale, *La terra trema* (Luchino Visconti, 1948, frame enlargement).

the two photographic genres, seeing one (the documentary) in terms of the other (the affective narrativizing of ties). The elegant blocking of actors among the architectural elements pertains to a deterministic outlook consistent with Visconti's theatricality. In a sense it serves to reconcile the *verista* and the Marxist conceptions of the inevitable outcome of social process: while in the former it is the return to an earlier order and in the latter it is a future revolutionary order that is bound to prevail, the deterministic suggestion of the decor allows Visconti to move from one to the other, complicating connotations in the process.

The *verista*-Naturalist notion of determinant cause-and-effect relations of milieu and character was akin, in Verga's thinking, to the ontology of photographic reproduction, whereby documentation from "a specific visual angle" not only inscribes the aspect by which we grasp phenomena, but accounts for and can thereby replace the denouement. Visconti's sense of the location as a fully controlled and contained space correlates to this deterministic conception of narrative and image. It is applied, we have seen, to the interior and built spaces of the town, but it is also at work, most daringly, in the use of exterior natural spaces grasped as stage-sets. In the desire for the perfectly controlled *mise-en-scène*, Visconti defied the heterogeneity of the location and, as Francesco Rosi recounts, even the contingent moods of the sea. A month passed before the shooting of the opening sequence – the fishermen returning from sea at dawn – was complete, as Visconti waited for perfect weather, light, and marine conditions, for the obedience of the sea itself to the exacting demands of the filmmaker. We witness here the process of filmmaking, as such, coming to constitute a mythicized creative moment when, as under the touch of Prospero, the island and the sea are forced to yield their imaginative burden. Clearly, the *verista* will to photographic-indexical "truth" and the realist depiction of quotidian detail in a quasi-documentary project were altogether permeated by Visconti's rich, controlled orchestration of materials, voices, places. These – while, in a sense, derived from actuality and drawing on visual and sociological data of documentary import – were designed to yield to a dominating artistic will, a firm vision that grasps them as ready materials for its own use in a theatrical chorale.

The accumulative effect of exterior panning and traveling shots delineates the topography's near and distant parts as interlocked centripetal spaces modeled, once again, on theatrical *tableaux*, with or without actors. And, just as the interior *tableaux* echo the delineation and containment of the film frame itself, so the theatricality of the natural landscape does not emerge as a random effect, but as the setting-up of a stage that bestows upon this world a sense of spatial determination and dramatic necessity. No differentiation here between landscape and the representation of landscape as image and discourse. The natural landscape of Aci Trezza participates in Visconti's choral spatiality: its forms, its proclivity, its prospects are made to appear *as if* they themselves direct the camera's framing and movement, its passages from one deliberate composition to another. The town in its entirety and its natural environment thus emerge as a set, a studio-stage, properly called in Italian *teatro di posa*.[35]

A succession of slow, wide panoramic shots over the landscape in the gradually increasing light of early dawn opens the film, under the credits. The camera finally rests as it comes to enframe the approaching fishing boats returning with their nightly burden between two of the *Faraglioni* (figure 14.6). These are the Rocks of the Cyclops that punctuate the curved coastline, harboring Aci Trezza's small fishing port and defining its view as if in parenthetical enclosure. The horizontal row of boat-lanterns may be seen as footlights in this theatrical set-up of the overture, as the light rises on the view of the small Sicilian town. Embraced by the easternmost slopes of Etna, the town descends, directing the look toward the perpendicular basalt rocks scattered along this coast – rocks that extend the volcanic embrace of the rough landscape. The monolithic *Faraglioni* may well have been perceived by a director immersed in the world of the theater as the *coulisses*, or the *paraskenia* of the classical open-air theater, the side scenery projecting frontally on both sides of the stage, concealing its wings as they define the site of dramatic action.[36]

As one acquires a sense of this place in the course of the film, one learns that this is the camera's most emblematic grasp of the undulation of the coastline and the *Faraglioni*, which appear in the film repeatedly from a limited variety of angles, but always referring back to this initial theatrical enframing. The natural landscape is made to interiorize the space of Aci Trezza and the cinematic location in its entirety. The camera obeys these apparent "dictates" of the topography; it will not leave these defined spaces

**Figure 14.6** Theatrically enframed view of Aci Trezza, *La terra trema* (Luchino Visconti, 1948, frame enlargement).

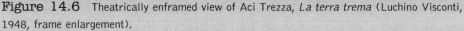

of social interaction within the town.[37] Against the dominant sense of enclosure, the comings and goings of characters – as if to the non-space of a backstage – punctuate the film: the fishermen's brief arrest, 'Ntoni's business in the Catania bank, the grandfather's move to the hospital, Lucia's disappearance. In response to the topography, as well, the camera simulates the position of a spectator in a vast theater, specifically the Greek or Hellenistic open theater, typically overlooking the stage below while backed by mountain slopes and the town.[38] The terraced alleys, sectioning the town's concave, tiered layout, descend toward the piazza overlooking the beach and the small fishing port. These are the sites of public action and exchange where the fishermen weave their nets and negotiate with the wholesalers. The town as a whole projects, then, toward this stage whose extension is the Ionian Sea, itself enframed by the *paraskenia* of the volcanic rocks. The natural landscape and its marine horizon are thus grasped as part of the town's theatrical layout, crystallized out of the materials and rhythms of the location. Like the architecture of classical theater, so Visconti's camera leads the eye via the angle and enclosure of descending tiers toward the orchestra below, commanding the view of the stage, echoing and complementing the landscape, bringing together culture and nature in dramatic reciprocity. Some Hellenistic cities have themselves been figured as great theaters, with mountains pressing up behind, while dramatic panoramas open before them, projecting across the Mediterranean landscape toward the sea.[39] In this way, the town embodies and articulates its site, figuring it as an intelligible entity with dramatic, anthropomorphic features. In a sense, its landscape comes to take the place of a Greek chorus, constituting a resonant spatiality in which the drama unfolds – a spatiality at once exteriorized yet as fully determined as a set. Its aesthetic is as fundamental to the film's ideology of representation as any character's action or narrative denouement.

Visconti, we have seen, was aware of the classical suggestiveness of this landscape; its theatricality must have appealed to him in this period, the inception of his work as director and designer for the stage, when he was experimenting with the spatial definition of the theater proper.[40] The choral landscape of *La terra trema* is distinct, yet its theatricality may be seen to prefigure Visconti's later film work, not quite contradicting but rather inflecting his exploration of cinema's realist impulse.[41] Following its opening plunge into an opera stage, *Senso*'s shots of a resonant, nocturnal Venice suggest a comparable identification of a theatrical space in the actual location. *White Nights*'s Livorno, replicated within a studio as an integral environment complete with canals and bridges, calls attention to theatrical machinery in panning shots that link disparate times and places in a simulated revolving stage. *La terra trema*'s cinematographic grasp of the location as already in itself enframed suggests a conception of nature as a contained, determinant, humanized stage – and a conception of reality as itself such a set. The movie camera, purporting in the *verista* tradition to register "as they are" human and social phenomena, the milieu's inscription of fate – as if these preceded consciousness, ideology, the act of representation – exhibits these conditions as natural. It finds in Aci Trezza a particular susceptibility to such a vision: an immanent figuration of nature even in its wildest aspect seems possible here.[42] *La terra trema*'s choral theatricality appears thus as *already* scripted into the location. Still committed to the Neorealist faith in the integrity of an authentic profilmic reality, the film betrays, like Verga's photographs, a need to anchor the aesthetic and ideological coherence of the work in an enhanced sense of nature's own participation in the production of art.

It is not, we have observed, direct influence that describes the relation between Visconti's adaptation and Verga's photographic project, but rather an oblique analogy. The seamless binding of photographic documentation with a determinate aesthetic and ideology, inflects Verga's realism and its claim to knowledge of the world. Visconti's crafting of his materials, most astonishingly in his molding of the actual location, adapts the chorale of *verità e poesia* that permeates the literary text, a chorale adapted, as well, by Verga's photography. Returning to the sites designated by the novel with a documentary film crew and no proper script, settling in Aci Trezza for some eight months, transforming the location of *I malavoglia* into an elaborate set in which the large, slow motions of the novel will be rehearsed, Visconti produces a work that quite exceeds the concern with the present state of Sicily as well as the practical needs of the Italian Communist Party. In the late 1940s, in the midst of a general effort of recovery from the devastation of Fascism and war, in the revival of art's nostalgia for a restored, unfractured reality that survived it all, we thus find Visconti exploring the foundations of realism, rehearsing a mythical grasp of nature as already humanized and coherent, amenable to the work of a camera. Even in this most humble location Visconti locates the forms that render the world as a winged, choral stage: a *tableau* not quite penetrable, but drawn to the measure of a screen.

---
## Notes
---

1   Barbaro's formulation concerns a silent film of 1914. Cited in Orio Caldiron (ed.), *Il lungo viaggio del cinema italiano: antologia di "Cinema" 1936–1943* (Padua: Marsilio, 1965), p. 423. Unless otherwise noted, translations in this chapter are mine, with the help of Paolo Barlera.

2   André Bazin, "The Ontology of the Photographic Image," in *What is Cinema?*, vol. 1, trans. Hugh Gray (Berkeley, CA: University of California Press, 1967), p. 15.

3   In English translation, Verga's novel also has the alternative title *The House by the Medlar Tree*. See Judith Landry's translation (1985; New York: Hippocrene, 1987).

4   Though distinctions between the practice of French Naturalism and of Italian *verismo* can certainly be made, these are not pertinent to the concerns of this chapter which focuses, in what follows, on select characteristics of Verga's *verismo* that were important to Neorealism.

5   Several excellent English-language commentaries on this film offer analyses of its relation to Verga's texts. See the chapter devoted to it by Millicent Marcus in *Filmmaking by the Book: Italian Cinema and Literary Adaptation* (Baltimore, MD: The Johns Hopkins University Press, 1993), pp. 25–44; and P. Adams Sitney's discussion in *Vital Crises in Italian Cinema: Iconography, Stylistics, Politics* (Austin: University of Texas Press, 1995), pp. 58–78.

6   Rosi's account of the production constitutes the Introduction to the published script in Luchino Visconti, *La terra trema* (Bologna: Cappelli Editore, 1977), pp. 9–17.

7   Alessandro Blasetti's cinema, specifically *Terra madre* (1931) and *1860* (1934), was the best that this rural ideology produced. The influence of Blasetti's work on Visconti is worthy of a separate consideration.

8   Biographical materials are largely drawn from Gianni Rondolino, *Luchino Visconti* (Turin: UTET, 1981).

9   As told by Gianni Puccini in "Storia di *Cinema*," in Caldiron, *Il lungo viaggio del cinema italiano*, p. lxxxiii.

10   Giovanni Verga, "Gramigna's Mistress," in *The She-wolf and Other Stories*, trans. Giovanni Cecchetti (Berkeley, CA: University of California Press, 1962), pp. 86–8.

11   Romano Luperini, *Simbolo e construzione allegorica in Verga* (Bologna: il Mulino, 1989).

12   From Verga's preface to *I malavoglia*, trans. Judith Landry (New York: Hippocrene, 1987), p. xviii (emphasis added).

13   Letter to Luigi Capuana, March 14, 1879, in Giovanni Verga, *Specchio e realtà*, ed. Wladimiro Settimelli (Rome: Magma, 1976), p. 174 (emphasis added).

14   Letter to Capuana, May 29, 1881, in *Specchio*, p. 175.

15   Verga must have encountered members of the *Macchiaioli* during his frequent visits to Florence beginning in 1865, followed by his residence there between 1869 and 1872. It is

there, as well, that he strikes up the friendship with Capuana. See "Chronology," in Verga, *I malavoglia*, p. iv.

16  From an 1852 *Vocabolario universale della lingua italiana*, cited by Norma Broude in *The Macchiaioli: Italian Painters of the Nineteenth Century* (New Haven, CT: Yale University Press, 1987), p. 4 (emphasis added). On the optical experiments of the *Macchiaioli*, see Broude, pp. 62 and 107. Consider, in particular, the example of such artists as Telemaco Signorini and Odoardo Borrani.

17  It is, of course, Verga's contemporary C. S. Peirce who categorized the indexical sign, using the photograph as one of his examples, in "Logic as Semiotic: The Theory of Signs," in Justus Buchler (ed.), *Philosophical Writings of Peirce* (New York: Dover, 1955), pp. 98–119.

18  Verga, "Gramigna," pp. 86–8.

19  Verga dedicated a copy of *I malavoglia* to Capuana, the "illustrious photographer" who had introduced him to photography. See the "Nota Bio-bibliografica" in Verga's *Tutte le novelle*, vol. 1, ed. Marco Buzzi Maresca (Milan: Mursia, 1986), p. 31.

20  The photographs have been published in *Verga Fotografo*, ed. Giovanni Garra Agosta (Catania: Giuseppe Maimone Editore, 1991). Compared with Verga's 400 extant photographs, Zola produced several thousand exposures with no fewer than ten cameras during the eight years between 1894 and his death in 1902. See François Emile-Zola and Massin, *Zola Photographer*, trans. Liliane Emery Tuck (New York: Seaver Books/Henry Holt, 1988), pp. 3–4.

21  I rely here on Roland Barthes's seminal analysis in "The Photographic Message," in *Image–Music–Text*, ed. and trans. Stephen Heath (New York: Hill and Wang, 1977), pp. 15–31.

22  See Gino Raya, *Verga e il cinema* (Rome: Herder Editore, 1984).

23  Luperini, *Simbolo e construzione allegorica*, p. 129.

24  Mario Alicata and Giuseppe De Santis, "Truth and Poetry: Verga and the Italian Cinema," in *Springtime in Italy: A Reader on Neo-Realism*, ed. and trans. David Overbey (Hamden, CT: Archon, 1979), pp. 134–5.

25  From the second part of Mario Alicata and Giuseppe De Santis's article, "Ancora di Verga e del cinema italiano," reprinted in Caldiron, *Il lungo viaggio del cinema italiano*, p. 446.

26  Alicata's text of 1942 is cited in Rondolino, *Luchino Visconti*, p. 98. His example of lyricizing – and thereby politically suspect – realism is Robert Flaherty's *Man of Aran*.

27  Luchino Visconti, "Tradizione e invenzione," cited in Rondolino, *Luchino Visconti*, p. 92. The *Faraglioni* are the perpendicular volcanic rocks scattered opposite the shore of Aci Trezza. I return to them below.

28  Gianni Puccini recounts this initial inspiration of the old postcard as having occurred just before Italy's entry into the war; he cites Visconti's statement: "dal paesaggio di quella cartolina mi nacque più tardi la voglia della *Terra trema*," in Caldiron, *Il lungo viaggio del cinema italiano*, p. lxxxiii.

29  "Tradizione e invenzione," quoted in Rondolino, *Luchino Visconti*, p. 91. I have added quotation marks to the phrase Visconti cites from Manzoni's description of the Lombard sky in Bruce Penman's translation, Alessandro Manzoni, *The Betrothed* (London: Penguin Books, 1972), p. 324. Millicent Marcus (*Filmmaking by the Book*, p. 26) cites Visconti's text, alongside Alicata and De Santis's writing on Verga, to support her analysis of the ideological contradictions at the heart of *verismo* and Neorealism.

30  The cultural connotations of the eastern shores of Sicily are numerous. We might count among them Antonello's *Crucifixion* (c.1460–5) against the background of Messina. Most eloquent

among Grand Tourists is Goethe whose interest in volcanic phenomena drew him to Aci Trezza; see *Italian Journey 1786–1788*, trans. W. H. Auden and Elizabeth Mayer (San Francisco: North Point Press, 1982). The consciousness of a tradition of representation free from the pretense of supplanting it under the imperatives of the moment is, one might say, the mark of Visconti's mature artistic awareness. Contrary to some views, I would claim that an approach that professes to expose a "reality behind the myth," independent of the layering of preceding representations, is often the more naïve and deluded one.

31   This is the title of Antonio Gramsci's seminal essay of the early 1920s. See the translation in *The Modern Prince and Other Writings*, trans. Louis Marks (New York: International Publishers, 1983), pp. 28–51.

32   Cf. Marcus, *Filmmaking by the Book*, pp. 38–9; Sitney, *Vital Crises in Italian Cinema*, pp. 72–7.

33   Accounts of the altering and interlacing of spaces may be found in Michele Mancini and Fiametta Sciacca (eds), *La città-set: La terra trema di Luchino Visconti. Reperti per una archeologia del cinema* (Rome: Theorema Edizioni, 1981). Rosi's account is in the introduction to Visconti, *La terra trema*, pp. 9–17. Visconti's sketches of settings and props may also be consulted here; see Lino Miccichè (ed.), *La terra trema di Luchino Visconti: Analisi di un capolavoro*, 2nd edn (Turin: Associazione Philip Morris Progetto Cinema, Centro Sperimentale di Cinematografia, Lindau, 1994).

34   I borrow this term from Bazin's characterization of theatrical, as juxtaposed with "centrifugal," cinematic space in "Theater and Cinema, Part Two," *What is Cinema?*, vol 1, pp. 95–124.

35   Cf. Allessandro Cappabianca, in Mancini and Sciacca (eds), *La città-set*, pp. 77–8: "The whole construction, in its globality of interiors and exteriors, places itself as a *total interior* (thus *studio*, thus *stage*) as opposed to the *radical exteriority represented by the sea* . . . It should then be the presence of the sea, of the "exterior-sea" set, that makes Aci Trezza in its entirety emerge as an interior, that renders it not only a set, but indeed a studio, a stage." Cappabianca does not associate the effect of interiority with Visconti's camerawork that, as I suggest, renders even the sea and, basically, reality as such, as a coherent and determinant theatrical space. This distinct conception is fundamental, in my mind, to Visconti's aesthetic and ideology at large.

36   While my evocation of the classical theater is deliberate, one may also consider here the stagecraft of Northern Italian Baroque theater; for example, the marine backdrops of designer Francesco Guitti where perspectival effect is enhanced by similar rocks that enframe the horizon. See Janet Southorn, *Power and Display in the Seventeenth Century: The Arts and their Patrons in Modena and Ferrara* (Cambridge: Cambridge University Press, 1988), pp. 133–9 and plates 99–111.

37   There are only two exceptions to this rule (thus proved): in a startling shift we are offered in those instances return shots, of sorts, from the viewpoint of the marine horizon, revealing the coast as a distant background: first in the celebratory image of 'Ntoni and his brothers fishing for the first time as their own masters. In the film's closing, a similar shot of liberating motion at the open sea is repeated, now with added pathos of 'Ntoni's gaining of class consciousness, despite individual failure and family tragedy.

38   Unlike Roman amphitheaters surrounded on all sides by tiers and stage buildings, the Greek and Hellenistic theaters project toward the stage, which is at least in part open to the landscape beyond.

39  Vincent Scully describes the remains of Greek and Hellenistic theaters scattered in comparable southern European sites and along this very coast. See *The Earth, the Temple and the Gods: Greek Sacred Architecture* (New Haven, CT: Yale University Press, 1962), pp. 192–4. John Brinckerhoff Jackson's "Landscape as Theater" also suggests the centrality of the theater to our grasp of the landscape in *The Necessity of Ruins and Other Topics* (Amherst: University of Massachusetts Press, 1980), pp. 67–75. Interestingly, in obeying the theatrical projection of the view, Visconti keeps the spectator's back to Etna, which must be visible from any point along these shores but makes only few ghostly appearances in the film, most prominently as a painted backdrop in the family photograph discussed above.

40  Following some unrealized plans to produce plays "off stage" by making use of garden vistas, courtyards, and *palazzi* windows as enframing devices, Visconti constructed in 1949 for a production of *Troilus and Cressida* a vast three-dimensional model of Troy for an outdoor staging of the Shakespeare play in the Boboli Gardens. This was a miniature city complete with walls, gates, towers, hanging bridges in rounded details, and a shifting perspective which allowed for this integral set to be seen from numerous points of view. The ambition of this experiment and its spectacular results (not to mention cost) were rather bold in the era of humble postwar productions. This "stretching" of theater sets toward the continuous, open, penetrable space available in principle for a film shot on location, is a matching reversal of *La terra trema*'s landscape grasped as a theater. See Luchino Visconti, *Il mio teatro*, vol. 1: *1936–1953*, ed. Caterina d'Amico de Carvalho and Renzo Renzi (Bologna: Cappelli, 1979).

41  My undertanding of Visconti diverges here from the view of Geoffrey Nowell-Smith, who posits the theatrical strain of *La terra trema* irreconcilably against its realist project. See his *Visconti* (Garden City, NY: Doubleday, 1968), p. 53.

42  Such a sense of landscape is suggested by Adrian Stokes's remark that, just as human works organize and resolve the Mediterranean landscape, so "upon this sea and land the creations of men look natural, acceptable to the play of Nature," in *Stones of Rimini* (1934; New York: Schocken, 1969), p. 64. In "Visconti a tourné *La Terre tremble*," *L'Ecran Français* 176 (November 9, 1948), 5, Jean-Charles Tacchella exhibits great foresight at a time when critics still measured the film by moralistic dichotomies: "For the author of *La terra trema* 'life is a work of art' ... Having chosen to 'take nature as a model' ... Visconti seeks to poeticize this nature." This before Visconti went on to explore even more boldly just what a notion of "life as a work of art" might entail in the cinema and beyond.

# Chapter 15

# The Devil's Parody

## Horace McCoy's Appropriation and Refiguration of Two Hollywood Musicals

## Charles Musser

> Have you ever noticed how many films are adaptations? Adaptations are the lifeblood of the film and television business.
>
> Linda Seger, *The Art of Adaptation*[1]

> These novels are a kind of Devil's parody of the movies . . .
>
> Edmund Wilson, *Classics and Commercials*[2]

**1.1** The Hollywood novel and the screenwriting manual boast a shared history. Both have typically been written by those claiming to be Hollywood insiders, whose access gives them behind-the-scenes insights. How-to manuals claim to offer the truth as they reveal little-known tricks of the trade. In explicating the ways of Hollywood (particularly its ways of telling stories), they at least imply that this way of life is "good work if you can get it." They may warn readers of the difficulties that they face, but the very act of writing these manuals presupposes a degree of optimism: that it is possible for readers to succeed in the film industry with talent, perseverance, and effective guidance. When it comes to Hollywood novels, the situation is generally the reverse. Richard Fine has detailed the ways in which those East Coast writers who came to Hollywood in the late 1920s and early 1930s felt profoundly alienated as they abruptly lost control over the fruits of their labor.[3] The Hollywood novel was a way for these writers to reassert their artistic integrity outside and in many ways against the Hollywood system. Written against the boss (though McCoy and others were always eager to sell the movie rights back to the studio), Hollywood novels generally offer a highly jaundiced view of the moving picture world out of which they come. (F. Scott Fitzgerald's *The Last Tycoon* [1940] with its celebration of a studio head modeled after Irving Thalberg is the exception. Far more typical is Budd Schulberg's *What Makes Sammy Run?* [1941] with its cynical, angry view of a system that ends up turning out films like sausages.) Taking the form of literary exposés, at least in certain periods these books spoke truth to power, or claimed to. Certainly this was the case with Horace McCoy's two Hollywood novels, *They Shoot Horses, Don't They?* (1935) and *I Should Have Stayed Home* (1938).

**1.2** The studio-era classical Hollywood film industry was a vacuum cleaner that sucked up stories from a wide variety of cultural practices and turned them into movies: plays, short stories, novels, news items, earlier films, and even comic strips were raw material for studio recycling, cannibalization, and adaptation. The largely uni-directional flow of narrative properties to Hollywood, which characterized the studio era, was due to a confluence of factors.[4] Some of these cultural forms (for example, short stories) offered a comparatively cheap source of story ideas. Novels and plays were generally more expensive, and the most expensive offered prestige and pre-sold popularity.[5] One exception to this general pattern of adaptation involved the novelizations of movies. This degraded literary form, of low prestige and modest remuneration, was one of many genres in the vast array of Hollywood ephemera.[6] Hollywood novelizations are thus closely related to fan magazines: indeed, the first fan magazine, *Motion Picture Story Magazine* (started in 1912) offered its readers short story versions of films. Both novelizations of Hollywood films and fan magazines, which frequently published short stories about Hollywood, had much in common with Hollywood novels. All three are nonfilmic cultural forms that owe their very existence to Hollywood. These affinities are particularly evident with McCoy's *They Shoot Horses, Don't They?* (1935) and *I Should Have Stayed Home* (1938), which cannibalize and borrow from – one is tempted to use the word "adapt" – popular Hollywood films for their own purposes. Aligned with the lowly novelizations of feature films, McCoy's efforts swam against the more respectable flow of literature-to-film adaptation. McCoy's embrace of a nonliterary form was an act of nihilism and rage that echoes the novels' narratives, but he used this process for serious artistic purposes.

## The Cultural Life of Adaptation

Most Academy Award- and Emmy Award-winning films are adaptations. Consider these amazing statistics:

*85% of all Academy Award-winning Best Pictures are adaptations.

Linda Seger, *The Art of Adaptation*[7]

"I'm working on a football story and I'm running a couple of college pictures in the projection room this afternoon. Just to make sure it isn't too similar."

"Which I suppose is a polite way of saying you're looking for something you can lift," I said.

He seemed actually pleased that I saw through his feeble euphemism. He grinned. "You'll be all right out here," he said. "You learn fast."

Budd Schulberg, *What Makes Sammy Run?*[8]

2.1 Adaptation, both as a poetics (a way of making films) and as a reading strategy (a way of interpreting them), has been an area of renewed interest in cultural studies (film, media, and literary studies in particular). This renaissance is doubtless tied to the importance of intertextuality as a theoretical and historical area of inquiry. To shock and so revive what has been widely recognized as, at least until recently, a moribund field of inquiry, scholars have retheorized and reconceptualized the topic in substantively new ways. Robert Stam has been a leader in this process of revitalization, providing us with liberatory ways of reimagining adaptation. As he suggests, "Adaptation theory has available a whole constellation of tropes – translation, reading, dialogization, cannibalization, transmutation, transfiguration, and signifying – each of which sheds light on a different dimension of adaptation."[9] This has proved invaluable as a way to think about texts (films, novels, and so forth) in relation to their antecedents. Nonetheless, we must also ask ourselves: what are the appropriate limits to adaptation theories? Adaptation involves a sustained relationship between a cultural work and its source or "hypotext." This relationship must not only be sustained and in certain respects systematic, but of a particular kind. Because adaptation is such a central creative process (if screenwriting guru Linda Seger is to be believed), its theorization is important not only in the world of academia but in the broader worlds of culture and commerce. There are other less literary or theoretical ways of thinking about this problem. One involves the nitty-gritty issues of copyright and legal ownership.

In the present intellectual climate, where intertextuality has become of crucial methodological importance for cultural theorists and historians, critics can be tempted to evoke the process of adaptation almost any time they uncover an intertexual reference. Taken to a daring and apparently logical extreme, intertextuality and adaptation are categories that become interchangeable. This has potential consequences in the real world, for media conglomerates are clearly eager to extend the reach of adaptation to include a wide range of textual referencing just as they have sought to extend the time frame covered by copyright. These enhance company revenues. Indeed, as cultural theorists have been busy pushing the traditional boundaries of adaptation theory, so have corporate lawyers.

If adaptation is increasingly understood as an overarching Ur category or process, we must then begin to think more carefully about its limits. What should and what should not be considered adaptation? Dudley Andrew has pointed to some ways to limit the domain of adaptation as a process: "The explicit, foregrounded relation of a cinematic text to a well-constructed original text from which it derives and which in some sense it strives to reconstruct provides the analyst with a clear and useful 'laboratory' condition."[10] Although the notion of "striving to reconstruct" might narrow the domain of adaptation too much, it nonetheless provides an important brake on a too-broad use of the term. Citation, limited (or literal) quotation, allusion, evocation are not, in fact, forms of adaptation as we should strictly define the term. They mobilize connections between two texts that are insufficiently sustained to involve adaptation. On the other hand, adaptation may involve a less reverent, more ambivalent, or cynical view toward the source material.

For many filmmakers, a source is merely that – a source, a convenient starting-point. One thinks of the process of adaptation depicted in Nicholas Ray's *In a Lonely Place*

(1950) as well as the actual adaptation of the Dorothy B. Hughes novel of that name (1947). Ray's screenwriter, played by Humphrey Bogart, does not even bother to read the novel before beginning to write his script. He listens to a hat-check girl recount its highlights. The relationship between Hughes's novel and Ray's film is far more complex than the screenwriter's attitude toward his source material might suggest. Both works are set in Los Angeles, but the novel's Dickson Steele is a sociopathic killer posing as a writer, while the film's Dixon Steele is a veteran Hollywood screenwriter burdened with a temper, wartime past, and self-destructive personality. (Their formal first names are spelled somewhat differently, though they have the same nickname – Dix.) The Bogart character is haunted not only by the police but also by the novel. His antecedent becomes the screenwriter's ghost-like doppelgänger.

The fact of adaptation can put two texts in a complex and rewarding relationship. Nonetheless, as a source is reimagined, various possible attitudes – as well as operations – can loosen the bonds that make one indebted to the other. In some respects, there can be a fine line between adaptations that are aggressive and those that are indifferent to their sources. Displacement, condensation, elaboration, and refiguration are among the operations that stretch these connections. Such operations are to some degree inevitable in any process of adaptation. Yet when they are pursued with casual indifference, the random or noncoherent nature of these changes can mean that the claim "x is an adaptation of y" becomes less and less interesting and important. In a Lonely Place is an interesting case because the film depicts a situation where the writer violates the wishes of the producer and is indifferent to (or rather contemptuous of) the source material. The film itself may appear to be indifferent and yet, in truth, it is both aggressive and, in some sense, systematic in its reworking. Its strategies of adaptation are anything but casual. In a Lonely Place is about the act of writing and other creative, imaginative acts such that the attenuated relationship between film and source generates powerful overtonal meanings. In the gap between what it seems to say, and what it actually does say, there is a powerful artistic statement. We can find aspects of this indirection at work in McCoy's novels as well.

**2.2** Certain sustained relationships between one text and its antecedent, such as parody, are generally not considered to be "adaptations." They try to make fun of the original text, to mock it. If parodies do not always destroy the originary text completely, they at least deflate it. When we think of Woody Allen's Everything You Wanted to Know About Sex (1972) as an adaptation of the best-selling sex manual of that name (for which he bought the rights), the result is comic. It is funny because the results mock or parody the process of adaptation itself. It forcefully presents this film as the definitive adaptation of a best-seller, only to show that this assertion is ridiculously inappropriate or empty.

Is a given work of art an adaptation of another art work or is it drawing on the prior text in a related but ultimately different way? The answer to such a question may not be easily resolved. It is often the gray areas between adaptation and evocation, generic similarity, parody, or critique that often intrigue us the most. Is Sergio Giral's The Other

*Francisco* (1972) an adaptation of Cuba's first anti-slavery novel, Anselmo Suárez y Romero's *Francisco: The Sugar-mill or the Delights of the Canefields* (1839) as Robert Stam suggests, or is it something else? Because the filmmaker seeks to ''deconstruct'' rather than ''reconstruct'' – to turn the novel inside out and deflate its sentimental pretensions – the film may be closer to parody than to traditional methods of adaptation. The film evokes the novel, not to embrace it but to interrogate it.

Because Suárez y Romero's novel is in the public domain, we do not have to be unduly concerned with defining the relationship between it and Giral's film with legalistic precision. It can be immensely useful to think of the relationship between the two texts as one characterized by adaptation. The assertion of adaptation activates a relationship between a text and its antecedent(s). This enables the scholar (or spectator/reader) to emphasize the parallels in order to explore the differences. It becomes a form of play, of liberation from too-familiar ways of analyzing. These issues, however, have had different implications with Alice Randall's novel *The Wind Done Gone*, a re-imagining of *Gone with the Wind* (1939). If this is an ''adaptation,'' which the Margaret Mitchell estate has argued that it is, then the estate could have blocked its publication by legal means. Because of its far-reaching deconstruction (labeled ''a parody'') of Mitchell's novel (and the David O. Selznick film adaptation), the courts decided that it did not violate copyright. If it can be productive to think of a film as a kind of adaptation even when it is not, sometimes – given copyright laws – it is necessary to take what we now commonly call an adaptation and imagine it as something else.

**2.3** Genre is another factor that limits the domain of adaptation. If one looks narrowly or naïvely at two films in the same genre, it may seem that one film is ''stealing'' a great deal from another. When examined generically, these correspondences are revealed to be less unique, less specific, less sustained, and so less close. As a result, the relationship between the two works may not be best – or most appropriately – characterized as one of adaptation.

Generic considerations are among the more respectable practices to limit the field of adaptation. Film cycles, studio style, fashion, fads, imitations, scriptwriting by committee, a profound absence of creativity, all haunt both Hollywood and the process of adaptation. Is ''adaptation'' truly the ''lifeblood'' of the movies or has the term been used to mask a wide range of less attractive and even more pervasive practices that were (and are today) routine in Hollywood? Whether these represent a cultural apocalypse or ''the genius of the system'' is an evaluation that remains much in debate. For our purposes, we merely note that many of these practices inform (or haunt) a full understanding of *They Shoot Horses, Don't They?*

At the very least it can be heuristic to think of Horace McCoy's novels *They Shoot Horses, Don't They?* (1935) and *I Should Have Stayed Home* (1938) as adaptations of Hollywood films. Certainly, to the extent to which these stories and the ways they are told often evoke processes of adaptations, McCoy encourages us to think along these lines. Nonetheless, Horace McCoy's estate owes Warner Brothers nothing for copyright infringement even though *They Shoot Horses, Don't They?* appropriates numerous elements from at least two of that company's films. In the end, its engagement with these films is perhaps something else: refigurations of tropes, characters, star personas, visual symbols, and figures of speech that reside not only in these films but in Hollywood culture more generally. Looked at from a slightly different perspective, McCoy's novel employs Hollywood's well-established practices of cannibalizing, recycling, and reworking elements from film to film. Max Horkheimer and Theodor Adorno would identify and condemn this "constant reproduction of the same thing" in their essay "The Culture Industry: Enlightenment as Mass Deception."[11] Material is endlessly recycled, recombined, and repeated so "nothing changes" and "nothing unsuitable will appear." McCoy understood not only the nature of this repetition but its radical potential, and he reprised or borrowed materials from films while giving them an acerbic, unexpected twist. Put another way, in writing novels about Hollywood, McCoy employed the methods of Hollywood against itself.

Charles Musser

## Sources and Intertexts

> Literally hundreds of persons who are unable to imagine plots or who, at least, are unable to imagine plots worth while, turn to adaptations that they may become participants in the wealth that is supposed to be gained through photoplay work.
>
> Epes Winthrop Sargent, *Technique of the Photoplay* [12]

> Talents can get you just so far . . . Then you got to start using your head.
>
> Budd Schulberg, *What Makes Sammy Run?*[13]

**3.1** Horace McCoy's *They Shoot Horses, Don't They?* and *I Should Have Stayed Home* use similar approaches to refigure high-profile Hollywood films of the 1930s and perform radical acts of "adaptation" that become forms of demystificatory critique.[14] *They Shoot Horses, Don't They?* reworks *42nd Street* (Lloyd Bacon, 1933) and *Gold Diggers of '33* (Melvyn LeRoy, 1933), while *I Should Have Stayed Home* does much the same for *A Star is Born* (William Wellman, 1937). These films were box-office hits: *42nd Street* and *Gold Diggers of '33* were the second and third top grossing pictures of 1933, while *A Star is Born* became the top grossing film of 1937 even as it was nominated for numerous Academy Awards.[15] Perhaps it is not entirely coincidental that these films were already part of an intertextual web based on a succession of adaptations and cannibalizations. As J. Hoberman details, *42nd Street* (the film) was an adaptation of the novel of that name by Bradford Ropes, though Rick Altman maintains that its plot was derived from *On with the Show* (1929).[16] In a clear case of cross-fertilization, *Gold Diggers of '33* recycled elements of *42nd Street* in combination with another, earlier Warner Brothers' film: *Gold Diggers of Broadway* (Roy Del Ruth, 1929). *Gold Diggers of Broadway* was

Chapter 15

a sound version of *The Gold Diggers* (Harry Beaumont, 1923). All three films were thus indebted to a David Belasco play, *The Gold Diggers: A Comedy in Three Acts* (written by Avery Hopwood), which was a Broadway hit in 1919. *A Star is Born*, which somewhat ironically won the Academy Award for "Best Original Story," is a reworking of *What Price Hollywood?* (George Cukor, 1932) and to a greater or lesser extent, a *film à clef*, incorporating incidents of Hollywood life. *I Should Have Stayed Home* is not only a systematic refiguration of *A Star is Born*, it recycles and reworks numerous elements of McCoy's *They Shoot Horses*. Drawing on some real-life elements from the author's own experiences, it was part of McCoy own literary cycle as well. Certainly, the intersection of multiple sources makes faithfulness to, or straightforward adaptation of, any one source more problematic. (Cross-fertilization and multiple sources force a more complex, attenuated notion of adaptation. In a culture that privileges monogamy, faithfulness to more than one source is an oxymoron.)

**3.2** In interpreting a film or novel, critics and historians must consider the ways in which that work has been constructed by or through its intertexts. Sources are often but not always active intertexts, just as there are many intertexts that are not sources. We can ask if a text's relationship to its source(s) is more or less explicitly acknowledged and how important this relationship appears to be for the spectator seeing the film or reading the novel. For example, credits clearly indicate that the movie *42nd Street* was an adaptation of the novel of that name by Bradford Ropes. Nonetheless, criticism of the time and subsequent scholarship suggest that knowledge of Ropes's novel would be unlikely to significantly enhance our understanding or enjoyment of the film. Ropes's novel was neither a bestseller nor a critical success. The fact that few copies of the novel survive tends only to confirm its negligibility. In his study of *42nd Street*, J. Hoberman gives us an interesting case study of the way in which a Hollywood studio went about the process of adaptation. He also demonstrates how a familiarity with the novel does little to enhance our appreciation of the film.

Many Hollywood film adaptations functioned quite differently from that of *42nd Street*, often by operating simultaneously on two levels. A general audience can view a given film as a more or less self-sufficient text, independent of any familiarity with its source. Indeed, many regular moviegoers consider other kinds of intertextual relationship to be much more compelling; for instance, generic considerations or the prior films of its stars. In others instances, viewers who lack direct acquaintance with a film's source may see the picture as an opportunity to gain useful cultural knowledge of its prestigious antecedent. (This is one reason why the issue of faithfulness and accuracy haunts studies of film adaptation.) At the same time, some of these pictures also address or acknowledge audiences that are already familiar with the source material. Interviews with the director, studio publicity, and film criticism all informed prospective moviegoers that Ernst Lubitsch's *Lady Windermere's Fan* (Warner Bros, 1925) could be better savored if they had read or seen the Oscar Wilde play. Spectators were actively encouraged to compare Lubitsch's visual wit with Wilde's verbal wit. Rather than a naïve, self-enclosed viewing of the film, this required an active comparison between the film and its source. Likewise, numerous moviegoers would have seen *Gold Diggers of '33* only a few months after *42nd Street*. One pleasure in seeing that second film came through an appreciation of the numerous variations, inversions, substitutions, repetitions, and differences with its immediate predecessor.

Not all aspects of a work's intertextual references are made explicit. Sometimes the intertexts are purposefully concealed by the author(s) as a kind of inside joke or private pleasure.[17] Or a clue may be half hidden. Like a stone half-submerged by windblown sand, it awaits discovery. In some cases this discovery is never made before it is completely buried underneath the sands of passing time. That is, to abandon the metaphor, the passage of time often obscures key intertextual connections, which the historian can help retrieve or occasionally even discover. For instance, the delay in a film's release or a book's publication may efface these connections before they are ever made publicly. Given the various clues (or cues) in McCoy's novel, a reader might be expected to relate *They Shoot Horses, Don't They?* to Warner Brothers' backstage musicals *42nd Street* and *Gold Diggers of '33*. Nonetheless, given the delay in publication (though essentially completed by November 1933, the novel was not published until 1935), the ever-shifting matrices of ephemeral culture had changed sufficiently so that these connections were no longer evident. And literary critics did nothing to reclaim them. Perhaps they were uninterested. Because most literati did not consider movies to be significant cultural works, these sources or intertexts went either unrecognized or unreported. Literary critics have customarily understood a novel in relationship to other novels not in relation to films.

**3.3** Horace McCoy is a key figure in the emergence of that specialized genre of literature known as the Hollywood novel. *They Shoot Horses* and *I Should Have Stayed Home* were written and published before Nathaniel West's *The Day of the Locust* (1939) and Budd Schulberg's *What Makes Sammy Run* (1941).[18] These Hollywood novels require their own intertextual framework for understanding: one in which knowledge of stars, films, the movie business, and recent gossip are as important as serious literature. Literary critics look at Horace McCoy as a writer of short stories and novels, while traditional film scholars tend to look at him as a struggling actor and screenwriter, who wrote novels (when they mention him at all). Yet McCoy not only moved freely between the realm of literature and film, he also had important experiences in the theater. To understand his oeuvre (to use a now quaint phrase) and any individual work within it requires moving across these too familiar disciplinary boundaries. It is not insignificant that the two films that McCoy sought to engage, *42nd Street* and *Gold Diggers of '33*, are both about the theater.

Neglecting the relationship of a cultural artifact to its intertexts and sources can profoundly affect our understanding of that work's style as well as its meaning, scope, and ambition. It not only impoverishes our grasp of the artist's aspirations and achievements, it frequently distorts our understanding. The problem here is a basic but still familiar one. Period criticism promptly aligned McCoy's with the "hard-boiled" writings of James

Cain and Dashiell Hammett. Reviewing *They Shoot Horses, Don't They?* for *The New York Times*, Robert van Gelder predicted that it "will be seen as both the best and worst of the hard-boiled novels."[19] This framework for interpretation was reiterated by subsequent commentators. Even today, the most influential criticism of *They Shoot Horses* and *I Should Have Stayed Home* probably remains Edmund Wilson's essay "The Boys in the Back Room," written in 1940 and expanded with a postscript in 1941. Wilson and other critics before and since situate McCoy squarely in the "tough guy," "hard-boiled" school of writing. Wilson calls Cain and McCoy "the poets of the tabloid murder"; certainly, murder, death, and suicide permeate the novels of both writers. The emphasis is on action and society's underbelly. The writing is lean. John Thomas Sturak, whose dissertation remains the definitive biographical study of McCoy, finds Wilson's characterizations of McCoy's fiction often misleading, but acknowledges that his novels were "hard-boiled" if that meant that he wrote "In a terse, objective, impersonal and implicational style."[20] Sturak does note the flashback style, another feature of some hard-boiled fiction and much *film noir*, as well as the novel's repetitive, circular structure, which mimes the "merry-go-round" circularity of the marathon dance.[21] Yet, the novel's style is hardly objective or impersonal. It is, I will argue in the following pages, metaphorical and grotesque – a fact most clearly seen in the relationship of the novel to its film sources.

There is, therefore, a more innovative dimension to Edmund Wilson's commentary. In his brief survey of fiction by Hollywood writers, he focuses on James Cain (*The Postman Only Rings Twice* [1934], *Serenade* [1937]) and several of his contemporaries. Discussing Cain while throwing in Horace McCoy's *They Shoot Horses* and *I Should Have Stayed Home* for good measure, he remarks, "These novels are a kind of Devil's parody of the movies." He goes on to explain that "All the things that have been excluded by the Catholic censorship: sex debauchery, unpunished crime, sacrilege against the Church – Mr Cain has let loose in these stories with a gusto of pent-up ferocity that the reader cannot but share."[22] Moreover, he suggests that certain storytelling techniques endemic to Hollywood movies are mobilized in their novels. They turn the Hollywood-style story upside down and inside out. These novels mock the product of Hollywood itself, in terms of form and content.[23] And yet while Cain focused on those tawdry elements of Los Angeles other than Hollywood, McCoy took Tinseltown as his subject. When Wilson claimed that McCoy's novels only "trifle with the fringes of Hollywood,"[24] he missed the many literary clues that signaled otherwise.

**3.4** McCoy, an ex-journalist, short-story writer, and theater actor, had moved to Hollywood in 1931. After two years struggling to make a living as an actor and/or writer, he finally landed a job at Columbia Pictures, then little more than a poverty row studio. During this period he wrote short stories about Hollywood, including one on marathon dancing that survives in two versions neither of which was ever published. He also tried to turn the idea into a screenplay. According to Sturak, who has read these manuscripts, they were short and largely underdeveloped, though McCoy had come up with the book's title (*They Shoot Horses, Don't They?*) by late 1932. In the course of 1933–4, he radically expanded and reworked that story, turning it into the tour de force that was finally published as a short novel in 1935.[25]

Hollywood was a dream factory at a time when the American dream had seemed to come to an end. Drawn to Hollywood by fantasies of success, McCoy and his characters found only failure.[26] Both *They Shoot Horses, Don't They?* and *I Should Have Stayed Home* take a critical look at the dream factory, in ways that show it to be nothing less than a nightmare. They reveal not just the tinsel that passes for glamor but the desperation underneath the tinsel. Seen in the day under the hot sun, Hollywood was "a cheap town filled with cheap stores and cheap people."[27] *They Shoot Horses* is the story of two aspiring extras, desperate to eat and just as desperate to be discovered. They sign up for a brutal dance marathon. Hollywood stars come to gawk at their tired, desperate performances, but it ends badly for all concerned. The novel's protagonist, Robert Syverten, finally shoots Gloria, his dance partner, because she finds life unbearable and asks him to "pinch hit for God." In his hallucinatory, sleep-deprived state, he recalls his youth on a farm: when horses are no good anymore, they shoot them, don't they?

*I Should Have Stayed Home* has another male protagonist, Ralph Carston, a man quite similar to Robert Syverten in name and personal qualities. (That their first names begin with R and their last names end in N only underlines the obvious.) Equally desperate, Ralph has a chance to move up into the Hollywood power scene by becoming the kept lover of an aging, well-connected Hollywood matron. He proves unequal to the task: when a friend quickly steps in and masters the situation, he ends up back on the streets, desperate to be discovered, perhaps ready to join in a dance marathon. These novels can be read as exposés of a world glamorized by the media: this is their manifest content. They mock the Hollywood version of this world – the one of fan magazines and films. In this way the term "Devil's parody" is apropos, but this phrase and the ways it applies to McCoy's novels can be pursued further than Wilson, a man of letters, realized. For McCoy is hardly derivative of Cain. And where he is "derivative," it is not of other writers, but of the movies. McCoy's two Hollywood novels mock "the lifeblood of the film and television business" (to use Linda Seger's phrase) because they evoke and pervert the very notion of adaptation. Their sources are simultaneously obvious and repressed. Even when their half-hidden sources are revealed, their status as adaptations is corroded.

---

### Two Warner Brothers' Musicals

---

During a recession, audiences probably won't want to watch films about a stock market crash.

Linda Seger, *The Art of Adaptation*[28]

> *Trixie*: What's the show about?
> *Barney*: It's all about the Depression.
> *Carol*: We won't have to rehearse that.
>
> *Gold Diggers of '33*

**4.1** At first glance, McCoy's decision to direct his acerbic attention to two Warner Brothers' musicals might seem surprising. Warner Brothers has been regularly characterized as the most progressive American motion picture studio of the early 1930s, one which made films that often acknowledged the Depression and the dislocations accompanying it. Films such as *Little Caesar* (Melvyn LeRoy, 1931), *The Public Enemy* (William Wellman, 1931), and *I am a Fugitive from a Chain Gang* (LeRoy, 1932) expressed and resonated with at least some of the alienation felt by many Americans. The backstage musicals *42nd Street* and *Gold Diggers of '33* seem to acknowledge the desperate conditions facing many ordinary people in general and aspiring actors and chorus girls in particular. For the young women at the center of these two musicals, a job on the chorus line could mean the difference between a decent life (food, clothes, and romance) and a fall into prostitution. Yet even those who were fortunate enough to have employment often gained or retained it through an informal (and usually continuing) exchange for sexual favors.

Darryl Zanuck proudly described *42nd Street* as a musical exposé that "dramatically endeavors to lift the curtain and reveal the strenuous, heart rending efforts of a well-known Broadway producer [Florenz Ziegfeld] to stage a musical comedy in this year of depression."[29] Andrew Bergman, who took the title of his book on Depression America and its films (*We're in the Money*) from the opening number of *Gold Diggers of '33*, has hailed the two films' Depression theme while simultaneously noting their celebration of success, with the Depression just increasing the stakes. That is, their criticism of American life is obviously softened somewhat as all ends happily: the romantic leads achieve both success and true love, while the secondary women characters find charming sugar daddies.[30]

*42nd Street* and *Gold Diggers of '33* clearly spoke to Americans as meaningful entertainment. Although these two musicals can easily be criticized for their ideological conformity (their suggestion of dreams fulfilled, of pluck, luck, and talent rewarded), they are complex, "ambiguous" texts that acknowledged the severity of the Depression and offered glimpses of the economic and sexual predicaments that confronted numerous people.[31] Moviegoers could readily generate diverse, even progressive interpretations, particularly when they interpreted the films somewhat against their narrative trajectory by placing them in relationship to their own lives. Indeed, audience recognition translated into box-office success, producing a whole cluster of Warner Brothers' backstage musicals usually starring Ruby Keeler and Dick Powell: *Footlight Parade* (1933), *Dames* (1934), *Gold Diggers of '35*, and *Gold Diggers of '37*.

**4.2** As a group, *42nd Street*, *Gold Diggers of '33*, *Footlight Parade*, *Dames*, *Gold Diggers of '35*, and *Gold Diggers of '37* pose interesting questions as to their relational definition. *Gold Diggers of '33* is certainly not a sequel to *42nd Street*: at least, the principal characters appearing in the former film do not reappear as "the story continues." But *Gold Diggers of '33* is clearly something more than just another film in a cycle of backstage musicals. Nor is it a traditional adaptation. In many respects it is a reconfiguration of *42nd Street*. Its relation to the earlier film involves a series of substitutions, displacements, and refigurations that closely bind the two films together. Certainly this enjoyed Hollywood precedent: for example, with the earlier DeMille grouping of remarriage comedies, such as *Don't Change Your Husband* (1919), *Why Change Your Wife?* (1920), *Bluebeard's Eighth Wife* (1923), and *Changing Husbands* (1924).[32] Although Theodor W. Adorno and Max Horkheimer have seen these kinds of films as pastiche that signal Hollywood's cultural bankruptcy (the industry's signal lack of originality), this analysis misses the ways that these reworkings could be playful and pleasurable, related to puns, word play, and jokes.[33]

**4.3** The pleasures of textual reconfiguration from film to film is only one area of textual dynamics that the spectator can mobilize in the process of watching a film such as *Gold Diggers of '33*. There are other kinds of correspondences, both within the film and between the film and the world beyond it. In fact, the *intertextual* refigurations that one finds in the movement from *42nd Street* to *Gold Diggers of '33* are consistent with the *intratextual* structures of each film. One set of substitutions involves the musical numbers. In *42nd Street*, the theatrical showstoppers from *Pretty Lady* resonate with, refigure, and abstract the world of those backstage. The song "Young and Healthy" certainly speaks for the chorines, Billy Lawler, and Pat Denning (if not for Julian Marsh or Abner Dillon). The many pairings of characters – with marriage in the wings – is articulated in "Shuffle Off to Buffalo." At the same time the initial pairings on stage do not match those backstage (Dick Powell is with Toby Wing in the "Young and Healthy" number, while Keeler is with the male ingénu (Clarence Nordstrom). Only in the final number, "42nd Street," do Peggy Sawyer and Billy Lawler get together and embrace. Indeed, this reflects a storyline in which preliminary pairings of characters (Denning/ Brent with Sawyer/Keeler and Brock/Daniels with Dillon/Kibbee) are eventually reshuffled. Only at the film's conclusion does the central couple on stage coincide with the central couple backstage (i.e. Keeler and Powell).

Until its utopic conclusion *42nd Street* underscores the slippage between life and representation – the lack of literal correspondences between the screen world and the "real world." (Just as the musical numbers are themselves transformed by Busby Berkeley and the cinematic technique.) In these films, the musical numbers gravitate toward the arch-typical, the abstract, and the utopic, while the backstage interactions are more mundane and depicted in a more realistic mode.[34] If the correspondences are mediated, it is not entirely clear which has precedent. Is there a certain natural order of things, which the stage musical articulates and to which the backstage world of the main characters naturally conforms? Or, does the musical world evolve organically from the world of its performers? Chronology and narrative might support the former, but the issue is never explicitly addressed. Utopically, they merge. It is the discovery of correspondences between these two modes of representation that provides the viewer with many of the film's pleasures.

Both *42nd Street* and *Gold Diggers of '33* are built around substitutions and displacements that oscillate between correspondences that are textual and others that point to the world beyond the screen. In *42nd Street*, Julian Marsh (Warren Baxter), the producer/ director, is a fictionalized version of Florenz Ziegfeld. Peggy Sawyer, played by Ruby Keeler, thus becomes a kind of stand-in for Keeler herself, since she had recently been a popular chorine for Ziegfeld Follies. Having come out of the chorus line, helped first by her mobster boyfriend and later in the movies by her lover and then husband Al Jolson, Keeler strengthened and enriched these parallels between life and art, even as the film offered a sanitized version of events.[35] Dick Powell, who had been singing at a Warner Brothers' theater in Pittsburgh, was finding his way to stardom in a manner not unlike Billy Lawler. Beyond this particular *film à clef*, in which the world on film refers to a prior world in the theater, *42nd Street* can be read allegorically in others ways as well. For instance, there is an implied self-referentiality: in a way that was already a well-established convention, the theater world portrayed in the film serves as a substitute for the film world, in particular the world of Warner Brothers. Thus Peggy Sawyer gets her big break in the theater even as Keeler gets a big, "real life" movie break by debuting in this film. The songwriters for *Pretty Lady*, who protest about having their song thrown out, are played by Harry Warren and Al Dubin, the actual song writers for *42nd Street* (and therefore of the stage musical as well).[36] Likewise in a kind of wish fulfillment, the theatrical producer (Marsh/Ziegfeld) has his counterpart in Darryl Zanuck at Warner Brothers. These films, it was said, helped rescue Warner Brothers from being broken up, much as *Pretty Lady* saved Julian Marsh. Moreover, Ginger Rogers did have a rather active sex life, not unlike the character she plays (Anytime Annie), at least according to Melvyn LeRoy.[37]

**4.4** There are still other levels of substitution, allegory, or identification in which the film moves beyond the world of theater and/or film to establish a synecdochic relationship to the larger society as a whole. Ruby Keeler is thus a kind of every girl. Perhaps cute, she is hardly a beauty. More than her talent, Keeler's charisma and her persona's friendly yet somewhat innocent determination provide the basis for success. Shop girls in the movie seats could pretend, that is imagine, they were *like* Sawyer/Keeler – that their life contained the possibility for that same larger-than-life drama. (I am looking for another term for, or a particular way of thinking about, the concept of "identification.") Dorothy Brock/Bebe Daniels offers another viewing position, which somewhat older women might occupy, authorizing them to give up work in exchange for a family (a choice relatively few actually had the luxury to make). Billy Lawler and Pat Denning (George Brent) perhaps played similar roles for men, though viewer mobility between characters and across gender should not be minimized. Certainly Julian Marsh is a Franklin Roosevelt-like figure, a strong benevolent leader who works his cast hard, but only so that he can rescue them – and himself. If others pair off, he is the solitary leader, hanging out by the stage door to overhear the parting remarks of opening nighters (like a man waiting for a handout).

*Gold Diggers of '33* replaces many of the real-world correspondences evident in *42nd Street* with textual ones, in a way designed to enhance and sustain spectatorial pleasure. The producer is Barney Hopkins, played by Ned Sparks who was also Barry, one of the producers (Jones and Barry) of *Pretty Lady* in *42nd Street*. A minor player in the earlier film, he becomes more prominent as the director/Julian Marsh character (now the dance director, Robert Agnew) withdraws into the background. Barney has a vision of putting on a musical about the Depression (like the film, which presents itself as being about the Depression). Ruby Keeler is now Polly Parker as opposed to Peggy Sawyer, though it is hard to keep the characters' names straight. (Please note that Keeler's characters share the same first and last letters of their full names – just like Robert Syverten and Ralph Carston.) Likewise, Dick Powell is now Brad Roberts as opposed to Billy Lawler. Here, both characters share the same first letter of their first names. The fact that Brad Roberts is a "stage name" for Robert Bradford draws further attention to the name game in these films and so McCoy's novel. And so on, and so on.

*Gold Diggers of '33* still retains its own distinct series of substitutions, which continue along a serious, quasi-historical trajectory. The chorus line displaces the bread line, which is a successor to the marching columns of soldiers from World War I – all of which the stage musical now presents as representations.[38] The hard work of the chorus line (in conjunction with the vision and entrepreneurship of Barney Hopkins as well as the money and talent of Brad Roberts) is offered as the way out of the Depression for these characters – and synecdochically for America. The perfect coordination of the chorusline dancers looks toward the productivity of the assembly line and prosperity. Likewise, the rich Bradfords from Boston find happiness and vitality with the New York based chorines. The haves and have-nots come together and find a way to work together in a new synthesis that overcomes the Depression. Of course, many of the interpretations readers can apply to *42nd Street* continue to work for *Gold Diggers of '33*, though not always with the same effectiveness and exactitude. (As briefly discussed above, McCoy adopts the same strategy with *I Should Have Stayed Home*.)

--------------------  McCoy's Textual Engagement  --------------------

> Dramatic structure of the screenplay may be defined by the linear arrangement of related incidents, episodes, or events leading to a dramatic resolution.
>
> Syd Field, *Screenplay: The Foundations of Screenwriting*[39]

> *Brad*: I just got the idea for it last night. I was down on Times Square watching those men on the bread line. Standing there in the rain, waiting for coffee and donuts. Men out of a job. Around the soup kitchen.
>
> *Barney*: Stop. That's it! That's what this show is about. Men marching, marching in the rain. Donuts and crullers. Man marching. Marching. Jobs. Jobs.
>
> *Gold Diggers of '33*

**5.1** Recognizing the textual dynamics operating in *42nd Street* and *Gold Diggers of '33*, Horace McCoy appropriated and perverted them in his Hollywood novel *They Shoot Horses, Don't They?* Like Barney, he wanted to create a work "about" the Depression; unlike Barney or his Warner Brothers' surrogates, he did not want to pull his punches. What authorizes us to see *They Shoot Horses* as an engagement with, and repudiation of, these two musicals? I confess that a single passage in the novel started me on this train of thought. But it was a powerful one. A variety of real-life Hollywood stars are given cameo appearances in *They Shoot Horses*, but only one stands out as much more than a kind of name dropping: Ruby Keeler. Well into the marathon and roughly halfway through the novel, Keeler makes an appearance in the stands. She shoots the gun that starts the dancers on their first derby, a nightmare race around the oval that will test their endurance; each night a derby will result in the elimination of a couple from the marathon dance contest. Keeler also provides a $10 prize for the couple that comes in first. She self-consciously functions as a role model for those in the marathon dance. Perhaps they, like she, can be discovered – or can find a sugar daddy; for, as McCoy slyly notes, she is not accompanied by her very successful husband, Al Jolson, at this event. Her trajectory is one that both Gloria Beatty and her marathon partner, Robert Syverten, hope will happen to them. "A lot of producers and directors go to those marathon dances. There's always the chance they might pick you out and give you a part in a picture," Gloria tells Robert (p. 10).[40] One might be discovered. In this respect, the marathon dance is the poor person's version of the chorus line. Being picked out seems unlikely to happen to Gloria, who radiates negative energy; but it almost happens to Robert.

Forging a key link between films and novel, McCoy splits and refigures the Ruby Keeler character. While retaining Ruby Keeler herself, he also creates his own Ruby. She is Ruby Bates (Ruby B, the second Ruby). Ruby is a veteran marathon dancer. She and her husband James have already won at least one marathon, taking home $1,500. Even though Ruby is noticeably (and soon disturbingly) pregnant, she and James seem poised to win the derby. They are routinely in first place (p. 96). Eventually, however, her condition offends the Mothers' League for Good Morals, whose leaders insist that she be ejected from the contest. It does not seem to concern them that her participation is a sign of obvious desperation. They have no wish to help her; they just want her out of sight. This Ruby is, McCoy subtly suggests, a real down-to-earth star; in fact, the *real* Ruby; that is, a real jewel. Likewise her husband James provides her with physical and moral support. He is with her constantly – in contrast to the absent Jolson.[41] Ruby Bates is a more fitting model for the ordinary American woman, McCoy seems to suggest. And when the reader pretends to be like Ruby Bates, it cuts much closer to the bone. It is less flattering, but more truthful. James Bates is the kind of person that Robert aspires to make a film about – "the life of an ordinary man – you know who makes thirty dollars a week and has to raise kids and buy a home and a car and a radio – the kind of guy bill collectors are always after" (p. 69). Robert Syverten is also, of course, a variant of Ruby (their first names share the same first letter).[42]

**5.2** Both *42nd Street* and *Gold Diggers of '33* devote considerable attention to the chorines' hopes of being discovered and/or finding a sugar daddy. In *42nd Street*, Dorothy Brock (Bebe Daniels) is able to star in *Pretty Lady* because she is sleeping with the musical's sole backer, Abner Dillon (Guy Kibbee). When she self-destructs, it appears that Dillon's new mistress, Anytime Annie, will take her place in the musical. Instead, Annie recognizes Peggy's talent, steps aside, and tells Marsh to cast Peggy/Keeler in the lead instead. Annie gets her sugar daddy, and Broadway gets its star. Success is possible because the two roles (performing in bed and performing on stage) are finally separated. In each case the best person gets the job.[43] In *Gold Diggers of '33* producer Barney Hopkins (Ned Sparks) overhears music wafting from a neighboring apartment and, courtesy of Polly Parker (Ruby Keeler), meets struggling composer Brad Roberts (Dick Powell). Barney quickly decides to use his music. Brad, who it turns out is rich, backs the musical – provided that Polly has a starring role. Now Robert Syverten appears to have exactly such a sponsor – Mrs Layden.

Mrs Layden is a cross between Abner Dillon in *42nd Street* and Brad Roberts in *Gold Diggers of '33*. Like Brad Roberts, Mrs Layden seems poor but is actually quite wealthy – just slumming or rather moving about under cover so that people will accept her for who she is. Like Abner Dillon, she is much older in age. Certainly she prides herself on her eccentricity. It is not clear to Robert or us if this "angel," who seems ready to fund his direction of a small independent film, is expecting a sexual quid pro quo or not. (It was not clear to Dorothy either until Abner Dillon makes the exchange explicit.) Mrs Layden does seem earnestly concerned about his future – a good woman, perhaps too good for this world. And so she dies. She is killed by a stray bullet from a gunfight in the Palm Garden – shot right between the eyes. The benevolent angel – which both Abner Dillon and Brad Roberts become for their respective Ruby Keeler characters – is too good to survive in McCoy's novel. She is killed in a *deus-ex-machina* fashion. She literally becomes an angel.

The trading of sex for money and the good life is pervasive in both films. Gold digging appears to be a highly enjoyable game for these chorines. In *Gold Diggers of '33* Carol King (Joan Blondell) digs money out of J. Lawrence Bradford (Warren William), and they discover mutual love in the process. Even the aging comedienne Trixie (Aline MacMahon) finds a safe haven with Fanny Peabody (Guy Kibbee). Both gold diggers ultimately succeed in marrying their well-to-do men, with these calculated exchanges softened by romantic and comic overtones. This happens, in a somewhat different way, to Geneva Tomblin in McCoy's novel. She is "discovered" by her future husband – a modestly well-to-do skipper who will marry her at once. Here such "happy outcomes" are made real. Geneva is marrying a man she does not know to live on a bait barge anchored three miles out in the Pacific Ocean. To the world desperate for romance and happy endings, she is presented as one of the lucky ones. To embrace such a choice, however, says something about Depression desperation that is excluded from the films.

Another variation on this type of arrangement is also depicted in these backstage musicals: in *42nd Street*, Loraine Fleming (Una Merkel) is having an affair with the assistant director or stage manager, Andy Lee (George Stone). Although this alliance secures her position in the chorus line, it also appears to be more than just a calculated exchange of favors. The other assistant stage manager, MacElroy (Allen Jenkins), lacks a steady girlfriend; he suggests that a little night work could help one or another chorine on her way to success. The objects of his sexual interest greet such propositions with different levels of credibility or cynicism – perhaps merely content to have a backstage protector. In *They Shoot Horses*, these two assistants are refigured as Rocky Gravo and Rollo Fingers, the assistant managers (announcer and floor judge, respectively). Fingers uses his position to extract a quickie from Gloria and other female marathoners amidst the filth and total darkness of the space under the grandstands. The romance and/or the fun as well as the benefits of this sex trade are, we might say, demystified. (In *42nd Street*, when Dorothy Brock wants a quickie on the side with her boyfriend, Pat Denning, it happens in all the comfort of her sugar daddy's luxury car.)

One of the few people seemingly not interested in sex is the marathon promoter, Vincent "Socks" Donald. Very much like the Julian Marsh and Barney characters, he is focused on pulling off the show. He is sleazier but knows his business. He is not evil, but skillfully exploits the participants in a logical, business-like, almost benevolent way. Gloria and others want "Hollywood" to come down to the dance hall on Santa Monica pier: it is the only way to be discovered. So they agree to the derby. In this respect, he is not the evil con artist of Sydney Pollack's 1969 movie adaptation. The marathon producer in that film is really a liar and deceiver (like Presidents Johnson and Nixon): Pollack's promoter has sex with the female contestants and never intends to pay the winner. McCoy deheroicizes the role of the promoter but he does not destroy it. A successful producer finds a way to attract an audience, saving "jobs" and putting food on the table. "Socks" Donald thus retains certain elements of benevolent paternalism. McCoy's novel is about survival and subsistence. Pollack's film is about something else (Vietnam).

**5.3** The contrasts between the backstage world constructed by the "dream factory" and the brutal realism of the dance marathon is the fulcrum around which McCoy builds his critique of Hollywood. The musicals offer a series of linear structures: the chorus line itself but also the films' narratives. Desperate though not dispirited men and women come together, share talent and resources, and ultimately overcome adversity. They learn about life and love. The films move toward a happy resolution as amateur actress Peggy Sawyer/Ruby Keeler becomes a chorus girl, then a star, and finally finds romantic fulfillment with Billy Lawler/Dick Powell. The star (Dorothy Brock/Bebe Daniels) finds herself by acknowledging her true love and throwing in her lot with her old partner (Pat Denning/George Brent). Anytime Annie/Ginger Rogers finds a sugar daddy (Abner Dillon/Guy Kibbee). And so on. All these individual solutions occur within the larger framework of the show's success. While acknowledging the Depression, the film offers an upward, upbeat trajectory.

*They Shoot Horses* has a circular structure which parallels the oval around which the derbies are run. In certain respects, it is not unlike Shakespeare's *Romeo and Juliet*: from the outset, we know how the story will turn out. Chapter 1 begins where the last chapter (number 13) ends, with Robert Syverten condemned to death for the murder of Gloria Beatty. In this opening chapter (one page), Robert recalls the moment he did Gloria a favor and shot her. It was the one moment he saw her happy and relaxed. Her intense despair and desire to end her own life are then threaded throughout the story. His present fate – his imminent execution for shooting Gloria – is also repeatedly interpolated throughout the book. We are never allowed to forget it. Hope, a linear unfolding of events, and the possibility of some upward trajectory are eliminated. Even the marathon, which might yield some victor who would walk away with $1,000, is terminated without any resolution. The organizers promise to divide the money among the remaining contestants – tomorrow. But tomorrow never comes in this novel, and it is quite possible that the organizers will skip town. Yet even if they do deliver the money or there had been a winner, it seems that nothing would really change for anyone. James and Ruby once won $1,500 (more than the present marathon) and yet they are as desperate as ever. As Gloria puts it, this whole business is a "merry-go-round." "When we get out of here we're right back where we started" (p. 44). The tone and flashback structure of *film noir* is fully developed in this novel.

The worst that *42nd Street* has to offer still contains a silver lining. Julian Marsh (Warren Baxter) tells his cast: "I'm going to work you day and night until you drop." In fact, our young trooper, Peggy Sawyer/Ruby Keeler, does pass out and is carefully carried back to a bench where she is ministered to by a number of concerned people, including the very debonair Pat Denning/George Brent. Held gently, she is handed a glass of water and sips it gratefully. Brent then takes the Keeler character out for dinner and, having lost her lodging room, back to his apartment where he gives her his double bed for a good night's sleep (she locks the door keeping him on the other side). Sawyer/Keeler is "dead tired," but clearly not in the way that Gloria or even the other dance marathoners are dead tired. Working on the chorus line gives the cast members a sense of community – of possibility enmeshed with danger and romance, of sex and money. (They are members of a cast – not outcasts.)

The marathon is a kind of waking nightmare that literally goes on endlessly as one sunset succeeds another, giving a new and more concrete meaning to Marsh's declaration: the marathon contestants do literally work day and night until they collapse. Every two hours the contestants are allowed to stop for ten minutes and eat/shave or sleep (and on cots rather than Pat Denning's double bed). They are awakened by ammonia. When contestants pass out after the derby, as Robert Syverten does at one point, they are dropped into a tub of water cooled by a 100-pound block of ice. This assistance, which Robert seems even to appreciate, can be contrasted to the attention that Peggy Sawyer/Ruby Keeler receives under comparable circumstances (the dainty glass of water). (As one observer of Syverten's dousing remarks, "that ice water fixes 'em right up" [p. 62].) Syverten is tossed into the tub and when he gets out, another contestant quickly follows. If there is a straight line in McCoy's novel, it is only the line of unconscious contestants waiting to be dunked so they can get back on the merry-go-round. Will Ruby lose her job if she takes that needed break after passing out – apparently not (and if she does, Pat Denning assures her that there will be something else). In the marathon, if you can't come right back, it is all over.

Something always happens at a marathon declares Rocky Gravo, the announcer, and passing out is part of the show. The contestants' agony is much of what people come to watch. That is why the derbies are the high points of each day. (Like the nightly Broadway performance for the chorines, they come at the end of the day.) Life, rehearsal, and show time are collapsed in the world of marathon dancing. People sleep and eat while dancing. They have sex within the ten-minute breaks they get every two hours. During the derbies, contestants are pushed to the very limits of endurance. They fall, collide, and keep the house doctor busy. Pain becomes spectacle. People come to see others who are more desperate than themselves, to see people struggle to stay standing, to ward off collapse. This spectacle is different from, indeed the reverse of, the spectacle offered by Warner Brothers' musicals. Not pain but pretty ladies with sexy legs, sexual vitality and utopic possibilities are on display. If the process of selecting dancers for the chorus line involves what is known in the business as a "cattle call," Syverten/McCoy suggest that the dance marathon is like a bull fight (p. 20). And the contestants are the bulls.

**5.4** Endings are important in cultural works. Neither *42nd Street* nor *Gold Diggers of '33* ends with a kiss, a choice that foregrounds the studio's social conscience and relates these personal solutions to the larger resolution (the show's success, the ending of the Depression). *42nd Street* ends with Julian Marsh alone, outside the theater, overhearing the reactions of the opening-night crowd. They are enthralled and the play is a success. He and his company are safe. In *Gold Diggers of '33*, the successful mounting of a musical that acknowledges the Depression (with "Brother, Can You Spare a Dime?") merely reverses the film's opening number ("We're in the Money") which hides it. Admitting that there is a crisis (like Franklin Roosevelt) is better than denying it or its severity (like Herbert Hoover). Only then can the community resolve it. In both cases, however, the kiss is shown or implied in the penultimate scene. Romantic union and marriage remain central to the resolution of the narrative (which involves a larger union – that of classes as well as performers and audience members).

Rather than the conventional Hollywood happy ending, McCoy's novel ends as it begins, with the protagonist shooting his dance partner (this occurs in both instances as a flashback recalled while the protagonist is being sentenced to death by the judge). The couple is united by death rather than by a kiss. And yet, the gunshot to the head is like a kiss: Robert sees Gloria's murder as the single most loving act that he does for her, fulfilling her deepest held desire – to die quickly. Moreover, like marriage, it is an act that unites Robert and Gloria – not until "death do us part" but in and through death. The judge's pronouncement of the death sentence is like that other pronouncement often spoken by the judge: the wedding ceremony in which he pronounces a couple man and wife. Narrative resolution is bleak, indeed.

**5.5** McCoy, a marginal Hollywood scriptwriter, directed his rage at Hollywood and its invidious ideological project: its pretense to heroically depict the Depression even as it pulls its punches. Refiguration, his means of ideological indictment, is systematic and devastating. Legs are a central and recurring motif in both *42nd Street* and *They Shoot Horses*. This is acknowledged by the very title of McCoy's novel, which as a question at least implies an explanation as to why or when they shoot the horses. When the horse has broken a leg, when it is in pain, and when it can no longer work (pp. 76–7). Gloria is in pain, she wants to get off the merry-go-round of life which is like the merry-go-round of the derby. Metaphorically, she has broken a leg and is, as she says, no good. In *42nd Street*, Dorothy Brock/Bebe Daniels also breaks a leg and is no good. She cannot perform for *Pretty Lady*, nor is she willing to perform for her sugar daddy. She soon realizes that this is a piece of good luck: her broken leg has actually saved her from a hypocritical situation. She is reunited with her true love, with Pat Denning/George Brent. Breaking a leg ensures her happy ending.

In the theater, of course, the expression "break a leg" is used to wish someone luck. Breaks and broken legs can move in opposite directions. People are broke but looking for a break.[44] This means looking for a good break – a breakthrough. But there are bad breaks, some of which leave people irredeemably broken. Bad luck or good luck. Ruby gets a break, a chance to star. She is told she cannot fail, she cannot "fall down." Even in the final, thirteenth chapter of McCoy's novel, Robert Syverten is still hoping for a break – that Mrs Layden's assistant will still help him out. Gloria mocks him: "Always tomorrow . . . The big break is always coming tomorrow" (p. 116). And so in McCoy's novel, a broken leg is what it is. People are treated like animals and some, like a horse with a broken leg, are killed. Not just by Robert in a sleep-deprived hallucinatory state. The state performs these acts as well. *They Shoot Horses* starts with the judge intoning, "The prisoner will stand." Syverten acknowledges that when it comes to his case, he "doesn't have a leg to stand on." His leg is also broken (metaphorically), and he too will be killed.

Dancing is a leg sport. The chorines' jams are the objects of Abner Dillon's delight. "I don't know about contracts, but it looks good to me," Dillon remarks at the beginning of the film as he looks at one of Dorothy Brock's legs in the mirror. During the cattle call, Julian Marsh starts out by looking at the girls' legs. After three weeks, Dillon has changed his tune: "A leg is nothing but something to stand on." Nonetheless, the Busby Berkeley production numbers focus on and fetishize the legs of the chorines, in keeping with the film's motif. The dance marathoners also depend on their legs. Their legs are not spectacles – at least until the derbies when they are put in shorts and made to run around the oval. Their legs are simply to stand on, to dance on, and to run on. Their worth is measured by their durability, valued like the leg of an animal – for the work they can deliver. The marathoners' legs swelled painfully during the first week, but no one sees them. (To avoid overheating, the women do shed their sweatshirts during the derbies, providing audiences with the spectacle of breasts bouncing in skimpy brassières [p. 63].)

Joblessness and bankruptcy – being broke and broken – haunted the Depression. Robert S. MacElvaine notes that crime and suicide were two responses to this desperation: both are present in the Warner Brothers' musicals and McCoy's novels. In *Gold Diggers of '33*, Polly Parker and her roommates have no reason to get up because there is no work. The alarm sounds and they turn over and go back to sleep. They steal a bottle of milk from the neighbor's fire escape. In McCoy's novel, the crimes are more serious. Giusippe Lodi robbed a drug store and killed the elderly proprietor. Perhaps, like Robert, he was just being nice – pinch hitting for God. Suicide rates rose in the 1930s; and, for many, it "seemed the only solution." "Can you be so kind as to advise me as to which would be the most human way to dispose of my self and my family, as it is about the only thing that I see left to do," wrote one advice seeker.[45] Although few actually took the fatal step, many considered it. Gloria thinks of it constantly. At the beginning of *42nd Street*, when Jones and Barry are talking to Marsh, the director tells them that he is broke and will give them a hit or die trying. Barry remarks that if he dies, there will be a triple funeral. That is, their situation is so desperate that they see suicide as the inevitable result of failure. If success is so important in these musicals, it is because the Depression grinds everyone down even as it keeps everyone on edge. Even a highly successful director like Marsh must risk everything on one roll of the dice. And the odds against him had never been higher, but not nearly as high as the odds against Gloria or the other marathoners. McCoy shifts the question of suicide from the well-to-do producers to those living truly on the edge. Socks Donald may fail, but he lives to try again. Failure to mount a successful dance marathon in no way seems to threaten his future. In contrast, a desperate contestant such as Gloria comes to recognize that there is no way off the merry-go-round but death.

If despair and suicide are pervasive, it becomes all the more urgent to produce the life-affirming events of love and marriage (but, as the pregnant Ruby Bates shows, not babies). *42nd Street* moves from casual if pragmatic promiscuity by the leading characters to more permanent pairings with marriage in the wings, echoed in the musical numbers ("Shuffle Off to Buffalo" and the section of "Young and Healthy" in which the chorines are all dressed in wedding gowns). Likewise in *Gold Diggers of '33*, the shift is from gold digging and seduction to serious involvement and marriage. In *They Shoot Horses*, marriage is a recurrent obsession. Despite the grind of the marathon, the promoters are eager to show that even here, under such circumstances, romance and marriage can flourish. They try to arrange a public wedding between one of the couples – tapping Robert and Gloria who refuse. When another couple accepts, they are protected from elimination in the nightly derbies. As already noted, the marriage of a contestant (Geneva) to a spectator (the skipper of a bait boat) is also ballyhooed. The promoters are too cynical to believe it. That is why Rollo Fingers gets knifed: he seduced a woman whose partner believes her to be his fiancée. Indeed, James and Ruby had a public wedding at an earlier marathon. *They Shoot Horses* does not rule out the possibility (McCoy married the daughter of a wealthy oil man in late 1933), but it exposes the hype – the commodification of marriage. Fairy-tale endings rarely occur – least of all in the midst of a marathon dance or a Depression.

As Robert Stam reminds us, "Central to the transformational grammar of adaptation are permutations in locale, time and language."[46] McCoy handles such displacements and substitutions in a variety of ways. If the marathon dance is a refiguration of the chorus line as a trope, McCoy sets his story in Hollywood to which the films so obviously allude. McCoy thus reverses one of the substitutions (New York for Hollywood or the world of theater for the world of film) on which the films are based, bringing the metaphorical signifier closer to the actual signified. Many of the dance marathoners are would-be extras who had used their legs walking from studio to studio looking for a job, hoping to be discovered but always on a treadmill. They cannot even get listed in Central Casting. Some are desperate enough so that they take the marathon because it offers food and a bed (even if it is only a bed for ten minutes every two hours). At least by being in a marathon, they can be extras – extras in so many ways. When the need arises, the marathoners are easily jettisoned: whether Mario, Freddy and the under-aged Manski girl, a pregnant Ruby Bates, or the anonymous couples eliminated by the derby on a daily basis.

---
### Ideology and Style
---

If you must kill off your main character (and I do not take the view that you must never do this – just be aware that it's a risky decision), make sure that there is some other emotional center to your story.

Linda Seger, *The Art of Adaptation*[47]

All you got to do to that story is give it the switcheroo.

Budd Schulberg, *What Makes Sammy Run?*[48]

**6.1** If *They Shoot Horses* is an anti-Hollywood novel, if McCoy takes *42nd Street* and turns the musical inside out, then it makes sense that the movie stars come down to the dance hall on Santa Monica pier to watch the people who normally would watch them on the big screen – contestants like Gloria, who came to Los Angeles because of the stories she read in a fan magazine. Out of curiosity or just a desire to reverse looking relations, they watch these ordinary people trying to succeed – to become like themselves.

Alice Faye, who was in the chorus line when she was discovered by Rudy Vallee, comes first. Vallee had her star in *George White's Scandals* (1934). Ruby Keeler is followed by many others. Some are stars like Bill Boyd, who had appeared in *Lucky Devils* and *Emergency Call* in 1933. He had been a popular star until another actor of the same name was involved in a gambling and liquor scandal, tarnishing his image. (His career began to revive in 1935, starring in the Hopalong Cassidy series.) Ken Murray, who had appeared in *Disgraced* and *From Headquarters* in 1933, would not have another major screen credit for the next three years. June Clyde – whose 1933 credits included *A Study in Scarlet*, *Her Resale Value*, and *Forgotten* – would be in England by 1935. She was in a group with her future husband, Thornton Freeland, who was known for his light, lively comedies and musicals. Sue Carol appeared in *Secret Sinners* (1933) and Tom Brown was in *Laughter in Hell* (1933) at Universal.

Many of these actors in the grandstands were themselves on the edge of Hollywood's star system – players with a handful of credits who could, and in some cases would, disappear, losing their livelihood in the film industry. They are watching ordinary people, whose efforts to stay standing perhaps can serve to remind them of their own struggles to stay afloat, while providing enough distance to put their own uncertainties in a more favorable light. If movie viewers frequently pretend that they are like people on the screen, characters who are idealized and upwardly mobile versions of themselves, these actors pretend that they are unlike these marathoners. They deny or suppress their affinities. They see these marathoners as distopic, grotesque versions of themselves. Although purportedly there to watch the dance marathon, they are still there to be looked at – by the more ordinary people in the seats as well as by the marathoners themselves. Those struggling to stay standing still aspire to be like them – like those celebrities in the grandstands who can sit, whose breaks have been of a different kind. Certainly the sense of community, which as Jane Feuer reminds us is constructed in the musical, is undone.[49]

**6.2** *They Shoot Horses, Don't They?* is a complex literary achievement. On an immediate level, McCoy's novel seems to offer a gritty realism related to its "hard-boiled" style. As Edmund Wilson remarked: "the first of his books is worth reading for its description of one of those dance marathons that were among the most grisly symptoms of the depression."[50] This documentary-like aesthetic can be highlighted for the contemporary reader by situating McCoy's novel against historical accounts of marathon dancing, such as the one by Carol Martin.[51] Nonetheless, *They Shoot Horses* is carefully constructed and highly stylized. Consider its use of numerology. There are thirteen chapters, for instance. The numbers assigned to the couples are also telling. James and Ruby Bates are "unlucky," drawing number thirteen: they lead the derby but are forced to quit by nosy reformers (the Mothers' League). Number 22 is Hollywood's lucky number: remember Rick (Humphrey Bogart) tells one young woman to play 22 at the roulette wheel in *Casablanca* (1942): she plays it twice and wins both times. The number 22 makes similar appearances in other, earlier Warner Brothers' films. Robert and Gloria are couple no. 22 in the marathon. Robert meets his female counterpart from that other lucky number: couple number 7

(Rosemary Luftus).[52] She is well bred and apparently comes from wealth. Robert and she have an instant connection and drift rapidly toward the dark area under the grand-stands, only to be interrupted by the sexual activities of Gloria and Rollo Fingers. This attraction, however, is never again pursued. Surviving takes priority. In fact, there is no clearer indication that *They Shoot Horses* is an anti-Hollywood novel than that the couple wearing 22 suffer the greatest series of blows. If they find luck, it is – as Gloria maintains – only in a quick death. Perhaps then they did get a good break after all.[53]

Hollywood is thus indicted in this novel. As a Hollywood allegory, *42nd Street* seems to say that, with a little luck, hard work, and some sexual quid pro quo, an extra can become a star – or at least live reasonably happily and comfortably. But the main characters in *They Shoot Horses* cannot even get extra work. They are not even eligible for walk-on parts as members of the chorus line in *42nd Street* (or any other backstage musical) because they cannot join Central Casting. (If the reader will allow me to indulge in an anachronism I've generally kept to the epigraphs, here is a real Catch-22.) Instead, these aspiring extras perform the only roles available to them. With food, a cot, and the faint hope of prize money as their only payment, they play themselves – objects of spec-tacle and pity for members of the Hollywood community whose films affirm the ideology of success, hard work, talent, and luck. They are the stars' alter egos: their opposites who are nonetheless acting out their drama of success. The systematic, extended nature of these oppositions forces a further reassessment of the novel's apparent realism. Rather than involving a simple correspondence with, description and assessment of, and engagement with the real world, McCoy employs a mode of description or writing that is situated in relation to, and stands in stark opposition to, Hollywood glamor.[54]

McCoy's novel is written in the style that Michael Denning has called the proletarian grotesque, an engaged and critical literary style of the Depression.[55] It is the grotesque, not realism that stands in strongest opposition to Hollywood glamor. Dumping contest-ants into bath tubs filled with 100-pound blocks of ice, and marathoners having sex amidst the dark filth under the grandstands, goes beyond realism, even as a realist component retains a credibility that is crucial to the impact of the novel. In fact, the Warner Brothers' musicals, by focusing on the lowly chorines and the cavernous backstage areas, provide a realism that ultimately supports the glamor.[56] Romantic realism is shared by both films and novel. Beyond that they move in different directions. McCoy responded to his des-perate encounter with Hollywood by countering its depiction of the world (Hollywood glamor) with the grotesque. And the grotesque, Kenneth Burke argues, is a style most appropriate to moments of crisis, one in which "the perception of form is perceived with-out smile or laughter."[57] The tendency to associate McCoy with the hard-boiled writing of Cain and Dashiell Hammett has also concealed the extent to which McCoy's first novel can be seen as part of the proletarian movement that "produced a counterculture to Ford-ism and its nascent machinery of advertising, journalism, and broadcasting."[58] Syverten, certainly an author surrogate, aspires to make a film about "the life of an ordinary man." With McCoy's novel, we can see how this variant of proletarian literature confronted the Hollywood dream factory and its way of depicting the world. In this respect, it is crucial that McCoy directed his devil's parody of the movies not at an easy target but at meaningful entertainment that claimed to be about the Depression.

------------------ Quotation, Appropriation, or Adaptation ------------------

> Why, I knew a guy who made a nice little pile out of one of De Maupassant's stories just the other day. And all he had to do was switch the hooker from a French carriage to a Western stagecoach. If you were smart you'd try to hit on something like that and write yourself an original.
>
> Budd Schulberg, *What Makes Sammy Run?*[59]

**7.1** To see the relationship of *They Shoot Horses* to the Warner Brothers' backstage musicals of 1933 as one of caustic transformation – of profound reconfiguration and even radical adaptation – is crucial to our understanding and full enjoyment of the novel. And yet, as I have already suggested, I feel some discomfort in situating this novel within theories of literary or filmic "adaptation," even as an inversion of Hollywood practices. Some of my unease can be explained by the history of its writing: the fact that earlier drafts were written even before these films were in production (as discussed above). At the very least, McCoy did not begin by secretly encoding and transforming these Warner Brothers' musicals into *They Shoot Horses*. Rather the films provided McCoy with crucial literary traction: a series of symbols, motifs and tropes, an ideology, and some characters that he could work with and against.

In making a case for or against *They Shoot Horses* as adaptation, the story itself is a crucial consideration. Even if we accept the transpositions of Los Angeles for New York and a dance marathon for a Broadway musical, there is real uncertainty or ambiguity here. Although all three works have people coming together to put on a show or a performance, this aspect is something that they share with many other backstage musicals. There are also a very large number of Hollywood films in which boy meets girl, boy and girl strive to make their lives or their projects a success, and, after twists and turns, boy gets girl. As in many Hollywood films, these backstage musicals involve a double movement in which work and romance are intertwined. The problems in one area interact with those in the other. Although there were some exceptions (for example, *I'm a Fugitive from a Chain Gang* and, in a less unexpected way, *Little Caesar*), most Warner Brothers' films – most Hollywood films – had a happy ending in which success and romance are achieved, more or less simultaneously (a double orgasm, if you will). *They Shoot Horses, Don't They?* is, at the very least, a story of double failure: an inverted romance and an inverted success story – a devil's parody of conventional Hollywood narratives. With the death of his sponsor, Syverten loses his chance to chase his dream and perhaps direct a film. The bullet he sends into Gloria's brain is a kiss of death and a negation of hope rather than an affirmation of life. Nonetheless, it is possible to assert that these two movie musicals offer a paradigm of one popular type of Hollywood story. Despite the numerous evocations of *42nd Street*, it is this paradigm that McCoy is engaging. Indeed, *42nd Street* is but one substantiation of it.

**7.2** At what point does quotation or appropriation become extensive enough to merit the term "adaptation?" And is refiguration necessarily adaptation? We have seen the various tropes and symbols that McCoy has appropriated and turned inside out as well as perhaps upside down: the break, leg art and breaking a leg, the wedding, the show, hard work, sex, success, stardom, sugar daddies, the producer, Ruby Keeler, and so forth. If Hollywood films are always simply reworkings and reconfigurations of what has been done before, as Adorno and Horkheimer insist in their analysis of Hollywood movie-making and Budd Schulberg suggests in his Hollywood novel *What Makes Sammy Run?*, then classical Hollywood filmmaking in general can be understood as a degraded and derivative substantiation of the process of adaptation. Genres, star personas, story lines, and so much else were constantly reworked and rehashed. If so, Edmund Wilson was right. McCoy does more than offer us a parody of the movies or, even, of this one movie (*42nd Street*). He takes the essence of Hollywood movie-making, its "lifeblood," and mocks it even as he brilliantly employs it against all that Hollywood represents. It is this perverse dialectic – McCoy's brilliant execution and simultaneous disparagement – that provides a devil's parody of, among other things, Hollywood adaptation.

---

Notes

---

1   Linda Seger, *The Art of Adaptation: Fact and Fiction into Film* (New York: Henry Holt, 1992), p. xi.

2   Edmund Wilson, "The Boys in the Back Room," in *Classics and Commercials* (New York: Farrar, Straus, 1950), p. 22.

3   Richard Fine, *West of Eden: Writers in Hollywood, 1928–1940* (1985; Washington, DC: Smithsonian Institution Press, 1993).

4   In today's post-classical, postmodern world, the direction of adaptation across media and forms has become more complex: new musicals are now more likely to be based on movie classics than the other way around (for example, *The Sweet Smell of Success*, *Sunset Boulevard*, and *The Producers*). Narrative properties shuttle back and forth between film and television (e.g. *Buffy the Vampire Slayer*, *Clueless*, and *Star Trek*).

5   See, for instance, Mikhail Iampolski, *The Memory of Tiresias: Intertextuality and Film* (Berkeley, CA: University of California Press, 1998), pp. 80–1, who explains the use of literary sources this way: "The cinema needs to refer to the Book as its source in order to legitimate its own textual status. A text acquires social authority only if it is produced by an author who enjoys a specific social and cultural credibility. The literary text has a particularly close link to the authorial instance. Unlike literature, a film produces photographic texts whose index of author-ship is lower. Its credibility is based on the photographic self-evidence of what it shows. Yet

this photographic self-evidence is not enough, within the framework of traditional cultural assumptions (above all in the early stages of film history), to secure cinema its legitimacy. It is precisely this that might explain, at least to some extent, why films generally acknowledge the book and writer that inspired them: both project onto the film the aura of additional legitimacy that written texts have enjoyed in our culture."

6 These adaptations are rarely considered by cultural historians. To offer one example: Arline de Hass, *The Jazz Singer: A Story of Pathos and Laughter* (London: The Readers Library Publishing Company, n.d.) from the play by Samson Raphaelson.

7 Seger, *The Art of Adaptation*, p. xi.

8 Budd Schulberg, *What Makes Sammy Run?* (1941; London: Allison and Busby, 1992), p. 46.

9 Robert Stam, "Beyond Fidelity: The Dialogics of Adaptation," in James Naremore (ed.), *Film Adaptation* (New Brunswick, NJ: Rutgers University Press, 2000), p. 62.

10 Dudley Andrew, "Adaptation," in Naremore (ed.), *Film Adaptation*, p. 29.

11 Max Horkheimer and Theodor W. Adorno, *Dialectic of Enlightenment* (1944; New York: Herder and Herder, 1972), p. 134.

12 Epes Winthrop Sargent, *Technique of the Photoplay*, 3rd edn (New York: The Moving Picture World, 1916), p. 244.

13 Schulberg, *What Makes Sammy Run?*, p. 139.

14 Robert Stam discusses aspects of these radical acts of adaptation in "Beyond Fidelity," p. 63.

15 "Box Office Champions of 1933," *Motion Picture Herald* (February 3, 1934), 16–17. (In fact, *Gold Diggers of '33* was tied for second and *42nd Street* was tied for third in this listing.) Patricia King Hanson (ed.), *The American Film Institute Catalog of Motion Pictures Produced in the United States, Feature Films, 1931–1940* (Berkeley, CA: University of California Press, 1993), pp. 2043–4.

16 J. Hoberman, *42nd Street* (London: British Film Institute, 1993); Rick Altman, *The American Film Musical* (Bloomington, IN: University of Indiana Press, 1987), p. 228.

17 Sometimes the author or filmmaker will feel the need to point out a textual reference that others have missed. Godard is one such example. See Iampolski, *The Memory of Tiresias*, pp. 31–2.

18 Although Bruce Chipman fails to mention *They Shoot Horses, Don't They?* in *Into America's Dream-dump: A Postmodern Study of the Hollywood Novel* (Lanham, MD: University Press of America, 1999), he considers *I Should Have Stayed Home* as the last of the "early Hollywood novels" (p. 45). The novel is dealt with in some depth in John Parris Springer, *Hollywood Fictions: The Dream Factory in American Popular Literature* (Norman: University of Oklahoma Press, 2000), pp. 152–7.

19 Robert van Gelder, *The New York Times* (July 25, 1935), 17. Writing in the Sunday book review section of *The New York Times*, Edith H. Walton remarked, "in pace and violence it may be inferior to the Cain–Hammett opuses, but its implications are far more deadly": "They Shoot Horses, Don't They?" (July 28, 1935), 6F. See John Thomas Sturak, "The Life and Writings of Horace McCoy," unpublished PhD dissertation, University of California at Los Angeles, 1966, p. 272.

20 Sturak, "The Life and Writings of Horace McCoy," p. 273.

21 If attentive to elements of the novel's style, Sturak concludes that "more than a symbolic comment upon the desperate socio-economic condition of the Western world in the thirties,

McCoy's marathon *danse macabre* is also an universally applicable parable of modern man's existential predicament" (Sturak, "The Life and Writings of Horace McCoy," p. 268). He wrongly concludes, I think, that McCoy "consciously minimized topical allusions to the Depression" (p. 269). Such approaches tend to examine the novel separately from both social and cultural contexts.

22  Wilson, "The Boys in the Back Room," p. 22.

23  While offering impressive insights, Wilson's essay also has serious limitations. Despite its publication date, McCoy had written *They Shoot Horses* long before the publication of Cain's *The Postman Only Rings Twice* (Sturak, "The Life and Writings of Horace McCoy," pp. 273–8). He also overlooked important works, notably *Double Indemnity*, which appeared in serial form in the mid-1930s, though it was not published as a novel until 1943. Likewise, he appears unaware of Horace McCoy's second novel, *No Pockets in a Shroud* (London: A. Barker, 1937), published only in England. More problematically, Wilson sees McCoy as secondary and subservient to Cain, making him, along with Richard Hallas (Eric Knight), a member of the Cain "school" of fiction, which he suggests is indebted to Ernest Hemingway.

24  Wilson, "Boys in the Back Room," p. 48.

25  Sturak, "Life and Writings of Horace McCoy," pp. 257–61.

26  Jopi Nyman, *Hard-boiled Fiction and Dark Romanticism* (Frankfurt, Germany: Peter Lang, 1998), pp. 57–8.

27  Horace McCoy, *I Should Have Stayed Home* (1938; London: Midnight Classics, 1996), p. 5.

28  Seger, *The Art of Adaptation*, p. 218.

29  Rudy Behlmer (ed.), *Inside Warner Bros (1935–1951)* (New York: Viking, 1985), p. 10.

30  Andrew Bergman, *We're in the Money* (1971; Chicago: Ivan R. Dee, 1992), pp. 62–3.

31  See Noel Burch, "Double speak: de l'ambiguïté tendancielle du cinéma hollywoodien: cinéma et réception," *Réseaux* 99 (2000), 99–130.

32  Charles Musser, "DeMille, Divorce and the Comedy of Remarriage," in Kristine Brunovska Karnick and Henry Jenkins (eds), *Classical Hollywood Comedy* (New York: Routledge, 1995), pp. 282–313. Griffith's films for Biograph might offer an earlier example of these principles.

33  Sigmund Freud, *Jokes and their Relation to the Unconscious* (London: Hogarth Press, 1960).

34  For an examination of musicals and the utopic, see Altman, *The American Film Musical*, esp. pp. 69, 77, 206. See also Jane Feuer, *The Hollywood Musical* (Bloomington, IN: University of Indiana Press, 1982), p. 17.

35  See Herbert G. Goldman, *Jolson: The Legend Comes to Life* (New York: Oxford University Press, 1988), pp. 157–8, 184, and Michael Freedland, *Jolson* (New York: Stein and Day, 1972), pp. 124–5. Nancy Marlow-Trump, *Ruby Keeler: A Photographic Biography* (Jefferson, NC: McFarland, 1998), pp. 44–5, 50–2, offers a cleaned-up account of Keeler's love life and rise. This conflation between life and art echoes an earlier Warner Brothers' film, *The Jazz Singer* (1927): Jake Rabinowitz (aka Jack Robin) evokes the story of Al Jolson, who also happens to be playing the role.

36  Gary Marmorstein, *Hollywood Rhapsody: Movie Music and its Makers 1900 to 1975* (New York: Schirmer Books, 1997), p. 57.

37  Melvyn LeRoy as told to Dick Kleiner, *Melvyn LeRoy: Take One* (New York: Hawthorn, 1974), p. 104.

38  Springer, echoing Sturak, suggests that McCoy's removal of references to bread lines in the novel version of *They Shoot Horses* (as opposed to the earlier short story) moves away from the specifics of the Depression to a more universal story. On the contrary, with bread lines mentioned in the Warner Brothers' musicals, these references became redundant and unnecessary (Springer, *Hollywood Fictions*, pp. 152–7).

39  Syd Field, *Screenplay: The Foundations of Screenwriting*, expanded edn (New York: Dell, 1994), pp. 14–15.

40  Horace McCoy, *They Shoot Horses, Don't They?* (1935; London: Serpent's Tail, 1995). Subsequent quotations by page number in parenthesis in the text will be to this edition.

41  Gaspar Gonzalez-Monzon, "Barnstorming American Culture: Traveling Entertainment as Work and Performance," unpublished PhD thesis, Yale University, 1999.

42  Their names share other letters as well, though there are some gaps (Robert Syverten lacks the "U" to have all the letters in "Ruby"). Robert has the potential to be a Ruby, but lacks something – perhaps luck, perhaps common sense or street smarts.

43  In this respect, it is crucial for both films that the director (Marsh) and producer (Barney) are asexual, without romantic attachment or interest.

44  As Al Jolson told *Motion Picture Classic Magazine*, "Not that I don't have a lot of fun in life, understand me. I'm always kidding. If I break a leg I enjoy that experience. If I make a million I enjoy that one" (quoted in Freedland, *Jolson*, p. 123).

45  Robert S. MacElvaine, *The Great Depression* (New York: Times Books, 1984), p. 174.

46  Stam, "Beyond Fidelity," p. 69.

47  Seger, *The Art of Adaptation*, p. 7.

48  Schulberg, *What Makes Sammy Run?*, p. 73

49  Feuer, *The Hollywood Musical*, p. 17.

50  Wilson, "The Boys in the Back Room," p. 20.

51  Carol J. Martin, *Dance Marathons: Performing American Culture of the 1920s and 1930s* (Minneapolis, MN: University of Mississippi Press, 1994).

52  In Sidney Pollack's film adaptation of this novel, the couples also wear numbers. The principal characters wear the numbers 65, 66, 67, and 68 – the years of the Vietnam War.

53  It is perhaps worth noting another difference between the McCoy novel and the Pollack film adaptation. In Pollack's film, the horse is running free when it falls in the hole and breaks a leg. In the novel, it is pulling a plow.

54  It has always intrigued me that the unemployed chorine played by Ruby Keeler at the beginning of *Gold Diggers of '33* wears perfectly applied lipstick in bed. Even though she is without a job and so without a reason to get out of that bed in the morning, her character must retain a glamorous sheen.

55  Michael Denning, *The Cultural Front: The Laboring of American Culture in the Twentieth Century* (London: Verso, 1996), pp. 118–21.

56  The realist thrust of *42nd Street* and *Gold Diggers of '33* is evident if we contrast them to later backstage musicals such as *Singin' in the Rain* (1952) or *Band Wagon* (1953).

57  Kenneth Burke, "Revolutionary Symbolism in America" (1935), quoted in Denning, *The Cultural Front*, p. 122.

58  Denning, *The Cultural Front*, p. 121.

59  Schulberg, *What Makes Sammy Run?*, p. 62.

# Chapter 16

# The Sociological Turn of Adaptation Studies
## The Example of *Film Noir*

## R. Barton Palmer

The screen adaptation of literary works has not emerged as a focus of cinema studies since the advent of theory began to organize (some might say create) the field in the late 1970s.[1] That film scholars have not been interested in what we might term adaptation studies has not gone unnoticed. In a widely influential survey of theoretical work, published twenty years ago, Dudley Andrew conceded that film adaptations constituted a "peculiar discourse," yet issued a strong call to arms: "We need to be sensitive to that discourse and to the forces that motivate it."[2] His colleagues, with a few exceptions, have not responded to the summons. This is surprising on theoretical grounds. For (post)structuralists otherwise display an enthusiasm for connections that transgress textual boundaries.

Intertextuality is a key element in the poststructuralist understanding of how texts are constructed and how they do their cultural work. It is essentially a relational concept that focuses not on texts *in se* but on the relations between them. Popularized by Julia Kristeva, following the work of M. M. Bakhtin, intertextuality thus contests the received notion of closed and self-sufficient "works," their borders impermeable to influence, their structures unwelcoming of alien forms. As an archly postmodernist critical protocol, intertextuality provides an ideal theoretical basis from which can proceed an account of the shared identity of the literary source and its cinematic reflex. This is because intertextuality emphasizes both constructiveness (as opposed to expressivity) and the conventionality of materials, seen not only as *parole*, but also as *langue*. Unlike the aesthetic of high modernism, it does not privilege textual self-containment or "spatial form." And this is important because any consideration of filmic adaptation means speaking of one text while speaking of another. Adaptation is thus by definition intertextual, or transtextual, to use Gérard Genette's more precise and inclusive taxonomic concept of textual relations.[3]

In fact, from a transtextual viewpoint, the filmic adaptation of literary texts is especially interesting since the borders transgressed involve divergent signifying systems and practices. Filmic adaptation, to describe it in terms of structuralist theory, is inter- (not intra-) semiotic. Because the signifying systems of the cinema are also mixed, including the specifically cinematic and non-specifically cinematic codes first identified by Christian Metz, adaptation studies should hold a special interest for (post)structuralist theory and critical practice. This would be especially true if adaptation studies took what Andrew identifies as a "sociological turn" toward a consideration of institutional and contextual issues.

The reason is simple. An embrace of the sociological would permit adaptation studies to do more than probe the relationship between a particular literary source and its filmic reflex. Adaptation studies, in other words, could be more than just another critical protocol, more than just another approach to a valued or interesting text. Sociologically conceived, the field Andrew suggests might attempt answering this central question: "How does adaptation serve the cinema?" A short answer, I suggest, is that adaptation provides the cinema not only with new texts, but with new norms and models (conceived, in the neoformalist sense, as systems of norms). Such inquiries might be especially useful in the writing of cinema history. For they might explain how exactly literary texts or the signifying practices they employ have come to be incorporated within the cinema. For the cinema, like the novel, as Robert Stam eloquently puts it, is not only a "summa" in the sense that it provides a structure within which competing or opposed forms can be included and reconciled. It has also become "a receptacle open to all kinds of literary and pictorial symbolism, to all types of collective representation, to all ideologies, to all aesthetics."[4]

Despite Metz's emphasis on mixed codes (the signifying reflex of the cinema as "receptacle"), an important thrust of the theory revolution his writing in large measure promoted, especially in the United States, has been to establish the specificity and independence of film as an art form. Much of this work (including the turn toward psychoanalysis, the incorporation of Althusserian re-thinking of ideology, the modeling of the cinematic apparatus) has responded to a felt need, following French and British initiatives, to theorize the medium's connection to politics. However constitutive of film studies as a separate discipline, such developments have had at least one unfortunate consequence. The linguistic, more properly discursive, impulse of the first wave of semiotic thinking was abandoned before it could be made to yield insight into the relationship between the two signifying practices, film and literature, that have much in common (most prominently, an orientation toward narrativity on the level of connotation). In any event, it now seems clear that the ideal complement to Metz's early and very productive work is in fact supplied by a Bakhtinian translinguistics, supplemented by concepts drawn from discourse analysis and the narratology of Genette. Unfortunately, this approach has not yet found wide acceptance in film studies.

The theory revolution contested much in the Western humanist tradition. But it also had its culturally conservative side. More or less unconsciously, theorizing the specificity of the medium's psychological motors and ideological apparatus constructed film as an object properly *sui generis*. This conceptualization (at least in some important ways) fell in line with the tradition of German idealist aesthetics formulated by Lessing and, pre-eminently, Kant. Such a move, not coincidentally, argued for the funding and foundation of cinema studies as a stand-alone academic discipline – not as one of several tangential areas, like linguistics and folklore, that could effectively be contained by the larger disciplinary embrace of English departments. There is no small irony in this effect of "grand" theory. For cultural materialism (or, less politically, cultural studies) took shape during the past two decades from similar theoretical underpinnings, especially Althusserian Marxism and Lacanian psychology. The enthusiasm and work of film scholars fueled this disciplinary innovation, in the United States and in Britain. Now recognized as a legitimate academic specialty, cultural materialism ignores the disciplinary boundaries between film and literature, even as it provides fertile ground for working on their interconnections. Thus, it is within the general disciplinary framework of cultural materialism that a sociologically oriented adaptation studies might find its most appropriate and welcoming home.

During the past three decades, cinema studies has aspired to, and been somewhat successful in establishing, a freedom from institutional ghettoizing. And this was perhaps the reason why a different defense of cinematic particularity (but *not* specificity), though achieving an international renown, was not much taken up by the theory revolutionaries. I refer to the identification of filmmaking as a form of writing (*écriture*) and the director as a writer (*auteur*), the theoretical and critical position promulgated by the *Cahiers du Cinéma* circle in the 1950s and generally known as the *politique des auteurs*. The *Cahiers* position, to simplify, views film and literature as analogs whose complementarity should not be dismissed on any *a priori* grounds. Though showing little enthusiasm for a pseudo-literary cinema of "quality" that had often been praised by others, the *Cahiers* critics, especially André Bazin, did not reject the interest or importance of studying film adaptation.

However, a nascent discipline eager to establish its independence perhaps could not afford such tolerance and breadth of critical vision. An approach that identified films as secondary, especially as derivative versions of valued literary texts, would enact in microcosmic form the institutional bondage of film to literature. It would also reinforce the notion that the cinema was an art form dependent on prior literary creation. In adaptation studies, the cinema's value often was implicitly located in the honored texts it recycled in versions now accessible to a mass audience. Providing popular abridgments of literary masterpieces (to make the obvious point) hardly argued for the cultural importance of the seventh art. To be sure, even André Bazin's ostensibly positive remarks about a filmic adaptation's status as a "digest" betray a lack of enthusiasm for such a secondary role.[5]

The standard view on adaptation positioned the source text as high art and its adaptation as mass culture. Little work was done when the opposite was the case; that is, when the dross of a pulp or mediocre novel was transmuted into cinematic gold, as, for example, when it was a question of such Hitchcock masterpieces as *Strangers on a Train*

(1951), *Rear Window* (1954), and *Vertigo* (1958). Thus, studies of filmic adaptation, whose objects were chosen by virtue of the source's literary value, microcosmically restaged the fall across what Andreas Huyssens appropriately terms "the great divide" between high and mass culture. The interest of the American cinema, even before the evolution of the feature film, in producing screen versions of literary masterpieces could also be seen as the leading edge of the decline lamented by the Frankfurt School theorists. For Hollywood was part of the "culture industry," as Theodor Adorno and Max Horkheimer termed it, that not only devoted itself to meaningless textual production, but victimized, in the manner of a greedy parasite, the high culture it displaced and replaced.

Studying filmic adaptation thus ran counter to the new theorizing about the cinema in the 1970s – not to mention the academic respectability and independence that such work implicitly argued for. Adaptation studies encountered disfavor on both intellectual and institutional grounds. In addition, there was also the considerable question of established practice. Analyzing the film versions of literary fiction or drama was a popular critical sideline of English professors who liked to go to the movies (but often had little or no academic training in the area). With the increasing turn of the profession toward the journal publication of interpretations in the late 1960s, such critical work even led to the founding of a specialized venue, *Literature/Film Quarterly*, in 1973, which was exclusively devoted to publishing the results of this research. Ironically, the enthusiasm of English professors for writing about the cinema as a kind of secondary literary form was one of the first signs in the United States of an awakening academic interest in film. But these studies of screen adaptation implicitly upheld humanist, neo-romantic values – which were a poor fit with the anti-humanism of semiotic and poststructuralist theorizing.

Actually, adaptation studies was also a poor fit with neo-romanticism. In the long run, this has proved even more problematic. Neo-romanticism can only understand adaptation as a fall from textual uniqueness and self-containment because it involves both the severing of the text's genetic connection with its creator and the confection of another version of what could not (should not?) be reproduced. In any analysis of adaptation, the neo-romantic view of the "great literary work" meant acknowledging, if only unconsciously, that what had been valued as a "creative" artifact (the material reflex of genius) could and did exist within a transtextual series. In short, the unique could find a second existence in another form. The literary work, it was undeniable, had been transformed from a text into a pretext, or, to use the Genettian term, into a hypotext.

This transtextual tie raised the uncomfortable possibility that the literary work itself might not be unsourced and unexampled, might in fact be, to use the Bakhtinian term, itself an "answer" to other texts whose voices, whose otherness might still be discovered within. In other words, the paradox of traditional screen adaptation studies is that the very fact of textual history that constitutes the focus of critical attention (the transtextual tie between fictional and filmic forms) threatens the values of neo-romanticism. Perhaps this accounts for the often directly expressed concession in such studies that no adaptation could "equal" the original. In any event, the neo-romantic theory of the artist locates meaning and form in the artist him or herself, thus reorienting the term "original," as Raymond Williams has shown, which comes to mean "having no origin." Isolated from any textual series, the literary text thus becomes personal property whose rights belong to its creator. Any texts that derive from it are *ipso facto* valueless, for they do not result from the originary, creative process that produced their model. Traditional adaptation studies thus strive to estimate the value of what, by its very nature, can possess no value.

This *aporia* is signified by the promotion of "faithfulness" as the most important criterion of evaluation. Faithfulness suggests that one way of looking at an adaptation is to see it as a kind of translation, as a "presence" that stands for and signifies the "absence" of the source text. Thus the act of translation produces the impossible co-presence of two texts with the same identity that are not the same. Fidelity promotes an evaluation of the target text's presence in terms of what it is not and what it could not be (that is, the source text) if it continued to be itself. Or, to put it another way, the better the adaptation is, the less it can be differentiated from what, in its otherness, it must replace. The most faithful adaptation would simply be the reinstantiation of the source text. But this would refine the adaptation out of existence and, not unimportantly, obliterate the textual series it constitutes.

Faithfulness thus becomes an eternally elusive Holy Grail, the obtaining of which should restore the adaptation to itself (i.e., to identity with its source). This state of unattainable purity would reverse the fall into transtextuality. In the familiar terms of post-structuralism, the traditional study of filmic adaptation treats the screen version as a disposable supplement to the literary text. Thus, an adaptation can be valued only if, through some kind of organic trope (principally reproduction), the separateness of, yet link between, source and adaptation can be figured. Jacques Derrida, to take a notable example, speaks of the "citational graft" that "belongs to the structure of every mark, spoken or written . . . engendering an infinity of new contexts in a manner which is absolutely illimitable."[6] The trope is well chosen and especially apt in regard to the traditional notion of adaptation. For a graft can produce something new when planted by itself (that is, if it becomes a "cutting") or suffer subordination to whatever it is properly joined to.[7]

As a trope, translation is useful because it emphasizes the (at least normally) shared identity of source and adaptation. But translation is also distorting, for it postulates a "carrying over" of some irreducible set of features or qualities from one text to another. There are two serious problems here. On the one hand, the source text is not altered through translation (nothing is removed from it, in the manner of an organ transplant). On the other hand, it is impossible to identify the irreducible features that establish a connection between any hypotext and its potential hypertexts, which can assume an unlimited number of forms. In other words, the same source text can sustain an infinite number of translations, each of which might select different aspects to "carry over." A correlative is that the reversal of the process cannot re-create the source text. This principle of irreversibility is a clear indication of the source text's priority, but it also signals the hypertext's freedom from "carrying over" something irreducible. Moreover, in postulating a material connection between the two texts, with what is shared coming from the source, translation makes it difficult to theorize any adaptation as a separate entity. Or, from a global perspective, it makes it difficult to theorize adaptation as an area of study worthy in its own right, as something that might be said to "serve" the cinema.

Invoking representation as a trope makes it much easier to do so. In Aristotle's oft-quoted formulation, representation depends on three terms: the object represented, the means by which representation is effected (language in the case of literature; the specific and non-specific codes of cinema in the case of film); and the manner of representation or the specific ways in which the means are employed (particular "styles" or sub-sets of conventions). For Aristotle, the artist's deployment of the means and manner of representation, in reference to its object, results in a representation that relates to the object in a way that can normally be defined by the concept of iconicity. In short, a representation can more or less resemble its object, just as an adaptation can more or less resemble its source text.

Following Aristotle's lead, we might say that such resemblance may serve, rhetorically but not essentially, to establish a shared identity of sorts. Or the resemblance between the object and its representation may be passed over in silence, even deliberately obscured. Fidelity is one of the protocols that, in different ways, affects such a process of representation. In the case of the filmic adaptation of literary texts, a sense of "faithfulness" is most often an aspect of affect, a favorable impression created for the spectator. It is not a criterion of value to be established by the re-presentation of something irreducible.

Lillian Hellman's play *The Children's Hour*, for example, has twice been adapted for the screen: once under its own name (*The Children's Hour*, directed by William Wyler in 1961) and once under another name (*These Three*, directed by William Wyler in 1936). The two versions differ considerably, perhaps in regard to what some might call an irreducible something. For Hellman's original conception of the play's action turns on the possibility, ultimately confirmed, that the two female protagonists share a homosocial, even homosexual connection. Though Hellman herself penned the rewritten screenplay, *These Three* substitutes a heterosexual dynamic (with the two women now competing for the love of a male friend). The later screen version, *The Children's Hour*, in contrast, resembles the original stage play more closely. Despite the arguably "central" revision of *These Three* from the original, both versions are equally adaptations of the same source text, with the differences between them to be accounted for "sociologically," in this case the unalterable opposition of the Production Code Administration in the 1930s (but not in the early 1960s) to any hint of a homosexual theme. As representations, the two versions differ in their degree of iconicity. But their value lies not simply in their identity with their object (with how "faithful" they are). It may be measured instead by whatever qualities they have as representations.[8] In fact, only by being "unfaithful" to its source could Hellman's play initially serve the cinema by providing it with new and interesting dramatic material.

Aristotle, of course, assumed that what is represented would be some aspect of the natural world (particularly "actions"), not another text from a different semiotic series.

But this different object poses no difficulties. Representation is a trope that usefully illuminates the process of adaptation without imposing an inappropriate *a priori* set of values for judging the relative value of hypotext and hypertext. From this perspective, the adaptation is part of a new and independent (if interconnected) textual order. As Dudley Andrew puts it, "in the case of those texts explicitly termed adaptations, the cultural model that the cinema represents is already treasured as a representation in another sign system."[9] I would offer only one correction to this formulation: the cultural model in question need hardly be treasured. The point is important. For valorizing "faithfulness" seems a desperate gesture at recuperating an outmoded concept of textual production whose foundational concept is the irreproducible original. This does not mean, however, that we can ignore fidelity. For it is a rhetorical force (or, alternatively, a norm or protocol) often of considerable importance in explaining the relationship between the source and its adaptation.

Abandoning traditional notions of fidelity, moreover, permits us to re-orient the question usually asked about film adaptations of literary sources. For, as Andrew rightly suggests, the sociological turn means that we no longer ask how the adaptation (pre)serves the source, but how adaptation, as a general phenomenon of intersemiotic relations, serves the cinema. In the remainder of this chapter, I will attempt an *in parvo* answer to that question by focusing on one of the Hollywood cinema's most intriguing and yet obscure developments, the advent and flourishing of what has come to be called *film noir*.

## *Film Noir* and Adaptation

What is perhaps best termed the "*film noir* phenomenon" is now acknowledged as the most important textual development of 1940s' and 1950s' Hollywood. The sudden advent of a "dark cinema" that, from within, contested Hollywood's textual optimism was a startling innovation. Or, at least, so it appears in retrospect. Some six decades later, it is now clear that *film noir* dialogized a storytelling tradition previously marked by ideological closure. The most important mark of that closure was the restoration of the social status quo: simply put, the resolution of the problem or disruption posed by the narrative in favor of conventional, mainstream values – social, sexual, moral, scientific, and political. It was such a "happy ending" that Hollywood's customers were thought to have wanted, at least most of the time.

*Film noir*, we might say, catered to a different taste, if not to a different audience. These films revealed in some depth the dark, often grotesque underside of American life. Thus they followed a representational protocol opposed to that of mainstream texts, which tended to identify the narrative problem with some easily explicable aberrancy, not an alternative world or mode of living. *Film noir*, however, did more than give diegetic shape to an alternative world. These films also refused to figure that dark underside within the context of appropriately "restorative" forces. In other words, these films resisted the imposition of poetic justice, the movement toward heterosexual coupling (and away from other forms of the sexual), the sharp and traditional delineation of gender roles, the endorsement of the American political and legal systems, the celebration of family life, and, perhaps above all, the exaltation of those values summed up in the term Horatio Algerism. In the grim cityscape limned by *noir* films, restorative forces sometimes lose their purchase and relevance entirely – even if at the very end these nightmare visions are recuperated as dream, fantasy, or psychopathology.

Such Caligarism, however, does not really save appearances. As the *Cahiers* critics in the later 1960s correctly observed, Hollywood films differ in the degree to which they display the contradictions inherent in their culturally derived materials. Following that typology, *film noir* may be most usefully understood as belonging to "Category E," or those films that seem, in a "normal" fashion, to repress the difficulties and incoherencies of ideology, but which, upon closer inspection, are "splitting under an internal tension which is simply not there in an ideologically innocuous film."[10] In the case of "progress-ive *auteurs*," as *Cahiers* termed them, it was easy to understand why their films self-deconstructed, that is, without the aid of critical analysis. *Film noir*'s refusal of socially conservative resolutions, the hallmark of ideological closure, proved more difficult to explain, absent (at least in many cases) a discernible authorial intention. And, I might add, absent as well any thoroughgoing study of the anti-establishmentarian literary sources of this emerging tradition.

Not surprisingly, *film noir* cannot be easily accommodated to the notion of the "classic Hollywood text," the inductively derived formulary that has dominated study of the Hollywood cinema for nearly three decades. Which is to say, *film noir* cannot be described or accounted fully for by either the Neoformalist (Bordwell and Thompson) or Realist models (Allen and Gomery). Though of immense descriptive value in the grand tradition of structuralist theory, these two approaches, with their strong emphasis on Hollywood "systems," prove less useful in providing explanations that must take into account the influence of other textual traditions, including those from literature and overseas cinemas.

In Bakhtinian terms, the explanations of the Neoformalists and Realists emphasize the monologic tendencies or centripetal self-regulation that characterize all semiotic prac-tices. Even when eschewing a purely synchronic orientation, such structural methods prove less useful in explaining changes that arise from outside the system. In the case of *film noir*, the two most important events are the "Germanization" of Hollywood following the collapse of the Weimar film industry; and the sudden upsurge in the popularity of those fictional genres of American middlebrow literature summed up in the term *roman noir* or "black novel." Such fictional texts deserve the designation "black" for they unremit-tingly portray an America rife with urban malaise, unrepentant criminality, and the break-down of traditional values. Now acceptable to a broad readership, these novels and stories were soon adapted for the screen by a Hollywood eager, as always, for narrative material of proven appeal. A third influence, certainly not negligible, came from both French cinema and cinema culture. These "outside" forces, often centrifugal in their pressure and effect, proved to be of crucial importance in the shaping of the textual tradition, often through literary adaptation in some sense.

Most often in film studies, looking at literary adaptation has meant an "atomist" focus on the relations between an admired fictional text and its cinematic reflex. In contrast, the kind of inquiry I propose must take a "global" perspective on the body of sub-literary and literary texts that constitute in some sense the literary origins of *film noir*. My purpose will be instead to suggest a direction that adaptation studies might take in explaining, if only in part, the advent and nature of *film noir*. Clearly, *film noir* is the result of developments in which literary and cinematic influences are difficult, even impossible to entangle. The transtextual connections between the two institutions, literary and cinematic, are multifarious, and, in the case of *film noir*, complexly international as well. The advent of this studio type is thus overdetermined – its history a veritable polyphony of harmonizing and competing "voices" from different cinematic and literary traditions. After a brief survey of this polyphony, I will conclude with some remarks about how an approach might be developed to analyzing one of these "voices."

Like adaptation, *film noir* is a relational, not an essential term, at least as far as the Hollywood cinema is concerned. We should recall that, used to describe some American films of the immediate postwar era, it was first intended to characterize a resemblance and a transtextual connection rather than to designate some defining and essential set of conventions. The "dark" Hollywood films in the 1940s were first identified as a group – and valued as an intriguing new departure – by French journalists who thought them similar to certain "dark" French films of the previous decade. Interestingly, this "resemblance" discovered by criticism was subsequently confirmed by a number of direct connections – literary/filmic adaptations that link the two cinemas. Fritz Lang adapted Zola's *La Bête humaine* in the *noir* style (*Human Desire*, 1954), but his film was an homage in part to Jean Renoir's classic screen version of the novel (*La Bête humaine*, 1938). Lang's adaptation of George de la Fouchardière's *La Chienne* as *Scarlet Street* (1945) is yet another homage to Renoir, who made the original screen version in 1931. Similarly, Otto Preminger's *The Thirteenth Letter* (1951) is also a double adaptation: a remake of Henri-Georges Clouzot's adaptation of Louis Chavance's *Le Corbeau* (1943). Finally, Anatole Litvak's *The Long Night* (1947) remakes Marcel Carné's classic *Le Jour se lève* (1939), perhaps the central text of the pre-war French *noir* series.

These four American *films noirs* not only adapted for the Hollywood screen certain classics of modern French literature (here the presence of Zola, who inaugurated the movement of literary naturalism, is defining), they also forged a transtextual tie between the French screen versions of such "dark" naturalist fiction and the American *film noir*, actualizing the perception of critics of a resemblance between the two cinemas. And, to analyze these connections from another point of view, the French naturalist texts in question are "selected" for adaptation along with so many American *romans noirs*. The two literary traditions are thereby shown to resemble one another, but only implicitly, for this resemblance, though not concealed, is not emphasized by the adaptation process.

Thus, Lang's *Human Desire* was marketed as neither a Renoir remake nor a Zola adaptation. One surmises therefore that the motive for adaptation was that Renoir/Zola provided material that could be readily assimilated to the series of *roman noir* adaptations and their imitations. Hence the original title, not useful for publicity, was discarded in favor of a *noir* emphasis on both a self-interested promiscuity and a more "normal" form of heterosexual predation (the protagonist's greater interest in a transgressive woman in need of protection than in the "good" girl who truly loves him). The original forms of the story, literary and cinematic, concern themselves with a sexual perversity that might not have passed PCA scrutiny and needed to be altered for the American screen. Yet Lang and screenwriter Alfred Hayes were also influenced greatly by the *roman noir*. Zola and Renoir share a naturalist interest in the iron rule of genetic inheritance and its irresistible thwarting of the moral and the rational in human behavior. For this, the Hollywood version substitutes an unfathomable fatality, the outward sign of the reign of the accidental in human affairs, which is so strong an element in the fiction of Cornell Woolrich, David Goodis, Dorothy Hughes, and other leading lights of the American *roman noir*. Like the other three Hollywood re-adaptations of French originals, *Human Desire* evidences the *rapprochement* of two literary traditions, the discovery of a common ground useful to the Hollywood cinema.

More important, however, may be the transference of value from one cinematic culture to the other. For it is the positive French valuation of Hollywood *film noir* that gave rise to an Anglo-American re-examination of these films, only then conceived as a series or genre. Another link between the French and American cinemas is that some of the émigrés from the Weimar cinema who eventually made American *films noirs* worked for a time in the French cinema, contributing to that country's tradition of dark film. Instructive examples are two films directed during his brief French exile by Robert Siodmak, who was later to become Hollywood's most prolific director of *film noir*. Both *Mister Flow* (1936) and *Cargaison blanche* (1937) offer much the same visual style and themes of such Siodmak American films as *Criss Cross* (1948) and *Christmas Holiday* (1944). *Mister Flow*, I might add, like some of Siodmak's other dark Weimar and French films, is a literary adaptation, based on the French *roman noir* of the same name by Gaston Leroux. The *roman noir*, we might recall, is itself an international phenomenon and flourished in all three countries in which Siodmak worked: Germany, France, and the United States.

And "dark fiction" had deep roots in English popular literature as well. The advent of *film noir* in the United States soon became even more broadly international. British *film noir* was a series inspired by native fictional traditions and also by a number of Anglo-American co-productions (for example, Jules Dassin's *Night and the City* [1950] and Joseph L. Mankiewicz's *Escape* [1948]). *Film noir* quickly became a staple of fifties' cinema in Britain. Many of that country's most noted postwar films, including Carol Reed's *The Third Man* (1949) and Joseph Losey's *The Sleeping Tiger* (1954), are deeply *noir*. Perhaps more important, French New Wave filmmaking offers an extended homage to American *film noir*, from Godard's *A bout de souffle* (1960) to Truffaut's *La Mariée etait en noir* (1968) and *La Sirène du Mississippi* (1969). This homage is not only cinematic, but also literary, involving a continuation of the screen adaptation that had fueled the American movement.

The two Truffaut films are quite faithful adaptations of forties' novels by Cornell Woolrich, *The Bride Wore Black* and *Waltz into Darkness*. Woolrich was the American master of the *roman noir*. His tales of mysterious fatality, disastrous coincidence, pervasive criminality, and female vengeance fascinated the American reading public of the 1940s. Woolrich's novels and stories were often the source of American *films noirs* during the period, the most notable of which, perhaps, is Alfred Hitchcock's *Rear Window*. Truffaut's work, then, is from this perspective an extension of the American dark cinema, and his films in turn did much to reinvigorate native French *noir* traditions, which were strong in the fifties and sixties. Such a multi-directional international transtextuality is one of the distinguishing features of the *film noir* phenomenon. It finds a reflex in the Anglo-American diversity of the literary sources. Britain's Graham Greene, Eric Ambler, and W. Somerset Maugham figure alongside America's Woolrich, Raymond Chandler, and James M. Cain as writers who have exerted a great influence on Hollywood's dark cinema.

Can *film noir* then be accurately described as a Hollywood phenomenon? Or does it more properly belong, energized by the play of international influences, literary and cinematic, to world cinema? Such questions become more pressing when we also take into consideration German influences on *film noir*. On the one hand, these influences are properly transtextual, exercised through the international popularity of German Expressionism, especially the later phase of that movement, the so-called *Kammerspielfilm* or "chamber play film." On the other hand, this Germanization is a feature of the partial transference of the cinematic means of production, the relocation of the Weimar directors, cameramen, art designers, actors, writers, and others who emigrated, virtually en masse, to Hollywood during the 1930s. "Adapting" themselves to a different set of cinematic institutions, these émigrés played an important role in the making of Hollywood *film noir*. A short list of relevant directors makes this plain: Robert Siodmak, Billy Wilder, Otto Preminger, Fritz Lang, Boris Ingster, Josef von Sternberg, Rudolph Maté, Edgar G. Ulmer, and Anatole Litvak. Obviously, the view that *film noir* is in some sense a Germanization of Hollywood has much to recommend it.

A complexly international development, *film noir* also differs from other Hollywood genres or series in that it was not a production category, or, at least, not until its selfconscious revival during the Hollywood Renaissance of the early 1970s. No Hollywood producer or director of the 1940s set out to make a *film noir*. This raises a question that has been variously answered during the past three decades. Is classic *film noir* a genre (like the Western) or a series (like the disaster film)? Is neither term an adequate description? What complicates this taxonomic inquiry is that several pre-existing genres, especially the detective film, the woman's picture, and the thriller, are "adapted," as it were, to a *noir* sensibility. Even the Western (for example, *Pursued* [1947], *Blood on the Moon* [1948], *Rawhide* [1951]) and the comedy film (for example, *Fly by Night* [1942], *Arsenic and Old Lace* [1944], *Unfaithfully Yours* [1948]) offer important texts marked deeply by *noir* elements. Perhaps ultimately unclassifiable, one of the most unusual Hollywood films of the immediate postwar era shows deep affinities with *film noir*: Charlie Chaplin's *Monsieur Verdoux* (1947), with its Bluebeard hero not only a serial killer but also a strangely comic figure. Though the modern city is the conventional setting of *film noir*, the period film (for example, *Gaslight* [1944], *The Tall Target* [1951]) also fell under its influence, so to speak. It would not be distorting to say that some pre-existent genres are "adapted" to a different kind of story, a different kind of ideological effect.

The familiar denizens of the *noir* universe – psychotic killers, faithless women, helpless victims of irresistible fatality – became stock characters across the breadth of forties' Hollywood production. Genres in the studio era, of course, were never separated by textual equivalents of a *cordon sanitaire*. They often dialogized one another, producing interesting hybrids. The genre system, to put it differently, was dynamic rather than static as it responded to unpredictable fluctuations in popular taste, the availability of literary sources, and the need to create star vehicles. Even so, *film noir* appears exceptional. No other genre (to use the term provisionally) seems so complexly balanced between self-sufficiency, on the one hand, and subordination to pre-existing formulas, on the other.

Either view of *film noir* can be plausibly argued, as the critical tradition amply exemplifies. Significantly, the first influential full-length study of *film noir*, Borde and Chaumeton's *Panorama du film noir américain* (1955) effectively straddles the question.[11] The two authors suggest that a new narrative type (the hard-boiled detective story) is most fully *noir*, but that a *noir* influence (the result of adaptation in some sense?) can be detected in several of the established genres as well, particularly the thriller and the crime melodrama. So *film noir*, to conclude, can be alternatively seen as something new (an innovative genre) or a different version of the familiar (a "period" in the detective film, woman's picture, and so on).

Even if this inquiry into genre is bracketed off, another difficult, and not unrelated, issue remains. Critics agree substantially on what films belong to the *film noir* category, but, rather confusingly, they differ just as substantially about what features of these films are normative. Such debate was inaugurated by Borde and Chaumeton, whose work emphasized the importance of narrative formulas. Because the narrative formulas of *film noir* are among the elements most obviously derived from literary sources, such a debate ultimately concerns what features to valorize as normative: those which are intersemiotic or those which are specifically cinematic. Thus, the debate about normative features engages the relative importance of literary adaptation.

A further complication is the formulaic diversity of the fiction termed *roman noir* or *série noire* in France (there is no adequate term in English to describe this important American and European tradition). The *roman noir* includes a number of narrative sub-types that, because they share a number of elements, prove impossible to differentiate clearly: the detective, thriller, and mystery stories, to name the three most prominent. For such important Anglo-American critics as James Damico and Amir Karimi, the diversity of *noir* narrative is the reflex of the diversity in the phenomenon's literary sources.[12] Arguably, however, such a view does not explain the influence of pre-existing Hollywood genres (such as the woman's picture) on the shape and reach of *film noir*. Here is another area, in short, that adaptation studies taking a sociological turn could fruitfully examine.

In any event, such an emphasis on narrative, and hence the importance of literary sources, did not go unchallenged. In fact, critical work after the French pioneers generally served to forestall further inquiry into the global connection between the filmic and literary traditions. Inaugurating American interest in *film noir* during the 1960s, the critic and director Paul Schrader advanced the view that *noir* is a distinctive visual style, with its roots in German Expressionism. This emergent, if derivative, style defines the cinematic realization of a diversity of fictional sources. In fact, it offers not only a means for realizing literary themes. That is, visual style is more than a specifically cinematic equivalent. Instead, *noir* style is to be valued *in se* as what is distinctive and important about the films. It is the source of meaning, not its enhancement. In such a formulation, the film's narrative becomes, if not disposable, at most the motivation for stylistic virtuosity.[13] Following the work of Raymond Durgnat, J. A. Place, and L. S. Peterson, the style position achieved prominence in American *noir* studies during the 1980s, with a corresponding de-emphasis on narrative patterns and, hence, literary sources.[14] It is thus not surprising that the most influential global treatment of *film noir*, by Alain Silver and Elizabeth Ward, is entitled *Film Noir: An Encyclopedic Reference to the American Style*.[15]

We can easily recognize that such an emphasis on *noir* style is part of the larger movement within film studies toward a valorization of cinematic specificity and, by extension, a bracketing off of literary influences. A few additional comments are needed here. In the fifties, the *Cahiers* circle in France advocated an *auteurism* that was accompanied by the implicit valorization of certain genres (for certain valued directors often worked in particular genres). The two trends happily coincided in *auteurist* work on the Westerns of John Ford and Howard Hawks, and on the *films noirs* of Anthony Mann, John Huston, Edward Dmytryk, Samuel Fuller, and Alfred Hitchcock. An interest in Hollywood genres was subsequently taken up by the *Movie* group in England. This body of Anglo-French critical work constitutes a veritable *politique des genres*, and bespeaks its close connection to the *politique des auteurs*. The two approaches emphasize style or, more inclusively, *mise-en-scène*, either that of the individual director, whose imagistic realization of narrative givens marks his creativity, or that of a group, collectively shaping a textual tradition. Thus, both *politiques* emphasize the iconographic and visual, while ignoring or, at least, undervaluing the non-cinematic. Auteurism privileges the director as a source of meaning and value rather than either the screenwriter or original source. And the *politique des genres* brackets off from more than superficial consideration the connection between film and literary genres. The two *politiques*, in fact, agree in finding little worth in what might be called a "literary" cinema. Unfortunately, much foundational work on *film noir* reflected such restrictive views of authorship and genre.

If contemporary film studies have been shaped by the theory revolution, they are also the inheritors of older Anglo-French approaches to Hollywood. In both cases, the result has been a general neglect of adaptation studies and, as far as work on *film noir* has been concerned, an underestimation of the influence of the *roman noir*.

But how to estimate that influence? How, in particular, can the adaptation of many different literary texts, events that are in an obvious sense serially "singular," be theorized as having a "global" influence on the advent of *film noir*?

An answer to this question (or more properly this series of questions, for such influence is multivalent) could be developed through the deployment of the polysystemic method. This structuralist approach has its roots in Russian Formalism, Tel Aviv narratology, and contemporary pragmatics. First developed as a theory of literary translation, polysystemics has been shown to be useful for the understanding of literary adaptation by Patrick Cattrysse in a book, published nearly a decade ago, whose importance has yet to be recognized.[16] Intriguingly, Cattrysse uses *film noir* as an extended illustration for his argument because "critics have generally associated *film noir* in an explicit fashion with a particular corpus of literary texts, that is the American *roman noir*." Yet "paradoxically, neither this literature, nor its relations with film *noir* have until now been examined in an extended or systematic way" (p. 45).

Before discussing polysystemics further, I will begin with a simple and illustrative example of how the approach works in practice. Let us consider Edward Dmytryk's *Murder, My Sweet*, a screen version of Raymond Chandler's bestselling novel, *Farewell, My Lovely*. The screenplay was written by John Paxton, probably with a fair amount of input from the director. Released in 1944, *Murder, My Sweet* was successful at the box office and received positive critical notice. Thus, the film proved important (along with John Huston's 1941 version of Dashiell Hammett's *The Maltese Falcon*) in establishing the hard-boiled detective story as a staple of what would be later termed the *noir* series. By this, I mean that it was imitated by films not based on published fiction (among other examples, by John Cromwell's *Dead Reckoning*, released in 1947). And it also cleared a path for the cinematizing of similar fiction, especially other Chandler novels (for example, Howard Hawks's *The Big Sleep*, released in 1946) and even an original screenplay by the novelist (George Marshall's *The Blue Dahlia*, released the same year). I will concentrate on one simple aspect of the adaptation process: the decision to alter Chandler's title.

Though Dmytryk's film was initially released in Minneapolis as *Farewell, My Lovely* (December 18, 1944), by its New York opening (March 8, 1945), the film's title had been changed to *Murder, My Sweet*. Before discussing the well-known explanation for this change, we should pay some attention to the underlying dynamics of the process, that is, to the semiotic systems involved and the contextual pressures that affected their deployment. Simplifying, we could say that novels use only one means of representation: words. The cinema, in contrast, mobilizes a more complex set of means. It uses words, in the forms of written language and speech, with both these categories further divisible into various diegetic and non-diegetic forms. The cinema also deploys various aspects of *mise-en-scène*, photographic realization, and non-linguistic sound. The means of the cinema thus include but exceed, in terms of variety, that of literary narrative.

The Sociological Turn: *Film Noir*

Chapter 16

In the case of titles, however, novels and films are exactly homologous, which is to say that they both use words. Thus, nothing in the different signifying systems of the two media prevents the film version in this case from precisely preserving the original title. Indeed, there would have been strong contextual pressures toward doing so since Chandler's novel was "pre-sold," a property whose popularity in fictional form might well be transferred to the screen version. But this transference could only occur were the original title retained. Fidelity, in short, would have been in this instance commercially desirable, a most important marketing consideration. However, such pressure toward fidelity (which was a general protocol) found itself in this instance in conflict with another general protocol, one also connected to marketing. It was that the titling of the classic Hollywood film should, as clearly as possible, indicate generic affiliations. Such indications, often rather general, would be clarified by poster iconography and, to some degree, by the performance histories of the principal players. In the case of *Murder, My Sweet*, the producers had decided to cast an established star, Dick Powell, very much against type, in the main role of Chandler's famous detective, Philip Marlowe. At the time of this film's release, Powell has become firmly established in Hollywood as a song and dance man, starring in musical and light comedy films such as *Dames* (1934), *Stage Struck* (1936), and *Varsity Show* (1937). Powell's presence in the film, along with the fact that Chandler's title was somewhat ambiguous, led to the decision that the film's release should continue under a different title, one that, explicitly referring to crime, would better indicate its genre. In other words, generic affiliation was in the end considered more important to the film's box office success than the fact that it was an adaptation of a well-known Chandler novel.

What this example makes clear is that the filmic adaptation of a literary source cannot simply be considered intersemiotically, as a negotiation, so to speak, between two signifying systems. The process must also be considered "sociologically," as the interplay between the norms or conventions of two semiotic systems *and* the contexts in which both hypotext and hypertext are located. As Cattrysse maintains, the proper approach to the filmic adaptation of literary sources must begin with "an instrument of analysis which permits the description and explanation, systematic as well as exhaustive, of the phenomenon" (p. 3). His preliminary analysis of certain aspects of the adaptation process in the case of *film noir* permits the identification, in the manner of the Russian Formalists, of norms and sets of norms (which may be termed systems or models). In the end, therefore:

> an approach in terms of norms and systems permits the study of the particular and the individual in a different fashion, that is, under the light of general practices and tendencies. After having discovered several general mechanisms . . . one can proceed to the study of the directors of individual films, seeing if they are "deviant" or "conventional." (p. 206)

Working in this way through several aspects of the global adaptation of the *roman noir* to the screen, Cattrysse is able to show that a number of themes from *roman noir* transfer more or less unchanged to the screen (for example, the use of dream and dream-like sequences, the unhappy ending, a misogynistic presentation of female characters). He can also show that, in one case, an accepted generalization about the global influence of the literary tradition on the filmic is not borne out by the evidence; in the body of principal texts he analyzes, flashback sequences are often suppressed in the screen versions. Cattrysse's study is full of interesting findings of this kind.

Interesting questions remain, however. In particular, a polysystemic approach does little to advance our understanding of the intersemiotic aspects of adaptation, that is, when it is a question of the film and literary versions making use of different materials. Cattrysse's study of *noir* features concentrates on narrative norms, which exist, semiotically speaking, on the level of connotation. Cattrysse acknowledges this limitation: "The differences between cinematic and literary materials of expression do not facilitate the comparison of fictional and filmic texts, the establishment of a 'third term of comparison,' and especially the metalinguistic description of such a comparison in terms of norms and systems" (p. 207). Some other theoretical approach must be devised to account for the ways in which the cinema functions as a "summa" of the other arts, as Robert Stam puts it. But the polysystemic approach to literary adaptation could "be inserted in turn into an intersystemic approach of greater generality which examines the historical connections of an intersystemic kind between the cinema and other systems of communication, artistic or non-artistic" (p. 210).

Polysystemics, furthermore, might be taken in a slightly different direction, one that Cattrysse, relying on an analysis that is basically structuralist, does not envision. For his reliance on the identification of norms and systems provides a means for determining the results of adaptation, seen in both its individual and global senses. But attention might be paid to how norms and systems are themselves changed through the adaptation process. Certainly, Cattrysse is right to suggest that a foundational element of the process is that the literary text is controlled by norms that are often quite different from those that shape its cinematic reflex. Adaptation, in other words, represents the conflict between, and subsequent negotiation of, divergent norms. As the example of *Murder, My Sweet* reveals, moreover, conflict can also occur within the norms of the filmic system, which, we might say, becomes "unbalanced" when presented with material from outside. What I mean here is that a generically ambiguous title for Dmytryk's film would never have emerged from a "pure" cinematic production process. Or, even had it emerged, there should have been no difficulty in altering it, for the conflict of norms arises only because Chandler and his publishers, responding to different values and norms within a strictly literary context, chose this particular title. We might observe that his novels (*The High Wall, The Big Sleep, The Long Goodbye* and *The Little Sister*, but *The Lady in the Lake*) generally, but not always, fail to give a strong indication that they are crime or detective fiction. Is this a deliberate effect to avoid notions of formulaic or generic pressure? If so, then there is some irony that the word "murder" (which is the titling signature of Agatha Christie, series writer par excellence) occurs in the re-titling of *Farewell, My Lovely*'s initial screen adaptation.

In any event, I would say that Cattrysse's strictly structuralist mode of analysis, based on the Saussurean model of *langue* and *parole*, would benefit from a Bakhtinian critique. The notorious blind spot of the Saussurean model is its strong emphasis on the product-ive regularity of the various codes of *langue*. If language is strictly the enactment of all-powerful rules, then how (or indeed why) does *langue* ever change? The Bakhtinian critique of this position, as is well known, emphasizes the generality of linguistic codes and the particularity of language use. To simplify, Bakhtin (and others) argue that the codes are shaped by use, responding to the needs of those who use them. Bakhtin envis-ages *langue* and *parole* as dialectic. The model of adaptation Cattrysse creates, though Saussurean in conception, is unbalanced in a fashion that goes far beyond this model. For the essence of the polysystemic model is the dialogical connection established between two signifying practices and two contexts. In short, an adaptation is by no means "generated" by this nexus of systems, but results instead from the fashion in which they interact with one another in particular cases (hence his insistence on pragmatics). This model suggests a way beyond the one Cattrysse has already eloquently described in which adaptation "serves" the cinema. For it is not only the case that texts are "translated" from one signifying practice to another, but that the norms or conventions of a literary series might be translated as well, becoming yet another element in that "mixed" body of signifying practices that constitutes the cinema. A properly dialogical polysystemics would show how adaptation, particularly of the global kind evident in the *film noir* phenomenon, can influence the medium's signifying practices.

*Murder, My Sweet* provides an interesting illustration. Though the novel's title is not retained, the screen adaptation is in at least two other aspects quite faithful to the ori-ginal. First, Chandler's verbal style is strikingly idiosyncratic, rich with rhetorical figures (irony, litotes, chiasmus), and this *préciosité* is perhaps best exemplified by the novel's taste for the outrageous simile: Marlowe, for example, at one point refers to an unpleas-ant woman as having "a face like a bucket of mud." In the novel, which uses first-person character narration, this highly mannered language functions not only as an element of dialogue, energizing the detective's acerbic interchanges with the gallery of venal and corrupt people, it is also the defining feature of the narrator's world-weary and cynical account of the weakness and blindness that he and the other characters fall victim to. To preserve this language, Dmytryk's film turns Marlowe into an embedded narrator (thus altering the specifics of the novel in order to remain faithful to it); he also emphasizes Marlowe's linguistic control of the tale through an often-excessive use of voice-over.

It is the second aspect of Dmytryk's fidelity to his source, however, that is of greater interest and influence. Though Cattrysse shows that often the adaptation process simpli-fies the intricate and complex plots of "dark fiction," in this case the novel's elaborate narrative is not simplified. Because the adaptation process from book to screen means that the average novel must be condensed, this faithfulness here creates a perhaps unexpected effect: the succession of scenes, their causal relations often unclear, moves forward with relentless speed. A certain incoherence is the result (perspicacious indeed is the first-time viewer who can recount the story accurately). Such incoherence and difficulty of processing violate the norms of classic Hollywood cinema as delineated in the standard Neoformalist account of Hollywood practice.[17] My point is this. In the adaptation of *Murder, My Sweet*, the literary norm of a complex narrative exerts a greater influence on the film version than the corresponding cinematic norm of narrative simplicity, presumably because of yet another norm, that of fidelity. Once exemplified in a popular film, such a norm was then adopted (at least as an alternative) by the emerging model of *film noir*. The effectivity of that norm, in fact, can be traced in later productions, especially another adaptation, Robert Siodmak's *The Killers* (1946), in which the literary model, Ernest Hemingway's short story of the same title, is simple, narratively speaking, only alluding to difficulties of motive and hence "backstory" that are never delineated, much less explained. Not only does Sidomak's film, benefiting from Hollywood veteran Anthony Veiller's expert screenplay, fill in Hemingway's backstory, providing an explanation for the hitherto inexplicable (why a man pursued by killers chooses not to flee), but, like *Murder, My Sweet*, the film version of *The Killers* follows an investigative model in which this story, in all its details, emerges only unchronologically, in bits and pieces of the truth that constitute the serial flashback narratives of a gallery of informants.

This striking feature of Siodmak's film has its strictly cinematic "causes" and antecedents (for example, Orson Welles's quite similar investigative biography of an enigmatic character, *Citizen Kane*, with its series of interconnecting flashback narratives). Arguably, such narrative complexity, an important element of *film noir* storytelling, can also be traced to adaptation – not of the literary text actually being reworked in this instance, but of a literary norm adopted by this emerging model, this genre or series, from an earlier and ground-breaking adaptation. By making possible new practices, this is how adaptation truly serves the cinema, permitting its norms and systems from becoming closed practices, opening them instead to productive influences from "outside."

---
## Notes
---

1   This neglect is eloquently addressed by the contributors whose work is collected in James Naremore (ed.), *Film Adaptation* (New Brunswick, NJ: Rutgers University Press, 2000). The present chapter carries further a number of the initiatives suggested there.

2   First published as one of the chapters in Dudley Andrew, *Concepts in Film Theory* (Oxford: Oxford University Press, 1984), conveniently reprinted in Naremore (ed.), *Film Adaptation*, pp. 28–37, under the title "Adaptation." I quote here from p. 37.

3   Robert Stam and I share an enthusiasm for the intersection between Genette's theory of transtextuality (with its illuminating taxonomy of intertextual and intratextual relationships) and Bakhtin's concept of the open, polyvalent, and polyphonic text. See Stam's ground-breaking essay "Beyond Fidelity: The Dialogics of Adaptation," in Naremore (ed.), *Film Adaptation*, pp. 54–76, which effectively uses Genette's concept of the hypotext/hypertext relationship to delineate different varieties of adaptation, leaving aside notions of fidelity which Stam, as do I, brackets off as a criterion of value. Because I am not concerned here with individual texts, but certain global aspects of filmic adaptation, I travel here a different but complementary

path, guided also by Bakhtin and Genette, but also making use of polysystemic theory, a borrowing from translation studies. For a discussion of transtextuality, see Gérard Genette, *Palimpsestes: La littérature au second degré* (Paris: Seuil, 1982).

4 Stam, "Beyond Fidelity," p. 61.

5 Bazin's defense of the cinema's ability to produce and widely exhibit simplified versions of great works of literature, previously known to and by intellectual elites alone, ostensibly emphasizes the democratization involved (which he says is a kind of progress). Yet his formulation betrays, I think, a certain disdain for what is after all also a kind of vulgarization: "In place of the classical modes of cultural communication, which are at once a defense of culture and a secreting of it behind high walls, modern technology and modern life now more and more offer up an extended culture reduced to the lowest common denominator of the masses," from "Adaptation, or the Cinema as Digest," in Naremore (ed.), *Film Adaptation*, p. 22.

6 Jacques Derrida, "Signature Event Context," *Glyph* 1 (1977), 185.

7 As such a trope, the notion of the textual process of "grafting" has a long history. For example, when the fourteenth-century French poet Eustache Deschamps praises Geoffrey Chaucer as a "great translator," he writes:

> And for a long time you've been building
> A garden, for which you have requested cuttings
> From those men who write to advance themselves,
> Great translator, noble Geoffrey Chaucer.

My translation, quoted in R. Barton Palmer, "Rereading Guillaume de Machaut's Vision of Love: Chaucer's *Book of the Duchess* as *Bricolage*," in David Galef (ed.), *Second Thoughts: A Focus on Rereading* (Detroit: Wayne State University Press, 1997), p. 182.

8 Stam makes a similar point working with the Genettian categories of hypotext and hypertext: "one way to look at adaptation is to see it as a matter of a source novel's hypotext's being transformed by a complex series of operations: selection, amplification, concretization, actualization, critique, extrapolation, analogization, popularization, and reculturalization. The source novel, in this sense, can be seen as a situated utterance produced in one medium and in one historical context, then transformed into another equally situated utterance that is produced in a different context and a different medium" ("Beyond Fidelity," p. 68). This last observation, we will see, anticipates the essence of the polysystemic approach to adaptation in the invocation of different contexts of production as well as different signifying systems.

9 Andrew, "Adaptation," p. 29.

10 Quoted in Sylvia Harvey, *May '68 and Film Culture* (London: British Film Institute, 1978), p. 35.

11 Raymond Borde and Etienne Chaumeton, *Panorama du film noir américain* (Paris: Editions de Minuit, 1955). The relevant chapter of their book, translated into English, is included in R. Barton Palmer (ed.), *Perspectives on Film Noir* (New York: G. K. Hall, 1996), pp. 59–65.

12 See Damico's "Film Noir: A Modest Proposal," reprinted in Palmer (ed.), *Perspectives on Film Noir*, pp. 129–40, and Amir M. Karimi, *Toward a Definition of the American Film Noir (1941–1949)* (New York: Arno, 1976).

13 "The fundamental reason for film noir's neglect, however, is the fact that it depends more on choreography than sociology, and American critics have always been slow on the uptake when

it comes to visual style. Like its protagonists, film noir is more interested in style than theme . . . Although, I believe, style determines the theme in every film, it was easier for sociological critics to discuss the themes of the western and gangster film apart from stylistic analysis than it was to do for film noir," from Paul Schrader, "Notes on Film Noir," reprinted in Palmer (ed.), *Perspectives on Film Noir*, pp. 108–9.

14  For further discussion of these critical developments, see R. Barton Palmer, *Hollywood's Dark Cinema: The American Film Noir* (New York: Simon and Schuster, 1994), ch. 1.

15  Alain Silver and Elizabeth Ward, *Film Noir: An Encyclopedic Reference to the American Style* (Woodstock, NY: Overlook, 1979).

16  Patrick Cattrysse, *Pour une théorie de l'adaptation filmique: le film noir américain* (Berne: Peter Lang, 1992). Specific references will be noted in the text.

17  David Bordwell, Janet Staiger, and Kristin Thompson, *The Classical Hollywood Cinema: Film Style and Mode of Production to 1960* (New York: Routledge, 1985).

# Chapter 17

# Adapting *Farewell, My Lovely*

## William Luhr

The credits for *The Falcon Takes Over* appear over a silhouette of an elegantly postured man sporting a top hat, an overcoat, and a walking stick. The story begins in Club 13, a 1940s' Manhattan nightclub so stylish that it requires formal evening attire. When a murder is committed there, the case is handily solved by a regular patron, the debonair Gay Lawrence. He is a wealthy amateur detective known as the "Falcon" and it is his silhouette that appears under the credits.

The film, released in May 1942, marked the earliest adaptation of a Raymond Chandler detective novel. The film's ideology, style, locale, approach to the detective genre, as well as its construction of its central character, of masculinity, of crime, and of mid-twentieth-century urban life, however, are virtually antithetical to comparable components in that novel. The film's very divergence from the novel's dominant image makes it a good place to begin this chapter on adaptation.

Much of traditional adaptation discourse engages in some fashion the notion of a film's "fidelity" to a prior text, in this case a novel. Such discourse often focuses primarily upon narrative and thematic parallels between film and novel and tends to, implicitly or explicitly, presume and evaluate some kind of transferability of aesthetic worth. It will speak of what was "left in" and "left out" of the novel, for example, or of alterations in the novel's themes. Such assumptions are often explicit in journalistic reviews of films based upon prestigious novels such as *Great Expectations* or *Howards End* in which reviewers commonly praise the filmmakers for having caught the "essence" of the novel, or condemn them for having missed it. Such discourse does acknowledge, in some limited way, the fundamental formal differences between literature and film. It might acknowledge quantitative reductions in the number of a novel's narrative events due to time constraints on a two-hour film, or even tolerate changes in time and locale, as with

Baz Luhrman's 1996 updating of *Romeo and Juliet* to contemporary Miami street culture, but is then likely to revert to asking whether or not the film is "true" to its source. One would be hard pressed to argue for any "essential" relationship between *The Falcon Takes Over* and Chandler's novel but, as this chapter will demonstrate, that does not mean that examining them from different critical perspectives cannot yield useful insights about the adaptation process.

Even beyond its essentialist underpinnings, much of traditional adaptation discourse tends to treat texts as fixed and closed entities. But regardless of such fundamental problems as the presumption of aesthetic transferability, of an identifiable and fixed "essence" to a text, and of the critical primacy of discussing the adaptation primarily, if not exclusively, in terms of direct parallels with the adapted text, such discourse remains widespread.[1] Such approaches have produced useful insights,[2] but are based upon highly questionable premises. Furthermore, the extent to which these presumptions pervade popular discourse has had the effect of profoundly delimiting the approaches one can take toward adaptations. Steven Spielberg raised precisely this issue in a discussion of negative reviews of his 1985 adaptation, *The Color Purple*: "That was a film where there was more ink shed on the comparison with the Alice Walker novel than there was on the merits or problems with the film. In fact, the film was not analyzed. Instead, a mirror of Alice Walker was held up to it" (quoted in Lyman, 2001: 24). But problems with traditional adaptation discourse go beyond a tendency to ignore or minimize the individuality of the adaptation; such approaches also minimize or ignore the complex institutional, cultural, intergeneric, and intertextual fertilizations present in any adaptation. An important question to ask when looking at adaptations is: "What is being adapted?" In all cases, it is more than the source work.

This chapter will examine the three Hollywood adaptations of Raymond Chandler's 1940 novel, *Farewell, My Lovely*, with greater attention to the influence of shifting trends in the film industry in narration, genre, and characterization, as well as of contemporary ideological and social constructions, upon the adaptations than to establishing direct parallels with Chandler's novel. It will show that the films "adapt" much more than Chandler's novel. Furthermore, it will treat the novel not as a *sui generis* construction, but rather as itself engaging and adapting both contemporary fictional trends and Chandler's own series formula, developed in his prior novel, *The Big Sleep*, and earlier novellas. None of these texts – novel or films – exists either in isolation or in a totalizing relationship with another text. Furthermore, just as the texts are not unitary entities, their significance is not fixed. Contemporary cultural theory has shown that texts continue to yield meanings with reference to both emerging critical approaches and cultural productions.

RKO purchased the film rights to *Farewell, My Lovely* from Chandler for $2,000 in July 1941 and produced two adaptations of it, vastly different in style, during the following three years. One reason for this unusually close grouping is the major shift in representational strategies for detective films that was then taking place in Hollywood. RKO's 1942 adaptation followed industry practice of the 1930s; its 1944 one, however, engaged the new strategies to such an extent that a casual spectator seeing both films might have no idea that they were adaptations of the same novel. Chandler's novel had not changed but film industry practices had. The very difference in the films points to extra-textual influences upon adaptations. Furthermore, the shift in film strategies was itself influenced by innovations in detective fiction that had begun roughly twenty years earlier.

The new trend in Hollywood was later called *film noir*; the earlier trend in detective fiction was called "hard-boiled" fiction. The two trends have become linked in the popular and critical imagination partly because many *films noirs* adapted hard-boiled novels. Furthermore, Chandler's work, perhaps more than that of any other author, has become widely associated not only with hard-boiled detective fiction but also with *film noir*. His Philip Marlowe detective novels have frequently been adapted into *films noirs* (or neo-*noirs*) such as *Murder, My Sweet* (1944), *The Big Sleep* (1946), *Lady in the Lake* (1947), *The Brasher Doubloon* (1947), *The Long Goodbye* (1973), and *Farewell, My Lovely* (1975). In addition to his novels, he wrote or co-authored screenplays for canonical *films noirs* such as *Double Indemnity* (1944) and *The Blue Dahlia* (1946). Films with which he had nothing to do as a writer and which are not based upon his fiction have been called "Chandleresque." His verbal style has become associated with the cynical, wisecracking dialogue of hard-boiled film detectives as well as with the subjective, voice-over narration often used in *films noirs*.

The first adaptation of Chandler's *Farewell, My Lovely*, *The Falcon Takes Over* (1942), reveals genre conventions of 1930s' detective films. The second adaptation, *Murder, My Sweet* (1944), employs representational strategies associated with *film noir*. The third, *Farewell, My Lovely* (1975), reflects a post-*noir* or neo-*noir* nostalgia for a Hollywood gone by.

## *The Falcon Takes Over* (1942)

Detective films are nearly as old as film itself. The first was possibly American Biograph's *Sherlock Holmes Baffled* in 1903, and the first detective feature possibly Essanay's *Sherlock Holmes* in 1916. In 1922, Samuel Goldwyn produced *Sherlock Holmes* starring John Barrymore. There were many others, and other detectives aside from Sherlock Holmes, but it was not until the sound era that the genre took off. In his *The Detective in Film* (1972), William K. Everson suggests a number of reasons for this development. One is the relative newness of the detective fiction from which the films drew extensively. The detective had only become a significant figure in fiction – primarily with Sherlock Holmes – in the last quarter of the nineteenth century. Many popular detectives did not appear in fiction until after 1925; examples are Hercule Poirot, Philo Vance, Ellery Queen, Charlie Chan, the "Saint," and Sam Spade. The magazine associated with the introduction of the hard-boiled detective story, *Black Mask*, first appeared in 1920. Dashiell Hammett first published in it in 1922 and Carroll John Daly introduced his popular private eye, Race Williams, to *Black Mask* in 1923. The American private eye, then, was only beginning to appear in fiction in the waning days of the silent era.

Early in the sound era, mystery and detective films experienced a boom in popularity. Many film detectives became so popular that they were made the basis for a series, often continuing with the same actor, but at other times switching the lead actor in the series. William Powell enjoyed great success as Philo Vance, and later as Nick Charles in the *Thin Man* series; Ronald Colman became identified with Bulldog Drummond; and, of course, starting in 1939, Basil Rathbone with Sherlock Holmes. As these series progressed, they often slipped from "A" to "B" status; sometimes, as with Sherlock Holmes, even changing studios. Many, indeed most, other detective series existed only in "B" formats. They were made cheaply, using a readily identifiable formula, and received only perfunctory critical attention.

By the 1940s, detective films had largely become synonymous with "B" films. Examples are the Ellery Queen and Boston Blackie series at Columbia; Charlie Chan, Mr Moto, and Mike Shayne at Twentieth Century Fox; the "Saint" and the "Falcon" at RKO; Philo Vance at Warner Brothers; and Bill Crane and Sherlock Holmes at Universal. In these films, the world of crime did little more than provide a context in which the brash, intelligent, elegant or two-fisted (sometimes both), and witty central character proved himself a hero. Many of the films were comedies with violence thrown in. Nearly all had as a central characteristic the ability of the hero to unravel complex mysteries, often after plodding police detectives had failed at the task. The films, however, seldom developed a sense of a genuinely corrupted social structure, and certainly did not present the hero as significantly jaded or even partially broken by that environment. Such was the context within which the first films based upon Chandler's fiction appeared.

*The Falcon Takes Over* was the third film in the "Falcon" series which (ostensibly based upon a Michael Arlen character) had begun in 1941 with *The Gay Falcon*. Interestingly enough, this series had a kind of origin in another RKO series, the "Saint." George Sanders had played the Saint in five films, starting with *The Saint Strikes Back* in 1939. After *The Saint in Palm Springs* in 1941, RKO used Sanders to begin the "Falcon" series, which was heavily indebted to the "Saint" series, not only for its star but also in style and format.

*The Falcon Takes Over*, as do many series films, presents a number of situations and relationships as already established, and they remain stable at the film's end, ready for revival in the next episode. The Falcon is widely known for his interest in crime, and when, at the film's beginning, he happens to be at a nightclub when a man is killed, the press assume he will pursue the case. A running gag in this and other films in the series is the fact that he is engaged to be married and yet continually becomes involved with attractive women, and often quickly abandons them to move on to others. He has a bumbling, often terrified chauffeur, Goldy (Allen Jenkins), who provides comic contrast to the elegant Gay Lawrence. Goldy's trademarks are his Brooklyn accent and continual malapropisms such as "corpus delicious" and "miscarriage of injustice." Gay Lawrence also has a relationship of genial antagonism with a wisecracking police detective, O'Hara

(James Gleason), and his dullard assistant, Bates. The setting for much of the action is the posh world of society nightlife in which all of the regulars except Lawrence are laughably out of place.

A look at industry norms for detective films of the 1930s and, more specifically, RKO's formulas for both the "Saint" and "Falcon" series, can give us greater insights into the workings of the film than a narrative and thematic comparison with components of Chandler's novel. It also shows that the film adapted much more than Chandler's novel.

In fact, the "Falcon" series embodied much of what Chandler hated about the detective genre, and much of what hard-boiled detective writers revolted against in British detective fiction. Chandler found particularly noxious the notion of the debonair, amateur detective who solves the crime between brunch and cocktails, as well as the notion of the world of murder and crime as little more than a context for a puzzle to be wittily solved. He even parodies it at the end of *Farewell, My Lovely*. Anne Riordan tells Philip Marlowe that he should have given an elegant dinner party for all of the suspects at which he wittily unraveled the mystery with "a charming light smile and a phony British accent like Philo Vance." Marlowe's response summarizes his sense of the difference between the British and American tradition: "It's not that kind of story . . . It's not lithe and clever. It's just dark and full of blood" (Chandler, 1976: 242).

Both Chandler's novel and the film begin with similar plot events, but differences in the contexts constructed around those events point to fundamental differences in the works and in their traditions. In both, Moose Malloy, a giant of a man just out of prison, is searching for his former sweetheart, Velma. He enters a bar in which he is clearly out of place and which has changed considerably since Velma worked there years before. He easily defeats men in the bar who try to throw him out and winds up killing the manager, Mr Montgomery. It is not a premeditated murder but simply the unfortunate result of Montgomery's trying to oppose a man who does not know his own strength. The detective simply happens to be there when the killing occurs and becomes involved more from idle curiosity than from anything else.

In Chandler's novel, the bar – Florian's – is in a run-down section of Los Angeles that has become an African American ghetto during the eight years Malloy has been in prison. Marlowe happens to be nearby on a petty case he neither solves nor gets paid for. Malloy is out of place not only because of his size and ostentatious clothes but also because he is white. Intense racial antagonism causes a bouncer to attempt to eject Malloy from the bar, and the manager tries to shoot him, leading to his own death. Nulty, the police detective assigned to the case, is resentful about the assignment, calling it "another shine killing" (Chandler, 1976: 12). He feels, accurately, that because the victim is a black man, the case will get no publicity for him and that no one in either the press or the police department cares very much whether or not it is solved.

*The Falcon Takes Over* opens as Malloy (Ward Bond) approaches Club 13. It is not a run-down bar in a Los Angeles ghetto but a stylish Manhattan nightclub. The Falcon is not there on a fruitless job, but is a well-known patron. The doorman tries to eject Malloy not for racial reasons (everyone in the club is white) but because evening clothes are required. Malloy stands out not because he is white but because he does not wear a tuxedo. When Detective O'Hara arrives, he is not resentful because the racial implications of the assignment indicate that his superiors hold him in low esteem; rather, he engages in witty banter with the Falcon, saying, "Oh, the great Falcon. Haven't seen you around for about half a dozen murders." While they talk, an attractive woman approaches the Falcon, calling him "Homer Bilky." He tells her that she must be mistaken, that his name is "Dittenfries," and quickly moves away from her, exchanging sly grins with O'Hara. This points to his habit of seducing women under false names while his fiancée is out of town.

In both novel and film, the murder victim (the manager) is virtually ignored, but for very different reasons. In the novel, the victim is black in a racist society. Marlowe even comments bitterly that the police treat his murder as a misdemeanor. The official indifference to the man's death points to a profound social problem. The film, however, ignores such social issues. Its murder victim receives scant attention simply because his death provides little more than a catalyst for the plot and an excuse for verbal banter between O'Hara and the Falcon.

The central detective characters in the two works are constructed along radically different lines. The Falcon is a tireless *bon vivant*, for whom everything, including this case, is a lark. He is rich and famous, apparently has no need to work, has a stylish apartment and servants, a fiancée, and as many other women as he wants. Marlowe, on the other hand, has not worked in a month and needs money. A lonely man, he has few friends and no sweethearts. He exists in an atmosphere of depravity and failure and has little more than his sense of integrity to sustain him.

The "Falcon" series formula reveals explicit presumptions about class and masculinity. Like the British detective tradition of the time, the series does not critique upper-class privilege, a privilege that it presents within a benign and stable social environment. Gay Lawrence's heroic status comes from the film's characterization of him as inherently superior to working detectives and working-class people with Brooklyn accents.

## Chandler's Novel

Much of American hard-boiled fiction critiqued the class presumptions of traditional British detective fiction and demonstrated an allegiance not with wealthy amateurs such as Lord Peter Wimsey, but rather with proletarian figures such as the Continental Op, Sam Spade, Race Williams, and Philip Marlowe. This critique often involved a broad indictment of existing class structures. Chandler's *Farewell, My Lovely* integrates the crimes of the privileged rich with those of the brutalized poor. Racism, municipal corruption, and murder are part of a complexly intertwined and dysfunctional social structure. The novel presents a crime like murder not as an aberrant eruption into a benign society (as was the case with British detective fiction of the era) but rather as symptomatic of a deranged one.

Class affiliations, as well as a sense of literary origins within Chandler's aesthetic for detective fiction, are evident in his praise for Dashiell Hammett as the pre-eminent writer of American detective fiction. In an essay, "The Simple Art of Murder," for the December 1944 *Atlantic Monthly*, Chandler wrote:

> Hammett was the ace performer, but there is nothing in his work that is not implicit in the early novels and short stories of Hemingway . . . You can take it clear back to Walt Whitman, if you like. But Hammett applied it to the detective story, and this, because of its heavy crust of English gentility and American pseudogentility, was pretty hard to get moving . . . Hammett took murder out of the Venetian vase and dropped it into the alley . . . Hammett gave murder back to the kind of people who do it for a reason, not just to provide a corpse; and with the means at hand, not with handwrought duelling pistols, curare and tropical fish. (Chandler, 1988: 14)

Chandler's allegiance to hard-boiled fiction was a conscious choice. Born in 1888 in Chicago, his family moved to England when he was seven and he was educated there. His first professional writing appeared before World War I and was very much of the high literary style of the Edwardian era, nearly the polar opposite of his later hard-boiled writing. He returned to the United States in 1912 and largely abandoned writing until the early 1930s when he found himself out of work. Determined to write for the "pulp" magazines, he slavishly imitated the works of authors such as Hammett and Erle Stanley Gardner as a way of teaching himself the trade. He published his first hard-boiled detective story, "Blackmailers Don't Shoot," in *Black Mask* in 1933.

His decision to write such fiction involved more than financial necessity. Sensitive to cultural trends, he knew that the postwar era was a breakthrough one for American writers. In the 1920s, for the first time, American authors dealing with American topics, sensibilities, and idioms achieved broad international respect. More than successful authors of the 1890s, like Stephen Crane, or even the Europeanized Henry James, writers of the 1920s, like Ernest Hemingway, F. Scott Fitzgerald, and Eugene O'Neill, were perceived as heralding the unapologetic arrival of the United States on the world literary stage.

Much was made of the literary expressivity of Hemingway's idiomatic vernacular, and some hard-boiled writers felt that, in using the rough language of the proletariat, they were following in his footsteps. Chandler even makes a joking reference to this in *Farewell, My Lovely* by having Marlowe call a barely articulate cop "Hemingway." Writers like Hammett and James M. Cain received quick praise among European critics. Chandler, among the second generation of hard-boiled detective writers, then, did not create the formula but drew upon established literary codes. He particularly cherished dealing with American vernacular, not as a debased but rather as a rich, virtually foreign language. After a number of novellas, he published his first novel, *The Big Sleep*, in 1939, not with a poverty-row publishing house, but with the prestigious Knopf. When he published *Farewell, My Lovely* the following year, he had already established narrative, thematic, and ideological structures for his detective fiction. *Farewell, My Lovely* drew upon these structures, as would Chandler's five succeeding Marlowe novels. Furthermore, the novel, in a process Chandler termed "cannibalism," incorporated plot elements from three novellas that he had published in the "pulp" magazines, *Black Mask* and *Dime Detective*, in the mid-1930s. The novel, then, was not a *sui generis* construction, but rather itself adapted contemporary literary trends as well as Chandler's earlier work.

Early hard-boiled fiction had a transgressive image, one associated with pulp magazines and with topics inappropriate for mainstream culture. When James M. Cain's *The Postman Always Rings Twice* was first published in 1934, it acquired the reputation of a daring and "dirty" book. Paramount purchased the rights to it, but, largely due to censorship anxieties, did not make its adaptation until 1946, when *film noir* had become fashionable. One way that Hollywood dealt with hard-boiled fiction was to avoid it, as with the Cain novel; another was to elide transgressive content and adapt the novel's narrative structure to another formula, as with the two adaptations of *The Maltese Falcon* (1931 and 1936) preceding the 1941 John Huston one, and with *The Falcon Takes Over*.

Chandler had spent much of the 1930s learning his craft as a hard-boiled fiction writer, and his first two novels placed him at the top of the field. *Farewell, My Lovely* is perhaps his best-plotted detective novel. However, it also reveals another component of his fictional career: his desire to move away from detective fiction. He resented the second-class category in which mainstream critics placed genre fiction, and at the same time was elated by the praise he received from prestigious literary critics such as J. B. Priestley and W. H. Auden. He entertained hopes of elevating the genre to that of "serious" literature and felt trapped writing formula detective novels. He wanted to be known as a "novelist," not placed in the ghetto of "detective novelist." By the late 1940s he realized that this was unlikely to happen in the United States.

Although *Farewell, My Lovely* works expertly as a hard-boiled detective novel of its era, it also shows Chandler experimenting with fictional styles uncharacteristic of the genre. John Steinbeck had written him an encouraging letter after having read *The Big Sleep*, and in *Farewell, My Lovely* Chandler experiments with a device Steinbeck had used in *The Grapes of Wrath* – the weaving of parallel but unconnected events in the natural world with those in the narrative. He structures chapter 31 around Marlowe's detailed observation of and identification with the fruitless movements of a shiny black bug on and beyond a police detective's desk. The bug has no relation to the narrative at all, although its presence in the novel clearly implies comparisons between human and non-human endeavors. It also develops Marlowe's subjectivity.

All of Chandler's novels are told from Marlowe's point of view and subjectivity was a central concern of modernist fiction writers. Hemingway famously claimed that American fiction sprang from Mark Twain's *The Adventures of Huckleberry Finn*, and much of the resonance of his statement comes from a major shift in nineteenth-century fiction from objective to subjective perspectives. Twain's novel presents not "objective truth," but the "truth" as Huck, its narrator, sees it. His perspective is often profoundly limited or wrong; at times the reader is better able to judge the significance of the events that he relates than he is. Much of Hemingway's fiction similarly explores the subjectivity of its narrating voice, and William Faulkner's *The Sound and the Fury* holds classic modernist status for its multiple and incomplete perspectives on shared events. Such high modernist novelists as James Joyce, Virginia Woolf, and Marcel Proust deal centrally with subjective perception.

Such subjectivity is central to *Farewell, My Lovely*, not only in lines that express desire ("It was a blonde. A blonde to make a bishop kick a hole in a stained glass window," 1976: 78) or disorienting pain ("I felt like an amputated leg," 1976: 55), but also in more ambitious places in which he uses "stream of consciousness" techniques important to modernism. Chapter 25 deals with Marlowe hallucinating in a drug-induced state and gives his detailed descriptions of things that clearly have no objective reality and include surreal distortions of space, causality, and time. The chapter closes as he exerts himself to keep awake by walking around a room until he can regain some coherence of reliable consciousness:

> I walked.
> They built the Pyramids and got tired of them and pulled them down and ground the stone up to make concrete for Boulder Dam and they built that and brought the water to the Sunny Southland and used it to have a flood with.
> I walked through it all. I couldn't be bothered.
> I stopped walking. I was ready to talk to somebody. (1976: 144)

This passage not only presents Marlowe's subjectivity but also his disordered subjectivity. And disorientation was a central trope of *film noir*.

---

## Murder, My Sweet (1944)

*Murder, My Sweet* opens with an unoriented shot of what we later learn is the reflection of a lamp on a desk-top. We soon hear dialogue, and it becomes evident that Marlowe (Dick Powell) is being interrogated by the police. His eyes are bandaged. The room is unevenly lit: we see harsh, stark contrasts from an overhead bulb and murky shadows in the background. When Detective Randall enters, Marlowe says, "The boys tell me I did a couple of murders. Anything in it?" Randall's face is grim, and he quietly advises Marlowe to tell the whole story from the beginning. "With Malloy, then," replies Marlowe. "Well, it was about seven. Anyway, it was dark." As he talks, the camera moves past him to, and then out of, the window to a montage sequence of Los Angeles at night.

On the sound track we hear Marlowe tell how he had been working on a petty case that he had accepted because he was broke. "I just found out all over again how big this city is." At the end of the city-at-night montage, we see Marlowe in flashback, alone, without the eye bandages, in his dark office. His voice-over tells us that he had been depressed, and that his office bottle had not helped him. The camera moves in on him as a flashing light outside intermittently illuminates the office in an eerie, lonely way. We hear Marlowe's voice-over: "There's something about the dead silence of an office building at night – not quite real – the traffic down below was something that didn't have anything to do with me."

Marlowe sits looking at the city below through a large window, and whenever the dully flashing light appears we see his reflection in it. Suddenly, we also see the reflection of a huge, sinister-looking man who seems to have come from nowhere. It is Moose Malloy (Mike Mazurki). He appears, disappears, and reappears with the flashing light. Marlowe sees him, represses his shock, and ultimately goes off with him to look for Moose's lost sweetheart, Velma.

The sequence establishes major patterns of formal and thematic disorientation for both the characters in the film and the spectator. The very first shot, of the lamp's reflection, is impossible to situate until the camera moves away. The spectator literally does not know what he or she is looking at: lamp, reflection of a lamp, blank wall, or abstract space. Marlowe is confused. Most obviously, he is blinded. Initially, he literally does not know whether or not Randall is in the room. We also learn later that he does not know how the major events of the story he relates turned out, since he was blinded and knocked unconscious by gunfire at the climax. He is literally and metaphorically "in the dark." When he refers to the inceptive moment of the series of events by saying, "Anyway, it was dark," the dialogue underlines the fact that the darkness extends far beyond the interrogation room in which the film opens.

Nothing in the opening sequence has any narrative parallel in Chandler's novel. The novel does not have an unresolved retrospective narration begun *in medias res*; Marlowe is never blinded, and Malloy never comes mysteriously to Marlowe's office. These things are understood not with reference to the novel but rather to the then-developing strategies of *film noir*. Many *films noirs*, such as *Double Indemnity*, *The Killers* (1946), and *D.O.A.* (1950), often opened with retrospective narrations by or about profoundly confused or doomed central characters, frequently placed them literally or metaphorically "in the dark," and frequently introduced the spectator, both visually and thematically, to a disturbing urban world.

Furthermore, the vulnerability and confusion of the detective, the disquieting menace and seediness of the environment, and the spectatorial disorientation have nothing to do with the adaptive strategies of *The Falcon Takes Over*. Here the detective is not a *bon vivant* bantering with the police detective, but a wounded and scared man who might very well be indicted for murder by the police. Little in *The Falcon Takes Over* implied a pervasive, sinister urban environment, or is spectatorially confusing. Although both films adapted the same novel, the extreme differences between them and their styles resulted not from the novel but from the very different film traditions they engaged.

Later in *Murder, My Sweet*, Marlowe's plight is capsulized when he stumbles into Ann Grayle's (Ann Shirley) house for refuge after having been beaten and drugged. She tells him: "You go barging around without a very clear idea of what you're doing. Everybody bats you down – smacks you over the head and fills you full of stuff, and you keep right on hitting between tackle and end. I don't think you even know which side you're on!" Marlowe replies: "I don't know which side anybody's on. I don't even know who's playing today." When in the opening scene, he joked to Randall: "The boys tell me I did a couple of murders. Anything in it?" it is not entirely a joke. At this point, he does not even know who has been killed or what his involvement was.

This disorientation is not confined to Marlowe. When he begins to tell his story and the camera moves out of the window for a series of shots of the city at night, there is no clear clue as to the temporality of the images of the city. At the end of the sequence, we see Marlowe's flashback of himself at an earlier time in his office, but the point of transition is uncertain. The spectator does not know whether those images show the city at the time of Marlowe's interrogation or at the time his retrospective story began. This lack of temporal specificity makes the images of the nocturnal city a continuous presence. Marlowe's statement, "I just found out all over again how big this city is," points to how easily one can lose one's bearings in it, as the spectator just has.

Early in the film, Lindsey Marriott, a client of Marlowe's, is murdered. Marlowe discovers the body and looks at Marriott's driver's license. We see a shot of the license in a man's hand. Then the camera cuts to show that it is Randall, and not Marlowe, who is looking at the license, and that we are no longer at the murder scene but are in a different time and place altogether. We see Randall looking out of a window at night-time Los Angeles. Since it is in the same room as the film's framing story, since it is at night, since Randall is dressed similarly and speaks in the same tone of voice, we are led to believe that the film has jumped back from the murder scene to the initial interrogation scene from which Marlowe is narrating the film. But it has not. Randall moves across the room and the camera pans with him. Suddenly we see Marlowe without bandaged eyes, and this fact places the scene not within the frame story but immediately after Marriott's death. These two minor dislocations of spectator expectation, as well as the early lack of temporal specificity in the city montage, point to the film's strategy of disorienting the spectator.

Another such scene occurs at the home of the drunken Mrs Florian. Seated across from Marlowe, she has just given him a picture that is supposed to show the missing Velma. The camera moves in to a close shot as she takes another drink and continues to talk to Marlowe. Then the camera pulls back and we suddenly see that Marlowe is no longer in the chair he sat in only seconds before. The spectator and Mrs Florian are surprised at about the same time. Marlowe has, in a way, fooled both the camera and Mrs Florian by sneaking into the room from which she got the picture to search for another.

At times, both the viewer and Marlowe are disoriented simultaneously. A prime example is the early appearance of the reflection of Moose Malloy, seemingly from nowhere and with shocking suddenness at the film's beginning. Malloy's image is reflected in Marlowe's window and consequently is superimposed over the city at night. When Marlowe describes "the dead silence of an office building at night – not quite real," and says "the traffic down below was something that didn't have anything to do with me," he establishes the city as a location for a highly subjective awareness of dark and disconnected forces. The association of the sudden appearance of Malloy – this doomed, apelike, strange man – with the image of the city at night indicates that the things that Marlowe feels have nothing to do with him will, in fact, have a great deal to do with him.

Malloy's reflected and ghostlike image is visible only when the eerie outside light flashes. A major disorienting strategy of the film is its use of lighting, especially low-key lighting, stark contrasts, and often visually jarring shadows. The film frequently suggests, by means of its visual textures, a nightmare-like world.

When Marlowe and Malloy enter Florian's bar, for example, one side of the bar is visually dominated by the sharp, criss-crossed shadows of stacked chairs reflected on the wall and ceiling. The shadows seem more substantial than the objects that cast them – and infinitely more sinister. Most of the film occurs at night, and its strange, and at times jarring, shadows suggest a greater darkness beyond.

When, early in the film, Marlowe accompanies Lindsey Marriott to ransom a stolen necklace, the meeting place resembles nothing urban but rather a primeval forest. It is wooded and murky, and mist rolls over the damp earth. The camera pans to follow the ghostly mist across the weird landscape. Marlowe is startled by a deer. He has no idea what lurks in the darkness and, as he looks around, is suddenly knocked unconscious. When he awakes, an unknown woman is shining a light in his face. She runs off. He finds Marriott beaten to death. It all seems like a crazed nightmare. The place at first seems very different from the city at night, and yet it also is dark, and the darkness contains unknown threats. But it is more than dark, it has an intensely subjective quality to it.

Most of the film is told from Marlowe's point of view. We see not so much what happens, as Marlowe's perception of what happens: things that occur only within Marlowe's mind are presented as though they were real events. When he hallucinates in a drugged state, we see the crazed and paranoiac images his mind conjures up. When he is knocked unconscious and describes the sensation – "a black pool opened up at my feet. I dived in. It had no bottom" – we see the frame slowly covered by spreading blackness, like an oil slick. The spectator knows that this is not an actual black pool, even though it appears to be one on screen, but its tangible presence underlines the fact that we see nearly everything in the film from Marlowe's recollected point of view. Just as that point of view does not discriminate between "objective" occurrences and hallucinatory perceptions, so there is no assurance that even the "objective" events may not be highly colored by Marlowe's perception.

Marlowe's personality dominates the film. We not only constantly see him on screen – almost nothing is shown in which he is not directly involved – but we also continually hear his narrating voice. The narrative comes to us not as an independently existent sequence of events but filtered through Marlowe's perception and remembrance. But how reliable an observer can he be? He is frequently beaten unconscious; he is drugged, blinded, wearied, compromised by poverty, and at times nearly hysterical with rage, desperation, and confusion. As in much of *film noir*, we explore with him a reality he does not fully – and may never – understand.

The film not only develops patterns of disorientation by means of strange camera angles, unexpected editing, and lighting strategies that evoke sinister forces, but it also continually places Marlowe in situations that are exotic or perverse. The settings for these situations seem to have very little in common. They vary from sleazy low-life dens – Mrs Florian's house and Florian's bar – to the dwellings of the ultra-rich – the high ceilings, wood paneling, and cavernous interiors of the Grayle mansion; the overlit, ultra-modern apartment of the suave professional psychic, Jules Amthor; the shadowy sensuality of the Grayle beach house – to Marlowe's shabby apartment and office; from Los Angeles at night to the primeval canyon where Marriott is killed.

Many of the settings into which Marlowe moves convey a sense of something gone wrong or perverse. Amthor's apartment and Dr Sonderborg's house are supposed to be medical establishments. However, Amthor suavely admits that he is a "quack," and we learn that he uses his psychic consultations to blackmail his patients; Dr Sonderborg permits his house to be used as a prison for the drugged detective. Both men clearly pervert their professions.

The thread connecting all of these diverse locales is sexual manipulation. As in much of *film noir*, the locus of the film's events is its "black widow," Mrs Helen Grayle (Claire Trevor), who is also Moose's lost Velma. The film presents her as intensely attractive and deadly. She acts seductively toward Marlowe, even boldly comes to his apartment, comments on his good build, and invites him to an exotic nightclub. In the beach house scene near the end, she is frequently photographed before a large and luxurious bed. During Marlowe's first time there, she disrobes before him to reveal a clinging slip, asks him to murder Amthor for her, and pleads with him to spend the night. She soon tries to kill him, and we learn that she had tried to kill him before they met.

Marlowe is the only major male character in the film (excepting detective Randall) to resist her allure, and live. All others are destroyed. Moose had been involved with her years before and still loves her; her husband's desperate love for her necessitates his continual humiliation and suicidal despair; Marriott had had an affair with her but had outlived his usefulness. All of these men, as well as Jules Amthor, who were powerfully attracted to her, die as a result of their involvement with her. The nature of Amthor's involvement with her is unclear. She claims to have gone to him for psychic consultation and to have been blackmailed by him. Whether or not they ever became sexually involved is never established, but it is not unlikely.

The film develops a strong association of perversity with sexuality. All of Mrs Grayle's sexual partners are unlikely choices for her: Moose is a grotesque gorilla of a man, whose dim-wittedness and criminal background would not fill her social needs; her husband is at least twice her age and frail; Marriott is foppish and ineffectual. Mrs Grayle's association with these men is clearly manipulative. She uses her sexuality to get what she wants from them, and then moves on to others.

The pervasive aura of sexual manipulation affects the one traditionally normative relationship in the film – that of Marlowe and Ann Grayle. After her father nearly commits suicide in humiliation over his wife's treachery, he pleads with Marlowe to abandon the case. Marlowe tells him he will but then goes with Ann to explore the beach house for evidence, telling her that things have gone too far to be dropped. At the beach house, they become affectionate and kiss. Suddenly, Marlowe suggests that, since her father could not buy him off the case, "you decided to be nice to me." She becomes insulted and bitter. Marlowe retracts the suggestion, but it still remains a possible motivation and taints the purity of her sexuality. It also points to Marlowe's suspicion of all sexual motives. And he is quickly justified, since Mrs Grayle has been watching him and Ann, and will soon attempt to seduce Marlowe and get him to murder Amthor.

The film develops areas of sexual perversity without parallel in the novel. The novel does have an Ann with whom Marlowe becomes romantically involved, but she is not Mr Grayle's daughter. In the film, Ann is profoundly upset by her father's sexual humiliation at the hands of his wife. When Ann first meets Marlowe, she takes pains to establish the fact that her father's wife is not her mother. When Marlowe comes to their mansion, she watches in agony as Helen flirts with him. Her pain comes from a dual sexual jealousy: she is developing a fondness for Marlowe, and she has an intense, possibly neurotic, desire for her father's affection. Here, she watches as her stepmother flirts with Marlowe to the abject humiliation of her father.

Ann feels that she and her stepmother are rivals for the affections of both her father and Marlowe – and that she is losing. When she and Marlowe find her father preparing to commit suicide because he thinks his wife has spent the night with Marlowe, he pathetically explains: "I am an old man. You can see that. I only have two interests in life – my jade and my wife." Although he quickly adds "And, of course, my daughter," it is obviously little more than a polite afterthought and indicative of a domestic situation that has caused his daughter anguish. Then, increasing her humiliation, he desperately pleads with Marlowe to agree with him that Helen is "beautiful and desirable."

Ann has lived, then, in the middle of a Freudian nightmare – one without parallel in Chandler's novel – and the climax of the film makes it worse. She sees her stepmother shot dead by her father, then her father and her stepmother's former lover kill one another, and then the man she cares for blinded. She soon appears at the police station to exonerate Marlowe, whose blindness, we learn, will only be temporary, and the film closes as they kiss in a taxi. But the "happy ending" barely covers over the film's atmosphere of manipulative and deadly sexuality, with overtones of incest and prostitution, which joins with other factors in suggesting a very disturbed world. That atmosphere was a major indication of the ways in which *film noir*, as had hard-boiled fiction a decade earlier, first challenged and then stretched censorship codes of the time.

---

### *Farewell, My Lovely* (1975)

---

*Farewell, My Lovely*, the third Hollywood adaptation of Chandler's novel, appeared in 1975 and reveals an adaptation strategy as different from that of *Murder, My Sweet* as that film's strategy differed from the earlier *The Falcon Takes Over*. Where *The Falcon Takes Over* engaged industry norms for adapting detective fiction in the 1930s, and *Murder, My Sweet* engaged tropes of the then-emerging *film noir*, *Farewell, My Lovely*, coming three decades later, demonstrates an intense nostalgia for the *films noirs* of the 1940s as well as for the long-gone, classical Hollywood era.

In the 1940s, *film noir* reflected a contemporary sensibility; the hard-boiled private detective was a man of his era. By the 1970s, however, the romanticized private eye, like the cowboy, was considered part of a past age. He was associated with value structures and styles of filmmaking that were as anachronistic as the fedora or Lucky Strike Green. Even when presented as contemporary men dealing with contemporary problems, they could not help but recall a past age, like modern-day cowboys in pick-up trucks.

There is considerable debate about whether or not *film noir* of the 1940s and 1950s is a genre. A problem that a number of critics have with calling it a genre is that the term was used primarily in European criticism until the 1960s. Many filmmakers who made *films noirs* in the postwar era, such as Edward Dmytryk (director of *Murder, My Sweet* and *Crossfire* [1947], among others), have claimed that they never heard of *film noir* during that time. They felt that they were making films in other genres, such as detective films, crime films, or melodramas. While the issue of intentionality does not necessarily deny genre status to these films, that issue simply does not apply to neo-*noir* films from the mid-1960s onward. Films like *Farewell, My Lovely*, *Chinatown* (1974), *Body Heat* (1981), *The Postman Always Rings Twice* (1981), and *Blood Simple* (1984) clearly position themselves within the *noir* tradition. Some, like *Farewell, My Lovely* and *The Postman Always Rings Twice*, are literal remakes of canonical *films noirs*, others, like *Chinatown*, are set in the *noir* era and others, like *Body Heat* and *Blood Simple*, are set at the time of their production, but all use visual and narrative strategies to evoke *film noir*.

Once more, the question arises as to what, exactly, is being adapted. In some cases one might say a novel, or an earlier film or films. But it goes beyond that. These films tend to engage not only individual texts but also a genre and an historically specific style of filmmaking. They display intense nostalgia for classical Hollywood filmmaking practices of the studio era and for American culture in the postwar era. This nostalgia perhaps marks the most significant change in mood from canonical *films noirs* to neo-*noir*. The films of the 1940s and 1950s were set at the time of their release and spoke in disquieting ways to their contemporary audiences about issues and sensibilities of their time. The post-1960s' films spoke not about the time of their release but about the remembered past, and even though many things within the films are disturbing and sleazy, those things are linked with problems and sleaze of the past, not the present. Consequently, they have a tone almost unthinkable in canonical *film noir* – nostalgia. While the themes of the recent films are dark and chilling, their tone often strives to construct a comfortable, not disquieting, reception climate of nostalgia for dark and chilling moments in old films.

Unlike the first two adaptations of Chandler's novel, *Farewell, My Lovely* is not set at the time of its production; rather, it is a "period" picture, set over three decades earlier in 1941. It appeared when nostalgic films set in the 1930s and 1940s – *Summer of '42* (1971), *Paper Moon* (1973), *The Sting* (1973), *Chinatown* – and films reprising genres associated with that era – *What's Up, Doc?* (1972), *That's Entertainment* (1974), *The Three Musketeers* (1974), *Young Frankenstein* (1975) – were popular. *Farewell, My Lovely* does both: it is set in 1941 and reprises *film noir*.

Much about the film, aside from the obvious period costuming, sets, automobiles, and other props, recalls 1940s' *film noir*. Most obviously, it stars Robert Mitchum in a trench coat as Marlowe. Mitchum was an important star in the 1940s who appeared in a number of *films noirs* such as *Undercurrent* (1946), *Out of the Past* (1947), and *Macao* (1952). Charlotte Rampling (who plays Mrs Grayle/Velma) is made up and costumed and acts in a way that recalls Lauren Bacall in *The Big Sleep*.

Both Mitchum and Rampling recall presences from the history of film, and because they do, their use in this film works in a different way from those presences in the original films: they cannot help but evoke a discrete historical period about which audiences might feel nostalgic. In fact, Mitchum himself could have played Marlowe in *Murder, My Sweet* in 1944 since he was under contract to RKO at the time. However, the presence of Mitchum in a 1940s' *film noir* and that of Mitchum in *Farewell, My Lovely* carry an entirely different significance. Furthermore, as in *Murder, My Sweet* and many *films noirs*, the detective tells the story in a retrospective voice-over narration. But, in 1975, not only did the device and the language recall an earlier era for audiences, but it is also Mitchum's voice, used as it was in *Out of the Past*.

Unlike *films noirs*, *Farewell My Lovely* is in color, but a highly stylized color. Cameraman John Alonzo made the film one of the first Hollywood films to use Fujicolor because he wanted the film dominated with "warm," intense colors – deep reds, browns, yellows – and a good deal of neon-type lighting. The color textures of the film resemble those of old color photographs and advertising posters of the early 1940s. *Farewell, My Lovely* opens with processed color shots of Los Angeles traffic and a shot of a neon marquee showing a woman's face. The cars, the colors, the depiction of the woman, all recall older styles, but the colors are a bit too intense, the movements a bit too slow, the stylization a bit too extreme – it recalls a dream of the past rather than a naturalistic depiction. The camera tilts up to show Marlowe looking out of a hotel window. His voice-over says, "This past spring was the first that I'd felt tired and realized that I was getting old." He says that things are now worse for him than they were in the spring and that his only pleasure comes from following the hitting streak of the 26-year-old Joe DiMaggio.

DiMaggio's streak is a central motif in the film: it gives Marlowe something heroic to believe in, in the face of almost universally depressing events, one of which is his own age. Throughout most of the film, he is confused and endangered by the events of the case, and world events provide no relief. At one point, a news vendor says, "Whaddya think of this guy Hitler? He invaded Russia." Marlowe replies, "So did Napoleon, and that's not as hard as hitting forty-two straight."

We frequently see Marlowe pick up a newspaper, ignore the world events on the front page, and turn to the back to learn of DiMaggio's progress. Georgie (Jimmy Archer), the ex-boxer news vendor, comments, referring to the increasing pressure upon DiMaggio during the streak, that he also knows what pressure is, that he once won nineteen straight fights. The pressure parallels the pressure on Marlowe. Things go poorly for him throughout the film, and, at the end, they look worse. His clients and a man with whom he sympathized are dead, DiMaggio's streak has been broken, and American involvement in World War II is imminent. He even gives away the money he earned.

But regardless of his circumstances, the film presents Marlowe in an unremittingly romanticized light. He maintains admirable integrity in the face of great danger and loss, and the very extent of his loss amplifies the courage it takes for him to go on. Although he identifies with DiMaggio, who is younger than he is and a "winner," he sympathizes with Tommy Ray (John O'Leary), even more of a "loser" than Marlowe. He involves Tommy Ray in the case by asking him about Moose Malloy's lost Velma. Soon, Tommy Ray is murdered. This event profoundly upsets Marlowe. Tommy Ray was white and married to a black woman, a fact that ruined his show business career. He and his wife appear devoted to one another, and Marlowe strikes up a friendship with their mulatto son, also a baseball fan.

The film climaxes on the gambling boat of Laird Brunette (Anthony Zerbe), a rich racketeer who wants Marlowe to bring Malloy (Jack O'Halloran) to him. Marlowe realizes that Brunette probably intends to murder them both if they go onto the boat, but he also realizes that only by taking that risk can he solve the case. He takes it because "otherwise that kid of Tommy Ray's will haunt me for the rest of my life for letting them kill his father." Marlowe's act of altruistic heroism inspires a comparable one from Detective Nulty (John Ireland). Nulty at first refuses to help Marlowe because Brunette has enormous political power. Suddenly, Nulty tells his driver to head for Brunette's boat. His thoroughly corrupt assistant, Billy Rolfe (Harry Dean Stanton), refuses to go, and Nulty screams, "Seven people are dead, Rolfe, seven, and the police are driving away." He risks his career, is morally rejuvenated, saves Marlowe's life, and scores a major triumph on the case.

At the end, Marlowe reads of the breaking of DiMaggio's streak. He still has money he had from Brunette and says, "I had two grand in my pocket that needed a home and I knew just the place." He goes to give the money to Tommy Ray's widow and son, and the film ends. Even the DiMaggio loss does not bring him to despair, but rather to a sense of admiration for the unexpected achievements of so-called losers. "Bagsby and Smith, a couple of run-of-the-mill pitchers, stopped DiMaggio. Perhaps they had a little extra that night, like Nulty had tonight."

Marlowe is presented as a man of prodigious integrity, an old-fashioned hero who gains nothing for himself but helps the underdog and inspires moral strength. There are no analogues to Tommy Ray's family, to Nulty's rejection of his corrupt past, to World War II, to Joe DiMaggio, or to Georgie in either of the earlier adaptations or in Chandler's novel, but they are central to the nostalgic strategies of this film. At the center of that nostalgia is the film's intensely romanticized presentation of Marlowe's "old-fashioned" masculinity. Marlowe's kindness to the family is presented as evidence of his radiant moral heroism, confirmed not only by the boy's fondness for him but also by its effect on Nulty's moral rejuvenation. Furthermore, nearly everyone in the film, even Brunette, respects Marlowe.

Unlike the two earlier adaptations and the novel, Marlowe has no significant romantic involvement, and the plot is not structured around a developing romance. In the novel and in the earlier adaptations, Ann provides a romantic interest for Marlowe. This film has no analogue to her, and the place she structurally supplies in the novel's plot is partially filled by the punchy news vendor, Georgie. Most women in the film are unappealing or evil. Marlowe's flashback begins as he searches for a runaway high-school girl in a dance hall. He has to get rid of a bloated, middle-aged woman who aggressively approaches him before he finds the runaway. When he delivers her to her parents, she hits him powerfully in his groin, and he doubles up in pain. His remaining experiences with women in the film are comparable.

He is not presented as a celibate and is obviously attracted to Mrs Grayle. When he leaves after her husband has discovered them kissing, she says, "You're old-fashioned, aren't you?" and he replies, "from the waist up." Later in the film, he invites her "to my place," and she says, "What for? You've got everything we need with you." The director then cuts to a long shot of Marlowe's car parked at the beach, and, although we only see them necking, the film implies that they have made love. Marlowe later tells Nulty, "She was incredibly beautiful. And she was something, Nulty, really something."

Mrs Grayle is the film's center of desire and is destructive or deadly to all of her lovers or consorts – her husband, Moose, Marriott, Brunette – except Marlowe. The film presents most sexual activity as destructive, and it is much more explicit about sexuality and sexual deviation than earlier adaptations. Marriott is presented as homosexual, and jokes are made about his sexual orientation. Florence Amthor (Kate Murtagh), the madam of a whorehouse in which Mrs Grayle once worked, is presented unattractively as a "butch" lesbian.

As in many neo-*noir* films, Marlowe finds himself surrounded by sexual excess and deviation. Hollywood's abandonment of the Production Code in the 1960s allowed many things to be shown and discussed that could only be hinted at in the 1940s. A curious pattern in neo-*noir* films, however, is that, permitted a freedom of sexual display unthinkable in the 1940s, many display attitudes about sexuality that would have been reactionary in the 1940s. The sexuality that is shown is often degenerate and punished severely, and a sign of the detective's integrity is the relative absence of sexuality from his life. In the 1940s, the "badness" of sexual excess and manipulation was often counterbalanced by the "goodness" of the hero's salvation of, and involvement with, a "good" heroine. The only way for Marlowe to deal with the world of "bad" sex in the post-1960 world seems to be either minimal involvement or abstinence. In this film, Marlowe does not wind up a lover, with a young woman of his own, as in the earlier adaptations, but as a kind of asexual uncle to the one traditional family unit in the film, that of Tommy Ray. The film never allows for the slightest hint of sexual attraction between Tommy Ray's widow and Marlowe; his generosity will be without recompense, and avuncular. Their relationship remains "pure."

And the family is black. Like sexuality, racism was a touchy topic for films of the 1940s, and neither of the earlier adaptations engages any of the racial material developed in the novel. *Farewell, My Lovely* gives that motif central importance. Marlowe warns Malloy as they approach Florian's, "Hey, this is a colored neighborhood." When they enter the bar, a bouncer tells them, "No white folks in here, just for the colored." The atmosphere, as in the novel, is racially antagonistic, and the film develops institutionalized racism as a social fact. Nulty tells Marlowe that Moose's killing of the black bar owner is irrelevant to the police but that they have to go through the motions of an investigation to avoid trouble from Eleanor Roosevelt.

Marlowe is aware of racial antagonism, but he himself shows no racial contempt and, furthermore, he becomes the champion of what in a racist society is a supreme sin: a "mixed" marriage. In the 1940s, miscegenation was explicitly forbidden as screen material by the Production Code. This film presents mixed marriage as an act of courage: the white Tommy Ray lost his show business career because of his marriage to a black woman. He and his family become the ultimate cultural underdog, and the film, made at the time of civil rights consciousness in the early 1970s, makes Marlowe, that defender of lost causes, their enlightened champion.

A central imperative of this chapter has been to indicate that the adaptation process is more complex than traditionally presented, and that adaptations adapt much more than their designated sources. Furthermore, even those sources adapt others. *Farewell, My Lovely* is certainly an adaptation of Chandler's novel and bears identifiable narrative, character, and thematic relations with it. However, it is only one of three films with comparable narrative, character, and thematic relations, and yet those three films are radically different. Each shows the influence not only of the novel but also of industry practice, as well as of cultural and ideological trends of the time in which it was made. When we speak of adaptations, we must ask what is being adapted – a novel, a contemporary industry formula, a new style, contemporary political formulations, or . . . ? Even when citing a specific source novel, we must ask what is being adapted from the novel – plot, themes, characters, or . . . ? Novels are complex entities, and themselves reveal multitudinous literary and cultural influences. Such an awareness makes the study of adaptations a rich and wide-ranging endeavor.

--- Acknowledgments ---

I have drawn some of the material in this chapter from previously published material, particularly my book, *Raymond Chandler and Film*, 2nd edn (Tallahassee: Florida State University Press, 1991), my article, "Pre-, Prime-, and Post-*Film Noir*: Raymond Chandler's *Farewell, My Lovely* and Three Different Film Styles," *The Michigan Academician* 15: 1 (Fall 1982), 125–31, and a textbook that I co-authored with Peter Lehman, *Thinking About Movies: Watching, Questioning, Enjoying*, 2nd edn (Oxford: Blackwell, 2003).

1 For a more extensive discussion of many of these issues, see Robert Stam, "Beyond Fidelity: The Dialogics of Adaptation," in Naremore (2000: 54–76). James Naremore's book does a fine job of outlining the history of adaptation discourse, including explanations for why it has long been marginalized within film studies, and charting some new directions for the field.

2 While this chapter discusses the limitations of traditional adaptation discourse, I do not want to dismiss that discourse. I disagree with some widespread premises within much of it, but also want to acknowledge that it contains a good deal of intelligent and helpful work, from George Bluestone's *Novels into Film* (1957), probably the first academic book in English on adaptations, through John Fell's *Film and the Narrative Tradition* (1974), work published in the *Literature/Film Quarterly* from 1979, to many more recent works.

## References

Bluestone, George (1957) *Novels into Film: The Metamorphosis of Fiction into Cinema.* Baltimore, MD: The Johns Hopkins University Press.

Chandler, Raymond (1976) *Farewell, My Lovely.* New York: Vintage.

—— (1988) *The Simple Art of Murder.* New York: Vintage.

Everson, William K. (1972) *The Detective in Film.* Secaucus, NJ: Citadel.

Fell, John (1974) *Film and the Narrative Tradition.* Norman: University of Oklahoma Press.

Hiney, Tom (1997) *Raymond Chandler: A Biography.* New York: The Atlantic Monthly Press.

Luhr, William (1991) *Raymond Chandler and Film*, 2nd edn. Tallahassee: Florida State University Press.

Lyman, Rick (2001) "A Director's Journey into a Darkness of the Heart," *New York Times*, Arts and Leisure Section (June 24), 24.

MacShane, Frank (1976) *The Life of Raymond Chandler.* New York: Dutton.

Naremore, James (ed.) (2000) *Film Adaptation.* New Brunswick, NJ: Rutgers University Press.

Phillips, Gene D. (2000) *Creatures of Darkness: Raymond Chandler, Detective Fiction, and Film Noir.* Lexington: University Press of Kentucky.

# Chapter 18

# Daphne du Maurier and Alfred Hitchcock

## Richard Allen

Born in London's East End in 1899 at the end of the Victorian era, Alfred Hitchcock, the son of a Catholic family in the greengrocery trade, made his first film, *The Pleasure Garden*, in 1925. Given his lower middle-class background, his facility as a graphic artist, his practical bent, and his interest in theater, it was unsurprising that this clever, ambitious young man should be drawn to the new medium of film. Daphne du Maurier was born in 1907 near London's Regent's Park, a distinctly posher side of the town than Hitchcock, to the most successful actor of the Edwardian period, Gerald du Maurier. Du Maurier hailed from a cultured and literary family with French Catholic ancestry, though the "du" in du Maurier was a fiction she subsequently exposed. Her grandfather was the renowned Victorian sketch artist and novelist George du Maurier. She wrote her first book, *The Loving Spirit*, in 1931.

Both the novelist and the filmmaker chose to work in popular narrative idioms that combined "romance" with "murder mystery" and achieved an unprecedented success with the public that was inversely proportional to the guarded response accorded to their work by arbiters of taste. It was for their popularity more than their perceived stature as artists that Hitchcock was knighted and du Maurier was made a Dame. However, both artists undercut the ostensibly conservative character of the popular romance by exploring dimensions of human perversity contained within it, not simply as a foil to dramatize the growth, development, and triumph of the heterosexual couple, but also as the primary source of fascination and allure. Furthermore, both authors used the short story format (Hitchcock through his TV shows) to circumvent and subvert the romance narrative altogether. Hitchcock inhabited and was partly responsible for the triumph of American popular culture in Europe in the decades after World War II; du Maurier, on the other hand, though she showed an interest in film, despised that culture, and satirized an American takeover of Britain in her last novel *Rule Britannia* (1972). Nonetheless, the culture that both witnessed emerge in the late 1960s was profoundly different from the one in which they grew up in and marked the twilight of their careers. Hitchcock, who died in 1980, made only two films in the 1970s; du Maurier, who died in 1989, completed only one novel in the last two decades of her life.

In this chapter I will seek to explain the nature and significance of du Maurier's influence on Hitchcock's work. Hitchcock's affinity for du Maurier is suggested by the fact that he adapted three of her stories in different phases of his career: *Jamaica Inn* in 1939 at the end of his "English period," *Rebecca* in 1940 at the beginning of his collaboration with Selznick, and *The Birds* in 1963, which is arguably the summation of his art. Each of these works, I will suggest, represents very distinct strategies of adaptation, and through mapping these strategies I will show how the aesthetic preoccupations of novelist and filmmaker converged. *Jamaica Inn*, du Maurier's romantic novel narrated from the point of view of its passionate heroine, is merely a pretext for an adaptation that abstracts from it key situations and plot points. Hitchcock "reduces" du Maurier's novel by submitting it to the kind of "masculine" strategies of storytelling he had perfected in his English sound films. However, in his adaptation of *Rebecca*, Hitchcock took du Maurier's narrative at its word, and, as a result, realized for the first time the "feminine" dimension of his own aesthetic. In *The Birds*, Hitchcock undertakes a unique adaptation – a kind of adaptation in reverse – where he fills out the scenes schematically portrayed in du Maurier's short story with a full-blown "family romance" narrative scripted by Evan Hunter in a way that makes explicit the manner in which du Maurier's short story undermines the conventions of the romance narrative that both he and du Maurier inhabited for most of their careers.

## Queer Author/Queer *Auteur*

Du Maurier and Hitchcock emerged as artists at a moment when the normative heterosexual feminine and masculine roles prescribed by the Victorian gender system had been threatened by an emergent feminism and by the trials of Oscar Wilde in 1895, which rendered visible male homosexuality as the "open secret." The impact of Wilde's trials for the social construction of homosexuality and the homophobic responses to it had, as its correlate, the trial of Radclyffe Hall's lesbian novel, *The Well of Loneliness*, for obscenity in 1928. Lesbianism was not outlawed, but it remained unacknowledged and invisible as the response to Hall's book attested. Both du Maurier and Hitchcock encountered, in their formative years as artists, the "queer conservative" milieu of the London stage of the 1920s represented by Coward and his circle – a culture that was conservative in the way it nostalgically celebrated the manners and mores of an urban drawing-room elite, yet queer in the way it explored the themes of deviant sexuality in the form of heterosexual promiscuity with a hint of something other.[1]

Du Maurier was immersed in the atmosphere of London theater through the acting career of her famous father Gerald, who perfected a modern, "naturalistic" style of stage acting, was a friend of Coward's, and who lived the double life that Coward portrayed on the stage: devoted husband by day, stage-door Johnny by night. Hitchcock was an inveterate theatergoer with his mother in the late teens and early twenties when Coward hit the London stage with *I'll Leave it to You* (1920), *The Young Idea* (1923), and *London Calling* (1923). Furthermore, Hitchcock's early career consisted of many play adaptations and collaborations with men and woman of the stage, including figures from Coward's circle. He collaborated with the matinee idol, Ivor Novello, who, like Coward, was homosexual, on two films: *The Lodger* (1926) and *Downhill* (1927), the latter based on a Novello play with a clear homosexual subtext. With scenario writer Eliot Stannard, Hitchcock adapted Noel Coward's 1925 play *Easy Virtue* in 1927 (with Novello's initial involvement), and conservative, lesbian, playwright Clemance Dane's *Murder!* for the screen in 1930. Intriguingly, Hitchcock invited Dane to write the original scenario of his film version of du Maurier's *Jamaica Inn*, but the collaboration failed. In the early 1930s, Hitchcock produced *Lord Camber's Ladies*, which starred Daphne's father, Gerald, who Hitchcock said later was "the leading actor in London at the time, and, in my opinion, the best actor anywhere."[2]

Du Maurier's particular mixture of conservatism and queerness as writer were bound together in her complex relationship to the du Maurier family lineage. Du Maurier's grandfather, George du Maurier, was author of the immensely popular novels of the *fin de siècle*, *Peter Ibettson* and *Trilby*, which celebrated the perpetual, wonderful folly of masculine youth. As Nina Auerbach has suggested, grandfather George, father Gerald, and family friend, J. M. Barrie, were all Victorian men who, like Peter Pan, wanted to remain boys, boys who would never grow up.[3] For du Maurier, the idea of inhabiting a never, never land of perpetual and unruly boyhood was a seductive one. She identified herself as a boy, Eric Avon, in her adolescence, and conceived her writerly persona as "the boy in the box" who was normally contained within the veneer of her ostensibly conventional femininity but liberated in the activity of writing. Du Maurier's identification with writing as a masculine activity took place in a culture where the appeal of masculine identity was strong among women who wished to free themselves from traditional femininity. But her identification with the "boy in the box" was deeper than a simple reversal of gender roles: it was also the way in which she conceived her passion for women. Du Maurier wrote to her unrequited epistolary love, Ellen Doubleday, that she was once a tomboy who, as a boy, fell in love with her French governess: "And then the boy realized he had to grow up and not be a boy any longer, so he turned into a girl . . . and the boy was locked in a box forever."[4] But then she met Ellen and found it difficult, for a while, to keep the boy in the box.

Psychologists of sexuality Havelock Ellis and Richard von Krafft-Ebbing made official the equation of lesbianism with inversion at the end of the nineteenth century, and the publication of *The Well of Loneliness* (1928) further consolidated this link in the public imagination and in the mind of those who identified – or who might identify – as lesbians. Stephen Gordon, the aristocratic lesbian writer "hero" of Hall's novel, is defined by her masculine good looks inherited from her father (her surname is Byron's last name), and by her strong identification with the father's line embodied in the patriarchal estate of Morton. She wears her masculinity at once as a badge of honor and self-loathing. It is her source of identity and strength, but it also reminds her that she is forever exiled from the world of Morton, the patriarchal family and the lineage it embodies. But while Radclyffe Hall identified as a lesbian, Daphne du Maurier did not.[5] Through her identification of her masculine self with writing, du Maurier defined herself as career woman as opposed to the role of mother and homemaker that she also assumed. Furthermore, through her fiction, she could at once imaginatively identify with her male first-person narrators and entertain or construct possibilities of experience and identity that "real life" did not afford. Indeed, at its best, du Maurier's writing destabilizes any fixed sense of identity in a manner that echoes, in a popular idiom, the more experimental fiction of Virginia Woolf. At the same time, since her transgressive identity and identifications were largely confined to fiction, du Maurier was able to maintain an allegiance to family and patriarchy. Indeed, even in her novels, du Maurier appears to celebrate the idea of the past and its continuity with the present in a manner that might be confused with high Toryism. But it is also the persistence of tradition that gives potency and energy to those unruly and irrepressible desires that threaten to shatter the world of the familiar and the normal, as if a life lived conforming to convention is merely a façade.

Scholars have identified a number of literary influences on du Maurier's work. As Alison Light observes, du Maurier closely identified with the literary romanticism of the Brontës, where primacy was given to the thoughts and feelings of the protagonist and where romantic love was "a potentially dangerous place where the individual, and especially the woman, might get taken 'beyond herself', uncover hidden desires and often destructive wants."[6] *Rebecca* (1938) follows quite closely the plot of *Jane Eyre*, and the darkly romantic hero, Jem Merlyn of *Jamaica Inn* (1936), who roams the "wuthering heights" of the Cornish moors, is modeled on Heathcliff. But du Maurier was also influenced by a different kind of literary romanticism, the boys' adventure stories of Robert Louis Stevenson and R. M. Ballantyne, which allowed her writing to break the bonds that tied femininity to orthodox domesticity and cast her heroines as well as her heroes in the role of vagrant and adventurer. Deracination is a prelude to self-realization in her novels, but in liberating repressed desires, it is also threatens psychic disintegration.

Both the Brontës and Stevenson were influenced by the gothic tradition, and, as Avril Horner and Sue Zlosnick argue, the imaginative landscape of the double takes center stage in du Maurier's work.[7] Where romance is at stake, the formation of the heterosexual couple is informed and even derailed by a male or female double, who in the manner that is characteristic of gothic fiction, seems to objectify or to make manifest feelings that are of a nature and intensity that conventional romance cannot accommodate. In the female-centered romances for which du Maurier is best known (although she wrote only three of them), and which include *Jamaica Inn* and *Rebecca*, the disruptive force of perverse desire embodied in the figure of the double is ultimately contained within the boundaries of the heterosexual romance. Where the central protagonist of du Maurier's novel is male, romantic love fails to bring satisfaction, often because an intense homosocial bonding between a younger and an older man mediates the hero's encounter with and perception of women in what du Maurier herself described as "conventional misogyny." For example, in *My Cousin Rachel* (1951) the ambivalent desire of a younger man, Philip, for an older woman, Rachel, is mediated by his intense attachment to a father figure and double, Ambrose, who raises him in a homosocial environment devoid of women. It is Ambrose who first loves Rachel, inflaming Philip's jealousy of her, and it is Ambrose's death, perhaps at Rachel's hands, that draws Philip and Rachel together in a pattern of deadly repetition. Although *My Cousin Rachel* manifests the logic of homosocial bonding at the expense of women that Eve Kosofsky Sedgewick finds endemic to the nineteenth-century novel, it also suggests the patterns of desire that lurk within homosocial bonds and the subversive, disruptive force of the powerful woman who eludes male control.[8]

In this respect, Rachel in *My Cousin Rachel* is an echo and reprise of du Maurier's earlier novel *Rebecca*: in both novels the heroine exerts an uncanny power over the protagonist and the formation of the romance through her deadly involvement in an earlier relationship with someone to whom the protagonist is also close. In both novels, the uncanny force of repetition that governs the formation of the romance and retards or delays the promise of futurity and the facile optimism that it embodies, lends that romance a sense of unreality, falseness, or impossibility, as if conventional courtship and romance were itself something acted out, a masquerade or mask. Narrative suspense in du Maurier's writing is tied to the imminent collapse of romance that seems founded on a lie that constantly threatens to be exposed. Du Maurier herself speaks of conventional femininity as a kind of mask when she writes in Jungian terms of "the boy in the box" as "her number 2 self" that causes her trouble as when "one makes up one's mind what one thinks of another person and takes no notice of their real character but treats them how one imagines they are, and then one pretends to be the sort of person one thinks they would like to be, so the whole thing is one ghastly sort of dressing up."[9] In her superb late novel, *The Scapegoat* (1957), the idea of life as a masquerade is given striking articulation when John, a shy bachelor and scholar of French literature, encounters his exact double, the flamboyant and irresponsible family patriarch Jean de Gue and assumes his existence in the family chateau. John eventually seeks to repair the damage done by Jean to the family, amongst other things, by restoring the authority and power of its female members. However, the force of the novel lies in its rendition of familial relationship as a masquerade and as a fiction. The only time that John feels real — that is, himself — is when he consummates an affair with Jean's Hungarian mistress. Yet he is also seduced by the masquerade and the power it affords him to affect the lives of the family members he comes to love. It is hard not to see John as a male surrogate for the author.

Despite Hitchcock's frequent adaptation of du Maurier, an explanation of the nature of du Maurier's influence upon Hitchcock has hitherto eluded Hitchcock scholars. Indeed, by and large, they have simply ignored it. Notoriously, Robin Wood, in his seminal book on Hitchcock, dismissed the "novelettish" ingredients of du Maurier's *Rebecca*, and hence its source of value for Hitchcock, in terms that echoed Hitchcock's own disparaging remarks upon the book in his interview with Truffaut.[10] In part, the reasons for the neglect of du Maurier lie in the general way in which *auteurist* studies of film foster a sense of directorial autonomy from "source" material that is considered to be merely an occasion for the director to produce the work of art. Furthermore, this imperious relationship between writer and director is fostered by an industry that self-consciously embraces *auteurism* in a manner that Hitchcock himself pioneered. Also, quite often, the source material may be written by a woman, whereas the filmmaker is more often than not male. In part, the invisibility of du Maurier in Hitchcock scholarship is due to the specific works adapted and the circumstances of the collaboration. *Jamaica Inn* is generally considered to be one of the least successful of Hitchcock's works, and the reasons for Hitchcock's failure to successfully adapt du Maurier's novel have not been explored. *Rebecca*, following Hitchcock's lead, tends to be considered as an anomaly in Hitchcock's canon in which its distinctive importance is said to lie in what it tells us about David O. Selznick's taste and his influence upon the filmmaker during that period. Finally, the significance of du Maurier's authorship of *The Birds* is dismissed because it was merely a short story idea for Hitchcock's feature film scripted by Evan Hunter.

However, Paula Marantz Cohen does indirectly address the influence of du Maurier on Hitchcock, through an account of the filmmaker's relationship to the nineteenth-century novel that was also du Maurier's inheritance.[11] Cohen's primary concern is the relationship between masculinity and femininity as it is figured through character in novel and film. She argues that while, as a number of critics have suggested, the ideology of domesticity in the nineteenth-century novel served to perpetuate and sustain patriarchal authority, the amplification and valorization of the "feminine" realm of imagination, self-reflection, and emotional depth by both male and female writers of the nineteenth-century novel for a largely female readership provided an unprecedented exploration of feminine subjectivity that tested the boundaries of the gender system it appeared to support. For example, the dramatization of romance in the work of the Brontës as a source of self-transcendence and self-transformation revealed patterns of desire that scarcely squared with the passive, domestic ideal of Victorian femininity. And while Dickens in early works such as *David Copperfield* appears to be an ideologue of domesticity, in later works the defiance of the domestic ideal is treated sympathetically and orthodox masculinity is called into question.

Cohen argues that the new medium of film, a medium of images rather than words, dispensed with the requirement that its audience be literate and thereby neutralized female literacy and the advantages that had accrued to women from readership. Films were designed to be consumed in a short space of time with simple plot lines that militated against the articulation of complex subjectivity, and the "limitations" of the medium with respect to the rendition of a reflective subjectivity were compounded in silent cinema with its absence of spoken dialogue and the cumbersome nature of intertitles. A medium in which character must be read at a glance through physiognomy and typing seemed better suited to rendering action rather than reflection. While film introduced the practice of consuming fictions and emotionally engaging with characters to a male audience for the first time, it did so at the expense of the novelistic conception of character and the idea of female consciousness and sensibility that it had served to elevate. Furthermore, as feminist theorists have pointed out, the tendency of the medium of film to render women as a spectacle for the gaze of the male agent reinforced the masculine orientation of the institution.

Hitchcock's early films, according to Cohen, partook of the tendency of the institution toward male-centered plots and a plot-centered conception of character: "Hitchcock's inclination was to favor humor over sentiment, action over reflection, the visual over the literary, the present over the past."[12] By the 1930s, Hitchcock had successfully developed a formula of light, fast-paced, comic, male-centered romantic thrillers epitomized by *The 39 Steps* (1935) that focused upon action and plot rather than on character and depth psychology. However, Cohen argues that Selznick's collaboration with Hitchcock was a turning point for the filmmaker because it alerted him to the challenge of rendering a more complex "feminine" conception of character in a medium that had hitherto been resistant to it. According to Cohen, under the influence of Selznick, Hitchcock used the cinematic techniques of the moving camera, point-of-view editing, and the close-up to develop a more novelistic conception of character. While he worked under Selznick, Hitchcock deployed this more complex conception of subjectivity in the context of the "woman's film" – traditionally the Hollywood genre that focused on female-centered narratives of feeling and response, rather than action and reflection. Later, Hitchcock was to adapt this feminine conception of character to the portrayal of masculinity, particularly in his collaboration with James Stewart in works such as *Rear Window* (1954) and *Vertigo* (1958) in a manner that defied and revised orthodox gender roles and offered to the male (and female) spectator a conception of subjectivity that approximated the emotionally richer, more self-conscious conception of character to be found in the novel.

Undoubtedly Selznick encouraged Hitchcock to develop a more feminine, novelistic conception of character, and this introduced a new seriousness of tone into his work. Notoriously, Hitchcock complained to Truffaut that his first American film, *Rebecca* (1939), made under Selznick's close supervision, was not a Hitchcock film: "The story is old-fashioned; there was a whole school of feminine literature at that period, and though I'm not against it, the fact is that the story is lacking in humor."[13] Later, when making *To Catch a Thief* (1955), Hitchcock complained to André Bazin about "the necessity of renouncing adult, masculine humor in order to satisfy American producers."[14] Du Maurier's influence on Hitchcock's work, then, can be understood in part according to the way in which Hitchcock learned from the process of adapting du Maurier's novel under Selznick's strict hand to portray and explore character emotion with an intensity and seriousness that had hitherto eluded him. But while Cohen accurately identifies the influence of a "feminine" novelistic conception of character upon Hitchcock's work when he moved to Hollywood, and by implication the importance of du Maurier's *Rebecca* in Hitchcock's development as a filmmaker, she nonetheless misunderstands the significance of this influence due to a failure to accurately discriminate the nature of Hitchcock's aesthetic before he arrived in Hollywood. As a result, Cohen, too, fails to grasp the distinctive influence of du Maurier upon Hitchcock's work.

While Hitchcock gained popular success with his Buchan-inspired plots of the 1930s, his interest in storytelling had long been informed by a particular fascination with the power of the image and performance to bestow and create meaning in excess of plot. In particular, he was interested in the ways in which aspects of human motivation could be suggested through techniques of performance, image composition, and image juxtaposition that could not be directly represented through a plot-driven conception of character. If film was a medium of surfaces that militated against the kind of depth characterization afforded by the novel, as Cohen argues, it also offered an advantage on account of that fact. This advantage was less the immediate comprehensibility that conventional forms of plotting and characterization in the cinema afforded, but, rather, the way in which cinema could be used to convey the sense that conventional forms of plotting and characterization were only skin deep, a pretext for the staging of a shadow world of perverse desire secreted beneath the veneer of orthodox values. The influence of German Expressionist film was of paramount importance for Hitchcock in this context, for Expressionist film offered Hitchcock both a stylistic vocabulary and a thematic universe that he could deploy alongside and within linear conventions of classical narrative technique, and the popular romance narrative those conventions served to support, to suggest the shadow world of perverse desire harbored within the world of appearances.[15]

Whatever the facts are about Hitchcock's own sexuality – and without a paper trail of letters and diaries there is plenty of room, but little grounds, for speculation – Hitchcock discovered in the relatively impersonal medium of film a way to dramatize a divided self in a manner that bears close comparison to du Maurier's staging of the self in fiction. The narrative universe of both artists is one of conventional romance that is subtended or doubled by a world of perverse desire. However, du Maurier's concerns, like those of the traditional novelist, are internal, they lie in the domain of feeling and the way in which feelings motivate and govern actions. The sense of the self as masquerade and the lure of perverse desire in du Maurier's writings are intensely felt dramas of lived experience. In contrast, Hitchcock's perspective upon the drama of self-division in his early films is, with significant exceptions, detached, external, and typically comic, even when the themes of human perversity are ostensibly quite serious. As I have argued in detail elsewhere, in this respect *The Lodger* (1926), which Hitchcock himself dubbed as "the first Hitchcock film," provides a model for the Hitchcockian aesthetic.[16] The romance narrative in *The Lodger* between the gentleman-hero and the daughter of the house provides a pretext for Hitchcock to entertain the audience with the thought that the gentleman-hero is, in fact, Jack the Ripper who harbors murderous desires toward the heroine, and that beneath her mask of virginal innocence, the heroine desires the hero on account of, rather than in spite of, her suspicion of him.

Contra Cohen, Hitchcock does not begin his career with a simplified conception of character or personal identity that can be grasped through image or appearances alone, only to progress to a more complicated portrayal of character subjectivity. For Hitchcock's portrayal of character is complicated from the beginning by the idea that conventional masculinity and conventional femininity are surface effects and that the male–female complementarity of the heterosexual romance is a fiction predicated upon the concealment of darker, perverse impulses. Hitchcock's aesthetic cannot be defined by his adherence to the romance narrative; rather, his interest in the romance narrative should be understood as a form of aestheticism or textual dandyism that affords a pretext for the staging of human perversity. Hitchcock's aesthetic, at its most articulate, exposes the "performative" quality of conventional gender identities and the lure of perverse desires that threaten to fracture or expose those identities in a manner that anticipates the speculations of recent theorists of gender.[17]

Cohen bases her understanding of Hitchcock's English films upon a passing reference to the thrillers of the 1930s, but this is simply too limited a corpus upon which to build an understanding of his early aesthetic. It is certainly true that *The 39 Steps* is adapted from the male-centered action adventure novel of John Buchan whose conception of character is entirely plot-centered.[18] Hitchcock's film and the formula it established modified Buchan's plot by introducing the plucky heroine as the hero's helper and companion, and thereby attenuated the masculine orientation of the novel in a manner that follows Buchan's own lead in other works.[19] However, these changes did little to render character more complex. However, while Hitchcock's expressionist visual style and the narrative doubling that it serves to orchestrate are muted in *The 39 Steps*, it seems to me that *The 39 Steps* and other thrillers like it still register the trace of Hitchcock's perverse aesthetic: for the attraction of the hero to the heroine is that he lies outside the law, the process through which the heroine becomes attached to him is not without force, and the line between conventional identity and its subversion remains paper thin.

By refusing seriousness, intimacy, and depth of feeling, and by embracing comedy, irony, and emotional detachment, Hitchcock's aesthetic may be termed "masculine" as both Cohen and Hitchcock himself maintain, but this adjective describes an aesthetic that, although lacking a novelistic conception of character, involves far from the orthodox portrayal of masculinity that Cohen imputes to Hitchcock. For his "masculine" comic aesthetic is linked to the portrayal of masculinity as a masquerade that conceals perverse desires. In this sense, his aesthetic is a "queer" aesthetic. The extent to which these perverse desires are homosexual is hinted at in the English works, most notably *Murder!* (1930), though a homosexual subtext is certainly discernible in the films he made with Ivor Novello, *The Lodger* and *Downhill* (1927). The theme of homosexuality receives a much fuller elaboration within the terms of Hitchcock's aesthetic in *Rope* (1948) and *Strangers on a Train* (1951).[20] In the writings of du Maurier, Hitchcock discovered a feminine double who explores similar themes through the vocabulary of the novelist. However, in his first adaptation of du Maurier for Erich Pommer, *Jamaica Inn*, Hitchcock failed to discern what is distinctive in du Maurier's writing. Hitchcock simply assimilated the novel to the practices and the aesthetic that he had hitherto established, and the results are very mixed. It was, paradoxically, only when Selznick forced Hitchcock to adopt the tone of *Rebecca* and to realize a cinematic rendition of the du Maurier novel, that Hitchcock was able discover, through du Maurier, and to make his own, a feminine version of his masculine aesthetic, one in which perverse desire was explored with an intimacy and intensity that had hitherto eluded him. *Rebecca*, far from representing an anomaly in the Hitchcock canon, paved the way for later works whose focus upon emotional intimacy of a quasi-incestuous, incipiently perverse quality is the hallmark of du Maurier's writing: These works include *Shadow of Doubt* (1943), *Under Capricorn* (1948), *Vertigo* (1958), and *Marnie* (1964).

## Novel as Pretext: The "Masculine" Aesthetic of *Jamaica Inn* (1939)

The power of *Jamaica Inn*, like all du Maurier's romances, lies in the way in which du Maurier dramatizes the shattering force of transgressive desire upon her smart, but naïve, young heroines. At the beginning of the novel, when the young heroine Mary Yellan, upon the death of her mother, leaves the comforting, verdant lowlands of Helford – with its "shining waters," "green hills," and "sloping valleys" – to go to live with her aunt on the bleak, rainswept moor of Bodmin, we realize immediately, as Alison Light observes, that we are entering the landscape of literary romanticism, the landscape of desire.[21] Jamaica Inn, perched on the moor and housing a band of pirates, condenses a Stevensonian romanticism of Caribbean adventure with an idea of racial otherness figured, as it is in Charlotte Brontë's *Jane Eyre*, as a site of unruly, unbounded, and potentially deadly, passions. Yet this dangerous exotic world is not located in a faraway place but right at home on the "wuthering heights" of Cornwall and in the confines of the heroine's family, the house of her mother's sister.

Joss Merlyn, the patriarch of the house and pirate leader, who opens the door of the inn to Mary, is a monstrous apparition of masculinity, bestial and obscene, a figuration of Mary's worst nightmare:

> He was a great husk of a man, nearly seven feet high, with a creased black brow and a skin the color of a gypsy. His dark hair fell over his eyes in a fringe and hung about his ears. He looked as if he had the strength of a horse, with immense powerful shoulders, long arms that reached almost to his knees, and large fists like hams . . . his head was dwarfed and sunk between his shoulders, giving that half-stooping impression of a giant gorilla, with his black eyebrows and his mat of hair.[22]

Yet within this obscene, bestial husk there remains an intimation of something more handsome, of a diamond in the rough, which Mary recognizes and responds to: "his mouth might have been perfect once but was now sunken and fallen . . . and there was still something fine about his great dark eyes" (p. 22). The man that Joss Merlyn might have been, and once was, in the eyes of her aunt has long been lost to alcohol and murderous rage, and Merlyn dominates Mary's aunt in a grotesque parody of patriarchy. The quest of Mary in the novel is to confront this figure of evil and rescue her aunt from his clutches.

But Joss has a double, his brother Jem, a horse thief rather than a murderer, who swaggers into the inn as if he owned it and brusquely orders Mary to serve him: "He had Joss Merlyn's eyes without the blood-flecked lines and without the pouches, he had Joss Merlyn's mouth, firm, though, where the landlord's was weak, narrow where his lower lip sagged." "Mary," narrates du Maurier, registering her nascent desire, "splashed the water onto the stone flags and began to scrub furiously, her lips pressed tightly together. What a vile breed they were, then, these Merlyns, with their studied insolence and coarseness, their rough brutality and manner" (pp. 73–4). In choosing Jem, Mary demonstrates her striking independence of spirit and yet, du Maurier intimates, her fate may be not so different from her aunt's who fell in love with the young Joss. Indeed, during the course of the novel, Mary begins to suspect that Jem is the brains behind the gang of wreckers, and when Joss and her aunt are found murdered she believes that he committed the act. She turns out to be mistaken. But how should we interpret the end of the novel when Mary chooses to run off with Jem rather than return to Helford and work as a domestic for the good-humored but dull-witted Squire Bassett, the local *éminence grise*? "If you come with me it will be a hard life, and a wild one at times, Mary, with no biding anywhere, and little rest and comfort. Men are ill companions when the mood takes them, and I, God knows, the worst of them" (p. 202).

The fascinating, sinister, androgyne vicar of Altarnun in *Jamaica Inn* is even more important than the doubled hero to the figuration of Mary's desire. Ageless and genderless, this compelling fictional creation holds a mesmerizing power over Mary: "how strange a freak of nature was this man, who might be twenty-one, who might be sixty, and who with his soft, persuasive voice would compel her to admit every secret her heart possessed" (p. 105). Until Mary realizes at the end of the novel that the vicar of Altarnun is, in fact, the criminal mastermind and murderer of her aunt and Joss Merlyn, he is her single source of comfort and solace. It is as if this ageless and genderless being represents a different utopian conception of human possibility, one not governed by the prison house of gender, unbound by the conventions of social life and somehow liberated from the temporality of a human life governed by death. When Mary discovers his real identity, she accuses him of using religion as a façade. He responds that he sought religion as a refuge from himself and "found it to be built upon hatred, and jealousy, and greed – all the man-made attributes of civilization," while the ancient pagan barbarism he identifies with is "naked and clean" (p. 278). Corruption, he implies, lies in the person who falsely identifies him or herself with the trappings of civilization, for man's true identity resides elsewhere. The vicar tries to lure Mary by identifying her spirit of adventure with his own and forcibly abducts her until they are hunted down on the moor and he flings himself from the highest tor. While Mary's resistance to Altarnun ultimately helps, shapes, and supports her self-determination, he also functions as a kind of double, mirroring to her a realm of possibilities that are not contained within the narrow range of choices presented to the heroine in the final chapter of the novel. In this respect, he anticipates the role played by Rebecca for the unnamed heroine of that novel.

More research needs to be done into the circumstances of the production of *Jamaica Inn* before the motivation behind Hitchcock's approach to the adaptation of du Maurier's book can be understood. However, what is clear from a comparison between novel and film is that the screenwriters, Sidney Gilliat, Joan Harrison, and Alma Reville with Hitchcock's collusion, made a fateful decision to translate du Maurier's dark, gothic romance into a version of the wrong-man thriller that had proved so successful for Hitchcock in the previous five years, where the patina of suspicion cast upon the wrong man is only of the most superficial kind. The dark character of Jem Merlyn is written out of the film and replaced by Jem Trehearne (Robert Newton), who plays an agent of the crown who has infiltrated the band of wreckers. There is not a hint of ambiguity to this wrong man: from his first appearance he is individuated from the gang of wreckers in accent, mannerisms, and complexion in a manner that seems intentionally comic and a dramatic counterweight to the Dickensian figure of Joss Merlyn (Leslie Banks). Rather than suggesting the potential for the moral contamination of the hero – his fall into a world of chaos – the class milieu of the wreckers serves instead to underscore the hero's difference, his unblemished, fresh-faced, wholesome, good nature.

The character of Mary Yellan is built up in the adaptation from novel to film, in the sense that she is a pluckier heroine. In the film, Mary's actions emphatically determine the outcome of the plot: first by rescuing Jem Trehearne from a lynching by Joss's gang, and then by single-handedly (and quite implausibly) foiling the wreckers' plans to ensnare one more ship. In the novel, by contrast, Mary fails to foil a hanging, while at the scene of the shipwreck she manages to escape a grim assault only to stare on helplessly at the murder and pillage taking place on the shoreline. The script turns Mary into a less passive and ostensibly more feminist heroine who complements the agency of the hero. Indeed, Mary Yellan of the film is the hero's equal in every respect. And yet this feminist re-writing of Yellan's character is of a piece with the compromise made in the film by flattening the character of the male lead. For Mary is rendered a "masculine" character in precisely the sense identified by Cohen. That is, the Mary Yellan of the film is an emphatically plot-centered character: little is conveyed to the spectator of the film of her feelings or desires. Both characterizations serve to turn the internal "feminine" point of view of the novel inside out. They suggest the extent to which Hitchcock transforms a novel whose concerns center upon the feelings of its heroine and the ambiguity of her desires that are figured in the gothic romantic milieu of the narrative into an adventure romance, though an adventure romance that is narrated in large part from the woman's point of view.

At the same time, Hitchcock was drawn to the role of the perverse criminal mastermind in the film. Presumably to anticipate the strictures of the censors, Hitchcock and his collaborators transposed the vicar of Altarnun role in the novel onto the figure of Squire Bassett, who is transformed into the sinister, malevolent Squire Pengallen. For Pengallen, Hitchcock made the brilliant casting choice of Charles Laughton who proceeded, according to Hitchcock, to amplify the role, with the help of dialogue writer, J. B. Priestley, into that of a puffed-up, perverted, Byron-quoting, Regency dandy who parades his favorite white horse through the dining-room like the Emperor Caligula.[23] As Donald Spoto has noted, Laughton's Squire Pengallen is the fullest realization of the figure of Jekyll and Hyde, of the gentleman dandy as "pervert," in Hitchcock's entire repertoire.[24] The space that is given to his performance recalls the earlier self-conscious performances of dandyism by Ivor Novello in *The Lodger* and Esme Percy in *Murder!*, and anticipates the cameo of Marlene Dietrich in *Stagefright*, twelve years later. The Dietrich comparison is especially illuminating since both in *Jamaica Inn* and in *Stagefright*, it is as if Hitchcock, in order to counter the flatness of a rather conventional wrong-man narrative, cedes authority to a queer performer in a manner that seems to rival his own directorial control. Laughton's character not only threatens the formation of the romantic couple in the film, but his characterization and Hitchcock's response to it as a director, interrupts the tone of the romance narrative. In *Jamaica Inn*, the romance narrative does not "contain" the portrayal of human perversity as it does in *The 39 Steps*; rather Hitchcock and Laughton's figuration of human perversity seems to belong to a different film altogether.

The two tendencies within Hitchcock's aesthetic within the British period – the ludic, queer aesthetic of *The Lodger* that centers on the ambivalent persona of the dandy gentleman and the feminist revision of the masculine Buchan adventure narrative – come into conflict, creating an aesthetic impasse. Hitchcock's evident indulgence of Charles Laughton's flamboyant performance in *Jamaica Inn* clearly suggests a dissatisfaction with the way in which his perverse aesthetic was contained in the formula of the adventure romance, but the film lacks the overall structure and rhetoric of doubling that would bring the two aspects of his aesthetic into line in the manner he achieved in *The Lodger* and was to perfect in American films such as *Shadow of a Doubt* (1943) and *Strangers on a Train*. Charles Laughton's character is too grotesque to be other than a source of strange fascination to the heroine. Because he lacks the allure of the gentleman dandy in other Hitchcock works, such as the Lodger, Bruno in *Strangers*, or Uncle Charlie in *Shadow*, he cannot serve as a double for the hero. Conversely, Robert Newton is too much of the boyish romantic hero, and contrasts too strikingly with the debased environment of *Jamaica Inn*, to be afflicted with the anodyne anonymity that characterizes the cop heroes in *The Lodger*, *Shadow* and *Strangers*. Furthermore, while *Jamaica Inn* displays a willingness to pursue a feminist/feminine point of view further than perhaps any Hitchcock film hitherto, this leads to a creative impasse, for that feminist point of view is restricted to an action-centered portrayal of character; it appears entirely divorced from the portrayal of human perversity through style that is arguably Hitchcock's central preoccupation as a filmmaker.

In retrospect, Hitchcock's failure in *Jamaica Inn* is clear. It is the failure to provide a cinematic rendition of the female point of view of the novel; that is, to provide a cinematic vocabulary for a novelistic conception of character that would connect the female point of view of the romance narrative with the exploration of human perversity. Such was the challenge raised by adapting du Maurier's works, but in his adaptation of *Jamaica Inn*, Hitchcock, governed by paths he had already trodden, was unable to meet it. Indeed, it is evident that he had not thought the problem through at all. Du Maurier was so dissatisfied with his treatment of her book that she was skeptical of the planned adaptation of *Rebecca* with Selznick.[25] Selznick, with his passion for fidelity, forced Hitchcock to confront the concerns of the novelist for the first time, and Hollywood furnished the technical resources for him to realize them.

───── ## Film as Novel: The "Feminine" Aesthetic of *Rebecca* (1940) ─────

Like *Jamaica Inn*, *Rebecca* is a novel that centers on the nascent desires and yearnings of its orphaned heroine who enters by marriage into the house of a brooding patriarch, Maxim de Winter. The heroine's deracination confronts her with a perverse family situation, but in *Rebecca* the perverse family situation involves the character of her husband's former wife, Rebecca, and the nature of her relationship to de Winter. Like Brontë's *Jane Eyre*, the house of the patriarch contains a "secret beyond the door" that is explicitly linked to the threat that female sexuality poses to patriarchal authority. Jane Eyre discovers that the Byronic hero of the novel, Rochester, was lured into marrying a dark-skinned Jamaican beauty whose surface charms disguised a "pigmy intellect," congenital madness, and unbridled promiscuity and that she remains his wife, locked away in the attic of Thornfield. But the secret of female sexuality that Rebecca represents is more threatening and subversive. Rebecca is polymorphously perverse: she is certainly sexually predatory and promiscuous toward men but she is also, declares Maxim in the novel, "not even normal."[26] Her "abnormality" is literalized in the novel by her doctor's diagnosis of sterility, of a "malformation of the uterus" (p. 367), which, as Rhona Berenstein points out, is a tell-tale indication of lesbianism.[27] Rebecca is also possessed of "beauty, breeding, and brains," the traits, Maxim acknowledges, of the ideal wife and of the grown-up women that the newlywed heroine aspires to be. But these virtues are an elaborate and wholly convincing façade wielded with a "masculine" autonomy, authority, and panache. The qualities of the ideal wife turn out to be performed by the female dandy, someone who is merely masquerading conventional femininity, and who maintains Manderley and all it stands for merely as a façade, someone for whom heterosexual monogamy is merely the necessary fiction that enables her to do the things that she enjoys doing in a boathouse down by the sea. Rebecca's perversity is not merely a source of female abjection, as in *Jane Eyre*, but also a source of power and allure that challenges the authority and naturalness of patriarchal law and the heterosexual "family romance" it supports.

In the novel, Rebecca's transgressive behavior unleashes the full force of violence that lurks beneath patriarchal authority. De Winter murders his first wife in cold blood and then covers up the crime with a false alibi. Furthermore, the representative of the patriarchal establishment, Colonel Julyan, colludes in covering up the crime even though he knows that de Winter's alibi is a false one. While de Winter's confession of his crime to his second wife paves the way for a restoration of romance by freeing de Winter from his guilt about the past and his wife from the burden she has felt to be like Rebecca, the romance that is restored is denuded of passion, devoid of heirs, and lived in exile. Hitchcock's *Rebecca* fails to deliver the extraordinarily downbeat ending of the novel, for in order to comply with the censors, de Winter turns out not to be a murderer. While the patriarchal establishment still colludes in covering up the truth in the film – de Winter kills Rebecca, albeit by accident, and he lies about what happened by inventing a false alibi – the cover-up seems more excusable given the ordeal that de Winter has already been through. Since the enormity of de Winter's crime is lessened and moral responsibility placed squarely with Rebecca, the film allows us to believe that passion might be restored between the couple.

Nonetheless, the fascination of the film, like the novel, turns not on the trajectory of the heterosexual romance but in the portrayal of the force that threatens to derail that romance, Rebecca herself, who is realized only as an evanescent ghost-like presence that haunts the house and the imagination of its occupants, in particular, the imagination of the narrator heroine. While the heroine's obsession with Rebecca is partly explicable by her desire to become the mistress of Manderley that she thinks her husband wants her to be, it is mediated by the sinister figure of Mrs Danvers, who harbors what novel and film portray as a "perverse" erotic attachment to her dead idol. In her identification with Rebecca, the heroine not only mimes the idolatry she imputes to her husband but she also mimes the idolatry of Danvers in a way that renders her own fascination with Rebecca "perversely" erotic. Although the heroine enters Manderley a married woman, both novel and film make clear that she is not grown up; like the heroine of *Jamaica Inn*, her experience in the patriarchal home away from home is one that educates her in her desire. In the figure of Rebecca she confronts her perverse double, who is at once a source of repulsion and compelling allure. As in *Jamaica Inn*, the threat of perverse desire is registered through the force of a deadly corrupting nature embodied in the figure of Danvers "whose prominent cheek bones and great, hollow eyes gave her a skull's face, parchment white, set on a skeleton's frame' (p. 66). The lesbian, as she is personified in the figure of Danvers, is a vampire, nurtured and sustained by drawing the life from the being to which it is attached. And the heroine is "recruited" by Danvers, her sense of agency, her identity, her life itself is drawn from her.[28] More generally, both in novel and film, Rebecca is associated with corrosive nature in the form of lashing sea, driving rain. In the novel, in the second Mrs de Winter's retrospective, nightmare vision, Rebecca has taken over Manderley completely as dead, corrupted nature, and this inscription of Rebecca's presence is preserved in the film by the projection of images of dead nature on the walls of Manderley.

Just as Altarnun and Merlyn in du Maurier's *Jamaica Inn* are associated with the wilds of the moors in contrast with the benign domesticated valleys of the coastal lowlands, the association of Rebecca with corrosive and deadly nature contrasts in du Maurier's novel with the ideal of a benign domesticated nature embodied in the English patriarchal family home. We surmise from the novel that Manderley is one of the last great English Cornish coastal estates. Manderley is Man of the ley or of the valley. The valley (Happy valley) plays an important symbolic role in the novel as the conduit between the house and the ocean (and the boathouse). Manderley connotes the civilization of feminine nature by a benign patriarchy as well as the redemption of civilization by feminine nature; in short, the garden of England as the Garden of Eden. Domesticated nature is embodied in the rose garden that grows under the second Mrs de Winter's rooms in the east wing of the house that she enters upon her arrival at Manderley. Maxim remarks to her: "I love the rose-garden. One of the first things I remember is walking after my mother, on very small, unsteady legs, while she picked off the dead heads of the roses" (p. 75). The film establishes this image of Manderley less insistently but it is nonetheless invoked in a fleeting image of the house framed by the garden and in the painstaking care de Winter (and Hitchcock) have taken to bedeck the heroine's newly furnished rooms with freshly cut flowers. The framing of the heroine against these flowers, which are echoed in the draperies of the room, forms a striking contrast to the arrangement of dead nature that frames Danvers as she first enters.

Yet if Rebecca's is a nature that is corrupting and deadly, its monstrousness also takes on a very different quality, not a nature that is dead but something natural that is more than nature. In the novel, as Maxim and his new bride arrive at Manderley, they pass through a serpentine driveway whose enclosed nature suggests a feminine, uterine, corridor. With trees arched "like the roof of a church" (p. 64), it has the sublime qualities of a religious place – "very silent, very still." The second Mrs de Winter suddenly catches sight of a bank of rhododendrons, "a wall of color, blood red, reaching far above our heads." She narrates:

> They startled me with their crimson faces, massed one upon the other in incredible profusion, showing no leaf, no twig, nothing but the slaughterous red, luscious and fantastic, unlike any rhododendron plant I had ever seen before . . . to me a rhododendron was a homely, domestic thing, strictly conventional, mauve or pink in color standing one beside the other in a neat round bed. And these were monsters, rearing to the sky, massed like a battalion, too beautiful I thought, too powerful, they were not plants at all. (p. 65)

Far from an image of corrupted or dead nature, du Maurier pictures the monstrosity of Rebecca as something more than nature, her "blood red" femininity is something sublime, "luscious and fantastic," it is a thing of overwhelming beauty and class, at once feminine and partaking in nature, yet masculine in power and force and self-expression, transcending nature. Furthermore, this display of artificial nature or natural artifice stands for Manderley itself; indeed, it frames the house: "with the blood-red wall still flanking us on either side; we turned the last corner, and so came to Manderley" (p. 65). Emerging at the end of the uterine corridor, Manderley, the man of/in the valley clearly stands not for de Winter but for the powerful "masculine" woman, Rebecca.

Late in the novel, de Winter makes clear that Rebecca is identified with all that Manderley stands for, house and garden together: "The gardens, the shrubs, even the azaleas in the Happy valley," Maxim tells the second Mrs de Winter, "Do you think they existed when my father was alive?"

> Half the stuff you see here in the rooms was never here originally. The drawing-room as it is to-day, the morning room – that's all Rebecca. Those chairs that Frith points out so proudly to the visitors on the public day, that panel of tapestry – Rebecca again . . . The beauty of Manderley that people talk about and photograph and paint, it's all due to her, to Rebecca. (pp. 274–5)

I would suggest that du Maurier proposes in *Rebecca* the thesis that English patriarchal aristocracy between the wars is a façade, a masquerade, maintained by "masculine women" like Rebecca (and du Maurier herself).[29] Its real foundation had already collapsed in the disaster of World War I. *Rebecca* is not nostalgic for English patriarchy, it is nostalgic for a moment when married lesbians, provided they masquerade their identity, could rule supreme and freely indulge their forbidden pleasure. This is, as it were, the female correlative of the establishment homosexual spy culture that so fascinated Hitchcock. Written in 1938, on the cusp of war, the era *Rebecca* describes is clearly coming to an end; indeed, it has already come to an end. The façade, both of the old class order and the masquerade of sexual identity that serves to support it, is no longer tenable. Danvers in the novel does not perish in the flames of Manderley; she is free, and the heroine wonders what she and Flavell are up to, as she lives with de Winter a life of exile. One imagines that something is clearly gained for du Maurier by the collapse of the old order but something, of a class nature, is also irretrievably lost. And certainly someone like the second Mrs de Winter is not equipped to take over or sustain the old order. Manderley, the memorial to Rebecca, must be burned to the ground rather than turned over to the safe-keeping of such a woman.

This peculiarly English configuration of class, gender, and sexuality between the wars is attenuated in Robert Sherwood's treatment of the novel in favor of a more fairy-tale atmosphere. This is something that Hitchcock appears to have regretted, though it is in keeping with the transposition of an English novel to the specifically American imaginary of Hollywood where Englishness, the garden of England, becomes a kind of aristocratic never, never land, and Joan Fontaine fulfills the fantasy of the young American princess who marries into English civilization and culture.[30] Furthermore, the suggestion that Rebecca's perverse identity is a lesbian one is also more heavily disguised. Nonetheless, by turning the visual resources of film to his advantage, in particular, of Hollywood technique, Hitchcock strikingly evokes Rebecca's powerful and subversive presence through the strategy of intensifying and dramatizing the surfaces. For the social order itself – embodied in Manderley – is revealed to be nothing but a façade inscribed and defined by Rebecca's presence. If Hitchcock's career in film is a celebration of the subversive power of surfaces to undercut the manifest or apparent content of the heterosexual romance narrative and the idea of the human social order it supports and articulates, *Rebecca* is of singular importance in Hitchcock's work because the subversive surface it manifests, its textual dandyism, is distinctly feminine, distinctly beautiful – as if the ghost-like presence of Rebecca, her evanescent, mercurial identity, were constructed out of the fabric of Hitchcock's film itself.

The identification of Rebecca with corrosive nature is at once registered in the film and rendered sublime. Hitchcock takes up the vaginal, uterine, and holy imagery of the winding driveway and makes it his own. The forces of corrosive nature, of water, and "dead nature" enter into the gothic arches and mullioned windows of the patriarchal house and transform it from within into a cathedral of awesome Sapphic power and beauty. This transformation is enacted the moment the second Mrs de Winter (Joan Fontaine) arrives at Manderley out of the rain and is met by Danvers (Judith Anderson) in her bedroom in the west wing.[31] As Fontaine leaves the bedroom on Danvers's cue, she enters diminutively, like a girl in a fairy tale, a hall filled with towering bulbous (feminine) forms projected as shadows onto the curved white plaster walls. And with Danvers following silently, as if her escort, Fontaine glides, with her back to Hitchcock's camera, through a long, cathedral-like corridor shimmering with watery light, echoed by the mystical strains of tremulous violins. The invasion of corrosive nature into Manderley may be corrupting but it is a delicious corruption that paralyzes the mind with its beauty. They stop at the top of the stairs, framed from behind in a two-shot as Danvers points out the doors of Mrs de Winter's room. First Danvers, then Fontaine, peel off, leaving Hitchcock's camera to venture, to be lured, a little closer to the gigantic doors that look like the entry gates to some masonic temple until, as it were, stopped from approaching any closer by Rebecca's dog, Jasper, who stands guard, a benign Cerberus at the gates of a delicious hell.

But there is a temporal as well as a spatial dimension to Hitchcock's queer aesthetic that is, again, adapted from du Maurier's novel. Early on in the film, when they are courting, Fontaine says to Maxim that she wishes that there was an invention to bottle up moments and stay the passing of time. Fontaine here is referring to their romance, but the moments of experience that Hitchcock chooses to bottle up, as it were, in the camera are the moments of Fontaine's encounter with Rebecca. Just before the scene between Fontaine and Danvers, we see a single shot of a grandfather clock signaling ten to seven, bathed in shimmering, watery light. This shot is realistically motivated in terms of the temporality of the unfolding story by the fact that, in the scene after the encounter I have just described, dinner is served. But given the scene that immediately follows this shot, the image of the clock suggests something else. Rather than cueing the subsequent meal that is the first communal meal at Manderley for the newly weds, the image of the clock, given the superimposition of the rain motif, also seems to cue the encounter of Fontaine with Danvers and with Rebecca's presence in the house. It suggests not simply the continuity of time and an anticipation of an unfolding romance, but also the suspension of time and the interruption of the heterosexual romance by forces of desire that subvert it. Fontaine's encounter with the presence of Rebecca seems to exist outside the forward-looking temporality of the heterosexual romance that is geared toward the anticipation of a happy future, most immediately embodied in the couple's first meal together. It is also an encounter that redefines the space of Manderley as a feminine space rather than the masculine, patriarchal space. It is as if, in the sequence, Hitchcock plunges the spectator into a universe of "perverse," deathly desire that exists alongside and subverts the facile, forward-looking optimism of the heterosexual romance narrative that is ultimately geared to the idea of a fertile, procreative future.[32]

In confirmation of the striking reversal of priorities that makes real the subversive temporality of perverse desire, when Hitchcock cuts at the end of the scene to the meal that has been announced by the clock to resume the thread of the romance narrative, he creates an image of marriage as entombment and the communal dinner table as a space of alienation. As the music abruptly shifts from the ethereal tremulous violins to a stately regal tune, the camera moves from a close-up on the "R" of Fontaine's napkin and gradually pulls pack to reveal her nervously smiling at de Winter, who sits at the other end of the long dining table obscured from our vision. Butlers, clad in black, enter and leave the room in silence, save for the clink of the soup bowls on their china plates. The table itself is positioned in the middle of a large, dark hall, in the corners of which are gigantic formal arrangements of flowers, their dark shadows projected upon the wall. As the camera reaches its greatest height, funeral urns frame the whole scene, left and right. It is true that his image represents the deathly presence cast by Rebecca on the romance. But to simply interpret it in this way would be to ignore the allure of Rebecca signaled in the previous scene. From the perspective of the reality of the polymorphous and perhaps lesbian desire suggested by Rebecca's presence, the deathliness of the scene describes the marriage itself that has only been made possible by the killing of Rebecca and the possibilities of desire she represents. From this perspective, it is the compulsory future-orientated logic of the heterosexual romance narrative that kills or eliminates difference and that obliterates the past that is itself deathly in character.

By rendering corrosive nature sublime, Hitchcock dismantles the opposition between a benign and a corrupted nature in a manner that has no direct precedent in the novel. To a similar end, but following more directly the lead of the novel, Hitchcock associates Rebecca with the formal, augmented, artificial nature embodied in du Maurier's rhododendrons. The floral arrangements that characterize Rebecca's presence are marked, like du Maurier's rhododendrons, by their giganticism, and, undoubtedly, if Hitchcock had deployed the resources of color, they would have been blood red. Of course, the monstrous quality of these arrangements is at once a source of awe and anxiety for the heroine. The assertive femininity of Rebecca only underscores Fontaine's lack. Twice in the film Fontaine emulates Rebecca by wearing dresses whose defining features are prominent formal floral arrangements. The first is a black dress with an enormous bouquet of rhododendron blossoms draped over her bosom that she wears to the screening of their honeymoon pictures. Fontaine manages to inhabit the dress in such a way that the blossoms appear as grotesque extrusions, as an absurd artifice that exposes the extent to which Fontaine falls short in her ability to successfully be Rebecca, to fully inhabit the feminine masquerade. She is condemned to be a poor imitation, to be the abject crea-ture we see in the holiday film surrounded by geese. Of course, Maxim does not wish her to try to be Rebecca, but to fail to try condemns Fontaine to a state of abjection and non-identity, manifest in her childish attempt to conceal the broken china cupid. The sec-ond time Fontaine puts on a floral dress it is the copy of the white floral dress worn by Lady Caroline de Winter that Danvers entices her to wear to the Manderley ball. When Rebecca wore this dress, connoting femininity and purity, she wore it as a triumphant masquerade in full knowledge that she was acting the part of the woman that she knew Maxim wished her to be. In disguising her perverse "masculine" identity through a masquerade of feminine passivity and purity, she was, simultaneously, asserting it. Her masquerade of femininity appears fully authentic because she is in command of the show. When Fontaine inhabits the dress, she simply wishes to please Maxim, believing that by wearing the dress and by comporting herself in a manner that befits it she will become the woman that she believes Maxim wishes her to be and hence desires to be herself. But rather than asserting herself through a masquerade of femininity, she only reveals her naïveté, insecurity, and lack of self-assurance, as Mrs Danvers, who prompted her to wear the dress in order to humiliate her, knew she would. Even when Fontaine manages to look like Rebecca, to the extent of being momentarily confused with her, her earnest-ness betrays her.[33]

A third pervasive feature of the work that identifies and inscribes Rebecca in the *mise-en-scène* of Manderley is Rebecca's elegant monogram: "R" or "R de W." Amplifying a motif of the novel, the Rebecca monogram, in the film, is embroidered on the surface of the fabrics used by Fontaine: a table napkin, a handkerchief, a blanket in the boathouse, Rebecca's pillow, even the elegant surface of Rebecca's writing book. The size and ele-gance of the "R," the emphasis it gives to the idea of writing, and the embroidered nature of the inscription indicate Rebecca's mastery of the presentation of self, her studied self-fabrication. As Horner and Zlosnick point out, in the novel Rebecca's handwriting is defined by its slope or slant and with a vibrant "masculine" vitality: "That bold, slanting hand, stabbing the white paper, the symbol of herself, so certain, so assured" (p. 43). In both novel and film, the gigantic "R" that combines a bold, slanting spine with dramatic curvature suggests the combination of masculine and feminine qualities that define the larger-than-life nature of Rebecca's self-fabrication, one that continues to evoke her pres-ence even after her death. And, once again, Rebecca's mastery of self-definition is in stark contrast to the bumbling second Mrs de Winter who is in search of a self to become. The "R" monogram also serves to connect Rebecca with the fabrics it appears upon. The hangings, the furnishings, and the covers of Manderley signify Rebecca. This identification of Rebecca with the furnishings of Manderley is literalized in the one time we actually see her in the film (though critics have always claimed that she never appears). As Danvers entices her to the window to jump to her death, Fontaine is framed in two-shot with Danvers at Rebecca's bedpost. However, the two-shot is, in fact, a three-shot: for inscribed in the fabric of the bed hangings, towering over Fontaine, is a female face of great power and beauty . . . the face of Rebecca?

All three features of *Rebecca*'s *mise-en-scène* – corrosive or dead nature rendered sublime through the play of light, nature as artifice, and the extension of nature as artifice in the fabrics and garments through which Rebecca performs her femininity – come together in the rendition of Rebecca's bedroom. When Fontaine finally enters the "forbidden room," it is again a moment of dead time in the romance narrative. Maxim has left Manderley, and Fontaine is distraught, at a loss. We hear a clock ticking and violins begin a rising crescendo as Fontaine pauses on the landing bathed in the light of a giant cathedral-like window and turns to Rebecca's door. Hitchcock films her approach using a backward-tracking reaction shot and a forward-tracking point-of-view shot, to evoke the mysterious lure of Rebecca's room and its compulsive grip upon Fontaine's imagination.

As she enters, a flute plays Rebecca's eerie theme, and Fontaine is framed against a gigantic gothic arch draped with luminous white muslin against which the shadows of "dead nature" are projected. These shadows are, in fact, cast in part by a gigantic formal flower arrangement in the foreground of the image. As Fontaine passes through the gap in another curtain of white muslin (entering a dark, womb-like space) a theremin augments the *Rebecca* theme, and she is transported, awestruck into the feminine space of Rebecca's inner room shrouded in darkness. She opens a giant curtain that casts a pool of light in the room, and then the window itself that allows the wind to enter. Fontaine goes to pick up Rebecca's brush on her nightstand but, surprised by seeing a picture of Maxim that seems incongruous in these surroundings, she withdraws her hand guiltily. This is a moment in the film where it is quite clear that Fontaine is being directed to perform an action whose significance she does not understand. That is, Fontaine does not understand why she withdraws her hand; she just withdraws it in a mechanical gesture. Thus, Hitchcock conveys the way in which Fontaine's actions are governed by forces beyond her control. Suddenly, Fontaine is cold and disconcerted as she passes in front of a large bunch of roses. The shutter bangs and Danvers materializes through the muslin gauze. She dramatically opens a second curtain and the camera pulls back to reveal a room bathed in light – "the loveliest room you have ever seen" – framed by roses on the left and orchids on the right, a temple to Rebecca, whose nightstand appears as an altar against the far window.

Danvers approaches Rebecca's closet. Framed by the dark fur on one side and a white dress on the other, Danvers pivots to face Fontaine with a kind of animal-like intensity: "This is where I keep all her clothes. You'd like to see them, wouldn't you?" Rebecca is defined by her wardrobe, her masquerade of femininity; when they share in caressing her furs in tight close-up, it is as if by touching them they are engaged in a shared experience of touching Rebecca's skin. Danvers shows Fontaine Rebecca's underwear, whispering that they were "made specially for her by the nuns of the convent of Saint Clair," enacts combing Rebecca's hair by pretending to comb Fontaine's, then, finally, as the culmination of Fontaine's initiation rite into lesbian desire, takes her over to Rebecca's bed to show her the exquisite silk case with its "R" monogram embroidered by Danvers that contains Rebecca's see-through negligee. At first Fontaine stands to the left of the two-shot, shadowed by dead nature; she had previously lingered over the photograph of de Winter, and she is now intensely trying to resist the positive lure of Rebecca in proportion as her desire and fascination are aroused. "Did you ever see anything so delicate?" asks Danvers, as Fontaine is irresistibly drawn toward her. "Look, you can see my hand," she softly murmurs as she places her hand inside the negligee in imitation of Rebecca's skin. Berenstein writes of this moment: "As Fontaine moves, so does the camera which pans around the outside of the bed. Fontaine stares at the black negligée. As she does so she is entrapped both within the frame and within the confines of the bed's posts; she is locked into the space that most explicitly signifies Rebecca's sexual activities."[34] Fontaine stands so close to her that she almost touches the untouchable Danvers as she gestures to reach, to reciprocate and mimic Danvers's gesture of caressing Rebecca's negligee from within, from without. But she recoils in horror, flees from the room and enjoins Danvers "to forget everything that happened this afternoon."

## Adaptation in Reverse: The "Queer Modernism" of _The Birds_ (1963)

Thus far, I have explained the influence of du Maurier on Hitchcock, mid-career, in terms of Hitchcock's embrace of a novelistic conception of character in film. However, I have argued that it is not the novelistic conception of character per se that was important to Hitchcock, for Hitchcock's interest in du Maurier took place against the common background of their shared concern to subvert the conventions of the romance narrative. Du Maurier's novelistic exploration of human perversity inspired Hitchcock to inflect and transform his own perverse aesthetic in the "feminine" direction of intimacy and affect. But Hitchcock's aesthetic in _Rebecca_ and after, although informed by a deeper conception of character, remains an aesthetic of surfaces in which the conventional romance affords a kind of pretext for the aestheticized staging of perverse desire. However, by the end of the 1950s, Hitchcock began to use the format of the television show to sidestep altogether the conventional romance narrative with its obligatory happy ending, in favor of stories with necessarily minimal characterization, criminal heroes, and amoral twists; this experimentation in the television medium began to influence his approach to feature filmmaking. _Psycho_ (1960) demonstrates the impact of television on Hitchcock's filmmaking aesthetic, for he is emboldened in that work to explode entirely the romance narrative and expectations about character development upon which the romance narrative is founded. He seduces the audience into complicity with the perverse deeds of a psychotic hero and into a spiraling freefall of character identification: Marion, Norman, Arbogast, Lila (the next Marion?). The figuration of human perversity as deadly nature through the imagery of the bird is, of course, a defining feature of _Psycho_. It is almost certain that Hitchcock was already familiar with du Maurier's short story before the filming of _Psycho_; written in 1952, _The Birds_ had been optioned for the television show, was featured in one of the literary anthologies that came out under his name, and was the inspiration for his next film. In this way, du Maurier was to have a decisive role in the final phase of Hitchcock's career that involved a turning away from character, but one that has been masked by the failure to grasp the common aesthetic preoccupations of author and *auteur*.

Du Maurier's own turn to the short story format in the 1950s allowed her to subvert more thoroughly the conventions of the romance formula that uphold the ideas of gender complementarity, family, and futurity in a manner that presaged the more experimental novels of her later career – and to a certain extent parallels Hitchcock's own turn to television work. In du Maurier's short story *Monte Verita*, a woman abandons sexual relationships with men altogether to join a community of women in the mountains in central Europe. In another story, *Kiss Me Again Stranger*, a taciturn young mechanic picks up a cinema usherette and begins to fantasize a future with her only to discover that she is a serial killer. In *The Apple Tree* a husband takes on the qualities of a dead wife whom he hated. He does everything to destroy the tree, but it keeps getting revenge upon him until, finally, when it is hacked to pieces, he trips over its roots and is trapped in the snow. While these stories do not jettison a novelistic conception of character altogether, they do dispense with the first-person narration of du Maurier's novels and they minimize characterization in favor of atmosphere and effect. In this context, *The Birds* can be understood as the limit point of du Maurier's experimentation with the form of the short story where plot and character is at a minimum. Du Maurier's short story of *The Birds* simply presents a situation – birds gather together and attack an isolated family homestead in Cornwall – with little plot or characterization. Within this overall setting, a series of smaller scenes are staged that center upon the sights and sounds of the bird attacks, the dreadful deathly silence that follows, the anticipation of the impending attacks, and the attempts by Nat Hocken (the Mitch Brenner character in the short story) to fortify the house and defend the homestead.

The force of du Maurier's short story lies in the absence of explanation for the birds' attack; nonetheless, it is clear in the novel what is being evoked. The birds are intent upon destroying human civilization, but human civilization specifically as it is embodied in the nuclear family, and, in particular, the offspring of the nuclear family. Birds, particularly the seagulls that figure prominently in the bird attacks, are a potent force in many of du Maurier's works. In one of her most conventional novels of bourgeois transgression, *Frenchman's Creek*, the heroine escapes for a brief moment the responsibilities of being a bourgeois wife and mother to steal away on a French pirate ship, *La Mouette* – the seagull. The seagull symbolizes a release from the familiar land-based constraints of conventional femininity to the dangerous uncharted waters of desire, and the heroine is consistently compared to a bird throughout the novel. At the core of du Maurier's first novel, *The Loving Spirit*, lies the unfulfilled yearning of her heroine, Janet Coombe: "all she understood was that the peace of God was unknown to her, and that she came nearer to it amongst the wild things in the woods and fields, or on the rocks by the water's edge."[35] Janet's unfulfilled desire is channeled in the quasi-incestuous spiritual bond she forms with her youngest son, Joseph, whom she spurs on to reckless adventure, in defiance of her husband, with whom she vicariously identifies. In one scene, Joseph goads his brothers to take a rowing boat out on the rough seas where he faces certain death until rescued by his mother, but the rescue is described by du Maurier in terms of a thrilling, death-defying passion:

> "I'm coming, Joseph" – she said, and she knew he was waiting for her. The sea sounded loud and cruel beneath her, the wind blew at her hair – the stones and the earth crumbled beneath her feet and hands. A gull screamed nearby, rousing his fellows, and they flew about her head – crying and beating their wings. She cursed them aloud, caring not at all. Her heart sang. This was danger. She loved it. (p. 54)

*Jamaica Inn* and *Rebecca* link avian imagery to more radical transgressions of desire and identity – and hence more closely to death. The androgynous vicar of Altarnun with his hooked nose, like a beak, appears as a gigantic bird of prey as he stands upon a granite tor and throws out his arms "as a bird throws his wings for a flight" as a prelude to his death (*Jamaica Inn*, p. 293). The mounting anxiety of the heroine of *Rebecca* once she has entered the boathouse by the sea, site of both Rebecca's transgression and her murder, is signaled in the novel by the wintry presence of the sea and the presence of the gulls driven inland: "They hovered above the house in circles, wheeling and crying, flapping their spread wings" (*Rebecca*, p. 119). *The Birds*, then, draws upon a rich reservoir of avian imagery in du Maurier's writings, in which the figure of the bird suggests emancipation from the chains of family and conformity. But where the alternative to conventional gender roles cannot be realized or imagined in a culture of compulsory heterosexuality, the birds become a figuration of deadliness. It is not humanity per se that is under attack in *The Birds*, but the nuclear family, insofar as it is considered to be the sole enshrinement of human value.

Until recently, the significance of du Maurier's short story for Hitchcock's film has been ignored because, in the film, scripted by Evan Hunter, the birds' attacks take place within the familiar contours of the romance narrative and family melodrama – the triangle of the mother, the son, and the woman he loves – that are entirely absent from the short story. Furthermore, in the film, it is this family melodrama that seems to provide a clue as to why the birds attack. But, as Bill Krohn points out, Hitchcock not only takes the basic idea from du Maurier's story, but also the rhythm and texture of the birds' attacks are transposed directly from story to film, together with many of the specific incidents, such as the siege of the isolated homestead, the birds gathering as the children leave school, and the attack and killing of the neighboring farmer.[36] Hitchcock had always approached film as a series of visual and aural set pieces and hired writers to fill in story and character around them, and his visual style is always in tension with his source material where his source is not a kindred spirit. But, in *The Birds*, the creative tension between set pieces and plot takes on an altogether heightened self-consciousness. From the perspective of Hunter's narrative, the birds' attacks appear to be motivated by human emotions, to represent forces that inhibit romance or emotional connection, and the romance narrative is thus one that is, in principle, redeemable if they can be staved off as they appear to be at the end of the story.[37] In this sense, the film seems to domesticate du Maurier's subversive tale. However, in fact, Hitchcock's work amplifies the resonance of the novel, for, as Slavoj Žižek has rightly pointed out, the naïve or spontaneous viewer of the film does not link the attack of the birds to the psychology of the family; instead, the viewer awaits the onslaught of the bird attacks that appear all the more vivid and traumatic when set against "an undifferentiated tissue of everyday incidents."[38]

In this sense, Hitchcock's film is not simply about the family and its continuation or not; it is a film that takes conventional storytelling itself, centered on the family, and subjects that story to an act of sabotage enacted by the onslaught of the birds. Hitchcock's *The Birds* is "an adaptation in reverse" which adds to the source material the novelistic details of the romance narrative and melodrama of family, of procreativity, in order to expose the conventional "fictive" nature of that story. By taking du Maurier's tale outside the conventions of the short-story format, which traditionally afford a license with form that the conventions of novelistic characterization preclude, and "framing" this tale with the elements of the family romance, Hitchcock dramatizes the radical implications of du Maurier's birds. He makes explicit the sense in which du Maurier's short story subverts the conventions of storytelling that both she and Hitchcock inhabited for so long and so successfully. Hitchcock's *The Birds* is a supremely self-conscious, modernist statement of Hitchcock/du Maurier's perverse aesthetic in which, as Lee Edelman has argued, the relentless, mechanistic, phallic aggression of the birds represents a "death drive" that signifies a form of sexual desire that shatters "the compulsory fantasy of an always impending future that only a fruitful heterosexual coupling manages to assure," one that is at once evoked and refused in the catchphrase that Hitchcock cannily devised for the film "*The Birds* is coming."[39]

I have pursued two main lines of argument in this chapter. The first argument is one that identifies the common aesthetic preoccupations of du Maurier and Hitchcock, considered as "queer" author and "queer" *auteur*, in the context of their explorations of different media – novel and film – whose traditions and forms fostered very different approaches to the portrayal of subjectivity and feeling. Hitchcock's silent-film aesthetic explored film as a medium of surfaces that dramatized the perverse core harbored beneath the heterosexual world of appearances. Du Maurier was also interested in approaching this perverse core but through the medium of character and feeling afforded by the conventions of the novel. *Jamaica Inn* (novel and film) illustrates the divergence of their aesthetic concerns – the contrast of their "feminine" and "masculine" aesthetics – but with *Rebecca*, Hitchcock squarely embraced du Maurier's "feminine" aesthetic. With *The Birds*, their aesthetic concerns converge in a different way: Hitchcock adds to du Maurier's short story in a manner that makes explicit the implications of her "abandonment" of character. *The Birds* marks a return to Hitchcock's "masculine," ludic, silent-film aesthetic, but in a way that registers the full force and destructive intensity of perverse desire, in which the birds break the boundaries of narrative form – the form of the romance narrative – itself.

The second argument of the chapter traces the strategies of adaptation that define the encounters between these two artists. The novel of *Jamaica Inn* is merely a pretext for the film, reduced to episodes and characters that are adapted to Hitchcock's pre-existing narrative formulas and representational strategies. In contrast, Hitchcock's *Rebecca* is a "faithful" adaptation whose success lies not simply in mimicking the plot of the novel, but in finding a cinematic vocabulary in which to realize du Maurier's aesthetic preoccupations. Hitchcock's *The Birds*, I have argued, marks a kind of adaptation in reverse, in which du Maurier's short story is endowed by the filmmaker with a "novelistic" context, in a manner that makes manifest its subversion of narrative form.

## Acknowledgment

Thanks to Lucas Hilderbrand for his comments on the manuscript.

## Notes

1. On this "queer conservative" culture of the London theater, see Alan Sinfield, "Private Lives/Public Theater: Noël Coward and the Politics of Representation," *Representations* 36 (Fall 1991), 43–63; and Terry Castle, *Noël Coward and Radclyffe Hall: Kindred Spirits* (New York: Columbia University Press, 1986).
2. François Truffaut, *Hitchcock* (New York: Simon and Schuster, 1985), p. 82.
3. Nina Auerbach, *Daphne du Maurier, Haunted Heiress* (Philadelphia: University of Pennsylvania Press, 2000), p. 38.
4. Quoted in Margaret Forster, *Daphne du Maurier* (New York: Doubleday, 1993), p. 222. Forster's book is an indispensable resource for understanding du Maurier.
5. Speaking of falling in love with her French tutor to Ellen Doubleday, du Maurier wrote "by God and by Christ if anyone should call that sort of love by that unattractive word that begins with 'L,' I'd tear their guts out" (Forster, *Daphne du Maurier*, p. 222).
6. Alison Light, *Forever England: Femininity, Literature and Conservatism between the Wars* (London: Routledge, 1991), p. 165.
7. Avril Horner and Sue Zlosnick, *Daphne du Maurier: Writing, Identity, and the Gothic Imagination* (London: Macmillan, 1998), pp. 21–30.
8. See Eve Kosofsky Sedgwick, *Between Men: English Literature and Male Homosocial Desire* (New York: Columbia University Press, 1985).
9. Quoted in Forster, *Daphne du Maurier*, pp. 276–7.
10. Hitchcock actually states: "Well, it's not a Hitchcock picture; it's a novelette, really" (Truffaut, *Hitchcock*, p. 127). Robin Wood writes: "In any case, the film fails either to assimilate or to vomit out the indigestible novelettish ingredients of Daphne de Maurier's book;" Robin Wood, *Hitchcock's Films Revisted* (New York: Columbia University Press, 1989),

p. 74. Wood recants his remarks and "rehabilitates" du Maurier's novel in "Rebecca Reclaimed for Daphne de Maurier," *CinéAction* 29 (Fall 1992), 97–100.

11  Paula Marantz Cohen, *Alfred Hitchcock: The Legacy of Victorianism* (Lexington, KY: University of Kentucky Press, 1995), pp. 10–28.

12  Paula Marantz Cohen, "James, Hitchcock, and the Fate of Character," in Richard Allen and Sam Gonzalèz (eds), *Alfred Hitchcock: Centenary Essays* (London: British Film Insitute, 1999), p. 16.

13  Truffaut, *Hitchcock*, p. 127.

14  André Bazin, "Hitchcock versus Hitchcock," in Albert J. LaValley (ed.), *Focus on Hitchcock* (Englewood Cliffs, NJ: Prentice Hall, 1972), pp. 65–6.

15  On the influence of German Expressionism on Hitchcock, see Theodore Price, *Hitchcock and Homosexuality: His 50 Year Obsession with Jack the Ripper and the Superbitch Prostitute – A Psychoanalytic View* (Metuchen, NJ: The Scarecrow Press, 1992), pp. 288–354; and Sid Gottlieb, "Early Hitchcock: The German Influence," in *Hitchcock Annual* (1999), pp. 100–30.

16  Richard Allen, "*The Lodger* and the Origins of Hitchcock's Aesthetic," *Hitchcock Annual* (2001–2), pp. 38–78. Hitchcock comments upon *The Lodger* as the first "true" Hitchcock film in Truffaut, *Hitchcock*, p. 43. See also my article, "Hitchcock, or the Pleasures of Metaskepticism," in Allen and Gonzalèz (eds), *Hitchcock: Centenary Essays*, pp. 222–4.

17  See, for example, Judith Butler, *Gender Trouble: Feminism and the Subversion of Identity* (New York: Routledge, 1990).

18  See Toby Miller, "39 Steps to the 'Borders of the Possible': Alfred Hitchcock, Amateur Observer, and the New Cultural History," in Allen and Gonzalèz (eds), *Hitchcock: Centenary Essays*, pp. 323–4.

19  On the role of romance in Hitchcock, see Lesley Brill, *The Hitchcock Romance* (Princeton, NJ: Princeton University Press, 1988).

20  For an extensive discussion of the theme of homosexuality in Hitchcock's work, see Price, *Hitchcock and Homosexuality*.

21  See Light, *Forever England*, p. 156.

22  Daphne du Maurier, *Jamaica Inn* (New York: Avon Books, 1936), pp. 21–2. All subsequent citations in parentheses in the text are to this edition.

23  Peter Conrad provides a wonderful and informed characterization of Laughton's performance in *The Hitchcock Murders* (London: Faber and Faber, 2000), p. 88.

24  Donald Spoto, *The Dark Side of Genius: The Life of Alfred Hitchcock* (New York: Da Capo Press, 1999), p. 184.

25  Ibid., p. 183.

26  Daphne du Maurier, *Rebecca* (New York: Avon Books, 1938), p. 271. All subsequent citations in parentheses in the text are to this edition.

27  Rhona Berenstein, "'I'm Not the Sort of Person Men Marry': Monsters, Queers and Hitchcock's *Rebecca*," in Cary K. Creekmur and Alexander Doty (eds), *Out in Culture: Gay, Lesbian and Queer Essays on Popular Culture* (Durham, NC: Duke University Press, 1995), p. 245. This article was originally published in *CinéAction* 29 (Fall 1992). Berenstein's insightful diagnosis of the lesbian subtext of the novel and film, one that has certainly inspired my own thoughts, has been all but ignored by those literary critics who have written on the subject of *Rebecca*. At the same time, feminist film critics have failed to take the literary source

and its authorship sufficiently seriously in their interpretations of the film. This undoubtedly helps to explain their blindness to the lesbian aspects of Hitchcock's film. This blindness is discussed, though not in these terms, by Patricia White in *Uninvited: Classical Hollywood Cinema and Lesbian Representability* (Bloomington, IN: Indiana University Press, 1999), pp. 64–8.

28   On the lesbian as vampire, see Sue Ellen Case, "Tracking the Vampire," *Differences* 3 (Summer 1991), 1–20. Terry Castle explores the related figure of the lesbian as a ghost-like or haunting presence in *The Apparitional Lesbian: Female Homosexuality and Modern Culture* (New York: Columbia University Press, 1993), pp. 28–65.

29   In a case of life imitating art imitating life, before writing *Rebecca*, du Maurier had long coveted the decaying country estate of Menabilly situated near the du Maurier family's country cottage in Cornwall. After marrying a soldier and writing *Rebecca*, du Maurier rented Menabilly on a twenty-year lease that required her to maintain and renovate the place for its absent owner, which she did. Her husband, who became Mountbatten's right-hand man during World War II and later served as the Duke of Edinburgh's treasurer, for many years visited only at weekends.

30   Hitchcock comments on Sherwood's contribution in the interview with Truffaut, see Truffaut, *Hitchcock*, p. 128.

31   Since the second Mrs de Winter remains nameless in the film (as she is in the novel), I shall refer to her, for the sake of simplicity, by the name of the actress who plays the character, Joan Fontaine.

32   My understanding of the relationship between the aestheticization of human perversity in Hitchcock and the way it challenges the logic of futurity that characterizes the romance narrative is indebted to the writings of queer theorist Lee Edelman, in particular his essay on *The Birds*, "Hitchcock's Future," in Allen and Gonzalèz (eds), *Hitchcock: Centenary Essays*, pp. 239–58.

33   See Horner and Zlosnick, *Daphne du Maurier*, pp. 117–19.

34   Berenstein, "Monsters, Queers and Hitchcock's *Rebecca*," p. 254.

35   Daphne du Maurier, *The Loving Spirit* (New York: Avon Books, 1931), p. 24. All subsequent citations in parentheses in the text are to this edition.

36   Bill Krohn, *Hitchcock at Work* (London: Phaidon Press, 2000), p. 240.

37   I analyze the significance of the bird imagery in great detail in "Avian Metaphor in *The Birds*," *Hitchcock Annual* (1997–8), pp. 40–67, reprinted in Sid Gottlieb and Christopher Brookhouse (eds), *Framing Hitchcock: Selected Essays from the Hitchcock Annual* (Detroit: Wayne State University Press, 2002), pp. 281–309.

38   Slavoj Žižek, "The Hitchcockian Blot," in Allen and Gonzalèz (eds), *Hitchcock: Centenary Essays*, p. 127.

39   Edelman, "Hitchcock's Future," p. 247.

# Chapter 19

# Running Time

## The Chronotope of *The Loneliness of the Long Distance Runner*

## Peter Hitchcock

> The rats are government who stave off death!
> Who plaster posters level with your eye
> Who make lugubrious demands for breath
> Obedient from you to fly
> To be X-rayed, immunized, enslaved
> Tested, docketed, depraved
> To keep your miserable machine in shape
> By giving for the maximum of years
> Protection from the wisdom that you ape
> Because you lacked necessity for tears . . .
> Death is the horrible, the terrible, the brute
> That sometimes floats from heaven by parachute.
> Death is the end, my friend, the narrow gate
> That never can be closed by a rat-run State.
>
> From Alan Sillitoe, *The Rats*

A standard quip about British cinema (apart from the observation that it is American cinema with different accents) is that it tends to excel at social engagement rather than entertainment. Although a plethora of exceptions comes to mind, the generalization has a ring of truth about it, as if Britain's niche in world cinema is the social problem film, the sociological treatise, or even some kind of socialist intervention with a human face. In the era of devolution and postcolonialism, of course, a burning question is whether it is useful anymore to write in terms of British cinema at all? One could make the argument, nevertheless, that British cinema has shown a consummate skill in representing social crises, more prominently during long periods of Conservative Party rule (the 1950s to early 1960s and the late 1970s to mid-1990s), and, now, when New Labour has assumed that mantle. This does not make it a necessarily political cinema, but how the social is narrated is never far from a politics of the possible. In the 1950s, for instance, socially conscious filmmaking was cast against a backdrop of political reorientation overdetermined by the end of empire and the emergence of postcolonial migration, relative prosperity coupled with the twilight of industrialism, and an inkling that, after the invasion of Hungary, revolution could no longer be conjured from the east.[1] It was not the case that artists sought a manifesto from these contradictory omens, but history underlined that the social might necessitate complex and more innovative expression.

The film I am going to discuss was born of this historical and social compulsion, but not in any unmediated or stark reflective fashion. Tony Richardson's *The Loneliness of the Long Distance Runner* (1962) was adapted from a short story of the same name (1959) by Alan Sillitoe (who also wrote the screenplay) and released to a British audience already well accustomed to film narratives heavily sedimented with the social concerns of the moment. The film stars Tom Courtenay as Colin Smith, a working-class youth who is sent to a Borstal (or reform school) for robbing money from a bakery. While in the Borstal, its governor discovers that Smith has a talent for long-distance running and encourages him to train for a cup competition with a local public school. On long training runs Smith recalls the circumstances of his youth, life at home, first loves, the death of his father, stealing, and getting caught. Later, in an impressive act of defiance, Colin stops just short of the finish line when he is about to win the big race. The film ends with Smith still defiant in the Borstal but now without his privileges.

My particular interest is in a specific logic of adaptation at work in the film which, I would argue, is highly dependent on the time/space of the social as a problem of cinematic representation. All adaptations are chronotopic to the extent that they are hypertextual reworkings of an anterior hypotext.[2] Obviously, this does not mean that the hypertext merely duplicates the time/space of its source text even if it can follow chronologically very quickly. Yet there are important differences in film adaptation that require further nuance in the form of chronotope at issue. I am going to approach this problem of time/space in adaptations in terms of variations of context using Richardson's film as my primary example. The first requires exploration of the broader or macrocontextual determinants in adaptation.

An adaptation is always already con-textual to the extent that it is simultaneously set *with* and *against* the text that is its very possibility. But we should keep alive other meanings of *con* put into motion in Latin compounds. In its older forms, *con* is a cognate both of *can* to be able and of *cun* which is linked both to knowledge and expression. *Cun*, incidentally, is the root of *cunning*, which is a key motif in *The Loneliness of the Long Distance Runner*. In general, context is about weaving and connecting, but it is important to stress that this links to what comes before a text *and* also what follows it. An adaptation not only transforms a text but also changes all subsequent interpretations of it. (It is difficult now, for instance, to think of Sillitoe's short story without also calling to mind Tom Courtenay playing its lead character.) Why *macro*? The *macro* in "macrocontextual" allows us to accentuate elements of the social circumstances of the adaptation rather than only the form and content of the adaptation itself. If all context were of the same nature, then *macro* would obviously be redundant. But adaptations are context-sensitive in different intensities. In this sense, an approach to macrocontextual adaptation emphasizes a sensitive dependence on the social coordinates in which the adaptation is enmeshed. Again, this does not assume that the macrocontext is identical to that of the source text – in this case, a short story published three years earlier – but it does draw attention to an adaptation's *active* negotiation of social contingencies which may indeed invoke the circumstances of the source text. In practical terms, of course, cinematic chronotope reveals that macro and micro-elements are deeply entwined (which is one reason that the socio-history of adaptation is so provocative). This practicality, nevertheless, has often dissolved into either formal/structural analysis or content/socio-logical critique with nary a time/space between the two. If the different intensities of context begin to merge in the following exegesis, it is in part because the differences at stake must not elide the necessity of foregrounding the embeddedness of both.

In contrast to the macrocontextual, the aesthetic or microcontextual determinants of forms of adaptation offer a different methodological concern: specifically, the elements of cinema that determine, to a degree, the actual form and content of the film and that ultimately represent the adaptation's achievement *as a film*. This is not an innocent dis-tinction because it stresses stark formal differences that may obtain (between fiction and film, for instance) and the film's interest in showing what film can do (in other words, it measures the extent to which the adaptation wishes to break from naïve notions of fidelity or faithfulness toward a text that has a different logic of composition and texture). Yet the concern for film as film does not obviate a need to consider context: what micro-contextual means in this instance, therefore, is the more immediate film context of the text, including stylistic influences, directorial idiosyncrasies, and the situation of the film industry itself in which the film is made. When film adaptation analysis focuses only on the relationship between the film and its source text a very denuded sense of context is implied; indeed, such criticism often aspires to a kind of cinematic formalism. By coor-dinating different levels of macro- and microcontextual concerns, however, a richer sense of chronotopic adaptation emerges. Mikhail Bakhtin thought of chronotope as the time/space in which the knots of narrative were tied and untied.[3] While this might not reveal the inner life of film, it nevertheless draws attention to the concreteness of its art, not just as an effect of time/space but as an ardent *producer* of chronotopes. And this is a *running time* shared by Colin Smith, the lead character in Richardson's film and the narrative itself.

The problem remains that an analysis of context in forms of adaptation rarely yields sharp distinctions in what we have been referring to as macro- and microcontextual deter-minants. Indeed, it would seem more useful to fathom the extent to which such elements are mutually imbricated rather than itemize their otherwise elusive independence. Perhaps a *chronotope* of adaptation means precisely this: the varying intensities of context deter-mined by and productive of the time/space of narrative. This sense of narrative includes both the source text and the adaptation itself but also maintains the difference in time/space between the two. Certainly we will register such differences between Sillitoe's short story and the subsequent film which may themselves be symptomatic of the quickly shifting sands of cultural relations in England at that time. But I want to press the point that such an approach is more than just an adjustment in the study of film adaptation: it also raises significant questions about the value of the chronotope for film history in general.

At first glance, chronotopes of aesthetic production seem bound by two parts inspiration and one part serendipity. For instance, in 1957 Alan Sillitoe and his wife, Ruth Fainlight, returned to England from Spain to drum up support for their writing. Sillitoe was still in the process of trying to place a novel in manuscript, *Saturday Night and Sunday Morning*, while Fainlight was attempting to get a broader audience for her poetry. They were enthusiastic that things would work out, even though Sillitoe had seen plenty of rejection slips both for novels (most abandoned) and for his articles and short stories. While in the army, Sillitoe had contracted tuberculosis and, by living in Majorca, he had been able both to recuperate and survive on a meager pension while honing his skills as a writer. Sillitoe was more certain than his agent that he could get a contract for *Saturday Night*, but as he waited for a decision he and Fainlight had the good fortune of being loaned a country cottage near Bishop's Stortford for a few weeks.

Sillitoe was heavily into Albert Camus's *L'Homme révolté* and decided to work on a different approach to the rebel's state of mind (different, that is, to Arthur Seaton in *Saturday Night*). At issue was his strong sense as a returning *exile* that Britain was mired in conformity and complacency. Sillitoe began a novel called *The Rats* aimed at upsetting what he saw as the deadening torpor of consensus culture. *The Rats* would eventually become the title piece in a book of his poems (quoted above) and is remarkable both for its content and for its anarchic tone. Working on the text one day, Sillitoe stared absent-mindedly out of his study window as a young lad ran along the lane in a vest and shorts. Sillitoe took out a fresh sheet of paper and wrote down the title of a new poem, *The Loneliness of the Long Distance Runner*. The poem was never written, but the following year Sillitoe found this sheet among other papers he was about to discard. Seeing the title, he set about writing a tale based on its associative effects. It remains his most significant short story.

These facts are unremarkable in themselves, and my point is not to make biography or chance the linchpin in macro- or microcontextual concerns. The journey from short story to film in this example, however, is informed by both Sillitoe's outsider status and a social desire that actively sought out this type of marginality. For a young, working-class person the path to writing as a profession is often daunting. Sillitoe's art was driven by an almost belligerent non-conformism coupled with a keen ear for dialogue and a fervent belief that the voices of the majority of British people were not being heard. Sillitoe has never subscribed to labels, either political or sociological. (It is no small irony of history that one of English literature's finest working-class writers has no truck with the term – a writer simply wants to be a writer, of course, not a standard bearer for a division which may be less than literary.) It has to be said, however, that without the very specific nature of Britain's class system, Sillitoe would not have found his footing in literary history. Why? The foregrounding of Sillitoe's literary expertise occurred in the late fifties at a moment when working-class narratives were celebrated as a cultural phenomenon or *event*.[4] This was not just a product of the crass tokenism of Britain's cultural elite seeking entertaining distractions from parlor-room fiction and stodgy farces. It also emerged out of the interpellation of the working class as notable and discerning cultural consumers. With rationing and postwar belt-tightening receding into the past, Britain's *lower orders* now had significant purchasing power. Popular culture, whatever else it meant, now meant big business. To be sure, much of this popular culture labored under the ideology of mindless materialism and commodity entertainment. Keep the masses bloated on thin TV programming, cheap fashion, Westerns, and sports, such thinking went, and there will be no more of the social ferment that Britain witnessed in the twenties and thirties. But the cultural event of working-class expression was more complicated than that, and indeed forever changed the landscape of the *sceptr'd isle*'s cultural coordinates. If this argument is about the intricate process of the film adaptation of Sillitoe's most famous story, *The Loneliness of the Long Distance Runner*, it is simultaneously focused on adaptation context and the specific logic of the culture industry of its day. This historical note, therefore, almost always carries some political and aesthetic import for chronotopic critique.

The cultural event that turns a moment of inspiration first into a story, then into a successful film is the phenomenon of the "Angry Young Men," a cultural formation that began in anti-establishment theater (the performance of John Osborne's *Look Back in Anger* in 1956 at the Royal Court Theatre is a crucial touchstone), proceeded quickly into fiction, and then flourished in British film up to 1963. The roots of the Angries go back further, of course, most immediately to the non-conformist poetry of the early fifties heralded as "the Movement" but more significantly to the protest literature of the pre-war years. The feeling was that with the Suez Crisis and the invasion of Hungary in 1956 there were, indeed, new reasons to be politically active on the cultural front (despite Jimmy Porter's cynicism in Osborne's play). Cultural events after the war did not require manifestos: they were overdetermined in a number of ways by mediatization, hype, iconoclasm, and consumption aesthetics. As it happens, the Angry Young Men had an anti-manifesto published in 1957, *Declaration*, edited and introduced by Tom Maschler who, incidentally, as an editor for MacGibbon and Kee, had rejected Sillitoe's manuscript for *Saturday Night* that year (a pointed example of irony, given the phenomenal success of the book and subsequent film).[5] *Declaration*, while deriding the "Angry Young Men" moniker, nevertheless tapped into its sense of *angst* and dissatisfaction with the cultural status quo. One of its contributors was Lindsay Anderson, who was busy reinvigorating British documentary filmmaking in a way that learned from and leaned toward Grierson through the notion of Free Cinema. Anderson's plea for British cinema in *Declaration* is direct:

> The number of British films that have ever made a genuine try at a story in a popular milieu, with working-class characters all through, can be counted on the fingers of one hand . . . this virtual rejection of three-quarters of the population of this country represents more than a ridiculous impoverishment of the cinema. It is characteristic of a flight from contemporary reality by a whole, influential section of the community. And, which is worse, by reason of their control of the cinema, they succeed in imposing their distorted view of the present on their massive and impressionable audience.[6]

These sentiments would be shared by another rising star of British cinema, Karel Reisz, whose major contribution to the Free Cinema movement, *We are the Lambeth Boys* (1959), not only answered Anderson's clarion call for working-class realism but was also a springboard for his Woodfall film the following year, *Saturday Night and Sunday Morning*.

The importance of Woodfall in what was adapted from working-class writing in the late fifties cannot be overemphasized. The Woodfall Company was specifically set up by Tony Richardson and John Osborne to produce the film adaptation of *Look Back in Anger*. Richardson had never directed a feature before (he had, however, co-directed a documentary, *Momma Don't Allow* with Karel Reisz, which appeared in 1956; he had also directed Osborne's play at the Royal Court) and it was only through the tenacious bargaining of the firm's producer, Harry Saltzman, that the film got made at all (some of the production costs were funded by Osborne's royalties). For Richardson, the aim of the company was as basic as Anderson's desire for British cinema: "It is absolutely vital to get into British films the same sort of impact and sense of life that what you can loosely call the Angry Young Man cult has had in the theatre and literary worlds."[7] On one level, this form of adaptation is premised on exploitation, cashing in on the cultural event; on another level, Richardson fervently believed that a "sense of life" was both necessary in itself and that it could be imaged. *Look Back in Anger* did not just build on the extraordinary success of Osborne's play, however; the adaptation showed that the film could maintain the emotional intensity of its forebear, enhanced in no small way by Richard Burton's portrayal of Porter, while providing the narrative with a broader, less solipsistic, rendering of youthful discontent (underlined by Richardson's agreement with Nigel Neale, the scriptwriter, that much of the action should occur outside Porter's flat in a variety of urban locations).

The macrocontextual determinants of Richardson's *Loneliness of the Long Distance Runner* are thus marked to a significant degree by the confluence of two otherwise distinct threads: (1) Sillitoe's exotopy or outsideness to the British literary establishment, evident in the nonconformism of his characters like Arthur Seaton and Colin Smith (who break other stereotypes, like those of the working-class, rogue male) and the anarchic pronouncements of poetry like *The Rats*; and (2) the specific concerns of Anderson, Richardson, and Reisz in their Free Cinema and Woodfall projects to tap the "Angry Young Man" as a cultural event, and, indeed, to recreate it, in order to break from the languor of the British film industry. What is fascinating about this cultural event is the interdependency of these elements, as if the true measure of, say, Sillitoe and Richardson cannot be adequately appreciated if separated from the logic of that moment. I have argued elsewhere that Sillitoe's writing career suffers appreciably when unhinged from the sociocultural conditions precipitate in the "Angry Young Man" phenomenon[8] and, although the case is more complicated for British film, it is clear that Richardson's fortunes are not unconnected to this logic, a sense accentuated even in the title of his posthumously published memoir, *The Long Distance Runner*.

The association of Smith's gritty determination and dogged anti-establishmentarianism with Richardson's career is not unfounded (and is a point usefully explored by William

Horne in his essay on the film),[9] although the class differences that obtain could not be more stark. Solidly middle class (in the British rather than American sense) Richardson distinguished himself at Oxford University by energizing its Dramatic Society. This paved the way for a brief sojourn with the BBC where Richardson felt stifled by its conservatism. Meeting George Devine, the Director of the English Stage Company and a key figure in the ascendancy of the Royal Court Theatre, Richardson not only learned about directing but also about the sheer power of visual culture in shaking up British quietism of the time. James Welsh suggests, however, in a chapter on Richardson pointedly titled "Running the Distance," that, while Richardson learned from Devine the art of nonconformism, he never believed that the stage could represent this as radically as film.[10] The difference was not one of degree, but of cinema's ability to grapple with the living texture of the everyday in a way that constantly moved the spectator's relationship to the real as real. The realism of the films of the "Angry Young Men" period is undeniably more problematic from the vantage point of today's prominent chronotope, the postmodern, and appropriately so, but this in itself may blind one to the distinctive character of Richardson's mode of adaptation which often took the real as socially contradictory expression from below. More than a class alliance, Richardson believed that this position revitalized the aesthetics of time and place.

Sillitoe's screenplay for *The Loneliness of the Long Distance Runner*, with significant directorial input, dramatically alters the conditions of his story. Buoyed by the success of Reisz's *Saturday Night and Sunday Morning* the narrative is less interested in the sharp idiosyncrasy of Smith's monologue than it is concerned to pitch Smith into a maelstrom of social and personal contradictions. Although the film begins with Smith's voice-over this technique is quickly dropped and the difference from the short story's inner speech could not be more stark. Sillitoe's story is deductive: it seeks to characterize Smith's existential substance from a range of general circumstances, those that produce what Smith calls "Out-laws." The film, however, is inductive: it jumps to the meaning of long-distance running before the title sequence. While some may read this simply as an exigency of form (films have to get on with it) or as a comment on Woodfall's populism, it is also Sillitoe's explanation to Richardson as well as the audience about the kernel of the story: "Running's always been a big thing in our family, especially running away from the police. It's hard to understand. All I know is that you've got to run, run without knowing why through fields and woods. And the winning post is no end, even though barmy crowds might be cheering themselves daft. That's what the loneliness of the long-distance runner feels like." Sillitoe captures both the isolation and *angst* of Smith and something of the allegory of the working-class writer at the edge of Britain's publishing world (a theme that runs throughout his memoir, *Life Without Armour*).[11] Yet the way in which this first sequence is shot underlines that the film is more interested in Smith's "Us and Them" polemic rather than his complex introspection. It is also clearly trading on the "Angry Young Men" phenomenon that had already provided Woodfall with a windfall. First, the film is in black and white (which is both an economic necessity and something of Britain's disputed New Wave nod to the French). It has a fast-film graininess very much in the spirit of Free Cinema's documentary realism that simultaneously allows for high contrast as stark opposition. Second, the opening sequence follows Smith as he runs along a country road (the fact that Smith probably would not be training on a road for a cross-country race is suspended for the convenience of a vehicle-mounted camera). Following Smith is a clever touch, since the field of vision shows Smith alone against the landscape and literally ahead of the film's point of view. It has the air of anthropological pursuit (or even a foxhunt) rather than the story's revelation of inner turmoil and existential dilemma. Indeed, one could argue that, in attempting to convey Smith's detachment, the film accentuates its own. The working class is on display.

Like his adaptation of his novel *Saturday Night and Sunday Morning*, for Karel Reisz, Sillitoe's second Woodfall screenplay strongly resists the "Exhibit A" tendencies of Richardson's realism. Indeed, one cannot help thinking as one watches *Loneliness* that the central tension between Colin Smith and the governor of the Borstal is a correlative of Sillitoe's relationship as writer to Richardson's as producer/director. Richardson had passed over the opportunity to direct the first film, opting to be the producer instead. This time around Richardson takes on both positions with gusto (and in the process displaced Anderson from the project). He had just returned from a brief sojourn in Hollywood, directing a lackluster adaptation of Faulkner's *Sanctuary* and clearly feels more at home with Woodfall's trademark grittiness and an opportunity for greater independence. But the space between Richardson's aesthetic sense of film and Sillitoe's existential reading of working-class life is often quite pronounced. Thus, while appreciating the obstinate individualism that Sillitoe's Smith exudes in almost every scene, Richardson's direction clings to less ambivalent sociological distinctions.

In Sillitoe's short story, Smith outlines a world of what he calls "In-laws" and "Out-laws."[12] The "In-laws" are conformists who follow the rules and know their place as if it were pre-ordained. For Smith, "In-laws" are not just the governors of the world, or the coppers (police), but people anywhere (in "shops, offices, railway stations, cars, houses, pubs") who place their faith in the status quo as the best way to live. "Out-laws" like Smith, on the other hand, are unconvinced that the world, as it is, is consonant with what makes a human alive. (I have always found it interesting of the class prerogatives of the review industry that Smith's position is often ascribed simply to a criminal pathology.) In the opening paragraphs of the story, Smith's first-person narration suggests that running alone at the break of dawn makes him feel like the first person on earth, a body that has come alive from what is otherwise dead (this sentiment, by the way, can also be found in the works of Sillitoe's Nottingham forebear, D. H. Lawrence). "In-laws," however, believe themselves to be alive but, because of their worldview, are dead inside.

While Smith's assessment does have connections to class antagonism, it does not represent class solidarity in any conventional manner. He talks of "millions like me" and uses "us" and "them" polemics, but these do not add up to unproblematic class *ressentiment*. If Smith is an "angry young man" it is because he sees a world in which those who are true to themselves are often held to be dishonest before the eyes of the law. His war against the governor of the Borstal is based on honesty. The governor is a representative of the law and yet he only favors Smith because he wants the Borstal to win the challenge cup for cross-country running, not because he truly believes it will make Smith a better person. For Smith, the governor is quintessentially dishonest and lacks basic human integrity, even though it is Smith who has robbed the baker's factory and will rob again if he has the chance. Both sides of this ethical divide are cunning but Smith is convinced that "Out-laws" like him are more cunning because they can see deeper into the governors of the world than the other way around. Smith ponders these feelings as he trains for the race, and the more he thinks, the greater the chasm between him and the governor becomes. It is clear, however, that Smith distrusts his own community just as much, especially in the immediate aftermath of the robbery when he fears that his neighbors will turn him in out of jealousy and greed. If there are millions of "Out-laws," then, they are essentially alone in their honesty to self and it is this sense, precisely, that informs the loneliness of the long-distance runner.

Sillitoe attempts to get as much of Smith's idiosyncratic rebelliousness into the film as he can, but what is closer to a kind of anarchic anomie is taken by Richardson to be simply class war of a more recognizable kind, in keeping with the "us" and "them" distinctions of the Angry Young Men phenomenon (William L. Horne notes that Sillitoe built Smith's interpretation of being "alive" into the script, but that Richardson dropped it from the narrative).[13] In part, Richardson wants to make sure that the film gets made and seen, and the recasting of Smith's idiosyncratic worldview is deemed essential to that end. Later in his memoir, *Life Without Armour*, Sillitoe invokes the macrocontextual as a ground for microcontextual adjustments which he understood and accepted: "I was under no illusion that the success of my first book – or my second – need be put down to no more that a socio-historical accident, and artistic success had to be striven for, and never lost sight of."[14] In the event, neither the exigencies of cinematic representation nor those of Sillitoe's art are socio-historical accidents but the tension in the film remains between Smith/Sillitoe's "Out-law" status and Richardson's populism.

Richardson, then, is obviously and absolutely influential on what Sillitoe's screenplay becomes. If the length of Sillitoe's novel *Saturday Night and Sunday Morning* hamstrings his earlier adaptation, for which Reisz's direction provides the cut and paste, then his short story provides another acute formal dilemma: that Smith's first-person narrative has neither enough content nor action for a feature-length film. One could argue, then, that Richardson's foregrounding of the social in and outside the Borstal is a microcontextual concern for cinematic imperatives: for the story to be a film it must be adapted as such. The difficulty is not one of fidelity to the prerequisites of the literary, but of a properly filmic realization of what the narrative could possibly mean visually. A consideration of at least some of the cinematic elements throws into relief the strengths and weaknesses of Richardson's vision of Sillitoe's story and screenplay.

Much of the debate about Richardson's *Loneliness* has focused on whether his style derives from the Free Cinema/Woodfall ethos, as a creative working out of the intervention *that* represents, or whether the film is simply derivative, by basing its aesthetic predilections on the *nouvelle vague*.[15] Both Anderson and Richardson held that Free Cinema

emphasized the poetry of cinema and the independence of the director in producing it.
Yet eschewing the profit and loss impulses of the big studios did not mean an aversion
to populism, conventional realism, or the realities of the market. It helped, of course,
that when Free Cinema reformed in Woodfall it was bankrolled both by the extraordinary success of Osborne's *Look Back in Anger* (and, as mentioned, by the money-raising
skills of Harry Saltzman), but the question of artistic creativity was attacked from another
angle. The influence of French cinema on British film of the time seems undeniable:
existential themes, outsiderism, black and white *auteurism*, and a kind of studied plot-
lessness abound. Two points can be made here with direct reference to Richardson's
*Loneliness*. First, viewers should not be surprised by the stylistic affinities between the
British and French New Waves. Richardson had been fascinated by the connections between
the two for some years; indeed, the Free Cinema film programs of the late fifties at the
National Film Theatre in London included both Free Cinema work *and* continental film
production (Truffaut, Franju, Varda). As James M. Welsh astutely notes, however, the
question of derivation in British film of the time is complicated by chronology. Anderson
and Gavin Lambert, for instance, had founded the film journal *Sequence* in 1947 and
laid out at least some of their *auteurist* principles before Truffaut made his more famous
contributions to *Cahiers du Cinéma*. Similarly, Richardson and Reisz had already completed their film *Momma Don't Allow* when Truffaut's *Les Mistons* appeared in 1957.
Yes, there are distinct parallels between Richardson's *Loneliness* and Truffaut's *Les Quatre
Cents Coups*, but an argument can also be made that what is "New Wave" in Richardson's
film is a logical outgrowth of stylistic and technical elements already at work in British
film and theory. One view does not cancel out the other but, to read most film histories,
Richardson's work with Reisz and Anderson seems not to matter.

Second, even if one sets aside the trusty Truffaut yardstick, there remains plenty of
hostility to Richardson's film style in *Loneliness*, in general based on class antagonism
and less patience for the, by then, fairly well-trodden ground of kitchen-sink cinema. This
line of attack also avers that *Loneliness* is not the fruition of a fully articulated "Angry"
technique but is rather its death-knell, and underscores the view that both the event and
its aesthetic have run their course. If the first critique emphasizes the derivative nature
of Richardson's film, the second underlines the opinion that even that derivation has become
something of a broken record: "There is much that is all too recognizable. We have already
witnessed the dingy family background, the parental misunderstanding and youthful resentment, the stark irreverent language, the general air of cynical defeatism."[16] On the face
of it, Richardson appears to have done his job too well, since these elements do, indeed,
represent certain *topoi* of "Angry" fiction and film. In general, however, framing the
film either by comparison to the French New Wave or to any other "Angry" film of the
period has tended to stigmatize Richardson's *Loneliness* both as art that cannot stand
alone and as an adaptation out of sorts with the moment in which it is precipitate. Again,
the study of adaptation is not simply a question of measuring the ability of the hypertext to match its hypotext, but to come to terms with the logic of context that structures
both, internally and in relation to one another.

The "New Wave" aspects of Richardson's film include: speeding up action or otherwise distorting film time at key moments (usually for comic effect); fast crosscutting to heighten tension or complicate diegesis; breaking up chronology through flashbacks; and an attempt to render the subjective elements of Smith's worldview in the film narrative as a whole. Both Welsh and Horne have argued that what is really at stake in assessing Richardson is not the stylistic influences but the thorny question of the director's *auteur* status. With critics harping so much on Richardson's derivative technical hodgepodge, his authorial stamp gets elided; indeed, the one pre-empts consideration of the other. I have already noted the tension in Richardson's relationship with Sillitoe and his story, but a deeper level of cinematic chronotope reveals a sharper sense of the power of Richardson's adaptation.

Seduced by an outsiderism measured by the "us" and "them" distinctions of class, Richardson makes the sports day in Sillitoe's story a contest between a Borstal and a public (meaning private) school, rather than a contest among several Borstals. Whereas Sillitoe's story emphasizes Smith's private battle with the governor as distinct from his identification with his fellow Borstal inmates, Richardson flattens out this aspect of the psychological complexity in Smith by casting Sillitoe's screenplay as class dysfunction writ large in the difference between Borstal boys and their public-school counterparts. Despite what Peter Stead has called the "fussy pretentiousness" of Richardson's film,[17] it is often quite modest in its narrative components. For instance, after the opening sequence recounted above, the soundtrack features a version of "Jerusalem," a somewhat parodic invocation of Blake's lyrics about the manifest destiny of Englishness thwarted by the "dark Satanic mills" of progress (again, my point in quoting Sillitoe's *Rats* is to accentuate the writer's difference from that destiny). As the wind instruments lament in the background, the camera offers close-ups of handcuffs and the gaunt expressions of disaffected working-class youths on their way to Ruxton Towers with its medieval turrets oddly signifying a social order that modernity conquered. Richardson is not nostalgic for the verities of that world; indeed, he precisely attacks an Establishment belief in English exceptionalism. Thus, he uses "Jerusalem" again in a later sequence in which the Borstal boys have to endure one of the governor's gala events that includes bad bird impressions and snippets of opera. Finally, they are asked to sing "Jerusalem." Again, there are close-ups of the boys' faces, yet this time they are lit up by a kind of devotional aura. Called on as proud Britons, the Borstal inmates belt out "Jerusalem" as if the lyrics are a justification rather than an indictment of their predicament. Just as the earlier juxtaposition asks the viewer to ponder the stark contradiction between handcuffs and national hubris, so Richardson's second deployment of the song contrasts the enthusiasm of the boys' singing with a scene from another part of the Borstal where a boy is prepared for a beating after having tried to run away. There is an obviousness to the motif and its manipulation, yet I would argue that in both sequences Richardson is showing how film itself can expand the social vocabulary of Sillitoe's first-person story.

This is not absolutely at odds with Sillitoe's own outsiderism and its refraction through Smith's idiosyncrasies of critique. It does, however, underline a key microcontextual difference between the social realism of the "Angry" fiction of the time and the specific logic of anti-Establishment filming in the British New Wave. We should not be taken aback that Richardson introduces the public-school theme since this is part of his own upbringing and a common thread among the theater and film community. (Lindsay Anderson's *If* offers a pertinent correlative here, particularly since, even though it was released in 1968, the screenplay on which it was based was written in 1960.) The main contrast, however, was that Woodfall, like Free Cinema, saw in working-class content and regionalism a way not just to open up a debate about the cloying conventions of Britain's class system, but also to forward a polemic on the ossified institutions of British cinema itself. This, of course, has a positive and negative valence. Richardson clearly encourages Sillitoe to expand on the pensive, thoughtful side of Smith in his screenplay by making this part of the active dialogue of the narrative. Smith comes across as a class rebel in two senses, both with respect to bourgeois institutions and with his intra-class isolationism. Tom Courtenay's Smith is quite brilliant in conveying this bleached-out cynicism, a dour individualism wrought by an environment of mistrust: mistrust for the governors of the world, the factory owners, the policemen, but also the local community ("informants"), his mother (bringing in a "fancy man" so soon after his father's death), and other Borstal boys like Stacey who toe the line to gain favor with the authorities. The difficulty, however, is in squaring Richardson's technical virtuosity with the implications of Smith's "loneliness." The adaptation makes the case for cinematic risk-taking but also at the risk of reducing the narrative to a symbolic practice of class anomie.

One way to explain this drawback is in the macrocontextual terms of the cultural event. By the late fifties, novelists and playwrights had proved that the representation of the working class was more than a nod to populism but was also a challenge to British culture's sense of itself in the aftermath of the Second World War. It was not simply a recognition of "how the other half lives" but of a sea change in how the intricacies of a community's existence might be told. Yes, this was a continuation of 1930s' realism, but there was also a belief that a different crisis was at stake that one might characterize as that between reflection and projection. By this I mean that writers like Shelagh Delaney, David Storey, and Alan Sillitoe were not only interested in honest reflections of the working class to itself (which, after all, might predictably flinch at already familiar misery once the novelty of representation itself wore off), but that they simultaneously struggled to disrupt the predilections of a predominantly middle-class readership and theater-going audience. Note the point of address in Smith's first-person narration in the short story:

> And when the governor kept saying how we wanted you to do this, and we wanted you to do that, I kept looking round for the other blokes, wondering how many of them there was. Of course, I knew there were thousands of them, but as far as I knew only one was in the room. And there *are* thousands of them, all over the poxeaten country, in shops, offices, railway stations, cars, houses, pubs: In-law blokes like you and them, all on the watch for Out-law blokes like me and us – and waiting to phone for the coppers as soon as we make a false move. (p. 10)

Here the second-person address is caught between Smith's suspicion of his own community and of that surveillance afforded by readers beyond his community, an audience with its own projections of what a working-class narrator might be. The complex nexus of reflection/projection is at the heart of Richardson's dilemma in taking up Sillitoe's story and screenplay. If the early stages of the cultural event had featured a flowering of working-class expression, the first films had nevertheless interpreted this as class content; Reisz, for instance, actually filmed at the bicycle factory where Sillitoe had worked in order to give a realistic feel to Arthur Seaton's milieu in *Saturday Night and Sunday Morning* (this is the documentary edge of Free Cinema). The reflection mode answers the question: "So this is what a working-class life looks like." But, increasingly, films that drew on working-class writing wanted to hold more than a mirror to the worlds presented. They also wanted to address what Smith would call an "In-law" question: "Why do these people do the things that they do?" As Richardson seeks to turn Sillitoe's short story into a feature film, his narrative appears compelled to supply as many reasons as possible.

Why does Smith lie? To protect himself. Why does Smith steal? It is better than working himself to death like his father. Why does Smith trick the governor? He wants to prove that he is more cunning than the authorities with their suspect moral code. Why is Smith wary of his mother? Because he believes she does not honor the memory of his father. And why, of course, does Smith lose the long-distance race? Because, as the fast and furious flashbacks pointedly remind us as he approaches the finishing line, of all of the above. Oddly, or symptomatically, Richardson's position in filming merges with that of the new housemaster and pseudo-psychologist at the Borstal, Brown, who picks away at Smith's brain for a kind of anthropological confirmation that juvenile delinquency is an entirely mappable psycho-pathology. Brown, armed with the latest in analytic techniques, tries to get at the "why?" of Smith through a game of word association. Thus:

> *Brown*: "Water" . . . *Smith*: "Football"
> Sky . . . Snow
> Girl . . . (pause) What are you trying to do?
> Girl . . . Boy
> Boy? You got a girlfriend, Smith?
> Gun . . . Horses
> Knife . . . Smoke
> Car . . . Crumpet
> Father . . . Dead
> Is your father dead? Ahhhh.

Brown's final exclamation is like the regulatory function of the Symbolic in Lacanian critique, as if the narrative has sutured the spectator to Brown's fatherly revelation. When the film takes this route its chronotope is at its weakest, for it forfeits the intricacies of both micro- and macrocontextual concerns for pat psychologism and classic class condescension. Yet surely such exchanges are so obvious that they are precisely the object of criticism, so that the film replays Smith's cruel hoax on the governor at every turn? Perhaps, but as I have already indicated, Richardson seems less inclined to suspend judgment on Smith than Sillitoe does. In part, this is the doubled/troubled function of the cultural event of the "Angries" itself which, in representing the British working class, finds in that representation the displaced desire of another class structured in dominance. As Robin Wood has provocatively suggested, this is particularly pertinent in terms of the representation of working-class squalor and sex.[18] There is one moment in the film narrative, however, when the question of desire in its chronotope is, if not sublated, then problematized significantly.

In one of the key flashbacks we watch the aftermath of Smith's father's death. Smith's mother, and indeed his siblings, are less concerned with mourning than they are with spending the money provided by the firm his father worked for as compensation for their loss. The light music and buoyant smiles as the family goes shopping are wonderfully evocative: the story records a primal scene of working-class consumption of which the film itself is a veritable symptom. This notion of reflexivity is so pronounced that Richardson even uses advertising gimmicks, like star-shaped transitions, to separate each scene of consumption, and advertising jingles ("Give me a girl in a Rollerroy / Wash and wear, easy care"). As the family gathers around the television for another round of consumption aesthetics, Colin goes to his parents' bedroom where his father died. As Colin looks around the room Richardson cuts in images from Colin's discovery of his father dead in bed. Colin then stares at himself in a mirror (it is the kind of existential glance that Reisz used in *Saturday Night and Sunday Morning* to convey the crisis of the working-class anti-hero). The soundtrack goes silent. No voice-over, no sound at all. Colin pulls out a pound note that his mother has given him and, in close-up, he sets light to it. Howard Slater believes that this is a prime example of symbolic resistance in working-class film, and there is little doubt that the open-endedness of meaning in the scene is precisely what makes it profound in the film as a whole.[19] If we think of this in terms of subject address, however, more than symbolic resistance is implied. Thus, if one level of the chronotope fixes Smith in the gaze of he who is to be represented, a sociological marker of those traditionally excluded from the screen in their own name, then the chronotope of *Loneliness* also displaces this self-same image by questioning a universal equivalent (money) that underpins this subject's emergence. In this scene at least, like the one in which Smith stops running before the winning tape, the adaptation doubts the very time/space of the cultural event that has nourished it.

As if to accentuate the ambivalence that Richardson's film eventually displays about Smith's representative status, the narrative also foregrounds the medium, quickly reconfiguring working-class presence on both sides of the screen: television. Richard Dyer has noted that the burgeoning of fiction and film representations of the working class in Britain was accompanied, on the one hand, by an intellectual critique spurred by Richard Hoggart's influential *The Uses of Literacy* (1957) and, on the other, by the impact of mass media like television on working-class self-perceptions (he has in mind the hugely successful TV series *Coronation Street* which first broadcast in 1960).[20] Both Sillitoe and Richardson share something of Hoggart's disdain for the effect of television on working-class culture in the main because it is seen to short-circuit traditional pastimes and activities. Yet even then, *Loneliness* questions assumptions about working-class passivity and ideological brainwashing before the great juggernaut of mediatization.

Again, the adaptation introjects important contextual elements that provide its chronotope with historical specificity. For instance, in order to gain acceptance with Colin's family, his mother's boyfriend buys them a television for twenty pounds (in the short story his mother buys it with the firm's settlement money) and it quickly becomes the center of attention as a status symbol and source of entertainment (his mother calls Colin and his friend Mike "the telly boys"). Perhaps this is why Colin treats the set with such contempt in the film but he acts out his rebellion in ways that refract a more complex sense of the place of television at the time. One game that he and Mike play is to turn down the sound when politicians are holding forth to the country. This not only plays with the technology but with the government's investment in it. In a sequence that features shot/reverse shot between the boys and the television, the film also plays with its own difference among available media. It begins with the televised speech of a politician delivered in clipped, Queen's English tones accompanied by the boys' commentary (in parentheses):

> I want to talk to you tonight about the challenge of prosperity. Patriotism is out of favor with the intellectuals now, but I believe that Britain is emerging into an age when she will be greater than ever. And I ask you to hold fast to this faith, because this is our strength. What I am looking for [I know what I'm looking for] is a spirit of rededication such as we feel at a coronation or at a royal birth [ooh dear, have a look at his crown]. In these days when we are enjoying greater luxury than ever before, with our unemployment benefits, and our family allowances, and our old age pensions [I wouldn't mind drawing mine now], I believe that a new mood of self-discipline is abroad in the land [take hold of yourself lad]. Our young people have never been infected by a disease of continental existentialism. Unlike the Americans, our cousins in affluence, we have shown ourselves strong in the face of the virus of . . .

At this point the sound is turned down. In the reverse shots we see the boys imitating the speaker and wagging their fingers at the screen in mock authority. Of course, this carnivalizing of the politician as talking head is laddish interactivity but it comes with a couple of interesting twists: first, the reference to "existentialism" as an intellectual force is a nod to Sillitoe's philosophical interest in Smith as a rebel; second, Richardson augments the comedy of the muted politician by speeding up his movements on the screen, a level of interactivity unavailable to the boys at the time but a nice comment on the myriad ways that film can create or enhance meaning. Indeed, rather than being true to Sillitoe's story, the adaptation constantly seeks out its possibilities for cinema at or beyond the enigma Sillitoe creates in Smith himself.

In the event, *Loneliness* remains a troubling adaptation not because of the creative differences between Sillitoe and Richardson, nor indeed because of the different aesthetic demands of fiction and film, but because it is so thoroughly embedded in the micro- and macrocontextual concerns of its time that its chronotopicity is barely distinguishable from them. While I have less trouble with the sociological content of the narrative than some of its critics (particularly those of the time who wanted all of this interest in the working class to go away) the film is ultimately too impatient with Smith's worldview and wants his motives spelled out, if only because Richardson believes his audience requires just this form of "literacy." Sillitoe, as intimated above, quickly understood how his work would be interpreted within this chronotope but, as a writer who had struggled for some years to gain an audience, he decided in the end that Richardson's view of class war as Borstal versus public school was a small price to pay if this might garner a broader readership for his fiction.

In fact, of course, literary recognition had already come Sillitoe's way since *Saturday Night and Sunday Morning* had won the Author's Club Award for the best English first novel of 1958 and his short story collection, *The Loneliness of the Long Distance Runner*, had won the Hawthornden Prize of 1959 for the best prose work of imagination. No one should doubt, however, the power of the cultural event to bolster book sales. The book tie-in to *Saturday Night and Sunday Morning* that appeared in 1960, for instance, took sales of the novel from a few thousand to six hundred thousand by the end of the film's first run. Sillitoe's *Loneliness* also benefited from interest in the film and at that level he regarded Richardson's efforts as a success. In a final twist, such was the reading of Sillitoe as a spokesperson for the English working class that Hollywood lured him with a scriptwriting offer of $50,000. But Sillitoe was never interested in being rich, and he chafed at the idea that his characters should be rendered in a single key. Just like Arthur Seaton, Colin Smith, and the voice of *The Rats*, Sillitoe's own desire cleaved closely to a kind of anarchism and, whatever Richardson's doubts about the state and cinema, that race was for him a non-starter. Yet Richardson clearly admired Sillitoe's feisty anti-Establishmentarian bent and *Loneliness*, along with *A Taste of Honey*, remain his most poignant, heartfelt films. It is perhaps the dedication to an emotion rather than to an anterior hypotext that makes *Loneliness* so striking, just as Richardson's adaptation as contextual articulation makes more sense than faithfulness. As Tom Courtenay's Smith stops before the finish line the fast-cut flashbacks barely hint at his motivations, cunning or otherwise, and now the full range of that ambivalence might be read back into the chronotope of the Angries as a whole.

--- Notes ---

1   For pertinent historical and social background on the period, see Eric Hobsbawm, *Age of Extremes* (London: Abacus, 1995), esp. chs 7–9; Arthur Marwick, *British Society since 1945* (London: Pelican, 1982); and Alan Sinfield (ed.), *Society and Literature* (London: Methuen, 1983).
2   For more on "hypotext" and "hypertext," see Gérard Genette, *Palimpsestes*, trans. Channa Newman and Claude Doubinsky (Lincoln, NB: University of Nebraska Press, 1997). See also Robert Stam, *Reflexivity in Film and Literature* (Ann Arbor: University of Michigan Press, 1985).

Running Time

Chapter 19

3   See Mikhail Bakhtin, *The Dialogic Imagination*, trans. Caryl Emerson and Michael Holquist, ed. Michael Holquist (Austin: University of Texas Press, 1981).

4   For a theoretical explanation of the historical axes of the cultural event, see Peter Hitchcock, *Working-class Literature in Theory and Practice* (Ann Arbor: University of Michigan Press, 1989).

5   See Tom Maschler (ed.), *Declaration* (New York: E. P. Dutton, 1958).

6   Ibid., pp. 140–1.

7   Quoted in John Hill, *Sex, Class and Realism: British Cinema 1956–1963* (London: British Film Institute, 1986), p. 40. In addition to providing a fine survey of the main currents of British film during this period, Hill also advances an argument about the limited range of innovation in films like those of Woodfall. While it is true that the social realism deployed was hardly revolutionary, much of the film production of this time problematized the social rather than just describing it.

8   See Hitchcock, *Working-class Literature*, esp. ch. 6.

9   See William L. Horne, "'Greatest Pleasures': *A Taste of Honey* (1961) and *The Loneliness of the Long Distance Runner* (1962)," in James M. Welsh and John C. Tibbetts (eds), *The Cinema of Tony Richardson* (Albany, NY: State University of New York Press, 1999), pp. 81–126.

10  See James M. Welsh, "Introduction: Running the Distance," in Welsh and Tibbetts (eds), *The Cinema of Tony Richardson*, pp. 1–22.

11  See Alan Sillitoe, *Life Without Armour* (New York: Harper Collins, 1995). Sillitoe's autobiography covers the period up to the point where he is working on the "Loneliness" screenplay.

12  See Alan Sillitoe, "The Loneliness of the Long Distance Runner," in *The Loneliness of the Long Distance Runner* (London: W. H. Allen, 1959).

13  See Horne, "'Greatest Pleasures'."

14  Sillitoe, *Life Without Armour*, p. 273.

15  Examples abound. Alexander Walker notes that the film review in *Time* is of this kind, but also betrays a fairly bald-faced class aversion to the likes of Colin Smith: Colin's father dies of "some nameless capitalist disease" and overall the film was "a piece of skilful but specious pleading for the British proletariat . . . the hero is too palpably prolier-than-thou, his case is too obviously rigged." See Alexander Walker, *Hollywood, England* (London: Harrap, 1986), pp. 125–6.

16  Quoted in Horne, "'Greatest Pleasures'," p. 117. Among other things, Horne's article provides an excellent sense of the reception of *Loneliness*.

17  See Peter Stead, *Film and the Working Class* (London: Routledge, 1989), p. 195. Despite his generally dismissive view of the "Angry" films of the late fifties and sixties, Stead's book breaks new ground in studying working-class representation in cinema, especially those films that foreground labor and labor organization in constructing their narratives.

18  Robin Wood, *American Nightmare* (Toronto: Festival of Festivals, 1979), p. 10.

19  See Howard Slater, "The New Wave Films and the Loneliness of a Long Distance Runner" (http://ourworld.compuserve.com/homepages/working_press).

20  Richard Dyer, "Introduction," in Richard Dyer et al., *Coronation Street* (London: British Film Institute, 1981); see also Richard Hoggart, *The Uses of Literacy* (London: Chatto and Windus, 1957).

# Chapter 20

# From Libertinage to Eric Rohmer
## Transcending "Adaptation"

## Maria Tortajada

Because of its use of speech, its proliferation of discourses, and the artificial "tone" of its dialogue and phrasing, the cinema of Eric Rohmer has often been labeled "modern." Although it would be wrong to call it a "literary cinema" – a stereotype best avoided because it dilutes the notion of both the filmic and the literary – it nevertheless remains true that Rohmer's cinema is *invested* in the written text, whether because he integrates the text into the medium itself or because he turns it into the source for the film or at least into an obligatory stage of creation.

Rohmer has made three adaptations in the conventional sense: *La Marquise d'O . . .* (1976), based on the work of the same title by Kleist; *Perceval le Gallois* (1978), based on Chretien de Troyes' *Le Roman de Perceval* or *Le Conte du Graal*; and, most recently, *L'Anglaise et le Duc* (2001) which stages the Grace Eliott memoirs. Even before becoming a filmmaker, Rohmer wrote *Elizabeth*, a novel which he never actually adapted. Rohmer writes his own scripts and dialogues, adopting diverse strategies in terms of his relation with the performers and with other collaborators. The six *Contes moraux* were published as short stories; some were written as such before being filmed, while others emerged from the filmmaking process. Rohmer's procedures are therefore quite diverse both in terms of the importance of writing for this filmmaker, and in terms of literary works as a source of inspiration.

This relationship with writing prior even to his filmic work, this literary anteriority, is precisely what defines the notion of adaptation, already implying notions of borrowings and reshapings of style and story, characters, and other recognized features of the source text. Whether referring to the process of filmmaking or to the film as a finished object, adaptation forms part of a genealogy, of an ancestral descent from a work constituted as origin. This ancestral view implies an essentialist valorization of an indispensable source text which then provides the touchstone for any evaluation of the film. One might, of course, reject this narrow conception in favor of Robert Stam's notion of adaptation as critical and creative reading of the source.[1] But expanding our conception of adaptation virtually obliges us to appeal to other terms such as "intertextuality," "transtextuality," and "hypertextuality," given that the term "adaptation" is completely caught up in the web of its own erroneous assumptions.

Here I will mention only two such assumptions. The first has to do with the hierarchization within the field of the arts and the practices implied by the hyper-valorization of origins, a hierarchization that can become linked to processes of cultural legitimation. The second concerns the heuristic value of the term: adaptation conceived as a "passage" from one singular text to another singular text lends itself to a comparative, evaluative approach which conforms, in a circular manner, to the same criteria that constitute the source text as origin, as a work closed in on itself. This interpretative grid closes off any form of questioning which might explode the very notion of the "work" in order to produce other forms of intelligibility. For even if we do not define the source text in an essentialist way, there remains a structural postulate which defines the source text as identifiable within its limits, limits which provide the basis for the notion of adaptation: the source text is *one*, a singled, bounded unit, and it can be named.

But one way to revivify adaptation, I would argue, is to place it in relation to intertextual practices that can explode the unity of the source text, so that the notion of source as origin no longer provides a foundational principle. This kind of analysis has the advantage of allowing us to rethink the relationship between different types of cultural production through a grid that bypasses notions of influence and genealogical contiguity in favor of a more epistemological approach. It becomes a question, then, of discerning structures, and their variations, of bringing these systems together for heuristic purposes, in order to better understand the schemas placed in relation through a *reciprocal* illumination of the cases analyzed.

While Rohmer has shown interest in adaptation in the traditional sense of the term, his creative activity – whether admittedly or not – works through the absorption and the transformation of a system of value and behavior borrowed from "libertinage." In this sense, it is not a question of a single work exercising its "influence." Rather, the literary reference becomes complex: here it is a question of the "libertine constellation," a model which needs to be elaborated on the basis of multiple texts, a model reworked in various ways by Rohmer's films. The source is not single or unique, just as the film is not single or unique. Rohmer's work is thus inscribed within a broader practice of re-reading a larger network of stories. By the same token, the result is also plural, realized through variations: and it is the model allowed by these variations that interests us here.

My focus, then, on the one hand, is on a practice which consists not so much in adapting a story (with its characters) but rather in reshaping the structural schema of the relations between subjects, seduction, and other actions as they operate within the "libertine constellation." On the other hand, my focus is on the process of appropriation of this cultural and anthropological model and Rohmer's reformulation of the model in his films. Thus, *Le Genou de Claire* (1970), which has sometimes been compared to Laclos's *Les Liaisons dangereuses*, might be analyzed in the same way as a "real" adaptation. Even though the film does not explicitly declare itself an adaptation (for example, in the credits), it can nonetheless be analyzed in terms of all the ways in which the film picks up on this pre-existing text (in the broad sense). Beginning our analysis in this way allows us to show the diverse structural elements bearing on transtextuality at work in Rohmer's cinema, while also taking us beyond the relations between single texts.

## The Case of *Le Genou de Claire*

*Le Genou de Claire* does not claim in any way to be an adaptation of *Liaisons dangereuses*. Unlike the 1960 Vadim film, which updates the Laclos novel for the twentieth century, the Rohmer film does not pick up the novel's characters, or their names or psychology, or their relationships and intrigues. Nor does it reconstitute an epoch, in the manner of Rohmer's own films *Perceval le Gallois* or *La Marquise d'O*. . . . In those two films, Rohmer stays close to the text even while he seeks an historical authenticity which transcends photographic realism, as he also does in the recent *L'Anglaise et le Duc*. *Le Genou de Claire*, for its part, creates an indirect link with literary works, providing only a few clues to its kinship with the Laclos novel.

The play between the characters and groups formed around a common project, for example, recalls a basic feature of the great libertine novel by Laclos. Two old friends, Jerome and Aurora, meet near Annecy shortly before Jerome's marriage. Aurora is a writer, currently living with a family including two adolescent girls, Claire and Laura. Jerome is fascinated by the two girls. Laura, meanwhile, is interested in him, but he feels rejected by Claire, who for her part loves only her boyfriend. The conversation between Jerome and Aurora quickly turns to his relationship with the two girls. The two adults become allies around an agreement, a kind of game or challenge: even though he is on the verge of getting married, Jerome will inform Aurora about the twists and turns of the games of seduction, so she can use the stories as material for her own novel.

Jerome's complicity with Aurora and all that comes with it places all the characters in a frame close to that of libertine mores. Seduction is implicit not only in Jerome's relationship with the young Laura, but also with his "friend" Aurora. Both the discourse and the gestures of complicity become caught up in a double-register game, of doubled signs, a kind of mechanism familiar from the eighteenth-century libertinage of Laclos and Crebillon Fils. In essence, the game consists in not naming the desire, or the taboo, and in using a substitute term to make oneself understood. The interlocutor, now become a partner in seduction, understands the erotic meaning hidden behind the respectable and decorous vocabulary. Libertinage often speaks of a "friend" who is really a lover, and of "love" as a substitute for physical desire. The basic principle is one of terminological ambiguity, but one based on a shared code. In a sense, Aurora and Jerome never stop playing with language, and while analyzing their relationship with third parties, enter themselves into a highly ambiguous relationship.

We are thus confronted by a case of criss-cross seduction: the seduction involving the two adults interferes with that of the third parties, the young girls, who are unaware of the contractual game instigated by Jerome and Aurora. It is this same back-and-forth shuttle that structures *Les Liaisons dangereuses*. Laclos's novel is entirely constructed around the game inaugurated by the grand libertines Madame de Merteuil and Valmont, and the attempts to seduce third parties such as Cecile, Madame de Tourvel, or Prevan. To put it somewhat schematically, if complicity and connivance are the rule between the two protagonists, mendacious seduction, lure, and entrapment are the rule for the seductions the protagonists carry out toward the naïve and the pure, or toward other, less experienced, libertines.[2]

Rohmer's film, for its part, does not stage a mendacious or malicious seduction of the two girls, although the scene where Jerome takes advantage of Claire's confusion, where he manipulates her to the point of tears through rather perverse confidences, suggests a less than honorable behavior. The hero's apparent, occasionally self-declared libertinage does not lead, in the Rohmer film, to the kind of violence sometimes implied by libertine seduction. That kind of violence nevertheless forms the substratum on which an earlier version of the script of *Le Genou de Claire* was based; it is what is in the background, something which is refused but the presence of which one discerns in the text, a kind of first version of the story. *La Roseraie*, published in *Cahiers du Cinéma* in 1951,[3] written by Rohmer in collaboration with Paul Gegauff, betrays a more dramatic and perverse libertine tendency.[4] The story involves a similar intrigue – a character of Jerome's age is fascinated by two young girl neighbors he observes playing tennis – but the general tone of the narration is different. The hero's behavior is associated with evil; he cultivates cynicism and the abuse of power.

The exhibition of writing as a practice constitutes another common point between film and novel. In the novel, the epistolary form mediates all actions and dialogue through writing; each event is presented to the reader through narration by a character. In the film, literariness is assumed a priori in what is by now a classic device, through titles which date the sequences, turning the film into the diary of a seduction.[5] But even more striking in the film is the literary nature of the dialogue – despite the sequence improvised by Fabrice Luchini, in the role of Laura's young friend, which creates a rupture in tone – and the diction of the characters who "carry" the words. The film places the act of saying in the very foreground of the filmic representation. It is one of the distinctive features of Rohmer's cinema to play with artifice in order to foreground the materiality of words. As both Rohmer himself and the critics have often pointed out, speech is of the essence in his cinema, and the relation with the libertine corpus also passes through this centrality of speech. Moreover, the narrative mechanism based in the story content also imposes the mediation of speech: the presence of the writer (Aurora) and the fact that Jerome's amorous adventures form part of a *literary* project to support the writing of Aurora's novel. In this sense, the film is structured around the alternation of the encounters with the young girls and Jerome's reports to his author-friend. Thus the film manifests the literarization of an action implicated in the tradition of the epistolary novel, where the reader never has direct access to events.

Although our rapprochement between Rohmer's work and adaptation gets at something essential about the film, we have not yet gone beyond the superficial level of recognition and transformation, the echoes of situations and procedures. The comparison becomes even more fruitful if we move on to the broader question of the "libertine constellation" as a broader explanatory principle for seductive behavior, for the place of the subject in relation to both behavior and desire.

## The Libertine System in Rohmer's Films

To move beyond the idea of a single source text to the notion of libertinage as a crucial reference within Rohmer's cinema requires that we first define more clearly the "contours" of this libertinage; for the term is defined precisely by its historical and literary complexity.[6] While libertinage was a social reality, what interests us here is the literary "modeling" of the social context in which it is inscribed. It is difficult to speak of a libertine genre, however, because its forms were extremely varied.

One essential feature of the eighteenth-century libertine novel, it has been argued, is a kind of "doubling:" "When one brackets the question of style and the writer designates things by their real name," as Henri Coulet puts it, "the novel is no longer libertine."[7] Whether in the representation of a licentious scene or of a seductive exchange, whether involving the discourse of the narrator or of the character, a kind of "gauze" comes to cover up anything shocking. Every word is submitted to a double register; every erotic scene is veiled. It is this kind of libertinage, one which emphasizes the game of seduction, which interests us here.

In defining a phenomenon like libertine discourse, however, this doubling is not the only important feature. Some novels said to be libertine neglect this ambiguous language, focusing instead only on stories which have to do with free sexual mores and the erotic satisfaction of desire. Libertine literature in this sense appears to be a series of licentious, even pornographic, representations, offered to a reader-voyeur. *Therese Philosophe*, for example, probably authored by Boyer d'Argens, or Fougeret de Monbron's *Margot la ravaudeuse* both exalt the flesh and proliferate in risqué situations.[8] Such literature is radically different from the kind of libertinage based on the doubling of signs, limited to the narrow, closed world of the aristocracy with its rules and conventions, its strategies of seduction, its games of word and gesture, within which the work of Laclos and Crebillon Fils is inscribed. Libertinage can even exist *without* any erotic dimension, detached from any sexual reference whatsoever. In this sense, the libertine novel is related to the philosophical novel.[9] As a novelistic genre, then, libertinage is difficult to pin down.

Within the frame of "gallant" libertinage, defined by the deployment of a double linguistic register, the subject is obliged to negotiate with the laws of society. If society tolerates libertine behavior, it is only to the extent that everyone hides behind the mask of social decorum. Freedom, within this eighteenth-century society, can only thrive within a regime where the participants accept a social role which dissimulates the realization of all desires. The preference for euphemistic doubling, then, is not at all gratuitous. At times, the practice of seduction becomes more important than its goal; the pleasure of the game and the manipulation of signs become more important than the satisfaction of desire.[10] Nevertheless, it is still true that the system of double registers is founded inevitably on the social functioning that regulates the relationship between the individual and his pleasure and his action. Summing up, the game of libertine seduction works through a double linguistic register. It is based on complicity and connivance rather than trickery, and it assumes a code which must remain implicit even at the very moment it is being used.

The kinds of games operative in Rohmer's films reference this form of libertinage even while "perverting" them even further. The characters are endlessly confronted with an ambiguity linked to a game of doubles. Obviously, the social world of these characters lacks the extremely codified nature of behavior that one finds in eighteenth-century society. But the films always manage to find ways to exacerbate and amplify double meanings. Adrien's reply to Haydee in *La Collectionneuse* (1966) offers a synthetic formulation of the kind of seduction staged in Rohmer's films:

ADRIEN:   What did he do to you?
HAYDEE:   Nothing.
ADRIEN:   Did he bother you?
HAYDEE:   Not at all. He invited me to go boating. Last night we went to a casino. Very, very charming . . .
ADRIEN:   So he didn't try anything that bothered you?
HAYDEE:   If I said I slept with him, would you believe me?
ADRIEN:   About you, I would believe anything. I know that if you say yes, it probably means no . . . but it might also mean yes. You're an immoral little whore.[11]

Confronted by the total ambiguity of a woman he regards as a dangerous seductress, the male character offers the key to the seduction. Saying "yes," for her, is the same thing as saying "no." The female character is so invested in the game of double registers, an essential feature of the "libertine constellation," that ambiguity exceeds the limits of a mastered code.

But the play of seduction is not without its hope of erotic satisfaction. Seduction does end by producing corporeal pleasure, and from a novelistic point of view, it does involve the portrayal of physical relations. However veiled or covered with "gauze," the erotic scene is nevertheless recounted and brought to life. Seduction gets played out in the essential act of the libertine universe; it is the horizon in relation to which seduction and play are staged. The game gives birth to the desire that is satisfied in the erotic scene, a standard *topos* of these novels that seem to privilege speech. In his brief dialogue *La Nuit et le moment*, Crebillon Fils offers the ideal functioning of libertine seduction which passes through the pleasure of speech.[12] Even if, unlike ribald or pornographic novels, the "gallant" novel privileges words and stratagems, the erotic act still retains an essential place. In fact, if one removes the sexual dimension, the text no longer works because the reader never stops postulating the physical dimension of the exchanges, thanks both to the double entendres of the characters and the commentaries of the narrator. So these texts never omit the licentious scene. Even in *Les Liaisons dangereuses*, which is entirely constructed around verbal artifice, the reader finds the account, however veiled, of the night where Valmot takes Cecile, or where Mme de Tourvel gives herself to her lover.

The seductive word dominates, but the act itself also takes place. If the double-register discourse is in the foreground, it is always by designating the moment of physical pleasure as the goal of the seduction. It is true that Crebillon, in some of his works, for example in *L'Ecumoire* or in the story of Mazulhim in *Le Sopha,* stages the failure through impotence of his characters.[13] Crebillon thus tests the limits of the act as he explores the limits of the game. But the act itself is never excluded; it too belongs to the libertine constellation. Failure is not elimination. Mazulhim manages, despite his difficulties, to generate the necessary energy required to surprise his mistresses. And if the moment of action is itself threatened, what does the reader get if not an erotic scene rendered in veiled terms, with all the allusions required to trigger his or her curiosity and excitement? Seduction, with the double register it installs, can only be conceived within a larger horizon of action.

But for most of Rohmer's characters, action as a consequence of seduction poses the major problem. It is precisely in this manner that Rohmer highjacks libertinage: his films are offered to the spectator in relation to a schema of behavior where the erotic act as the goal of seduction is essential, and no longer only in relation to a precise antecedent text with its own narrative economy. The first series of Rohmer's films, *Les Contes moraux*, installs a system where the coherence of seduction and its sequels are questioned. The male heroes, whom we take to be the narrators of the stories, take great risks by engaging in seduction. They are attracted to one woman, although they are practically or emotionally involved with another. Such is the narrative schema that each film picks up only in order to propose a new variation. Seduction based on the ambiguity of play leads directly to involvement with the second woman. As far as the libertine constellation is concerned, then, this series of films installs a veritable system. The protagonist, who is almost always the narrator of the story, always ends up rejecting the person who plays the role of the second woman. Distancing himself, he refuses to get involved. But this renunciation brings with it the deliberate erasure of the erotic scene. Frederic, in *L'Amour l'après-midi* (1972), literally flees to the staircase, while Cloe, naked and available, waits for him in the next room. We find the same pattern in the case of the guilty seducer played by Trintingnant in *Ma nuit chez Maud* (1969): having fallen asleep next to a superb brunette, protected by his bedcovers, he brusquely rejects her at the precise moment when he is about to give in to temptation. *Maud* proposes a variation on the paradoxical situation explored in *La Nuit et le moment*, which places the lovers in bed without having gone through the stages of seduction. Except that Rohmer draws out something quite different from the situation, which is very significant since in the film nothing actually happens. The erotic scene does not take place.

In fact, this is true of all the heroes of the series. In *La Collectionneuse*, Adrien abandons Haydee on the road, just at the point when he is in a position to possess her, after having only been a witness to her affairs. In *La Carrière de Suzanne*, similarly, the shy hero spends an entire night with the woman who fascinates him. Despite his scorn for her, which actually betrays his ambiguous desire, he sleeps peacefully in his bed, while she naps in an armchair. In the end, nothing, emptiness. The male seducers in the *Contes moraux* do not go to the end point of seduction. Only Jerome actually makes an attempt: he caresses Claire's knee, the young woman he desires. But this gesture, carefully staged by the film, seems rather pathetic in comparison with the erotic scene in the libertine tradition: he turns away from the essential, satisfying himself with only a small part of the desired woman. And it is not so much impotence at the moment of truth that is stigmatized here as the refusal of the act itself.

At the very kernel and system of Rohmer's narrative in *Contes moraux* one finds lack, the non-event.[14] Nevertheless, this "nothing" is central to the Rohmerian schema reproduced in the *Contes moraux*. The conversation (at the end of the June 30 sequence) between Jerome and Aurora, the writer in *Le Genou de Claire*, clarifies the mechanism:

AURORA: You will sleep with a schoolgirl on the eve of your marriage, but that doesn't mean you'll provide me with a good story.
JEROME: And if I don't sleep with her?
AURORA: The story will be much better, because it is not necessary that something happens.

And later (at the beginning of the Wednesday July 1 sequence):

AURORA: For me to write our story, it has to happen.
JEROME: And if it doesn't happen . . . ?
AURORA: Something always happens, if only your refusal to let something happen.

Emptiness is at the center of the story that Aurora wants to write about Jerome's adventures with the young girls, which implies that the character's refusal of the act and the film's elision of the erotic scene provide the key to the *Contes moraux*. But this device can only be read as the inversion of a libertine logic which would make the act itself the *telos* of the story and of the seduction. In this sense, the *Contes moraux* are not really libertine stories at all, despite their staging of doublings and games of seduction.

The dialogue with the libertine model found in Rohmer's films is based on a veritable reappropriation of the libertine system. As a constructed model rather than an actualization of a single source text, libertinage forms the substratum that allows the films to re-elaborate the place of the subject within the game of seduction, especially at the moment of truth. The idea of "adaptation," in contrast, usually closes off this kind of perspective.

Two phenomena are linked to the refusal of action. The first has to do with the "*detournement*" or highjacking of the game. The heroes, caught up in the process of seduction, refuse to recognize the seriousness of the game and its implications, and turn playful behavior into a pretext that empties their words of meaning. We see this with Jerome, when he flirts with the young Laura during a mountain hike. The play of double registers allows him to suggest that their relationship is only one of friendship even as he maintains an attitude that undermines the purity of his feelings. When he tries to kiss her (during the Monday July 6 sequence), she exclaims:

> LAURA:   Let me go.
> JEROME:   Why should I let you go, can't we play anymore?
> LAURA:   No, I would like to really be in love.

If Laura interrupts Jerome so brutally, it is because she senses the danger of seduction, because these verbal doublings have consequences and she pretends to opt out of the game rather than take the risk of the erotic act. Jerome's attitude is different, because he does not see the game as serious. It is his excuse; his gesture has no importance because it is all just a game. Thus we find two opposite conceptions of the game: one recognizes its seriousness; the other uses the game, while making sure that the seduction never becomes anchored in the reality of action.

The second phenomenon that arises from the Rohmerian refusal of action bears on one of the essential points in the transformation of the libertine system: the function of words in relation to actions. Instead of the erotic scene, we are given the words of the hero, as a kind of re-evaluation. It is necessary to speak of the act, whether in order to turn refusal into a real "event" or in order to affirm one's freedom within the refusal. The methods vary, but speech is always present. Sometimes the protagonist soliloquizes; or speaks as a voice-over narrator, or confides to the other characters. He reflects on what happened, or what did not happen, and analyzes his choice, his decision to refuse or he speaks of some meaningless event that occurred at the same time.[15]

That is precisely what happens at the end of *La Collectionneuse* when Adrien leaves Haydee on the road, thus deciding not to possess her:

> But I quickly understood that I would not stop to pick her up, and in doing so I was, for the first time, really making a decision. This story has to do with my changes . . . Calm, solitude, I had them. They weren't simply given to me. I gave them to myself through a decision which affirmed my own freedom. I enjoyed my success, and gave the credit to myself and not just to chance. I let myself be invaded by a feeling of delicious independence, of total control of my destiny.[16]

The commentary here represents the opposite of the libertine principle which sees the satisfaction of desire as the key to the conquest of independence. Adrien believes that he finds independence through renunciation, when he escapes from seduction. He substitutes for erotic investment a discourse on freedom which turns his choice into a symptom of superiority. But the film soon reveals the deficiencies of his analysis, since it is clear that he will not be able to tolerate solitude. The voice-over comments: "But when I came back, in the emptiness and silence of the big house, I felt full of anxiety. I couldn't sleep." Then he goes to London to find the woman whom he thought he had forgotten.

*Le Genou de Claire* juxtaposes the pathetic substitute for the erotic scene, the caressing of the knee, with the long sequence (Tuesday July 28) where Jerome tells Aurora about his time with Claire.

> In short, she was sitting in front of me, one leg stretched out, the other bent, the sharp angular knee, thin, smooth, fragile, available, within reach. My arm was in a position that made it easy to simply extend it to touch her knee. Touching her knee was the most extravagant thing to do, the only thing that shouldn't be done, and at the same time the easiest thing in the world. At the same time that I felt the . . . facility, the simplicity of the gesture, I was also aware of its impossibility. You know, as if . . . you are on the edge of a cliff, and it would take only one step to jump into the abyss, and even if you want to do it, you can't? It took a lot of courage, you know, really a lot of courage. In all my life, I never did anything as heroic, or anything so voluntary and deliberate. It's even the only time that I accomplished an act of pure will. I have never had such a strong feeling that I had done something because it had to be done. Because it had to be done, that's right, since I had promised to you that I would do it.

It is through words that Jerome manages to raise to the acme of all possible actions the one which, worthy of a true Hero, consisted in placing his hand on a knee. The film is thus extremely ironical. But even while he tries to idealize this substitute for the erotic act, Jerome curiously evacuates desire, as if pleasure were somehow contrary to his own freedom, to his autonomy as a rational subject capable of analyzing everything that happens to him even as it is occurring. It is duty, as he explains, that makes him touch Claire's knee, to fulfill the contract he has made with Aurora and which obliges him to provide material for her novel. And as with the hero of *La Collectionneuse*, his justification contradicts basic libertine principles.[17]

What is striking here is the gap between the nothingness of the act that the story could have staged and the words of the character-narrator that lift this nothing to the summits of real action. On the basis of the connection made by the stories between the words and what they reflect on, the *Contes moraux* propose a basic narrative schema which supports a model of behavior. Thus a matrix is constituted which will dominate, with variations, all the subsequent films. Other films revolve around an absent event, whether directly linked to eroticism or not. At the heart of *Conte de printemps* (1990) is the disappearance of the necklace, which the characters never stop recounting and commenting on. Unlike *Contes moraux*, where the erotic denouement is excluded, in *La Marquise d'O . . .* the act is only elided, ceding place to speech. In *Pauline à la plage* (1982), we find the same problem, but the person concerned with re-evaluation is the chance witness, the one who by definition does not act but only takes note of action. Even in *L'Anglaise et le Duc*, which would seem a priori to have less to do with stories of seduction than with history, even here the filmmaker slips in a reference to the erotic scene, which obviously never takes place, and substitutes the evaluation of the event, a substitution which has a double value. To protect the wounded man sought by soldiers, who ransack the house, Grace hides him *in her bed*. The act this time is really heroic, since the young woman is risking her life. Moreover, before her protégé, she launches into a long appreciation of his heroism, which she nevertheless describes as ambiguous. She claims to have reacted in some ways to the sighs of the person sleeping next to her, under the covers. If, on one level, the sigh is the sign of the wounded man's suffering, the erotic ingredients that Rohmer introduces into the situation should not be overlooked: the man is in bed with a woman, who is wearing very little – she will later confide to the Duke of Orleans that she was almost naked – the sigh comes, along with the violence of the soldiers with their rude looks and gestures in the intimacy of the chamber. Given these elements, and the ambiguity that they impose on a second level, a pseudo-erotic scene and the evalutation of the situation, we can conclude that the libertine schema, and its subversion, penetrate even this film about the French Revolution.

Narrative speech is also operative in libertine stories, along with evaluation: which is what demonstrates the pre-eminence of the word in staging intimate events in front of the interlocutor. Within the libertine model, the representation of the erotic scene by the characters themselves is of the essence. In *La Nuit et le moment*, Clitandre keeps telling seduction stories to Cidalese, who cannot get enough of them. The stories become the exchange currency of their bargaining: you can stay as long as you tell stories. But in the end, the overall narrative schema of *Contes moraux* is closest to that of *Les Liaisons dangereuses*, since, like Laclos's epistolary novel, it makes the re-evaluation of action a distinct moment. The correspondence between Valmont and Merteuil is the secret place where the two libertines reveal to each other their descriptions of erotic scenes and their seduction strategies. These epistolary exchanges escape seduction and action, since they distance both seduction and action, submitting them to the test of judgment. Obviously, speech can be recuperated by another form of doubling play, the one that takes place between Valmont and Merteuil, as is also the case, as we have seen, between Jerome and Aurora: but here speech pretends to be something different, a discourse of mastery. The subject who takes up this discourse occupies the position of a third party in relation to the scene he describes. One of the particularities of the libertine, as of Rohmerian heroes, is that he ultimately goes off alone, in order to turn his adventure into a story.

Nevertheless, an essential difference separates Rohmer's films from the characters of *Liaisons*: the position of re-evaluation confronts the hero with the *absence* of the erotic act. The great libertines recount what they have really done: never does the Laclos novel cast doubt on the content of the letters. Valmont might be mistaken in his judgments about what has transpired with his mistress – since he does not know or refuses to recognize that he loves her – but the erotic act has in fact taken place, and the proposed version of the facts does not change. While *Les Liaisons dangereuses* adds speech to action within the economy of the story, the *Contes moraux* propose a substitution, to the point of inverting the very principle of libertinage, since it is through renunciation that the characters believe they are gaining their freedom.

Nevertheless, in evaluating this absence, the hero takes up a very problematic position, one which confronts him with his own irrationality, which he tries to escape by attributing an arbitrary value to this nothing. By suppressing the erotic act, the *Contes moraux* produce a defocalization in the libertine system, which makes of this moment the essential stakes of the freedom of the subject. Obviously, this engagement is often problematic; at times, it becomes banal, an easy way of augmenting the list of one's conquests. When he no longer obeys desire but rather social necessity, the libertine ends up, paradoxically, by losing himself in fickleness. The impotence of certain Crebillon characters can also appear as the testing of the libertine act par excellence. It is not in action that the subject risks himself, but elsewhere, in the place of the third-person witness that he claims to adopt, of the one who evaluates, judges, dictates his laws. The heroes of Rohmer's films are characters who incarnate their own principles. In sum, the films problematize the position of the subject himself when the subject is presented as witness, guarantor, or spectator of his own act.

But the third-person witness is a pivotal figure within the constellation of libertinage. In the gallant aristocratic society of the eighteenth century, this observer is the instance which founds the double-register game, he is the privileged guarantor that the characters of this closed world call the public. In Crebillon Fils's *Les Egarements du coeur et de l'esprit*, Versac defines its function in relation to one of his adventures:

> He has the eyes that one cannot trick: the public saw despite ourselves, that we loved each other; even though we were not indiscreet, he thought it appropriate to speak of what he had seen; It didn't matter that I wanted to maintain decorum, to sacrifice myself, they thought me in love, because in fact I was in love: and sometimes we thus find the kinds of engagements which one can dissimulate better.[18]

The public is represented by society in general and by each of its members in particular. The public sets itself up as a guarantor of decorum; it is from the public that the characters hope to hide. The public is the censor that surveys their behavior and which appears "behind" their discourses, hidden behind that indefinite and impersonal entity called "people say." Indeed, the turn of phrase "they" or "people" is common in their discourse. Here is Cidalese: "only having been weak, perhaps they will think me gallant, or at least born with great hopes of being gallant." Or Clitandre: "Eraste has an advantage over me in terms of attractiveness, but I dare say that they regard my way of thinking as different from his."[19]

Although the films inscribe seducers within the libertine schema, they do not integrate in any definitive way this essential pivot of social functioning, for the rules of decorum are formulated by the hero himself in relation to himself. (Thus we find a kind of individualization of the codes of decorum.) Unlike the libertine public, which gives voice to the law even while slandering it, and which takes someone else as its target, the hero of the *Contes moraux* expresses principles which apply only to himself. His position is not, however, that of the libertine, the position of the Versacs, Valmonts, and Merteuils who, in their will to power and mastery, also define for themselves the rules of behavior; they are in concurrence with the established morality incarnated by the public. The libertine is obliged to juggle social decorum and his own principles at the same time. The liberatory impulse which pits him against society is never completely effaced. The narrator-hero of the *Contes moraux*, in contrast, takes as his own the law he formulates; by respecting that law, he believes, he can achieve freedom. He places himself in the position of guarantor, while claiming to be outside that which he is evaluating. The hero of *Contes moraux*, in sum, chooses to occupy the precise space that libertinage reserved for the public.

This choice can only bring him problems, however. While libertines veil their behavior in the face of conventional morality, the Rohmerian hero can only escape himself when he becomes involved in seduction. It is therefore understandable that he transforms the nature of the game in order to flee from its seriousness. For his position is ultimately untenable; he is simultaneously the one who possesses and defends the law, and the one who is presumed to dodge it and subvert it. He takes up, within the libertine constellation as re-envisioned by Rohmer, two incompatible positions.

The *Contes moraux* propose a curious interpretation of libertinage. While the eighteenth-century texts elaborate a seduction based on doublings, articulated together with the erotic act as the quintessence of action, and with the public as certifying third party or guarantor, the system of seduction staged by Rohmer creates a vacuum: the act is insignificant, a pathetic gesture or even the refusal to act; the third party, the external judge incarnated by the others, gives way to the law as chosen individually by the hero. Indeed, the place of the guarantor seems to be freed so that the subject can lose himself in it. When he proposes to occupy it, but without giving up the idea of seduction, the hero is himself seduced, caught up in the web of his own ambiguity. That is when he becomes a kind of unstable third party caught in the seduction. Here we find a basic principle of Rohmer's cinema, which also has to do, as I argue in *Le Spectateur séduit*, with the seduction of the spectator, which in its turn opens up new perspectives in terms of the theory of representation. That is the very kernel of Rohmer's cinema, which through the multiple variations found in the films, interrogates the significance of seduction and the role of action in the constitution of the subject.

Rohmer's practice of adaptation, and the structural analogies between a single film and a single literary source (for example, the relation between *Le Genou de Claire* and *Les Liaisons dangereuses*), I have tried to show, should not distract us from the larger transtextual processes that bring in elements that acquire a heuristic dimension which we could have not attained had we limited ourselves to a logic of "adaptation." The process enables us not only to illuminate the indirect historical context – it is not exactly an issue of influence – in which the films are inscribed, but also, especially, to clarify a social practice, a certain kind of seduction bearing on the structuration of the subject, and his relation to action, desire, and language. In this sense, this process touches on a deeper and more abstract dimension, on a behavioral paradigm, a system of relations between actors within a social group, a hierarchy of values which subjects actions to a specific *telos* and thus justifies the actions of the individuals participating in it. This system, which we have called the "libertine constellation," has to be constructed on the basis of the convergences noted within a coherent corpus. It is not discernible from the outset as a plot from a specific story, but rather as the continuous bass note, a bass note that structures the texts of an entire epoch precisely because these texts play out again the interrogations linked to this system. This is what creates the force and value of the libertine culture.

The New Wave in which Rohmer's earliest films are inscribed has also often been associated, whether accurately or not, with libertinage; indeed, the idea has become a kind of cliché. But in Rohmer's films, the libertine dimension is deployed as a kind of cultural schema against which the latent structure of Rohmer's films is constructed. It is not sufficient therefore to simply mention a few obvious traits, a few claims made by the seducers themselves, nor even the similarity of situation between, for example, *Le Genou de Claire* and *Les Liaisons dangereuses*. Libertinage is a larger system of comprehension that needs to be well understood before we talk about the ways in which it has been subsequently transformed. Such a method goes beyond cliché, but, more important, it also goes beyond any strict notion of "adaptation." Adaptation assumes an antecedent text, while we assume a plural textuality as a substratum of the model to be constituted. Adaptation also implies a product text, while we see a text multiplied into numerous variations over a series of films. If "the source" is given in the evidence of the origin it represents, whether manifest or as something that needs to be found in the form of the transtextuality as we have developed it here, the model of reference also has to be constructed. Thus, having lost its "visibility," the very idea of a "source" loses its prerogatives.

*Translated by Robert Stam*

---

### Notes

1 See Robert Stam, "Introduction: The Theory and Practice of Adaptation," in Robert Stam and Alessandra Raengo (eds), *Literature and Film: A Guide to the Theory and Practice of Film Adaptation* (Oxford: Blackwell, 2005), pp. 1–52.

2    Naturally, the novel does not freeze these two different axes.

3    *La Roseraie* (a film subject by Eric Rohmer and Paul Gegauff), *Cahiers du Cinéma* 5 (September 1951), 4–12.

4    Gegauff's influence is not without importance in terms of the libertine drift of the subjects, not only for Rohmer but also for all the New Wave filmmakers. Gegauff also worked with Chabrol on *Les Cousins* and *Les Godelureaux*. A real "character," Gegauff himself incarnated the image of the seducer who inspired the *Cahiers* directors.

5    The titles also recall the intertitles of silent film.

6    For a more elaborate discussion of these issues, see my *Le Spectateur séduit: le libertinage dans le cinéma d'Eric Rohmer et sa fonction dans une théorie de la représentation filmique* (Paris: Editions Kimé, 1999). Apart from all the works referenced in the aforementioned text, the reader should also consult Michel Delon, *Le Savoir Libertin* (Paris: Hachette, 2000).

7    See Henri Coulet, *Le Roman jusqu'à la Révolution* (Paris: Armand Colin, 1991), p. 386.

8    Raymond Trousson (ed.), *Romans libertins du dix-huitième siècle* (Paris: Robert Lafont, 1993). Henri Coulet calls attention to a "cynical genre" within the larger group of libertine novels: "those basically realist novels (but more aggressively so) whose heroes are adventurers, prostitutes and kept women . . ." (*Le Roman jusqu'à la Révolution*, p. 388).

9    One might also see libertinage as linking philosophy and eroticism, within a current of thought where the theorization of pleasure becomes the key to the freedom of mind and behavior. Inconstancy thus finds its natural explanation.

10   Raymond Trousson surveys various definitions, including the following: "Retracing the path that leads from the first encounter to amorous possession, [the libertine novel] is more interested in strategy than results; it abandons the description of the defeat of the enemy in favor of the description of the manoeuvres in the amorous war" (*Romans libertins*, p. ix).

11   Dialogue transcribed from the film. The published script is slightly different. See *L'Avant-scène du Cinéma* 69 (April 1967), 33. When the scripts of cited extracts are published, I reproduce the dialogue according to the transcription, unless it differs from what is said in the film, though without retaining the description of the visuals in italics.

12   Crebillon Fils, *La Nuit et le moment: le hasard au coin du feu* (Paris: Desjonqueres, 1981).

13   See Yves Citton, *Impuissances: défaillances masculines et pouvoir politique de Montaigne à Stendhal* (Paris: Aubier, 1994), pp. 227–300.

14   *La Collectionneuse*, as *Le Royons vert*, which belongs to the series *Comedies et proverbes*, offers erotic scenes, but they appear only in the margins of the central story since in both cases they form part of the prologue, thus, in a way, within another temporality, outside the logical sequence of actions.

15   All the films in the series, except *Le Genou de Claire*, are narrated by male protagonists, with off-screen narration more or less present. Thus *Ma nuit chez Maud* includes only two sequences with off-screen narration, while *La Collectionneuse* systematically frames its dialogues with commentaries from the hero as narrator.

16   *L'Avant-scène du Cinéma* 69 (April 1967), 33–4.

17   The motivation for the act varies, for Jerome later in the same sequence inverts his own position: "The gesture, which I believed to be motivated by desire, she understood as a gesture of consolation."

18   Crebillon Fils, *Les Egarements du coeur et de l'esprit* (Paris: Flammarion, 1985), p. 137.

19   Crebillon Fils, *La Nuit et le moment*, p. 62.

From Libertinage to Eric Rohmer

Chapter 20

# Chapter 21

# The Moment of Portraiture
## Scorsese Reads Wharton

## Brigitte Peucker

While she approved of the adaptations of her fiction to the theater, Edith Wharton, we are told, had little or no use for the cinema. Wharton's experience of the movies was probably limited to one visit in Bilbao, Spain, in 1914, a visit that may have given rise to the brief rendering of cinematic spectatorship we find in Wharton's novella *Summer*, published three years later. Insofar as *Summer*'s evocation of cinematic experience emphasizes visual sensations such as "swimming circles of heat and blinding alternations of light and darkness," it participates in an attitude of the times that sees the moving images of cinema as waging an assault on the human sensorium.[1] From this point of view, cinema constitutes one aspect of the "chaos" of urban experience, of which the crowds constitute another. In *Summer*, interestingly, Charity Royall's act of spectatorship merges the images on the screen with those of the crowd around her, whose faces "became part of the spectacle, and danced on the screen with the rest."[2] Wharton may have absorbed this contemporary perspective on cinematic images, but it is also likely that the traumatic merging of screen images with those of real world experience has its origins in Wharton's personal abhorrence for a "spectacle shared by a throng of people."[3] In any case, in 1917 Wharton shared the American attitude toward cinema that stressed its entertainment rather than its artistic values. It would not be until D. W. Griffith released *Broken Blossoms* as a "European art film" in 1919 that the expectations of the public would begin to change.

But Wharton's attitude toward the cinema appears to have remained constant. Though not averse to the income derived from the screen – proceeds from film and stage adaptations of her work were substantial, her primary source of support during the Depression – Wharton had no interest in what Hollywood now calls "the product" and did not see either of the two movie versions of *The Age of Innocence* that were released during her lifetime.[4] Had Wharton been able to see Martin Scorsese's 1993 adaptation of her novel, however, she might have experienced a conversion. Shot with the most minute attention to visual surface, Scorsese's film is suffused with "high art" values and subtleties: it is, as he has put it, shot and composed for "the purists."[5] Scorsese seems intuitively to grasp that the intriguing issue of cinematic adaptation is most appropriately viewed against the backdrop of a broader approach to the interrelation of the arts in cinema, since it is that interrelation that determines film as a medium. Scorsese's *Age of Innocence* substantiates the claim that, as a latecomer among the arts, film alludes to, absorbs, and undermines the language of the other arts in order to create its own idiom.[6] Borrowing from literature and painting equally, the medium of film is an amalgam of image and narrrative that renders film heterogeneous, a hybrid that emerges out of traditionally sanctioned cultural forms. Seen in this light, as the convergence of literary and painterly concerns, film as a medium might very well have appealed to Edith Wharton, for the conjoining of language and image is figured in Wharton's fiction: a preoccupation with the visual is central to her writing.

Indeed, this interest in the visual is central even to the plot of *The Age of Innocence*, which it may be useful briefly to recall here. When the beautiful and nonconformist Countess Ellen Olenska, a woman around whom scandalous rumors circulate, returns from Europe to her proper and socially prominent New York family, the family rallies around her to safeguard her reputation. In a gesture of solidarity, Newland Archer, scion of another such family, hastily announces his engagement to Ellen's cousin, May Welland. From this point on, the die is cast. Archer, one of Wharton's "collectors" and a man of sensibility, customarily escapes from the strict decorum and from what he takes to be the stifling lack of imagination of New York society into a world of literature and painting. A reader of Ruskin and Walter Pater, Archer reads in Ellen an "incarnation of the life of art,"[7] and falls deeply in love with her, but society impedes their union at every turn. The conflict between social codes and the yearning to break free plays itself out both in the arena of the erotic and in the desire to lead a more unconventional – read "artistic" – life, but emotional turmoil remains contained beneath the surface of manners and mores. Wharton's world is a world represented by the objects that populate it, a world in which bringing out the Sèvres and the George II plate are significant acts. As Wharton's narrator puts it, "in reality they all lived in a kind of hieroglyphic world, where the real thing was never said or done or even thought, but only represented by a set of arbitrary signs" (p. 44).

Not surprisingly, then, in this novel as elsewhere Wharton makes use of painting in order to delineate her characters. It tells us a great deal about the dashing Julius Beaufort that he "ha[s] the audacity to hang 'Love Victorious'" – a painting that Wharton calls "the much-discussed nude of Bouguereau" – in his drawing room (p. 23). It is telling, too, that the portrait executed of Mrs Henry van der Luyden twenty years ago is still "a perfect likeness" of this lady who, as Wharton puts it, "has been gruesomely preserved in the airless atmosphere of a perfectly irreproachable existence," entombed like the image of the portrait in a kind of "life-in-death" (p. 52). Somewhat predictably, Newland falls in love with the Countess Olenska in part because she represents the "decadent" European world of culture and also because, as her grandmother notes, she is a woman whose portrait has been painted nine times. Since, for Newland, art is the suppressed realm both of the imagination and of the erotic, it is not surprising that he chooses the art museum as the location of their tryst.

In keeping with these concerns, Scorsese frames Wharton's characters in painterly effects: in the profilmic, of course, the actors are arranged in painterly compositions, but Scorsese goes far beyond these arrangements. Using color in film as though it were paint, Scorsese tells us in a compelling interview that "the camera moves in on the back of Newland's head, music comes up, and the wall goes red, like a blush."[8] The film's syntax, in paying homage to the syntax of silent cinema with its irises, masking, and fades, was also designed to reinforce Scorsese's painterly aesthetic: instead of fading to black at the end of scenes, he chose to fade to red and yellow because, as he says, he "was interested in the use of color like brushstrokes throughout the film."[9] Editing procedures also contribute to the painterly look of this film, Scorsese tells us; he chose to shorten many of its shots in order to suggest "a brush coming through and painting bits and pieces of color, swishing by."[10] Sometimes camera movement, too, is used to suggest the sweep of the artist's paintbrush, as when a slow tracking shot from left to right gradually reveals – to Newland's eye and to ours – the long landscape painting that hangs in the Countess's drawing room.[11]

Literary concerns also suffuse this film. Its visual surface, its minute attention to detail, have been termed "fetishistic" by critics,[12] and Scorsese's style does indeed mirror and emphasize the attention to objects and ceremonies that function emblematically in Wharton's novel. But Scorsese's attention to the world of things is also an attempt to render Wharton's language which – to borrow a phrase from Walter Benjamin – is a language "heavy with material display."[13] Likewise, Scorsese's almost slavish attention to detail is not simply a bow to realism and period style, or a recognition of the importance of *mise-en-scène* in Wharton, be its function fetishistic or not. It is also a means of transposing novelistic description into the imagistic terms of film, an attempt to bridge what Scorsese calls the "schism" between novelistic and filmic description.[14] Further, the use of Joanne Woodward's third-person voice-over is designed to give the impression of the narrator's voice – or actually of Wharton's voice, Scorsese tells us – and therefore to simulate the experience of reading the novel.[15] Thus the voice of a woman is superimposed upon our experience of the film, constituting an aural dimension that both distances and draws the spectator in,[16] and reinforces the spectatorial position that Scorsese strove to create. The emotional power of melodrama to entangle the spectator is to be tempered, according to the director, by the distance achieved through the conscious aestheticization of the film's surface.[17] Scorsese's critics, however, have tended primarily to fix their gaze upon the impression of distance that the film conveys;[18] Amy Taubin puts it aptly in suggesting that "Scorsese's desire was somehow 'to present' Wharton's novel."[19]

Film understood as a medium in which different representational systems – specifically those of painting and writing – at times collide, at times replace, but always supplement one another, makes film a medium particularly congenial to the artistic concerns of Wharton, whose fiction not only manifests a pronounced interest in the visual, but whose mode of allusion is so frequently intermedial, so frequently involves the multiple layering of painterly and writerly references. As Cynthia Griffin Wolff has pointed out, *The Age of Innocence* derives its title from a Joshua Reynolds portrait of the same title and is connected by this means – "a private pun" – to Henry James's *Portrait of a Lady*, thus making Newland Archer the subject of Wharton's "portrait of a gentleman."[20] And Candace Waid has allowed us to see that Wharton's *The House of Mirth*, which features a Reynolds portrait in a *tableau vivant*, alludes via Reynolds's painting both to the Ariosto story of Angelica and Medora and to the many artists – Tiepolo among them – who have chosen to depict it.[21] Both of these instances of intertextuality – and there are many similar moments in Wharton's writing – are intermedial: they draw simultaneously upon painting and literature, creating a textual overlay, a palimpsest of sorts, that is at once imagistic and verbal.

Any filmmaker who, in adapting Wharton's text to film, had done his or her home-work – and Martin Scorsese has – would certainly have noticed this method of layering representational systems in Wharton's work. It is precisely this stylistic feature that makes adapting Wharton's work to film cinematically challenging – a working out of what it means to transpose one medium into another – for this layering of allusions necessitates a conscious working-through of the relation of film to writing and painting. Scorsese mentions other filmic influences on his work,[22] but the manner in which Scorsese addresses these concerns makes it quite evident that, in preparation for shooting *The Age of Innocence*, Scorsese had not only seen Philip Moeller's 1934 adaptation, but also Eric Rohmer's *The Marquise of O* (1976), another film that is notable for the manner in which it approaches a literary text suffused with references to the visual arts, the novella of that title by Heinrich von Kleist. The relation of the visual to the literary and their transumption by film is the central preoccupation of Rohmer's *Marquise*. And Rohmer, like other French New Wave directors a writer on film as well as a filmmaker, in his turn learned a great deal from the films of F. W. Murnau, the German art historian-turned-filmmaker of the 1920s from whose work the French New Wave directors developed their theory of the filmmaker as *auteur*. Indeed, Rohmer himself wrote a book about Murnau's *Faust* (1926) that remains one of the most sustained meditations on the relation of painting and literature to cinema.[23]

But what do these relationships have to do with Scorsese's adaptation of Wharton? By my next example, I would like to suggest that they have a great deal to do with it. If they suggest a complex genealogy, they also suggest the essential forces that shaped Scorsese's adaptation. At one decisive moment in Wharton's novel – in Newport, after the honeymoon that marks his marriage to May Welland – Newland is sent down to the water to fetch Ellen, the Countess Olenska, who is standing near a "pagoda-like sum-merhouse" facing the bay (p. 215). Newland pauses at a distance, contemplating Ellen as a spectator might view a sculpture, and decides that he will go to her only if she turns before a certain sailboat reaches Lime Rock. He will go to her only, that is, if her inan-imate figure – her body as sculpture – will, like Pygmalion's Galatea, come magically to life.[24] But this crucial moment in which Newland watches Ellen by the bay takes on an additional significance in Scorsese's film. In imitation of Wharton, Scorsese uses painting to evoke social position, taste, and the historical moment that he is representing. But he uses it also to say something about his chosen medium of film as when, for instance, the camera sweeps across the long canvas that hangs in Ellen's house as though in imitation of a brushstroke, emphasizing by this means that film has the diegetic flexibility and the temporal dimension that painting lacks. Predictably, then, when Scorsese approaches Newland's decisive moment in Newport, he makes it decisively and complexly cinematic.

Whereas Wharton tells the reader that the immobile Ellen is "gazing at a bay furrowed with the coming and going of sailboats, yacht-launches, fishing-craft and trailing black coal barges hauled by noisy tugs" (p. 215), Scorsese radically reduces this scene to the movement of a single sailboat – not out to sea, as in Wharton – but very slowly from right to left across the cinematic frame. In this scene, Scorsese's film is very pointedly quoting *Nosferatu*, Murnau's 1922 classic, a film known among film directors, scholars, and fans alike for its painterly beauty. A hallmark of Murnau's visual style – pointed out by Alexandre Astruc, one of the contributors to the *Cahiers du Cinéma*, is what Astruc termed the "invasion of the frame," a moment in which a moving object is represented slowly and deliberately entering an otherwise static cinematic frame. Imagine a large nineteenth-century sailboat as it enters the frame from right to left, a frame devoid of anything but a seemingly motionless sea and sky: the effect of this "invasion" is to call attention to the introduction of movement – and therefore narrrative, story – into the stasis of painting, thus creating the narrative of moving images that is film.

As I mentioned earlier, Murnau was trained as an art historian and derived many of his images from painting. The image of the sailboat, for instance, is based on the coastal paintings of Caspar David Friedrich, one of Murnau's favorite sources. More pointedly than other filmmakers, Murnau calls attention to the manner in which film subsumes pictorial moments within the flow of its narrative. Although his carefully composed frames must of necessity give way to one another – since that is the nature of the medium – the tension between the static images of painting and film's capacity for animating those images is one of the motivating forces of Murnau's film. In *The Age of Innocence*, Scorsese's allusion to Murnau – no doubt mediated by Rohmer – is not only an homage to a filmmaker of the silent period, but comments on film's indebtedness to the compositional practices of painting while flaunting film's capacity for movement, and hence for storytelling. Very often in film such moments present the medium as triumphing over the other visual arts.

In Scorsese's *Age of Innocence*, however, this scene in Newport takes on an additional significance. Not only does the image of the sailboat recall the paintings of Caspar David Friedrich, but the motionless figure of Ellen, her back to her spectators – both to Newland and to the spectator of the film as well – is an example of Friedrich's famous *Rückenfigur*, a human figure in the act of looking, viewed from behind. At this moment in Scorsese's film, then, the figure of the woman is multiply encoded as a figure of art. At once (1) an enactment of a scene from a novel, (2) a reference to Ovid's

*Metamorphoses*, notably to a story which is itself a parable of art in which the sculpted female figure comes to life, (3) a quotation of another scene in *Nosferatu* in which a woman sits motionless in a seaside graveyard, gazing out at the sea, and hence (4) a cinematic allusion already a quotation of another Friedrich painting. Finally, all of these layered allusions, so much in the mode of Wharton's textual layering, are suddenly intensified as we realize that in this scene from Scorsese's film Michelle Pfeiffer, performing the role of Ellen Olenska, is herself enacting a *tableau vivant* – a point to which I will return.

In this scene at the bay and elsewhere in his film, Scorsese consciously adapts Wharton's technique of layering one representational mode with another: he alludes to his precursors in the art of "painterly" film – to Murnau and to Rohmer – via the painting of Caspar David Friedrich. At this point it will be useful to recall the manner in which, as Cynthia Griffin Wolff puts it, Wharton uses a "private pun" in order to allude to Henry James's novel by way of Reynolds's painting. The pun, or what we might call, in allusion to *The House of Mirth*, "the word which made all clear" is, of course, "portrait." Indeed, *The Age of Innocence* retains in its title a residual trace of the *tableaux vivants* so central to Wharton's earlier novel, *The House of Mirth* (1905). (Wharton's readers will recall that in this novel an entire evening is devoted to this form of entertainment, a parlor game in which costumed participants pose in stillness to enact well-known paintings.)[25] Once again, the key to the solution is through another text: this time it is *Vanity Fair*, in which a series of what Thackeray calls a "*charade tableau*" are performed in a picture gallery. In Thackeray's novel the *charade tableau* is a form of visual representation – helped along by music – that uses the human body as a vehicle to spell out syllables of words. Here images, as one might put it, serve as riddles whose solution is verbal. This is precisely the nature of Lily Bart's tableau in *The House of Mirth*, a *tableau vivant* which, as Candace Waid has pointed out, dramatizes a painting whose subject is writing.[26]

But Michelle Pfeiffer's *tableau vivant* in Scorsese's film is not only yet another sign of this director's involvement with Wharton's writing and its complicated conjunction of literature with painting. Film, too, has an abiding interest in *tableau vivant*, for *tableau vivant* moments in film – moments of arrested motion, by and large – remind us by contrast that the "motion picture" is the first medium able to animate visual representation, to make painting "come to life." From the point of view of the human perceptual apparatus, it is motion that confers the impression of three-dimensionality upon the image. *Tableau vivant* moments in film set up a tension between the two- and three-dimensional, between stasis and movement, between the "death" of the human body in painting and its "life" in cinema. Further, since *tableau vivant* exists at the nodal point that joins painting, sculpture, and theater, its evocation in film is a moment of intensified intermediality.

Siegfried Kracauer has contended that there are no films on the subject of art in which the camera is not featured.[27] And, indeed, flashy camerawork is everywhere apparent in Scorsese's film. Interestingly, it is Michael Ballhaus, Rainer Werner Fassbinder's erstwhile cameraman, who is Scorsese's cinematographer here. Fassbinder, also very much concerned with the conjunction of literature, painting, and theater, is a director in whose films artifice and formal arrangements can be understood as erotic display. The ostentatious movement of the camera in *The Age of Innocence*, so typical of films Ballhaus shot for Fassbinder, calls attention to itself, underlining the way in which the camera virtually generates space and gestures toward the three-dimensionality of that space in the process. Camera motion also affects our perception of the human body in film: in *The Age of Innocence*, the camera's striking mobility forms a pronounced contrast to the relative immobility of the characters, as when, for instance, the members of New York society are seated in formally scripted places at table in shots that suggest arranged displays. At such times the camera zooms in and moves in circles, tracking around the actors as though to expose the painterly stasis that emblematizes the fixed social hierarchy in which they are trapped.

But Ballhaus's camerawork has yet another point of connection to Wharton. Designed by Saul and Elaine Bass (best known for their work for Hitchcock, to whom we shall return), the film's opening credits superimpose a text being writtten in cursive over the image of a flower, thus aptly figuring the conjunction of the literary – the flow of writing – with the imagistic. With its operatic soundtrack and the repeated erotic image of an unfolding flower shot in stop-action photography first opening, then finally going to seed, this credit sequence is followed by the first diegetic shot of the film, a close-up of a chrysanthemum. The camera then tracks back to reveal a bunch of chrysanthemums, part of the stage set of Gounod's *Faust*. One of these flowers is plucked, and the camera pulls back to reveal the garden scene with Marguerite holding the flower by means of which she will symbolically deflower and dismember herself. After this operatic "defloration," the camera, in what we discover to be an extreme close-up of Newland Archer's evening attire – the frame is black – pans to the left to focus on his boutonnière, on the white gardenia in his lapel. A few shots later, Newland's gaze through opera glasses (another citation of spectatorship with antecedents in film and painting),[28] followed by shots from his point of view, establishes Newland's gaze and the sensibility of the connoisseur and spectator as the determining sensibility of the camera. The shots that follow, of several men looking through opera glasses – Larry Lefferts, arbiter of style in Wharton's novel, is the most prominent among them – confirm the conjunction of camera and opera glass in joint connoisseurship. Under their gaze the woman as flower must ever be aestheticized and, like Goethe's and Gounod's Marguerite and her model, Ophelia, consigned to death – if not to an actual death, then to death in art.

A brief look at the other extant film version of *The Age of Innocence*, a film to which Scorsese referred while planning his own, provides additional insight into the trope of the woman dying into art. Like Scorsese's film, Philip Moeller's 1934 adaptation simultaneously addresses concerns of Wharton's writing and of filmmaking, perhaps most clearly in the scene in the Metropolitan Museum. Moeller's version of this scene – in marked distinction from the novel – begins in a room that contains a few classical sculptures of male and female nudes among which the Countess Olenska and Newland Archer wander: in this film, too, there is a suggestion of Pygmalion and Galatea. Soon the couple enters the room containing the Egyptian collection, where they converse among Egyptian sculptures and encounter a mummy, labeled "A Woman who Lived in Egypt."[29] This label functions as an interesting diversion from the factuality of the female corpse and its "mummification," its preservation in art. In Egyptian culture, of course, art and the preservation of the body go hand in hand: Egyptian art at once defies and is complicit with death, expressing, as André Bazin has put it, "the mummy complex," or what he has called the "psychological ambition" of all art to "embalm time."[30] By means of this Egyptian Room setting, the film version of 1934 addresses the issues implicit in Scorsese's summer-house sequence in which Ellen stands immobile: the issues posed by the Galatea story and in *tableau vivant*, the "bringing to life" of painting or the "killing off" of the living body into the stasis of sculpture. Again, the fate of Lily Bart in *The House of Mirth* looms large. Displayed in death, her corpse is a still life or rather, as the French put it, a "*tableau mort*."[31]

But in what sense may this scene in the Egyptian collection be understood as self-consciously cinematic? On the one hand, it may very well allude to an early Hitchcock film, *Blackmail*, released in 1929, which includes an astonishing chase sequence through the Egyptian collection of the British Museum. *Blackmail* contains the first of several museum sequences in Hitchcock's films, many of which are concerned with precisely the issues which we have been discussing, with the conjunction of film, narrative, and painting, and with the "killing off" of the female body into the aesthetic: *Vertigo* (1958) is a prime instance of this obsession.[32] On the other hand, we recall that for early writers on film, such as Vachel Lindsay, film images are best understood as "hieroglyphics": Lindsay develops his notion of "photoplay hieroglyphics" as analogous to "Egyptian Picture-writing."[33] Moeller's scene in the Egyptian collection, then, additionally serves as a reminder that film is indeed a "mixed medium," a form of picture writing.[34] As the term "picture writing" could reasonably serve as another metaphor for the simultaneously verbal and imagistic allusions in Wharton, as a metaphor for the multiple layering of visual and verbal allusion, it seems a particularly resonant choice. Paradoxically, perhaps, in this scene "hieroglyph" is "the word that makes all clear," lending another dimension to the "hieroglyphic world" described by the novel's narrator (p. 44).

In conclusion, I shall briefly call to mind the scene at the end of Scorsese's film, the moment at which the golden light shining on the Countess's Paris window recalls Newland Archer's "decisive moment" at Newport to his memory. Wharton tells her readers that for Newland "by some queer process of association, that golden light became for him the pervading illumination in which she lived" (p. 359). Wharton's readers recognize that light as the auratic glow of the aesthetic: this moment in Paris serves as Wharton's private tribute to Henry James.[35] But in his film Scorsese elaborates on this moment to play once again on the painterly quality of his earlier, multivalent scene. When, this time, in Pygmalion-like fashion, Newland Archer succeeds in making his Galatea come to life — she turns, if only briefly, in his imagination — we realize that at this moment, for Scorsese, film has triumphed over painting's entombment of the human figure by its capacity for rendering movement and thus for rendering *life*.

My thanks to the editors of the *Edith Wharton Review* for allowing me to expand here an earlier essay entitled "Rival Arts? Filming *The Age of Innocence*," *Edith Wharton Review* 13: 1 (Fall 1996), 19–22. A truncated version appears in Candace Waid (ed.), *Edith Wharton's The Age of Innocence: The Norton Critical Edition* (New York: W. W. Norton, 2002), pp. 504–14.

————————————————— Notes —————————————————

1   Edith Wharton, *Summer* (New York: Bantam, 1993). See Scott Marshall's excellent compendium, "Edith Wharton on Film and Television: A History and Filmography," *Edith Wharton Review* 13: 2 (Spring 1996), 15–26.

2   Wharton, *Summer*, p. 97.

3   From "A Little Girl's New York," quoted from Marshall, "Edith Wharton on Film and Television," 16. Walter Benjamin's "The Work of Art in the Age of Mechanical Reproduction" (1935) later famously theorized this attitude. Benjamin's essay is anthologized in Leo Braudy and Marshall Cohen (eds), *Film Theory and Criticism: Introductory Readings* (New York: Oxford University Press, 1999), pp. 731–51.

4   For that matter, she did not see the stage version starring Katharine Cornell, either. *The Age of Innocence* was first filmed in 1924 by Wesley Ruggles, with Beverly Bayne as the Countess Olenska and Eliot Dexter as Newland Archer. Unfortunately, this silent film was lost. In 1934, Wharton's novel was filmed again, this time by Philip Moeller, with Irene Dunne as the Countess and John Boles as Archer. For further information, see Marshall, "Edith Wharton on Film and Television," 17, 22.

5   Gavin Smith, "Martin Scorsese Interviewed by Gavin Smith," *Film Comment* 29: 6 (1993), 15–26, at p. 22.

6   I make this argument about film at greater length in *Incorporating Images: Film and the Rival Arts* (Princeton, NJ: Princeton University Press, 1995).

7   R. W. B. Lewis, "Introduction," in Edith Wharton, *The Age of Innocence* (New York: Scribner's, 1968), p. xi. All subsequent references in parentheses in the text will be to this edition.

8   Smith, "Martin Scorsese," 16.

9   Ibid.

10   Ibid., 18.

11   The landscape painting chosen by Scorsese is a divergence from Wharton's novel, in which "a couple of Italian-looking pictures in old frames" (p. 69), mounted on red damask, take center stage in the Countess's drawing room. Scorsese relinquishes the erotic resonance of these paintings in favor of the long landscape painting that allows a "brushstroke" tracking shot.

12   Amy Taubin, "Dread and Desire," *Sight and Sound* 3: 12 (1993), 6; see also Pam Cook, "Review of *The Age of Innocence* by Martin Scorsese," *Sight and Sound* 4: 2 (1994), 45.

13   Walter Benjamin, *The Origin of the German Tragic Drama* (New York: Verso, 1977), p. 200.

14   Smith, "Martin Scorsese," 21. It should be noted, further, that Scorsese made one major visual change in his film: May Welland, as played by Winona Ryder, is not a blonde and blue-eyed athlete, just as the Countess Olenska as played by Michelle Pfeiffer is not dark and frail.

Brigitte Peucker

Chapter 21

Scorsese does not code these women as convention would dictate with the "dark lady" (the Countess) as literally dark-haired, as well as dangerously alluring.

15 Smith, "Martin Scorsese," 18.

16 I am usually a great admirer of Joanne Woodward, but her accent and inflection do not seem appropriate to Wharton's narrrator.

17 This is a balancing act familiar to us from the films of R. W. Fassbinder, to whom we shall return below.

18 It is interesting that *The New York Times* critic of Philip Moeller's earlier film adaptation also makes the point that his "photoplay" "leaves the spectator curiously cold and detached from the raging emotions of the story," *The New York Times Film Reviews, 1932–38*, vol. 2 (New York: New York Times Press, 1970), p. 1105.

19 Taubin, "Dread and Desire," 8.

20 Cynthia Griffin Wolff, *A Feast of Words: The Triumph of Edith Wharton* (New York: Oxford University Press, 1977), p. 312.

21 Candace Waid, *Edith Wharton's Letters from the Underworld: Fictions of Women and Writing* (Chapel Hill, NC: University of North Carolina Press, 1991), p. 29.

22 Among these are New York City films, including some very early Otoscope rolls whose images are reminiscent of the pages of a flipbook; Max Ophüls's *Letter from an Unknown Woman* (1948) and *Lola Montez* (1955); William Wyler's *The Heiress* (1949; based on *Washington Square* by Henry James); and Dreyer's *Gertrud* (1964). See Ian Christie, "The Scorsese Interview," *Sight and Sound* 4: 2 (1994), 10–15.

23 Eric Rohmer, *L'Organisation de l'espace dans le "Faust" de Murnau* (Paris: Union Générale d'Editions, 1977).

24 Pygmalion, the sculptor of classsical antiquity, fell in love with his own work of art and, as Ovid tells us, took the sculpture to bed with him.

25 The *tableau vivant* scene in Wharton's *House of Mirth* closely recalls that of Goethe's novel, *Elective Affinities* (1808), which established the real-life fashion for such entertainments in the nineteenth century. Wharton herself was a reader of Goethe.

26 Waid, *Edith Wharton's Letters*, pp. 27–31.

27 Siegfried Kracauer, *Theory of Film: The Redemption of Physical Reality* (Oxford: Oxford University Press, 1960), p. ix.

28 Most notably it occurs in Fritz Lang films, but it is generally a self-conscious reference to another lens, that of the camera.

29 The novel refers to the "vista of mummies and sarcophagi" through which the museum guard wanders "like a ghost stalking through a necropolis" (p. 311).

30 André Bazin, "The Ontology of the Photographic Image," *What is Cinema?* vol. 1 (Berkeley, CA: University of California Press, 1967), pp. 9–11.

31 Waid, *Edith Wharton's Letters*, p. 38.

32 As we recall, Saul Bass designed the famous credit sequence for *Vertigo*, as well as for many other Hitchcock films.

33 Vachel Lindsay, "Hieroglyphics," in *The Art of the Moving Picture* (New York: Liveright, 1970), p. 203.

34 For a thought-provoking reading of film's various forms of "Egyptomania," see Antonia Lant, "The Curse of the Pharaoh, or How Cinema Contracted Egyptomania," *October* 59 (1992), 87–112.

35 Wolff, *A Feast of Words*, pp. 333–4.

# Chapter 22

# The Talented Poststructuralist

## Hetero-masculinity, Gay Artifice, and Class Passing

## Chris Straayer

To con someone is to seduce him. If one's persona gives pleasure to others, especially if it flatters their self-estimates, an unwitting complicity will drive their assumptions in the deceptor's direction. Perhaps the pleasure of being seduced relies on a willing suspension of disbelief not entirely unlike that sexual economy in which men pay women for "sincere" compliments. Perhaps the mistake of Anthony Minghella's 1999 *The Talented Mr Ripley* is that its allegiance to "truth" ultimately jilts its viewers.

Ripley, the film's protagonist, is willing to kill for upward mobility. Twice before, Ripley has gone on killing sprees: first, in the 1955 source novel, Patricia Highsmith's *The Talented Mr Ripley*; second, in René Clément's 1960 filmic adaptation *Purple Noon*. The present chapter, which is concerned with talented passing, focuses primarily on these two earlier texts. In Minghella's more recent film, passing becomes a tortured process. Homosexuality is rendered through a combination of pre-Stonewall discourse on gender inversion and post-Stonewall discourse on "the closet." The closet figures as a dominant motif in the film both visually via shots of doors, for example, and verbally via Ripley's references to secrets in the basement of his self. Thus Minghella delivers a post-gay-liberation Ripley who suffers deeply from his inauthentic pose. Homosexual "character" is updated to reflect identity politics, within which coming out ensures health, and remaining in the closet ensures the ills of internalized homophobia. The film's opening title presents a rapid sequence of adjectives before briefly landing on "The Talented Mr Ripley." In this sliding signification, "talented" shares its host with "mysterious, yearning, secretive, lonely, troubled, confused, loving, musical, gifted, intelligent, beautiful, tender, sensitive, haunted, passionate." Rather than a promise of poststructuralism, however, this slippery title forecasts the film's conventional attempts at psychological depth. Highsmith's 1955 Ripley carries no such investment in authenticity, and I will argue below that freedom from core identity underwrites his greater talent. More seduced by the pleasure than the guilt of passing, I now put aside discussion of Minghella's film until the conclusion of this chapter.

One man kills a second man for his money. This familiar plot anchors both René Clément's 1960 film *Purple Noon* and the novel on which it is based, Patricia Highsmith's *The Talented Mr Ripley*. However, while the film concludes with Ripley's impending capture by police, in the novel he gets away with murder. These divergent endings are the result of contradictory attitudes toward class identity. This chapter analyzes the two texts in relation to masculinity, homosexuality, and class and argues that, in these realms, the novel, unlike the film, endorses a freedom from determination and fixity that is compatible with both the existentialism of the 1950s and contemporary poststructuralism.

Tom Ripley's victim in *Purple Noon* and *The Talented Mr Ripley* novel is Philippe/ Dickie Greenleaf,[1] a rich American who has lived in Italy for several years supported by his trust fund. Back in the United States, Greenleaf's father locates a prior acquaintance of his son, Ripley, and sponsors his trip to Italy for the purpose of influencing Greenleaf to return home. Very soon after meeting up with Greenleaf, Ripley reveals his travel arrangement to him, and they get on with enjoying Italy. Although they had not been close friends in the United States, now Greenleaf is amused by Ripley's displays of forgery and mimicry, and Ripley savors Greenleaf's higher-class lifestyle. At first, Greenleaf's female companion, Marge, also an American living abroad,[2] is the only hindrance to the men's bonding. However, when Greenleaf does not write an encouraging, if insincere, letter to his father – as he promised Ripley he would do – Ripley's expense account is cut off. Ripley, who covets upward class mobility more than anything, kills Greenleaf. At first Ripley impersonates his wealthier victim, wearing his monogrammed clothes, spending his family money, traveling in his style. To protect this acquired identity, he even commits a second murder when Freddie Miles, one of Greenleaf's old friends, pays an unexpected visit. The real Greenleaf, who is missing but presumed still alive, is blamed for the murder. At this point Ripley forges Greenleaf's will to his own advantage and resumes using the name Ripley. This summarizes that portion of the plot shared by film and novel. Before analyzing the texts in more detail, I must note several significant discrepancies, especially with regard to homosexuality and class. My general purpose in comparing the texts is not to measure the adaptation's accuracy, but rather to explore the consequences for identity of their different portrayals of repressed homosexuality.

Both texts use homosexuality to provide depth to the story, but because homosexuality is not analyzed but rather connoted via literary tropes and cultural stereotypes, I cannot really describe this depth as properly psychological. Yet I think this undercurrent of homosexuality offers mainstream viewers/readers an opportunity to utilize popularized psychology for their interpretive efforts in at least two areas: the association of repressed sexuality with violence, and the association of homosexuality with narcissism.

In the film *Purple Noon*, homosexuality remains subtextual, coded primarily (but not entirely) through triangles involving the two men and a woman. For example, early in the film, Ripley and Greenleaf are visiting Rome. During a game of pretending to be blind, Greenleaf induces a woman to join them. They take her on a buggy ride during which she is positioned between them as they both kiss and fondle her.[3] Eve Kosofsky Sedgwick (1985) has argued that such triangulation is an instance of "homosocial desire" in which the desire of two (assumed heterosexual) men for each other is exchanged through a woman.[4] Later in the film, when Greenleaf, Marge, and Ripley are boating together, Ripley reacts jealously to Greenleaf and Marge's private lovemaking below deck. In light of the earlier scene in the buggy, one might understand this as Ripley's jealousy of Greenleaf's desire for Marge, of Marge's desire for Greenleaf, or of the couple that excludes him (that is, as his desire to join them).

By contrast, in the novel *The Talented Mr Ripley*, Ripley will not tolerate any such triangulation. Women disgust him as does any semblance of heterosexuality. This is attributable to a homosexuality that he resolutely resists and denies. He wants Greenleaf to travel only with him, to leave Marge behind in Mongibello. He fantasizes a committed, idyllic bond between Greenleaf and himself that transcends sexuality. In other words, Ripley adamantly seeks an exclusively male homosociality with Greenleaf.

Traditionally understood as heterosexual male bonding in male-only social environments (such as sports, the military, and so on), the concept of *homosociality* precludes homosexuality. Homosociality assumes that men desire to emulate one another but do not desire to have one another sexually. Homosociality is the ideal platonic bond. Taking issue with this, Sedgwick's (1985) theorization of *homosocial desire* posits a continuum between homosociality and homosexuality, despite heterosexuality's pertinacious espousal of a distinct separation that would maintain a normative masculinity regulated by heterosexuality.

In "On Narcissism," Freud assigned the ego ideal (of heterosexuals) to one's own sex and the object of desire to one's opposite sex. In accordance with this schema, homosociality reinforces heterosexual masculinity by providing manly role models as ego ideals. Against Ripley's will, however, Greenleaf is both his ego ideal and the object of his (forbidden) desire. In such a case – when ego ideal and object of desire are located in a single sex – Freud finds a basis for homosexuality: narcissism. Michael Warner (1990) has astutely critiqued this equation of homosexuality with narcissism. Warner not only interrupts Freud's collapse of same sex into sameness, and sameness into self, but also reveals the arbitrariness of Freud's sex-specific scenarios, thus indicating the equal possibility of heterosexuals locating ego ideals in the same sex that they desire. In *The Talented Mr Ripley*, Ripley wants to become Greenleaf and he also desires to couple with him. As Ripley will learn, homosociality can precipitate homosexual panic in the repressed homosexual. And, as we will learn, murder is not the enactment of homosexual panic but the means by which Ripley avoids it.

In the novel, Ripley's passing as Greenleaf is absolutely convincing. In fact, I will argue later that Ripley not only impersonates Greenleaf but becomes him. This transformation is made possible by Ripley's total lack of allegiance to any former identity. By contrast, the film binds Ripley to identity by enforcing class difference. When Ripley claims to be a close friend from Greenleaf's past, Greenleaf not only denies it to Marge but points to the visible signs of class to disprove it. Correcting the way Ripley holds his silverware, Greenleaf not only performs a classist infantilization but also implies that, because Ripley is of the working class, they could not possibly have been close friends. Cutting both ways, Greenleaf also criticizes Ripley's class performance by declaring that the sure sign of someone not being upper class is his effort to act as such. "If you're trying to look well bred, which is a sign of bad breeding, don't use the knife to cut fish, and don't hold the knife that way. Hold it this way. I'm telling you this for your own good." After Ripley kills Greenleaf and is traveling under his name, film viewers (as opposed to diegetic characters) see Ripley in his private luxurious space eating chicken from the baking pan instead of at a properly set table. This portrays Ripley as ultimately unable to become upper class.

While the film nods toward what the novel calls Ripley's "talent," it ultimately forbids his mutability through this essentialist discourse on class. Despite temporarily passing as Greenleaf, Ripley remains a common crook. According to *Purple Noon*, class is natural and unchangeable, located in certain people, not in their possessions. Even though Ripley obtains Greenleaf's money, he can never assume his class. Hence the novel and film produce different discourses about both class identity and (repressed) homosexuality.

Notwithstanding its blazing sunlight and European holiday location, *Purple Noon* is *film noir* at heart.[5] Like the classic *femme fatale*, the film's central agency, Ripley (Alain Delon), pursues upward mobility via charm and murder. He is an *homme fatal*: handsome, covetous, enticing, duplicitous, unknowable, and fatal. His soon-to-be-victim, Greenleaf (Maurice Ronet), although aware of Ripley's intentions, is irresistibly drawn to him. This attraction is Greenleaf's downfall. After Greenleaf invites Ripley to join him and Marge (Marie Laforet) on his yacht, Ripley plants in Greenleaf's pocket an earring taken from the woman they kissed together in the buggy in Rome. Just as he hopes, Marge finds the earring, and it causes a rift between her and Greenleaf. Less explainable is why, rather than trying to make up with Marge, Greenleaf then thoroughly ruptures the relationship by throwing her book manuscript overboard during their argument. Marge asks to be put ashore, and both men seem helpless and unwilling to change her mind.

In concert, Ripley and Greenleaf have arranged for the two of them to be alone. And, without a female intermediary, they proceed toward physical contact. Prior to eliminating Marge from their company, Greenleaf had discovered some of his bank statements among Ripley's clothes. He even asked Ripley if he had felt like killing him, and Ripley did not deny it. So, why did Greenleaf not put Ripley ashore instead of Marge? Alone now on the yacht, Greenleaf and Ripley sit at a small table playing poker. Against Ripley's watch, his most precious possession, Greenleaf bets $2,500, one-half the reward that his father would have paid Ripley for bringing his son home. They pretend to be joking as they continue discussing the murder scheme. When Greenleaf declares his love for Marge, Ripley averts his eyes. Then, in a shot/reverse-shot pattern, the camera alternates between the men as they smile at one another and look intensely into each other's eyes. Camera positioning and focal length bring the two faces even nearer to each other. Greenleaf cheats so that Ripley can win the poker game, but Ripley catches him cheating. A discarded card lies on the floor between their feet. Ripley tells Greenleaf that he cannot be bought, not for $2,500, not even for $5,000 now. As Greenleaf bends to retrieve his card from the floor, Ripley nimbly swings a dagger off the bench by his hip and stabs Greenleaf in the chest. More than a psychological cliché calls for reading this scene as sexual desire displaced onto violence: Greenleaf's attraction to Ripley, his active complicity in Ripley's attempt to rid them of Marge, the hypocritical foreplay in their card playing, the final penetration. Did Greenleaf think he could buy Ripley as if he were trade?

Ripley's life ambitions exceed those of a working-class thief. He cannot settle for money when the opportunity for upward mobility is facing him. He lusts for the kind of class that comes complete with identity, with being, with family, with blood. Thus, Ripley kills Greenleaf and exceeds his formerly inept class passing by assuming Greenleaf's identity. Later, when suspicions about Greenleaf's disappearance begin to impinge on Ripley's confidence, he forges a will, leaving Greenleaf's money to Marge, whom he then seduces. Here lies another triangle in *Purple Noon*. Greenleaf's money passes through Marge to her new partner, Ripley. By replacing Greenleaf in the heterosexual couple, Ripley *inherits* Greenleaf's money. In this transaction, Ripley makes himself the recipient of homosocial desire and achieves his ego ideal. Ripley becomes Greenleaf's "family."

Unfortunately for Ripley, the film's containing discourse on class ultimately will not abide such status-shaking success. In retrospect, the ominous ending of *Purple Noon*, in which Ripley sips a cool drink on the beach unaware that at that very moment Greenleaf's body has been found nearby in circumstances that incriminate him, seems foreshadowed by an earlier scene in which Ripley is apprehended wearing Greenleaf's clothes. Upon returning from vacationing together, Greenleaf expels Ripley from the living room, where he is attempting to soothe the grudging Marge with tender kisses and hugs. Upon entering Greenleaf's bedroom, Ripley begins trying on Greenleaf's clothes before a full-length mirror. Even Greenleaf's shoes fit Ripley as he lies on the floor, pulling them on and tilting his feet in the air in a quite feminine gesture. Ripley recombs his hair in Greenleaf's style as the film cuts to a closer image of him. Finally, Tom Ripley leans into the mirror, pointing his finger at the image and murmuring: "My Marge. Marge, my love. My little Marge knows I love her and that I won't go with that nasty Tom to San Francisco." Ripley kisses the image before him. "My love for Marge is blind" (figure 22.1).

Obviously this scene enacts a third instance of triangulation in the film: Marge serves as intermediary in an otherwise same-sex kiss. Yet the scene is complex and offers numerous readings: Ripley is kissing Marge; Greenleaf is kissing Marge; Ripley is kissing Greenleaf (via Marge); Greenleaf is kissing Ripley (via Marge). At the level of pure image, however, we cannot help but see Ripley kissing Ripley. In relation to the film's understanding of homosexuality, this image of a man kissing his mirror reflection is the most forceful moment in the film. It fixes viewers' memories and effectively manages the film's homosexual subtext. First, the audio indexing of Marge is inconsequential next to the powerful visual semiotics of the shot. In a sense, the audiovisual construction of this scene ejects Marge, just as Greenleaf and Ripley later evacuate her from the yacht. If we privilege the central image – an isolation the film executes by cutting to medium close-up and then tracking closer – it contains only one person, who kisses his mirror image. Hence

**Figure 22.1** Alain Delon as Ripley in *Purple Noon* (*Plein soleil*, René Clément, France, 1960).

we move inward from a *scene* that contained both Ripley dressing up as Greenleaf and then kissing him in the mirror, while speaking to Marge, to the *image* of a single person kissing himself. While we might understand Ripley's donning of Greenleaf's clothes as feigning his ego ideal, and his subsequent kissing that image of Greenleaf as expressing desire for Greenleaf via Marge, the dominance of the scene by his mirrored image privileges a reading of homo-narcissism. This accusation of homo-narcissism, which locks Ripley within his own identity, is amplified when Greenleaf walks into the room, interrupting our gaze at the mirror and prohibiting Ripley's actions.

Let us compare the above filmic scene, which I have related as the modification of a triangle of homosocial desire toward homo-narcissim, to its rendering in *The Talented Mr Ripley* novel. To contextualize the written scene, it must be noted that Greenleaf's heterosexuality is subdued in the novel, so much so that it remains in question. That Greenleaf is very private about his (hetero)sexuality, that he is latently homosexual, and that he is nearly asexual are all plausible conclusions. In Mongibello, Marge and Greenleaf rent separate houses but are very friendly neighbors, sharing their privileged life almost on a daily basis. In the novel, the mirror scene quoted below occurs after Ripley, standing outside Marge's window, has surreptitiously observed Greenleaf in a rare moment embracing her and kissing her cheeks. Shocked, Tom Ripley runs back to Dickie Greenleaf's house.

He wondered when Dickie was coming back? Or was he going to stay and make an after-noon of it, really take her to bed with him? He jerked Dickie's closet door open and looked in. There was a freshly pressed, new-looking grey flannel suit that he had never seen Dickie wearing. Tom took it out. He took off his knee-length shorts and put on the grey flannel trousers. He put on a pair of Dickie's shoes. Then he opened the bottom drawer of the chest and took out a clean blue-and-white striped shirt.

He chose a dark-blue silk tie and knotted it carefully. The suit fitted him. Tom re-parted his hair and put the part a little more to one side, the way Dickie wore his.

"Marge, you must understand that I don't *love* you," Tom said into the mirror in Dickie's voice, with Dickie's higher pitch on the emphasized words, with the little growl in his throat at the end of the phrase that could be pleasant or unpleasant, intimate or cool, according to Dickie's mood. "Marge, stop it!" Tom turned suddenly and made a grab in the air as if he were seizing Marge's throat. He shook her, twisted her, while she sank lower and lower, until at last he left her, limp, on the floor. He was panting. He wiped his forehead the way Dickie did, reached for a handkerchief and, not finding any, got one from Dickie's top drawer, then resumed in front of the mirror. Even his parted lips looked like Dickie's lips when he was out of breath from swimming, drawn down a little from his lower teeth. "You know why I had to do that," he said, still breathlessly, addressing Marge, though he watched himself in the mirror. "You were interfering between Tom and me – No, not that! But there is a bond between us!" (Highsmith, 1992: 78–9)[6]

Three points drastically distinguish this scene from its articulation in the film and point us to significant qualities of the novel. First, Ripley does not kiss the mirror but instead uses it to appraise his impersonation of Greenleaf. Ripley is never reduced to an image as he is in the film, but rather retains a looking agency. This, along with his frequent movements, maintain his presence in three-dimensional space. Second, Ripley exhibits complete competence in transforming himself into Greenleaf. Not only do Greenleaf's clothes fit him physically, but they fit his taste. His body can stand in for Greenleaf's, naturally performing his gestures and expressions. Ripley's automatic movements in locat-ing Greenleaf's clothes suggest that he would know just how to handle and arrange such a wardrobe, that his own preferences and instincts about personal space are *simpatico* with Greenleaf's. His attention to detail, appreciation of nice materials, and quick decisions suggest a natural affiliation with the finery of this class. Ripley is not a clumsy "wannabe" as in *Purple Noon,* but a fully malleable person. To a degree impossible with the visually denotative language of film, readers are able to receive Ripley as Greenleaf here. By the time he talks to Marge, Ripley *is* Greenleaf. When Ripley looks in the mirror and sees Greenleaf's likeness, he reaps another benefit from his impersonation. Rather than being reduced to homo-narcissism, he has produced Greenleaf and himself as a *couple*. Ripley populates this couple as both himself and Greenleaf. Or, in other words, Ripley has succeeded in both being and having Greenleaf. When he speaks as Greenleaf and looks at Greenleaf, it is as if they were standing right next to each other, Greenleaf defending him against Marge. And not only that: in this configuration, Ripley has ascended to Greenleaf's class. He has obtained an identity that would warrant Greenleaf's acceptance and desire.[7]

The third significant difference between this scene and its rendering in the film is that Ripley strangles Marge instead of (suggesting verbally that he is) kissing her. There is no homosocial triangulation that safely conducts desire between the two men without exposing it as such. Instead, Ripley imagines an outright accusation of homosexuality from Marge. As it happens (one page later), Greenleaf does tell Ripley that Marge thinks he is queer. But here, Ripley (speaking as Greenleaf to the imaginary Marge) denies any homosexuality between the men while nevertheless claiming (without elaboration) a primary bond between them.[8] More important, he says this to Marge after supposedly killing her. His non-comprehension of death in this imaginary scenario foreshadows his later reaction to Greenleaf's death.

It is because Ripley is rebuffed by Greenleaf that he murders him. During their last trip together in the novel, Greenleaf says that next time he wants to travel alone with Marge.[9] On the train he seems bored, distant, only politely cheerful like a "host who has loathed his guest and is afraid the guest realizes it, and who tries to make it up at the last minute" (p. 96). Later, when Ripley points out a group of young male acrobats on the beach (wearing yellow G-strings),[10] Greenleaf makes a sour remark that fills Ripley with shame. Ripley remembers Marge thinking he was queer and his aunt calling him a sissy when he was a boy. When Greenleaf attempts to leave him there, Ripley's hurt turns to anger. "Damn him anyway, Tom thought. Did he have to act so damned aloof and superior all the time? You'd think he'd never seen a pansy! Obvious what was the matter with Dickie, all right! Why didn't he break down, just for once? What did he have that was so important to lose?" (p. 99). The suddenness of this shift from inward guilt to outward anger is typical of Ripley. Soon after the incident with the acrobats, Ripley quickly proceeds from fantasizing to enacting murder. In San Remo, he suggests that they take out a motor boat and, when they have reached a secluded spot, he beats Greenleaf to death with the oar and throws him overboard.

This murder was not fate. Things could have happened differently. Upon reaching the decisive moment in which Ripley hits Greenleaf, the text abruptly tells us that Ripley could have "sprung on him, or kissed him, or thrown him overboard" (p. 103). Russell Harrison has written about the influence of French existentialism on Patricia Highsmith's work in the 1950s. This postwar philosophy insisted on the necessity of choice even when no choice can be transcendentally justified or meaningful. Even when choice is absurd, it is unavoidable. Harrison argues that Highsmith took a positive stance toward irrationality and even motiveless behavior (1997: 3–7). Although I have repeatedly characterized Ripley as desiring upward mobility, the kiss-or-kill moment described above complicates any assumption that this is *the* reason he kills Greenleaf. Indeed, it acknowledges an equally forceful alternate desire and the necessity to choose between these two desires. Ripley makes the decision instantly. This is an integral part of his "talent." Combined with his practical play-acting skills, extensively rendered in the novel, Ripley's ability to react quickly to situations, to seize immediate opportunities, to take advantage of the

The Talented Poststructuralist

Chapter 22

present is what makes him successful. Adaptability, not deliberation, makes a con man.[11] This talent of Ripley's springs into action in the absence of any essential identity. Ripley's refusal of any past formation grants him freedom. As Harrison (1997: 6) states, "Reacting against the literature of the 1930s, especially that which depicted people as overwhelmingly determined by their circumstances, Highsmith's fiction pushed 'choice' to a solipsistic extreme."

Was Ripley panicked when he killed Greenleaf? Certainly at that moment he closely resembles the profile for the *psychiatric* understanding of acute homosexual panic during the 1950s: he is severely defensive if not actually repressed about his homosexuality; he is horrified by heterosexuality; he senses an impending separation from a same-sex friend to whom he is emotionally attached; he feels an outsider (Marge) is trying to negatively influence his life; and he is self-derogative. Numerous times throughout the novel Ripley succumbs to severe depression and hopelessness when made to face up to what he judges to be his own inadequacy. Shortly before their trip to San Remo, Ripley and Greenleaf have an argument. Greenleaf disapproves of a scheme for making money in which Ripley wants to involve them. Greenleaf says that Ripley is being taken in by a dirty crook. Tom Ripley resents Dickie Greenleaf's smug attitude. Suddenly he feels an unbearable estrangement and inferiority:

> Tom felt a painful wrench in his breast, and he covered his face with his hands. It was as if Dickie had been suddenly snatched away from him. They were not friends. They didn't know each other. It struck Tom like a horrible truth, true for all time, true for the people he had known in the past and for those he would know in the future: each had stood and would stand before him, and he would know time and time again that he would never know them, and the worst was that there would always be the illusion, for a time, that he did know them, and that he and they were completely in harmony and alike. For an instant the wordless shock of his realization seemed more than he could bear. He felt the grip of a fit, as if he would fall to the ground. It was too much: the foreignness around him, the different language, his failure, and the fact that Dickie hated him. (p. 89)

Ripley has become gravely dependent on Greenleaf's attention. For Greenleaf to rebuff Ripley is to threaten his stability. Certainly Ripley is panicked before he kills Greenleaf.

Gary David Comstock (1992) convincingly demonstrates the critical differences between the psychiatric category of homosexual panic and its misappropriation by the courts as a legal defense.[12] The latter, homosexual panic defense, is the more familiar to a contemporary public. A strategy to defend men who have murdered homosexuals, it presents the following narrative: a (latently gay) heterosexual-identified man responds to a sexual solicitation from a homosexual with a violent psychotic reaction. The argument presented is that the defendant was temporarily unable to distinguish right from wrong, and so should be absolved of responsibility. As Comstock makes clear, this narrative and argument severely distort the psychiatric theory (and actual cases) on which its authority depends. In psychiatric homosexual panic, the patient has uncontrollable homosexual urges that compete against his socially accepted goals. These homosexual urges are precipitated or strengthened by same-sex environments or the loss of a same-sex friend to whom the patient has become attached. In addition, the patient intensely fears heterosexuality. Already, the illogic of the homosexual panic defense is obvious: practicing heterosexuals do not demonstrate sufficient fear of heterosexuality. Furthermore, in order to gain sympathy from jurors, lawyers generally downplay or deny any latent homosexuality in the defendants. Most important to disputing the homosexual panic defense, however, is the total absence of outward violence in its psychiatric basis. Patients are not aggressive, but rather self-punishing, sometimes to the point of suicide. So, we see that although Ripley does seem a likely candidate for homosexual panic before the murder, by murdering he actually avoids it. Instead, he enacts an equally psychotic scenario: acute aggressive panic. By killing Greenleaf, Ripley saves himself. But not simply himself.

In his murder and subsequent impersonation of Greenleaf, Ripley consummates a corporeal union and reproduction that simultaneously rids him of the Ripley he so detests, transforms him into Greenleaf, makes him worthy of Greenleaf's approval, and produces them as a couple. Surely Greenleaf had become the ego ideal beside which Ripley's ego was deficient. But Ripley did not kill Greenleaf to save his ego. As the quote above illustrates so pitiably, Ripley could not have survived with himself alone. Homosexual panic would have destroyed him. Instead, he survives psychologically by abandoning rather than reprimanding his ego, by becoming his ego ideal.

Impersonating Greenleaf, Ripley is exceedingly happy. He travels about the country, staying at expensive hotels, eating the foods that he knows Greenleaf liked, wearing the rings he often admired on Greenleaf's hands. He buys two Gucci suitcases that Greenleaf would surely have liked: "one large, soft suitcase of antelope hide, the other a neat tan canvas with brown leather straps. Both bore Dickie's initials" (pp. 138–9). Competent in his new identity, he telephones Greenleaf's family and friends. He almost forgets how to talk like Ripley. "It was impossible ever to be lonely or bored, he thought, so long as he was Dickie Greenleaf" (p. 122). And he *is* Greenleaf. And yet he also is always *with* Greenleaf. Ripley feels no remorse about killing Greenleaf, because Greenleaf still lives for Ripley. And Ripley lives for Greenleaf. He sings in the shower "in Dickie's loud baritone that he had never heard, but he felt sure that Dickie would have been pleased with" (p. 180). Ripley's living as Greenleaf creates him. Ripley relishes life with Greenleaf in harmonious unity. Celebrating his good fortune, he goes to a Roman nightclub and orders a superb dinner "which he ate in elegant solitude at a candlelit table for two" (p. 133). Ripley is psychotic.[13]

One of the paramount benefits Ripley gains by killing Greenleaf is heteronormativity. In the novel, despite Greenleaf's ability to shame him, Ripley is proficient at passing. *The Talented Mr Ripley* novel never states whether or not Ripley is homosexual. Highsmith's reliance on gay stereotypes and codes produces a text that, in its opacity, resembles Ripley's personality. Such a gay stereotype links Ripley's performative ability to his proclivity for artifice. The affectation and affection for style that are often described as effeminacy in the gay male subject are simply attributed to class in the wealthy heterosexual male. Thus one can argue that Ripley's "homosexuality" actually facilitates his class passing. His fondness for jewelry and exquisite clothing suits the upper-class masculinity of Greenleaf. Ironically, once achieved, this upper-class masculinity then facilitates Ripley's passing as straight. It was only his desire for Greenleaf that ever interrupted Ripley's heterosexual attitude and cracked his façade. By killing Greenleaf, he eliminated that vulnerability. Now, he *has* Greenleaf. And he has Greenleaf's heterosexuality. Together they form his ideal homosocial *couple*, two heterosexual men (with the woman excluded).

As long as Ripley is Greenleaf, he does not have to worry about being called a sissy. But when Freddie unexpectedly arrives at his door one day and Ripley has to revert to the position of Greenleaf's unsanctioned friend, paranoia returns. How did Freddie know his address? From an Italian fellow, Freddie says, a young kid whom he met at the Greco. Freddie asks if Ripley is living here. No. Ripley tries to send Freddie off to a restaurant where he claims Greenleaf is having lunch. Even though Freddie has already seen too much – Greenleaf's shoes and jewelry on Ripley's person – Ripley reckons he can pack hastily and disappear before Freddie returns. As Freddie is leaving the building, however, he asks the landlady about Greenleaf's apartment and, upon hearing "only Signor Greenleaf," returns to the apartment. Again Ripley murders without forethought. He clubs Freddie over the head with an ashtray, pours gin down him, carries his slouching body to the car, and dumps it along the Appian Way.

It seems logical that Ripley kills Freddie because Freddie has discovered his fraud. Perhaps Ripley kills too quickly and carelessly, but Freddie is on the verge of realizing that Ripley has killed Greenleaf. But what really happens to make Ripley kill? The following thoughts, which run through Tom Ripley's head as he stands over Freddie's body, scream out another reason.

> [H]ow sad, stupid, clumsy, dangerous and unnecessary his death had been, and how brutally unfair to Freddie. Of course one could loathe Freddie, too. A selfish, stupid bastard who had sneered at one of his best friends – Dickie certainly was one of his best friends – just because he suspected him of sexual deviation. Tom laughed at that phrase "sexual deviation." Where was the sex? Where was the deviation? He looked at Freddie and said low and bitterly: "Freddie Miles, you're a victim of your own dirty mind." (pp. 146–7)

Ripley has been caught wearing Greenleaf's identification bracelet and tie clip. *Why* do men exchange jewelry? Freddie's reference to the Italian kid shamed Ripley. What was Freddie insinuating when he asked if Ripley lived here too? What did he suspect Ripley and Greenleaf of *doing*? One of two things was going to happen if Freddie had been allowed to go on. He would either discover that Ripley was passing as Greenleaf, or that Ripley and Greenleaf had been passing as straight. Freddie's discovery would explode Ripley's beautiful union of ego ideal and lover: "Freddie and his stinking, filthy suspicions" (p. 146). Ripley kills Freddie because Freddie sees homosexuality in him. But Ripley's

Chris Straayer

Chapter 22

incarnation is so replete that he feels Freddie arraigning Greenleaf as well. Ripley kills Freddie for sneering at the man Ripley recently killed. Ripley is a psychopath.

Robert J. Corber describes the discursive construction of the homosexual in postwar US culture as "an extended ideological struggle among competing political interests" (1993: 67). Homosexuals were considered to have both a fundamental identity different from heterosexuals and an unstable identity (or no identity at all). They were both recognizable via an established paradigm of gender inversion and, contradictorily, unidentifiable due to a lack of physical markers. Because of their ability to pass, homosexuals were considered national security risks. The Kinsey studies, which divulged that a large percentage of heterosexuals had engaged in homosexual behaviors, contributed to a perception of sexual identity as precarious. This indicated that both homosexuals and heterosexuals required surveillance and regulation, and exacerbated an already emergent heterosexual panic (Corber, 1993: 63). Homosexuals were denied government jobs not only because they were susceptible to blackmail, but also because heterosexuals were susceptible to their sexual advances. Rather than offer clarification or redress, psychology depoliticized and personalized the "problem" of homosexuality. "Psychoanalysis was itself one of the major tropes of the postwar period" (Corber, 1993: 10). As theories and diagnoses proliferated and contributed to the popular imagination, passing homosexuals became more "dangerous," their subversiveness presumed.

No wonder Ripley would want to be heterosexual. Patricia Highsmith also eshewed the identity of homosexual. Her lesbian novel *The Price of Salt* was published under the pseudonym Claire Morgan in 1952. She did not come out publicly until after the gay liberation movement. In 1984, the lesbian-identified Naiad Press republished *The Price of Salt* with the title *Carol* and under Highsmith's name. According to Brooks Peters, Barbara Grier (of Naiad Press), who never met her in person but corresponded with her frequently, says Highsmith suffered acutely from "internalized homophobia," which was not surprising, she adds, considering the era in which she was raised. Highsmith's own attitude is put rather succinctly in a postscript to *The Price of Salt,* in which she states, "I like to avoid labels" (Peters, 1995: 150). We would be wrong to seek a clear discourse on or picture of homosexuality in *The Talented Mr Ripley* novel. What we can find is a shameless exploitation of cultural perplexity, in which, with existential absurdity, I choose to see a poststructural disobedience with regard to identity.

When it becomes necessary for Ripley to retreat from his impersonation of Greenleaf, there is no return to a former self. Ripley's second murder of Greenleaf is nothing but a name change. True, he can no longer lay claim to his life as Greenleaf. The suitcases he bought belong to Greenleaf (p. 160). But, then, so does the guilt of Freddie's murder (p. 194). Fortunately, while Ripley was Greenleaf, he forged a will leaving everything to Ripley. This means that Ripley, unsuccessfully interpellated by the US work ethic, will continue in his travels: a rich man's "pleasant, rewarding, life's work" (p. 289). It is not this fortune, however, that qualifies Ripley for his elite station in life. Rather, it is his poststructuralist recognition of artifice, which the novel indulges. Whereas Greenleaf's body resurfaces to ensnare Ripley in *Purple Noon,* surface evidence is an unreliable signifier in *The Talented Mr Ripley* novel. When police retrieve Greenleaf's suitcases, the finger-prints they reveal match those of Freddie's murderer: Greenleaf. Whereas the *homme fatal* must meet his fate at the end of the film, the poststructuralist of the novel has learned how to survive by being Greenleaf. "If you want to be cheerful, or melancholic, or wistful, or thoughtful, or courteous, you simply had to *act* those things with every gesture" (p. 193).

I have argued that the film *Purple Noon* maintains a notion of fixed identity in relation to class, while *The Talented Mr Ripley* novel asserts identity as artificial and flexible. What in the film is class passing is a matter of becoming in the novel. Returning to the more recent film with which I began this chapter, Anthony Minghella's *The Talented Mr Ripley*, I must point out a fixity in relation to sexual orientation.

In some ways, Minghella's film creatively echoes my reading of Highsmith's novel. That Ripley (Matt Damon) desires to *become* Greenleaf (Jude Law) is suggested by his will-ingness to assume Greenleaf's responsibility for impregnating his mistress. The scene in which Ripley-as-Greenleaf celebrates Christmas by giving presents to himself suggests a couple. However, to an even greater extent than *Purple Noon* before it, this film prefers fixed identity. Despite Ripley's saying that he would rather be a fake somebody than a real nobody, identity is deeply psychological here, and homosexuality highly visible.

In terms of my argument, the most important change that the 1999 film makes is its creation of a wholly new, identifiably gay character, Peter Smith-Kingsley (Jack Davenport). The relationship between Ripley and Peter precludes understanding Ripley's murders as the result of homosexual panic, whether medically or legally defined. The film misses an opportunity, however, when it disallows any similar, reciprocal desire between Ripley and a second newly created character, Meredith Logue (Cate Blanchett), who meets him while he is passing as Greenleaf. One of Highsmith's more perverse moves occurs when she marries off her Ripley character in a later novel.[14] The bisexuality achieved in her Ripley series as a whole is consistent with her disregard for sexual identity in this novel.

In Minghella's film, the plot structure would allow a similar bisexuality. Both Meredith and Peter desire Ripley. In fact, the film's conclusion positions him between them. Ripley-as-Ripley is traveling with Peter when Meredith arrives on the same boat and recognizes him as Greenleaf. To avoid exposure as a murderer, Ripley kills Peter. Ripley is left with Meredith, but since his romantic demonstrations toward her have been totally insincere, her character cannot convincingly point to Ripley's heterosexual future in Highsmith's series. This, of course, severely qualifies the success of his escape.

One might say that Ripley gets away with murder in Minghella's film, but this would be to ignore the film's implication of self-destruction. Whereas previously in the film mirrors have been Ripley's playground for gender inversion, in the final scene Ripley sits alone in his cabin trapped by their surface reflections in the sadness of a closeted existence. Ironically, the post-gay-liberation mentality of Minghella's film both pushes its protag-onist into the closet and insists on explicit representations of homosexuality.

This contradiction is economically portrayed in an earlier scene when Ripley uses the reflection of a train window to enact a simulated kiss while Greenleaf sleeps. Seeing

Greenleaf's face reflected in the window, Ripley quietly repositions himself so that his own reflection kisses Greenleaf's. If we compare this image with the one of Ripley kissing the mirror in *Purple Noon*, we see how the protagonist's psychology has moved from narcissism to secrecy, and the film's rhetoric from suggestion to explicitness. In the 1999 film, Ripley sings "My Funny Valentine" to Greenleaf in a bar and watches a nude Greenleaf bathing. He even has a male lover in Peter Smith-Kingsley. Perhaps this explicitness provides a certain satisfaction to contemporary viewers. In the end, however, like *Purple Noon* before it, *The Talented Mr Ripley* film falls short of Highsmith's nerve. Neither film consummates the freedom that readers feel at the end of the novel when, surrounded by police, Ripley realizes that no one is looking for him.

Highsmith's narration in *The Talented Mr Ripley* holds tightly to Ripley's experience. This then holds viewers tightly to Ripley. We find ourselves desiring his victory despite his abhorrent crimes. Amy Taubin makes the connection between this reading encounter and Ripley's passing. "Highsmith suggests that the ability to lose oneself in writing or reading a novel has something in common with Ripley's 'talent' and with his perverse ability to picture himself leading someone else's life – and that such identifications can lead to murder" (Taubin, 1999). Although consistently focused on Ripley via a visual structure that parallels Highsmith's restricted narration, both *Purple Noon* and *The Talented Mr Ripley* film discipline viewers for their complicity with Ripley. We are not allowed to get away with surrogate murder. For whatever reason, filmic adaptations often assume a moral agenda not present in their literary sources.[15] Lamentably, this ruptures the seduction.

In Highsmith's *The Talented Mr Ripley,* murder produces the perfect poststructuralist twosome. Ripley not only becomes rich and heterosexual but also couples with Greenleaf. This is possible because, for Patricia Highsmith, homosexuality and heterosexuality, like being, are not things. Now Ripley can love himself the way that he loves Greenleaf. And Greenleaf will love him back. For the couple lives on. "It was his! Dickie's money and his freedom. And the freedom, like everything else, seemed combined, his and Dickie's combined" (p. 294).

--- **Acknowledgment** ---

This chapter slightly amends and expands an earlier version published in Peter Lehman (ed.), *Masculinity: Bodies, Movies, Culture* (New York: Routledge, 2001).

--- **Notes** ---

1   Greenleaf's first name is Philippe in the film, but Dickie in the novel. Throughout this chapter I will generally refer to Ripley and Greenleaf by their last names. This has the disadvantage of formalizing them in relation to those characters referred to by first names.

I must ask the reader to overlook this unfortunate repercussion and bear in mind that my intent is simply to avoid the confusion caused by Greenleaf's varying first name.

2   The European setting is not inconsequential. Pierre Bourdieu (1984) has noted how, from a US perspective, Europe's cultural difference reads as class distinction. In addition, to US homosexuals of the 1950s it offered a respite from the oppression of Cold War labeling. Patricia Highsmith was also an American who lived much of her life in Europe.

3   A corresponding scene occurs in the novel, but without the kissing, when the two men escort a woman home in a taxi. "Dickie and Tom sat very properly on the jump seats with their arms folded like a couple of footmen" (p. 67). After dropping her off, Tom conjectures that other Americans would have raped her. This thought productively collapses the class enhancement of living abroad with heterosexual restraint.

4   Although Sedgwick is describing a triangulation in mid-eighteenth to mid-nineteenth century English novels, I believe her model and arguments offer insight here. In chapter 2 of *Deviant Eyes, Deviant Bodies* (Straayer, 1996), while discussing what I call the hypothetical lesbian heroine, I investigate a triangle formed by a man between two women. I argue that this male intermediary separates the women and prohibits homosexuality even as he connects them and eroticizes their relationship. I see this contradictory function of the intermediary operating in *Purple Noon*, not so much within specific triangulations but in their contrast to the murder scene, which seems to require Marge's absence for the men to achieve direct physical contact.

5   The original French title for the film was *Plein soleil*. The literal translation used for the Australian release was *Full Sun*. In the UK, the film was released under the title *Blazing Sun*. The English translation offered in *Variety* was *Broad Daylight* (March 23, 1960). *Purple Noon* was the title given the film upon its US re-release by Miramax in 1996. Whereas the previous titles ring of Tom's getting away with crime in the novel, the darkening that occurs in the change of title to *Purple Noon* might appropriately suggest the *noir* element I attribute to the film.

6   Subsequent references by page number in parenthesis in the text will be to this edition.

7   Mirror images that substantiate my reading of this scene are abundant in the novel. As if disassociated from himself, Tom frequently surveys himself in mirrors. After Greenleaf's father first talks with him in a bar: "Slowly [Tom] took off his jacket and untied his tie, watching every move he made as if it were somebody else's movements" (p. 10). During his visit to Greenleaf's father's Park Ave home near the beginning of the novel: "Several times Tom got up with his drink and strolled to the fireplace and back, and when he looked into the mirror he saw that his mouth was turned down at the corners." Also, Tom observes himself and Greenleaf as mirror images when they are together. During their trip to Rome: "They sat slumped in the carrozza, each with a sandalled foot propped on a knee, and it seemed to Tom that he was looking in a mirror when he looked at Dickie's leg and his propped foot beside him. They were the same height, and very much the same weight, Dickie perhaps a bit heavier, and they wore the same size bathrobe, socks, and probably shirts" (p. 67).

8   In the novel, Tom's belief in this primary bond early on is explicitly bound with the homosocial. "[Marge] seemed to know that Dickie had formed a closer bond with [Tom] in twenty-four hours, just because he was another man, than she could ever have with Dickie, whether he loved her or not, and he didn't" (p. 70).

9   In the novel, soon after the scene in which Greenleaf catches Tom wearing his clothes before the mirror, Tom explicitly asks Greenleaf if he is in love with Marge. He answers, "No, but

I feel sorry for her. I care about her. She's been very nice to me. We've had some good times together. You don't seem to understand that . . . I haven't been to bed with her and I don't intend to, but I do intend to keep her friendship" (p. 82). So, Tom was correct when, in his fantasy before the mirror, he/Greenleaf tells Marge that he doesn't love her. However, by now Tom is (possibly) fantasizing more than actually exists between Greenleaf and Marge. This is not outlandish since Greenleaf is buying perfume to take back to Marge. Late in the novel, Tom looks back on this as one of his imaginary fears, "which, a couple of weeks later, he was ashamed that he *could* have believed. Such as that Marge and Dickie were having an affair in Mongibello, or were even on the brink of having an affair" (p. 247).

10  Much earlier, when first arriving in Mongibello, Tom had bought himself a black and yellow bathing suit "hardly bigger than a G-string" (p. 44).

11  In the novel, when Greenleaf asks Tom what kind of work he does, the answer seems to be anything but holding down a job. "'Oh, I can do a number of things – valeting, baby-sitting, accounting – I've got an unfortunate talent for figures. No matter how drunk I get, I can always tell when a waiter's cheating me on a bill. I can forge a signature, fly a helicopter, handle dice, impersonate practically anybody, cook – and do a one-man show in a nightclub in case the regular entertainer's sick. Shall I go on?' Tom was leaning forward counting them on his fingers. He could have gone on" (p. 58). Tom then springs up and, with one hand on his hip, one foot extended, impersonates Lady Assburden, which enchants Greenleaf. But, of course, Tom's "talents" are more sophisticated when it comes to murdering and impersonating Greenleaf and to murdering Freddie.

12  For a history of the psychiatric category "acute homosexual panic," Comstock draws heavily on the work of Burton S. Glick, MD, in the 1950s. Interesting to my discussion here, Glick (1959) observes already in the 1950s many variegated descriptions of homosexual panic in the psychiatric discussions, although not among case studies. (Homosexual panic as a psychiatric disorder was introduced in 1920.)

13  In "Mourning and Melancholia," Freud (1989) describes melancholia as the refusal to let go of a lost love object. This contrasts with normal grieving in which one eventually gives up the lost object and redirects one's desire. In melancholia, the absorption of the esteemed object is associated with a deflated ego or self-hate. Ripley's happiness within a melacholic structure, however, suggests the possibility of a radical re-evaluation of psychosis. For an interesting argument about the relations among melancholia, the illegitimacy of the lost love object, and Freud's admitted lack of knowledge about nonnormative relations see Gideon van Frank (2002).

14  *The Talented Mr Ripley* is the first in a series of five novels by Highsmith with the Ripley protagonist, although in the later novels Ripley is less problematically heterosexual. In addition to the two films named in this article, the Ripley series also generated *The American Friend* (Wim Wenders, 1977) and *Ripley's Game* (Liliana Cavani, 2002), both based on Highsmith's novel *Ripley's Game*.

15  In "The Subversive Ms Highsmith," Michael Bronski (2000) addresses this in relation to films adapted from Highsmith's novels and offers an especially sharp critique of the changes made to her *Strangers on a Train*. Similarly, he sees the changes made to Highsmith's *The Talented Mr Ripley* as an effort to render the film more palatable to mainstream audiences. "Highsmith rejects the entire assumption upon which Western ethical systems are based, that humankind has the potential and the will to act morally, leading her to singularly subversive insights."

Bourdieu, Pierre (1984) *Distinction*. Cambridge, MA: Harvard University Press.

Bronski, Michael (2000) "The Subversive Ms Highsmith," *The Gay and Lesbian Review* 7 (2): 13–16.

Comstock, Gary David (1992) "Dismantling the Homosexual Panic Defense," *Law and Sexuality* 2 (81): 81–102.

Corber, Robert J. (1993) *In the Name of National Security: Hitchcock, Homophobia, and the Political Construction of Gender in Postwar America*. Durham, NC: Duke University Press.

van Frank, Gideon Querido (2002) "The Shadow of Disavowal: Queer Desire, the Fantasmatic and the Performances of Melancholia," unpublished Master of Arts thesis in Cultural Studies and Literature, University of Utrecht.

Freud, Sigmund (1953–74) "On Narcissism," in James Strachey (ed.), *The Standard Edition of the Complete Psychological Works of Sigmund Freud,* 24 vols. London: Hogarth Press.

—— (1989) "Mourning and Melancholia," in John Rickman (ed.), *A General Selection from the Works of Sigmund Freud*. New York: Anchor Books.

Glick, Burton S. (1959) "Homosexual Panic: Clinical and Theoretical Considerations," *Journal of Nervous and Mental Disease* 20: 20–7.

Harrison, Russell (1997) *Patricia Highsmith*. New York: Twayne.

Highsmith, Patricia (1992) *The Talented Mr Ripley*. New York: Vintage Books (originally published 1955).

Peters, Brooks (1995) "Stranger than Fiction," *Out* (June): 70, 72, 150.

Sedgwick, Eve Kosofsky (1985) *Between Men: English Literature and Male Homosocial Desire*. New York: Columbia University Press.

Straayer, Chris (1996) *Deviant Eyes, Deviant Bodies: Sexual Re-orientations in Film and Video*. New York: Columbia University Press.

Taubin, Amy (1999) "From Riches to Rags: Ugly Americans and Plucky Irish," *Village Voice* (December 22–28) (http:www.villagevoice.com/issues/9951/taubin.php).

Warner, Michael (1990) "Homo-narcissism; or Heterosexuality," in Joseph A. Boone and Michael Cadder (eds), *Engendering Men: The Question of Male Feminist Criticism*. New York: Routledge.

Chris Straayer

Chapter 22

# Chapter 23

# From Bram Stoker's *Dracula* to *Bram Stoker's "Dracula"*

## Margaret Montalbano

Though it cannot claim to be the first, the longest, or even the most bizarre, *Dracula*, written by Bram Stoker (1897), is perhaps the best known of all vampire texts and is certainly the one that has the strongest connection to cinema. Perhaps this is because the birth of *Dracula* and that of the cinema were coincident and because their histories and lifespans are eternally synchronized: Thomas Edison received a patent on his moving picture camera and projector the year that Stoker's novel was first published. Whatever the reason, *Dracula* has become a prime source of material for cinematic rearticulation. Since its inception, cinema has enjoyed a close relationship with literature, exploiting it primarily for financial gain. Early films were often based on condensed adaptations of popular fiction or stage plays; and if the novel provided both topic and audience for the film, the film could in turn be used to create a larger audience for the written work. Vampire tales have provided a steady stream of source material for cinematic adaptation, and Stoker's immortal novel – never out of print since its initial publication – returns to life on screen again and again, spawning more cinematic retellings of the vampire myth than all other vampire novels and stories combined. Even for those who have not read the novel, "Dracula" has become synonymous with the cultural conception of a "vampire," and *Dracula* has become the key point of reference for all vampire texts that follow. Arguably, the most interesting cinematic version of this novel, however, is Francis Ford Coppola's *Bram Stoker's "Dracula"* (1992).[1]

Coppola has repeatedly claimed that *Bram Stoker's "Dracula"* is "closer to Stoker's novel than anything done before . . . Aside from the one innovative take that comes from history, . . . we were scrupulously true to the book."[2] Yet *Bram Stoker's "Dracula"* differs from Bram Stoker's *Dracula* to such an extent that it permitted a novelization of the film entitled *Bram Stoker's Dracula*, whose cover proclaims that it is the "official movie edition," and whose frontispiece advises that what follows is:

> BRAM STOKER'S
> *Dracula*
> The Novel of the Film directed by
> FRANCIS FORD COPPOLA
> By FRED SABERHAGEN and JAMES V. HART
> Based on the Screenplay by
> JAMES V. HART
> From the Bram Stoker Novel

The novelization requires the further disclaimer on the first page that "what follows here is not Bram Stoker's 1897 novel . . . but Fred Saberhagen's retelling of the motion picture called *Bram Stoker's 'Dracula'* . . . based on [James V. Hart's] screen adaptation of that classic story."[3]

As Robert Stam notes, "An adaptation consists in an interested reading of a novel and the circumstantially shaped 'writing' of a film."[4] Although it is tempting to discuss and evaluate a cinematic adaptation of a literary text in terms of the former's fidelity to the latter, as Stam's statement implies, what emerges in the transition between the literary and the cinematic is *a* reading of the literary text, one of an infinite number of possible readings, yet one which is eternally put into play with the "source" text as well as with other adaptations of that text. Thus Coppola's film enters into a dialogue with Stoker's novel and other cinematic adaptations of the novel in which the existence of each affects the meaning of the others, referencing its predecessors and defining itself in its similarities to, and differences from, them. A viewer's experience of *Bram Stoker's "Dracula"* is conditioned and inflected by encounters with these other texts as well.

This dialogic relationship that prevails in the adaptation process may be further explicated by Mikhail Bakhtin's concept of "heteroglossia," which asserts the "primacy of context over text" so that the meaning of every utterance – every text – is determined by the social, historical situation in which it is produced and received. From this perspective, even a word-for-word reproduction of a given text could not be considered identical to the original as a result of the differing temporalities in which each was produced and received; it would be considered, instead, a new text to be put into dialogue with its predecessors.[5] Thus while *Bram Stoker's "Dracula"* claims to be "scrupulously true" to Bram Stoker's *Dracula*, the film functions as a critical reading of the novel – one which, in light of Coppola's claims, proves an instructive example of the dialogic relationship of adaptation.

Although the transition from novel to film changes the medium of communication, *Bram Stoker's "Dracula"*, through its method of presentation, does come closest of all the cinematic retellings of *Dracula* to providing cinematic equivalents of key elements of Stoker's novel which are emphasized by its fragmented and polyphonic narrative style:

a multiplicity of voices and points of view; an acknowledgment of influences which inform the novel's structure and narrative style; a linking of present and past as exemplified, in part, by a fascination with the capabilities of modern technology tempered with a respect for the proven value of seemingly "primitive" technologies. Yet this adaptation also manifests the specific social, historical moment in which it was produced and thus embodies the ideological issues of that moment in complex and contradictory ways, so that Stoker's novel is refracted through twentieth-century concerns with, among other things, gender roles and sexuality. This refraction is most apparent in Coppola's acknowledged amendment to Stoker's novel; the "one innovative take that comes from history" constructs an entirely new narrative, structuring Coppola's film and providing both the framework on which the elements of Stoker's novel are hung and the frame through which they are viewed. This "innovation" also brings the film into dialogue with the pressing concerns of the twentieth century by moving back in time, narratively, to the fifteenth century for a prologue which provides the lens through which Coppola's reading of Stoker's novel is filtered. As elements of the prologue resonate throughout *Bram Stoker's "Dracula"* and climax in the representation of the blood exchange that typically defines a vampire text, the discussion that follows focuses primarily on these two scenes.

*Dracula* was read as a horror tale by Stoker's contemporaries. More than 75 years passed before the novel was read through the respective disciplines of literary theory, psychoanalysis, feminism, and cultural studies; even then, *Dracula* was often read as a morality tale: the crime and punishment of a voracious female sexuality. The novel's representation of female protagonists is well within the bounds of the stereotypes of Victorian sexuality until the vampire's bite unleashes a sexual aggression that must be contained and punished. *Dracula* represents the relationship between vampire and victim both as one of dominance and submission (in which the survival of either victim or vampire is made possible only by the death of the other) and, metaphorically, as the spread of a virulent and contagious disease that must be contained and eradicated.

Coppola's reading problematizes the dichotomy of Stoker's novel – innocence and guilt are not necessarily mutually exclusive or easy to define – and sets into motion all of the polarities that enabled the novel to pass as an unambiguous morality tale. The "innovative take" that structures Coppola's film paves the way for the change in the representation of the relationship between vampire and "victim" as the prologue provides motivation for Dracula's actions and thereby sets the stage for the representation of *Bram Stoker's "Dracula"* as a tragic romance. Coppola adopts Stoker's narrative structure to introduce the point of view and discourse of the only major character who is not permitted a narrative voice in *Dracula*, the title character. Diegetically situated 400 years prior to the initial entry of Jonathan Harker's journal that opens *Dracula*, the prologue of *Bram Stoker's "Dracula"* simultaneously posits "woman" as the metaphysical "cause" of vampirism and initiates the motif of blurred boundaries and overlapping categories that defines an hysterical text.[6] While the warrior prince Dracula is defending Christendom from the Moslem Turks, his bride receives a message announcing his death at the hands of the enemy. Distraught at the prospect of life without him, she leaps to her death. Her lack of faith in her husband's return (an unfaithful wife?), her gullibility in the face of the enemy's trickery, and her willingness to flout the laws her husband was fighting to uphold (as a suicide, she could never be reunited for eternity with a husband who died in battle) precipitate Dracula's reactions upon his return to find her lifeless body, barred from eternal life in the hereafter by the interdiction of the laws of a God he was pledged to defend. Enraged with grief, he renounces God, desecrates the chapel, and vows to rise from his own death to avenge hers with the powers of darkness. The end of this sequence is punctuated by the only opening title of the film, "Bram Stoker's Dracula," as if to acknowledge the separation and difference of this prologue from the source text, Bram Stoker's *Dracula*.

In this opening segment the hero is turned to villain through the actions of a woman, and the dividing line between good and evil is blurred. Dracula's actions, prompted by grief and passion (traditionally acceptable and sympathetic motivation), characterize him as (human) lover as well as (non-human) monster; and both elements of this characterization are maintained and developed throughout *Bram Stoker's "Dracula"*. This characterization is in direct contrast to the unquestionably and unrepentantly evil figure in *Dracula* for whom the novel provides neither past nor psychologized character traits to render him sympathetic. In addition, this segment introduces the film's motif of representing its female characters as possessed of active, sexual desire in their initial on-screen appearances as Elizabeta kisses her husband aggressively as he departs for battle, hanging on his armor, clutching his hand.[7] The prologue also sets the stage for a particularly contemporary take on the contagion spread through the bite of the vampire. Vera Dika notes that Coppola's reading of *Dracula* emphasizes the potentially fatal consequences of love and desire, linking love to "death and loss." She further suggests that the fantasies, both deadly and erotic, that play out on the screen resonate with the AIDS crisis in that Coppola represents the spread of such disease through "passion, desire [and] love."[8] While Stoker's nineteenth-century narrative certainly encompasses the spread of a strange malady associated with the vampire's bite, it is Coppola's fifteenth-century prologue that connects that contagion to love and passion. Thus the imbrication of the narrative penned by Stoker in the nineteenth century with that inspired by an historical figure of the fifteenth century results in a reading of *Dracula* that resonates with one of the overriding concerns of the late twentieth century.

Formally, the prologue of *Bram Stoker's "Dracula"* also serves to introduce the various aural and visual motifs through which the traditionally stable polarities – good and evil, guilt and innocence, masculine and feminine – are set into flux as excess repressed in the film's narrative is returned to the body of the text. An unidentified voice-over narrates the history of Dracula's condemnation to a life of darkness as the musical theme that signals and accompanies Dracula's subsequent appearances is introduced for the first time. This theme is superseded by several other dramatic themes with multiple and repeated crescendos emphasizing different families of musical instruments that underscore climactic moments in the narrative (strings for the massacres of war; brass for Dracula's victory over the Moslem Turks; drums for Elizabeta's plunge to her death; and a combination of full instrumentation, a mixed vocal chorus, chants, and Diamanda Galas's vocal effects as Dracula discovers Elizabeta's body). Visually, many of the motifs of *mise-en-scène* that structure the film are introduced in quick order: highly detailed settings (the chapel, filled with stone angels, snarling dragons, and metal arch supports in the shape of wolf heads; before the prologue ends it is bathed in a sea of red as the stone angels cry tears of blood, a stone cross bleeds from the wound inflicted by Dracula's sword, candles produce blood drippings, and a font of holy water sends a bloody red tide washing across the chapel floor); the use of color to define settings or scenes (the fiery oranges and yellows that characterize the battle scenes and the maps that chart them, and which reappear in the flame-like motif that provides the background for the opening title); and the use of shadows (the shadow of a crescent moon that sits atop the chapel dome moves across a map to indicate victory at war; battle scenes are highly stylized and played out in silhouette and shadow puppets, foreshadowing the divergent movements of figures and the shadows they cast later in the film). The cinematography includes dissolves (from the opening shot of the cathedral dome shrouded in clouds to a stone cross smashing to the ground and raising a cloud of dust and then back to the dome and clouds), super-impositions (Elizabeta's face over Dracula's shoulder as he has a premonition of her danger), multiple exposures (Elizabeta's body falls endlessly along the margin of her suicide note as Dracula reads), slow motion (the falling cross), and extreme high-angle shots (the camera pulls back from a close-up of Elizabeta's lifeless face to a view from the top of the chapel's high ceiling). These motifs and other variations on them continue after the opening titles, functioning primarily to underscore the differences between the source novel and the film.

Unlike the majority of novels which employ an omniscient and deified narrator and thereby define a single position from which the text "makes sense" for an ideal and univocal reader, *Dracula* is constructed through multiple voices and points of view, incorporating third-person, objective narration with the first-person accounts provided by the novel's protagonists: Jonathan Harker keeps a journal in shorthand, detailing his impressions of his travels; Mina, his betrothed, also keeps shorthand and typewritten journals of her daily activities, while she and Lucy engage in voluminous correspondence on the topic of their respective romantic entanglements. Newspaper clippings (imitating both the sensationalism of tabloid journalism and the "objective" recital of facts of the respectable press) furnish accounts of events that occasionally overlap with those described in various journal entries and letters. Telegrams convey plot developments succinctly while Dr Seward's phonograph diary provides a scientific record, and the captain's log of a sailing ship provides a similarly straightforward account of events. Although the constraints of the literary format confine Stoker's representational prac-tice to a single medium, the novel references visual as well as verbal cues in the con-struction of its narrative as characters consult rail and maritime schedules, examine maps, and "take views" with Kodak cameras. Additionally, in the course of his investigation/ examinations, Professor Van Helsing reads the text mapped out on Lucy's body, and encourages Dr Seward to do the same.

*Bram Stoker's "Dracula"* adheres to this polyphonic narrative format, employing the multitrack capabilities of film to reproduce journal entries in both visual image and voice-over, and to display the newspaper clippings, telegrams, letters, maps, and schedules referenced by the characters. In addition, the film provides its own illustrative "views" of the materials described, occasionally elaborating on Stoker's polyphonic structure, as when the frame is composed of pages from Jonathan's journal entry written en route to Transylvania: a miniature train chugs along the top margin of the journal, and Jonathan's voice-over narration of this entry is overlaid with the sound of the train's engine and whistle. *Bram Stoker's "Dracula"* also utilizes the cinematic equivalent of the cubist narrational style that provides accounts from varying perspectives on the same event, as well as information on different events which occurred at the same time, as narrators relate their individual experiences. Though such accounts are placed sequentially in the novel, Coppola employs parallel editing and crosscutting to indicate the simultaneity of certain events and to permit each to comment on the other. The most emphatic instance of this technique is the intercutting of Jonathan and Mina's somber wedding in Buda-Pest with Dracula's final assault on Lucy as the wolf crashes through the doors of her bedroom and tears at her throat. The chants that are part of the wedding service grow in volume and intensity and are heard over both spaces, joined, as the scene progresses, by the howls of a wolf. Mina and Jonathan's modest, downcast glances are contrasted with Lucy's screams of pain and of passion as she grasps at the wolf savaging her throat. The solemn religious ritual contrasts with the violent bestial coupling; and the sequence ends with crashing waves of splattering blood that meet in the middle of the frame/image of Lucy's bedroom, the furiously intense union of blood to blood (underscored by the multiple crescendos of the chants, howls, and brass instruments) juxtaposed with Harker and Mina's chaste kiss. After a fade to black and abrupt break to silence, the next image is of Lucy, in the bridal attire absent from the wedding scene, in her glass coffin.

Stoker acknowledges the literary antecedents of *Dracula* within the polyphonic narrative structure of the novel as he combines elements of the epistolary, travel, and gothic novel genres. And the novel's self-proclaimed conceit of setting forth a set of documents for a reader's examination "so that a history almost at variance with the possibilities of later day belief may stand forth as simple fact" may be read as a reference to the folkloric, anecdotal, and official accounts of vampire activity that were typically hawked by the itinerant peddlers more than a century before the publication of *Dracula*. Possibly an allusion to that method of obtaining knowledge about vampires, Stoker's collection of documents was intended to enable readers to come to conclusions about this particular vampire in much the same way as the peddlers' accounts enabled listeners to come to conclusions about vampires in general. Thus Stoker's text engages in a dialogic relationship with both literary genres and earlier traditions of acquiring information about vampires.

Coppola also acknowledges the antecedents of his text with a survey of film styles and histories that begins in the film's prologue, in which the battle between the Romanians and the Turks is staged with shadow puppets and silhouettes characteristic of early cinema and pre-cinema spectacles. The cinematograph visited by Mina and Dracula includes several pre-cinema magic illusions (a coffin containing a woman's corpse that appears to decompose to skeletal form, a glimpse of the puppeteers who control the silhouette soldiers for the battle sequence), as well as Lumière's *Arrival of a Train at the Station* and some period pornography/erotica. Additionally, the formal composition of *Bram Stoker's "Dracula"* acknowledges specific cinematic vampire texts, including previous adaptations of Stoker's novel. The dramatic, looming shadow effects – a vivid reminder that the very essence of cinema is the play of light and shadow – while harking back to German Expressionism and certainly playing a large part in vampiric *mise-en-scène*, also reference the first surviving version of *Dracula*, *Nosferatu* (Murnau, 1922), as does Dracula's abrupt rise from his coffin to a standing position, witnessed by Jonathan in the decaying chapel. The vampire's shadow moving independently of his body serves as a repeated quotation of *Vampyr* (Dryer, 1927), the use of the "historical" prologue harks back to *Dracula* (Curtis, 1973), and the foregrounding of special effects resonates with the negative color superimpositions used in *Dracula* (Saville, 1977). As if to acknowledge the cinematic sources that influenced his presentation of the romance between Mina and the vampire, Coppola pays homage to *Beauty and the Beast* (Cocteau, 1946) in his use of sconces in the shape of human arms to light Dracula's castle, the diamond tears that Mina weeps in the company of the vampire, and the vampire's very countenance – the face of a beast – as he weeps purple tears at Mina's parting.

The cinema technology that Coppola both represents and utilizes in *Bram Stoker's "Dracula"* echoes Stoker's approach to the technology available at the time he was writing *Dracula*. Stoker's characters avail themselves of telegraphy, "traveler's typewriters," shorthand, phonograph dictaphones, Kodak cameras, Winchester repeating rifles, and blood transfusions. Yet in the midst of such modern technology, the protagonists of *Dracula* rely on Bowie and Kukri knives to destroy the vampire, a method characterized as "medieval" by a contemporary review of the novel.[9] *Bram Stoker's "Dracula"* catalogs Stoker's "modern" technology within the diegetic space of the film and adds to it as Mina and the vampire visit the cinematograph, a nascent technology not referenced by Stoker although contemporary with the publication of his novel. But the film also reaches back to reference the time period between 1897 and 1992 – the lifespan of both cinema and *Dracula* at the time of this production. *Bram Stoker's "Dracula"* utilized the state-of-the-art technology available at the time of its production and was the first "major motion picture to go through editing and post-production entirely in the electronic domain – that is, to be cut and sound-edited on videotape with the aid of computers."[10] Yet it also employs many of the optical tricks that characterized cinema's initial years to represent the vampire's "magical" powers, utilizing vintage projectors, cameras, and paraphernalia that provided the ability to process effects in the camera rather than relying on the current standard of computer animation, morphing, and blue-screen technology.[11] *Bram Stoker's "Dracula"* avails itself of film technologies that were considered avant garde at the time of *Dracula's* initial publication as well as those that were "cutting edge" at the time of the film's production, with equal respect for the capabilities of each to address the specific needs of the production.

Yet the cinematic techniques of adaptation analogous to those devices employed by Stoker must be read in dialogue with the narrative frame Coppola sets up in the prologue. This results in an entirely different reading of the blood exchange between Dracula and Mina from that described in Stoker's novel and from that assumed by earlier representations of vampirism. A brief comparison of the representation of the exchange of blood between Dracula and Mina in two film versions of *Dracula* can foreground the contrasting representational practices and highlight the changing perspectives on gender roles and sexuality that inform Coppola's representations of vampirism. Stoker's novel narrates the incident through Dr Seward's diary entry:

> With his left hand he held both Mrs Harker's hands, keeping them away with her arms at full tension; his right hand gripped her by the back of the neck, forcing her face down on his bosom . . . The attitude of the two had a terrible resemblance to a child forcing a kitten's nose into a saucer of milk to compel it to drink . . . The Count turned his face, and the hellish look I had heard described seemed to leap into it . . . the white sharp teeth, behind the full lips of the blood-dripping mouth, champed together like those of a wild beast. Her face was ghastly . . . her eyes were mad with terror. (pp. 298–9)

The incident is not imaged in *Dracula* (Browning, 1931) but is noted only in a line of Mina's explanatory dialogue to Jonathan Harker: "Dracula, he came to me, opened a vein in his arm. He made me – drink." In both Stoker's novel and Browning's film the incident is framed as horrific. In the novel, Dr Seward is so "appalled" by the sight that he "felt [his] hair rise like bristles on the back of [his] neck, and [his] heart seemed to stand still" (p. 298); while in Browning's film Mina faints from the strain of recounting the incident in which Dracula's wound has somehow migrated from his chest to his arm.

*Bram Stoker's "Dracula"*, however, makes the blood-exchange scene the centerpiece of the film, the erotic climax, representing it as the consummation of the relationship between Dracula and Mina – and one which occurs at Mina's request. Mina murmurs in her sleep, as though in the throes of an erotic dream, as a trail of green mist enters the bedroom window and tunnels under her blankets. Dracula emerges from the bedding, beside her; she welcomes him with a kiss, wrapping her legs around his waist, laying her head in the hollow of his neck, confessing her love for him: "I want to be with you always . . . I love you . . . I want to be what you are, see what you see, love what you love . . . You are my love – and my life. Always." This moment of union, rather than representing a relationship of dominance and submission, positions Mina in the role of a desiring subject. The vampire is positioned as both object of desire and object of identification in relation to Mina; and it is, in part, Mina's identificatory love of the vampire – the desire to be like him – that spurs her desire for him. Mina desires Dracula and desires to be like him, not in terms of his masculinity, but in terms of his vampiric "otherness" (for although the vampire differs from Mina in terms of gender, the greater difference between the two lies in the status of each as human or non-human). Their coupling is choreographed to conform to the traditional signifiers of the cinematic "love scene" as Dracula and

Mina kiss, caress, and undress each other. Although she grimaces briefly as he fastens upon her neck, her soft moan signifies both pain and passion. Opening a vein above his heart so that Mina may drink, the vampire hesitates, pushing her away – "I love you too much to condemn you" – but Mina pleads with him, forcing her mouth back to his chest, and he relents with a groan of pleasure, arching his body and holding her close to him. At this moment of "orgasm," the sound of a door being forced open signals a cut to a wide-angle shot of the bedroom door, framing the Crew of Light, expressions of shock and horror on their faces.[12]

In this reading of *Dracula*, the "danger" unleashed by the vampire's bite is more than that of sexual aggressiveness: it is the confusion of traditionally fixed boundaries that prescribe socially acceptable gender-based behavior. It is Mina's active, passionate desire for the vampire that effectively defines the narrative of *Bram Stoker's "Dracula"* and distinguishes it from Stoker's novel, blurring the boundaries between vampire and "victim," guilt and innocence, and those between masculine and feminine, usually mapped onto the dichotomy of active/passive. This representation suggests that, rather than one of the pair surviving at the expense of the other, both can move beyond death to an eternal life in which the roles each may play are not subject to binary structures. In their embrace, overlapping gender characteristics are further mobilized and rendered fluid. As Mina sucks at Dracula's breast, imbibing the fluid necessary for her new life, the image echoes that of a child suckling at the mother's breast for the nourishment of milk. Yet Dracula's ecstatic response to Mina's sucking his bodily fluid permits the image to be read as one of fellatio, while the bleeding wound at which she sucks also allows for a reading of the act as cunnilingus. In this act, signifiers of both masculinity and femininity converge in each figure. In the exchange of blood, each embodies both traditionally "masculine" and traditionally "feminine" qualities, and each functions as both parent and child in relation to the other. As Mina nurtures Dracula with her blood, he suckles like a child at the mother's breast; and in providing his blood, he "gives birth" to her (in her new life as a vampire) and suckles the fledgling infant. Such "gender confusion" may be read as liberation from the entrapment of a binary structure of prescribed gender roles; ostensibly opposing traits and characteristics may be held in tension with one another, both readily accessible to an individual. This state of tension and accessibility may be considered homologous to the flexible identificatory capacities characteristic of a subject's early life before the Oedipal phase introduces the tyranny of binary structure in the form of heterosexual complementarity.

The end of the narrative of *Bram Stoker's "Dracula"* introduces yet another blurring of boundaries in relation to the union of the couple that traditionally marks the conclusion of film narratives and which marks the end of Stoker's novel. *Dracula* concludes with a "note" from Jonathan Harker, seven years after Dracula's death at the hands of Morris and Harker. Mina and Jonathan are the parents of a son; by all accounts good has vanquished evil, the couple has been reunited, and the traditional family unit preserved. *Bram Stoker's "Dracula"* is not able to fix the meaning of its ending as securely. The party closes in on Dracula at his castle at the moment of sunset, but the men are not successful in their attempt to kill the monster. Though they wound him, Mina defends him, pointing a rifle at her husband and the others, querying, "When my time comes . . . will you do the same to me?" She follows the wounded, aged Dracula into the chapel where her kiss restores his youthful countenance; at his request, she plunges the dagger through his heart and severs his head, releasing him to death. Mina's point of view frames the final shot of the film: the chapel ceiling's mosaic of Dracula and Elizabeta united in each other's arms. Given the visual similarities between Elizabeta and Mina, arguably this may be read as an image of Mina united with her lover. There is no final corresponding image of Jonathan and Mina, no sign of their unification as a couple. Though Mina's final query could be read as an indication of her plan to return to her husband and the possibility that he might have to put her to rest in the same fashion as she does Dracula, it might also be read as an indictment of Harker's cruelty and savagery in his pursuit of the vampire. In any event, the narrative cannot achieve the traditional closure of the happy reunited couple – that closure is displaced onto the *mise-en-scène* and the mosaic representation of Dracula and Elizabeta/Mina.

But the novelization of the film, *Bram Stoker's Dracula*, works hard to achieve closure, although the effort is not entirely successful. The traditional narrative structure of the novelization may be read as an attempt to recuperate some of the strangeness of the film, to provide a "preferred" reading of events for those who might have experienced difficulty following the form of the film. It also recuperates some of the consequences of Coppola's "one innovative take" as the novel's omniscient narration can direct a reader's interpretations of events presented on the screen. There is, however, a significant rupture of omniscience and recuperative power at the close of the narrative. *Bram Stoker's Dracula* follows the film narrative for the final scene as Mina defends her lover against her husband at rifle point, then plunges a dagger through his heart and severs his head, releasing him to death. Rather than reproducing or describing the ambiguity concerning Mina's future with Jonathan that marks the end of the film, the novelization takes pains to achieve closure as Mina kills Dracula and rises to her feet, walking toward the door of the chapel: "At that moment, Jonathan, unable to wait any longer, pushed the barrier open and rushed in to take his wife in his arms. And Mina knew, by the joy in her husband's face when he beheld her, that the snow was not more stainless than her own forehead . . ."[13] Yet the omniscient narrator who has been chronicling Mina's emotions throughout the text, providing detailed descriptions of her love for, and anguish over, the slain vampire, remains conspicuously silent on the topic of her response to this embrace and this knowledge, as the embrace of the couple that provides traditional closure elides this final gap in the narrative.

Coppola's "minor innovation" appears to open up a liberatory space for the expression of forbidden or taboo desire in *Bram Stoker's "Dracula"*. Unbridled sensuality and sexual excess abound: Lucy and Mina share a kiss in the rain, giggle speculatively over the illustrations in *Arabian Nights*, joke about the endowments and passions of each of their suitors. In this atmosphere, the film appears to break new ground as (arguably for the first time in a major motion picture) the "victim" expresses her desire for the vampire.

Further, Mina defends Dracula as she raises a shotgun against her husband, raising the possibility that the formation of a vampire couple will mark the fade-out of this tale, that Dracula and Mina (the true love he has crossed "oceans of time" to find) will be united as a couple, that desire will be given free rein – unconstrained by the demands of classical narrative or family values – that their reunion as the vampire couple will rhyme neatly with their earlier pairing as mortal lovers at the opening of the film.

Ultimately, the film cannot support or reward such ravenous female desire within the "reality" of the diegetic space. The eternal union of this couple is displaced to the representational realm of the *mise-en-scène* as the camera pans from the now-dead Dracula to the ceiling mosaic of Dracula and Elizabeta/Mina, simultaneously representing desire as both timeless and eternal – and contained and recuperated. Further, the voracious female (hetero)sexuality depicted in *Bram Stoker's "Dracula"* might be read as the result of the repression of the exploration of same-sex sexual relations. The visual excess and attention devoted to the erotic orgiastic spectacle of Harker's encounter with the three vampire brides effectively undercuts and distracts from the potential of a sexual interaction between Dracula and Harker – as does the added narrative of Dracula's infatuation with Mina/Elizabeta. Additionally, Dracula's relationship with Renfield is never explicitly discussed, elided by the emphasis placed on Dracula's quest for Mina. Though at one point Renfield protests that the eternal life promised to him is to be given to "the pretty woman," he functions primarily as a touchstone for Dracula's infatuation with Mina, repeatedly identifying her as "the bride my master covets." Coppola's film also opens up the possibility of an erotic relationship between Mina and Lucy with a kiss in the sudden storm that precedes Dracula's appearance. This theme is never developed, and the incident is not present in the novel or novelization, yet it raises the question of Lucy and Mina's friendship. Were Lucy to offer "eternal life" to her fiancé, why not to her "dearest friend," her "sister," Mina? And what of the brides? Although they are apparently in the habit of sharing the objects of their desire, their voracious sexual appetites seem to be activated by the presence of a male, Jonathan, in those episodes in which they appear on screen. When they call Mina to join them, they refer to her as "sister," safely moving the relationship away from the erotic to the sororital – they will not complete her transformation, but she may assume her "proper" place and join them.

While female agency and desire may be given free rein, the cost of such freedom is prohibitive, both in terms of the other sexualities and modes of desire that the representation of such aggressive heterosexual female desire represses and elides and in the role such desire is assigned in the origin of vampirism. In the dialogic relationship between *Bram Stoker's Dracula* and *Bram Stoker's "Dracula"*, Stoker's novel may punish the aggressive assertion of female desire and sexuality, but it is left to *Bram Stoker's "Dracula"* to assign responsibility and blame to such desire. *Bram Stoker's Dracula* provides neither an originary explanation of vampirism nor an explanation for the vampire's journey to London. The sympathetic monster of *Bram Stoker's "Dracula"*, however, is effectively brought to London by a woman, in this instance, Mina – an echo of the earlier function of the woman as bringing him to vampirism.[14] *Bram Stoker's "Dracula"*, the advertising for which describes the film with the tag-line "Love Never Dies," posits the originary responsibility for both with a woman's uncontrollable desire and willingness to die for love.

---

Notes

---

1   In this discussion, Coppola's 1992 film shall be referred to as *Bram Stoker's "Dracula"* and Stoker's 1897 novel as *Dracula* without further annotation as to director/author and date. All quotations are taken from the Bantam Books edition of *Dracula* published in 1989.

2   Francis Ford Coppola and James V. Hart, *Bram Stoker's "Dracula": The Film and the Legend* (New York: New Market Press, 1992), p. 3. Coppola's one "innovative take" is "the love story between Mina and the Prince." He is apparently referring both to the historical exist-ence of Vlad Tepes and to McNally and Florescu's work linking this historical figure to the Dracula myth: Raymond T. McNally and Radu Florescu, *In Search of Dracula: The History of Dracula and Vampires* (New York: Houghton Mifflin, 1972). But the context of Coppola's comment appears to legitimate, under the cloak of "history," the love story represented between this historical figure and a fictional character whose story time is separated from his era by at least 400 years, problematizing the definition of what might "properly" be considered historical.

3   Fred Saberhagen and James V. Hart, *Bram Stoker's Dracula* (New York: Signet, 1992).

4   Robert Stam, "Introduction: The Theory and Practice of Adaptation," in Robert Stam and Alessandra Raengo (eds), *Literature and Film: A Guide to the Theory and Practice of Film Adaptation* (Oxford: Blackwell, 2005), p. 46.

5   For elaboration of these concepts, see M. M. Bakhtin, *The Dialogic Imagination*, trans. Caryl Emerson and Michael Holquist, ed. Michael Holquist (Austin: University of Texas Press, 1981); and *Speech Genres and Other Late Essays*, trans. Vern W. McGee, ed. Caryl Emerson and Michael Holquist (Austin: University of Texas Press, 1986).

6   My use of the term "hysterical" in this discussion is determined by the use of the term in the work of film theorists such as Geoffrey Nowell-Smith, who discusses the symptomatic embod-iment of such "hysterical tendencies" in the formal elements of the film text, i.e., the inabil-ity of one term to successfully suppress or exclude the other. Nowell-Smith, in his work on melodrama, argues that film texts may participate in a process similar to the formation of hysterical symptoms as described by Freud, in which that which was repressed or could not be expressed in language would re-emerge as a bodily symptom. In the case of the film text, such somatization may frequently be expressed in terms of the sound track and *mise-en-scène*, providing an outlet for the repressed sexual desires, emotional excess, and unresolved con-tradictions of the narrative in music, color, camera angles, composition, and so on. In this fashion, that which cannot be explicitly spoken by the film text for reasons of censorship, narrative logic, and so forth, returns as a symptom in its formal construction; see Geoffrey Nowell-Smith, "Minelli and Melodrama," *Screen* 18: 2 (1977), 113–19.

7   This scene also sets the stage for Mina's function as a double for Elizabeta as, in her initial appearance in the film, she responds petulantly to the news that Harker must leave for Transylvania immediately, kissing him passionately as he glances impatiently toward the garden gate. The doubling is further reinforced in scenes that trace the "courtship" of Mina

and the vampire: she styles her hair as Elizabeta did and, in her ability to describe Dracula's homeland, seems to share Elizabeta's memories. The cinematography in these interludes underscores the linking of the two across "oceans of time" in the style in which these incidents are represented, spanning the 400-year gap in chronological continuity within a single image, condensing space and time in the representation of temporal relations in a spatial format. In a double exposure, Mina shares the frame first with Dracula's castle and then with Elizabeta's plunge to her death; thus it is possible to see the events she describes/"remembers" and her emotional reactions to them simultaneously as past and present are represented in a single frame.

8　　Vera Dika, "From Dracula – with Love," in Barry Keith Grant (ed.), *The Dread of Difference: Gender and the Horror Film* (Austin: University of Texas Press, 1996), pp. 388–400. Within the diegetic space of the film, the "mysterious" properties associated with the blood and bite of the vampire are couched in the contemporary rhetoric of AIDS research, diagnoses, and transmission. Van Helsing, whose initial on-screen appearance establishes him as an expert in venereal blood diseases as he (and viewers through his point-of-view shot) examines a microscopic view of a blood sample, pronounces Lucy's strange ailment a "disease of the blood unknown to all medical theory." Complete with moral undertones that often characterized discussion of AIDS transmission, Van Helsing interrogates Harker about his "infidelities" with the vampire brides, asking if he "ever tasted of their blood"; Harker's negative response permits Van Helsing to declare, diagnostically, that Harker has not "infected" his bloodstream. In addition, Frank Rich opines that the wounds inflicted by the vampire's bite "seen in close up look like the lesions of Kaposi's sarcoma;" see Frank Rich, "The New Blood Culture," *The New York Times* (December 6, 1992), 9: 1

9　　Review of *Dracula* in *The Spectator* 79 (1897), 150–1.

10　Coppola and Hart, *Bram Stoker's "Dracula"*, p. 149.

11　The London street scene where Dracula and Mina first meet was shot with a Pathé camera and features the slightly jerky movement of silent film shown at sound speed, the lighting flickering and somewhat uneven; the clicking sound of a projector is audible as are indistinct crowd noises, but there is no synchronized sound. The use of irises to fade in and out of shots is also reminiscent of the style of early cinema. Multiple exposures were used to process effects in the camera; a combination of rear projection and live action (rather than computer/blue screen manipulation) was used for several of Harker and Dracula's encounters at the castle; film was run in reverse to provide Lucy's eerie writhings in her bedroom and her return, snarling and hissing, to her coffin. One of the most spectacular visual effects, Dracula's approaching Mina in the form of green mist, was literally the product of smoke and mirrors (the purview of the stage magicians who were among the earliest cinema pioneers) – "dry ice smoke, lit green, and superimposed on the set with a 50/50 mirror" (Coppola and Hart, *Bram Stoker's "Dracula"*, p. 133). In addition, the film relies on the use of models and miniatures for exterior shots of Hillingham and Dracula's castle.

12　This representation of the exchange of blood between the pair also encapsulates the issues surrounding the AIDS crisis in 1992. The taboo exchange of bodily fluids is represented as a life-ending act (although it does not result in death; in fact, Mina pleads for the act in order to be taken away "from all this death" that surrounds her). The vampire, torn between his physical desire for Mina – for her blood – and his love for her, is hesitant to engage in the physical act that will "condemn" her to his fate. Mina, for her part, fully aware of the consequences, is resolved to pay with her mortal life for the desire she cannot control. And the expressions of horror on the onlookers' faces are, perhaps, the reactions of those who watch someone actively choose to sacrifice life for passion, to die for love. Yet, the figure of the vampire also comments on the AIDS crisis in a way resonant with a "safe-sex" message promulgated in the 1987 music video for George Michael's "I Want your Sex." The video features Michael, whose appearance remains relatively static throughout the video, in a series of sensual encounters with a woman whose appearance changes radically (with the help of costuming, wigs, makeup) from one encounter to the next. Michael scrawls the safe-sex slogan "Explore Monogamy" on her bare skin in lipstick, while repeating the refrain "sex is best when it's one on one." If the point, from the subjective perspective of Michael's character/persona, is that one can have relations with several "different" partners while in a monogamous relationship, imagine the possibilities offered by the various incarnations of the vampire – as young prince, old man, beast, mist, bat – for a monogamous union.

13   Saberhagen and Hart, *Bram Stoker's Dracula*, p. 298.

14   It is Mina's image, a daguerreotype carried by Jonathan Harker, that catches Dracula's eye, motivating his plans for a speedy departure to London.

# Chapter 24

# The Bible as Cultural Object(s) in Cinema

## Gavriel Moses

His hand managed the packing so that it never touched the Bible that had sat like a rock in the bottom of the bag in the last few years.

Flannery O'Connor, *Wise Blood*

One of the most striking film sequences in recent American cinema, from *The Apostle* (Robert Duvall, 1997), effectively encapsulates the focus of this chapter. The sequence brings to life a confrontation between Sonny Dewey, a Pentecostal preacher, at the head of his small congregation, and the local racist redneck who, furious at the sight of whites and blacks praying side by side, interrupts the Sunday church picnic by arriving with his huge bulldozer ready to tear down the church building. To stop him, and rather than call the police, the preacher places his Bible on the ground, in the path of the mechanical dragon, and dares his opponent to drive over the holy book. When members of the congregation start placing their own Bibles on the ground in a circle around the bulldozer, the troublemaker's henchmen, ordered to remove the Book, do not dare touch it. At last, having climbed down from the vehicle to do so himself, and confronted by Sonny Dewey's quiet faith and firm determination, the troublemaker crumbles and is converted.

A great deal has been written about films based on the Bible. Some studies examine films set in the modern world that in some allegorical, typological, or merely allusive way reference the Bible as the source of their narrative pattern. *The Apostle*, on the other hand, illustrates another way in which the Bible is present in cinema: as literal and cultural object. Easy to miss in its significance when it is present (a witness, after all, *would* normally be sworn in on a Bible) and just as easy to remember as being on screen when it is not (wasn't that US Senate chaplain so famous for his sermons always shown with the Bible open in front of him?), the Bible as a productive instance of material culture in cinema has not yet been the subject of any extensive study.

Yet the sequence in Duvall's film eloquently shows how the Bible can play a crucial role (and even rise to the status of a character) through its mere material presence. In this chapter, I want to call attention to a kind of book-to-film relationship that is not rooted in the adaptation or translation of one kind of text into another, at least not in the traditional sense. Sonny Dewey's Bible in the sequence described above may at first appear as a passive material presence, merely forbidding in its authority. The preacher wields it almost in the manner of Catholic exorcists. Confronted by the Book, the ringleader's friends, menacing though they may be, beat a comical retreat. Yet, before the confrontation is over, the Book's role in the conversion of a man transforms it into an active agent. Neither Sonny nor any of the others at the scene are the prime movers in the spiritual shift we are witnessing. For his sidekicks, the retreat may have to do quite simply with superstition, or a passive acceptance of the authority of the Bible. Yet what goes on during the quiet and whispered exchanges between the two men is quite different. It presupposes the Bible as third partner in a conversation, thus vividly illustrating one of the differences between the presence of books in general as objects in film, and that of the Bible.

While objects in the cinema by and large "are" content, books as objects "have" content, however generic the content may be. The books that prodigal son and aspiring writer Dave Hirsh picks out of his bag in *Some Came Running* (Vincente Minnelli, 1958), for example, constitute a veritable reading list signaling "modernist writer at hand." But a conflict between "my" Hemingway and "your" Hemingway pales by comparison to the stakes involved in the bibliographical signal of *The Apostle*. The Bible comes to the screen charged with centuries of variously transmitted contents, versions, interpretations, and cultural usages. The vast majority of Western spectators (and not only Western spectators) share this repertory in some measure. Despite variations in spectatorial knowledge, the book on screen plays a very different role when it is Genesis, rather than, say, *Manhattan Transfer*.

Because of this, the Bible on screen can convey a great deal, without abandoning the narrative unfolding of its immediate contact with plot, with characters, and with other screen objects. Such contact always already implies all kinds of previous translations and adaptations: translations presupposed by differing cultural codes, different historical moments, differing social contexts; adaptations driven by differing creative agendas, both formal and ideological. Even the episode in *The Apostle* articulates a series of topics all in their own way engaged in a dialogue with the Bible: from the clash between multi-racial worship and the threat of racist violence in the American South, to the contrast between the civil authority represented by the police (a power Sonny Dewey chooses not to invoke) and divine authority as mediated through a charismatic leader.

The Bible can enter into dialogue as an entire discursive repository when confronted with alternative cultural "bibles." The final moments of *Inherit the Wind* (Stanley Kramer, 1960) derive their force from the simple action performed by liberal lawyer Mathew Brady who, about to leave the empty courtroom after the trial of school teacher Cates for teaching evolution, seizes a volume of the Bible and a volume of Darwin, compares their weight, and then tucks them both under the same arm and walks out. The two volumes, by the end of the film, have acquired the meaning of cultural objects whose mere presence and juxtaposition convey a complex dialogue. During the film, Brady, in defending freedom of thought, and Henry Drummond, defending biblical literalism, come to personify two incompatible readings of the Bible. The adversaries' eloquence and passion is not merely didactic. The nature of the confrontation, and its possible consequences, are anything but abstract and conceptual. Even more extensively than in *The Apostle*, the opposition engulfs the secular as well as the spiritual life of a whole community, all rendered in the vivid and specific terms of cinematic representation.

Yet, questions arise even in sequences where the presence of the Bible as cultural object constitutes an expected part of the *mise-en-scène*. The case of courtroom scenes, for instance, is instructive. Even the most straightforward instances of "I swear to tell the truth . . ." are not always simple and routine. Apart from the inescapable proairetic complications these words contribute to the narrative (is it the truth or not?), we often reach such moments well into a story; by which time doubts have been raised about the definition of "truth" itself, or the possibility of ever knowing "all" of it, or even the nagging problem of "nothing but." A case in point is the moment in the trial in *Inherit the Wind* when the defendant's fiancée, who is also the daughter of the local minister, is sworn in. Having taken the oath, she has to face her individual conscience, to deal with the conflict between her duty to tell the truth, on the one hand, and her duty to obey her father by lying to protect his narrow and prescriptive reading of the Bible.

---
### "Nothing but the Truth"
---

> I would much rather believe a man who puts his hand on that Bible and swears to support and defend the Constitution of the United States against all enemies foreign and domestic, I would feel safer believing that that individual will adhere to his oath than I will have faith in an individual who has no manifestation of religion whatsoever or who has no religion.
>
> Senator Robert Byrd, *Congressional Record, Ashcroft Nomination Debate*

Courtroom oaths taken on the Bible underline how much we take for granted in such matters: the extent to which the mere presence of the Book brings elements already translated into our common cultural discourse. For one thing, the actual onscreen presence of a witness taking the oath is less frequent than one might imagine. Often we assume the presence of this discursive genre simply because of the context.[1] We also tend to forget the variety of ways in which the Bible is used: hand raised, hand touching/not touching the Bible; oaths taken in the presence of books that are not the Bible; oaths taken with no Bible present at all. The verbal formulas also vary. Distinctions may be relevant to the courtroom procedure as it happens in the situation as a whole (as it articulates, in other words, the culture code(s) at work in the scene), as well as relevant to the way in which the film chooses to represent the act dramatically. An episode of the television series *ER* illustrates the former case when the English surgeon Dr Corday, in the process of being sworn in for a deposition, inquires with puzzled astonishment: "What, no Bible?" She is told, "Just raise your hand" (*ER* 7: 144 "The Dance We Do"). In one quick stroke, the moment evokes the still-existing cultural differences separating the judicial systems in England and the United States as well as the way contemporary Americans discount religion as a guarantee in telling the truth. Again and again in court-room scenes, witnesses are reminded about the "civil" penalties for perjury. Only rarely in recent American cinema and television is a witness warned about the "religious" implications of lying under oath.[2]

Leave it to the inhabitants of Cicely, Alaska, characters endowed in equal parts with the contrarianism of Thoreau and the cultural savvy of *New Yorker* subscribers, to provide a fleshed out and humorous dramatization of the dilemmas facing the upstanding American citizen asked to tell the truth, Bible in hand (*Northern Exposure* 6: 10 "Crime and Punishment"). The oath in this episode is administered in what seems the standard way: the bailiff holds up the Bible for the witness who, left hand on the Bible and right hand raised, is asked to recite the usual words. Unlike most other cases in which this happens, the camera angle allows the Bible to disappear between bailiff and witness very rapidly indeed. This elision is in keeping with the politics of the series as a whole, which stresses the virtues of Americans in a secular context, in no need of the institutional guarantees of religion. Town disk jockey and philosopher, Chris Stevens is testifying in an extradition hearing caused by his long-standing West Virginia parole violation. He explains his reluctance to swear by slipping into a homespun version of postmodern discourse: "When push comes to shove I'd as soon not go to jail, and I don't think I can keep that from influencing my testimony, if only at the subconscious level, you see." He may have talked over what to say at the trial with his lawyer, he points out, and it is pretty persuasive, "but is it the whole truth? It's a slice of truth, a morsel, a refraction, it's . . . it's a piece of the pie, certainly not the whole enchilada, and now . . . now that I'm thinking about it I don't think I could tell the whole truth about anything." Swearing to tell the truth is "a pretty heavy burden because we all just see the world through this . . . little distorted piece of Coke bottle. Is there such a thing as . . . Objective Truth? I wonder . . . don't you?" One notices that the issue is not the usual civic protest against swearing on a religious volume. Nor is it the claim that US courts do not have any legitimacy for those who follow common law. Chris Stevens colloquializes postmodern philosophical argot with comical relish, a move reinforced by his lawyer's plan to defeat extradition by deconstructing the very notion of individual identity, mug-shot and fingerprints notwithstanding.[3]

In the context of a multidenominational society where even the right translation of the Bible is the concern of regular folk, rather than just scholars, what is a comic diversion in Alaska can acquire meanings fraught with history and emotions elsewhere. In John Ford's *Sergeant Rutledge* (1960) we encounter a witness who resists being sworn-in unless she is reassured that it is on a copy of the King James Version. Cordelia Fosgate's pedantic disruptiveness may well be taken as an odd moment of eccentricity. Yet, the religious conflicts and intolerance quickly evoked by the witness come into play as a foil to the racism that is the ostensible topic of the film.[4]

John Ford's Western courtroom drama about racially motivated accusations of rape and murder also illustrates another way in which the cultural status of the Bible and the claims of representational economy come into conflict. It is as if the fact that it is the Bible being invoked in the repetitive preliminaries of courtroom drama forces directors to show action they would normally abridge. Ford's solution in this case is to use the oaths to advance the psychological characterization of the witnesses. Defense counsel lieutenant Tom Cantrell, as he is sworn in because of a surprise move by the prosecutor, cuts the bailiff off before the formula is fully read to him: a vivid depiction of lawyerly entitlement. Sergeant Matthew Luke Skidmore, born a slave, and thus in possession of a culture-specific attitude about the Bible, reiterates his answer with emphasis and feeling saying, "I do!" twice over. Mr Hubbel, who ultimately turns the tide with information prompted by an inborn sense of honesty, actually sulks when asked, having had his say from the gallery, to swear an oath on the witness stand. He has said his piece, prompted only by common decency and civic duty. How could taking an oath on the Bible change any of that?

As opposed to Ford, Otto Preminger's *Anatomy of a Murder* (1959) resorts to the more common, and less productive, method of dramatic *variatio*. While a few oaths are filmed in full, more commonly the oaths are taken while lawyers talk to each other in the foreground, as the camera cuts to an oath already in progress. What is of special interest in Preminger's film is precisely what determines the reliability of an oath. From the Bible, the focus is displaced onto a religious object – in this case a rosary – that acquires the Book's inhibiting power. This creates a great deal of drama when the prosecutor repeatedly returns to the fact that the wife of the accused had sworn to her husband "on a rosary" that she had been raped. She is a Catholic, divorced, excommunicated, he insists at one point, so why on a "rosary"? For the prosecutor, this choice casts doubt on her integrity. Here it is the religious implications of taking an oath that come into play, including the denominationally specific importance of objects over the Bible in the religious practice of Catholics.[5]

## The Bible as Commodity

> What a freak! And why does he dress like a Bible salesman?
>
> Angela Hayes in *American Beauty* (1999)

At its inception in American culture, attention to the Bible as material object developed as part of a good faith effort to spread its content. It was assumed, perhaps naïvely, that literacy and the commerce in books would attract readers exclusively to books of piety, foremost among them the Bible. The increasing stress on the variety of forms of the Bible, its many available sizes and decorations, suited to a variety of tastes and occasions, was designed to stimulate the interest of as many prospective readers as possible. It was not envisaged at the time that this endeavor would result in the very first instance of mass media, and that commodification would bring the inevitable compromising of spiritual goals. Even the scenes of violence, sex and corruption for which films on religious topics are often condemned have long-standing precedents.[6] Early promoters of the printing press, again often in good faith, thought nothing of publishing ancillary texts (fictional, biographical, and in many other genres) the contents of which would have scarcely cleared the Hays Code. These factors help us to contextualize a film such as *Salesman* (Albert and David Maysles, 1969), popular for its congruence with contemporary views about the commercial exploitation of religion. At the very least, they should remind us that the practices illustrated by the film are not merely the creation of postwar American capitalism.[7]

As a film, *Salesman* is the most famous instance of the translation of the cultural discourse of the Bible as commodity into film terms.[8] This work of *cinéma vérité* follows a group of Bible salesmen as they go about their business. This non-fiction film, which strives to reveal unmediated situations surrounding the promotion of the Bible as commodity, markedly exposes the cultural codes that get attached to the Book when commercial agendas prevail.[9] As they move from target to target, the eager pack of salesmen spins a whole repertory of discourse genres around the Bible as cultural object.

Given the fact that the selling routines of the Badger, the Gipper, the Rabbit, and the Bull are carefully pre-programmed and rehearsed, the film lays bare the cultural buttons that the salesmen try to press. Their own self-awareness in turn leads to a steadily escalating contempt for the customers, a disregard seen especially in their passive-aggressive jokes. The Badger is most egregious in this sense. By the end, he even turns the sales-effective notion that one needs to be "mature" to appreciate the Bible into a dig at the age of a customer. Not to speak of the music we hear throughout the film: Badger again, humming "If I Were a Rich Man," between visits, during which he and the others stress that what they are selling should not be thought of in terms of money: "Quit figuring and start writing [a cheque]," he tells Mr Baker. Or, he says reassuringly, "Don't worry, they don't repossess the Bible." If, in the end, taking people's money must be acknowledged, it is trimmed with reassuring characterizations of the debt collector: "I'll send Paul down to pick up the down payment . . . he's a very devout Catholic." Even "This Land is my Land" pops up on the car radio while Badger (rich source of racist commentary throughout) is trying to find his way among streets, avenues, and boulevards called Sharazad, Ahmad, Sesame, Sinbad, Ali Baba, Harem.

The racism denied in the very act of expressing it works to displace the salesmen's feelings about the constant need to address the denominational diversity of prospective customers. While their Bible discourse seems primarily aimed at Catholics, one never knows where a Protestant (or even a Jewish wife) might lurk. This stands out most clearly in the training session for the salesmen: "I'm just a Bible salesman, not a theologian or a missionary" is one of the disclaimers they are taught. Or they are encouraged to appeal to masculine superiority (the Mrs might be reluctant, you see) by saying: "You're the man of the house . . . this is for your use." More charged (and most un-American) is the question: "Would it please you if [your wife] came to your religion?" Note the use of the word "came," so much more easygoing than the proselytizing it implies. Even worse is the suggested ploy of asking the husband in an interdenominational marriage about children raised by a heathen mother. In fact, come to think of it, wouldn't buying the Bible put pressure on the wife to convert? The didactic occasion also encapsulates many of the overt elements of discourse surrounding the Bible as cultural object. The sensitive and unpredictable matter of faith is sidestepped by reframing it as a matter of culture, while the discourses of culture and of commodity must be carefully separated.

It is in the name of culture that the salesmen appeal to received values such as prestige, beauty, education, great literature, and great art. Only then do they mention the recommendation of his Holiness the Pope, and the *nihil obstat* of the Catholic Church. Are culture and curia un-American perhaps? No fear: beyond the say-so of these foreigners, we have even ("see here on the title page") the guarantee provided by a well-known American prelate. As per instructions, the Bible *sub specie* commodity rears its head only after the prospective buyer has been cornered into conceding that there is no reason not to put down his money. Things now move quickly, as the salesmen carefully avoid any discursive transition that opens up the possibility of refusal. Even the "brother in law," who seems to throw the transaction into question, is dealt with summarily. He is subjected to rude and confrontational challenges to his claim to family status (no blood relation, is he?) and to shared economic stakes ("does he work for you?"). In the field, though, creativity is essential, for they may have to contend with family Bibles one hundred years old, for example, that obviate the need for any updated upstart elbowing its way onto the bookshelf. From central casting comes to the rescue the lady with a PhD, who owned fifteen Bibles already, yet "found comfort just from looking at the pictures" of yet another new one sold to her by yours truly. Commercial desperation can outrun the still somewhat dignified guarantees of canonical approval and lead to improvisations such as: "the fathers have it blessed because if it is not blessed you won't get the benefit of it." To bag a mark it may even be necessary to state (a novel theology this) that mere "exposure" to the physical presence of the Bible (the book, not its content) might bring benefits to the children. They can "catch Bible" just as they catch a cold, and in the end it is the "utility" of the Bible that matters: "Christ is something that doesn't enter into it at all."[10]

Should all of this seem, more than thirty years later, a somewhat obvious and easy target, we can find newly updated and even more outrageous strategies of salesmanship in the recent *The Bible and Gun Club* (Daniel J. Harris, 1997). Here a group of salesmen resort to selling, as a set, the Collectors' Edition Bible and a Defender 500 Pump-action Shotgun. Their pitch is: "A well-read family and a well-armed home." These are, after all, the cornerstones upon which America was built, and thus have a lasting appeal for the national collective unconscious. The film (clearly a mockumentary) may well push over the edge situations analogous to those in the Maysles Brothers' film. Yet there is no question that their timeliness (even the grafting of the gun lobby mentality to the topic of Bible as commodity) is fully confirmed by a recent infomercial entitled *Charlton*

*Heston Presents the Bible* (GT Merchandising and Licensing, 2000). In this effort, the actor tries to sell us a multimedia resurrection (a kind of transubstantiation) of what Badger and Gipper and Rabbit and Bull were peddling in 1968. Running for almost half an hour, the document confirms that cinema as an institution has caused a sea change: the Bible as cultural object in movies has usurped the canonical *authority* of Rome and the blessing of the fathers-without-which-we-won't-get-the-benefit-of-the . . . video cassettes and CDs. For why is it Charlton Heston who speaks to us with such authority? Priests, preachers, and rabbis are relegated to the role of satisfied customers providing genre-appropriate on-camera testimonials. It is Heston's movie role as Moses, we soon realize, that anoints him as *auctoritas*. The *nihil obstat* is Heston's. He even recounts the anecdote about the filming of *The Ten Commandments* (1956) sequence in which he realizes, as he brings the tablets down from the mountain, that the hundreds of extras who do not dare to look up at him are whispering "Moses . . . Moses . . ." in a variety of exotic languages. They took him for the real thing, you see, he explains. Why should not we as well?

What is remarkable in Heston's pitch is the fact that the discursive practice of the Bible as cultural object in cinema now blends seamlessly with that of the Bible as commodity. The sales techniques have not changed since they were applied to the printed book in the sixties (or, for that matter, in the nineteenth century). Yet this infomercial is, in a way, a movie about Moses himself as Bible salesman, Moses as Bogdanovich's Mose Pray, as the Maysles's Four Headed Beast.

---

## Gideon Bibles

> "Is there a Bible here?" "Here . . . the Gideons love us!"
>
> *Just Cause* (Arnie Glimsher, 1995)

Elmer Gantry, in the homonymous film (Richard Brooks 1960), rivets his congregation with his own conversion story by opening his sermon with words that trigger a network of discursive associations in his listeners' imagination. "I found me a Gideon Bible," he says, casting himself as the American Everyman journeying from hotel to hotel, aimless and lost until – Thank you Gideon! It is indeed Gantry's evangelical brethren who made it their mission to supply every night table, from luxury hotels to the seediest roadside motel, with a bound-together and available, Old and New Testament, a Gideon Bible.

The Gideon Bible is thus an instance of mass distribution untainted by commodification. What is more, its ubiquitous presence in the American landscape allows the Bible to meet individuals at a variety of personal moments, rather than during the enforced context of a sales pitch. The fact that we find it at hand while we travel does catch us at moments of particular openness to external influence and novel experience. But the specific moment in life and stage in personal development is dictated by the variety of individual histories. In film terms, such a range of personal experience is usually broken down into the terms of different film genres, each dedicated to isolating and amplifying a particular cross-section of human experience. Thus, this bit of Americana has allowed cinema to develop situations in which the Bible as cultural object appears in unexpected genre contexts. So ingrained is the expectation of its presence, and so intimately linked to the practice of opening the Sacred Book's pages for spiritual hints, that even Perry Mason, searching a motel room, goes straight for the Gideon Bible to look for clues, even though it turns out that this time the clue left behind by the victim is in the telephone books instead (*Perry Mason* 1: 13 "The Case of the Moth-eaten Mink").[11]

Few films actually use the Gideon Bible for its intended purpose. But in one film, *The Rapture* (Michael Tolkin, 1991), a chance discovery does indeed lead to the hoped-for conversion. Like many other American films that address the topic of faith, be it religious, political, utopian, *The Rapture* often dares to skirt the ridiculous a bit more than most other American films. However awkward and visually trivialized, the sequence in which the protagonist is converted by reading a Bible found in a nightstand drawer is nonetheless effective in making its point. After yet another unsatisfying and dangerous night of sex and booze with a stranger, in an anonymous motel, Sharon picks up a Gideon Bible from under the junk she had randomly dumped into the nightstand drawer. We see an ashtray (overflowing), a Whisky bottle (empty), a handgun (discovered in the stranger's backpack and confiscated), all of which cover the Bible. Yet Sharon now pulls it out and starts to read. As reviews and Internet summaries (some seriously inaccurate) of the film testify, spectators have trouble deciding whether Tolkin is taking all this at face value or providing cultural satire. In present-day America, it seems, any strongly expressed belief that is not secular is felt to be a transgression. Militant and fastidious religious belief suggests to the average secular spectator some form of mental aberration.[12]

The association of religious belief with mental aberration probably explains the quantity of films in which the villain, always in some way embroiled with Bibles, turns out to be psychotic. This even happens in films, such as *Household Saints* (Nancy Savoca, 1993), that are convincingly positive about religious faith. But more often than not we are among the criminally deranged. *Just Cause* (Arnie Glimsher, 1995) provides an interesting example, in that the turning point in the story hinges on a Gideon Bible. Paul Armstrong, an idealistic law professor, has agreed to defend a man he believes was falsely condemned for a rape and murder he did not commit. But suddenly, and well into the film, Armstrong, as well as the spectators, have to deal with an abrupt switch in genre, when it becomes evident that Bobby Earl, victim of judicial misconduct and police corruption, may in fact be involved in the crimes of prison-mate Blair Sullivan, an obsessive, Bible-spouting psycho. Armstrong's frantic reach for a Bible ("Here . . . the Gideons love us!," the prison guards reassure him, as he dashes from the interview with Sullivan searching for a copy) marks the shift. By the end of the film, Bible-marked psychosis and steamy swamps have taken over, as Armstrong stomps around in alligator habitat, wet to his knees, Bible in hand, trying to solve the mystery; trying to "read the signs" (as Sullivan in his pedantic doggedness has glossed for the lawyer, the portion for today is Ecclesiastes 2: 1).

What is hidden in Bibles may vary a great deal, and most of these treasures are of minor importance for the totality of the films in which they appear. Exceptions do exist, however, and what is hidden may be far more concrete than a clue. An example is the very effective use of the rock-hammer hidden in Andy's Bible in *The Shawshank Redemption* (Frank Darabont, 1994). Here the significance of what the Bible hides compounds the spiritual and the material. Andy's escape, the central element of the plot, hangs on the hammer he has hidden in the Gideon Bible in his cell, and on the importance of it not being found. Wondering when the hammer was placed in the Bible provides rich narrative extrapolation, especially when the warden orders a search and takes the Bible from Andy. Narrative tension mounts because we do not know if it contains the tool. Yet even greater narrative complexity emerges from the scene because if the warden does not open the Bible, it is only because Andy challenges him to a contest revolving around memorizing biblical passages. Incorporating the words of the Bible into memory becomes the means to protect the "incorporation" into the Book of Andy's means of escape. Physical freedom with its material means and spiritual freedom with its discursive ones enter in this way into a strange (and narratively rich) alliance.[13]

---

## Voicing the Bible

By mapping the text of the Bible into memory, Andy in *The Shawshank Redemption* "embodies" the book. His memorized personification is only a step away from the characters who, in François Truffaut's *Fahrenheit 451* (1966), "become" the books they have memorized, living as they do in a world in which books have been banned. Such somatic articulation of the text sometimes goes beyond mere memorizing. Voicing the Bible aloud, for one, often drives whole segments of a film and sometimes even an entire film. An example is Heisler's *Journey into Light* (1951), especially interesting in the way in which it sets up the evolving relationship between Bibles on screen and the protagonist, a Protestant minister who grows from arrogant narcissist to ideal minister through the course of the film. At the outset, as he preaches to his wealthy congregation, the Bible is not even visible on his pulpit. He is clearly very proud of his own rhetorical brilliance, which he seems to have honed with little, if any, recourse to the Book he is supposed to be preaching. Having lost his congregation, he goes to church to pray one last time and, in keeping with his relationship to the sacred text, the camera places him in long shot, erect, with legs apart, almost fitting into the decorative design of the building. He faces the altar from a direction that hides the side of the lectern on which the Bible would rest. The pastor subsequently abandons his calling altogether and drifts from place to place, until he ends up on skid row. There, he is finally forced, much against his will, to take up again his role as preacher. We watch with his congregation of derelicts as with great reluctance he gets behind the pulpit, its lectern graced with an outsized Bible. As invisible as it was in his church at the outset, the Book now is an imposing presence. Yet he is at a loss for words as he opens the Bible. The open pages seem to offer only half an answer to his need for language, since one of the two visible pages is an image. Finally, as the silence protracts expectation, one of the crowd sets him straight: "It don't have to be a fancy book reading, just a prayer."[14]

One would not expect the painter Vincent Van Gogh to join such company. Yet the early sequences of *Lust for Life* (Vincente Minnelli, 1956) depict the young Van Gogh's troubled attempts to become a minister. His speech impediments convince his superiors that he is not equipped to be a preacher. The final decision to send him to the provinces, as a kind of missionary among destitute miners, betrays his church leaders' lack of commitment to the poor and to the marginalized. We watch Van Gogh fail to reach even these people because of his inability to read from a text and deliver a coherent sermon. But in *Lust for Life*, congregation and minister at least share a language as well as a culture, contested in its details as may be, which is not the case if we look at the many movie-missionaries operating in colonial settings. While the barriers for Van Gogh are merely of a personal and somatic nature, in places such as Africa and China the obstacles derive from almost insurmountable linguistic and cultural chasms.

*The Left Hand of God* (Edward Dmytryk, 1955), for example, tells of the fake Jesuit priest Jim Carmody, an American pilot who has crashed behind enemy lines in China, and been taken prisoner by a local warlord. He escapes disguised as a priest, yet once safe at the nearest Mission, he finds he cannot reveal his identity. It is thus an unwelcome surprise to be asked to give the Sunday sermon at church. Uneasy behind the pulpit, Carmody takes his cue from the New Testament text open in front of him. He clings to the Book in its physical presence as if it were a life raft protecting him from exposure. As he starts to read, his tone seems to draw from the text the authority and self-assurance that he needs in order to maintain his cover. He seems to hope that by voicing the text as is, it will bear witness to his own authenticity. Yet, it is his very clinging to the words on the page that renders him suspect in the eyes of the European missionaries in the congregation. A sermon, after all, does not consist in the mere voicing of the words of the Bible. Especially in a Catholic mission it requires the priestly mediation of official interpretation, extrapolation, and gloss. Rather than attempt this route, Carmody's way out of his quandary turns out to be even more unorthodox than his bare, unadorned textual delivery. Free to see clearly, as the appointed missionaries do not seem to be, whom he is speaking to, Carmody finds a way to deliver the Bible to his exotic congregation with an effectiveness that is obviously new to this Mission. Noticing the lack of participation by the Chinese members who constitute the majority of the listeners, he suddenly jumps into Chinese, translating the text, discussing it in an accessible and colloquial way. The linguistic shift gives life to the words of the Bible by acknowledging the true cultural identity of the congregation. The success is immediate and banishes any resistance among the spiritual colonizers officially in charge. Perhaps they can excuse the Jesuit's odd behavior by recalling the traditions of his own religious order, notoriously theatrical and mimetic in furthering the missionary agenda of its priests.

Rev. Samuel Sayer, the missionary in *The African Queen* (John Huston, 1951), in contrast, lacks this ability to perform a seductive mimesis of the culture to be conquered. He fails in his clumsy attempts to guide the native flock through the religious service that opens the film, not least because he seems to believe that, by resorting to singing the Bible, the faithful will voice the text in music, if not in words. Such an appeal to the expressive faculties of the body are, after all, invoked by Psalm 150, cited by apostle Sonny Dewey: to *really* play the instruments, *really* sing and dance in the House of the Lord. The problem, for the geographically deracinated Anglican, derives from the choice of music. These tunes, like the foreign words on the pages placed in their hands, are totally alien to the musical sensibility of the Africans. In this Huston is more credible than Henry King who, in *Stanley and Livingstone* (1939), forces us to listen to a choir of native people singing, in the middle of the jungle, with improbable and absurd canonical perfection.

Yet the conflict between the language of the colonizers and that of the colonized is not a problem limited to colonial settings. As we know all too well, similar value-laden tensions also persist in a multicultural society. A priest or a minister may well feel like a missionary in his own country. As a result, a film like Fellini's *Le notti di Cabiria* (1957) turns out to be very different from its American adaptation. Fellini's protagonist may be cut off from her culture's religious discourse, yet she is not separated from the language that she needs in order to engage with it. When Cabiria joins the pilgrimage to the Shrine of the Madonna she may be skeptical, then overwhelmed, then resentful. But she understands the terms in which she is being addressed and can counter effectively. Transposed to counter-culture America in *Sweet Charity* (Bob Fosse, 1969), the dialogue between individual and church cannot occur at all. The congregation speaks a different language and their minister, like a missionary, has to translate.

Sammy Davis Jr, in the sequence in Fosse's film that parallels Fellini's pilgrimage, is transformed from Roman Catholic priest into a New Age preacher who relies on the singing and dancing of the Evangelical American tradition (forms of somatization more complex than simple voicing) to get the attention of his flock. But he too has to confront a linguistic and cultural chasm almost as deep as those faced by Jim Carmody and Rev. Samuel Sayer. His congregation may be made up of Americans, but they are alienated from the master language no less than the native people in the Huston and Dmytryk films. He thus warns his charges that time is short "on that big LP called life," and that eternity – "that big coffee break in the sky" – is just the "flip side of life." Not to speak of the Ten Commandments, notable among which is: "Thou shall not swing with another cat's chick." Although played for laughs, something serious lurks behind the song and dance. The very multicultural and pluridenominational richness of American culture hides the makings of colonial reductiveness.

> The book is virtually the central character of this movie.
>
> Roman Polanski about *The Ninth Gate* (1999)

As Polanski noted about *The Ninth Gate* (1999), one could regard the rare book at the center of his film as the protagonist. A satanic bible, which, if correctly re-collated after disassembling the only three extant exemplars, *The Nine Gates* is believed to allow the owner to bring forth Lucifer himself. Vague as Polanski's claim may be, it is true that all the characters in the film react to the existence and power of the book, much as they might have done had the protagonist been human. In its powerful agency, *The Nine Gates* is far more than just an influence upon those characters who happen to read it. It comes to control their lives. It is important less for what it says (in fact, the illustrations matter more than the text) but for what it can cause to happen. In similar fashion, *The Frisco Kid* (Robert Aldrich, 1979) features at its center a Torah scroll that a Polish rabbi named Avram Belinski is charged with carrying all the way from 1850 Poland to the burgeoning city of San Francisco. The manifold comical adventures of the film bring us repeatedly back to what happens to the sacred scroll, and what it causes to happen, as it is carried across the American West by the protagonist. Much like a character whose status and vision determine what happens in a story, the Bible as cultural object takes center stage in the fiction.

Belinski's Torah scroll has a physical presence as palpable as that of a human being. When the American Indians who capture the rabbi are about to burn him, noticing his protectiveness of the scroll, they offer to burn the Bible instead of him, as if human being and Book were an even match. The Indians' growing respect for Belinski and his scroll derives from his courage in being prepared to sacrifice himself rather than have the Bible destroyed. So impressed are the Indians by the rabbi's steadfast loyalty to the inscribed records of his faith, that they free him (as well as his less-deserving buddy, bank-robber Tommy Lillard) and invite him to their religious festivities. During these festivities, Avram, besotted by hallucinogenic mushrooms whose potency he has underestimated, teaches the tribe to dance the way tipsy Hassidim do on the Sabbath in the old country.

Belinski carries the scroll, fondles it, often cradling it like an infant, its vulnerability rendered like that of a human body. Especially in the sequence in which rabbi and scroll (stripped of their finery) are thrown from a wagon out onto the dusty trail, the film underscores the human physicality of both book and body. Belinski is left in his underwear face down in the dirt and has to retrace the wagon's trail back to his Torah. The sequence uses familiar comedy tropes to link the wounded physicality of the stripped Torah scroll to the equally stripped humanity of the rabbi. He stumbles toward us over a rise on the horizon, barefoot on the unforgiving pebbles of the trail. As he slowly gathers up his clothes, he haltingly bandages his human nakedness. Finally, he finds the Bible, barren

*The Bible as Cultural Object(s) in Cinema*

*Chapter 24*

of its own ceremonial breastplate, lying abandoned in the middle of the road. As he lifts it and cradles it lovingly, he even kisses it as one might kiss a baby abandoned in the dust. He even quickly checks under its cloth cover, as if to see whether the diapers are still dry. The brilliance of the sequence resides in its careful balance between the genre-appropriate elements of comedy and the serious articulation of the human-like presence of the scroll.

The body-like physicality of the anti-Bible in Polanski's satanic thriller is just as pronounced as it is in Aldrich's mock Western. In genre-appropriate manner, *The Ninth Gate* ultimately dissects, rather like bodies subject to medieval torture, the three volumes that book collector Boris Balkan manages to gather into his hands. The purpose of this dismemberment is the reconstitution of the relevant members of the three victims into a single body, quite like the stitching together of a Frankenstein monster. Balkan believes that, when laid out together in front of him, they will allow him access to unheard of satanic powers. The body language of the book collectors, dealers, and restorers handling these books, moreover, suggests that they are handling more than inanimate objects. The satanic prints in the three books, furthermore, all contain human figures, some actually foreshadowing the grotesque physical fate and ultimate metamorphosis of the characters. Bernie (of Bernie's Rare Books) is hanged, his body contorted precisely as in the illustration in *The Nine Gates*, and The Girl, Corso's ambiguous guardian angel, as she finally rides him naked to sexual frenzy, suddenly looks quite like the Whore of Babylon in the book's plate.

The tactile experience of the books, the frenzy to own, possess, and maintain control of them, drives most of the characters' actions. Such depths of obsession force collector Victor Fargas to sacrifice everything, quite like the ruined yet still besotted sex-slave of a Parisian coquette. The two book-restorers Pablo and Pedro Ceniza behave around their books like two dirty old men. Baroness Kessler has actually been crippled by her contact with *The Nine Gates*. And, finally Balkan's supercilious behavior, as he snatches the book away from Liana Tefler in the middle of her satanic ceremony, pits them against each other like two mutually contemptuous, bickering parents in a deadly custody battle.

## Objects as Bible

In such films, mechanisms of displacement (whether tropical or fetishistic) often take over the role of Bible as cultural object. From the Bible as *object*, in other words, one often passes to *objects as Bible*. I have already mentioned Moses descending from Mt Sinai carrying the tablets in *The Ten Commandments*. The stone tablets are, in fact, the kind of object I mean, since they are not yet part of the Bible itself. In the very same film we also find (far less spectacularized than the tablets but perhaps more important) the sacred objects destined for the Ark of the future Temple in Jerusalem. Moses places these in the hands of Eliezer so that he may, once having reached the destination with-held from the Prince of Egypt, place them in the Ark of the Covenant next to the Tables of the Law. These final moments of the film tend to be overlooked, especially after the preceding *son et lumière*. By contrast, they are quiet and brief, and as narrative they do not even attempt to clarify what is happening. Yet here we have a rare case in which the Bible as cultural object is shown at an early stage of its formation. Scrolls and stone tablets are treated by Moses as a collection of cultural objects to be preserved within another object (the Ark of the Covenant) which will soon acquire a spiritual charge all its own. Even more than the tablets bearing the Ten Commandments, the Ark has a spe-cial place in the *mise-en-scène* of the Jewish religion. Its presence, its absence, what it contains, what will happen when it is opened, the verbal formula necessary to open it, all of these have stimulated the imagination, especially a filmic imagination more epic than historical, more melodramatic than spiritual. To such a point that the Ark can become the narrative McGuffin of a spectacular mega production such as *Raiders of the Lost Ark* (Steven Spielberg, 1981). Yet the same Ark also turns out to be a narrative device in a more recent film, intellectually far more ambitious, entitled *Π* (Darren Aronofsky, 1997).[15]

In the latter film, more than the Bible itself, the commentaries, the numerological tradition of Judaism, the sacred object itself, become the protagonists of what turns out to be the final narrative subtext of the film. The opening situation does not take us far beyond the premise of the mathematician Max Cohen, genius or madman, engaged in a compulsive search for the numerical sequence first conceived by the medieval mathematician Fibonacci. Yet this narrative starting-point is not further developed and we soon find ourselves in a *film noir* in which sinister Wall Street traders try to kidnap the protagon-ist, convinced as they are that the Fibonacci sequence is the key to cracking the stock market. Yet this genre-specific narrative soon shifts when an earlier encounter with an Orthodox Jewish student of Old Testament Gematria turns out to have been more than just an anecdotal instance of the traditional juxtaposition of science and religion. The student saves Max from the ticker-thugs only to disclose that he belongs to an extrem-ist mystical sect whose members believe that Fibonacci's numerical sequence (since all Hebrew letters have a numerical equivalent) translates into the lost true name of God. This word was uttered once a year by the High Priest in the Inner Sanctum of the First Temple in Jerusalem in order to open the Ark. The members of this sect fully intend to rediscover the word and proceed to do likewise. Thus, this rabble of scholars suddenly turns into the cast of a Messianic End-of-Days potboiler. The long scene in which all of this becomes clear is played out in front of what one must assume to be the true Ark of the Covenant somehow delivered to Brooklyn, New York. Yet the scene derives its dramatic interest and intensity from a very different area of film discourse than that employed by the bland didactic finale of *The Ten Commandments*, not to speak of the grandly overdetermined means applied to the uncovering of the sacred biblical receptacle in *Raiders of the Lost Ark*. We are simply riveted by the long monologue of a rabbi who methodically explains all of this facing the camera.

Yet a carefully considered contrast between *Π* and Spielberg's raiders suggests that one must not summarily relegate the latter to the storeroom of despised potboilers. *Raiders of the Lost Ark* attains fascination superior to predecessors such as *The Ten Commandments* by transcending the shock effect of sexually transgressive content with a discursive productivity derived from the clash of familiar cinematic conventions. Rather than relying on the directness of the spoken word like Aronofsky's film, Spielberg produces a text so excessive at the formal level that language-based content diminishes in relevance. In the sequence where the Ark is opened by the Nazi officer and self-appointed High Priest, the film is taken over by the generic conventions of horror film and the formal conventions of special effects. Rather than mediating the fury of an angry God through the mimic expressiveness of the body of the prophet according to Heston, rather than reifying the divine anger through a hydraulic earthquake worthy of a provincial opera stage, Spielberg opts for a "Baroque wonder." Well known as an effective vehicle for spiritual spectacle since the Catholic Reformation, this technique works by directly implicating the physiological balance of spectators. The exaggerated and excessive emotional intensification provoked in the spectator by such formal evocations of the supernatural, illustrates the extent to which these formal "stand ins" for the textual content of the Bible assume the characteristics of a fetish. Our senses, bombarded by 70mm images and digital sounds, respond by investing the object on the screen with all the physiological intensity appropriate to the revelation of divine power. That which is "too much" in the film, that which "goes beyond" good taste, in other words, suggests that the film is hinting at something well beyond the proairetic impulse to show "what would have happened if . . ." The energies unleashed by the sinister German archeologist lead to an apocalyptic apotheosis in which the mystical tradition shines through the basic elements of the apparatus that is creating the cinematic illusion. Meanwhile, the erotic energies usually sublimated within such mystical crescendos are not here translated, as with DeMille, into the naked sexuality of burlesque strippers, but are rather displaced onto a more dignified iconographic matrix.

The erotic symbolism is initially mediated by the image of Indiana Jones and his partner Marion Ravenwood tied back to back to a stake against the backdrop of a cosmic fire. Spectators schooled in the classics might flashback to Renaissance lovers, both sacred and profane, also tied back-to-back on emblematic stakes. But popular culture has often resuscitated such iconography, from pop versions of the Petrarcan *Fire and Ice*, to comic strip Buffalo Bills and Calamity Jaynes burnt at the stake by bloodthirsty Indians, to Wendy and Peter Pan tied to the mast of Captain Hook's pirate ship as Big Chief Sitting Bull intones "Hana Mana Ganda," over the sealed casket with inaccessible treasure at his feet. Admittedly, my demented montage forms a scandalous pastiche of erroneous elements. But the point is that, quite apart from the fact that iconographic traditions do in fact evolve – rather like the broken telephone game – along the lines of dyslexic roller-coasters such as mine, they nevertheless continue to carry the associations of Once Upon a Time. Need I point to the inescapable puberty of Wendy Darling or to the continuity between her and Marion? Or even to the connection between both and Ariosto's

Sofronia? Whether classically schooled or not, it is hard to miss the abstract eroticism of Spielberg's fiery ejaculations, as they emerge from the tip of the volcano, penetrate through the soft opening in the clouds, then recede and, all energy spent, fall back into the hollow of the island.

Displacements of erotic mysticism aside, the Ark as cultural object is also a type of metonymy – container for the contained in this case – which encloses the kernel of the original sacred texts (I trust we paid attention at DeMille's Bible class). Yet this content, we discover in *Raiders of the Lost Ark*, has turned to dust. The Book as cultural object, therefore, appears on the screen in this version with redoubled presence precisely because of the discovery, upon opening the Ark, that it is gone. Of course, on one level, this objective absence is made up for by what pops out of the box. But the Spielberg sequence exemplifies a general tendency to trope the Bible; to substitute or displace the book with other objects. More mysterious and theoretically complex, for instance, is the case of the Jewish *tefilìn*, in evidence in the Aranofsky film. In a long scene, Max Cohen is instructed by his scholarly friend on how to bind them, before prayer, to the upper left arm, so as to place them nearest to the heart, and affix them to the forehead, so as to better remember what they contain – the fragments of a consecrated Bible. In other words, these small boxes are miniaturized versions of the Ark of the Temple. They thus form a cultural object that functions as a visual onomatopoeia; an objective displacement, moreover, that actually *contains* metonymies of the Bible.[16]

---

## Film Genres and Multicultural Accessibility

> The Bible is a book. It's a good book, but it is not the only book.
>
> Henry Drummond in *Inherit the Wind* (1960)

Within the context of films driven by strong genre rules (comedies such as *The Frisco Kid*, satanic thrillers such as *The Ninth Gate*), the Bible often acquires functional over-determinations and shades of meaning dictated less by content than by the symbolic and iconographic characteristics of the film genre in which the story is embedded. This allows filmmakers to compensate for the lack of a common and predictable canonical subtext in a multicultural and multi-faith society such as ours. Spectators informed about their own religious background may not know much about that of others. The specialized discourse-types of genre films can be used to translate for a broader audience meanings and implications created by the presence of the Bible as cultural object in the film.

The scene on Mount Sinai in Cecil B.DeMille's 1956 *The Ten Commandments* is more than just the adaptation of an episode from the Bible. Here we witness the actual "writing" of a segment of the Bible itself in a way that the biblical text does not provide. We are witnessing, in other words, a moment in the creation of the Bible in the most material sense of the word; something made possible only by the medium-specific features of cinematography. And when Moses breaks the tablets on which the Ten Commandments are carved, we are also looking at an image accessible to all. The immense importance and sacredness of the Commandments have just been underlined by the fiery finger carving them into the stone. That this is supernatural intervention is made clear, if only by the special effects endured by Moses on the mountain. The specific canonical meaning of the Commandments matters to the success of the sequence less than what is suggested about them. The juxtaposition of the tablets with the genre-specific orgy that unfolds at the foot of the mountain is also universally understandable as an index of sacrilege, even if the focus of attention is not, as in the Bible, on the fact that the people are now worshiping an idol.

This form of "translation," transposing elements of content into genre components, travels easily from genre to genre. In *History of the World, Part I* (Mel Brooks, 1981), the genre-specific comic effect is achieved through extensive knowledge of the Judeo-Christian tradition. In fact, the possibility that even those in the know may be wrong becomes the point of the joke. Clumsy Moses/Brooks, it turns out, drops and shatters ("*oy!*") one of the *three* tablets that had contained the original *Fifteen* Commandments. Even if the spectator does not remember the precise number of Commandments (nothing about them in Confucian or Buddhist texts or in the Native American tradition), the joke relies on the apparent arbitrariness: why ten indeed?

If the Ten Commandments, then why not the Seven Deadly Sins? In *Se7en* (David Fincher, 1995), genre-appropriate solutions respond to the fact that even many nominal Catholics cannot remember the specifics of all seven. The helpful police blackboard that lists them under the guise of clues, as in any other crime film, takes care of that. Cutting deeper still, Fincher addresses the fact that well-informed Catholics have come to regard the horrors of hell as metaphors, as abstractions.[17] It takes a psychotic killer, whose biblical obsession drives him to stage each one of the deadly sins as a gruesome charade, to bring back to concrete life what has long ago dropped into the deep recesses of the Christian imagination. John Doe's translation of the word into flesh, echoing as it does in its parodic exaggeration a tendency inherent in Catholicism in general, overflows the margins of the imaginable. His victims become literal personifications of the *contrapasso* they should receive for their deadly sins. While the translation is here undertaken by a character, as well as by the film-text itself, so much specialized cultural context is evoked that the police investigators have to run to the library and check out a pile of books ancillary to the Bible. This need for scholarship is not likely to alienate spectators in this film, as it might in others, since research into esoteric knowledge is part of the generic convention in complicated police investigations.

The film may at first appear to be merely sensationalistic. Yet ultimately it is a very intelligent attempt to screen the Bible as cultural object in a way that explores the narrative productivity of the Catholic notion of incarnation, while at the same time reactivating the effectiveness of tired genre tropes.[18] Fincher uses tropes deriving from conventional *horror* and similar genres (elements that have lost effectiveness because of repetition and overuse) yet manages to inject them with new energy by reifying a specific cultural discourse, which he also opens up into a broader cultural commentary. After opening with the typical moves of a genre film, *Se7ven* ends by implicating the spectator in ethical dilemmas that pit our most primitive emotions against principles still operative within everyday, secular life. Should spectators miss this as they flinch their way through the film's horrors, Fincher forces them to reflect on it. What happens at the end of this film is so extreme that we are moved to compromise our own better principles and go along with Brad's instinctive wish to kill John Doe right there and then. The resolution awakens fraught and contradictory emotions. Indeed, the alternative endings of *Se7en*, several filmed and/or storyboarded, bear witness to the difficult struggle of deciding between the primitive wish for retribution and the civilized principles of justice.

## Denominational Specificity

> Very well. Now, when a man collects books on a subject, they're usually grouped together, but notice, your King James Bible, your Book of Mormon, and Koran are separate, across the room in fact, from your Hebrew Bible and Talmud, which sit on your desk. Now these books have a special importance for you not connected with a general study of religion, obviously. The nine-branched candelabrum on your desk confirms my suspicion that you are of the Jewish faith; it is called a menorah, is it not?
>
> Sherlock Holmes in *The Seven-per-cent Solution* (1976)

The manner in which *Se7en* translates the textual tradition into bodies and objects is, as I have already pointed out, more typical of films set in Catholic than those in Protestant or Jewish environments. Films in Protestant settings, especially those about charismatic preachers in the Bible Belt, use the Bible as cultural object far more dramatically (even histrionically) than films set among Catholics and Jews. The Elmer Gantries in these films use Bibles as veritable theatrical props. But even when not burned, or waved around by a monkey, even when the films limit themselves to citing the actual words from the Bible, a Protestant context tends to elicit a more intensely expressive and melodramatic rendering of the text than is found in films set in other denominational milieux. Take, for instance, the overcharged elocution of Elmer Gantry, performed with an intensity worthy of Shakespearean tragedy, during the sermon that starts with a triple reiteration of the word "sin." The sermon even provokes a member of the congregation to break out into grotesque howling. In a Catholic context, on the other hand, even in a film as overblown and bizarre as *The Exorcist* (William Friedkin, 1973), even at the apex of the battle between sacred and profane, the recitation of the words designed to exorcise Satan is not as histrionic as the film's *mise-en-scène*. The actual Bible is barely present on screen, and the reading is anything but theatrical. And the reading of the Bible in films set in Jewish contexts features even less dramatic verbal flourishes, as can be seen in films such as *A Price Above Rubies* (Boaz Yakin, 1988) or *A Stranger Among Us* (Sidney Lumet, 1992).[19]

Both the voicing and the presence of the Book on screen are treated in denominationally specific ways. One of the early scenes in the Lumet film takes place in a Brooklyn synagogue, ending with the rabbi reading from the Torah scroll open on the *bimà*. One notes an effort to keep the view of this Bible just off the bottom of the screen. The camera floating at the edge of the visible paradoxically attracts attention. The hierarchy of Jewish texts places the Torah scroll above the regularly bound volumes used by the congregation. In terms of the Jewish religion, it is the scroll that constitutes the object closest to the true original Bible.[20] In fact, throughout *A Stranger Among Us*, other kinds of book and sacred objects appear on screen unimpeded. Among them a copy of the *Kabbalah* that the rebellious protagonist reads avidly, although men of his young age are not allowed to read it lest they be aroused by the mystical eroticism of some of the passages. Even more extensively, the central narrative in *Yentl* (Barbra Streisand, 1983) has to do with the protagonist's inability to so much as acquire the books she wants to read. Personal possession of the Bible and of associated sacred texts, not to mention who can use them and how, are matters secondary to the main plot in the Lumet film. Yet they drive the whole plot in Streisand's film. Much of the drama places the Bible as cultural object at the center of scenes; for example, the one in which Yentl tries to buy from the traveling salesman a book forbidden to her as a woman, or the moments depicting her transgressive evening blessing. In this light, the shots of Yentl caressing the spines of her father's religious books with evident yearning constitute an obscenity some may resist as firmly as the nakedness that movie cameras so often used to keep just beyond the frame. It is, in fact, the polemical spirit of the film that renders the riotous horsing around of the students in the Yeshiva's library such a powerful apotheosis of biblical volumes on screen.

## Conclusion

Stanley Cavell concludes his brief remarks about the question of "what becomes of things in film" by saying that the function of objects on screen is simply to represent themselves. Given this quality of cinema, much is often made in films of the simple physical presence of the Bible.[21] Its visibility, the angle from which it is filmed, whether it is new or old, illustrated or not – these and many other characteristics of the Bible generate meaning. If not the Bible itself, then objects deriving from the text, or standing in for it, often form the center of episodes and plot. Even when it is not the thematic center of a whole film or a sequence, the Bible is often intertwined with the cultural discourse present in films. The intertwining often goes unnoticed, or is simply taken for granted. Precisely because of its relative invisibility, one tends to discount the Bible's formative presence in many films.

But, given the cultural role of the Bible, the translation of textual elements raises special problems when this involves the expressive faculties of the body. Voicing the words, singing them, even dancing the Bible, in other words the somatic performance of the Bible, raises important issues especially in the context of cinematic representation. Similarly, the overwhelming presence of genres in cinema creates daunting yet productive challenges when directors have to deal with a book that, on the one hand, contains all genres and, on the other, is a genre unto itself. In films governed by strong genre rules, the Bible often acquires functional overdeterminations and shades of meaning dictated not so much by the specific details of its content, as by the symbolic and iconographic characteristics of the film genre in which it is embedded. In a multicultural society, one cannot count on a shared and predictable canonical subtext. The specialized discourse-types of genre films allow filmmakers to compensate for this lack of common knowledge. Genre elements in films can be used to translate meanings and implications that might otherwise be lost, created by the presence of the Bible as cultural object in the film.

The Bible, by virtue of its mere presence on screen, conveys a great deal, even in the absence of any overtly "biblical" narrative. Through its juxtaposition with plots, characters, and other screen objects, the Bible as cultural object renders accessible to a vast public – mostly secular – a cultural history and discursive repertoires closed off by current modes of thought, polarized as they are by secular and fundamentalist extremes. Filmed in this way, the Bible returns into circulation the multiple *kinds* of meaning that, thanks in no small part to the Bible and its cultural history, can be articulated within contemporary culture.

## Acknowledgments

This chapter is a partial overview of a book I am in the process of writing on the topic of the Bible as cultural object in cinema. See also my "La Bibbia nel cinema Americano contemporaneo," in Stefano Socci (ed.), *Il cinema e la Bibbia: atti del convegno internazionale (Genova 1999)* (Brescia: Morcelliana, 2001), pp. 97–116. And, floating in cyberspace, see also: www.biblia.org/pubblica.html and www.biblia.org/relacine.html.

## Notes

1   As *genre of discourse*, even the usual formulation can change in its details. Notably in films about the Nuremberg trials and trials devolving from war crimes committed during World War II, one notices the addition of the words "God the all-seeing and all-knowing" to the formula. Another significant element in these films is the matter of who is shown taking an oath and who is not. In *Judgment at Nuremberg* (Stanley Kramer, 1961) only the victims are shown swearing in. The recent TNT mini-series *Nuremberg* (Yves Simoneau, 2000) treats us to the spectacle of Goering taking the oath ("I swear by God the almighty and omniscient

that I will speak the pure truth and will withhold and add nothing.") Clearly such differences have more to do with a cultural evolution in dramatic practice than with the facts. Former Nazis were normally asked to take an oath when on the witness stand and when giving written depositions, and Eichmann as we know "swore by God to tell the truth" yet "refused to take the oath on the Bible;" Gideon Hausner, *Justice in Jerusalem: The Trial of Adolf Eichmann* (London: Thomas Nelson, 1967), p. 374. For the notion of "genres of discourse," see Christine Brooke-Rose, "Historical Genres/Theoretical Genres: A Discussion of Todorov on the Fantastic," *New Literary History* 8: 1 (1976), now in *Rhetoric of the Unreal* (Cambridge: Cambridge University Press, 1981); Tzvetan Todorov, *Introduction à la littérature fantastique* (Paris: Seuil, 1970); and Tzvetan Todorov, "The Origin of Genres," *New Literary History* 8: 1 (1976), now in Tzvetan Todorov, *Genres of Discourse* (Cambridge: Cambridge University Press, 1990). For a discussion of film theory as genre of discourse in literature, see Gavriel Moses, *The Nickel Was for the Movies: Film in the Novel Pirandello to Puig*, ch. 6 and passim (Berkeley, CA: University of California Press, 1995).

2   It does happen, for instance, when children, and others who are vulnerable, are the victims. Such is the case in an episode of *Law and Order* in which a mother who, albeit abused herself, had stood by and failed to protect her children from her husband's abuse. She is one of the rare witnesses shown taking the oath in the series (*Law and Order* 1: 9 "Indifference"). See also the episode entitled "Volunteers" (*Law and Order* 4: 2) in which a group of condo-vigilantes almost kill the mentally disturbed transient who lives in "their" downstairs alley. When questions arise about the victim's reliability in taking the oath, the man volunteers: "I am a very religious man, your Honor." "This is enough for me," concludes the judge.

3   Chris does this here, just as in another episode he calls the bluff of postmodern theory in the context of literary analysis. *Northern Exposure* 6: 17 "The Graduate."

4   The very real, if not always obvious, link between religious strife and racism is brought into focus by Bruce Lincoln's entry entitled "Conflict," pp. 55–69 in the recent methodological dictionary *Critical Terms for Religious Studies*, ed. Mark C. Taylor (Chicago: University of Chicago Press, 1998).

5   The unusual stress on the spiritual weight of the courtroom oath for Catholics is also present in *The Verdict* (Sidney Lumet, 1982). Here it is exploited by the lead lawyer, who is defending a Catholic hospital in a malpractice suit. Nurse Kaitlin Costello Price is brought in as surprise rebuttal witness, and her testimony undermines the plan to exonerate the defendants. So far in the trial there has been no Bible in sight, yet this time we get the whole ceremony. Subsequently, the defense lawyer (James Mason at his most slimy and most riveting) lays a carefully escalating and broadly histrionic guilt trip on the deeply religious nurse. He even tries to extend the reach of her innate fear of God by making a false analogy between a courtroom oath and the act of putting her initials on a hospital admissions form.

6   Recent films such as *Bad Lieutenant* (Abel Ferrara, 1992) should thus be seen in this light, for they are part of the long-standing American cultural tradition that does not presume moral fiber to be derived from ignorance about the nature of sin.

7   See R. Laurence Moore, *Selling God: American Religion in the Marketplace of Culture* (Oxford: Oxford University Press, 1994), pp. 14–15, 34–5, and 253–4. See also Paul C. Gutjahr, *An American Bible: A History of the Good Book in the United States, 1777–1880* (Stanford: Stanford University Press, 1999), and ch. 10 of Christopher de Hamel, *The Book: A History of the Bible* (London: Phaidon, 2001).

8   There are, indeed, also fiction films on the subject, such as *Paper Moon* (Bogdanovich, 1973). They do not capture, however, as fully as the Maysles Brothers film, the full range of the topic.

9   Most of the contemporary responses to the film failed to address this. The comments had to do, rather, with how and whether the film succeeds in being true to reality and/or whether this is even possible. John Simon, for instance, asked "is it unfair to the poor, decent fellows who happen to be selling Bibles instead of Fuller brushes, and are therefore pilloried as Pharisees?" John Simon, "A Variety of Hells," in Lewis Jacobs (ed.), *The Documentary Tradition* (New York: Hopkinson and Blake, 1971), p. 466.

10  Outrageous as their contagion theology sounds, and surely unbeknown to them, the salesmen come close to some of the views expressed in the nineteenth century by Henry Ward Beecher and others. Paul C. Gutjahr, in his discussion of Scottish common-sense philosophy, points out that the Bible "could be read as . . . an object whose mere presence infused its surroundings with a sense of the moral and the sacred, helping to make the home into an environment of moral nurture" (*An American Bible*, p. 47 and passim).

11  The practice of looking into the Bible for clues is used as the central organizing principle of a film such as John Ford's 1949 Western *3 Godfathers*.

12  "A secular society understands the religious mind less and less. It becomes more and more difficult in America to make belief believable, which is what the novelist has to do. It takes less and less belief acted upon to make one appear fanatic. When you create a character who believes vigorously in Christ, you have to explain his aberration." Flannery O'Connor, "The Catholic Novelist in the South," in *Collected Works* (New York: The Library of America), p. 857.

13  In a lighter vein, but still firmly anchored in the cultural context of the Gideon Bible, we may also remember Sister Sarah, the Salvation Army missionary in *Guys and Dolls* (Joseph L. Mankiewicz, 1955). She is surprised when she loses a bet to Sky the gambler, who turns out to be right about the source of a biblical citation displayed on one of her banners. Yet the contest winner explains to Sister Sarah that his knowledge derives from the fact that every motel in the country has a Gideon Bible. While waiting for the next card game, often a very long wait, he kills time by reading the omnipresent Book. One is led to ponder the quality and discernment of this knowledge: does Sky's knowledge, clearly of the agonistic kind that would lead to success on *Jeopardy*, make him into an exemplary Christian? And Sister Sarah? She seems to be worried less about a sinner's presumed ignorance of the Bible, than hurt in her self-righteous claim to authority; and wounded in her pride. In its odd genre-driven way, *Guys and Dolls* alludes to the necessary, and often forgotten, continuities between pulpit and street.

14  Very much in the same vein is *A Man Called Peter* (Henry Koster, 1955), a hagiographic biography of the Scottish minister, famed for his sermons, who rose to be chaplain to the US Senate. It provides us with a perhaps inadvertent, but not for that less significant, articulation of the issues inherent in the relationship between preacher and Bible.

15  For a recent description of the ark as cultural material object, see Ilana Pardes, *The Biography of Ancient Israel: National Narratives in the Bible* (Berkeley, CA: University of California Press, 2000), pp. 85–90.

16  In *The Apostle* we can actually witness the process of the Bible "releasing" some of the objects that it has generated in culture and cinema; objects that retain the full spiritual resonance of the Book from which they derive. These are the musical instruments that are invoked in Psalm 150, as those instruments that we should play when celebrating in the House of the Lord. As

Sonny Dewey reads them out, one by one, during the inauguration of his restored church building, he looks up and, gesturing to his parishioners, he seeks out those instruments in their hands. The transition from words on the page, to Sonny's gestural emphasis on the page as origin but also as limit, and to the discovery of real instruments in the hands of the faithful, occurs as a totally natural progression. This is not a "lesson" about the Bible in the world. It is a culturally internalized understanding of the productive translation into material culture of the words of the Bible. Similar in its discursive transition, but quite different in meaning, is the trumpet that appears in the hands of a congregant and is used to mock Elmer Gantry during the riot that leads to the fire that consumes the circus-like tent of his traveling religious show. As the latter instance demonstrates, the reifications of the biblical text, once launched into the world, pass easily into a parody of the source, not to speak of uses quite other than celebratory of the spirit of the Bible.

17  There still was a great deal of controversy (and perhaps regret?) when in 1999 the Pope made it known that, colorful and vivid as Dante may have been in his descriptions of hell, such things are not to be taken literally.

18  Another film that uses such subject matter (transubstantiation in this case), if in a different genre, is *The Wanderers* (Philip Kaufman, 1979). In the sequence in which the Polish street gang goes to church, the Duckie Boys' alienation from their community is vividly staged when, having taken communion, they proceed to chew with crackling ostentation the consecrated Host.

19  The exception to this may be found in musicals. See the overwrought singing and chanting in *The Jazz Singer* (Alan Crosland, 1927), or the singing of Barbra Streisand in *Yentl* (Barbra Streisand, 1983).

20  It is this fact that amplifies the horror, but also the interest, of what happens to the Bible scroll in the hands of a Jewish Nazi and his friends in the disturbing film *The Believer* (Henry Bean, 2001).

21  Stanley Cavell, "What Becomes of Things in Film?," in *Themes Out of School* (San Francisco: North Point Press, 1984), pp. 173–83. See also *Philosophy and Literature* 2: 2 (Fall 1978).

# Chapter 25

# All's Wells that Ends Wells

## Apocalypse and Empire in
## *The War of the Worlds*

## Julian Cornell

The waning moments of the nineteenth century were an auspicious time in European history. As the continent stood anxiously upon the precipice of a new epoch, momentous advances in the sciences were defining already a world yet to be born. In 1895, a young writer, Herbert George Wells fabricated his own wondrous machine, one that captivated the imagination of the reading public. With the publication of *The Time Machine*, the author, a biologist by training, issued a powerful rebuke to the optimistic view of technological progress precipitated by the scientific innovations of the fading century. A cautionary fable, Wells's novel was a bleak, allegorical rendering of an increasingly technological society, one whose future was already imperiled by growing class divisions and political ideologies which placed capital accumulation ahead of ethical considerations.[1] Two years later, Wells scripted *The War of the Worlds*, an equally powerful work that was just as adamant in its critique of British society as its predecessor. The novel envisions a malevolent Martian attack on Earth, during which the intergalactic aggressors lay waste to London before they succumb to a humble virus from which their extraterrestrial immune systems have no defense. An extremely rich and layered text, the narrative engages fears of a coming war on the continent and anxieties regarding technology unfettered by moral concerns, as it critiques both Social Darwinist and colonialist ideologies.

*The War of the Worlds* is, in Mike Davis's words, "Wells's great anti-imperialist allegory . . . which stood white supremacy on its head by depicting the English as helpless natives being colonized and slaughtered by technologically invincible Martians."[2] The story was serialized in 1897, the year of Queen Victoria's Diamond Jubilee, and its compelling allegorical critique of Britain's colonialist policies can be read against a rising tide of nationalist sentiment.[3] Wells's critique of this national mood is enacted through the figure of the merciless Martians who, as creatures of pure imagination, are multi-valent. In addition to allegorizing imperialism, the aliens have been said to narrativize fears of technology, (d)evolution, foreign invasion, colonization, and capitalism run amok.[4] While these purely textual monsters provide a powerful means through which Wells analyzes imperialism, they also produce a work whose semiotic openness and associative free play leaves the narrative readily available to appropriation.

As one of the most memorable creations in English literature, Wells's Martians spawned a seemingly infinite progeny, and served as the prototype for an impressive array of bug-eyed monsters in fiction and film. Until such films as *2001: A Space Odyssey* (1968), *Close Encounters of the Third Kind* (1977), and *E.T.: The Extraterrestrial* (1982), Wells's space creatures served as the primary model for science fiction treatments of alien encounters.[5] In a less positive vein, in the months following its stateside serialization, the story was bastardized by a number of American magazines and newspapers that fabricated strikingly similar tales of Martian destruction of American cities.[6] These "versions" typically deleted the parts of the story that were not action oriented, thus effacing the text's unnamed narrator's reflections on technology, evolution, and, crucially, what the Martians might "mean." The plagiarized renditions presage, in a sense, the book's adaptation to the cinema by privileging action and spectacle at the expense of social critique. However, in retaining the basic scenario and plot structure, the filmic adaptations, paradoxically, preserve Wells's rendering of his story in terms of the specific constellation of power relationships that inform the imperialist enterprise, though with often radically different emphases.

Despite the novel's uninterrupted popularity and prestige, the first adaptation, the 1938 Halloween CBS radio broadcast by Orson Welles and the Mercury Theater, did not appear until forty years after initial publication.[7] This famous (some might say infamous) retelling of Wells's tale followed the pattern established by the plagiarized renditions and denuded the narrative of much, if not all, of its political significance. The radio version was a virtuoso performance of audio technology. It presented the narrative in the form of broadcast interruptions, on the spot news reports, interviews with eyewitnesses, and other techniques familiar to listening audiences. Welles also made the crucial decision to relocate the story from Victorian England's near future to contemporary Depression Era New Jersey and New York City. Many of the pivotal characters of the novel were deleted and the first-person narrator was replaced by a complex multi-layered sonic narration. Despite the changes in characters, setting, and time frame, the radio version hewed closely to the original plot, following the narrative trajectory from initial extraterrestrial landing to resolution.

Furthermore, the radio drama replicated the stylistics of the novel. The book is an exemplary instance of Wells's technique; his intermingling of documentary-like detailed descriptions and far-fetched imaginings prompted his friend Joseph Conrad to label him a "realist of the Fantastic."[8] It is the interplay between the precise geographic delineation of actual locations, pseudo-scientific rumination, and often-lurid descriptions of bizarre intrusions into the peaceful, bourgeois idyll that gives the work much of its force.

The radio adaptation recapitulates this approach, pitting realism in the deployment of the medium's aural codes and conventions of reception, especially those of the newscast, against the fabulous in the portrayal of the Martians and their onslaught.

Beginning with its sole official cinematic appearance, the George Pal/Byron Haskin "faithful" 1953 adaptation, through the numerous B-movie alien invasions of the 1950s, to the 1996 "intertextual homage films" *Independence Day* and *Mars Attacks!*, on-screen versions of the novel have also consistently stressed the spectacle of domestic destruction over social critique. While the films typically have duplicated one of the great pleasures of the novel, the gripping spectacle of Martian conquest, they have rendered it as normative, downplaying or ignoring altogether Wells's ruminations on evolution, technology, power dynamics, and colonialism. This is not to suggest that these versions and adaptations have diverged completely from the source material. Indeed, many of the films based upon Wells's tale have articulated similar sets of xenophobic fear and technological foreboding. Cinematic versions have taken the cue from Wells's source material and lavished attention upon the invaders' grotesque, unearthly physiognomy, murderous designs, and alien technology. For instance, the Pal/Haskin version, with its Oscar-winning special effects directed by film pioneer Gordon Jennings, elegantly beautiful renderings of Martian spacecraft, complex and inventive soundscapes, and a visually stunning spectacle of terrestrial destruction, remains an exemplary instance of 1950s' Hollywood science fiction cinema on the strength of its shimmering Technicolor surface. However, in placing emphasis on these specific surface features of the story, its status as spectacle, the filmed versions have time and again appeared to favor empire building, rather than critique it. Nevertheless, by replicating or referencing Wells's narrative, these filmed texts often evince an ambivalent relationship to those structures of power that Wells interrogates.

Both the book and the 1953 filmed adaptation announce their greatly different intentions, and allegorical engagement with contemporary concerns, in their opening sections. Wells's critique of colonialism is sounded explicitly in the novel's powerful opening chapter. Regarding the Martians' imperial ambitions the first-person narrator comments:

> And before we judge of them too harshly we must remember what ruthless and utter destruction our own species has wrought, not only upon animals, such as the vanished bison and the dodo, but upon its inferior races. The Tasmanians, in spite of their human likeness, were entirely swept out of existence in a war of extermination waged by European immigrants, in the space of fifty years. Are we such apostles of mercy as to complain if the Martians warred in the same spirit? (I, 1)[9]

The text proclaims its status as allegory immediately, drawing explicit comparison between the narrative and the actual history of imperialist conquest and extermination. Positioning the reader along a continuum of power, with the Martians supplanting humans at the top of the chain, as well as drawing reference to, and deriving authority from, the natural world, Wells seeks to question the ideology of colonialism. Wells places England in the place of the indigenous Tasmanians and describes the Martians' view of humankind as analogous to "infusoria under the microscope" (I, 1). This is underscored by the narrator's assertion that if people thought of Mars before the invasion it was as a possible colony and "fancied there might be other men upon Mars, perhaps inferior to themselves and ready to welcome a missionary enterprise" (I, 1). Wells turns this Social Darwinist ethic on its head, reversing a supposed evolutionary hierarchy and forcing the bourgeois reader to confront the implications of imperialism based upon flawed, self-serving notions of evolution.[10]

Throughout the text, Wells expands upon these themes, attempting to undermine the reader's belief in the supremacy and invulnerability of the British war machine, by placing him or her in a position subordinate to its might.[11] The narrator's point of view, as expressed through his vivid recounting of his flight from the aliens' onslaught, is from the vantage point of the oppressed, of the colonized subject's helplessness before a technologically superior military force. Thus, *The War of the Worlds* is involved, through its spectacle of Martian bombardment, in examining the use and display of political power, specifically in relation to the formation, and perpetuation, of empire.

The prologue of the 1953 film also engages contemporary issues and, like the novel and the radio play before it, taps into a number of cultural anxieties regarding a coming conflict. After a black and white, Paramount logo, the intertitle "World War I" appears on screen followed by archival footage of troop, cavalry, and tank movements. Over these black and white images, an unseen "authoritative" announcer relates that, for the first time in human history, a conflict engulfed the entire globe, as nation warred against nation with the "crude weapons of those days." Another intertitle appears heralding the next conflagration, "World War II." In overheated newsreel style, the unseen voice recites that "men turned to science for new devices of warfare which reached an unparalleled peak in their capacity for destruction" as the audience observes warplanes, bombers and fighters, aircraft carriers and destroyers in combat. The prelude concludes with a long shot, a long take of an ICBM lifting off as the commentator grimly predicts: "And now, fought with the terrible weapons of super-science menacing all mankind and every creature on earth comes . . ." the final title card, in brilliant color, The *War of the Worlds*.

As with the novel, the introduction positions the film inside the lived history of prior conflict, providing an interpretative framework for the work of fiction to follow; unlike the novel, the film constructs an allegory of the future *in* the present as the phrase "and now" suggests. On a certain level, marshaling the archive in the service of the fictive provides the film with a measure of authority; in another sense, the change to vivid Technicolor spectacle after the credits seeks to validate its status as allegory. However, the film limits "conflict" to considerations of weaponry, rather than politics or colonialism, activating fears of atomic bombings. As such, rather than echoing the novel's critique of social institutions, government policies, and prevailing ideologies, the film text is engaged in anticipating the contours of the *next* battle, which for most Americans meant a seemingly inevitable nuclear war with the USSR; 1953, after all, was the year in which the Russians successfully tested their first hydrogen bomb.[12] With allegorical symmetry, Red Communist can be easily rendered as Red Planet and fears of invasion transferred from Bolsheviks to Martians.[13] The film is also an atomic bomb film text, "a vision of World War III" according to David Hughes and Harry Geduld,[14] with the seemingly indestructible extraterrestrial articulating fears of nuclear detonation, on the one hand, while the ultimately futile use of the bomb in the film problematizes the efficacy of such weapons. Rather than presenting a mindless reflection of Cold War propaganda, as Hughes and Geduld and many others have argued (a criticism often leveled at 1950s' science fiction), the film contains a muted critique of science and technology. While war itself may not be questioned, technology is figured as the locus of escalating terror, as the prologue suggests when it frames weaponry in terms of science rather than politics.

Changes in setting and time period also mark the divergences between film and source text. The filmmakers explicitly followed the precedent set by Welles and moved the story from England to present day Los Angeles.[15] Wells, who was angered by the liberties taken with the novel by the radio play, would probably have disapproved of transposing the story to present-day California.[16] Indeed, the author felt that Welles's changes diluted his original intentions. For example, in the novel, as far as the reader and narrator know, England is the only country that is invaded.[17] Limiting the scope of the conquest to Britain is crucial for the author's specific intent: to criticize Victorian bourgeois complacency and support of empire. In changing the locale, omitting crucial characters, and placing the story in the present day, Welles's adaptation downplayed the critique of empire and Social Darwinism, producing a tale that was more an articulation of native fears of a coming European conflict than a study of imperialism. Similarly, moving the principal place of action to the United States, and framing the story in terms of weaponry, allows the film to be rendered as Cold War atomic parable.

One essential alteration seldom noted by commentators is the temporal change. Wells's war takes place in an indeterminate near future, "early in the twentieth century" (I, 1),[18] aligning the text with *fin-de-siècle* cultural expression.[19] In a book lauded for its detailed descriptions of the geography of suburban London, it is curious that the author chose to remain vague about the time frame of his scenario. Like the radio broadcast before it, and the numerous films that would follow it, the Pal/Haskin version places the action in the present day. Wells's narrator relates his version of events from an uncertain point in the future, in a flashback, when the cataclysm is past, England has learned its evolutionary destiny, and witnessed imperialism in action. As Frank McConnell argues, the "Martians represent not just an invasion from space, but an invasion from time, from the future of man himself."[20] By transporting his bloodthirsty agents of our hypothetical future into the bourgeois present, Wells seeks to confront the reader with the political implications of empire building.[21] The ambiguous use of temporality, of time *as* place, leaves the reader with the sense that the future is still undecided, still open to reorientation and reinterpretation. In the film version and its progeny, the Martians do not typically represent our pre-ordained future but imagine an Other in our present who needs to be vanquished in order to affirm "our" values.

The Pal/Haskin film and the Wells novel both draw explicit reference to a literary mode in which their audiences would have been well versed: the apocalyptic. In both texts, the use of the apocalyptic literary genre can be understood in political terms. In *The Sense of an Ending,* Frank Kermode has argued that one of the essential types of the Western apocalyptic literary imagination is "empire." Oppression by the forces of imperialism was frequently the motivation for the prophets' issuance of their doomsday proclamations; thus, the apocalyptic was formed in opposition to empire, as a reaction to its articulations of knowledge and power. The mode "empire" was a form of protest literature that expresses a revenge fantasy against the conqueror by the disenfranchised.[22] Consequently, the spectacle of destruction, the utter decimation of one's persecutors, and the survival of the elect accounted for much of the pleasure of the genre. Furthermore, since the apocalyptic renders history as allegory – the past, present, or future is configured as a series of signs, rather than political events – it demands an active decoding on the part of the reader or audience. The intermingling of history and symbolism is integral to the apocalyptic narrative; indeed, it is constitutive of it and serves to legitimize it. Pleasure is also located in the reader/audience's ability to interpret the narrative, to read their beliefs into history and find the truth of the material world, of the visible, to see allegory as history and history as allegory.[23]

Apocalyptic narrative is often about the exercise of power, about the relationship between structures of domination and control, particularly as embodied in the institutions of military, church, and government. The apocalyptic is located not only in the plot, in the (super)natural cataclysm or spectacle of destruction and rebirth, but in the manner in which it depicts power relationships between these institutions which it often figures in terms of radical Otherness. *The War of the Worlds* addresses these aspects of the apocalyptic form, emerging as an extended meditation on the dynamic and deployment of political power, how it is created and nurtured by technological means. Ultimately, it is Wells's call for the "commonweal of mankind" (II, 10) in the epilogue that aligns his work with the millennial tendency of the apocalyptic, with the desire to avert cataclysm by creating a better world here on earth. However, since the apocalyptic mode is so heavily dependent upon allegorized spectacles of empire, upon visuality and the representation of destruction, displays of cataclysm can impart the sign with an excess of meaning that threatens to overwhelm the social critique.

Wells's story can also be read intertextually against another class of the apocalyptic tale of empire: the imaginary war genre. The fantastic popularity of the future military conflagration narrative was inaugurated with the publication of Sir George Chesney's *The Battle of Dorking* in 1871. Written in the immediate aftermath of the brutal Franco-Prussian War, Chesney's novella of an England pillaged and decimated by a ruthless, efficient, and technologically superior German military spawned a legion of imitators.[24] For Chesney, a former army officer who had served in India, the story was a warning to English society regarding the expansionist designs of Prussian chancellor Otto von Bismarck and the imperialist ambitions of other European states.[25] For the next four decades, the British pulp press issued innumerable retellings of Chesney's novella, in which a militarily unprepared England is ambushed by a deceitful foreign country, normally France or Germany, and forced to fend off massive land and sea invasions which result in humiliating defeat and the massacre of civilians.[26] Both the basic scenario of *The War of the Worlds* and its dramatic vision of London's ruin draw overt intertextual reference to *The Battle of Dorking* and the future war tale. To a British public well versed in the formal codes of the genre, according to McConnell, and for readers who were especially familiar with the depiction of fearsome, futuristic military technologies, Wells's allusion would have been readily apparent.[27]

The fears articulated by imaginary war literature can be seen as a by-product of guilt feelings engendered by Britain's own colonialist foreign policy.[28] At the same time, it is possible to apprehend these tales as being justifications *for* imperialism and military expansionism. On an elementary level, to heed Chesney's "warning" is to see empire as the solution to economic and political differences, to understand history in Social Darwinist terms: as a terminal struggle between states for scarce resources. To see oneself as the victim of colonialism when one is, in fact, an imperialist, is to justify one's reading of history, of one's own apocalyptic allegory regardless of whether one's narrative is sanctioned by nature or divinity, and to see conflict between empires as the natural order of things.

In another sense, *The Battle of Dorking* goes deeper, to the heart of the apocalyptic, to the complex relationship of imperialism to Otherness, and to the issue of appropriation of the mode of empire for purposes of legitimization rather than resistance. It marks the point at which empire becomes what we might term, following Kermode, "colonial," where the oppressor assumes the position of the oppressed. The dependence of the apocalyptic narrative on signs, and its allegorical re-envisioning of history, renders it indeterminate, available to support as well as critique empire. In the apocalyptic the enemy is, unsurprisingly, seen as Other, but in the allegorical sign system, the oppressor becomes *radically* Other, transformed from impersonal political entity and power structure into existential, supernatural signifier.

Wells's great innovation is to play with the conventions of the genre to reconfigure the future war tale. By having his invaders be radically Other, rather than familiar Other, such as German or French, Wells's inversion calls attention to the process of Other-ing and to the point at which the Other becomes recognizable *as* oneself. In the Martians, Wells takes the radical Otherness of the apocalyptic imaginary battle to a fanciful extreme, to the point at which the signifiers of difference break down. Wells envisions a dramatic spectacle of the exercise of power by a seemingly invulnerable enemy who is at once completely unlike, and exactly the same as, imperial England. When the narrator is first confronted by the Martians, he describes a creature whose resemblance to humanoids is tangential and can only be expressed through analogy to human features.

> Two large dark-colored eyes were regarding me steadfastly. The mass that framed them, the head of the thing, was rounded, and had, one might say, a face. There was a mouth under the eyes, the lipless brim of which quivered and panted, and dropped saliva. The whole creature heaved and pulsated convulsively. A lank tentacular appendage gripped the edge of the cylinder, another swayed in the air.

> Those who have never seen a living Martian can scarcely imagine the strange horror of its appearance. The peculiar V-shaped mouth with its pointed upper lip, the absence of brow ridges, the absence of a chin beneath the wedgelike lower lip, the incessant quivering of this mouth, the Gorgon groups of tentacles, the tumultuous breathing of the lungs in a strange atmosphere, the evident heaviness and painfulness of movement due to the greater gravitational energy of the earth — above all, the extraordinary intensity of the immense eyes — were at once vital, intense, inhuman, crippled and monstrous. (I, 4)

Later, the narrator speculates that these creatures which seem so radically Other from humans are actually our evolutionary destiny: "To me it is quite credible that the Martians may be descended from beings not unlike ourselves," their lack of emotion the consequence of their over-evolved intellects and shriveled bodies (II, 2).[29]

Wells does not present a simple tale of conflict between two species competing for scarce resources, since, as McConnell has suggested, "the Martians are not, after all, aliens. They are ourselves, mutated beyond sympathy, though not beyond recognition."[30] This configuration attempts to destabilize the notion of evolution as having culminated in the ascent of man to the acme of the evolutionary chain. It is the bacteria, the infusoria, the "humblest of things" (II, 8) who ultimately defeat the mightiest, the Martians. By depicting Martians as likely descended from humans, and placing their defeat at the hands of humanity's ancestral forebears, Wells counters the naturalization of power relationships that formed the basis of Social Darwinism. Establishing this evolutionary continuum also allows the author to figure Otherness as the interplay of radical similarity and difference, the effect of which is to profoundly decenter the imperial subject.

In both film and novel, the engagement with power structures underlying the apocalyptic empire narrative is depicted through the reactions to the Martian invasion of the characters who can be said to represent the institutions of state, church, and military. In the novel, these competing, often conflicting, voices pose responses not just to Social Darwinism and empire but to their function as stabilizing worldviews. Thus, both book and film are little concerned with psychology and, instead, use paradigmatic figures to allegorize institutional structures, character types who become part of the text's allegorical sign system. This holds true even in the film where granting proper names to the characters reduces their anonymity and makes it easier for the audience to identify with them.

In the novel, the character who evinces the greatest inability to come to terms with the Martian conquest is the curate. The cleric is painted as a self-serving coward who slowly loses his grip on his sanity, becoming a danger to his and the narrator's well-being. Before he is killed by the narrator, when his screaming and gesticulating threatens to attract the attention of the Martians, he constantly complains, selfishly consumes more than his share of their meager rations, and struggles with the narrator over the small portal through which they are able to observe the machinations of the invaders. The curate's interpretation of the war is derived from apocalyptic scripture. Almost immediately after meeting the narrator, the curate wonders aloud about the symbolic aspects of the attack saying, "What do these things mean?" (I, 13). As the narrator attempts to plan their next move, the cleric descends into a fatalistic apocalyptic understanding of the conflict: "'This must be the beginning of the end,' he said, interrupting me. 'The end! The great and terrible day of the Lord! When men shall call upon the mountains and the rocks to fall upon them and hide them – hide them from the face of Him that sitteth upon the throne!'" (I, 13). The curate pays little heed to the narrator's rational attempts to explain what he has seen and his conjecture about the Martians, their vulnerability and their intentions. Exasperated, the narrator exclaims: "What good is religion if it collapses under calamity? Think of what earthquakes and floods, wars and volcanoes, have done before to men! Did you think God had exempted Weybridge? He is not an insurance agent" (I, 13). The curate refuses the narrator's attempts at reason and explanation, referring to the Martians as "God's ministers," seeing them as agents of heaven's apocalyptic intention, and misreading the signs of empire as expressions of divine will.

Through his attempt to interpret the Martian assault in the light of a pre-existing ideological and totalizing framework, the curate refuses to evolve and adapt to new, catastrophic circumstances. His quest for meaning, the attempt to understand the invasion as an extension of an established worldview, is a doomed attempt at keeping central his subjectivity. This attempt, to narrate the Martians as a projection of one's subjectivity, reflects the curate's fatal desire to see the marauders as Other. Since the invasion has decentered the white male subject, the curate's attempt cannot hold; there is little left for him but to go mad. Wells depicts the apocalyptic reading of history as being inadequate for dealing with "real" cataclysm; the institution of religion is viewed by the text as wanting when confronted with the moral issues raised by empire and Social Darwinism.

Perhaps the most critical change in the re-envisioned power structure of the film occurs in its depiction of religion. Pastor Collins (Lewis Martin) presents a religious personage who is the diametrically opposite of the curate. In fact, the film's affirmative view of Christianity represents its greatest divergence from the source novel. While the military prepares to engage the Martians following their obliteration of the three sheriff's deputies, Collins quietly attempts to intercede on the aliens' behalf. He tells his niece that since the Martians are superior to humans, they must also be closer to God. The compassionate cleric approaches the Martians, crucifix emblazoned Bible held high, and recites Psalm 23. In response to his display of goodwill, faith, and plea for cross-cultural understanding the Martians incinerate him. As Hughes and Geduld note, while this scene highlights the Martians' cruelty, it also positions them as virulently anti-Christian.[31] Interestingly, his failure also leads to the rout of the military: in response to Collins's murder, General Mann (Les Tremayne) gives the order to fire, with the result being the army's defeat. If the Martians are allegorical Russians, then, this scene further underscores the supposed malevolence of Godless Communists. The film is not completely uncritical of Collins, however.[32] When he decides to approach the Martians, his eyes are wide, making him appear insane. His action leaves Sylvia (Anne Robinson) without a figurative father; he is viewed as having abandoned her. The reactions of Mann, the colonel and Dr Forrester (Gene Barry) to his attempt at diplomacy depict him as misguided at the least, his actions completely inappropriate for the situation.

Another marked divergence between novel and film lies in its portrayal of the military. We first meet the novel's soldier, the artilleryman, as he wanders into the narrator's garden looking for temporary shelter from the Martians' deadly laser-like Heat Ray (I, 11). Toward the end of the novel, when the narrator and military man meet again, the soldier repeatedly exclaims that humanity has been routed. "This isn't a war," he argues, "It never was a war, any more than there's war between man and ants" (II, 7). With a degree of spite he remarks, "Cities, nations, civilization, progress – it's all over. That game's up. We're beat" (II, 7). As he converses further with the narrator, it becomes clear that he is partaking of an apocalyptic rhetoric not entirely dissimilar from the type expressed by the curate. In barely concealed glee, he says:

> There won't be any more blessed concerts for a million years or so; there won't be any Royal Academy of Arts, and no nice little feeds at restaurants. If it's amusement you're after, I reckon the game is up. If you've got any drawing-room manners or a dislike to eating peas with a knife or dropping aitches, you'd better chuck 'em away. They ain't no further use. (II, 7)

The artilleryman's class-based resentment voices the desirability of destruction that is constituent of the apocalyptic. Unlike the fatalism of the curate, the soldier's apocalyptic imagining sees the attack as an opportunity to purify and reinvent society. As he imagines a resistance movement against the colonizers, he says, "we form a band – able-bodied, clean-minded men. We're not going to pick up any rubbish that drifts in. Weaklings go out again." Furthermore, he espouses a blunt survival-of-the-fittest ideology that jells with Social Darwinist thinking.

> Able-bodied, clean-minded women we want also – mothers and teachers. No lackadaisical ladies – no blasted rolling eyes. We can't have any weak or silly. Life is real again, and the useless and cumbersome and mischievous have to die. They ought to die. They ought to be willing to die. It's a sort of disloyalty, after all, to live and taint the race. (II, 7)

Initially, the soldier's invigorating vision of humanity re-emerging triumphant sways the narrator. He soon learns that the apocalyptic artilleryman is as ineffectual as the curate. The soldier's plan is mere talk; he is interested only in gluttony, self-aggrandizement, and scheming. As McConnell argues, the artilleryman's plan is "a selfish and a self-defeating plan, a revolutionary philosophy not for the sake of the survival of the species, but rather for the sake of the survival of class hatred and class warfare."[33]

Furthermore, while the soldier's imaginings are exhilarating and evocative, they are ultimately viewed by Wells as an oversimplification of evolutionary theory and fascist in their intent. As John Huntington notes, the artilleryman's rhetoric pales in contrast to the narrator's ruminations in the first book of the novel. Time and again, the narrator draws unfavorable comparisons between the Martian invasion and imperialist destruction of animals and indigenous populations, leading the reader to be skeptical of the indiscriminate use of Darwin's theories.[34] To live by a simplistic evolutionary ethos, such as the artilleryman's, is to mimic the Martians uncritically, to project one's centered subjectivity upon natural processes in order to justify a reactionary reorganization of society. The artilleryman views the Martians as wholly Other, failing to recognize their similarity to imperial Britain; thus, his response is not a radical divergence from the curate's. Instead, this figure allegorizes another institution of the state, the military, and demonstrates the apocalyptic underpinnings of its worldview that have contributed to the spread of empire.

In the film, Wells's brusque artilleryman is replaced by the admirable, if beleaguered, General Mann, who leads a military that provides a great deal more, though ultimately futile, resistance to the invaders than their literary counterparts. Indeed, the military is presented as benign. An interlude halfway though the film shows the effects of the conflagration on the far-flung corners of the globe and lauds the brave militaries of the world in their futile struggle against the conquerors. Archival scenes of, we are told, Indian, Turkish, Chinese, Finnish, and Bolivian armies are superimposed against images of Martian spacecraft and Heat Rays. Though these combatants fail to halt the invasion, their efforts are heroic.

The reports of the experiences of the narrator's brother present a different way of allegorizing social institutions and power relationships under duress. The narrator's brother bears witness to the breakdown of another pillar of civilization: the government. In the fourteenth to seventeenth chapters of Book One, Wells suddenly shifts from a first-person account to the third, from the thoughtful, if frightened narrator, to a detached, if frenetic, account. This movement produces a credible witness who is not only not implicated in the dissolution of the state, but is symbolic of the heroic potential of the unassuming, ethically minded citizen.[35] In the brother's escape from London under siege, Wells paints an indelible, vivid picture of society in chaos.

> By three, people were being trampled and crushed even in Bishopsgate Street, a couple of hundred yards or more from Liverpool Street station; revolvers were fired, people stabbed, and the policemen who had been sent to direct the traffic, exhausted and infuriated, were breaking the heads of the people they were called out to protect. (I, 16)

In the frantic exodus from the city, the brother also witnesses the death of the Chief Justice, innumerable fights between refugees, Londoners murdered by their fellow citizens, trampled by horses, and all manner of uncivilized behavior. It is a memorable vision of apocalypse, a scene of undeniable power that would be endlessly repeated in screen and literary adaptations of Wells's novel. The brother, however, retains his dignity, as he helps two women, strangers to him, escape first from assault by cowardly gentlemen and then from the country. Against the collapse of the state, Wells poses the "institution" of the common man through the figure of the brother; the brother's character attempts to balance the class hatred of the artilleryman with that of the anonymous citizen willing to help his fellows.

Importantly, the brother is also present for a military confrontation that represents a morally desirable contrast to the artilleryman's philosophy. In the *Thunder Child* episode, which concludes the first book, the brother sees a selfless act, a suicide mission, in which the ironclad ship sacrifices itself to fell two of the Martian war machines (I, 17). Thomas Renzi has argued that the emphasis on anonymity in the brother's narrative, and in the actions of the *Thunder Child*, privileges collective action over individual effort and humanity over a single heroic male or group.[36] Here Wells's tale reflects, rather than rebukes, the apocalyptic narrative in its emphasis on collectivity, rather than individuality. This seems to suggest the collective salvation posed by the apocalyptic narrative. However, by refusing closure, and declining to sanctify an elect for salvation, the novel resists simple apocalypticism. While one can identify the same concerns of the apocalyptic scripture and its deployment of the institutions of church, state, and military, Wells locates power not in these structures, or in divinity, but in the common man and the collective, and, thus, not the forces that support empire.

The interlude in the middle of the film parallels the *Thunder Child* episode but with different emphasis.[37] In this segment, a voice-over by noted British actor Sir Cedric Hardwicke serves to provide a similarly enlarged picture of the invasion. Like the *Thunder Child*, the world's armies fight the good fight though their efforts have little impact on the marauders. During the commentary, the film emphasizes the comparison by directly quoting Wells. Hardwicke intones "It was the beginning of the rout of civilization, of the massacre of humanity."[38] In addition to the military movements, the Martians are shown creating a refugee panic, which also echoes the paragraph from which this preceding quotation was extracted. Stock footage of World War II again draws continuity between that conflict and the nuclear conflagration prophesied by pundits and politicians at home. The curious statement that the Martians "appreciated the strategic significance of the British Isles" and the assertion that "the people of Britain met the invaders magnificently" conjures images of World War II and the Battle of Britain, while alluding to the source text. At the same time, the voice-over decisively excludes the Soviet bloc in its list of countries combating the Martians and states "a great silence fell over half of Europe," alluding to the Russian hegemony over Eastern Europe. Taken together, this narrative trajectory extends the analogy of Martians through Nazis to Soviets, providing an historical framework for interpreting the film: the coming conflict will be like World War II, only more so. In this manner, the film anticipates *Independence Day* and countless other future combat films; just as Chesney's *The Battle of Dorking* refought the Franco-Prussian War, the film of *The War of the Worlds* recapitulates World War II. Furthermore, the overall effect of the film's three Hardwicke voice-over segments is to move the narrative away from the interpretative template of historical reality that it has established and into the realm of metaphysical morality play; that is, into the apocalyptic.

Governments take a larger, more active role in the film than in the novel. The interlude makes a point of showing governments intact and functioning as they attempt to beat back the invasion, in contrast to Wells's picture of social disintegration. The audience watches the Indian cabinet meet in a railway car, French ministers gather in Switzerland, the British Parliament remains in session despite the obliteration of London. The sequence ends with a shot of an untouched Capitol Building. When Mann explains the situation to city officials, they assure him that an evacuation of Los Angeles is planned, feasible, and in their capable hands. Learning of the Martians' military strategy, the Secretary of Defense calmly gives the order to use the atomic bomb. The very institutions Wells criticized are depicted as rational, benevolent, and in control, even though they are ultimately inadequate to halt the conquest. However, inadequacy is quite another thing from actively nurturing and supporting empire. Unlike the curate and the artilleryman, or the municipal government of London, the representations of the central power structures of the apocalyptic narrative are absolved of blame for creating empire.

The film adds a fourth term to this configuration: the scientist. When the nuclear assault on the aliens fails, Mann tells Forrester that hope for humanity rests in the hands of the scientist and his colleagues. In a sense, the scientific community becomes an arm of the military in the attempt to develop an even more powerful super-weapon, a move that tacitly supports the arms race. Unlike the institutions of government, religion, and military, the scientists – Forrester and his colleagues at Pacific Tech – do not even get a chance to engage the enemy: a mob hijacks their buses and destroys their equipment before they can conduct their research. The film limits representations of science to explanation of the Martians, and critically, to the atomic bomb itself. As noted, the film is ambivalent about science and implicates it in creating the atmosphere of native paranoia, again eliding the role of political process.

Forrester functions similarly to Pierson, Orson Welles's Princeton scientist, to replace the narrator and facilitate both the narrative movement, from invasion to resolution, and audience identification. In the novel, the narrator is a professor of philosophy, a man of metaphysics rather than physics. The interplay between his geographically detailed "realistic" account of the Martian invasion, his bearing witness to their plans and weaponry, and his theorizing about what the Martians mean positions him at a distance from the apocalyptic narratives of the curate and the artilleryman, and empire. He interprets the Martians scientifically, rationally, allowing the reader to comprehend them both politically and allegorically. His recourse to reason also positions him as removed from the institutions of power, which, as we have seen, present little in the way of viable solutions to the problem posed by the Martians, and with the collective posited by the brother. His refusal to view the Martians as completely Other, but as embodying similarity and difference, allows him to resist apocalyptic interpretation. There is no apocalypse for the narrator or his brother. These characters mark a refusal of the apocalypse of empire, rather than the embrace suggested by the curate and the artilleryman.

In the film, Dr Clayton Forrester,[39] is a celebrated "astro and nuclear" physicist rather than an anonymous philosopher. Forrester has graced the cover of *Time* magazine and invented an "atomic engine"(!) and is sufficiently famous to be recognized by the media, civilians, and the military without introduction. Echoing the narrator's theories about Martian anatomy, Forrester appears on the radio to present the film's only depiction of Wells's central concern with evolution: he guesses that the aliens, due to "precedent in our own evolution" may have more than one brain. Unlike Wells's narrator who has had first-hand empirical observation and six years to reflect upon the invasion, Forrester's hypothesis is "only speculation" since it precedes his physical encounter with the Martians. Forrester further serves a narrator function, as he is able to explain the Martians' technology.[40] Coupled with his capacity as interpreter and source of knowledge, it is also through his eyes that we experience the mass panic and horrifying destruction of Los Angeles as he races through Martian-demolished streets in search of Sylvia. In providing the reader's means for understanding the attackers, Forrester's role is analogous to that of the narrator. Unlike Wells's philosopher, a passive observer struggling to stay alive, Forrester is an active participant, motivating narrative action: he calls in the military, assesses the invaders' technology and capabilities, works with his colleagues to understand the enemy, romances an admirer, and searches for his love in the film's emotional climax.

The critical difference lies in what he does *not* do. Unlike the narrator, Forrester provides no evaluation of what the invasion *means*, either narratively or allegorically, and fails to consider the Martians' connection to human history. They remain different from the humans, for that is Forrester's understanding of them. In omitting this key function for the "hero," the film's narrative declines to consider the Martians' ultimate similarity to us, and keeps the aliens positioned as Other, as agent of tribulation. In addition, the scientists and military men spend little time trying to ascertain what the Martians want, or what they mean. Indeed, their speculation revolves solely around the military capabilities of the Martians' weaponry. Thus, the film reverts to the external threat mode and attempts to disavow Wells's view of internal power dynamics as engendering an external threat. In this Cold War allegory, the threat is thoroughly Other and alien.

Indeed, the substantial changes from the source material that coalesce around the Martians highlight the differing treatments of Otherness in film and novel. Instead of Wells's anthropomorphic tripods and cyborgs, the film's Martians rain death upon the entire planet via their beautiful flying machines. The Heat Ray and Black Smoke are replaced by laser beams that cut a wide swath of devastation across their paths. Where Wells's Martians are briefly deterred by some fortunate cannon blasts and the defiant *Thunder Child*, the film's conquerors' electromagnetic "protective blisters" render them impervious to all military strikes. The film also excludes some of the horrific aspects of the Martians, principally their means of feeding themselves, through a form of vampirism through intravenous ingestion of human blood, and the suggestion that they intend to enslave humanity. Removing these details certainly lessens one's ability to read the Martians as an allegory of capitalism and colonialism.[41]

Instead of the "heads – merely heads" (II, 2), the film's sole glimpse of a Martian is, as Renzi describes it, as a small lumbering creature whose "head looks like a large misshapen potato, lumpy, flat, and horizontally elongated" with "pink skin, long spindly arms and three fingers like jointed knitting needles tipped with suction cups."[42] The film's Martians are more like mutated octopuses than highly evolved brains, more evolutionary dead-end than future for humanoids. Furthermore, the sole "close encounter" with a Martian casts their species as Other in a more conventional manner than the book. Perhaps inevitably for a Hollywood production with a substantial budget,[43] the filmmakers added a pivotal, action-motivating love story. The romance between Sylvia and Forrester moves along a predictable, "coupling" trajectory, but, at the same time, Sylvia can be said to replace the narrator's brother as the second witness to the destruction. Her presence in the narrative plays a critical role in the film's "wrecked house" scene, which mirrors the imprisonment of the narrator and curate under similar circumstances. As the couple enjoys a respite from the chaos, and Sylvia reminisces about her childhood with Collins, a momentary idyll of a happy bourgeois home is afforded to the protagonists. This normative coupling is violently interrupted by the crash of a Martian cylinder into the house. When we finally receive a glimpse of a flesh-and-blood Martian, it is reaching for Sylvia, attempting to capture the heroine. It would seem that the enemy is interested in possessing the blonde woman in addition to destroying the planet; instead of vampirism, the film gives us an implicit threat of miscegenation. The alien can be read, in this instance, as trying to usurp Forrester's rightful place as husband to Sylvia. Changing the aliens' intentions restates the colonizer's fear that the oppressed will desire "their women," a projection of the imperialist's sexual fantasies onto the Other. The physicality of the Martians, their sexualized desire, and the film's lack of theorizing of their evolutionary heritage renders their Otherness as Otherness, omitting the play of similarity and difference that is central to Wells's tale.

Another readily apparent change from the novel is the absence of a first-person narrator. In fact, the narrator function is split between Forrester and two unseen commentators. The film's three Hardwicke segments and near direct quotations of Wells's narrator's words remain in these framing devices, which begin and end the narrative proper. A sentence from the novel also appears in the interlude in the middle of the film. Where the source material alternates between first- and third-person narration in the brother's episode, the film can be said to engage in a similar process in the commentary segments through the alternation between Hardwicke and Forrester. On another level, the wrecked house scene features a complementary, more cinematic, version of the same dialectic movement. Here Sylvia and/or Forrester's subjective points of view of the Martians' movements and the searching eye of the alien probe can be said to engage in an interplay of first and third person that is a feature of the book.

Following the main title sequence, Hardwicke's first segment paraphrases Wells's opening paragraphs. Hardwicke intones: "No one would have believed in the middle of the twentieth century that human affairs were being watched keenly and closely by intelligences greater than man's. Yet across the gulf of space, on the planet Mars intellects vast and cool and unsympathetic, regarded our earth with envious eyes, slowly and surely drawing their plans against us."[44] Thus, the film omits Wells's comparisons between the Martians' activities and humanity's view of the animal kingdom, the prior view of Mars as a possible colony for earthlings, as well as the human race's blissful ignorance of the oncoming tempest. It also deletes the critical concluding sentence of the first paragraph, the one that places the decentering of hegemonic subjectivity squarely at the center of the narrative: "And early in the twentieth century came the great disillusionment" (I, 1). Like the novel, this is followed by a description of a dying red planet, providing a motivation for the Martian conquest. Where Wells proceeds to engage in some scientific speculation regarding the implacable Second Law of Thermodynamics and its role in the enervation of Mars, the film discusses the composition of the other planets of the solar system and their inability to support human or Martian life. A series of stunning matte paintings illustrates each planet (except, inexplicably, Venus) and its unsuitability as a colony for the Martians. Not surprisingly, Wells's narrator's caution about judging the Martians harshly for their colonial designs is elided. The film's Martians remain allegorical colonizers from the red planet, which erases the insinuation that they are "us" and keeps them in a position of being totally Other. The science lesson about the solar system mirrors the prologue with its intimations of authenticity and veracity, and while this seems to reflect Wells's interplay of science and fiction, the film's mode of "edification" does not contain the narrator's sociological digressions into the meaning of colonization. Again, this serves to diffuse the colonial allegory, but does not remove it from the realm of the apocalyptic.

Ultimately, the film does not unequivocally support the three-part structure of apocalyptic narrative. All the pillars of Western might and supremacy – religion, military, government, and science – are given their successive chance to engage and defeat the enemy. All fail. Thus, the film is not the simple travesty of the novel that its critics maintain. As the film's final scene and prologue suggest, there is a subtle critique of military science that is muted but still available. It is not the military or science that will forestall a Russian invasion, but something else entirely. As Hughes and Geduld note, "by implication, if America (and the rest of the world) is to be saved it must be through some ever-greater (i.e. 'Higher') power."[45]

The apocalyptic is clearly and succinctly reinforced by the emotional conclusion. The film's final scene, though it utilizes the same plot device as the novel, a literal *deus ex machina*, if you will, is only tangentially related to the intentions of Wells's novel. After the scientists have failed to provide a weapon to combat the invaders, the Martians begin their final assault on Los Angeles. Separated from his love, Forrester journeys from one church to another looking for Sylvia. Assembled in each house of worship are groups of citizens who have been unable to escape. As Martian lasers incinerate the city, and congregations pray for salvation, Sylvia and Forrester share an emotional reunion. Moments later, a Martian war bird collapses to the ground in the street outside the church. Forrester examines the ship's pilot and finds it deceased, killed by a microscopic virus. "We were all praying for a miracle," says Forrester, one that God has provided. When all of humanity's technological knowledge and military might have proved insufficient to stop the invasion, divine intervention saves the species. Hardwicke delivers a rendering of Wells's original text: "After all that men could do had failed, the Martians were destroyed and humanity was saved by the littlest things which God, in his wisdom, had put upon this Earth."[46] The final shot of the film is a church overlooking Los Angeles, set against a background of choral music and singers intoning "Amen." Significantly, the film's denouement places the death of the Martians in the final frames, pre-empting Wells's bleak and poignant coda, suggesting a hopeful, transcendent, that is to say, apocalyptic, ending that Wells's powerful Dead London chapter strenuously assails. The microbes that fell the Martians in the book are part of an evolutionary continuum from which no organism is exempt; in the film, bacteria are agents of God. The cinematic version of the Martian invasion replaces evolution with God, attempting to reinstall the hierarchy of being that Darwin's theories decisively dismantled. Rather than resisting apocalypse, the film embraces it; a savior "appears" at the end to deliver the elect, to rescue the chosen people, the Americans, from their tormentors.

It can also be said that what saves America is not just God, but its culture – its difference from the invaders. This allegory of political difference from the atheistic Soviets presents the defeat of the structures of Western political might but the simultaneous assertion of the power of belief in native culture. The essential, unbridgeable difference between the Red Other and the Americans is the invulnerability of the American system of values. *The War of the Worlds* film enacts a narrative of besiegement with the United States as the last outpost;[47] the halfway interlude concludes with Hardwicke saying "here was the only remaining unassailed strategic point" over images of the Statue of Liberty and Capitol Building. Positing an attack on the entire non-aligned globe renders the planet as fort under siege, attempting to assert the universality of American values. The miraculous rescue at the end of the film substitutes *Calvary* for *Cavalry*. Apocalypse, as enduring narrative mode for understanding historical process, is present in the original text; it has not been added by the filmmakers. The film chooses to emphasize it, to embrace it, rather than refute it. It delivers apocalypse and redemption and reveals its allegorical version of imperialism, that the transcendent meaning behind history is the supremacy of American values. The apocalyptic spectacle, with its fulfilled promise of divine intervention, confirming the status of America and its culture as "elect," becomes a justification of the nation's chosen status, of its political policies, of its Cold War self-surveillance. Though advanced, seemingly impotent thermonuclear devices may not provide defense against the red hordes, the film proposes that American society's core values and structures of power, though imperfect, are its best defense against the world's "colonization."

Spectacles of destruction are as central to Wells's novel as they are to the apocalyptic and the film. Here lies, however, one of the principal, unresolved tensions of the text, the one that would be exploited by subsequent versions of the tale. While the narrator and his brother resist apocalyptic self-definitions, the text as a whole does not. According to J. P. Vernier, Wells's envisioned war, and the devastating weaponry of the Martians, "clearly symbolizes a desire for purification through destruction"[48] that is constituent of the apocalyptic. At the same time, Wells himself was clearly aware of the appeal of the spectacle of destruction. While composing his story, he was simultaneously enjoying bicycling, and spent time journeying around Surrey "marking down suitable places and people for destruction by my Martians."[49] In a letter to his friend Elizabeth Healey, Wells remarks: "I'm doing the dearest little serial for Pearson's new magazine, in which I completely wreck and destroy Woking – killing my neighbors in painful and eccentric ways – then proceed via Kensington and Richmond to London, which I sack, selecting South Kensington for feats of peculiar atrocity."[50] As these quotes attest, Wells was certainly aware of the pleasures of cataclysm. Thus, the text is conflicted in terms of its dialectical refusal and embrace of many of the contours of apocalypticism. It is this tension, along with the establishment of the invasion story's paradigmatic use of power relationships as embodied in institutions and social structures, that has been taken up by the cinematic adaptations of his work.

The key difference between literary and filmed apocalyptic spectacle is in the use of special effects. Due to the specular nature of the cinema, it seems reasonable that the cataclysm should be the centerpiece of the apocalyptic film. Certainly, *Independence Day* was marketed on the strength of breathtaking images of aliens blasting our national landmarks to bits. More than just attracting audiences, the special effects become an integral signifying practice of the apocalyptic narrative itself, the spectacle of the spectacle. The reliance on spectacle underscores the essential destructive nature of the apocalyptic, how it is critical for the affirmation of transcendent reality. Unveiling truth alone does not produce apocalypse; it must be accompanied by purifying violence, with an attendant justice. In the novel, the special effect is defamiliarization, the implosion of the familiar and the intense portrayal of the mysterious Martians. While the specific manifestations of destruction in the film are markedly similar to the book, the removal of the intertwined narratives of evolution and empire reduces the spectacle to a function of the film's Cold War ideology. Where the narrator's reflections in the book's temporal present are strikingly contrasted with his visions and experiences in the novel's past, the film's univocal temporality makes differentiation between spectacle and explanation difficult. The overwhelming, exotic images of the film overtake, in a sense, the critiques implicit in the cinematic text itself and threaten to render meaning as visceral spectacle, to become the entirety of the text.

Wells's *The War of the Worlds* places a different narrative of vision at the center of the text. Again, this is established at the outset: the Martians are engaged in an act of observation and surveillance, as "this world was being watched keenly" by "envious eyes" much as we observe bacteria in a petri dish (I, 1). When the narrator watches in horror as the Martian appears from the cylinder, he describes the first thing to appear as "two luminous disks – like eyes" which were "regarding me steadfastly" (I, 4). About its alien visage the narrator recalls "above all, the extraordinary intensity of the immense eyes – were at once vital, intense, inhuman, crippled and monstrous" (I, 4). When trapped in the wrecked house, the curate and narrator observe the Martians, their wondrous technology and murderous vampirism, from a peephole-like slit, thus reversing the surveillance of the opening chapter. The narrator's reports have the validity of scientifically based direct observation and the authority of personal "visions." Finally, the book ends, not with the Martian defeat, but with the narrator's poignant reflection on the ghost-like images of devastation wrought by the invaders.

The novel *The War of the Worlds*, which is itself an intertextual parody of a popular narrative mode, has become a keystone intertextual document for many subsequent invasion stories. In the summer of 1996, nearly a hundred years after the novel's serialization, two films appeared which betrayed a heavy debt to Wells's visions. One, *Independence Day*, was an extravagantly produced and marketed grafting of Wells's tale onto the combat film and video games, while the other, *Mars Attacks!*, was an equally lavish production based upon a 1962 Topps trading set. Both films draw equal reference to Wells's novel and the Pal/Haskin adaptation. Again, each film highlights the power structures of America, particularly the government and the military. While *Mars Attacks!* lampoons these hierarchies and *Independence Day*, as Michael Rogin has astutely argued, refights World War II for the sake of national unity and racial harmony, both films end up where the 1953 version does – affirming the viability and hegemony of American culture.[51] They are quite different imaginings of Wells's source text, with messages that the pioneering author would certainly not have endorsed. On his tombstone, Wells joked, he wanted the epitaph: "God Damn You All; I Told You So." And as Frank McConnell notes:

> And what, after all, did he tell us? Well, just this: that the major disease of modern man is that his scientific and technological expertise has outstripped his moral and emotional development; that the human race, thanks to its inherited prejudices and superstitions and its innate pigheadedness, is an endangered species; and that mankind must learn – soon – to establish a state of worldwide cooperation by burying its old hatreds and its ancient selfishness, or face extinction.[52]

## Notes

1 Wells's fiction is not simply engaged with grappling with grand existential questions, but with political ones as well. One of Wells's express purposes in his scientific romances was to ridicule bourgeois complacency, to force the middle class to confront its unstated assumptions regarding technology and society. As author and scholar Darko Suvin notes, Wells's "What if?" scenarios are an attack on bourgeois presumptions, particularly the ideology of Social Darwinism, which provided a supportive rationale for Britain's imperialist adventures. See Darko Suvin, "Wells as the Turning Point of the SF Tradition," in John Huntington (ed.), *Critical Essays on H. G. Wells* (Boston: G. K. Hall, 1991), p. 27. Social Darwinism, of course, consecrated the continuation of class, race, and gender inequality by replacing the godhead at the top of the evolutionary chain with white men and reducing the cultural characteristics of whiteness to an immutable, eternal "nature." As the scientific theory of evolution entered the public discourse it was integrated into existing capitalist structures of power, control, and domination as a vehicle for "naturalizing" the ideological constructs that created these

institutional structures in the first place. Thus, the adherents of Social Darwinism configure the actions of social institutions, especially those that are based upon competition and aggression, as natural, and, thus, eternal and universal. If a gross oversimplification of evolution is the story of strong subjects vanquishing weak ones in an implacable competition for scarce natural resources, then the American conquest of the West, or the European project of imperialism, is a sign of the "natural" supremacy of the white, male subject. Imperialism, of course, pre-dates Darwin but the ease with which his theories were incorporated into other narratives of colonialism demonstrates notions of science-as-text as detailed by Donna Haraway and Andrew Ross. See Donna Haraway, *Primate Visions: Gender, Race and Nature in the World of Modern Science* (New York: Routledge, 1989); Andrew Ross, *The Chicago Gangster Theory of Life: Nature's Debt to Society* (New York: Verso, 1994).

   Unlike Jules Verne, with whom he was been traditionally compared, Wells was little interested in science for its own sake. Similarly, in the science fiction film, science itself is often a pretext for narrative action and the treatment of issues that coalesce around technology and/or otherness. Indeed, Wells saw his fiction as a form of social criticism, whose scientific conjecture was a pretext for interrogating and articulating concerns about the relationship between technology, society, and ethics. This is not to suggest that science is not important in science fiction films and novels. Rather, science fiction texts are often less about science than *scientism*. For Wells, this means rationalist ideologies as embodied by their physical, visible manifestations – technology – especially those that are willfully ignorant of, or divorced from, moral considerations. In much "soft" science fiction, deployment of science, particularly in the form of explanatory passages or dialogue, attempts to confer believability to the story, to provide causal justification for plot and action as well as to help facilitate narrative closure. Consequently, Wells's scientific romances can be understood as an important precursor to science fiction film.

2  Mike Davis, *The Ecology of Fear: Los Angeles and the Imagination of Disaster* (New York: Henry Holt, 1998), p. 290.

3  Bernard Bergonzi, *The Early H. G. Wells: A Study of the Scientific Romances* (Toronto: University of Toronto Press, 1961), p. 134.

4  David Hughes and Harry Geduld, *A Critical Edition of The War of the Worlds: H. G. Wells's Scientific Romance* (Bloomington, IN: Indiana University Press, 1993), pp. 24, 30–1.

5  Furthermore, Suvin notes: "*The War of the Worlds* also contains striking and indeed prophetic insights such as the picture of modern total warfare, with its panics, refugees, quislings, underground hidings, and an envisaged Resistance movement, as well as race-theory justifications, poison gas, and a 'spontaneous' bacteriological weapon" (Suvin, "Wells as the Turning Point," p. 28).

6  Davis, *The Ecology of Fear*, pp. 290–1; Suvin, "Wells as the Turning Point," p. 28.

7  The great Soviet director Sergei M. Eisenstein had some interest in adapting the novel when he was associated with Paramount Studios, which had optioned Wells's work. Jay Leyda, in the appendix to Eisenstein's *Film Sense*, states that the Wells project was abandoned because it was "too costly." See Sergei M. Eisenstein, *The Film Sense*, trans and ed. Jay Leyda (New York: Harcourt Brace Jovanovich, 1975), p. 223. See also Hughes and Geduld, *Critical Edition*, p. 246.

8  Hughes and Geduld, *Critical Edition*, p. 25

9  The mention of the genocide of the Tasmanians by English colonizers refers to the genesis of the idea for the book. As Wells reported in a 1920 *Strand Magazine* interview, he and his

brother Frank were wandering through pastoral Surrey discussing the annihilation of the indigenous population of Tasmania when Frank wondered aloud: "Suppose some beings from another planet were to drop out of the sky suddenly, and begin laying about them here!" (quoted in Bergonzi, *The Early H. G. Wells*, p. 124). For the purposes of this chapter, I have utilized the quotation system common to Wells scholars. Given the substantial number of editions of the book, scholars have employed the convention of using a Roman numeral to refer to Book One or Two of the text and an Arabic numeral to denote the chapter.

10   Suvin, "Wells as the Turning Point," p. 27.

11   As Mike Davis notes, when the novel was released it "stunned British readers, who . . . were forced to confront, for the first time what it might be like to be on the receiving end of imperial conquest" (*The Ecology of Fear*, p. 290).

12   Joyce Evans, *Celluloid Mushroom Clouds: Hollywood and the Atomic Bomb* (Boulder, CO: Westview Press, 1998), p. 17. Ironically, perhaps, it is Wells who is commonly held to have prophesied the invention of nuclear weapons. His novel *The World Set Free* (1914) features a war fought with super-weapons which are even called "atomic bombs." Though Wells is normally granted credit for predicting and naming atomic weapons, Davis reports that Upton Sinclair thought of them seven years earlier, though his work *The Millennium (A Comedy of the Year 2000)* was not published until 1924 (see Davis, *The Ecology of Fear*, pp. 312–13).

13   Indeed, there was a return of interest in the Red Planet in the early 1950s as Hollywood churned out a number of Mars-inflected movies (see Hughes and Geduld, *Critical Edition*, p. 246).

14   Hughes and Geduld, *Critical Edition*, pp. 247–8

15   In an interview in 1975 director Haskin remarked that "a recent writer on science fiction films said it was bad to have removed the story from its identifiable background, but it was identifiable to Americans, and that's who we were making the picture for. In making our choice, we did as Orson Welles had done. We transposed it to a modern setting, hoping to generate some of the excitement that Welles had with his broadcast." Quoted in Thomas C. Renzi, *H. G. Wells: Six Scientific Romances Adapted for Film* (Metuchen, NJ: Scarecrow Press, 1992), p. 121.

16   Wells, according to Hughes and Geduld (*Critical Edition*, p. 243) was "deeply incensed by the extensive changes" scripted by Welles. To the author, the radio play's infidelity to his text produced a completely different narrative. Claiming that they had been misled by CBS, Wells and his attorney Jacques Chambrun, demanded, and received, an apology and financial remuneration from the radio network. Welles, for his part, maintained that the play was "a legitimate dramatization of a published work" (*Critical Edition*, p. 244).

17   However, the brief ambiguous appearance of the Martian flying machine at the end of Book One suggests that the aliens may have gained the capability of expanding their enterprise beyond Britain's borders.

18   Wells intentionally keeps the exact date of the invasion ambiguous. This is in sharp contrast to the rest of the book's dependence on precise geographic detail: spatial detail is not supported by temporal details in the novel. Since the first astronomological abnormality is observed by scientists at the Lick Observatory in 1894 and the narrator relates that the invasion took place six years prior to his recording of the conflict, my conjecture is that the invasion took place not long after 1900.

19   The insistence on physical destruction leads Bernard Bergonzi to interpret Wells's early work as symptomatic, or reflective, of many of the cultural currents of *fin-de-siècle* Europe (Bergonzi, *The Early H. G. Wells*, p. 131). According to Bergonzi, "In its widest sense *fin*

de siècle was simply the expression of a prevalent mood: the feeling that the nineteenth century – which had contained more events, more history than any other – had gone on too long, and that sensitive souls were growing weary of it" (The Early H. G. Wells, p. 3). In Great Britain, many intellectuals had become impatient with the lengthy Victorian age, and the values that characterized it. At the same time, there was great trepidation about the coming century especially in relation to continental military expansionism. "The result could be described as a certain loss of nerve, weariness with the past combined with foreboding about the future" (p. 4). The cultural mood engendered an apocalyptic sensibility that Bergonzi characterizes as fin du globe, a feeling amongst artists and intellectuals that the prevailing social order could not hold, that it was destined for disaster and dissolution (p. 4). Indeed, Bergonzi contends that the "fin du globe motif is predominant in The War of the Worlds" (p. 15).

20 Frank McConnell, The Science Fiction of H. G. Wells (Oxford: Oxford University Press, 1981), p. 128.

21 Ibid.

22 Frank Kermode, The Sense of an Ending: Studies in the Theory of Fiction (Oxford: Oxford University Press, 1966), p. 29.

23 One might say that, through this mode of perceiving history, the subjugated attempts to re-allocate power from the oppressor to the reader.

24 As Warren Wagar relates, The Battle of Dorking attempts to communicate the "lesson" of the Franco-Prussian conflict, that "any country that is unprepared for combat, whether politically or militarily or psychologically, will collapse, just as Louis Napoleon's France collapsed before the war machine of the House of Hohenzollern." In W. Warren Wagar, Terminal Visions: The Literature of Last Things (Bloomington, IN: Indiana University Press, 1982), p. 119.

25 McConnell, Science Fiction, p. 132.

26 The popularity of this literary form was not confined to England; versions of the story surfaced throughout Europe and in the United States. Not surprisingly, perhaps, each country fantasized that it was the docile and defenseless victim of an unprovoked invasion by one or more of its rivals (McConnell, Science Fiction, p. 132).

27 McConnell, Science Fiction, p. 132.

28 Bergonzi, The Early H. G. Wells, p. 134; Hughes and Geduld, Critical Edition, p. 20.

29 The narrator concludes that the insensitivity of the Martians is a result of being at the end of evolution: "Without the body the brain would, of course, become a mere selfish intelligence, without any of the emotional substratum of the human being" (II, 2).

30 McConnell, Science Fiction, p. 130.

31 Hughes and Geduld, Critical Edition, p. 248.

32 For critics such as Hughes and Geduld, and Renzi, the film is unequivocally pro-religion.

33 McConnell, Science Fiction, p. 140.

34 John Huntington, The Logic of Fantasy: H. G. Wells and Science Fiction (New York: Columbia University Press, 1982), p. 84.

35 Renzi, Six Scientific Romances, pp. 136–7.

36 Ibid., p. 136.

37 For Renzi, the global view of the holocaust of the brother's chapters anticipates this interlude, as it can be conceived of as cinematic in form, with its hypothetical subject position ascribed to an imaginary balloonist surveying the devastation providing a parallel to crane shots and bird-eye views in cinema (Six Scientific Romances, p. 6).

38 The passage reads: "If one could have hung that June morning in a balloon in the blazing blue above London every northward and eastward road running out of the tangled maze of streets would have seemed stippled black with the streaming fugitives, each dot a human agony of terror and physical distress. I have set forth at length in the last chapter my brother's account of the road through Chipping Barnet, in order that my readers may realise how that swarming of black dots appeared to one of those concerned. Never before in the history of the world had such a mass of human beings moved and suffered together. The legendary hosts of Goths and Huns, the hugest armies Asia has ever seen, would have been but a drop in that current. And this was no disciplined march; it was a stampede – a stampede gigantic and terrible – without order and without a goal, six million people unarmed and unprovisioned, driving headlong. It was the beginning of the rout of civilisation, of the massacre of mankind" (I, 17).

39 The name Dr Clayton Forrester was appropriated by the *Mystery Science Theater 3000* production team as the moniker for the evil scientist who conducts mind-control experiments on captives Joel Robinson and Mike Nelson, and their robot companions Tom Servo and Crow T. Robot, by forcing them to watch horrible movies.

40 Save for the biologist Duprey's investigation of the extraterrestrials' blood and Mann's analysis of their military plan, Forrester is the character who explains the enemy's technology and intention.

41 Mark Rose makes this argument in "Filling the Void: Verne, Wells and Lem," *Science Fiction Studies* 8: 24 (1981), 121–42 (cited in Hughes and Geduld, *Critical Edition*, p. 19). Colin Manlove makes a similar point in "Charles Kingsley, H. G. Wells and the Machine in Victorian Fiction," *Nineteenth-century Literature* 48: 2 (September 1993), 212–39.

42 Renzi, *Six Scientific Romances*, pp. 124–25.

43 According to the Internet Movie Database, the film cost approximately $2 million to complete (see http://www.imdb.com).

44 Wells's complete opening paragraph is as follows: "No one would have believed in the last years of the nineteenth century that this world was being watched keenly and closely by intelligences greater than man's and yet as mortal as his own; that as men busied themselves about their various concerns they were scrutinised and studied, perhaps almost as narrowly as a man with a microscope might scrutinise the transient creatures that swarm and multiply in a drop of water. With infinite complacency, men went to and fro over this globe about their little affairs, serene in their assurance of their empire over matter. It is possible that the infusoria under the microscope do the same. No one gave a thought to the older worlds of space as sources of human danger, or thought of them only to dismiss the idea of life upon them as impossible or improbable. It is curious to recall some of the mental habits of those departed days. At most terrestrial men fancied there might be other men upon Mars, perhaps inferior to themselves and ready to welcome a missionary enterprise. Yet across the gulf of space, minds that are to our minds as ours are to those of the beasts that perish, intellects vast and cool and unsympathetic, regarded this earth with envious eyes, and slowly and surely drew their plans against us. And early in the twentieth century came the great disillusionment" (I, 1).

45 Hughes and Geduld, *Critical Edition*, p. 248.

46 The original text reads as follows: "In another moment I had scrambled up the earthen rampart and stood upon its crest, and the interior of the redoubt was below me. A mighty space it was, with gigantic machines here and there within it, huge mounds of material and strange shelter places. And scattered about it, some in their overturned war-machines, some in the

now rigid handling machines, and a dozen of them stark and silent and laid in a row, were the Martians – DEAD! – slain by the putrefactive and disease bacteria against which their systems were unprepared; slain as the red weed was being slain; slain, after all man's devices had failed, by the humblest things that God, in his wisdom, has put upon this earth" (II, 8).

47  The narrative of besiegement manifests itself in both Westerns and combat films. As previously noted, the film stages World War III as a recapitulation of World War II; thus, it alludes and enlarges upon the platoon film. There is a strain of Westerns, combat films, and colonial adventure stories in which a tiny band has to hold its position against an anonymous, mostly unseen, dark Other. For example, as Robert Stam and Ella Shohat have stated, "the Indian raid on the fort, as the constructed bastion of settled civilization against nomadic savagery . . . became a staple topos in American westerns." See Ella Shohat and Robert Stam, *Unthinking Eurocentrism: Multiculturalism and the Media* (New York: Routledge, 1994), p. 116. In these films, such as *The Lost Patrol* (1934), *Bataan* (1943), *Ulzana's Raid* (1972), or *Platoon* (1986), the group, depicted as a microcosm of society, fights the dark Other, which threatens not just to win the battle but to overrun civilization entirely. Though most of the characters in films of this type do not survive the narrative, the values of Western society, which they symbolically depict, are, nonetheless, affirmed. This is connected to apocalypse, as a desirable way to purge civilization of the unsavory, Other elements. The narratives of besiegement allow the films to work through the characteristics of national identity through contrast to a ruthless, faceless, undifferentiated, resolutely evil enemy.

In American narratives of imperialism, this mode of besiegement is played out through the myth of the frontier. Therefore, the film *The War of the Worlds* is intertextually consonant with a distinctly American configuration of the apocalyptic narrative. In the popular American imagination, and the cinema by extrapolation, empire's equation between oppressed and colonizer was inverted and became an instrument of the powerful against the marginalized. The apocalyptic expressed empire, not resistance to it, perhaps inevitably in the context of an affluent society, which was itself sometimes viewed as a New Jerusalem. As Richard Slotkin has extensively argued, the Puritans produced an impressive literature of the apocalyptic through which they filtered their experiences in North America. Indeed, Increase and Cotton Mather proved adept at finding apocalyptic biblical interpretations for contemporary events. See Richard Slotkin, *Regeneration Through Violence: The Mythology of the American Frontier 1600–1860* (Middletown, CT: Wesleyan University Press, 1973). The Native Americans were viewed as extensions of the physical landscape, as demons of the apocalypse, and their presence allowed the colonizer an outlet for a struggle against their own moral deficiencies. King Philip's War, during which the Puritans committed atrocities against the Pequot Indians, was interpreted as evidence of the onset of the Tribulation. Increase Mather suggested that the war was prophesied in the book of Revelations as the red horse of the Apocalypse. See Paul Boyer, *When Time Shall Be No More: Prophecy Belief in Modern American Culture* (Cambridge, MA: Harvard University Press, 1992), p. 69. Indeed, in the American colonial period, religious themes and secular events were increasingly intermingled in popular writings before the Revolution. As Richard Slotkin argues, the Puritans viewed the frontier as an existential landscape, and their purpose was to impose order upon a "formless" world. Thus, colonial discourse is necessarily predicated on the body of the Other and *regeneration through violence*, a reflection of the purifying destruction of the apocalypse, which becomes a justification for imperialism. See Richard Slotkin, *Gunfighter Nation: The Myth of the Frontier in Twentieth Century America*

(New York: Athenaeum, 1992), p. 12. The polysemic vagueness of Revelation permits an easy inscription of the Other within the crisis subjectivity of the colonizer as constituted by the apocalyptic.

48  J. P. Vernier, "Evolution as a Literary Theme in H. G. Wells's Science Fiction," in Darko Suvin and Robert Philmus (eds), *H. G. Wells and Modern Science Fiction* (Lewisburg, PA: Bucknell University Press, 1977), p. 82.

49  Quoted in Hughes and Geduld, *Critical Edition*, p. 1.

50  Quoted in Bergonzi, *The Early H. G. Wells*, p. 125.

51  See Michael Rogin, *Independence Day: Or How I Learned to Stop Worrying and Love the Enola Gay* (London: British Film Institute, 1998).

52  McConnell, *Science Fiction*, p. 11.

# Index

Printed and bound in the UK by
CPI Antony Rowe, Eastbourne